T0324958

Data Management for Multimedia Retrieval

Multimedia data require specialized management techniques because the representations of color, time, semantic concepts, and other underlying information can be drastically different from one another. The user's subjective judgment can also have significant impact on what data or features are relevant in a given context. These factors affect both the performance of the retrieval algorithms and their effectiveness. This textbook on multimedia data management techniques offers a unified perspective on retrieval efficiency and effectiveness. It provides a comprehensive treatment, from basic to advanced concepts, that will be useful to readers of different levels, from advanced undergraduate and graduate students to researchers and professionals.

After introducing models for multimedia data (images, video, audio, text, and web) and for their features, such as color, texture, shape, and time, the book presents data structures and algorithms that help store, index, cluster, classify, and access common data representations. The authors also introduce techniques, such as relevance feedback and collaborative filtering, for bridging the "semantic gap" and present the applications of these to emerging topics, including web and social networking.

K. Selçuk Candan is a Professor of Computer Science and Engineering at Arizona State University. He received his Ph.D. in 1997 from the University of Maryland at College Park. Candan has authored more than 140 conference and journal articles, 9 patents, and many book chapters and, among his other scientific positions, has served as program chair for ACM Multimedia Conference'08, the International Conference on Image and Video Retrieval (CIVR'10), and as an organizing committee member for ACM SIG Management of Data Conference (SIGMOD'06). In 2011, he will serve as a general chair for the ACM Multimedia Conference. Since 2005, he has also been serving as an associate editor for the *International Journal on Very Large Data Bases* (*VLDB*).

Maria Luisa Sapino is a Professor in the Department of Computer Science at the University of Torino, where she also earned her Ph.D. There she leads the multimedia and heterogeneous data management group. Her scientific contributions include more than 60 conference and journal papers; her services as chair, organizer, and program committee member in major conferences and workshops on multimedia; and her collaborations with industrial research labs, including the RAI-Crit (Center for Research and Technological Innovation) and Telecom Italia Lab, on multimedia technologies.

DATA MANAGEMENT FOR
MULTIMEDIA RETRIEVAL

K. Selçuk Candan
Arizona State University

Maria Luisa Sapino
University of Torino

CAMBRIDGE
UNIVERSITY PRESS

Shaftesbury Road, Cambridge CB2 8EA, United Kingdom

One Liberty Plaza, 20th Floor, New York, NY 10006, USA

477 Williamstown Road, Port Melbourne, VIC 3207, Australia

314–321, 3rd Floor, Plot 3, Splendor Forum, Jasola District Centre, New Delhi – 110025, India

103 Penang Road, #05–06/07, Visioncrest Commercial, Singapore 238467

Cambridge University Press is part of Cambridge University Press & Assessment,
a department of the University of Cambridge.

We share the University's mission to contribute to society through the pursuit of
education, learning and research at the highest international levels of excellence.

www.cambridge.org
Information on this title: www.cambridge.org/9780521887397

First published 2010

A catalogue record for this publication is available from the British Library

Library of Congress Cataloging-in-Publication data
Candan, K. Selçuk (Kasim Selçuk)
Data management for multimedia retrieval / K. Selçuk Candan, Maria Luisa Sapino.
    p. cm.
Includes bibliographical references and index.
ISBN 978-0-521-88739-7 (hardback)
1. Multimedia systems. 2. Database management. I. Sapino, Maria Luisa. II. Title.
QA76.575.C287 2010
005.74–dc22   2009043206

ISBN   978-0-521-88739-7   Hardback

Contents

Color plates follow page 38

Preface

Database and multimedia systems emerged to address the needs of very different application domains. New applications (such as digital libraries, increasingly dynamic and complex web content, and scientific data management), on the other hand, necessitate a common understanding of both of these disciplines. Consequently, as these domains matured over the years, their respective scientific disciplines moved closer. On the media management side, researchers have been concentrating on media-content description and indexing issues as part of the MPEG7 and other standards. On the data management side, commercial database management systems, which once primarily targeted traditional business applications, today focus on media and heterogeneous-data intensive applications, such as digital libraries, integrated database/information-retrieval systems, sensor networks, bioinformatics, e-business applications, and of course the web.

There are three reasons for the heterogeneity inherent in multimedia applications and information management systems. First, the semantics of the information captured in different forms can be drastically different from each other. Second, resource and processing requirements of various media differ substantially. Third, the user and context have significant impacts on what information is relevant and how it should be processed and presented. A key observation, on the other hand, is that rather than being independent, the challenges associated with the semantic, resource, and context-related heterogeneities are highly related and require a common understanding and unified treatment within a multimedia data management system (MDMS). Consequently, internally a multimedia database management system looks and functions differently than a traditional (relational, object-oriented, or even XML) DBMS.

Also acknowledging the fact that web-based systems and rich Internet applications suffer from significant media- and heterogeneity-related hurdles, we see a need for undergraduate and graduate curricula that not only will educate students separately in each individual domain, but also will provide them a common perspective in the underlying disciplines. During the past decade, at our respective institutions, we worked toward realizing curricula that bring media/web and database educations closer. At Arizona State University, in addition to teaching a senior-level

"Multimedia Information Systems" course, one of us (Prof. Candan) introduced a graduate course under the title "Multimedia and Web Databases." This course offers an introduction to features, models (including fuzzy and semistructured) for multimedia and web data, similarity-based retrieval, query processing and optimization for inexact retrieval, advanced indexing, clustering, and search techniques. In short, the course provides a "database" view of media management, storage, and retrieval. It not only educates students in media information management, but also highlights how to design a multimedia-oriented database system, why and how these systems evolve, and how they may change in the near future to accommodate the needs of new applications, such as search engines, web applications, and dynamic information-mashup systems. At the University of Torino, the other author of this book (Prof. Sapino) taught a similar course, but geared toward senior-level undergraduate students, with a deeper focus on media and features.

A major challenge both of us faced with these courses was the lack of an appropriate textbook. Although there are many titles that address different aspects of multimedia information management, content-based information retrieval, and query processing, there is currently no textbook that provides an integrated look at the challenges and technologies underlying a multimedia-oriented DBMS. Consequently, both our courses had to rely heavily on the material we ourselves have been developing over the years. We believe it is time for a textbook that takes an integrated look at these increasingly converging fields of multimedia information retrieval and databases, exhaustively covers existing multimedia database technologies, and provides insights into future research directions that stem from media-rich systems and applications. We wrote this book with the aim of preparing students for research and development in data management technologies that address the needs of rich media-based applications. This book's focus is on algorithms, architectures, and standards that aim at tackling the heterogeneity and dynamicity inherent in real data sources, rich applications, and systems. Thus, instead of focusing on a single or even a handful of media, the book covers fundamental concepts and techniques for modeling, storing, and retrieving heterogeneous multimedia data. It includes material covering semantic, context-based, and performance-related aspects of modeling, storage, querying, and retrieval of heterogeneous, fuzzy, and subjective (multimedia and web) data.

We hope you enjoy this book and find it useful in your studies and your future endeavors involving multimedia.

K. Selçuk Candan and Maria Luisa Sapino

Introduction

Multimedia Applications and
Data Management Requirements

Among countless others, applications of multimedia databases include personal and public photo/media collections, personal information management systems, digital libraries, online and print advertising, digital entertainment, communications, long-distance collaborative systems, surveillance, security and alert detection, military, environmental monitoring, ambient and ubiquitous systems that provide real-time personalized services to humans, accessibility services to blind and elderly people, rehabilitation of patients through visual and haptic feedback, and interactive performing arts. This diverse spectrum of media-rich applications imposes stringent requirements on the underlying media data management layer. Although most of the existing work in multimedia data management focuses on content-based and object-based query processing, future directions in multimedia querying will also involve understanding how media objects affect users and how they fit into users' experiences in the real world. These require better understanding of underlying perceptive and cognitive processes in human media processing. Ambient media-rich systems that collect diverse media from environmentally embedded sensors necessitate novel methods for continuous and distributed media processing and fusion schemes. Intelligent schemes for choosing the right objects to process at the right time are needed to allow media processing workflows to be scaled to the immense influx of real-time media data. In a similar manner, collaborative-filtering–based query processing schemes that can help overcome the semantic gap between media and users' experiences will help the multimedia databases scale to Internet-scale media indexing and querying.

1.1 HETEROGENEITY

Most media-intensive applications, such as digital libraries, sensor networks, bioinformatics, and e-business applications, require effective and efficient data management systems. Owing to their complex and heterogeneous nature, management, storage, and retrieval of multimedia objects are more challenging than the management of traditional data, which can easily be stored in commercial (mostly relational) database management systems.

Querying and retrieval in multimedia databases require the capability of comparing two media objects and determining how similar or how different these two objects are. Naturally, the way in which the two objects are compared depends on the underlying data model. In this section, we see that any single media object (whether it is a complex media document or a simple object, such as an image) can be modeled and compared in multiple ways, based on its different properties.

1.1.1 Complex Media Objects

A complex multimedia object or a document typically consists of a number of media objects that must be presented in a coherent, synchronized manner. Various standards are available to facilitate authoring of complex multimedia objects:

- **SGML/XML.** Standard Generalized Markup Language (SGML) was accepted in 1986 as an international standard (ISO 8879) for describing the structure of documents [SGML]. The key feature of this standard is the separation of document content and structure from the presentation of the document. The document structure is defined using *document type definitions (DTDs)* based on a formal grammar. One of the most notable applications of the SGML standard is the HyperText Markup Language (HTML), the current standard for publishing on the Internet, which dates back to 1992.

  Extensible Markup Language (XML) has been developed by the W3C Generic SGML Editorial Review Board [XML] as a follow-up to SGML. XML is a subset of SGML, especially suitable for creating interchangeable, structured Web documents. As with SGML, document structure is defined using DTDs; however, various extensions (such as elimination of the requirement that each document has a DTD) make the XML standard more suitable for authoring hypermedia documents and exchanging heterogenous information.

- **HyTime.** SGML and XML have various multimedia-oriented applications. The Hypermedia/Time-based Structuring Language (HyTime) is an international multimedia standard (ISO 10744) [HyTime], based on SGML. Unlike HTML and its derivatives, however, HyTime aims to describe not only the hierarchical and link structures of multimedia documents, but also temporal synchronization between objects to be presented to the user as part of the document. The underlying event-driven synchronization mechanism relies on timelines (Section 2.3.5).

- **SMIL.** Synchronized Multimedia Integration Language (SMIL) is a synchronization standard developed by the W3C [SMIL]. Like HyTime, SMIL defines a language for interactive multimedia presentations: authors can describe spatiotemporal properties of objects within a multimedia document and associate hyperlinks with them to enable user interaction. Again, like HyTime, SMIL is based on the timeline model and provides event-based synchronization for multimedia objects. Instead of being an application of SGML, however, SMIL is based on XML.

- **MHEG.** MHEG, the Multimedia and Hypermedia Experts Group, developed a hypermedia publishing and coding standard. This standard, also known as the MHEG standard [MHEG], focuses on platform-independent interchange and presentation of multimedia presentations. MHEG models presentations as a collection of objects. The spatiotemporal relationships between objects and the interaction specifications form the structure of a multimedia presentation.

- **VRML and X3D.** Virtual Reality Modeling Language (VRML) provides a standardized way to describe interactive three-dimensional (3D) information for Web-based applications. It soon evolved into the international standard for describing 3D content [Vrml]. A VRML object or world contains various media (including 3D mesh geometry and shape primitives), a hierarchical structure that describes the composition of the objects in the 3D environment, a spatial structure that describes their spatial positions, and an event/interaction structure that describes how the environment evolves with time and user interactions. The Web3D consortium led the development of the VRML standard and its XML representation, X3D standard [X3D].

- **MPEG7 and MPEG21.** Unlike the standards just mentioned, which aim to describe the content of authored documents, the main focus of the MPEG7 (Multimedia Content Description Interface) [MPEG7] is to describe the content of captured media objects, such as video. It is a follow-up to the previous MPEG standards, MPEG1, MPEG2, and MPEG4, which were mainly concerned with video compression. Although primarily designed to support content-based retrieval for captured media, the standard is also rich enough to be applicable to synthetic and authored multimedia data. The standard includes content-based description mechanisms for images, graphics, 3D objects, audio, and video streams. Low-level visual descriptors for media include color (e.g., color space, dominant colors, and color layout), texture (e.g., edge histogram), shape (e.g., contours), and motion (e.g., object and camera trajectories) descriptors. The standard also enables description of how to combine heterogeneous media content into one unified multimedia object. A follow-up standard, MPEG21 [MPEG21], aims to provide additional content management and usage services, such as caching, archiving, distributing, and intellectual property management, for multimedia objects.

Example 1.1.1: As a more detailed example for nonatomic multimedia objects, let us reconsider the VRML/X3D standard, for describing virtual worlds. In X3D, the world is described in the form of a hierarchical structure, commonly referred to as the scene graph. The nodes of the hierarchical structure are expressed as XML elements, and the visual properties (such as size, color, and shine) of each node are described by these elements' attributes. Figure 1.1 provides a simple example of a virtual world consisting of two objects. The elements in this scene graph describe the spatial positions, sizes, shapes, and visual properties of the objects in this 3D world. Note that the scene graph has a *tree* structure: there is one special node, referred to as the root, that does not have any ancestors (and thus it represents the entire virtual world), whereas each node except this root node has one and only one parent.

The internal nodes in the X3D hierarchy are called grouping (or transform) nodes, and they bring together multiple subcomponents of an object and describe their spatial relationships. The leaf nodes can contain different types of media (e.g., images and video), shape primitives (e.g., sphere and box), and their properties (e.g., transparency and color), as well as 3D geometry in the form of polyhedra (also called meshes). In addition, two special types of nodes, sensor and script nodes,

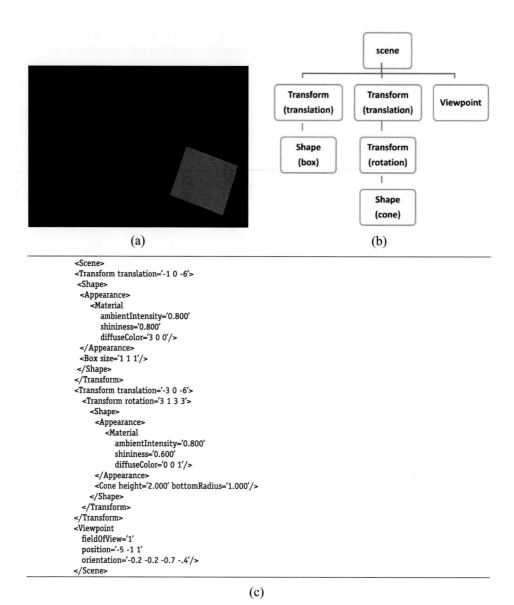

Figure 1.1. An X3D world with two shape objects and the XML-based code for its hierarchical scene graph: (a) X3D world, (b) scene graph, (c) X3D code. See color plates section.

can be used to describe the interactivity options available in the X3D world: sensor nodes capture events (such as user input); script nodes use behavior descriptions (written in a high-level programming language, for example, JavaScript) to modify the parameters of the world in response to the captured events. Thus, X3D worlds can be rich and heterogeneous in content and structure (Figure 1.2):

■ *Atomic media types:* This category covers more traditional media types, such as text, images, texture maps, audio, and video. The features used for media-based retrieval are specific to each media type.

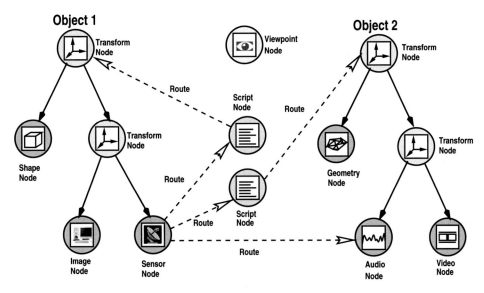

Figure 1.2. The scene graph of a more complex X3D world.

- *3D mesh geometry:* This category covers all types of polyhedra that can be represented using the X3D/VRML standard. Geometry-based retrieval is a relatively new topic, and the features to be used for retrieval are not yet well understood.
- *Shape primitives:* This category covers all types of primitive shapes that are part of the standard, as well as their attributes and properties.
- *Node structure:* The node structure describes how complex X3D/VRML objects are put together in terms of the simpler components. Because objects and subobjects are the main units of reuse, most of the queries need to have the node structure as one of the retrieval criteria.
- *Spatial structure:* The spatial structure of an object is related to its node structure; however, it describes the spatial transformations (scaling and translation) that are applied to the subcomponents of the world. Thus queries are based on spatial properties of the objects.
- *Event/interaction structure:* The event structure of a world, which consists of sensor nodes and event routes between sensor nodes and script nodes, describes causal relationships among objects within the world.
- *Behaviors:* The scripting nodes, which are part of the event structure, may be used for understanding the behavioral semantics of the objects. Because these behaviors can be reused, they are likely to be an important unit of retrieval. The standard does not provide a descriptive language for behaviors. Thus, retrieval of behaviors is likely through their interfaces and the associated metadata.
- *Temporal structure:* The temporal structure is specified through time sensors and the associated actions. Consequently, the temporal structure is a specific type of event structure. Because time is also inherent in the temporal media (such as video and audio) that can be contained within an X3D/VRML object, it needs to be treated distinctly from the general event structure.

■ *Metadata:* This covers everything associated with the objects and worlds (such as the textual content of the corresponding files or filenames) that cannot be experienced by the viewers. In many cases, the metadata (such as developer's comments and/or node and variable names) can be used for extracting information that describes the actual content.

The two-object scene graph in Figure 1.2 contains an image file, which might be used as a surface texture for one of the objects in the world; an audio file, which might contain the soundtrack associated with an object; a video file, which might be projected on the surface of one of the objects; shape primitives, such as boxes, that can be used to describe simple objects; and 3D mesh geometry, which might be used to describe an object (such as a human avatar) with complex surface description. The scene graph further describes different types of relationships between the two nodes forming the world. These include a composition structure, which is described by the underlying XML hierarchy of the nodes constituting the X3D objects, and events that are captured by the sensor nodes and the causal structure, described by script nodes that can be activated by these events and can affect any node in the scene graph. In addition, temporal scripts might be associated to the scene graph, enabling the scene to evolve over time. Note that when considering the interaction pathways between the nodes in the X3D (defined through sensors and scripts), the structure of the scene graph ceases to be a tree and, instead, becomes a *directed graph*.

Whereas an X3D world is often created and stored as a single file, in many other cases the multimedia content may actually not be available in the form of a single file created by a unique individual (or a group with a common goal), but might in fact consist of multiple independent components, possibly stored in a distributed manner. In this sense, the Web itself can be viewed as a single (but extremely large) multimedia object. Although, in many cases, we access this *object* only a page (or an image, or a video) at a time, search engines treat the Web as a complex whole, with a dynamic structure, where communities are born and evolve repeatedly. In fact, with Web 2.0 technologies, such as blogs and social networking sites, which strongly tie the users to the content that they generate or annotate (i.e., tag), this vast object (i.e., the entire Web) now also includes the end users themselves (or at least their online representations).

1.1.2 Semantic Gap

It is not only the complex objects (described using hypermedia standards, such as X3D, SMIL, MPEG7, or HTML) that may necessitate structured, nonatomic models for representation. Even objects of relatively simple media types, such as images and video, may embed sub-objects with diverse local properties and complex spatiotemporal interrelationships. For example, an experimental study conducted by H. Nishiyama *et al.* [1994] shows that users are viewing paintings or images using two primary patterns. The first pattern consists of viewing the whole image roughly, focusing only on the layout of the images of particular interest. The second pattern consists of concentrating on specific objects within the image. In a sense, we can view a single image as a compound object containing many sub-objects, each

Figure 1.3. Any media object can be seen as a collection of channels of information; some of these information channels (such as color and shape) are low-level (can be derived from the media object), whereas others (such as semantic labels attached to the objects by the viewer) are higher level (cannot be derived from the media object without external knowledge). See color plates section.

corresponding to regions of the image that are visually coherent and/or semantically meaningful (e.g., car, man), and their spatial relationships.

In general, a *feature* of a media object is simply any property of the object that can be used for describing it to others. This can include properties at all levels, from low-level properties (such as color, texture, and shape) to semantic features (such as linguistic labels attached to the parts of the media object) that require interpretation of the underlying low-level features at much higher semantic levels (Figure 1.3). This necessity to have an interpretive process that can take low-level features that are immediately available from the media and map to the high-level features that require external knowledge is commonly referred to as the *semantic gap*.

The semantic gap can be bridged, and a multimedia query can be processed, at different levels. In content-based retrieval, the low-level features of the query are matched against the low-level features of the media objects in the database to identify the appropriate matches (Figure 1.4(a)). In semantic-based retrieval, either the high-level query can be restated in terms of the corresponding low-level features for matching (Figure 1.4(b)) or the low-level features of the media in the database can

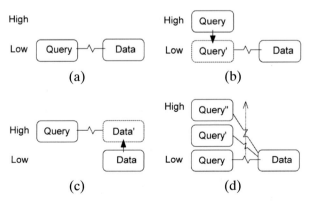

Figure 1.4. Different query processing strategies for media retrieval: (a) Low-level feature matching. (b) A high-level query is translated into low-level features for matching. (c) Low-level features are interpreted for high-level matching. (d) Through relevance feedback, the query is brought higher up in semantic levels; that is, it is increasingly better at representing the user's intentions.

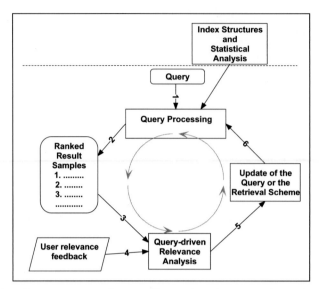

Figure 1.5. Multimedia query processing usually requires the semantic gap between what is stored in the database and how the user interprets the query and the data to be bridged through a relevance feedback cycle. This process itself is usually statistical in nature and, consequently, introduces probabilistic imprecision in the results.

be interpreted (for example through classification, Chapter 9) to support retrieval (Figure 1.4(c)). Alternatively, user relevance feedback (Figure 1.5 and Chapter 12) and collaborative filtering (Sections 6.3.3 and 12.8) techniques can be used to rewrite the user query in a way that better represents the user's intentions (Figure 1.4(d)).

1.2 IMPRECISION AND SUBJECTIVITY

One common characteristic of most multimedia applications is the underlying uncertainty or imprecision.

1.2.1 Reasons for Imprecision and Subjectivity

Because of the possibly redundant ways to sense the environment, the alternative ways to process, filter, and fuse multimedia data, the diverse alternatives in bridging the semantic gap, and the subjectivity involved in the interpretation of data and query results, multimedia data and queries are inherently imprecise:

- *Feature extraction algorithms that form the basis of content-based multimedia data querying are generally imprecise.* For example, a high error rate is encountered in motion-capture data and is generally due to the multitude of environmental factors involved, including camera and object speed. Especially for video/audio/motion streams, data extracted through feature extraction modules are only statistically accurate and may be based on the frame rate or the position of the video camera related to the observed object.
- *It is rare that a multimedia querying system relies on exact matching.* Instead, in many cases, multimedia databases need to consider nonidentical but *similar*

Table 1.1. Different types of queries that an image database may support

Find all images created by "John Smith"

Find all images that look like "query.gif"

Find top-5 images that look like "im_ex.gif"

Find all images that look like "mysketch.bmp"

Find all images that contain a part that looks like "query.gif"

Find all images of "sunny days"

Find all images that contain a "car"

Find all images that contain a "car" and a man who looks like "mugshot.bmp"

Find all image pairs that contain similar objects

Find all objects contained in images of "sunny days"

Find all images that contain two objects, where the first object looks like "im_ex.gif," the second object is something like a "car," and the first object is "to the right of" the second object; also return the semantic annotation available for these two objects

Find all new images in the database that I may like based on my list of preferences

Find all new images in the database that I may like based on my profile and history

Find all new images in the database that I may like based on access history of people who are similar to me in their preferences and profiles

---

features to find data objects that are reasonable matches to the query. In many cases, it is also necessary to account for semantic similarities between associated annotations and partial matches, where objects in the result satisfy some of the requirements in the query but fail to satisfy all query conditions.

■ *Imprecision can be due to the available index structures, which are often imperfect.* Because of the sheer size of the data, many systems rely on clustering and classification algorithms for sometimes imperfectly pruning search alternatives during query processing.

■ *Query formulation methods are not able to capture the user's subjective intention perfectly.* Naturally the query model used for accessing the multimedia database depends on the underlying data model and the type of queries that the users will pose (Table 1.1). In general, we can categorize query models into three classes:

  – *Query by example (QBE):* The user provides an example and asks the system to return media objects that are similar to this object.

  – *Query by description:* The user provides a declarative description of the objects of interest. This can be performed using an SQL-like ad hoc query language or using pictorial aids that help users declare their interests through sketches or storyboards.

  – *Query by profile/recommendation:* In this case, the user is not actively querying the database; instead the database predicts the user's needs based on his or her profile (or based on the profiles of other users who have similar profiles) and recommends an object to the user in a proactive manner.

For example, in Query-by-Example (QBE) [Cardenas *et al.*, 1993; Schmitt *et al.*, 2005], which features, feature value ranges, feature combinations, or similarity notions are to be used for processing is left to the system to figure out through feature significance analysis, user preferences, relevance feedback [Robertson

---

```
select image P, imageobject object1, object2 where
        contains(P, object1) and contains(P, object2) and
        (semantically_similar(P.semanticannotation, "Fuji Mountain") and
        visually_similar(object1.imageproperties, "Fujimountain.jpg")) and
        (semantically_similar(P.semanticannotation, "Lake") and
        visually_similar(object2.imageproperties, "Lake.jpg")) and
        above(object1, object2).
```

Figure 1.6. A sample multimedia query with imprecise (e.g., semantically_similar(), visually_similar(), and above()) and exact predicates (e.g., contains()).

and Spark-Jones, 1976; Rui and Huang, 2001] (see Figure 1.5), and/or collaborative filtering [Zunjarwad *et al.*, 2007] techniques, which are largely statistical and probabilistic in nature.

1.2.2 Impact on Query Formulation and Processing

In many multimedia systems, more than one of the foregoing reasons for imprecision coexist and, consequently, the system must take them into consideration collectively. Degrees of match have to be quantified and combined, and results have to be filtered and ordered based on these combined matching scores. Figure 1.6 provides an example query (in an SQL-like syntax used by the SEMCOG system [Li and Candan, 1999a]) that brings together imprecise and exact predicates. Processing this query requires assessment of different sources of imprecision and merging them into a single value for ranking the results:

Example 1.2.1: Figure 1.7(a) shows a visual representation of the query in Figure 1.6. Figures 1.7(b), (c), (d), and (e) are examples of candidate images that may match this query. The values next to the objects in these candidate images denote the similarity values for the object-level matching. In this hypothetical example, the evaluation of spatial relationships is also fuzzy (or imprecise) in nature.

The candidate image in Figure 1.7(b) satisfies object matching conditions, but its layout does not match the user specification. Figures 1.7(c) and (e) satisfy the image layout condition, but the features of the objects do not perfectly match the query specification. Figure 1.7(d) has low structural and object matching. In Figure 1.7(b), the spatial predicate and in Figure 1.7(d), the image similarity predicate for the lake, completely fail (i.e., the degree of match is 0.0). A multimedia database engine must consider all four images as candidates and must rank them according to a certain unified criterion.

The models that can capture the imprecise and statistical nature of multimedia data are many times fuzzy and probabilistic in nature. Probabilistic models (Section 3.5) rely on the premise that the sources of imprecision in data and query processing are inherently statistical and thus they commit onto probabilistic evaluation. Fuzzy models (Section 3.4) are more flexible and allow different semantics, each applicable under different system requirements, to be selected for query evaluation.

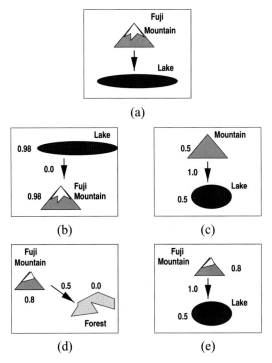

Figure 1.7. Four partial matches to a given query: (a) Query, (b) Match #1, (c) Match #2, (d) Match #3, (e) Match #4.

Therefore multimedia data query evaluation commonly requires fuzzy and probabilistic data and query models as well as appropriate query processing mechanisms. In general, we can classify multimedia queries into two classes based on the filtering criterion imposed on the results by the user based on the matching scores:

- *Range queries:* Given a distance or a similarity measure, the goal of a range query is to find matches in the database that are within the threshold associated with the query. Thus, these are also known as similarity/distance threshold queries. The query processing techniques for range queries vary based on the underlying data model and available index structures, and on whether the queries are by example or by description. The goal of any query processing technique, however, is to prune the set of candidates in such a way that not all media data in the database have to be considered to identify those that are within the given range from the query point.

    In the case of *query by profile/feedback*, the query, query range, and appropriate distance measure, as well as the relevant features (or the dimensions of the space), can all be set and revised transparently by the system based on user feedback as well as based on feedback that is provided by the users who are identified as being similar to the user.

- *Nearest neighbor queries:* Unlike range queries, where there is a threshold on the acceptable degree of matching, in nearest neighbor queries there is a threshold on the number of results to be returned by the system. Thus, these are also known as top-*k* queries (where *k* is the number of objects the user is interested in). Because the distance between the query and the matching media data is not known in advance, pruning the database content so that not all data objects are considered as candidates requires techniques different from range queries (Chapter 10).

As in the case of range queries, in *query by profile/feedback*, the query, the distance measure, and the set of relevant features can be set by the system based on user feedback. In addition, the number of matches that the user is interested in can be varied based on the available profile.

These query paradigms require appropriate data structures and algorithms to support them effectively and efficiently. Conventional database management systems are not able to deal with imprecision and similarity because they are based on Boolean logic: predicates used for formulating query conditions are treated as propositional functions, which return either true or false. A naive way to process multimedia queries is to transform imprecision into true or false by mapping values less than a cutoff to false and the remainder to true. With this naive approach, partial results can be quickly refuted or validated based on their relationships to the cutoff. Chaudhuri *et al.* [2004], for example, leverage user-provided cutoffs for filtering, while maintaining the imprecision value for further processing. In general, however, cutoff-based early pruning leads to misses of relevant results. This leads to data models and query evaluation mechanisms that can take into account imprecision in the evaluation of the query criteria. In particular, the data and query models cannot be propositional in nature, and the query processing algorithms cannot rely on the assumption that the data and queries are Boolean.

1.3 COMPONENTS OF A MULTIMEDIA DATABASE MANAGEMENT SYSTEM

As described previously, multimedia systems generally employ content-based retrieval techniques to retrieve images, video, and other more complex media objects. A complex media object might itself be a collection of smaller media objects, interlinked with each other through temporal, spatial, hierarchical, and user interaction structures. To manage such complex *multimedia* data, the system needs specialized index structures and query processing techniques that can scale to structural complexities. Consequently, indexing and query processing techniques developed for traditional applications, such as business applications, are not suitable for efficient and effective execution of queries on multimedia data.

A multimedia data management system, supporting the needs of such diverse applications, must provide support for specification, processing, and refinement of object queries and retrieval of media objects and documents. The system must allow users to specify the criteria for objects and documents to be retrieved. Both media object and multimedia document retrieval tasks must be similarity-based. Furthermore, while searching for a multimedia object, the structure as well as various visual, semantic, and cognitive features (all represented in different forms) have to be considered together.

Example 1.3.1: Let us reconsider the Extensible 3D (or X3D) language for describing virtual worlds [X3D]. Figure 1.8 offers an overview of some of the functionalities

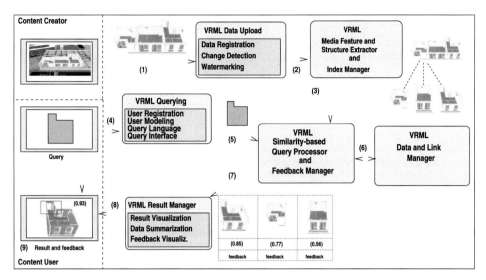

Figure 1.8. Components of a VRML/X3D database.

a VRML/X3D data management system would need to provide to its users [Yamuna *et al.*, 1999]. The first of these functionalities is data registration (1). During registration, if the input object is a newer version of an object already in the repository, then the system identifies possible changes in the object content, eliminates duplicates, and reflects the changes in the repository. Next (2), the system extracts features (salient visual properties of the object) and structure information from the object and (3) updates the corresponding index and data structures to support *content-based retrieval*. Users access the system through a visual query interface (4). Preferences of the users are gathered and stored for more accurate and personalized answers. Queries provided using the visual interface are interpreted (subcomponents are weighed depending on the user preferences and/or database statistics) and evaluated (5) by a similarity-based query processor using (6) various index and data structures stored in the system. The matches found are ranked based on their degrees of similarity to the query and passed to the results manager along with any system feedback that can help the user refine her original query (7). The results are then presented to the user in the most appropriate form (8). The visualization system, then, collects the user's relevance feedback to improve results through a second, more informed, iteration of the retrieval process (9).

We next provide an overview of the components of a multimedia data management system. Although this overview is not exhaustive, it highlights the major differences between the components of a conventional DBMS and the components of a multimedia data management system:

■ *Storage, analysis, and indexing:* The storage manager of a multimedia data management system needs to account for the special storage requirements of different types of media objects. This component uses the characteristics of the media objects and media documents to identify the most effective storage and indexing plan for different types of media. A *media characteristics* manager keeps

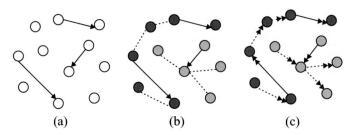

(a)   (b)   (c)

Figure 1.9. (a) A set of media objects and references between them, (b) logical links between them are established, and (c) a navigation network has been created based on information flow analysis.

metadata related with the known media types, including significant features, spatial and temporal characteristics, synchronization/resource/QoS requirements, and compression characteristics.

Given a media object, a *feature/structure extractor* identifies which features are most significant and extracts them. The relative importance of these features will be used during query processing. If the media object being processed is complex, then its temporal, spatial, and interaction structures also have to be extracted for indexing purposes. Not only does this enable users to pose structure-related queries, but many essential data management functionalities, such as object prefetching for interactive document visualization, result summarization/visualization, and query processing for document retrieval, depend on the (1) efficiency in representing structural information, (2) speed in comparing two documents using their structures, and (3) capability of providing a meaningful similarity value as a result of the comparison.

For large media objects, such as large text documents, videos, or a set of hyperlinked pages, a *summarization* manager may help create compact representations that are easier to compare, visualize, and navigate through. A multimedia database management system may also employ mechanisms that can *segment* large media content into smaller units to facilitate indexing, retrieval, ranking, and presentation. To ensure that each information unit properly reflects the context from which it was extracted, these segmented information units can be further *enriched* by propagating features between related information units and by *annotations* that tag the units based on a semantic analysis of their content [Candan *et al.*, 2009]. Conversely, to support navigation within a large collection of media objects, a *relationship extractor* may use association mining techniques to find linkages between individual media objects, based on their logical relationships, to create a navigable media information space (Figure 1.9).

Multimedia objects and their extracted information units need to be indexed for quick reference based on their features and structures. An *index/cluster/classification manager* chooses the most appropriate indexing mechanism for the given media object. Because searching the entire database for a given query is not always acceptable, indexing and clustering schemes reduce the search space by quickly eliminating from consideration irrelevant parts of

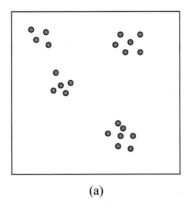 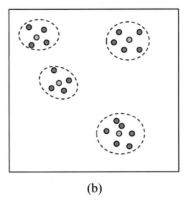

(a)   (b)

Figure 1.10. (a) A set of media objects in a database (each point represents an object (closer points correspond to media objects that are similar to each other). (b) Similar objects are clustered together, and for each cluster a representative (lightly shaded point) is selected: given a query, for each cluster of points, first its representative is considered to identify and eliminate unpromising clusters of points.

the database based on the order and structure implicit in the data (Figure 1.10). Each media object is clustered with similar objects to support pruning during query processing as well as effective visualization and summarization. This module may also classify the media objects under known semantic classes for better organization, annotation, and browsing support for the data.

A semantic network of media, wherein media objects and their information units are semantically tagged and relationships between them are extracted and annotated, would benefit significantly from additional domain knowledge that can help interpret these semantic annotations. Thus, a *semantics manager* might help manage the ontologies and taxonomies associated with the media collections, integrate such metadata when media objects from different collections are brought together, and use such metadata to help semantically driven query processing and navigation support.

■ *Query and visualization specifications:* A multimedia database management system needs to allow users to pose queries for multimedia objects and documents. A *query specification* module helps the user pose queries using query-by-example or query-by-description mechanisms. Because of the visual characteristics of the results, query specifications may also be accompanied with visualization specifications that describe how the results will be presented to the user.

■ *Navigation support and personalized and contextualized recommendations:* A *navigation manager* helps the user browse through and navigate within the rich information space formed by the multimedia objects and documents in the multimedia database. The main goal of any mechanism that helps users navigate in a complex information space is to reduce the amount of interaction needed for locating a relevant piece of information. In order to provide proper navigational support to users, a guidance system must identify, as precisely as possible, what alternatives to provide to the user based on the user's current navigational context (Figure 1.11). Furthermore, when this context changes, the system

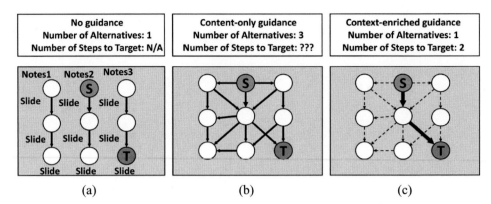

Figure 1.11. Context- and task-assisted guidance from the content user is currently accessing (S) to the content user wishes to access (T): (a) No guidance, (b) Content-only guidance, (c) Context-enriched guidance.

should adapt to this change by identifying the most suitable content that has to be brought closer to the user in the new navigational context. Therefore, the logical distance between where the user is in the information space and where the user wishes to navigate to needs to be dynamically adjusted in real time as the navigation alternatives are rediscovered based on user's context (see Figure 1.11). Such dynamic adaptation of the information space requires an indexing system that can leverage context (sometimes provided by the user through explicit interventions, such as typing in a new query), as well as the logical and structural relationships between various media objects. An effective recommendation mechanism determines what the user needs precisely so that the guidance that the system provides does not lead to unnecessary user interaction.

■ *Query evaluator:* Multimedia queries have different characteristics than the queries in traditional databases. One major difference is the similarity- (or quality-) based query processing requirement: finding exact matches is either undesirable or impossible because of imperfections in the media processing functions. Another difference is that some of the user-defined predicates, such as the media processing functions, may be very costly to execute in terms of the time and system resources they require.

A multimedia data management system uses a *cost- and quality-based query optimizer* and provides query evaluation facilities to achieve the best results at the lowest cost. The traditional approach to query optimization is to use database statistics to estimate the query execution cost for different execution plans and to choose the cheapest plan found. In the case of a database for media objects and documents, the expected quality of the results is also important. Since different query execution plans may cause results with different qualities, the quality statistics must also be taken into consideration. For instance, consider a multimedia predicate of the form image_contains_object_at(Image, Object, Coord), which verifies the containment relationship between an image, an object, and image coordinates. This predicate may have different execution patterns, each corresponding to a different external function, with drastically different *result qualities*[1]:

- image_contains_object_at(Image I, Object *O, Coord C) is likely to have high quality as it needs only to search for an object at the given coordinates of a given image.
- image_contains_object_at(Image I, Object O, Coord *C), on the other hand, is likely to have a lower quality as it may need to perform non-exact matches between the given object and the objects contained within the given image to find the coordinates of the best match.

In addition, query optimizers must take into account expensive user-defined predicates. Different execution patterns of a given predicate may also have different execution costs.

- image_contains_object_at(Image *I, Object O, Coord *C) may be very expensive, as it may require a pass over all images in the database to check whether any of them contains the given object.
- image_contains_object_at(Image I, Object *O, Coord C) may be significantly cheaper, as it only needs to extract an object at the given coordinates of the given image.

The query evaluator of a multimedia data management system needs to create a cost- and quality-optimized query plan and the index and access structures maintained by the index/cluster manager to process the query and retrieve results. Because media queries are often subjective, the order of the results needs to reflect user preferences and user profiles. A *result rank manager* ensures that the results of multimedia queries are ordered accordingly. Because a combination of search criteria can be specified simultaneously, the matching scores results with respect to each criterion must be merged to create the final ranking.

■ *Relevance feedback and user profile:* As discussed earlier, in multimedia databases, we face an objective-subjective interpretation gap (Li *et al.*, 2001; Yu *et al.*, 1976):

- Given a query (say an image example provided for a "similarity" search in a large image database), which features of the image objects are relevant (and how much so) to the user's query may not be known in advance.
- Furthermore, most of the (large number of) candidate matches may be only marginally relevant to the user's query and must be eliminated from consideration for efficiency and effectiveness of the retrieval.

These challenges are usually dealt with through a *user relevance feedback process* that enables the user to explore the alternatives and that learns what is relevant to the user through the user feedback provided during this exploration process (see Figure 1.5): (1) Given a query, using the available index structures, the system (2) identifies an initial set of candidate results; since the number of candidates can be large, the system presents a small number of samples to the user. (3) This initial set of samples and (4) the user's relevance/irrelevance inputs are used for (5) learning the user's interests (in terms of relevant features), and this information is provided as an input to the next cycle for (6) having the retrieval algorithm suitably update the query or the retrieval/ranking scheme.

---

[1] Arguments marked with "*" are output arguments; those that are not marked are input arguments.

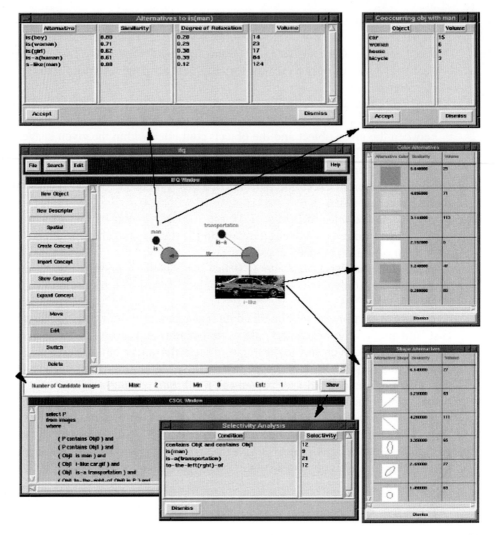

Figure 1.12. The system feedback feature of the SEMCOG multimedia retrieval system [Li and Candan, 1999a]: given a user query, SEMCOG can tell the user how the data in the database are distributed with respect to various query conditions. See color plates section.

Steps 2–6 are then repeated until the user is satisfied with the results returned by the system.

Note that although the relevance feedback process can be leveraged on a per-query basis, it can also be used for creating and updating a long-term interest profile of the user.

■ *System support for query refinement:* To eliminate unnecessary database accesses and to guide the user in the search for a particular piece of information, a multimedia database may provide support for *query verification, system feedback,* and *query refinement* services.

Based on the available data and query statistics, a *query verification and refinement manager* would provide users with system feedback, including an estimated number of matching images, strictness of each query condition, and alternative

query conditions (Figure 1.12). Given such information, users can relax or refor-
mulate their queries in a more informed manner. For a keyword-based query, for
instance, its hypernyms, synonyms, and homonyms can be candidates for replacement, each with different penalties depending on the user's preference. The system must maintain aggregate values for terms to calculate expected result sizes and
qualities without actually executing queries. For the reformulation of predicates
(for instance, replacing color_histogram_match(Image1, Image2) with the predicate
shape_histogram_match(Image1, Image2)), on the other hand, the system needs to
consider correlations between candidate predicates as well as the expected query
execution costs and result qualities.

1.4 SUMMARY

In this chapter, we have seen that the requirements of a multimedia database management system are fundamentally different from those of a traditional database
management system. The major challenges in the design of a multimedia database
management system stem from the heterogeneity of the data and the semantic gap
between the raw data and the user. Consequently, the data and querying models as
well as the components of a multimedia database management system need to reflect the diversity of the media data and the applications and help fill the semantic
gap. In the next chapter, we consider the data and query models for multimedia data,
before discussing the multimedia database components in greater detail throughout
the remaining chapters of the book.

2

Models for Multimedia Data

A *database* is a collection of data objects that are *organized* in a way that supports *effective* search and manipulation. Under this definition, your personal collection of digital photos can be considered a database (more specifically an image database) if you feel that the software you are using to organize your images provides you with mechanisms that help you locate the images you are looking for easily and effectively.

Effective access, of course, depends on the data and the application. For example, in general, you may be satisfied if the images in your collection are organized in terms of a timeline or put into folders according to where they were taken, but for an advertising agency which is looking for an image that conveys a certain feeling or for a medical research center which is trying to locate images that contain a particular pattern, such a *metadata-based* organization (i.e., an organization not based on the content of the image, but on aspects of the media object external to the visual content) may not be acceptable. Thus, when creating a database, it is important to choose the right organization model.

A *data model* is a formalism that helps specify the aspects of the data relevant for their organization. For example, a *content-based model* would describe what type of content (e.g., colors or shape) is relevant for the organization of the data in the database, whereas a *metadata-based model* may help specify the metadata (e.g., date or place) relevant for the organization. A model can also help specify which objects can be placed into the database and which ones cannot. For example, an image data model can specify that video objects cannot be placed in the database, or another data model can specify that all the images in the collection need to be grayscale. The constraints specified using the model and its idea for organizing the data are commonly referred to as the *schema* of the database. Intuitively, the data model is a formalism or a language in which the schema constraints can be specified. In other words, *a database is a collection of data objects satisfying the schema constraints specified using the formalism provided by the underlying data model and organized based on these constraints.*

2.1 OVERVIEW OF TRADITIONAL DATA MODELS

A media object can be treated at multiple levels of abstraction. For example, an image you took last summer with your digital camera can be treated at a high level for what it represents for you (e.g., "a picture at the beach with your family"), at a slightly lower level for what it contains visually (e.g., "a lot of blues and some skin-toned circles"), at a lower level as a matrix of pixels, or at an even lower level as a sequence of bits (which can be interpreted as an image if one knows the corresponding image format and the rules that image format relies on). Note that some of the foregoing *image models* are closer to the higher, semantic (or conceptual) representation of the media, whereas others are closer to the physical representation. In fact, for any media, one can consider a spectrum of models, from a purely conceptual to a purely physical representation.

2.1.1 Conceptual, Logical, and Physical Data Models

In general, a *conceptual model* represents the application-level semantics of the objects in the database. This model can be specified using natural language or using less ambiguous formalisms, such as the unified modeling language (UML [UML]), or the resource description framework (RDF [Lassila and Swick, 1999]). A *physical model*, on the other hand, describes how the data are laid down on the disk. A *logical model*, or the model used by the database management server (DBMS) to organize the data to help search, can be close to the conceptual model or to the physical model depending on how the organization will be used: whether the organization is to help end users locate data effectively or whether the organization is to help optimize the resource usage. In fact, a DBMS can rely on multiple logical models at different granularities for different purposes.

2.1.2 Relational Model

The *relational* data model [Codd, 1970] describes the constraints underlying the database in terms of a set of first-order predicates, defined over a finite set of predicate variables. Each relation corresponds to an n-ary predicate over n attributes, where each attribute is a pair of name and domain type (such as integer or string). The content of the relation is a subset of the Cartesian product of the corresponding n value domains, such that the predicate returns *true* for each and every n-tuple in the set. The *closed-world* assumption implies that there are no other n-tuples for which the predicate is true. Each n-tuple can be thought of as an unordered set of attribute name/value pairs. Because the content of each relation is finite, as shown in Figure 2.1, an alternative visualization of the relation is as a table where each column corresponds to an attribute and each row is an n-tuple (or simply "*tuple*" for short).

Schema and Constraints
The predicate name and the set of attribute names and types are collectively referred to as the schema for the relation (see Figure 2.1). In addition, the schema may

SSN	Name	Job

SSN	GPA

Figure 2.1. A simple relational database with two relations: *Employee* (*ssn, name, job*) and *Student* (*ssn*, gpa) (the underlined attributes uniquely identify each tuple/row in the corresponding table).

contain additional constraints, such as *candidate key* and *foreign key* constraints, as well as other integrity constraints described in other logic-based languages.

A candidate key is a subset of the set of attributes of the relation such that there are no two distinct tuples with the same values for this set of attributes and there is not a proper subset of this set that is also a candidate key. Because they take unique values in the entire relation, candidate keys (or keys for short) help refer to individual tuples in the relation. A foreign key, on the other hand, is a set of attributes that refers to a candidate key in another (or the same) relation, thus linking the two relations. Foreign keys help ensure referential integrity of the database relations; for example, deleting a tuple referred to by a foreign key would violate referential integrity and thus is not allowed by the DBMS.

The body of the relation (i.e., the set of tuples) is commonly referred to as the extension of the relation. The extension at any given point in time is called a state of the database, and this state (i.e., the extension) changes by update operations that insert or delete tuples or change existing attribute values. Whereas most schema and integrity constraints specify when a given state can be considered to be consistent or inconsistent, some constraints specify whether or not a state change (such as the amount of increase in the value a tuple has for a given value) is acceptable.

Queries, Relational Calculus, and SQL

In the relational model, queries are also specified declaratively, as is the case with the constraints on the data. The *tuple relational* and *domain relational calculi* are the main declarative languages for the relational model. A domain relational calculus query is of the form

$$\langle\langle X_1, \ldots, X_m \rangle \mid f_{domain}(X_1, \ldots, X_m)\rangle,$$

where X_i are domain variables or constants and $f_{domain}(X_1, \ldots, X_m)$ is a logic formula specified using atoms of the form

- $(S \in R)$, where $S \subseteq \{X_1, \ldots, X_m\}$ and R is a relation name, and
- $(X_i \ op \ X_j)$ or $(X_i \ op \ constant)$; here, op is a comparison operator, such as $=$ or $<$,

and using operators $\wedge$, $\vee$, and $\neg$ as well as the existential ($\exists$) and universal ($\forall$) quantifiers. For example, let us consider a relational database with two relations,

Employee(*ssn*, *name*, *job*) and *Student*(*ssn*, *gpa*), as in Figure 2.1. The first of these relations, *Employee*, has three attributes, and one of these attributes (*ssn*, which is underlined) is identified as the key of the relation. The second relation, *Student*, has two attributes, and one of these (*ssn*, which is underlined) is identified as the key. The domain calculus formula

$$\{\langle name \rangle \mid (salary \in Employee) \wedge (name \in Employee) \wedge$$
$$(ssn \in Employee) \wedge (salary < 1000) \wedge$$
$$(gpa \in Student) \wedge (gpa > 3.7) \wedge (ssn \in Student))\}$$

corresponds to the query "find all student employees whose GPAs are greater than 3.7 and salaries are less than 1000 and return their names."

A tuple relational calculus query, on the other hand, is of the form $\langle t \mid f_{tuple}(t) \rangle$, where t is a tuple variable and $f_{tuple}(t)$ is a logic formula specified using the same logic operators as the domain calculus formulas and atoms of the form

- $R(v)$, which returns true if the value of the tuple variable v is in relation R, and
- $(v.a \ op \ u.b)$ or $(v.a \ op \ constant)$, where v and u are two tuple variables, a and b are two attribute names, and op is a comparison operator, such as $=$ or $<$.

The two relational calculi are equivalent to each other in their expressive power; that is, one can formulate the same query in both languages. For example,

$$\{t.name \mid \exists_t \exists_{t_2} \ Employee(t) \wedge (t.salary < 1000) \wedge$$
$$Student(t_2) \wedge (t_2.gpa > 3.7) \wedge (t.ssn = t_2.ssn)\}$$

is a tuple calculus formulation of the preceding query.

The subset of these languages that returns finite number of tuples is referred to as the *safe relational calculus* and, because infinite results to a given query are not desirable, DBMSs use languages that are equivalent to this subset. The most commonly used relational ad hoc query language, SQL [SQL-99, SQL-08], is largely based on the tuple relational calculus. SQL queries have the following general structure:

```
select <attribute_list>
from <relation_list>
where <condition>
```

For instance, the foregoing query can be formulated in SQL as follows:

```
select t.name
from employee t, student t2
where (t.salary < 1000) and
      (t2.gpa > 3.7) and
      (t.ssn = t2.ssn)
```

Note the similarity between this SQL query and the corresponding tuple calculus statement.

Relational Algebra for Query Processing

Whereas the relational calculus gives rise to declarative query languages, an equivalent algebraic language, called relational algebra, gives procedural (or executional) semantics to the queries written declaratively. The relational algebra formulas are specified by combining relations using the following relational operators:

- selection (σ): Given a selection condition, Θ, the unary operator $\sigma_\Theta(R)$ selects and returns all tuples in R that satisfy the condition Θ.
- projection (π): Given a set, A, of attributes, the unary operator $\pi_A(R)$ returns a set of tuples, where each tuple corresponds to a tuple in R constrained to the attributes in the set A.
- Cartesian product ($\times$): Given two relations R_1 and R_2, the binary operator $R_1 \times R_2$ returns the set of tuples

$$\{t, u | t \in R_1 \land u \in R_2\}.$$

In other words, tuples from R_1 and R_2 are pairwise combined.
- set union ($\cup$): Given two relations R_1 and R_2 with the same set of attributes, $R_1 \cup R_2$ returns the set of tuples

$$\{t \mid t \in R_1 \lor t \in R_2\}.$$

- set difference ($\setminus$): Given two relations R_1 and R_2 with the same set of attributes, $R_1 \setminus R_2$ returns the set of tuples

$$\{t \mid t \in R_1 \land t \notin R_2\}.$$

This set of primitive relational operations is sometimes expanded with others, including

- rename (ρ): Given two attribute names a_1 and a_2, the unary operator $\rho_{a_1/a_2}(R)$ renames the attribute a_1 of relation R as a_2.
- aggregation operation (Γ): Given a condition expression, θ, a function f (such as count, sum, average, and maximum), and a set, A, of attributes, the unary operator $_\theta\Gamma_{f,A}(R)$ returns

$$f(\{t[A] | t \in R \land \theta(t)\}).$$

- join ($\bowtie$): Given a condition expression, θ, $R_1 \bowtie_\theta R_2$ is equivalent to $\sigma_\theta(R_1 \times R_2)$.

The output of each relational algebra statement is a new relation.

Query execution in relational databases is performed by taking a user's ad hoc query, specified declaratively in a language (such as SQL) based on relational calculus, and translating it into an equivalent relational algebra statement, which essentially provides a query execution plan. Because, in general, a given declarative query can be translated into an algebraic form in many different (but equivalent) ways, a relational query optimizer is used to select a query plan with small query execution cost. For example, the preceding query can be formulated in relational algebra either as

$$\pi_{name}(\sigma_{gpa>3.7}(\sigma_{sal<1000}(Employee \bowtie_{Employee.ssn=Students.ssn} Students)))$$

or, equivalently, as

$$\pi_{name}((\sigma_{gpa>3.7}(Students)) \bowtie_{Students.ssn=Employee.ssn} (\sigma_{sal<1000}(Employee))).$$

It is the responsibility of the query optimizer to pick the appropriate query execution plan.

Summary

Today, relational databases enjoy significant dominance in the DBMS market due to their suitability to many application domains (such as banking), clean and well-understood theory, declarative language support, algebraic formulation that enables query execution, and simplicity (of the language as well as the data structures) that enables effective (though not always efficient) query optimization.

The relational model is close to being a physical model: the tabular form of the relations commonly dictates how the relations are stored on the disk, that is, one row at a time, though other storage schemes are also possible. For example, column-oriented storage [Daniel J. Abadi, 2008; Stonebraker *et al.*, 2005] may be more desirable in data analysis applications where people commonly fetch entire columns of large relations.

2.1.3 Object-Oriented and Object-Relational Models

As we mentioned previously, a major advantage of the relational model is its theoretical simplicity. Although this simplicity helps the database management system optimize the services it delivers and makes the DBMS relatively easy to learn and use, on the negative side, it may also prevent application developers from capturing the full complexities of the real-world applications they develop. In fact, relational databases are not computationally complete: although one can store, retrieve, and perform a very strictly defined set of computations, for anything complex (such as analyzing an image) there is a need for a host language with higher expressive power. Object-oriented data models, on the other hand, aim to be rich enough in their expressive power to capture the needs of complex applications more easily.

Objects, Entities, and Encapsulation

Object-oriented models [Atkinson *et al.*, 1989; Maier, 1991], such as ER [Chen, 1976], Extended ER [Gogolla and Hohenstein, 1991], ODMG [ODMG], and UML [UML], model real-world entities, their methods/behaviors, and their relationships explicitly, not through tables and foreign keys. In other words, OODBs map real world entities/objects to data structures (and associate unique identifiers to each one of them[1]), their behaviors to functions, and relationships to object references between separate entities (Figure 2.2). Each object has a state (the value of the attributes); each object also has a set of (methods/interfaces) pairs to modify or manipulate the state. Consequently, object-oriented databases provide higher computational power: the users can implement any function and embed it into the

---

[1] Whereas the keys of a relation uniquely identify rows only in the corresponding relation, the unique object identifiers identify the objects in the entire database.

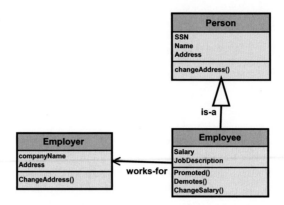

Figure 2.2. A simple object-oriented data schema created using the UML syntax. Rectangles denote the entities, and each entity has a set of attributes and functions (or behaviors) that alter the values of these attributes. The edges between the entities denote relationships between them (the IS-A relationship is a special one in that it allows *inheritance* of attribute and functions: in this example, the *employee* entity would inherit the attributes and functions of the *person* entity).

database as a behavior of an entity. These functions can then be used in queries. For example,

```
SELECT y.author
FROM Novel y
WHERE y.isabout("war").
```

is a query posed in an object-oriented query language, OQL [Cattell and Barry, 2000]. In this example, *isabout()* is a user-defined function associated with objects of type *Novel*. Given a topical keyword, it checks whether the novel is about that topic or not, using content analysis techniques.

Object-oriented models also provide ways to describe complex objects and abstract data types. Each object, except for the simplest ones, has a set of attributes and (unlike relational databases where attributes can only contain values) each attribute can contain another object, a reference to an object, or a set of other objects. Consequently, object-oriented models enable creation of *aggregation hierarchies* where complex objects are built by aggregating simpler objects (Figure 2.3(a)). Objects that share the same set of attributes and methods are grouped together in classes. Although each object belongs to some class, objects can migrate from one class to another. Also, because each object has a unique ID, references between objects can be implemented through explicit pointers instead of foreign keys. This means that the user can navigate from one object to another, without having to write queries that, when translated into relational algebra, need entire relations to be put together using costly join operators.

Object-oriented data models also provide *inheritance hierarchies*, where one type is a superclass or supertype of the other and where the attributes and methods (or behaviors) of a superclass can be inherited by a subclass (Figure 2.3(b)).

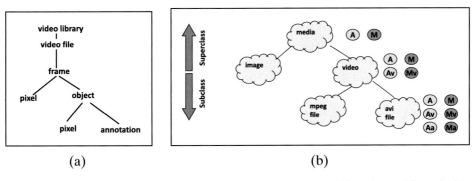

(a)   (b)

Figure 2.3. (a) A multimedia aggregation hierarchy and (b) a sample inheritance hierarchy (*A*s stand for the attributes and *M*s stand for the methods or functions).

This helps application developers define new object types by using existing ones. Figure 2.4 shows an example extended entity-relationship (EER) schema for a X3D/VRLM database. The schema describes the relevant objects, attributes, and relationships, as well as the underlying inheritance hierarchy.

Object-Relational Databases

Object-oriented data models are much higher level than relational models in their expressive power; thus they can be considered almost as conceptual models. This means that application developers can properly express the data needs of their

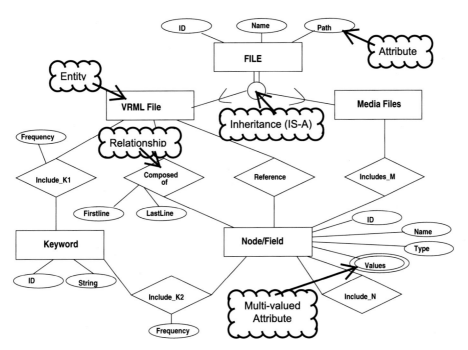

Figure 2.4. A sample extended entity-relationship (EER) schema for a X3D/VRLM database. This schema describes the relevant entities (i.e., objects), their attributes, relationships, and inheritance hierarchies.

applications. Unfortunately, this also means that (because object-oriented models are further away from physical models) they are relatively hard to optimize and, for many users, harder to master.

Object-relational databases [Stonebraker *et al.*, 1990] (also referred to as extended-relational databases) aim to provide the best of both worlds, by either extending relational models with object-oriented features or introducing special row (tuple) and table based data types into object-oriented databases. For example, the SQL3 standard [SQL3, a,b] extends standard SQL with object-oriented features, including user-defined complex, abstract data types, reference types, collection types (sets, lists, and multisets) for creating complex objects, user-defined methods and functions, and support for large objects.

2.1.4 Semi-Structured Models

Semi-structured data models, which were popularized by OEM [Papakonstantinou *et al.*, 1995] and which gained wider audience by the introduction of XML [XML], aim to provide greater flexibility in the structure of the data. A particular challenge posed by the relational and object-oriented (as well as object-relational) models is that, once the schema is fixed, objects that do not satisfy the schema are not allowed in the database. Although this ensures greater consistency and provides opportunities for more optimal usage of the system resources, imposing the requirement that all data need to have a schema has certain shortcomings. First of all, we might not know the schema of the objects in the database in advance. Second, even if the schemas of the objects are known in advance, the structures of different objects may be different from each other. For example, some objects may have missing attributes (a book without any figures, for example), or attributes may repeat an unspecified number of times (e.g., one book with ten figures versus another with fifty).

Semi-structured data models try to address these challenges by (a) providing a flexible modeling language (which easily handles missing attributes and attributes that repeat an arbitrary number of times, as well as disjunction (i.e., alternatives) in the data schema) and by (b) eliminating the requirement that the objects in the database will all follow a given schema. That is why semi-structured data models are sometimes referred to as *schemaless* or *self-describing* data models, as well.

Extensible Markup Language (XML) is a data exchange standard [XML] especially suitable for creating interchangeable, structured Web documents. In XML, the document structure is defined using BNF-like document type definitions (DTDs) that can be very flexible in terms of the structures that are allowable. For example, the following XML DTD

```
<!ELEMENT article title, (section+)>
<!ATTLIST article venue CDATA #REQUIRED>
<!ELEMENT section (title,(subsection| CDATA )+)>
<!ELEMENT subsection (title,(subsubsection| CDATA )+)>
<!ELEMENT subsubsection (title, CDATA)>
<!ELEMENT title CDATA>
```

states that

- an article consists of a title and *one or more* sections;
- all articles have a corresponding publication venue (or character sequence, i.e., CDATA);
- each section consists of a title and one or more subsections or character sequences;
- each subsection consists of a title and one or more subsubsections or character sequences;
- each subsubsection consists of a title and character sequence; and
- title is a character sequence.

Furthermore, the XML standard does not require XML documents to have DTDs; instead each XML document describes itself using tags. For example, the following is an XML document:

```
<book>
  <authors>
     <author>K. Selcuk Candan</author>
     <author>Maria Luisa Sapino</author>
  </authors>
  <title>
  Multimedia Data Management Systems
  </title>
...
</book>
```

Note that even though we did not provide a DTD, the structure of the document is self-evident because of the use of open and close tags (such as ⟨author⟩ and ⟨/author⟩, respectively) and the hierarchically nested nature of the elements. This makes the XML standard a suitable platform for semi-structured data description.

OEM is very similar to XML in that it also organizes self-describing objects in the form of a hierarchical structure. Note that, although both OEM and XML allow references between any elements, the nested structure of the objects makes them especially suitable for describing tree-structured data.

Because in semi-structured data models the structure is not precise and is not necessarily given in advance,

- users may want to ask queries about the structure;
- the system may need to evaluate queries without having precise knowledge of the structure;
- the system may need to evaluate queries without having any prior knowledge of the structure; and
- the system may need to answer queries based on approximate structural matching.

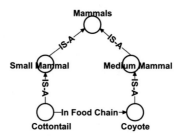

Figure 2.5. A basic relationship graph fragment; intuitively, each node in the graph *asserts* the existence of a distinct concept, and each edge is a constraint that *asserts* a relationship (such as IS-A).

These make management of semi-structured data different from managing relational or object-oriented data.

2.1.5 Flexible Models and RDF

All of the preceding data models, including semi-structured models, impose certain structural limitations on what can be specified and what cannot in a particular model. OEM and XML, for example, are better suited for tree-structured data. A most general model would represent a database, D, in the form of (a) a graph, G, capturing the concept/entities and their relationships (Figure 2.5) and (b) associated integrity constraints, IC, that describe criteria for semantic correctness. Resource Description Framework (RDF [Lassila and Swick, 1999]) provides such a general data model where, much as in object-oriented models, entities and their relationships can be described. RDF also has a class system much like many object-oriented programming and modeling systems. A collection of classes is called a schema. Unlike traditional object-oriented data models, however, the relationships in RDF are first class objects, which means that relationships between objects may be arbitrarily created and can be stored separately from the objects. This nature of RDF is very suitable for the dynamically changing, distributed, shared nature of multimedia documents and the Web.

   Although RDF was originally designed to describe Web resources, today it is used for describing all types of data resources. In fact, RDF makes no assumption about a particular application domain, nor does it define the semantics of any particular application domain. The definition of the mechanism is domain neutral, yet the mechanism is suitable for describing information about any domain. An RDF model consists of three major components:

- *Resources:* All things being described by RDF expressions are called resources.
- *Properties:* A property is a specific aspect, characteristic, attribute, or relation used to describe a resource. Each property has a specific meaning and defines its permitted values, the types of resources it can describe, and its relationship with other properties.
- *Statements:* A specific resource together with a property plus the value of that property for that resource is an RDF statement (also called an RDF triple). The three individual parts of a statement are called the subject, predicate, and object of the statement, respectively.

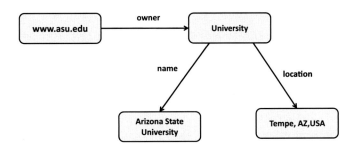

Figure 2.6. A complex RDF statement consisting of three RDF triples.

Let us consider the page http://www.asu.edu (home page of the Arizona State University – ASU) as an example. We can see that this resource can be described using various page-related content-based metadata, such as *title* of the page and keywords in the page, as well as ASU-related semantic metadata, such as the *president of ASU* and its *campuses*. The statement "*the owner of the Web site http://www.asu.edu is Arizona State University*" can be expressed using an RDF, this statement consisting of (1) a resource or subject (http://www.asu.edu), (2) a property name or predicate (owner), and (3) a resource (university_1) corresponding to ASU (which can be further described using appropriate property names and values as shown in Figure 2.6). The RDF model intrinsically supports binary relations (a statement specifies a relation between two Web resources). Higher arity relations have to be represented using multiple binary relations.

Some metadata (such as property names) used to describe resources are generally application dependent, and this can cause difficulties when RDF descriptions need to be shared across application domains. For example, the property *location* can be called in some other application domain an *address*. Although the semantics of both property names are the same, syntactically they are different. On the other extreme, a property name may denote different things in different application domains. In order to prevent such conflicts and ambiguities, the terminology used by each application domain can be identified using namespaces. A namespace can be thought of as a context or a setting that gives a specific meaning to what might otherwise be a general term.

It is frequently necessary to refer to a collection of resources: for example, to the list of courses taught in the Computer Science Department, or to state that a paper is written by several authors. To represent such groups, RDF provides containers to hold lists of resources or literals. RDF defines three types of container objects to facilitate different groupings: a *bag* is an unordered list of resources or literals, a *sequence* is an ordered list of resources or literals, and an *alternative* is a list of resources or literals that represent alternatives for the (single) value of a property.

In addition to making statements about a Web resource, RDF can also be used for making statements about other RDF statements. To achieve this, one has to model the original statement as a resource. In other words, the higher order statements treat RDF statements as uniquely identifiable resources. This process is called reification, and the statement is called a reified statement.

2.2 MULTIMEDIA DATA MODELING

Note that any one or combination of the foregoing models can be used for developing a multimedia database. Naturally, the relational data model is suitable to describe the metadata associated with the media objects. The object-oriented data model is suitable for describing the application semantics of the objects properly. The content of a complex-media object (such as a multimedia presentation) can be considered semi-structured or self-describing as different presentations may be structured differently and, essentially, the relevant structure is prescribed by the author of the presentation in the presentation itself. Lastly, each media object can be interpreted at a semantic level, and this interpretation can be encoded using RDF.

On the other hand, as we will see, despite their diversity and expressive powers, the foregoing models, even when used together, may not be sufficient for describing media objects. Thus, new models, such as fuzzy, probabilistic, vector-based, sequence-based, graph-based, or spatiotemporal models, may be needed to handle them properly.

2.2.1 Features

The set of properties (or *features*) used for describing the media objects in a given database is naturally a function of the media type. Colors, textures, and shapes are commonly used to describe images. Time and motion are used in video databases. Terms (also referred to as keywords) are often used in text retrieval. The features used for representing the objects in a given database are commonly selected based on the following three criteria:

- *Application requirements:* Some image database applications rely on color matching, whereas in some other applications, texture is a better feature to represent the image content.
- *Power of discrimination:* Because the features will be used during query processing to distinguish those objects that are similar to the user's query from those that are different from it, the features that are selected must be able to discriminate the objects in the database.
- *Human perception:* Not all features are perceived equivalently by the user. For example, some colors are perceived more strongly than the others by the human eye [Kaiser and Boynton, 1996]. The human eye is also more sensitive to contrast then colors in the image [Kaiser and Boynton, 1996].

In addition, the *query workload* (i.e., which features seem to be dominant in user queries) and *relevance feedback* (i.e., which features seem to be relevant to a particular user or user groups) need also be considered. We will consider feature selection in Section 4.2 and relevance feedback in Chapter 12.

2.2.2 Distance Measures and Metrics

It is important to note that measures used for comparing media objects are critical for the efficiency and effectiveness of a multimedia retrieval system. In the following chapters, we discuss the similarity/distance measures more extensively and discuss efficient implementation and indexing strategies based on these measures. Although these measures are in many cases application and data model specific, there are certain properties of these measures that transcend the data model and media type. For instance, given two objects, o_1 and o_2, a distance measure, Δ (used for determining how different these two objects are from each other), is called *metric* if it has the following properties:

- Distances are non-negative: $\Delta(o_1, o_2) \geq 0$
- Distance is zero if and only if the two objects are identical: $(\Delta(o_1, o_2) = 0) \leftrightarrow o_1 = o_2$
- Distance function is symmetric: $\Delta(o_1, o_2) = \Delta(o_2, o_1)$
- Distance function satisfies *triangular inequality*: $\Delta(o_1, o_3) \leq \Delta(o_1, o_2) + \Delta(o_2, o_3)$

Although not all measures are metric, metric measures are highly desirable. The first three properties of the metric distances ensure consistency in retrieval. The last property, on the other hand, is commonly exploited to prune the search space to reduce the number of objects to be considered for matching during retrieval (Section 7.2). Therefore, we encourage you to pay close attention to whether the measures we discuss are metrics or not.

2.2.3 Common Representations: Vectors, Strings, Graphs, Fuzzy and Probabilistic Representations

As we discussed in Section 1.1, features of interest of multimedia data can be diverse in nature (from low-level content-based features, such as color, to higher-level semantic features that require external knowledge) and complex in structure. It is, however, important to note that the diversity of features and feature models does not necessarily imply a diversity, equivalent in magnitude, in terms of *feature representations*. In fact, in general, we can classify the representations common to many features into four general classes:

- *Vectors:* Given n independent properties of interest to describe multimedia objects, the vector model associates an n-dimensional vector space, where the ith dimension corresponds to the ith property. Intuitively, the vector describes the composition of a given multimedia data object in terms of its quantifiable properties. Histograms, for example, are good candidates for being represented in the form of vectors. We discuss the vector model in detail in Section 3.1.
- *Strings/Sequences:* Many multimedia data objects, such as text documents, audio files, or DNA sequences, are essentially sequences of symbols from a base alphabet. In fact, as we see in Section 2.3.6.4, strings and sequences can even be used to represent more complex data, such as spatial distribution of features, in a more compact manner. We discuss string/sequence models in Section 3.2.
- *Graphs/Trees:* As we have seen in the introduction section, most complex media objects, especially those that involve spatiotemporal structures, object composition hierarchies, or object references and interaction pathways (such as hyperlinks), can be modeled as trees or graphs. We revisit graph and tree models in Section 3.3.

■ *Fuzzy and probabilistic representations:* Vectors, strings/sequences, and graphs/ trees all assume that the media data have an underlying precise structure that can be used as the common basis of representation. Many times, however, the underlying regularity may be imprecise. In such a case, fuzzy or probabilistic models may be more suitable. We discuss fuzzy models for multimedia in Section 3.4 and probabilistic models in Section 3.5, respectively.

In the rest of this section, we introduce and discuss many commonly used content features, including colors, textures, and shapes, and structural features, such as spatial and temporal models. We revisit the common representations and discuss them in more detail in Chapter 3.

2.3 MODELS OF MEDIA FEATURES

The low-level features of the media are those that can be extracted from the media object itself, without external domain knowledge. In fact, this is not entirely correct. However low level a feature is, it still needs a *model* within which it can be represented, interpreted, and described. This model is critical: because of the finite nature of computational devices, each feature instance is usually allocated a fixed, and usually small, number of bits. This means that there is an upper bound on the number of different feature instances one can represent. Thus, it is important to choose a feature model that can help represent the space of possible (and relevant) feature instances as precisely as possible. Furthermore, a feature model needs to be intuitive (especially if it is used for query specification) and needs to support computation of similarity and/or distance values between different feature instances for similarity-based query processing. Because basic knowledge about commonly used low-level media features can help in understanding the data structures and algorithms that multimedia databases use to leverage them, in this section we provide an overview of the most common low-level features, such as color, texture, and shape. Higher level features, such as spatial and temporal models, are also discussed.

2.3.1 Color Models

A color model is a quantitative representation of the colors that are relevant in an application domain. For the applications that involve human vision, the color model needs to represent the colors that the human eye can perceive.

The human eye, more specifically the retina, relies on so-called *rods* and *cones* to perceive light signals. Rods help with night vision, where the light intensity is very low. They are able to differentiate between fine variations in the intensity of the light (i.e., the gray levels), but cannot help with the perception of color. The cones, on the other hand, come into play when the light intensity is high. The three types of cones, R, G, B, each perceive a different color, red, green, and blue, respectively.[2] Therefore, color perception is achieved by combining the intensities recorded by these three different base colors.

---

[2] The human eye is least sensitive to blue light.

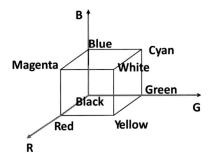

Figure 2.7. The RGB model of color.

RGB Model

Most recording systems (cameras) and display systems (monitors) use a similar additive mechanism for representing color information. In this model, commonly referred to as the RGB model, each color instance is represented as a point in a three-dimensional space, where the dimensions correspond to the possible intensities of the red, blue, and green light channels. As shown in Figure 2.7, the origin corresponds to the lack of any color signal (i.e., black), whereas the diagonal corner of the resulting cube corresponds to the maximum signal levels for all three channels (i.e., white). The diagonal line segment connecting the origin of the RGB color cube to the white corner has different intensities of light with equal contributions from red, green, and blue channels and, thus, corresponds to different shades of gray.

The RGB model is commonly implemented using data structures that allocate the same number of bits to each color channel. For example, a 3-byte representation of color, which can represent 2^{24} different color instances, would allocate 1 byte each to each color channel and thus distinguish 256 (including 0) intensities of pure red, green, and blue. An image would then be represented as a two-dimensional matrix, where each cell in the dimension contains a 24-bit color instance. These cells are commonly referred to as *pixels*. Given this representation, a 1,000 × 1,000 image would require 24 × 1,000 × 1,000 bits or 3 million bytes. When the space available for representing (storing or communicating) images of this size is not as large, the number of bits allocated for each pixel needs to be brought down.

This can be achieved in different ways. One solution is to reduce the precision of the color channels. For example, if we allocate 4 bits per color channel as opposed to 8 bits, this would mean that we can now represent only $2^{3\times4} = 2^{12} = 4,096$ different color instances. Although this might be a sufficient number of distinct colors to *paint* an image, because the color cube is partitioned regularly under the foregoing scheme, this might actually be wasteful. For example, consider an image of the sea taken on a bright day. This picture would be rich in shades of blue, whereas many colors such as red, brown, and orange would not necessarily appear in the image. Thus, a good portion of the 4,096 different colors we have might not be of use, while all the different shades of blue that we would need might be clustered under a single color instance, thus resulting in an overall unpleasant and dull picture.

An alternative scheme to reduce the number of bits needed to represent color instances is to use a *color table*. A color table is essentially a lookup table that maps from a less precise color index to a more precise color instance. Let us assume that we can process all the pixels in an image to identify the best 4,096 distinct 24-bit colors (mostly shades of the blue in the preceding example) needed to paint the picture. We can put these colors into an array (i.e., a lookup table) and, for each pixel in the image, we can record the index of the corresponding color instance in the array (as opposed to the 24-bit representation of the color instance itself). Whenever this picture is to be displayed, the display software (or hardware) can use the lookup table to convert the color indexes to the actual 24-bit RGB color instances. This way, at the expense of an extra $4,096 \times 3 \simeq 12,000$ bytes, we can obtain a detailed and pleasant-looking picture. A commonly used algorithm for color table generation is the *median-cut* algorithm, where the R, G, and B channels of the image are considered in a round-robin fashion and the color table is created in a hierarchical manner:

  (i) First, all the R values in the entire image are sorted, the median value is found, and all color instances[3] with R values smaller than this median are brought together under index "0" and all color instances with R values larger than the median are collected under index "1".
 (ii) Then, the resulting two clusters (indexed "0" and "1") of color instances are considered one at a time and the following is performed for both $X = 0$ and $X = 1$.
   ■ Let the current cluster index be "X". In this step, the median value for the color instances in the given cluster is found, and all color instances with G values smaller than this median are brought together under index "X0" and all color instances with G values larger than the median are collected under index "X1".
(iii) Next, the four resulting clusters (indexed "00", "01", "10", and "11") are considered (and each partitioned into two with respect to B values) one-by-one.
 (iv) The above steps are repeated until the required number of clusters are obtained.

Through the foregoing process, the color indexes are built one bit at a time by splitting the color instances into increasingly finer color clusters. The process is continued until the length of the color index matches the application requirements. For instance, in the previous example, the min-cut partitioning will be repeated to the depth of 12 (i.e., each one of the R, G, B channels contributes to the partitioning decision on four different occasions).

A third possible scheme one can use for reducing the number of bits needed to encode the color instances is to rely on the properties of human perception. As we mentioned earlier, the eye is not as sensitive to all color channels equally. Some colors are more critical in helping differentiate objects than others.[4] Therefore, these colors need to be maintained more precisely (i.e., using a higher number of bits) than the others which may not contribute much to perception. We discuss this next.

---

[3] *Nondistinct:* that is, if the same color instance occurs twice in the image, then the color instance is counted twice.

[4] In fact, in Section 4.2, we discuss the use of this "ease-of-perception" property of the features in indexing.

YRB, YUV, and YIQ Models

It is known that the human eye is more sensitive to contrast than to color. Therefore, a color model that represents grayscale (or luminance) as an explicit component, rather than a combination of RGB, could be more effective in creating reduced representations without negatively affecting perception. The luminance or the amount of light (Y) in a given RGB-based color instance is computed as follows:

$$Y = 0.299R + 0.587G + 0.114B.$$

This reflects the human eye's color and light perception characteristics: the blue color contributes less to the perception of light than red, which itself contributes less than green.

Given the luminance component, Y, and two of the existing RGB channels, say R and B, we can create a new color space YRB that can represent the same colors as the RGB, except that when we need to reduce the size of the bit representation, we can favor cuts in the number of bits of the R and B color components and preserve the Y (luminance) component intact to make sure that the user is able to perceive contrast well.

An alternative representation, YUV, subtracts the luminance component from the color components (and scales the result appropriately):

$$U = 0.492(B - Y)$$
$$V = 0.877(R - Y)$$

This ensures that a completely black-and-white picture has no R and B components that need to be stored or communicated through networks. In contrast, the U and V components reflect the *chrominance* of the corresponding color instance precisely.

Further studies showed that the human eye does not prefer either U (blue minus luminance) or V (red minus luminance) strongly against the other. On the other hand, the eye is shown to be less sensitive to the differences in the purple-green color range as opposed to the differences in the orange-blue color range. Thus, if these purple-green and orange-blue components can be used instead of the UV components, this can give a further opportunity for reducing the bit representation, without much affecting the human perception of the overall color instance. This is achieved simply by rotating the U and V components by 33°:

$$I = -0.492(B - Y)sin33° + 0.877(R - Y)cos33°$$
$$Q = 0.492(B - Y)cos33° + 0.877(R - Y)sin33°$$

In the resulting YIQ model of color, the eye is least sensitive to the Q component and most sensitive to the Y component (Figure 2.8).

CIE, CIELAB, and HSV

The YUV and YIQ models try to leverage the human eye's properties to separate dimensions that contribute most to the color perception from those that contribute less.

The CIELAB model, on the other hand, relies on the characteristics of the human perception to shape the color space. In particular, the CIELAB model relies on Weber's law (also known as the Weber–Fechner law) of perception of stimuli. This

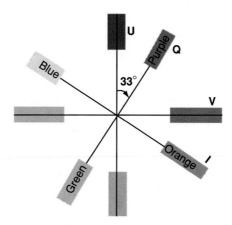

Figure 2.8. The relationship between UV and IQ chrominance components. See color plates section.

law, dating to the middle of the nineteenth century, observes that humans perceive many types of stimuli, such as light and sound, in logarithmic scale. More specifically, the same amount of change in a given stimulus is perceived more strongly if the original value is lower.

The CIELAB model builds upon a color space called CIE, consisting of three components, X, Y, and Z. One advantage of the CIE over RGB is that, as in the YUV and YIQ color models, the Y parameter corresponds to the brightness of a given color instance. Furthermore, the CIE space covers all the chromaticities visible to the human eye, whereas the RGB color space cannot do so. In fact, it has been shown that no three-light source can cover the entire spectrum of chromaticities described by CIE (and perceived by the human eye).

The CIELAB model transforms the X, Y, and Z components of the CIE model into three other components, L, a, and b, in such a way that in the resulting *Lab* color space, any two changes of equal amplitude result in an equal visual impact.[5] In other words, the distance in the space quantifies differences in the perception of chromaticity and luminosity (or brightness); i.e., the Euclidean distance,

$$\sqrt{(L_1 - L_2)^2 + (a_1 - a_2)^2 + (b_1 - b_2)^2},$$

between color instances $\langle L_1, a_1, b_1 \rangle$ and $\langle L_2, a_2, b_2 \rangle$ gives the perceived different between them. Given X, Y, Z components of the CIE model and given the color instance $\langle X_w, Y_w, Z_w \rangle$ corresponding to the human perception of the white color, the L, a, and b, components of the CIELAB color space are computed as follows:

$$L = 116 \, f\left(\frac{Y}{Y_w}\right) - 16$$

$$a = 500 \left[f\left(\frac{X}{X_w}\right) - f\left(\frac{Y}{Y_w}\right) \right]$$

$$b = 200 \left[f\left(\frac{Y}{Y_w}\right) - f\left(\frac{Z}{Z_w}\right) \right],$$

---

[5] There is a variant of this model, where two other components, $a*$ and $b*$, are used instead of a and b. We ignore the distinction and the relevant details.

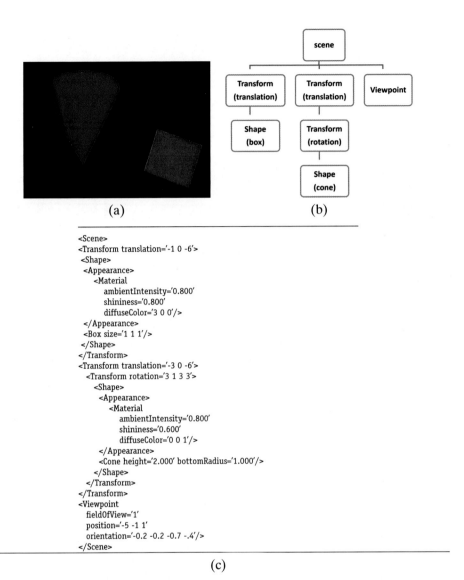

```
<Scene>
<Transform translation='-1 0 -6'>
 <Shape>
  <Appearance>
    <Material
        ambientIntensity='0.800'
        shininess='0.800'
        diffuseColor='3 0 0'/>
  </Appearance>
  <Box size='1 1 1'/>
 </Shape>
</Transform>
<Transform translation='-3 0 -6'>
  <Transform rotation='3 1 3 3'>
    <Shape>
      <Appearance>
        <Material
            ambientIntensity='0.800'
            shininess='0.600'
            diffuseColor='0 0 1'/>
      </Appearance>
      <Cone height='2.000' bottomRadius='1.000'/>
    </Shape>
  </Transform>
</Transform>
<Viewpoint
  fieldOfView='1'
  position='-5 -1 1'
  orientation='-0.2 -0.2 -0.7 -.4'/>
</Scene>
```

(c)

Figure 1.1. An X3D world with two shape objects and the XML-based code for its hierarchical scene graph: (a) X3D world, (b) scene graph, (c) X3D code.

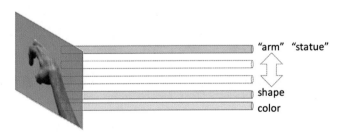

Figure 1.3. Any media object can be seen as a collection of channels of information; some of these information channels (such as color and shape) are low-level (can be derived from the media object), whereas others (such as semantic labels attached to the objects by the viewer) are higher level (cannot be derived from the media object without external knowledge).

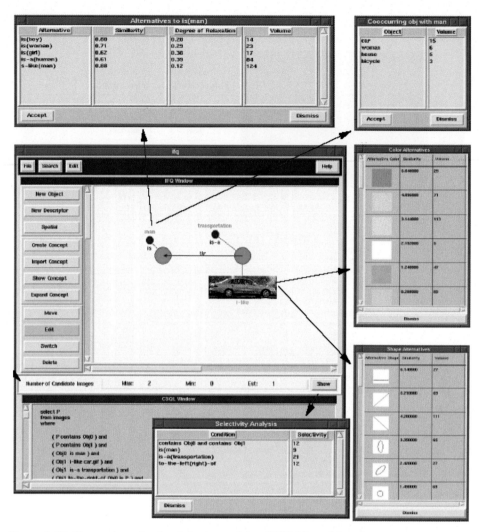

Figure 1.12. The system feedback feature of the SEMCOG multimedia retrieval system [Li and Candan, 1999a]: given a user query, SEMCOG can tell the user how the data in the database are distributed with respect to various query conditions.

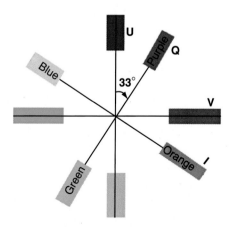

Figure 2.8. The relationship between UV and IQ chrominance components.

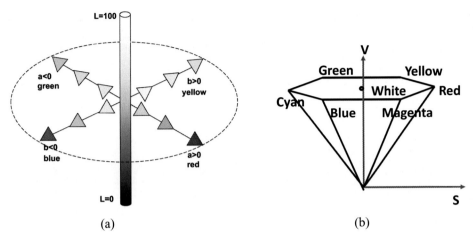

(a)   (b)

Figure 2.9. (a) The CIELAB model of color and (b) the hexconic HSV color model.

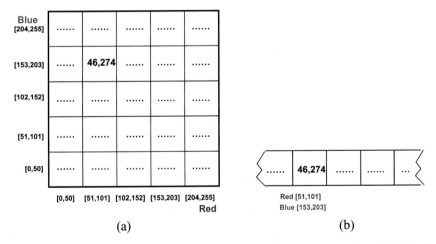

(a)   (b)

Figure 2.10. A color histogram example (only the dimensions corresponding to the "red" and "blue" color dimensions are shown). (a) According to this histogram there are 46,274 pixels in the image that fall in the ranges of [51, 101] in terms of "red" and [153, 203] in terms of "blue" color. (b) In the array or vector representation of this histogram, each position corresponds to a pair of red and blue color ranges.

Figure 2.11. (a) A relatively smooth and directional texture; (b) a coarse and granular texture; (c) an irregular but fractal-like (with elements self-repeating at different scales) texture; (d) a regular, nonsmooth, periodic texture; (e) a regular, repeating texture with directional elements; and (f) a *relatively* smooth and uniform texture.

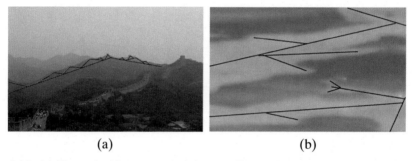

Figure 2.13. (a) Mountain ridges commonly have self-repeating triangular shapes. (b) This is a fragment of the texture in Figure 2.11(c).

Figure 2.16. Sample images with dominant shapes.

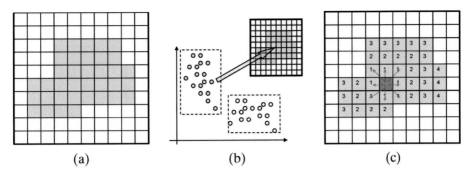

(a)   (b)   (c)

Figure 2.17. (a) An image with a single region. (b) Clustering-based segmentation uses a clustering algorithm that identifies which pixels of the image are similar to each other first, and then finds the boundary on the image between different clusters of pixels. (c) Region growing techniques start from a seed and grow the region until a region boundary with pixels with different characteristics is found (the numbers in the figure correspond to the distance from the seed).

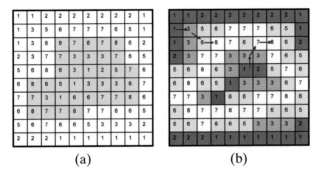

(a)   (b)

Figure 2.18. (a) Gradient values for the example in Figure 2.17 and (b) the topographical surface view (darker pixels correspond to the highest points of the surface and the lightest pixels correspond to the watershed) – the figure also shows the quickest descent (or water drainage) paths for two flood starting points.

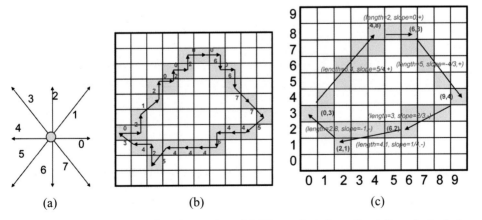

(a)   (b)   (c)

Figure 2.19. (a) The eight direction codes. (b) (If we start from the leftmost pixel) the 8-connected chain code for the given boundary is "0212020222626776754464445243." (c) Piecewise linear approximation of the shape boundary.

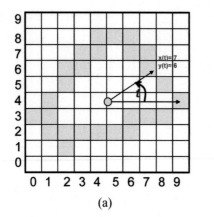
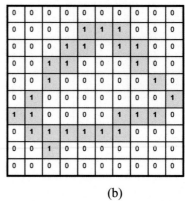

(a)   (b)

Figure 2.20. (a) Time series representation of the shape boundary. The parameter t represents the angle of the line segment from the center of gravity of the shape to a point on the boundary; essentially, t divides 360° to a fixed number of equi-angle segments. The resulting $x(t)$ and $y(t)$ curves can be stored and analyzed as two separate time-dependent functions or, alternatively, may be captured using a single-complex valued function $z(t) = x(t) + iy(t)$. (b) Bitmap representation of the same boundary.

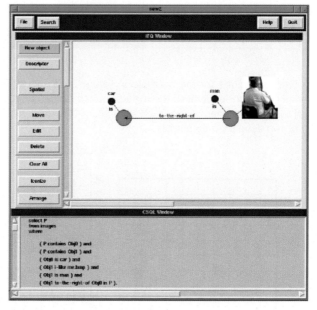

Figure 2.44. The IFQ visual interface of the SEMCOG image and video retrieval system [Li and Candan, 1999a]: the user is able to specify visual, semantic, and spatiotemporal predicates, which are automatically converted into an SQL-like language for fuzzy query processing.

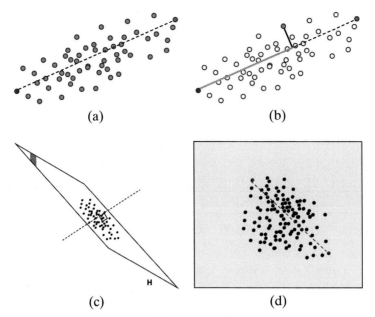

Figure 4.18. (a) Find two objects that are far apart to define the first dimension. (b) Project all the objects onto the line between these two extremes to find out the values along this dimension. (c) Project the objects onto a hyperplane perpendicular to this line. (d) Repeat the process on this reduced hyperspace.

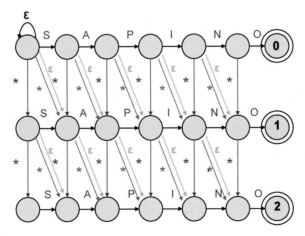

Figure 5.9. The NFA that recognizes the sequence "SAPINO" with a total of up to two insertion, deletion, and substitution errors.

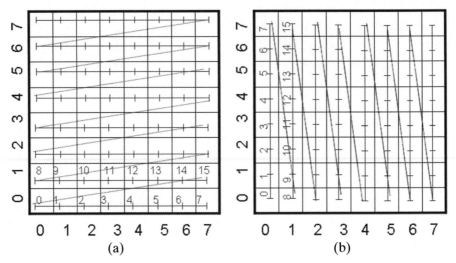

Figure 7.4. (a) Row- and (b) column-order traversals of 2D space.

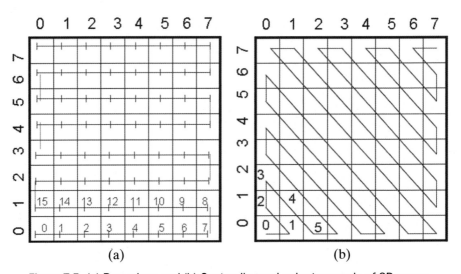

Figure 7.5. (a) Row-prime- and (b) Cantor-diagonal-order traversals of 2D space.

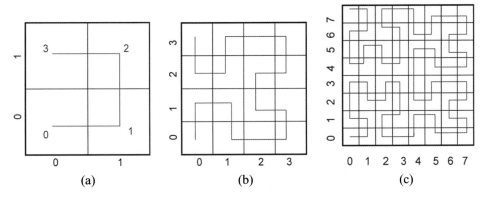

Figure 7.6. Hilbert curve: (a) First order, (b) Second order, (c) Third order.

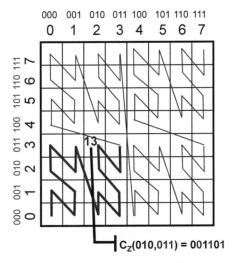

Figure 7.7. Z-order traversal of 2D space.

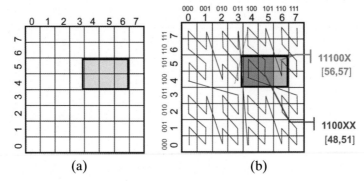

Figure 7.8. (a) A range query in the original space is partitioned into (b) two regions for Z-order curve based processing on a 1D index structure.

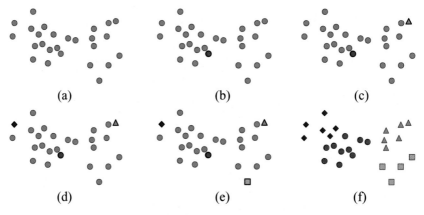

Figure 8.5. Max-a-min approach: (a) given a number of clusters, first (b,c,d,e) leaders that are sufficiently far apart from each other are selected, and then (f) the clustering is performed using the single-pass scheme.

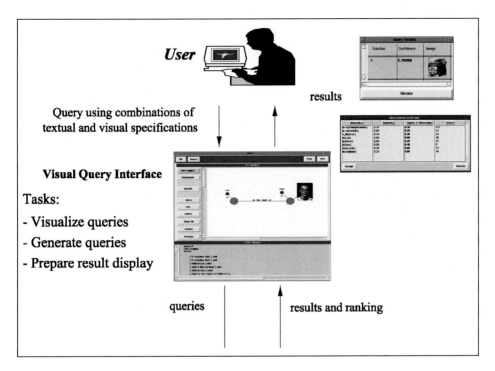

Figure 12.1. User relevance feedback process.

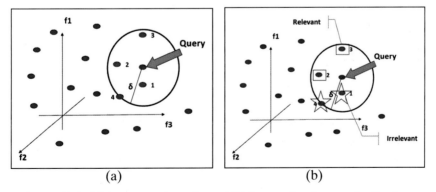

(a)   (b)

Figure 12.2. (a) A query and results and (b) the user's relevance feedback.

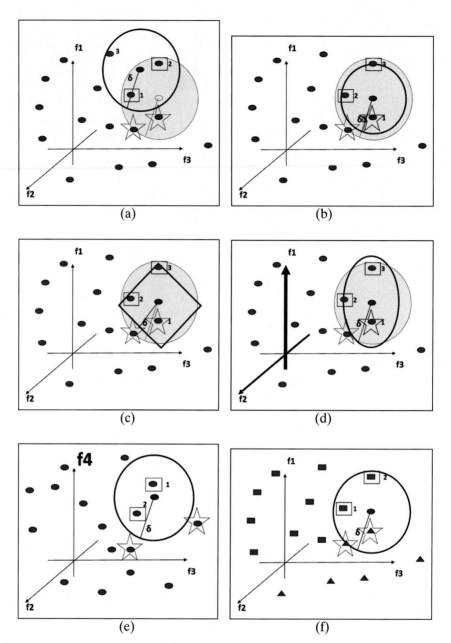

Figure 12.3. Alternative mechanisms for relevance feedback based adaptation: (a) Query rewriting, (b) query range modification, (c) modification of the distance function, (d) feature reweighting, (e) feature insertion/removal, and (f) reclassification (the numbers next to the matching data objects indicate their ranks in the result).

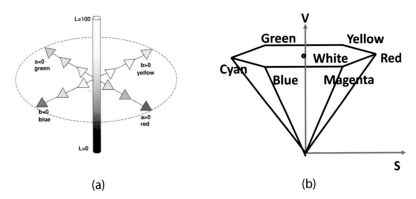

(a)   (b)

Figure 2.9. (a) The CIELAB model of color and (b) the hexconic HSV color model. See color plates section.

where

$$f(s) = s^{1/3} \qquad \text{for } s > 0.008856$$

$$f(s) = 7.787s + \frac{16}{116} \quad \text{otherwise.}$$

The first thing to note in the preceding transformation is that the L, a, and b components are defined with respect to the "white" color. In other words, the CIELAB model normalizes the luminosities and chromaticities of the color space with respect to the color instance that humans perceive as white.

The second thing to note is that L is a normalized version of luminosity. It takes values between 0 and 100: 0 corresponds to black, and 100 corresponds to the color that is perceived as white by humans. As in the YUV model, the a and b components are computed by taking the difference between luminosity and two other color components (normalized X and Z components in this case). Thus, a and b describe the chromaticity of the color instance, where $\sqrt{a^2 + b^2}$ gives the total energy of chroma (or the amount of color) and $tan^{-1}\frac{b}{a}$ (i.e., the angle that the chroma components form) is the hue of the color instance: when $b = 0$, positive values of a correspond to red hue and negative values correspond to green hue; when $a = 0$, positive values of b correspond to yellow and negative values correspond to blue (Figure 2.9(a)).

A similar color space, where the spectrum (*value*) of gray from black to white is represented as a vertical axis, the amount of color (i.e., *saturation*) is represented as the distance from this vertical, and the *hue* is represented as the angle, is the HSV (hue, saturation, and value) color model. This color model is commonly visualized as a cylinder, cone or hexagonal cone (hexcone, Figure 2.9(b)). Like CIELAB, the HSV color space aims to be more intuitive and a better representative of the human perception of color and color differences. Unlike CIELAB, which captures colors in the XYZ color space, however, the HSV color model captures the colors in the RGB color space.

Color-Based Image Representation Using Histograms

As we have seen, in almost all models, color instances are represented as combinations of three components. This, in a sense, reflects the structure of the human retina, where color is perceived through three types of *cones* sensitive to different color components.

An image, then, can be seen as a two-dimensional matrix of color instances (also called pixels), where each pixel is represented as a triple. In other words, if X, Y, Z denote the sets of possible discrete values for each color component, then a digital image, I, of w width and h height is a two-dimensional array, where for all $0 \leq x \leq w - 1$ and $0 \leq y \leq h - 1$, $I[x, y] \in X \times Y \times Z$. Matching two images based on their color content for similarity-based retrieval, then, corresponds to comparing the triples contained in the corresponding arrays.

One way to achieve this is to compare the two arrays (without loss of generality, assuming that they are of the same size) by comparing the pixel pairs at the same array location for both images and aggregating their similarities or dissimilarities (based on the underlying color model) into a single score. This approach, however, has two disadvantages. First of all, this may be very costly, especially if the images are very large: for example, given a pair of $1,000 \times 1,000$ images, this would require 1,000,000 similarity/distance computations in the color space. A second disadvantage of this is that pixel-by-pixel matching of the images would be good for looking for almost-exact matches, but any image that has a slightly different composition (including images that are slightly shifted or rotated) would be identified as mismatches.

An alternative representation that both provides significant savings in matching cost and also reduces the sensitivity of the retrieval algorithms to rotations, shift, and many other deformations is the *color histogram*. Given a bag (or multiset), B, of values from a domain, D, and a natural number, n, a histogram partitions the values in domain D into n partitions and, then, for each partition, records the number of values in B that fall into the corresponding range. A color histogram does the same thing with the color instances in a given image: given n partitions (or *bins*) of the color space, the color histogram counts for each partition the number of pixels of the image that have color instances falling in that partition. Figure 2.10 shows an example color histogram and refers to its vector representation.

In Section 3.1, and later in Chapter 7, we discuss the vector model of media data, how histograms represented as vectors can be compared against each other, and how they can be efficiently stored and retrieved. Here, we note that a color histogram is a compact and nonspatial representation of the color information. In other words, the pixels are associated with the color partitions without any regard to their localities; thus all the location information is lost in the process. In a sense, the color histogram is especially useful in cases where the overall color distribution of the given image is more important for retrieval than the spatial localities of the colors.

2.3.2 Texture Models

Texture refers to certain locally dominant visual characteristics, such as *directionality* (are the lines in the image pointing toward the same direction? which way do the lines in the image point?), *smoothness* (is the image free from irregularities and interruptions by lines?), *periodicity* (are the lines or other features occurring in the image recurring with a predetermined frequency?), and *granularity* (sandiness,

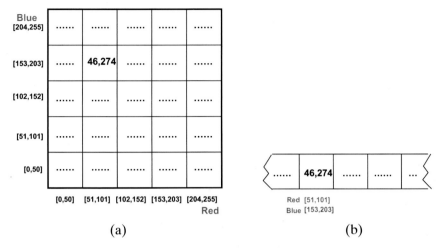

(a)   (b)

Figure 2.10. A color histogram example (only the dimensions corresponding to the "red" and "blue" color dimensions are shown). (a) According to this histogram there are 46,274 pixels in the image that fall in the ranges of [51, 101] in terms of "red" and [153, 203] in terms of "blue" color. (b) In the array or vector representation of this histogram, each position corresponds to a pair of red and blue color ranges. See color plates section.

opposite of smoothness), of parts of an image (Figure 2.11). As a low-level feature, texture is fundamentally different from color, which is simply the description of the luminosity and chromaticity of the light corresponding to a single point, or pixel, in an image.

The first major difference between color and texture is that, whereas it is possible to talk about the color of a single pixel, it is not possible to refer to the

(a)   (b)   (c)

(d)   (e)   (f)

Figure 2.11. (a) A relatively smooth and directional texture; (b) a coarse and granular texture; (c) an irregular but fractal-like (with elements self-repeating at different scales) texture; (d) a regular, nonsmooth, periodic texture; (e) a regular, repeating texture with directional elements; and (f) a *relatively* smooth and uniform texture. See color plates section.

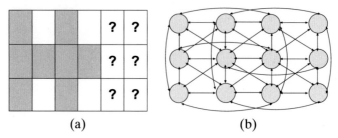

(a)   (b)

Figure 2.12. (a) Can you guess the luminosities of the missing pixels? (b) A random field probabilistically relates the properties of pixels to spatially close pixels in the image: in this figure, each node corresponds to a pixel, and each edge corresponds to a conditional probability distribution that relates the visual property of a given pixel node to the visual property of another one.

texture of a single pixel. Texture is a *collective* feature of a set of neighboring pixels in the image. Second, whereas there are standard ways to describe color, there is no widely accepted standard way to describe texture. Indeed, any locally dominant visual characteristic (even color) can be qualified as a texture feature. Moreover, being dominant does not imply being constant. In fact, a determining characteristic for most textures is the fact that they are nothing but patterns of change in the visual characteristics (such as colors) of neighboring pixels, and as thus, describing a given texture (or the pattern) requires describing how these even lower-level features change and evolve in the two-dimensional space of pixels that is the image. As such textures can be described best by models that capture the rate and type of change.

Random Fields

A random field is a stochastic (random) process, where the values generated by the process are mapped onto positions on an underlying space (see Sections 3.5.4 and 9.7 for more on random processes and their use in classification). In other words, we are given a space, and each point in the space takes a value based on an underlying probability distribution. Moreover, the values of adjacent or even nearby points also affect each other (Figure 2.12(a)). We can see that this provides a natural way for defining texture. We can model the image as the stochastic space, pixels as the points in this space, and the pixel color values as the values the points in the space take (Figure 2.12(b)). Thus, given an image, its texture can be modeled as a random field [Chellappa, 1986; Cross and Jain, 1983; Elfadel and Picard, 1994; Hassner and Sklansky, 1980; Kashyap and Chellappa, 1983; Kashyap *et al.*, 1982; Mao and Jain, 1992]. Essentially, random field-based models treat the image texture as an instance or realization of a random field. Conversely, modeling a given texture (or a set of texture samples) involves finding the parameters of the random process that is most likely to output the given samples (see Section 9.7 for more on learning the parameters of random processes).

Fractals

As we further discuss in Section 7.1.1, a fractal is a structure that shows self-similarity (more specifically, a fractal presents similar characteristics independent

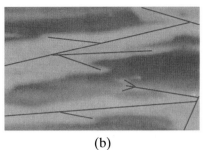

(a)   (b)

Figure 2.13. (a) Mountain ridges commonly have self-repeating triangular shapes. (b) This is a fragment of the texture in Figure 2.11(c). See color plates section.

of the scale; i.e., details at smaller scales are similar to patterns at the larger scales). As such, fractals are commonly used in modeling (analysis and synthesis) of natural structures, such as snowflakes, branches of trees, leaves, skin, and coastlines, which usually show such self similarity (Figure 2.13). A number of works describe image textures (especially natural ones, such as the surface of polished marble) using fractals. Under this texture model, analyzing an image texture involves determining the parameters of a fractal (or *iterated function system*) that will generate the image texture by iterating a basic pattern at different scales [Chaudhuri and Sarkar, 1995; Dubuisson and Dubes, 1994; Kaplan, 1999; Keller *et al.*, 1989].

Wavelets

A wavelet is a special type of fractal, consisting of a mother wavelet function and its scaled and translated copies, called daughter wavelets. In Section 4.2.9.2, we discuss wavelets in further detail. Unlike a general-purpose fractal, wavelets (or more accurately, two-dimensional discrete wavelets) can be used to break any image into multiple subimages, each corresponding to a different frequency (i.e., scale). Consequently, wavelet-based techniques are suitable for studying frequency behavior (e.g., change, periodicity, and granularity) of a given texture at multiple granularities [Balmelli and Mojsilovic, 1999; Feng *et al.*, 1998; Kaplan and Kuo, 1995; Lumbreras and Serrat, 1996; Wu *et al.*, 1999] (Figure 2.14).

Texture Histograms

Whereas texture has diverse models, each focusing on different aspects and characteristics of the pixel structure forming the image, if we know the specific textures we are interested in, we can construct a texture histogram by creating an array of specific textures of interest and counting and recording the amount, confidence, or area of these specific textures in the given image.

Because most textures can be viewed as edges in the image, an alternative to this approach is to use *edge histograms* [Cao and Cai, 2005; Park *et al.*, 2000]. An edge histogram represents the frequency and the directionality of the brightness (or luminosity) changes in the image. Edge extraction operators, such as the Canny [Canny, 1986] or the Sobel [Sobel and Feldman, 1968], look for pixels corresponding to significant changes in brightness and, for each identified pixel they report the

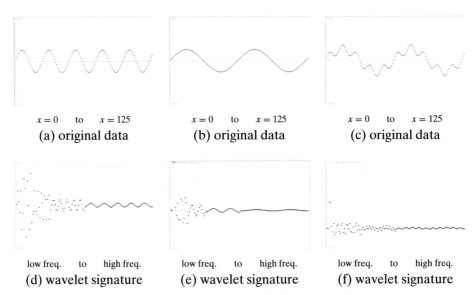

Figure 2.14. Wavelet-based texture signature for one-dimensional data. (a) Data with a high frequency pattern have nonnegligible high-frequency values in its wavelet signature. (b) Data with lower frequency, on the other hand, have highest values at low-frequency entries in the corresponding wavelet signature. (c) If the data are composed of both low-frequency and high-frequency components, the resulting signature has nonnegligible values for both low and high frequencies. (All the plots are created using the online Haar wavelet demo available at *http://math.hws.edu/eck/math371/applets/Haar.html*.)

magnitude and the direction of the brightness change. For example, the Sobel operator computes the convolution of the matrices

$$\delta_x = \begin{bmatrix} -1 & 0 & +1 \\ -2 & 0 & +2 \\ -1 & 0 & +1 \end{bmatrix} \quad \text{and} \quad \delta_y = \begin{bmatrix} +1 & +2 & +1 \\ 0 & 0 & 0 \\ -1 & -2 & -1 \end{bmatrix}$$

around each image pixel to compute the corresponding degree of change along the x and y directions, respectively. Given δ_x and δ_y values for a pixel, the corresponding magnitude of change (or gradient) can be computed as $\sqrt{\delta_x^2 + \delta_y^2}$, and the angle of the gradient (i.e., direction of change) can be estimated as $tan^{-1}\left(\frac{\delta_y}{\delta_x}\right)$ (Figure 2.15).

Once the *rate and direction of change* is detected for each pixel, noise is eliminated by removing those pixels that have changes below a threshold or do not have pixels showing similar changes nearby. Then, the edges are thinned by maintaining only those pixels that have large change rates in their immediate neighborhood along the corresponding gradient. After these phases are completed, we are left with those pixels that correspond to significant brightness changes in the image. At this point, the number of edge pixels can be used to quantify the *edginess* or *smoothness* of the texture. The sizes of clusters of edge points, on the other hand, can be used to quantify the *granularity* of the texture.

Once the image pixels and the magnitudes and directions of their gradients are computed, we can create a two-dimensional edge histogram, where one dimension corresponds to the degree of change and the other corresponds to the direction of

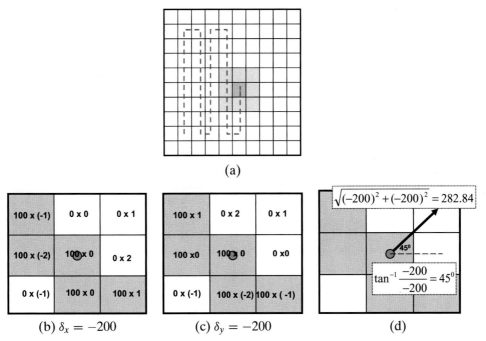

(a)

100 x (-1)	0 x 0	0 x 1
100 x (-2)	100 x 0	0 x 2
0 x (-1)	100 x 0	100 x 1

(b) $\delta_x = -200$

100 x 1	0 x 2	0 x 1
100 x0	100 x 0	0 x0
0 x (-1)	100 x (-2)	100 x (-1)

(c) $\delta_y = -200$

$$\sqrt{(-200)^2 + (-200)^2} = 282.84$$

$$\tan^{-1} \frac{-200}{-200} = 45^0$$

(d)

Figure 2.15. Convolution-based edge detection on a given image: (a) the center of the edge detection operator (small matrix) is aligned one by one with each and every suitable pixel in the image. (b,c) For each position, the x and y Sobel operators are applied to compute δ_x and δ_y. (d) The direction and length of the gradient to the edge at the given image point are computed using the corresponding δ_x and δ_y.

change. In particular, we can count and record the number of edge pixels corresponding to each histogram value range. This histogram can then be used to represent the overall directionality of the texture. Note that we can further extend this two-dimensional histogram to three dimensions, by finding how far apart the edge pixels are from each other along the change direction (i.e., gradient) and recording these distances along the third dimension of the histogram. This would help capture the *periodicity* of the texture, that is, how often the basic elements of the texture repeat themselves.

2.3.3 Shape Models

Like texture, *shape* is a low-level feature that cannot be directly associated to a single pixel. Instead it is a property of a set of neighboring pixels that help differentiate the set of pixels from the other pixels in the image. Color and texture, for example, are commonly used to help segment out shapes from their background in the given image. The three sample images in Figures 2.16(a) through (c) illustrate this: in all three cases, the dominant shapes have colors and textures that are consistent and different from the rest of the image. Thus, in all three cases, color and texture can be used to segment out the dominant shapes from the rest of the image. The sample image in Figure 2.16(d), on the other hand, is more complex: although the dominant human shape shows a marked difference in terms of color and texture from the rest

(a)   (b)   (c)   (d)

Figure 2.16. Sample images with dominant shapes. See color plates section.

of the image, the colors and textures internal to the shape are not self-consistent. Therefore, a naive color- and texture-based segmentation process would not identify the human shape, but instead would identify regions that are consistently red, white, brown, and so forth. Extracting the human shape as a consistent atomic unit requires external knowledge that can help link the individual components, despite their apparent differences, into a single human shape. Therefore, the human shape may be considered as a high-level feature.

There are various approaches to the extraction of shapes from a given image. We discuss a few of the prominent schemes next.

Segmentation

Segmentation methods identify and cluster together those neighboring image pixels that are visually similar to each other (Figure 2.17). This can be done using clustering (such as K-means) and partitioning (such as min-cut) algorithms discussed later in Chapter 8 [Marroquin and Girosi, 1993; Tolliver and Miller, 2006; Zhang and Wang, 2000]. A commonly used alternative is to *grow homogeneous regions* incrementally, from seed pixels (selected randomly or based on some criteria, such as having a color well-represented in the corresponding histogram) [Adams and Bischof, 1994; Ikonomakis *et al.*, 2000; Pavlidis and Liow, 1990].

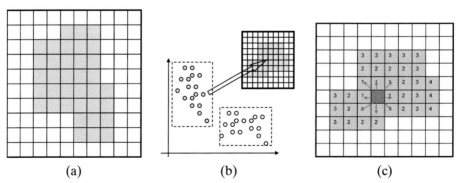

(a)   (b)   (c)

Figure 2.17. (a) An image with a single region. (b) Clustering-based segmentation uses a clustering algorithm that identifies which pixels of the image are similar to each other first, and then finds the boundary on the image between different clusters of pixels. (c) Region growing techniques start from a seed and grow the region until a region boundary with pixels with different characteristics is found (the numbers in the figure correspond to the distance from the seed). See color plates section.

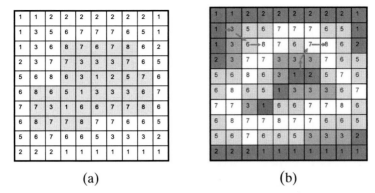

(a)   (b)

Figure 2.18. (a) Gradient values for the example in Figure 2.17 and (b) the topographical surface view (darker pixels correspond to the highest points of the surface and the lightest pixels correspond to the watershed) – the figure also shows the quickest descent (or water drainage) paths for two flood starting points. See color plates section.

Edge Detection and Linking

Edge linking–based methods observe that boundaries of the shapes are generally delineated from the rest of the image by edges. These edges can be detected using edge detection techniques introduced earlier in Section 2.3.2. Naturally, edges can be found at many places in an image, not all corresponding to region boundaries. Thus, to differentiate the edges that correspond to region boundaries from other edges in the image, we need to link the neighboring edge pixels to each other and check whether they form a closed region [Grinaker, 1980; Montanari, 1971; Rosenfeld et al., 1969].

Watershed Transformation

Watershed transformation [Beucher and Lantuejoul, 1979] is a cross between edge detection/linking and region growing. As in edge-detection–based schemes, the watershed transformation identifies the gradients (i.e., degree and direction of change) for each image pixel; once again, the image pixels with the largest gradients correspond to region boundaries. However, instead of identifying edges by suppressing those pixels that have smaller gradients (less change) than their neighbors and linking them to each other, the watershed algorithm treats the gradient image (i.e., 2D matrix where cells contain gradient values) as a topographic surface such that (a) the pixels with the highest gradient values correspond to the lowest points of the surface and (b) the pixels with the lowest gradients correspond to the highest points or plateaus. As shown in Figure 2.18, the algorithm essentially *floods* the surface from these highest points or plateaus (also called *catchment basins*), and the flood moves along the directions where the descent is steepest (i.e., the change in the gradient values is highest) until it reaches the minimum surface point (i.e., the watershed).

Note that, in a sense, this is also a region-growing scheme: instead of starting from a seed point and growing the region until it reaches the boundary where the change is maximum, the watershed algorithm starts from the pixels where the gradient is minimum, *that is, the catchment basin*, and identifies pixels that *shed* or *drain*

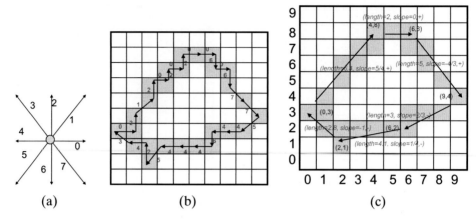

Figure 2.19. (a) The eight direction codes. (b) (If we start from the leftmost pixel) the 8-connected chain code for the given boundary is "0212020222626776454464445243." (c) Piecewise linear approximation of the shape boundary. See color plates section.

to the same *watershed lines*. The watershed lines are then treated as the boundary of the neighboring regions, and all pixels that shed to the same watershed lines are treated as a region [Beucher, 1982; Beucher and Lantuejoul, 1979; Beucher and Meyer, 1992; Nguyen *et al.*, 2003; Roerdink and Meijster, 2000; Vincent and Soille, 1991].

Describing the Boundaries of the Shapes

Once the boundaries of the regions are identified, the next step is to describe their boundary curves in a way that can be stored, indexed, queried, and matched against others for retrieval [Freeman, 1979, 1996; Saghri and Freeman, 1981]. The simplest mechanism for storing the shape of a region is to encode it using a string, commonly referred to as the *chain code*. In the chain code model for shape boundaries, each possible direction between two neighboring edge pixels is given a unique code (Figure 2.19(a)). Starting from some specific pixel (such as the leftmost pixel of the boundary), the pixels on the boundary are visited one by one, and the directions in which one traveled while visiting the edge pixels are noted in the form of a string (Figure 2.19(b)). Note that the chain code is sensitive to the starting pixel, scaling, and rotation, but is not sensitive to translation (or spatial shifts) in the image.

In general, the length of a chain code description of the boundary of a shape is equal to the number of pixels on the boundary. It is, however, possible to reduce the size of the representation by storing piecewise linear approximations of the boundary segments, rather than storing a code for each pair of neighboring pixels. As shown in Figure 2.19(c), each linear approximation of the boundary segment can be represented using its length, its slope, and whether it is in positive x direction ($+$) or negative x direction ($-$). Note that finding the best set of line segments that represent the boundary of a shape requires application of curve segmentation algorithms, such as the one presented by Katzir *et al.* [1994], that are able to identify the end points of line segments in a way minimizes the overall error [Lowe, 1987].

When the piecewise linear representation is not precise or compact enough, higher degree polynomial representations or B-splines can be used instead of the

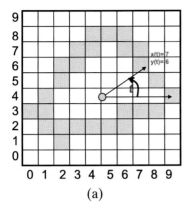
(a)

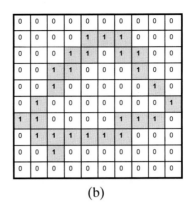
(b)

Figure 2.20. (a) Time series representation of the shape boundary. The parameter t represents the angle of the line segment from the center of gravity of the shape to a point on the boundary; essentially, t divides $360°$ to a fixed number of equi-angle segments. The resulting $x(t)$ and $y(t)$ curves can be stored and analyzed as two separate time-dependent functions or, alternatively, may be captured using a single-complex valued function $z(t) = x(t) + iy(t)$. (b) Bitmap representation of the same boundary. See color plates section.

linear approximations of boundary segments [Saint-Marc *et al.*, 1993]. Alternatively, the shape boundary can be represented in the form of a time series signal (Figure 2.20(a)), which can then be analyzed using spectral transforms such as Fourier transform (Section 4.2.9.1) and wavelets (Section 4.2.9.2) [Kartikeyan and Sarkar, 1989; Persoon and Fu, 1986]. As shown in Figure 2.20(b), the boundary of a region (or sometimes the entire region itself) can also be encoded in the form of a bitmap image. An advantage of this representation is that, since the bitmap consists of long sequences of 0s and 1s, it can be efficiently encoded using run-length encoding (where a long sequence of repeated symbols is replaced with a single symbol and the length of the sequence; for example, the string "110000000001111" is replaced with "2:1;9:0;4:1") or quadtrees (Section 7.2.2). This *compressibility* property makes this representation attractive for low-bandwidth data exchange scenarios, such as object-based video compression in MPEG-4 [Koenen, 2000; MPEG4].

Shape Histograms

As in color and texture histograms, shape histograms are constructed by counting certain quantifiable properties of the shapes and recording them into a histogram vector. For example, if the only relevant features are the 8 directional codes shown in Figure 2.19(a), a shape histogram can be constructed simply by counting the number of 0s, 1s, ..., 7s in the chain code and recording these counts into a histogram with 8 bins.

Other properties of interest which are commonly used in constructing shape histogram vectors include *perimeter length*, *area*, *width*, *height*, *maximum diameter*, *circularity*, where

$$circularity = \frac{4\pi \; area}{perimeter\_length^2},$$

number of holes, and *number of connected components* (for complex shapes that may consist of multiple components).

A number of other important shape properties are defined in terms of the *moments* of an object. Let $\bar{x}$ and $\bar{y}$ denote the x and y coordinates of the center of gravity of the shape. Then, given two nonnegative integers, p and q, the corresponding *central moment*, $\mu_{p,q}$, of this shape is defined as

$$\mu_{p,q} = \sum_i \sum_j (i - \bar{x})^p (j - \bar{y})^q s(i, j),$$

whereas $s(i, j)$ is 1 if the pixel $\langle i, j \rangle$ is in the shape and is 0, otherwise. Given this definition, the *orientation* (i.e., the angle of the major axis of the shape) is defined as

$$orientation = \frac{1}{2} \tan^{-1}\left(\frac{2\mu_{1,1}}{\mu_{2,0} - \mu_{0,2}}\right).$$

Eccentricity (a measure of how much the shape deviates from being circular) of the object is defined as

$$eccentricity = \frac{(\mu_{0,2} - \mu_{2,0})^2 + 4\mu_{1,1}}{area},$$

whereas the *spread* of the object is defined as

$$spread = \mu_{2,0} + \mu_{0,2}.$$

Hough Transform

Hough transform and its variants [Duda and Hart, 1972; Hough, 1962; Kimme *et al.*, 1975; Shapiro, 2006; Stockman and Agrawala, 1977] are *voting*-based schemes for locating known, parametric shapes, such as lines and circles, in a given image.

Like most shape detection and indexing algorithms, Hough transform also starts with an edge detection step. Consider for example the edge detection process described in Section 2.3.2. This process associates a "magnitude of change" and an "angle of change" to each pixel in the image. Let us assume that this edge detection process has identified that the pixel $\langle x_p, y_p \rangle$ is on an edge. Let us, for now, also assume that the shapes we are looking for are line segments. Although we do not know which specific line segment the pixel $\langle x_p, y_p \rangle$ is on, we do know that the line segment should satisfy the line equation

$$y_p = m x_p + a,$$

or the equivalent equation

$$a = y_p - x_p m,$$

for some pair of m and a values. This second formulation is interesting, because it provides an equation that relates the possible values of a to the possible values of m. Moreover, this equation is also an equation of a line, albeit not on the (x, y) space, but on the (m, a) space.

Although this equation alone is not sufficient for us to determine the specific m and a values for the line segment that contains our edge pixel, if we consider that all the pixels on the same line in the image will have the same m and a values, then we may be able to recover the m and a values for this line by treating all these pixels collectively as a set of mutually supporting evidences. Let us assume that $\langle x_{p,1}, y_{p,1} \rangle$, $\langle x_{p,2}, y_{p,2} \rangle, \ldots, \langle x_{p,k}, y_{p,k} \rangle$ are all on the same line in the image. These pixels give us the set of equations

$$
\begin{aligned}
a &= y_{p,1} - x_{p,1}\, m, \\
a &= y_{p,2} - x_{p,2}\, m, \\
\cdots \quad \cdots &\quad \cdots \cdots \cdots \cdots \\
a &= y_{p,k} - x_{p,k}\, m,
\end{aligned}
$$

which can be solved together to identify the m and a values that define the underlying line.

The preceding strategy, however, has a significant problem. Although this would work in the ideal case where the x and y values on the line are identified precisely, in the real world of images where the edge pixel detection process is highly noisy, it is possible that there will be small variations and shifts in the pixel positions. Consequently, the given set of equations may not have a common solution. Moreover, if the set of edge pixels are not all coming from a single line but are from two or more distinct line segments in the image, then even if the edge pixels are identified precisely, the set of equations will not have a solution. Thus, instead of trying to simultaneously solve the foregoing set of equations for a single pair of m and a, the Hough transform scheme keeps a two-dimensional *accumulator* matrix that accumulates votes for the possible m and a values.

More precisely, one dimension of the accumulator matrix corresponds to the possible values of m and the other corresponds to possible values of a. In other words, as in histograms, each array position of the accumulator corresponds to a range of m and a values. All entries in the accumulator are initially set to 0. We consider each equation one by one. Because each equation of the form $a = y_{p,i} - x_{p,i}\, m$ defines a line of possible m and a values, we can easily identify the accumulator entries that are on this line. Once we identify those accumulator entries, we increment the corresponding accumulator values by 1. In a sense, each line, $a = y_{p,i} - x_{p,i}\, m$, on the (m, a) space (which corresponds to the edge pixel $\langle x_{p,i}, y_{p,i} \rangle$) *votes* for possible m and a values it implies. The intuition is that, if there is a more or less consistent line segment in the image, then (maybe not all, but) most of its pixels will be aligned and they will all vote for the same m and a pair. Consequently, the corresponding accumulator entry will accumulate a large number of votes. Thus, after we process the votes implied by all edge pixels in the image, we can look at the accumulator matrix and identify the m and a pairs where the accumulated votes are the highest. These will be the m and a values that are most likely to correspond to the line segments in the image. Note that a disadvantage of this scheme is that, for vertical line segments, the slope m would be infinity, and it is hard to design a bounded accumulator for the unbounded (m, a) space. Because of this shortcoming, the following alternative equation for lines is commonly preferred when building Hough accumulators to detect lines in images:

$$
l = x \cos \Theta + y \sin \Theta,
$$

where l is the distance between the line and the origin and Θ is the angle of the vector from the origin to the closest point. The corresponding (l, Θ) space is more effective because both l and Θ are bounded (l is bounded by the size of the image and Θ is between 0 and 2π).

If we are looking for shapes other than lines, we need to use equations that define those shapes as the bases for the transformations. For example, let us assume that we are looking for circles and that the edge detection process has identified that the pixel $\langle x_p, y_p \rangle$ is on an edge. To look for circles, we can use the circle equation,

$$(x_p - a)^2 + (y_p - b)^2 = r^2.$$

This equation, however, may be costly to use because it has three unknowns a, b, and r (the center coordinates and the radius) and is nonlinear. The alternative circle representation

$$x_p = a + r\cos(\Theta),$$
$$y_p = b + r\sin(\Theta),$$

where Θ is the angle of the line from the center of the circle to the point $\langle x_p, y_p \rangle$ on the circle, is likely to be more efficient. But this formulation requires the gradient Θ corresponding to point p. Fortunately, because the edge detection algorithm process described in Section 2.3.2 provides a gradient angle for each edge point $\langle x_p, y_p \rangle$, we can use this value, Θ_p, in the foregoing equations. Consequently, leveraging this edge gradient, the equations can be transformed to

$$a = x_p - r\cos(\Theta_p) \quad \text{and}$$
$$b = y_p - r\sin(\Theta_p).$$

or equivalently to

$$b = a\tan(\Theta_p) - x_p\tan(\Theta_p) + y_p.$$

This final formulation eliminates r and relates the possible b and a values in the form of a line on the (a, b) space. Thus, a vote accumulator similar to the one for lines of images can be used to detect the centers of circles in the image. Once the centers are identified, the radii can be computed by reassessing the pixels that voted for these centers.

Finally, note that the Hough transform can be used as a shape histogram in two different ways. One approach is to use the accumulators to identify the positions of the lines, circles, and other shapes in the image and create histograms that report the numbers and other properties of these shapes. An alternative approach is to skip the final step and use the accumulators themselves as histograms or signatures that can be compared to one another for similarity-based retrieval.

2.3.4 Local Feature Descriptors (Set-Based Models)

Consider the situation in Figure 2.21, where three observation planes are used for tracking a mobile vehicle. The three cameras are streaming their individual video frames into a command center where the frame streams will be fused into a single combined stream that can then be used to map the exact position and trajectory of the vehicle in the physical space. Because in this example the three cameras themselves are independently mobile, however, the images in the individual frames need

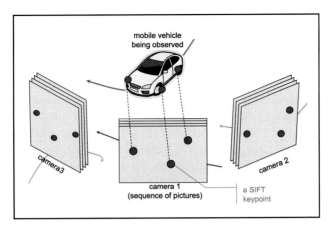

Figure 2.21. A multicamera observation system.

to be calibrated and aligned with respect to each other by determining the correspondences among salient points identified in the individual frames. In such a situation, we need to extract local descriptors of the *salient points* of the images to support matching. Because images are taken from different angles with potentially different lighting conditions, these local descriptors must be as invariant to image deformations as possible.

The *scale-invariant feature transform* (SIFT) [Lowe, 1999, 2004] algorithm, which is able to extract local descriptors that are invariant to image scaling, translation, rotation and also partially invariant to illumination and projections, relies on a four-stage process:

(i) *Scale-space extrema detection:* The first stage of the process identifies candidate points that are invariant to scale change by searching over multiple scales and locations of the given image. Let $L(x, y, \sigma)$, of a given image $I(x, y)$, be a version of this image smoothed through convolution with the Gaussian, $G(x, y, \sigma) = (1/2\pi\sigma^2)e^{-(x^2+y^2)/2\sigma^2}$:

$$L(x, y, \sigma) = G(x, y, \sigma) * I(x, y).$$

Stable keypoints, $\langle x, y, \sigma \rangle$, are detected by identifying the extrema of the difference image $D(x, y, \sigma)$, which is defined as the difference between the versions of the input image smoothed at different scales, σ and $k\sigma$ (for some constant multiplicative factor k):

$$D(x, y, \sigma) = L(x, y, k\sigma) - L(x, y, \sigma).$$

To detect the local maxima and minima of $D(x, y, \sigma)$, each value is compared with its neighbors at the same scale as well as neighbors at images up and down one scale.

Intuitively, the Gaussian smoothing can be seen as a multiscale representation of the given image, and thus the differences between the Gaussian smoothed images correspond to differences between the same image at different scales. Thus, this step searches for those points that have largest or smallest variations with respect to both space and scale.

(ii) *Keypoint filtering and localization:* At the next step, those candidate points that are sensitive to noise are eliminated. These include those points that have low contrast or are poorly localized along edges.

(iii) *Orientation assignment:* At the third step, one or more orientations are assigned to each remaining keypoint, $\langle x, y, \sigma \rangle$, based on the local image properties. This is done by computing orientation histograms for the immediate neighborhood of each keypoint (in the image with the closest smoothing scale) and picking the dominant directions of the local gradients. In case there are multiple dominant directions, then multiple keypoints, $\langle x, y, \sigma, o \rangle$ (each with a different orientation, o), are created for the given keypoint, $\langle x, y, \sigma \rangle$. This redundancy helps improve the stability of the matching process when using the SIFT keypoint descriptors computed in the next step.

(iv) *Keypoint descriptor creation:* In the final step of SIFT, for each keypoint, a local image descriptor that is invariant to both illumination and viewpoint is extracted using the location and orientation information obtained in the previous steps.

The algorithm samples image gradient magnitudes and orientations around the keypoint location, $\langle x, y \rangle$, using the scale, σ, of the keypoint to select the level of the Gaussian blur of the image. The orientation, o, associated to the keypoint helps achieve rotation invariance by enabling the keypoint descriptors (coordinates of the descriptor and the gradient orientations) to be represented relative to o. Also, to avoid sudden changes in the descriptor with small changes in the position of the window and to give less emphasis to gradients that are far from the center of the descriptor, a Gaussian weighing function is used to assign a weight to the magnitude of each sample point.

As shown in Figure 2.22, each keypoint descriptor is a feature vector of 128 ($= 4 \times 4 \times 8$) elements, consisting of 16 gradient histograms (one for each cell of a 4×4 grid superimposed on a 16-pixel by 16-pixel region around the keypoint) recording gradient magnitudes for eight major orientations (north, east, northeast, etc.). Note that, because a brightness change in which a constant is added to each image pixel will not affect the gradient values, the descriptor is invariant to affine changes in illumination.

Mikolajczyk and Schmid [2005] have shown that, among the various available local descriptor schemes, including shape context [Belongie *et al.*, 2002], steerable filters [Freeman and Y, 1991], PCA-SIFT [Ke and Sukthankar, 2004], differential invariants [Koenderink and van Doom, 1987], spin images [Lazebnik *et al.*, 2003], complex filters [Schaffalitzky and Zisserman, 2002], and moment invariants [Gool *et al.*, 1996], SIFT-based local descriptors perform the best in the context of matching and recognition of the same scene or object observed under different viewing conditions. According to the results presented by Mikolajczyk and Schmid [2005], moments and steerable filters perform best among the local descriptors that have lower number of dimensions (and thus are potentially more efficient to use in matching and retrieval). The success of the SIFT algorithm in extracting stable local descriptors for object matching and recognition led to the development of various other local feature descriptors, including the *speeded-up robust*

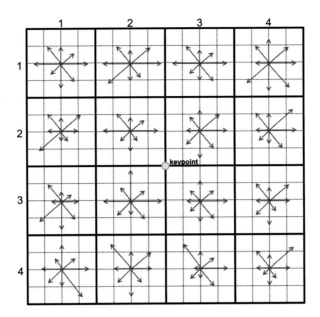

Figure 2.22. 128 (= 4 × 4 × 8) gradients which collectively make up the feature vector corresponding to a single SIFT keypoint.

features (SURF) [Bay *et al.*, 2006] and *gradient location and orientation histogram (GLOH)* [Mikolajczyk and Schmid, 2003, 2005] techniques, which more or less follow the same overall approach to feature extraction and representation as SIFT.

2.3.5 Temporal Models

Multimedia documents (or even simple multimedia objects, such as video streams) can be considered as collections of smaller objects, synchronized through temporal and spatial constraints. Thus, a high-level understanding of the temporal semantics is essential for both querying and retrieval, as well as for effective delivery of documents that are composed of separate media files that have to be downloaded, coordinated, and presented to the clients, according to the specifications given by the author of the document.

2.3.5.1 Timeline-Based Models

There are various models that one can use to describe the temporal content of a multimedia object or a synthetic multimedia document. The most basic model that addresses the temporal needs of multimedia applications is the *timeline (or axes-based) model* (Figure 2.23). In this model, the user places events and actions on a timeline.

Basic Timeline Model

Figure 2.23(a) shows the temporal structure of a multimedia document according to the timeline model. The example document in this figure consists of five media objects with various start times and durations. Note that this representation assumes

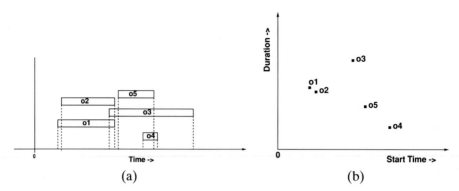

Figure 2.23. (a) Specification of a multimedia document using the timeline model and (b) its representation in 2D space.

that no implicit relationships between objects are provided. Therefore, the temporal properties of the objects can be represented as points in a 2D space, where one of the dimensions denotes the start time and the other denotes the duration. In other words, the temporal properties of each presentation object, o_i, in document, D, is a pair of the form $\langle s_i, d_i \rangle$, where

- s_i denotes the presentation start time of the object and
- d_i denotes the duration of the object.

The temporal properties of the multimedia document, D, is then the combination of the temporal properties of the constituent multimedia objects. Figure 2.23(b), for example, shows the 2D point-based representation of the temporal document in Figure 2.23(a).

Because of its simplicity, the timeline model formed the basis for many academic and commercial multimedia authoring systems, such as the Athena Muse project [Bolduc *et al.*, 1992], Macromedia Director [MacromediaDirector], and QuickTime [Quicktime]. MHEG-5, prepared by the Multimedia and Hypermedia information coding Expert Group (MHEG) as a standard for interactive digital television, places objects and events on a timeline [MHEG].

Extended Timeline Model

Unfortunately, the timeline model is too inflexible or not sufficiently expressive for many applications. In particular, it is not flexible enough to accommodate changes when specifications are not compatible with the run-time situations for the following reasons:

- Multimedia document authors may make mistakes.
- When the objects to be included in the document are not known in advance, but instantiated in run-time, the properties of the objects may vary and may not be matching the initial specifications.
- User interactions may be inconsistent with the initial temporal specifications.
- The presentation of the multimedia document may not be realizable as specified because of resource limitations of the system.

Hamakawa and Rekimoto [1993] provide an extension to the timeline model that uses *temporal glues* to allow individual objects to shrink or stretch as

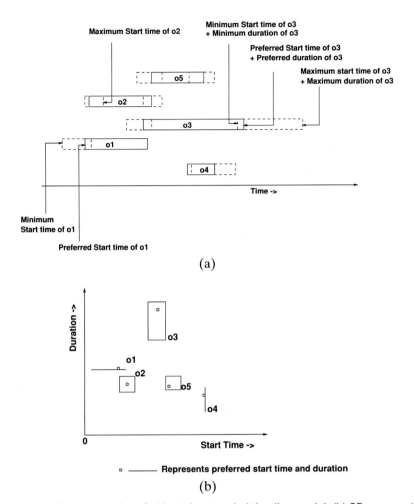

Figure 2.24. (a) Representation of objects in extended timeline model. (b) 2D representation of the corresponding regions.

required. Candan and Yamuna [2005] define a flexible (or extended) timeline model as follows: As in the basic timeline model, in the extended timeline model each presentation object has an associated start time and a duration. However, instead of being scalar values, these parameters are represented using ranges. This means that the presentation of an object can begin anytime during the valid range, and the object can be presented for any duration within the corresponding range. Furthermore, each object also has a preferred start time and a preferred duration (Figure 2.24(a)). Objects in a document, then, correspond to regions, instead of points, in a 2D temporal space (Figure 2.24(b)). More specifically, Candan and Yamuna [2005] define flexible presentation object, o, as a pair of the form $\langle S_{\{s_{min},s_{pref},s_{max}\}}, D_{\{d_{min},d_{pref},d_{max}\}}\rangle$, where $S_{\{s_{min},s_{pref},s_{max}\}}$ is a probability density function for the start time of o such that

$$\forall_{x<s_{min}} S_{\{s_{min},s_{pref},s_{max}\}}(x) = \forall_{x>s_{max}} S_{\{s_{min},s_{pref},s_{max}\}}(x) = 0$$

$$\forall_x S_{\{s_{min},s_{pref},s_{max}\}}(x) \leq S_{\{s_{min},s_{pref},s_{max}\}}(s_{pref}).$$

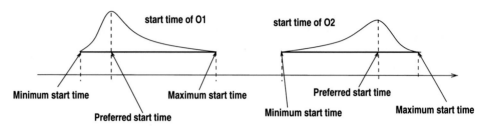

Figure 2.25. Start times of two flexible objects and the corresponding probability distributions.

$D_{\{d_{min}, d_{pref}, d_{max}\}}$ is a probability density function for the duration of o with similar properties. Figure 2.25 visualizes the start times of two example flexible objects. Intuitively, the probability density functions describe the likelihood of the start time and the duration of the object for taking specific values. These functions return 0 beyond the minimum and maximum boundaries, and they assign the maximum likelihood value for the preferred points. Note that document authors usually specify only the minimum, maximum, and preferred starting points and durations; the underlying probability density function is picked by the system based on how strict or flexible the user is about matching the preferred time.

Note that although the timeline-based models provide some flexibility in the temporal schedule, the objects are still tied to a timeline. In cases where the temporal properties (such as durations) of the objects are not known in advance, however, timeline-based models cannot be applied effectively: if the objects are shorter than expected, this may result in gaps in the presentations, whereas if they are too long, this may result in temporal overflows. A more flexible approach to specifying the temporal properties of multimedia documents is to tie the media objects to each other rather than to a fixed timeline using logical and constraint-based models. There are two major classes of such formalisms for time: *instant-* and *interval-*based models. In instant-based models, focus is on the (instantaneous) events and their relationships. Interval-based models, on the other hand, recognize that many temporal constructs (such as a video sequence) are not instantaneous, but have temporal extents. Consequently, these focus on intervals and their relationships in time.

2.3.5.2 Instant-Based Logical Models

In instant-based models, the properties of the world are specified and verified at points in time. There are three temporal relationships that can be specified between instants of interest: *before*, $=$, and *after* [Vilain and Kautz, 1986].

The temporal properties of a complex multimedia document, then, can be specified in terms of logical formulae involving these three predicates and logical connectives ($\wedge$, $\vee$, and $\neg$).

Difference Constraints

One advantage of the instant-based model is that the three instant based temporal relationships can also be written in terms of simple, *difference constraints* [Candan *et al.*, 1996a,b]: let e_1 and e_2 be two events, then the constraints of the form ($e_1 - e_2 < \delta_1$) can be used to describe instant-based relationships between these two events. For instance, the statement *"event, e_1, occurs at least 5 seconds before e_2"* can be described as $(e_1 - e_2 < -5) \vee (e_1 - e_2 = -5)$. Thus, under certain conditions this model enables efficient, polynomial time solutions. Instant-based models and their difference constraint representation are leveraged in many works, including the *CHIMP* system [Candan *et al.*, 1996a,b], the Firefly system by Buchanan and Zellweger (1993a,b) and works by Kim and Song [1995, 1993] and Song *et al.* [1996].

Situation and Event Calculi

Other logical formalism that describe the instant-based properties of the world include situation calculus and the event calculus. Situation calculus [Levesque *et al.*, 1998] views the world in terms of actions, fluents, and situations. In particular, values of the fluents (predicates or functions that return properties of the world at a given situation) change as a consequence of the actions. A finite sequence of actions is referred to as a situation; in other words, the current situation of the world is the history of the actions on the world. The rules governing the world are described in second-order logics [Vaananen, 2001] using formulae that lay down the preconditions and effects of the actions and certain other facts and properties that are known about the world.

Event calculus [Kowalski and Sergot, 1986] is a related logical formalism describing the properties of the world in terms of fluents and actions. Unlike the situational calculus, however, the properties of the world are functions of the time points (*HoldsAt(fluent, time_point)*). Actions also occur at specified time points (*Happens(action,time_point)*), and their effects are reflected to the world after a specified period of time.

Causal Models

Because it allows modeling effects of actions, the event calculus can be considered as a causal model of time. A more recent causal approach to modeling the synchronization and user interaction requirements of media in distributed hypermedia documents is presented by Gaggi and Celentano [2005]. The model deals with cases in which the actual duration of the media is not known at the design time. Synchronization requirements of continuous media (such as video and audio files) as well as noncontinuous media (such as text pages and images) are expressed through various causal synchronization primitives:

- *a* plays with *b*: The activation of any of the two specified media *a* and *b* causes the activation of the other, and the (natural) termination of the first media (*a*) forces the termination of the second (*b*).
- *a* activates *b*: The natural termination of the first media (*a*) triggers the playback or display of the second media (*b*).
- *a* terminates *b*: When the first media (*a*) is forced to terminate, a forced termination is triggered on the second media (*b*).
- *a* is replaced by *b*: if the two media *a* and *b* can use the same resources (channel) to be delivered, this synchronization rule specifies that the activation of the second object (*b*) preempts the first one, that is, it triggers its forced termination. The channel resource used by *a* is made available to the second media (*b*).

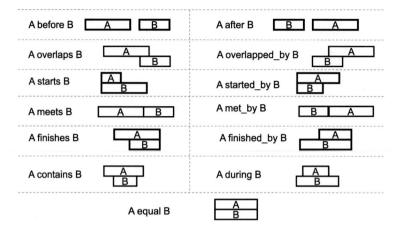

Figure 2.26. The thirteen binary relationships between pairs of intervals.

■ *a* has priority over *b* with behavior α: the activation of the first object (*a*) forces the second media (*b*) to release the channel it occupies, to make it available for *a*, if needed. According to the specified behavior (α), the interrupted media *b* can be *paused and waiting to be resumed*, or *terminated*.

Notice that the underlying hypothesis of this approach is that the actual duration of the media is known only at run time, given the fact that media are distributed on the Web, and their download and delivery times also depend on the available network resources. Therefore, Gaggi and Celentano [2005] rely on event-driven causal relationships between media. This also facilitates specification of the desired behavior in the cases of user interaction events.

2.3.5.3 Interval-Based Logical Models

Interval-based temporal data management was introduced by Allen [1983] and studied by many researchers [Adali *et al.*, 1996; Snoek and Worring, 2005]. Unlike an instant, which is given by a time point, an interval is defined by a pair of time points: its start and end times. Since the pair is constrained such that the end time is always larger than or equal to the start time, specialized index structures (such as interval trees [Edelsbrunner, 1983a,b] and segment trees [Bentley, 1977] can be used for searching for intervals that intersect with a given instant or interval. Allen [1983, 1984] provides thirteen qualitative temporal relationships (such as *before, meets,* and *overlaps*) that can hold between two intervals (Figure 2.26). A set of axioms (represented as logical rules) help deduce new relationships from the initial interval-based specifications provided by the user. For example, given intervals, I_1, I_2, and I_3, the following two rules are axioms available for inferring relationships that were not initially present in the specifications:

■ $before(I_1, I_2) \wedge before(I_2, I_3) \rightarrow before(I_1, I_3)$,
■ $meets(I_1, I_2) \wedge during(I_2, I_3) \rightarrow overlaps(I_1, I_3) \vee during(I_1, I_3) \vee meets(I_1, I_3)$.

Further axioms help the system reason about *properties*, *processes*, and *events*. For example, given predicates p and q (such as *media_active*() or *media_paused*()), describing the properties of multimedia objects, the axioms

- $holds(p, I) \leftrightarrow \forall_i(in(i, I) \rightarrow holds(p, i))$
- $holds(and(p, q), I) \leftrightarrow holds(p, I) \wedge holds(q, I)$
- $holds(not(p), I) \leftrightarrow \forall_i(in(i, I) \rightarrow \neg holds(p, i))$

can be used to reason about when these properties hold and when they do not hold. Such axioms, along with additional predicates and rules that the user may specify, enable a logical description of multimedia semantics.

Note that while the binary temporal relationships (along with logical connectives, $\wedge$, $\vee$, and $\neg$) are sufficient to describe complex situations, they fall short when more than two objects have to be synchronized by a single, atomic temporal relation. Consider, for example, a set $\{o_1, o_2, o_3\}$ of three multimedia objects that are to be presented simultaneously. Although this requirement can be specified using the conjunction of pairwise relationships that has to hold,

$$equal(o_1, o_2) \wedge equal(o_2, o_3) \wedge equal(o_1, o_3),$$

this approach is both expensive (requires larger constraints than needed) and also semantically awkward: the user's intention is not to state that there are three pairs of objects, each with an independent synchronization requirement, but to state that these three objects form a group that has a single synchronization requirement associated with it. This distinction becomes especially important when user requirements have to be prioritized and some constraints can be relaxed to address cases where user specifications are unsatisfiable in run-time conditions because of resource limitations. In such a case, an n-ary specification language (for example $equal(o_1, o_2, o_3)$) can capture user's intentions more effectively. Little and Ghafoor [1993] propose an interval-based conceptual model that can handle n-ary relationships among intervals. This model extends the definitions of *before*, *meets*, *overlaps*, *starts*, *equals*, *contains*, and *finished_by* to capture situations with n objects to be atomically synchronized.

Schwalb and Dechter [1997] showed that, when there are no disjunctions, interval based formalisms are, in fact, equivalent to the instant-based formalisms. On the other hand, in the presence of disjunctions in the specifications, the interval-based formalisms are more expressive than the instant-based models. van Beek [1989] provides a sound and complete algorithm for instant-based point algebra. Aspvall and Shiloach [1980] and Dechter *et al.* [1991] present graph theoretical solutions for the various instances of the temporal constraint satisfaction problem. Vilain and Kautz [1986] show that determining the satisfiability of interval-based assertions is NP-Hard. Interval scripts [Pinhanez *et al.*, 1997], a methodology proposed to describe user interactions and sensor activities in an interactive system, benefits from a restriction on the allowed disjunction combinations in rendering the problem more manageable [Pinhanez and Bobick, 1998].

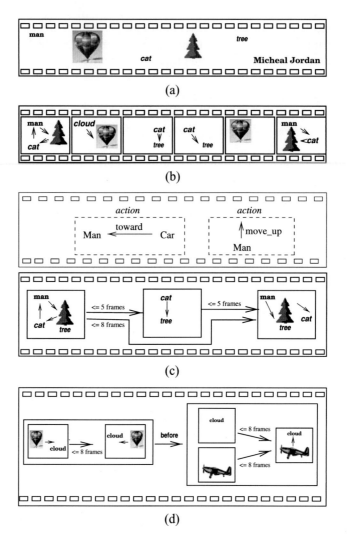

(a)

(b)

(c)

(d)

Figure 2.27. Four-level description of the temporal content of videos [Li and Candan, 1999a]: (a) Object level, (b) Frame level, (c) Simple action level, (d) Composite action level.

2.3.5.4 Hybrid Models

Instant-based and interval-based formalisms are not necessarily exclusive and can be used together. For example, Li and Candan [1999a] describe the content of videos using a four-level data model (Figure 2.27):

- *Object level:* At the lowest level of the hierarchy, the information modeled is the semantics and image contents of the objects in the video. Example queries that can be answered by the information at this level include "*Retrieve all video clips that contain an object similar to the* example image" and "*Retrieve all video clips that contain a submarine.*"
- *Frame level:* At the second level of the hierarchy, the concept of a video frame is introduced. The additional information maintained at this level are spatial relationships among objects within a frame and other meta-information related to

frames, such as "being a representative frame for a shot or a preextracted action" and frame numbers (a representative or key frame of a shot is the frame that describes the content of a shot the best). An example query that can be answered by the information at this level is *"Retrieve all video clips that contain a frame in which there are a man and a car and the man is to the right of the car."*

■ *Simple action level:* The next level of the hierarchy introduces the concept of time, that is, the temporal relationships between individual frames. The temporal relationships are added to the model through implication of frame numbers. Because each frame corresponds to distinct time points within the video, the temporal relationships introduced at this level are instant based. Multiple frames with temporal relationships construct actions. For example, an action of *"a torpedo launch from a submarine"* can be defined as a three-frame sequence: a frame with a submarine, followed by a frame with a submarine and a torpedo, followed by a frame with only a torpedo. Another example of an action, *"a man moving to the right,"* can be defined as a frame in which there is a man on the left followed by a frame with a man on the right side. Actions are defined as video frame sequences that have associated action semantics. The sequence of frames associated with an action definition is called an *extent*.

An example query that can be answered by the information at this level is *"Retrieve all video clips that contain two frames where the first frame contains a submarine and a torpedo and the second frame contains an explosion, and these two frames are at most 10 seconds apart."* Two more complicated queries that can be answered by the information modeled at this level are *"Retrieve all video clips that contain an action of torpedo launch from a submarine"* and *"Retrieve all video clips that contain an extent in which a man is moving to the right."*

■ *Composite action level:* This level introduces the concept of *composite actions*. A composite action is a combination of multiple actions with instant- or interval-based time constraints. For example, a composite action of *"a submarine combat"* can be represented with combinations of actions *"submarine moving to the right,"* *"submarine moving to the left,"* *"a torpedo launch from a submarine,"* *"explosion,"* and interval-based time constraints associated with these actions.

Other logic- and constraint-based approaches for document authoring and presentation include Özsoyoğlu *et al.* [Hakkoymaz and Özsoyoglu, 1997; Hakkoymaz *et al.*, 1999; Özsoyoğlu *et al.*, 1996], and Vazirgiannis and Boll [1997]. Adali *et al.* [1996], Del Bimbo *et al.* [1995], and others used temporal logic in retrieval of video data. More recently, Adali *et al.* [1999], Baral *et al.* [1998], de Lima *et al.* [1999], Escobar-Molano *et al.* [2001], Mirbel *et al.* [1999], Song *et al.* [1999], and Wirag [1999] introduced alternative models, interfaces, and algebras for multimedia document authoring and synchronization.

2.3.5.5 Graph-Based Temporal Models

Although logic- and constraint-based specifications are rich in expressive power, there are other more specialized models that can be especially applicable when the goal is to describe synchronization requirements of multimedia documents. These include the *Petri net*s model and its variations, time-flow graphs, and timed automata.

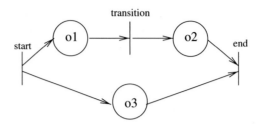

Figure 2.28. An interval-based OCPN graph for a multimedia document with three objects. Each place contains information about the duration of the object.

Timed Petri Nets

A Petri net is a concise graph-based representation and modeling language to describe the concurrent behavior of a distributed system. In its simplest form, a Petri net is a bipartite, directed graph that consists of places, transitions, and arcs between places and transitions. Each transition has a number of input places and a number of output places. The places hold tokens, and the distribution of the tokens is referred to as the marking of the Petri net. A transition is enabled when each of its input places contains at least one token. When a transition fires, it eliminates a number of tokens from its input places and puts a number of tokens to its output places. This way, the markings of the Petri net evolve over time. More formally, a Petri net can be represented as a 5-tuple (S, T, F, M_0, W), where S denotes the set of places, T denotes the transitions, and F is the set of arcs between the places and transitions. M_0 is the initial marking (i.e., the initial state) of the system. W is the arc weights, which describes how many tokens are consumed and created when the transitions fire. Petri nets allow analysis of the various properties of the system, including *reachability* (i.e., whether a particular marking can be reached or not), *safety/boundedness* (i.e., whether the places may contain too many tokens), and *liveliness* (i.e., whether the system can ever reach a situation where no transition is enabled).

Timed Petri nets (TPN) extend the basic Petri net construct with timing information [Coolahan and Roussopoulos, 1983]. In particular, Little and Ghafoor [1990] propose an interval-based multimedia model, called Object Composition Petri Nets (OCPN, Figure 2.28), based on the timed Petri net model. In OCPN, each place has a duration (and possibly resources) associated with it. In effect, the places denote the multimedia objects (and other intervals of interest) and the transitions denote the synchronization specifications. Unlike the basic Petri net formalism, where the transitions can fire asynchronously and nondeterministically, whenever they are enabled, the transition firing in OCPNs is deterministic: a transition fires immediately when each of its input places contains an available token. Because the places have durations, however, a token put into a place is not immediately available, but *locked*, for the duration associated with the place. A further restriction imposed on OCPNs is that each place has one incoming arc, and one outgoing arc.[6] This means that only one transition governs the start of each object. Little and Ghafoor [1990] showed that each of the thirteen pair-wise relationships

---

[6] This type of Petri nets are also referred to as marked graphs [Commoner *et al.*, 1971].

between intervals depicted in Figure 2.26 can be composed using the OCPN formalism. Note that although OCPN can be used to describe interval-based specifications based on Allen's formalism, its expressive power is limited; for example, it is not able to describe disjunctions.

Other relevant extensions of timed Petri nets, especially for imprecise multimedia data, include fuzzy-timing Petri nets (such as Fuzzy-Timing Petri-Net for Multimedia Synchronization, FTNMS [Zhou and Murata, 1998], and stochastic Petri nets [Balbo, 2002], which add imprecision to the durations associated to the places or to the firing of the transitions. Also, whereas most Petri net–based models assume that the system proceeds without any user intervention, the Dynamic Timed Petri Net (DTPN) model, by Prabharakan and Raghavan, enables user inputs to alter the execution of the Petri net by, for example, preempting an object or by changing its duration temporarily or permanently [Prabhakaran and Raghavan, 1994].

Time Flow Graph

Timed Petri Nets are not the only graph-based representations for interval-based reasoning. Li *et al.* [1994a,b] propose a Time-Flow Graph (TFG) model that also is based on intervals. Unlike timed Petri nets, however, TFG is able to represent (*n*-ary) temporal relationships between intervals, without needing advance knowledge about their durations. In the TFG model, temporal relationships are split into two main groups: parallel and sequential relationships. A time-flow graph is a triple $\{\Delta_N, N_t, E_d\}$, where Δ_N is the set of nodes corresponding to the intervals and nodes that describe parallel relations, N_t, are the transit nodes that describe sequential relationships, and E_d is a set of directed edges, which connect nodes in Δ_N and N_t.

Timed Automata

Timed automata [Alur and Dill, 1994] extend finite automata with timing constraints. In particular, they accept the so-called timed words. A timed word (σ, τ) is an input to a timed automaton, where σ is a sequence of symbols (representing events) and τ is a monotonically increasing sequence of time values. Intuitively, if σ_i is an event occurrence, then τ_i is the time of occurrence of this event. When the automaton makes a state transition, the next state depends on the event as well as the time of the input relative to the times of the previously read symbols. This is implemented by associating a set of clocks to the automaton. A clock can be reset to 0 by any state transition, and the reading of a clock provides the time elapsed since the last time it was reset. Each transition has an associated clock constraint, δ, inductively defined as

$$\delta := x \leq c | c \leq x | \neg \delta | \delta_1 \wedge \delta_2,$$

which determines whether the transition can be fired or not. Here x is a clock and c is a constant. Note that, effectively, clock constraints evaluate differences between the current time and the times of one or more of the past state transitions and allow the new transition occur only if the current time satisfies the associated difference constraints.

logO [Sapino *et al.*, 2006] is an example system that relies on timed automata for representing temporal knowledge. Unlike many of the earlier formalisms that aim to help content creators to declaratively synthesize multimedia documents, *logO* tries to analyze and represent (i.e., learn) temporal patterns underlying a system from its event logs. For this purpose, *logO* represents the *trace* of a system using a timed finite state automaton, described by a 5-*tuple* $AUT = \langle S, s_0, S_f, TR, next \rangle$:

- S is the set of observed states of the system. Each state is a pair of the form $\langle id, AM \rangle$, where *id* is a globally unique identifier of the state, and *AM* is the set media that are active in the state.
- s_0 is the initial state, $s_0 = \langle id_0, \emptyset \rangle$.
- The set of final states is the singleton $S_f = \{s_f = \langle id_f, \emptyset \rangle\}$.
- *TR* is the set of symbols that label possible state transitions. A transition label is a pair $\langle ev, inst \rangle$, where *ev* is an event and *inst* is the time instant in which the event occurs. Examples of events include the activation of a new media, or the end of a previously active one.
- $next : S \times TR \rightarrow S$ is the transition function. Intuitively, if a transition from the state s to the state s' occurs, the new state s' is obtained from s by taking into account the events occurring at time instant *inst* and updating the set of active media by reflecting the changes on the media affected by such events. In particular, those media that have terminated or have been stopped at time instant *inst* will not appear in the set of active media in s', whereas the media that are starting at the same time are inserted in the set of active media in s'.

The trace automaton created using a single sequence of events is a chain of states. It recognizes a single word, which is exactly the sequence of records appearing in the log. Thus, to construct an automaton representing the underlying structure of the system, *logO* merges related trace automata created by parsing the system logs. In general, *logO* relies on two alternative schemes for merging:

- *History-independent merging:* In this scheme, each state in the original automata is considered independently of its history. Thus, to implement history-independent merging, an equivalence relation ($\equiv_{log}$), which compares the active media content of two given states, s_i and s_j, is necessary for deciding which states are compatible for being merged. The merge algorithm produces a new automaton in which the media items in the states are (representatives of) the equivalence classes defined by the $\equiv_{log}$ relation. The label of the edge connecting any two states s_i and s_j includes (i) the event that induced the state change from a state equivalent to s_i to a state equivalent to s_j in any of the merged automata, (ii) the duration associated to the source state, and (iii) the number of transitions, in the automata being merged, to which (i) and (ii) apply.

    The resulting automaton may contain cycles. Note that the transition label includes the counting of the number of logged instances where a particular transition occurred in the traces. The count labels on the transitions provide information regarding the likelihood of each transition. In a sense, the resulting trace automaton is a *timed* Markov chain, where the transitions from states have not only expected trigger times, but also associated probabilities. Therefore, given the current state, the next state transition is identified probabilistically (as in Markov chains, see Section 3.5.4 for more details) and the corresponding state transition is performed at the time associated with the chosen state transition.

■ *History-dependent merging:* In this scheme, two states are considered identical only if their active media content *as well as* their histories (i.e., past states in the chains) are matching. Thus, the equivalence relation, $\equiv_{log}$, compares not only the active media content of the given states s_i and s_j but also requires their histories, $hist_i$ and $hist_j$, to be considered identical for merging purposes. In particular, to compare two histories, $logO$ uses an edit distance function (see Section 3.2.2 for more detail on edit distance). Unlike history-independent merging, the resulting merged automaton does not contain any cycles; the same set of active media can be represented as different states, if the set is reached through differing event histories.

2.3.5.6 Time Series

Most the of the foregoing temporal data models are designed for describing authored documents or temporal media, analyzed for events [Scher *et al.*, 2009; Westermann and Jain, 2007] using media processing systems, such as MedSMan [Liu *et al.*, 2005, 2008], ARIA [Peng *et al.*, 2006, 2007, 2010], and others [Nahrstedt and Balke, 2004; Gu and Nahrstedt, 2006; Gu and Yu, 2007; Saini *et al.*, 2008], which implement complex analysis tasks by coupling sensing, feature extraction, fusion, and classification operations and other stream processing services. In most sensing and data capture applications, however, before the temporal analysis phase the data is available simply as a raw stream (or sequence) of sensory values. For example, as we discuss later in this chapter, audio data can often be viewed as a 1D sequence of audio signal samples. Similarly, a sequence of tuples describing the surface pressure values captured by a set of floor-based pressure sensors or a sequence of motion descriptors [Divakaran, 2001; Pawar *et al.*, 2008] encoded by a motion detector are other examples of data streams. Such *time series* data can often be represented as arrays of values, tuples, or even matrices (for example when representing the temporal evolution of the Web or a social network, each matrix can capture a snapshot of the node-to-node hyperlinks or user-to-user friendship relationships, respectively). Time series of matrices are often represented in the form of *tensors*, which are essentially arrays of arbitrary dimensions. We will discuss tensors in more detail in Section 4.4.4. Alternatively, when each data element can be discretized into a symbol from a finite alphabet, a time series can be represented, stored, and analyzed in the form of a sequence or string (see Chapter 5).

The alphabet used for discretizing a given time series data is often application specific: for example, a motion application can discretize the capture data into a finite set of motion descriptors. Alternatively, one can rely on general purpose discretization algorithms, such *symbolic aggregate approximation (SAX)* [Lin *et al.*, 2003], to convert time series data into a discrete sequence of symbols. Consider a time series, $T = t_1, t_2, \ldots, t_l$ of length l, where each t_i is a value. In SAX, this time series data is first normalized so that the mean of the amplitude of values is zero and the standard deviation is one and then the sequence is approximated using a *piecewise aggregate approximation (PAA)* scheme, where T is reduced into an alternative series, $\bar{T} = \bar{t}_1, \bar{t}_2, \ldots, \bar{t}_w$, of length $w < l$ as follows:

$$\bar{t}_i = \frac{w}{l} \sum_{j=\frac{l}{w}(i-1)+1}^{\frac{l}{w}i} t_j$$

Table 2.1. SAX symbols and the corresponding value ranges

Symbol	A	B	C	D
Range	-inf ~ -1.64	-1.64 ~ -1.28	-1.28 ~ -1.04	-1.04 ~ -0.84
Symbol	E	F	G	H
Range	-0.84 ~ -0.67	-0.67 ~ -0.52	-0.52 ~ -0.39	-0.39 ~ -0.25
Symbol	I	J	K	L
Range	-0.25 ~ -0.13	-0.13 ~ 0	0 ~ 0.13	0.13 ~ 0.25
Symbol	M	N	O	P
Range	0.25 ~ 0.39	0.39 ~ 0.52	0.52 ~ 0.67	0.67 ~ 0.84
Symbol	Q	R	S	T
Range	0.84 ~ 1.04	1.04 ~ 1.28	1.28 ~ 1.64	1.64 ~ inf

Lin *et al.* [2003] showed that, once normalized as above, the amplitudes in most time series data have Gaussian distributions. Thus a set of pre-determined breakpoints, shown in Table 2.1, can be used for mapping the normalized data into symbols of an alphabet such that each symbol is equi-probable. Moreover, for ease of indexing and search, the PAA representation maps the longer time series into a shorter one in such a way that the loss of information is minimal.

2.3.5.7 Temporal Similarity and Distance Measures

Because multimedia object retrieval may require similarity comparison of temporal structures, a multimedia retrieval system must employ suitable temporal comparison measures [Candan and Yamuna, 2005]. Consider, for example, the five OCPN documents shown in Figure 2.29. In order to identify which of the temporal documents in Figures 2.29(b) to (e) best matches the temporal document specified in Figure 2.29(a), we need to better understand the underlying model and the user's intention.

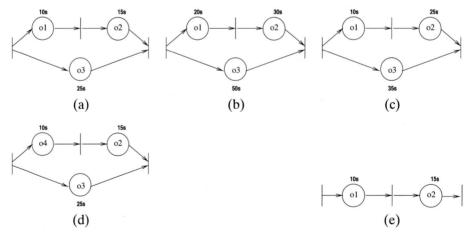

Figure 2.29. Five OCPN documents. Can we rank documents (b) to (e) according to their similarity to (a)? Hints: (b) has all object durations multiplied by 2, (c) has two objects with different and one object with the same duration as (a), (d) has all object durations intact, but one of the object IDs is different, and (e) has a missing object.

One way to perform similarity-based retrieval based on temporal features is to represent the temporal requirements (such as a temporal query) in the form of a fuzzy logic statement (Section 3.4) that can be evaluated against the data to obtain a temporal similarity score. A number of multimedia database systems, such as SEM-COG [Li and Candan, 1999a], rely on this approach. An alternative approach is to rely on the specific properties of the underlying temporal model to develop more specialized similarity/distance measures. In the rest of this section, we consider different models and discuss measures appropriate to each.

Temporal Distance – Timeline Model

As introduced earlier in Section 2.3.5, the timeline model allows users to place objects on a timeline with respect to the starting time of the presentation. It is one of the simplest models and is also the less expressive and less flexible.

One advantage of the timeline model is that a set of events placed on a timeline can be seen as a sequence, and thus temporal distance between two sets of events can be computed using edit-distance–based measures (such as dynamic time warping, DTW [Sakoe, 1978]), where the distance between two sequences is defined as the minimum amount of edit operations needed to convert one sequence to the other. We discuss edit-distance computation in greater detail in Section 3.2.2. Here, we provide an edit-distance–like distance measure for comparing temporal similarity/distance under the timeline model.

SCALE. The first issue that needs to be considered when comparing two multimedia documents specified using a timeline is the durations of the documents. Temporal scaling is useful when users are interested in comparing temporal properties in relative, instead of absolute, terms. Let σ be the temporal scaling value applied when comparing two documents, D_1 and D_2. If the users would like the document similarity/distance to be sensitive to the degree of scaling, then we need to define a scaling penalty, $\Upsilon(\sigma)$, as a function of the scaling value.

TEMPORAL DIFFERENCE BETWEEN A PAIR OF MEDIA OBJECTS. Recall from Figure 2.23(b) that the temporal properties of presentation objects mapped onto a timeline can be represented as points in a 2D space. Consequently, after the documents are scaled with scaling degree, σ, the temporal distance, $\Lambda(o_i, o_j, \sigma)$, between two objects $o_i \in D_1$ and $o_j \in D_2$, can be computed based on their start times (s_i and s_j after scaling) and durations (d_i and d_j after scaling) using various distance measures, including the Minkowski distance ($[\ |s_i - s_j|^\gamma + |d_i - d_j|^\gamma\ ]^{\frac{1}{\gamma}}$), the Euclidean distance ($[\ |s_i - s_j|^2 + |d_i - d_j|^2\ ]^{\frac{1}{2}}$), or the city block distance ($[\ |s_i - s_j| + |d_i - d_j|\ ]$).

UNMAPPED OBJECTS. An object mapping between the two documents may fail to map some objects that are in D_1 to any objects in D_2 and vice versa. These unmapped objects must be taken into consideration when calculating the similarity/distance between two multimedia documents. In order to deal with such unmapped objects, we can map each unmapped object, $o_i = \langle s_i, d_i \rangle$, to a null object, $o_i^* = \langle s_i, 0 \rangle$. The temporal distance values, $\Lambda(o_i, o_i^*)$ and $\Lambda(o_i^*, o_i)$, depend on the position of s_i and d_i. Figure 2.30 shows an example where some objects in the documents are mapped to virtual objects in the others.

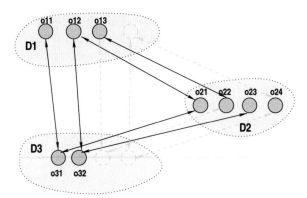

Figure 2.30. Three multimedia documents and the corresponding mappings. The dashed circles and lines show missing objects and the corresponding missing matchings.

OBJECT PRIORITIES AND USER PREFERENCES. In some cases, different media objects in the documents may have different priorities; that is, some media objects are more important than the others and their temporal mismatches affect the overall result more significantly. Let us denote the priority of the object o as $pr(o)$. Given two objects $o_i \in D_1$ and $o_j \in D_2$, we can calculate the priority, $pr(o_i, o_j)$, of the pair based on the priorities of both objects using various fuzzy merge functions, such as the arithmetic average ($\frac{pr(o_i)+pr(o_j)}{2}$, Section 3.4.2).

COMBINING ALL INTO A DISTANCE MEASURE. Given two objects $o_i \in D_1$ and $o_j \in D_2$, we can define the prioritized temporal distance between the pair of objects, o_i and o_j, as follows:

$$pr(o_i, o_j) \times \Lambda(o_i, o_j, \sigma).$$

In other words, if the objects are important, then any mismatch in their temporal properties counts more.

Let σ be a scaling factor and $\Upsilon(\sigma)$ be the corresponding scaling penalty, and let μ be an object-to-object mapping from document D_1 to document D_2. Then, the overall temporal distance between multimedia documents D_1 and D_2 can be computed as

$$\Delta_{timeline,\sigma,\mu}(D_1, D_2) = \Upsilon(\sigma) + \sum_{\langle o_i, o_j \rangle \in \mu} pr(o_i, o_j) \times \Lambda(o_i, o_j, \sigma).$$

Let σ' and μ' be the scaling value and the mapping such that the value of $\Delta_{timeline,\sigma,\mu}(D_1, D_2)$ is smallest; that is,

$$\langle \sigma', \mu' \rangle = \underset{\langle \sigma, \mu \rangle}{argmin} \, \Delta_{timeline,\sigma,\mu}(D_1, D_2).$$

Then, we can define the timeline-based distance between the temporal documents D_1 and D_2 as

$$\Delta_{timeline}(D_1, D_2) = \Delta_{timeline,\sigma',\mu'}(D_1, D_2).$$

Note that this definition is similar to the definition of edit distance, where the edit cost is defined in terms of the minimum-cost edit operations to convert one string

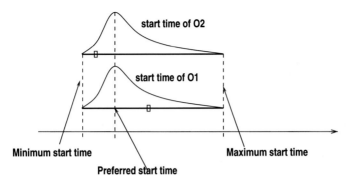

Figure 2.31. Start times of two identical flexible objects (note that the minimum, preferred, and maximum start times of both objects are identical). The two small rectangles, on the other hand, depict a possible scenario where the two objects start at different times.

to the other; in this case the edit operations involve temporal scaling and temporal alignment of the media objects in two documents.

Temporal Distance – Extended (Flexible) Timeline Model

As mentioned in Section 2.3.5, the basic timeline model is too rigid for many applications. This means that the presentation of the object cannot accommodate unexpected changes in the presentation specifications or in the available system resources. Consequently, various extensions to the timeline model have been proposed [Hamakawa and Rekimoto, 1993] to increase document flexibility. In this section, we use the extended timeline model introduced in Section 2.3.5.1, where a flexible presentation object, o, is described using a pair of probability density functions, $\langle S_{\{s_{min}, s_{pref}, s_{max}\}}, D_{\{d_{min}, d_{pref}, d_{max}\}} \rangle$.

Similar to the simple timeline model, the main component of the distance measure is the temporal distance between a pair of mapped media objects. However, in this case, when calculating the distance, $|S_i - S_j|$, between the start times and the distance, $|D_i - D_j|$, between durations, we need to consider that they are based on probability distributions. One way to do this is to compare the corresponding probability distribution functions using the KL-distance or chi-square test, introduced in Section 3.1.3 to assess how different the two distributions are from each other. This would provide an *intentional* measure: if two distributions are identical, this means that the intentions of the authors are also identical; thus the distance is 0.

On the other hand, when defining the distance *extensionally* (based on what might be observed when these documents are played), since the start time of a flexible object can take any value between the corresponding s_{min} and s_{max}, this has to be taken into consideration when comparing the start times and durations of two objects. The reason for this is that even though the descriptions of the start times of two objects might be identical in terms of the underlying probability distributions, when presented to the user, these two objects do not need to start at the same time. For example, although their descriptions are identical, the actual start times of two objects, o_1 and o_2, shown in Figure 2.31 have a distance value larger than 0. Hence, although *intentionally* speaking the distance between the start times should be 0, the observed difference might be nonzero. Consequently, even when a flexible document is compared with itself, the document distance may be nonzero. Therefore, we can define the distance between start times of two objects o_i and o_j as

$$| s_i - s_j | \quad = \quad \int_{s_{i,min}}^{s_{i,max}} \int_{s_{j,min}}^{s_{j,max}} S_{i\{s_{i,min},s_{i,pref},s_{i,max}\}}(x) \times$$

$$S_{j\{s_{j,min},s_{j,pref},s_{j,max}\}}(y) \times |x - y| \; dxdy.$$

The distance between the durations of the objects o_i and o_j can be defined similarly using the duration probability functions instead of the start probability functions. The rest of the formulation is similar to that of the simple timeline model described in Section 2.3.5.7.

Temporal Distance/Similarity – Constraint-Based Models

In general, the temporal characteristics of a complex multimedia object can be abstracted in terms of a temporal constraint, described using logical formulae over a 4-tuple $\langle \mathcal{C}, \mathcal{I}, \mathcal{E}, \mathcal{P} \rangle$, where

- $\mathcal{C} = \{C_1, \ldots\}$ is an infinite set of temporal constants,
- $\mathcal{I} = \{I_1, \ldots, I_i\}$ is a set of interval variables,
- $\mathcal{E} = \{E_1, \ldots, E_e\}$ is a set of event variables,
- $\mathcal{P} = \{P_1, \ldots, P_p\}$ is a set of predicates, where each P_i takes a set of intervals from $\mathcal{I}$, a set of events from $\mathcal{E}$, and a set of *constants* from C, and evaluates to *true* or *false*.

Example 2.3.1: Let $\mathcal{C} = \{Z^+\}$, $\mathcal{I} = \{int(o_1), int(o_2)\}$, $\mathcal{E} = \{pres_{st}, pres_{end}, st(o_1), st(o_2), end(o_1), end(o_2)\}$. The following constraint might specify temporal properties of a presentation schedule[7]:

$$T = (before(int(o_1), int(o_2))) \wedge$$
$$((0 \leq st(o_1) - pres_{st} \leq 3) \vee (0 \leq st(o_2) - pres_{st} \leq 20)) \wedge$$
$$(pres_{end} = end(o_2)).$$

Given this constraint-based view of temporal properties of multimedia documents, we can define temporal similarity and dissimilarity as follows:

- *Temporal similarity:* A temporal specification is satisfiable only if there is a variable assignment such that the corresponding formula evaluates to *true*. If there are multiple assignments that satisfy the temporal specification, then the problem has, not one, but a set of solutions. In a sense, the *semantics* of the document is described by the set of presentation solutions that the corresponding constraints allow. In the case of the timeline model, each solution set contains only one solution, whereas more flexible models may have multiple solutions among which the most suitable is chosen based on user preferences or resource requirements. For example, Figure 2.32(a) shows the solution sets of two documents, D_1 and D_2. Here, C is the set of solutions that satisfy both documents,

---

[7] In this example, the events in $\mathcal{E}$ and intervals in $\mathcal{I}$ are not independent; for instance, the beginning of the interval $int(o_1)$ corresponds to the event $st(o_1)$. These require additional constraints, but we ignore these for the simplicity of the example.

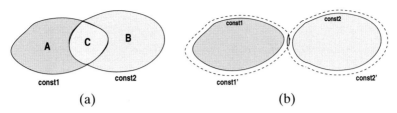

Figure 2.32. Constraint-based (a) similarity and (b) dissimilarity.

whereas A and B are the sets of solutions that belong to only one of the documents. We can define the temporal similarity of the documents D_1 and D_2 as

$$similarity(D_1, D_2) = \frac{|C|}{|A| + |B| + |C|}.$$

■ *Temporal dissimilarity:* The similarity semantics given above, however, has some shortcomings: if an inflexible model (such as the very popular timeline model) is used, then (because there is only one solution for a given set of constraints), $\frac{|C|}{|A+B+C|}$ will evaluate only to 1 or 0; that is, two documents either will match perfectly or will not match at all. It is clear that such a definition is not useful for *similarity*-based retrieval. Furthermore, it is possible to have similar documents that do not have any common solutions, yet they may differ only in very subtle ways. A complementary notion of dissimilarity (depicted in Figure 2.32(b)) captures these cases more effectively:

– Let us assume that two documents D_1 and D_2 are consistent. Because there exists at least one common solution, these documents are similar to each other (*similarity* = 1.0).

– If the solution spaces of these two documents are disjoint, then we can modify (edit) the constraints of these two documents until their solution sets overlap.

Based on this, we can define the *dissimilarity* between these two documents as the minimum extension required in the sizes of the solution sets for the documents to have a common solution:

$$dissimilarity(D_1, D_2) = (|A'| + |B'|) - (|A| + |B|),$$

where A' and B' are the new solution sets.

The two measures just given are complementary: one captures *the degree of similarity between mutually consistent documents* and the other captures *the degree of dissimilarity between mutually inconsistent documents*.

Let us consider two temporal documents, D_1 and D_2, and their constraint-based temporal specifications, $C(D_1)$ and $C(D_2)$. As described previously, if these documents represent nonconflicting intentions of their authors, then when the two constraints, $C(D_1)$ and $C(D_2)$, are combined, the resulting set of constraints should not contain any conflicts; that is, the combined set of constraints should be satisfiable. Figure 2.33 shows two temporal documents, an object-to-object mapping between these two documents, and the corresponding merged document. In this example, the combined temporal specification is not satisfiable: there is a conflict caused by the existence of the unmapped object. Given an object mapping, μ, the *temporal conflict*

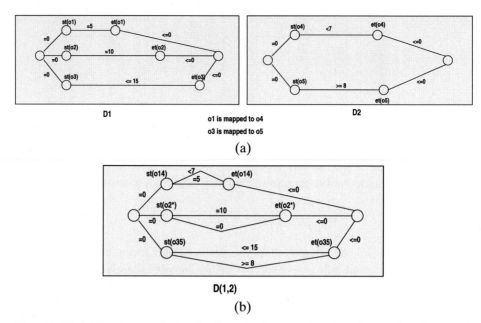

Figure 2.33. (a) Two temporal specifications (*st* denotes the start time and *et* denotes the end time of an object) and (b) the corresponding combined specification. Note that the object o_2 in document D_1 does not exist in document D_2 (i.e., its duration is 0); therefore the resulting combined specification has a conflict.

distance between two documents, D_1 and D_2, can be defined as

$$\Delta_{conflict}(D_1, D_2)_\mu = total\_number\_of\_conflicts\_in(C(D^{\mu}_{(1,2)})), \qquad (2.1)$$

where $C(D^{\mu}_{(1,2)})$ denotes the constraints corresponding to the combined document. A disadvantage of this measure, however, is that it is in general very expensive to compute. It is shown that in the worst case, the number of conflicts in a document is exponential to the size of the document (in terms of objects and constraints) [Candan *et al.*, 1998]. Therefore, this definition may not be practical.

Candan *et al.* [1998] showed that, under certain conditions, it is easier to find an optimal set of constraints to be relaxed (i.e., removed) to eliminate all conflicts than to identify the total number of conflicts in the constraints. Therefore, it is possible to use this minimum number of constraints that need to be removed to achieve consistency as an indication of the reasons of conflicts. Based on this, the *relaxation distance* between two documents, D_1 and D_2, is defined as

$$\Delta_{relaxation}(D_1, D_2)_\mu = cost\_of\_constraints\_removed(C(D^{\mu}_{(1,2)})). \qquad (2.2)$$

The cost (or the impact) of the constraints removed may be computed based on their number or user-specified priorities.

2.3.6 Spatial Models

Many multimedia databases, such as those indexing faces or fingerprints, need to consider predefined features and their spatial relationships for retrieval

Figure 2.34. Whereas some features of interest in a fingerprint image can be pinpointed to specific points, others span regions of the fingerprint.

(Figure 2.34). Spatial predicates and operations can be broadly categorized into two based on whether the information of interest is a single *point* in space or has a spatial extent (e.g., a *line* or a *region*). The predicates and operators that are needed to be supported by the database management system depend on the underlying spatial data model and on the applications' needs (Table 2.2). Some of the spatial operators listed in Table 2.2, such as *union* and *intersection*, are set oriented; in other words, their outcome is decided based on the memberships of the points that they cover in space. Some others, such as *distance* and *perimeter*, are quantitative and may depend on the characteristics (e.g., Euclidean) of the underlying space. Table 2.2 also includes *topological* relationships between contiguous regions in space. Spatial data can be organized in different ways to evaluate the above predicates. In this section, we cover commonly used approaches for representing spatial information in multimedia databases.

2.3.6.1 Fields and Their Directional and Topological Relationships
In *field-based* approaches to spatial information management, space is described in terms of three complementary aspects [Worboys *et al.*, 1990]:

- *A spatial framework*, which is a finite grid representing the space of interest;
- *Field functions*, which map the given spatial framework to relevant attribute domains (or features); and
- *Field operations*, which map subsets of fields onto other fields (e.g., union, intersection). For *local* field operations, the value of the new field depends only on the values of the input fields (e.g., color of a given pixel in an image). For *focal* field operations, the value of the new field depends on the neighborhood of the input fields (e.g., image texture around a given pixel). *Zonal operations* perform aggregation operations on the attributes of a given field (e.g., average intensity of an image segment).

Field-based representations can be used to describe *feature locales* and *image segments*.

Example 2.3.2 (Feature Locales): Let us be given an image, *I*. The two-dimensional grid defined by the pixels of this image is a *spatial framework*.

Table 2.2. Common spatial predicates and operations

	Name	Input 1	Input 2	Output
Topological predicates	contains, covers, covered by, disjoint, equal, inside, meet, and overlap	region	region	{true, false}
	inside, outside, on-boundary, corner	region	point	{true, false}
	touches, crosses	line	region	{true, false}
	endpoint, on	point	line	{true, false}
Directional predicates	north, east, south, west, northeast, northwest, southeast, southwest	region, point, line	region, point, line	{true, false}
Quantitative/ measurement operations	distance	region, point, line	region, point, line	numerical value
	length	line		numerical value
	perimeter	region		numerical value
	area	region		numerical value
	center	region		point
Data set/search operations	nearest	region, point, line		region, point, line
Set operations	intersection	region, line	region, line	region, line, point
	union	region	region	region
	difference	region	region	region

Let F be the set of features of interest; for example, "red" $\in F$. This feature set is an attribute domain and "red" is an attribute of the field.

Let the *tile* [Li and Drew, 2003] associated with a feature, $f \in F$, be a contiguous block of pixels having the feature f. For example, the set of pixels belonging to a red balloon in the scene may be identified as a "red" tile by the system. Let a *locale* be the set of tiles in the image all representing the same feature f. Each locale is a field on the spatial framework, defined by image, I.

Image processing functions, such as *returnLocale*("red", I), are the so-called field functions.

Feature extraction functions, such as *centroid*(), *eccentricity*(), *size*(), *texture*(), and *shape*(), can all be represented as zonal field operations.

Example 2.3.3 (Image Segments): Note that a locale is not necessarily connected, locales are not necessarily disjoint, and not all pixels in the image belong to a locale.

Unlike feature locales, *image segments* (obtained through an image segmentation process – see Section 2.3.3) are usually connected, segments are disjoint, and

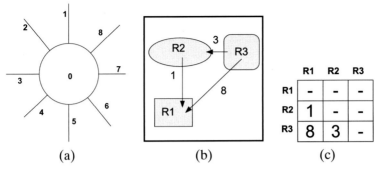

Figure 2.35. (a) The nine directions between two regions (0 means "at the same place") [Chang, 1991]. (b) An image with three regions and their relationships (for convenience, the relationships are shown only in one direction). (c) The corresponding 9DLT matrix.

the set of segments extracted from the image usually cover the entire image. Despite these differences, segments can also be represented in the form of fields.

Because field-based representations are very powerful in describing many commonly used spatial features, such as feature locales and image segments, in the rest of this section we present representations of directional and topological relationships between fields identified in an image.

Nine-Directional Lower-Triangular (9DLT) Matrix

Chang [1991] classifies the directional relationship between a given pair of image regions into nine classes as shown in Figure 2.35. Given these nine directional relationships, all directional relationships between n regions on a plane can be described using an $n \times n$ matrix, commonly referred to as the *nine-directional lower-triangular (9DLT) matrix* (Figures 2.35(a) and (b)).

UID-Matrix

Chang *et al.* [2000a] encode the topological relationships between each and every pair of objects in a given image explicitly using a *UID-matrix*. More specifically, Chang *et al.* [2000a] consider the $169 (= 13 \times 13)$ unique relationships between pairs of objects (13 interval relationships along each axis of the image) and assigns a unique ID (or *UID*) to each one of these 169 unique relationships. Given an image containing n objects, an $n \times n$ UID-matrix, enumerating the spatial relationships between all pairs of objects in the image, is created using these UIDs.[8]

In general, however, the use of the UIDs for representing spatial reasoning suffers from the need to make UID-based table lookups to verify which relationships are compatible with each other. The need for table lookups can, on the other hand, be eliminated if UIDs are encoded in a way that enables verification of compatibilities and similarities between different spatial relationships. Chang and Yang [1997] and Chang *et al.* [2001], for instance, encoded the unique IDs corresponding to the

---

[8] This is similar to the 9DLT-matrix. The 9DLT representation captures the nine directional relationships between a pair of regions, and given an image with n objects, an $n \times n$ 9DLT-matrix is used to encode the directional information in the image.

169 possible relationships as products of prime numbers. As an example consider the "<" relationship shown later in Table 2.3. Chang and Yang [1997] compute the UID corresponding to this relationship as 2×47; in fact, each and every spatial relationship that would imply some form of "*disjointness*" is required to have 2 as a factor in its unique ID and no relationship that implies "*intersection*" is allowed to have 2 as a factor of its UID. Consequently, the *mod 2* operation can be used to quickly verify whether two regions are disjoint or not. The other prime numbers used for computing UIDs are also assigned to represent fundamental topological relationships between regions.

The so-called PN strategy for picking the prime numbers, described by Chang and Yang [1997], requires 20 bits per relationship in the matrix. The GPN strategy presented by Chang *et al.* [2001] reduces the number of required bits to only 11 per relationship. Chang *et al.* [2003] propose an alternative encoding scheme that uses a different bit pattern scheme. Although this scheme requires 12 bits (instead of the 11 required by GPN) for each relationships, spatial reasoning can be performed using bitwise-and/bitwise-or operations instead of the significantly more expensive modulo operations required by PN and GPN. Thus, despite its higher bit length, this strategy has been shown to require much shorter time for query processing than the prime number-based strategies, PN and GPN.

Note that reducing the number of bits required to represent each relationship is not the only way to reduce the storage cost and the cost of comparisons that need to be performed for spatial reasoning. An alternative approach is to reduce the number of relationships to be considered: given an image with n objects, all the matrix-based representations discussed earlier need to maintain $O(n^2)$ relationships; Petraglia *et al.* [2001], on the other hand, use certain equivalence and transitivity rules to identify relationships that are redundant (i.e., can be inferred by the remaining relationships) to reduce the number of pairwise relationships that need to be explicitly maintained.

Nine-Intersection Matrix

Egenhofer [1994] describes topological relationships between two regions on a plane in terms of their interiors (^{o}), boundaries (δ), and exteriors ($^-$). In particular, it proposes to use the so-called *nine-intersection matrix* representation

$$\begin{pmatrix} o_1{}^o \cap o_2{}^o & o_1{}^o \cap \delta o_2 & o_1{}^o \cap o_2{}^- \\ \delta o_1 \cap o_2{}^o & \delta o_1 \cap \delta o_2 & \delta o_1 \cap o_2{}^- \\ o_1{}^- \cap o_2{}^o & o_1{}^- \cap \delta o_2 & o_1{}^- \cap o_2{}^- \end{pmatrix}$$

for capturing the $2^9 = 512$ different possible binary topological relationships[9] between a given pair, o_1 and o_2, of objects. These 512 binary relationships include eight common ones: *contains, covers, covered by, disjoint, equals, inside, meets,* and *overlaps.* For example, if the nine-intersection matrix has the form

$$\begin{pmatrix} \geq 1 & \geq 1 & \geq 1 \\ 0 & \geq 1 & \geq 1 \\ 0 & 0 & \geq 1 \end{pmatrix},$$

---

[9] Each binary topological relationship corresponds to one of the 2^9 subsets of the elements in the nine-intersection matrix.

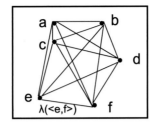

Figure 2.36. A sample spatial orientation graph.

we say that o_1 *covers* o_2. Similarly, the statement, o_1 *overlaps* o_2, can be represented as

$$\begin{pmatrix} \geq 1 & \geq 1 & \geq 1 \\ \geq 1 & \geq 1 & \geq 1 \\ \geq 1 & \geq 1 & \geq 1 \end{pmatrix}$$

using the nine-intersection matrix.

The nine-intersection matrix can be extended to represent more complex topological relationships between other types of spatial entities, such as between regions, curves, polygons, and points. In particular, the definitions of interior and exterior need to be expanded (or replaced by "not applicable") when dealing with curves and points. For example, the definition of *inside* will vary depending on whether one considers the region encircled by a closed polygon to be its interior or its exterior.

2.3.6.2 Points, the Spatial Orientation Graph, and the Plane-Sweep Technique

Whereas field-based approaches to organization are common because of their simplicity, more advanced image and video models apply object-based representations [Li and Candan, 1999a; MPEG7], which describe objects (based on their spatial as well as nonspatial properties) and their spatial positions and relationships. Also, field-based approaches are not directly applicable when the spatial data are described (for example using X3D [X3D]) over a real-valued space that is not always efficient to represent in the form of a grid. In this section, we present an alternative, point-based, model to represent spatial knowledge.

Spatial Orientation Graph

Without loss of generality,[10] let us consider a 2D space $[0, 1] \times [0, 1]$ and a set, $F = \{\langle f, x, y \rangle \mid f \in features \wedge 0 \leq x, y \leq 1\}$ of feature points, where *features* is a finite set of features of interest. The spatial orientation graph [Gudivada and Raghavan, 1995] one can use for representing this set of points is an edge-labeled clique (i.e., a complete undirected graph), $G(V, E, \lambda)$, where each $v_i \in V$ corresponds to a $f_i \in F$ and for each edge $\langle v_i, v_j \rangle \in E$, $\lambda(\langle v_i, v_j \rangle)$ is equal to the slope of the line segment between v_i and v_j (Figure 2.36):

$$\lambda(\langle v_i, v_j \rangle) = \frac{x_i - x_j}{y_i - y_j} = \frac{x_j - x_i}{y_j - y_i}.$$

---

[10] The algorithms discussed in this section can be extended to spaces with a higher number of dimensions or to spaces where the spaces have different, even discrete spans.

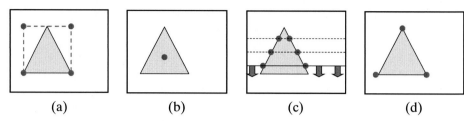

Figure 2.37. Converting a region into a set of points: (a) minimum bounding rectangle, (b) centroid, (c) line sweep, and (d) corners.

Given two spatial orientation graphs, G_1 and G_2, whether G_1 directionally matches G_2 can be decided by comparing the extent to which the edges of the two graphs conform to each other.

Plane Sweep

If the features are not points but regions (as in Figure 2.39) in 2D space, however, point-based representations cannot be directly applied. One way to address this problem is to convert each regional feature into a set of points collectively describing the region and then apply the algorithms described earlier to the union of all the points obtained through this process. Figure 2.37 illustrates four possible schemes for this purpose. (a) In the minimum bounding rectangle scheme, the corners of the tightest rectangle containing the region are used as the feature points. This scheme may overestimate the sizes of the regions. (b) In the centroid scheme, only a single data point corresponding to the center mass of the region is used as the feature point. Although this approach is especially useful for similarity and distance measures that assume that there is only one point per feature, it cannot be used to express topological relationships between regions. (c) The line sweep method moves a line[11] along one of the dimensions and records the intersection between the line and the boundary of the region at predetermined intervals. This scheme helps identify points that tightly cover the region, but it may lead to a large number of representative points for large regions.

A fourth alternative (d) is to identify the corners of the region and use these corners to represent the region. Corners and other intersections can be computed either by traversing the periphery of the regions or by modifying the sweep algorithm to move continuously and look for intersections among line segments in the 2D space. Whenever the sweep line passes over a corner (i.e, the mutual end point of two line segments) or an intersection, the algorithm records this point. To find all the intersections on a given sweep line efficiently, the algorithm keeps track of the ordering of the line segments intersecting this sweep line (and updates this ordering incrementally whenever needed) and checks only neighbors at each iteration (Figure 2.38). This scheme, commonly referred as the *plane sweep* technique [Shamos and Hoey, 1976], runs in $O((n+k)logn)$ time, where n is the number of line segments and k is the number of intersections, whereas a naive algorithm that compares all line segments against each other to locate intersections would require $O(n^2)$ time.

---

[11] Although this example shows a vertical sweep, in many cases horizontal and vertical sweeps are used together to prevent omission of data points along purely vertical or purely horizontal edges.

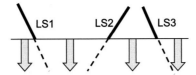

Figure 2.38. Plane sweep: Line segment LS_1 need to be compared only against LS_2 for intersection, but not for LS_3.

2.3.6.3 Exact Retrieval Based on Spatial Information

Exact query answering using spatial predicates involves describing the data as a set of facts and the query as a logical statement or a constraint and checking whether the data satisfy the query or not [Chang and Lee, 1991; Sistla *et al.*, 1994, 1995]. Specific cases of the exact retrieval problem can be efficient to solve. For example, if we are using the 9DLT matrix representation to capture spatial information, then an exact match between two images can be verified by performing a matrix difference operation and checking whether the result is the 0 matrix or not [Chang, 1991]. In general, however, given a query and a large database, the search for exact matches by comparing query and image representation pairs one by one can be very costly.

Punitha and Guru [2006] present an exact search technique, which requires only $O(log|M|)$ search time, where M is the set of all spatial media (e.g., images) in the database. In this scheme, each object in a given image is represented by its centroid. Let $F = \{\langle f, x, y\rangle \mid f \in features \wedge 0 \leq x, y \leq 1\}$ be a set of object centroids, where *features* is a finite set of features of interest. The algorithm first selects two distinct objects, $\langle f_p, x_p, y_p\rangle$ and $\langle f_q, x_q, y_q\rangle$, that are farthest away from each other and $f_p < f_q$.[12] The line joining $\langle x_p, y_p\rangle$ to $\langle x_q, y_q\rangle$ is treated as the *line of reference* and its direction from $\langle x_p, y_p\rangle$ is selected as the *reference direction*.[13] In particular, given

$$\alpha = tan^{-1}\left(\frac{y_q - y_p}{x_q - x_p}\right), \quad \text{and}$$

$$\beta = sin^{-1}\left(\frac{y_q - x_q}{\sqrt{(y_q - y_p)^2 + (x_q - x_p)^2}}\right),$$

the reference direction, θ_r, is computed as

$$\theta_r = \begin{cases} \alpha + \pi & \text{if } \alpha < 0 \wedge \beta > 0 \\ \alpha - \pi & \text{if } \alpha > 0 \wedge \beta < 0 \\ \alpha & \text{otherwise.} \end{cases}$$

The reference direction, θ_r, is used for eliminating sensitivity to rotations: After any rotation, the furthest objects in the image will stay the same and, furthermore, the

---

[12] This is only to have a consistent method of selecting the direction of the line joining these two centroids.

[13] If there are multiple object pairs that have the same (largest) distance and the same (lowest) feature-labeled centroid, then the candidate directions of reference are combined using vector addition into a single direction of reference.

relative positions of the other objects with respect to this pair will be constant. Thus, given two identical images, except that one of them is rotated, the spatial orientation graphs resulting after the respective directions of reference are taken into account will be the same. To achieve this effect, given two distinct objects, $\langle f_i, x_i, y_i \rangle$ and $\langle f_j, x_j, y_j \rangle$, the corresponding spatial orientation, θ_{ij}, is chosen as the direction of the line joining $\langle x_i, y_i \rangle$ to $\langle x_j, y_j \rangle$ relative to the direction of reference, θ_r.

Let N be the number of distinct spatial orientation edges in the graph (in the worst case $N = O(|F|^2)$). Instead of storing N direction triples (i.e., edges) in the spatial orientation graph explicitly, one can compute a unique key for each edge and combine these into a single key for quick image lookup. Given a spatial orientation edge, labeled θ_{ij}, from f_i to f_j, Punitha and Guru [2006] compute the corresponding unique key, k_{ij} as follows:

$$k_{ij} = D\left((f_i - 1)|F| + (f_j - 1)\right) + (C_{ij} - 1).$$

Here, D is the number of distinct angles the system can detect (i.e., $D = \frac{2\pi}{\epsilon}$, where ϵ is the angular precision of the system) and C_{ij} is the discrete angle corresponding to θ_{ij}. Given all N key values belonging to the spatial orientation graph of the given image, Punitha and Guru [2006] compute the mean, μ, and the standard deviation, σ, of the set of key values and stores the triple, $\langle N, \mu, \sigma \rangle$ as the representative signature of the image. Punitha and Guru [2006] showed that given two distinct images (i.e., two distinct spatial orientation graphs), the corresponding $\langle N, \mu, \sigma \rangle$ triples are also different. Thus these triples can be used for indexing the images, and exact searches on this index can be performed using a basic binary search mechanism [Cormen *et al.*, 2001] in $O(log|M|)$ time, where M is the set of all spatial media (e.g., images) in the database.

For more complex scenarios that also include topological relationships in addition to the directional ones, the problem of finding exact matches to a given user query is known to be NP-complete [Tucci *et al.*, 1991; Zhang, 1994; Zhang and Yau, 2005]. Thus, although in some specific cases, the complexity of the problem can be reduced using logical reduction techniques [Sistla *et al.*, 1994], in general, given spatial models rich enough to capture both directional and topological relationships (also considering that end users are most often interested in partial matches as well), most multimedia database systems choose to rely on approximate matching techniques.

2.3.6.4 Spatial Similarity
Retrieving data based on similarity of the spatial distributions (e.g., Figure 2.39) of the features requires data structures and algorithms that can support spatial similarity (or difference) computations. One method of performing similarity-based retrieval based on spatial features is to describe spatial knowledge in the form of rules and constraints that can be evaluated for consistency or inconsistency [Chang and Lee, 1991; Sistla *et al.*, 1994, 1995].

Another alternative is to represent spatial requirements in the form of probabilistic or fuzzy constraints that can be evaluated against the data to obtain a spatial matching score. Although the definitions of the spatial operators and predicates

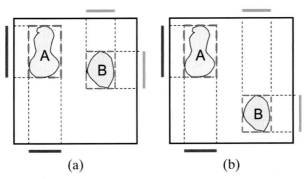

(a)   (b)

Figure 2.39. (a,b) Two images, both with two objects: *B* is to the right of *A* in both images; on the other hand, while *B* overlaps with *A* in the vertical direction in the first image, it is simply below *A* in the other. How similar are the object distributions of these two images?

discussed in the previous section are all *exact*, they can be extended with probabilistic, fuzzy, or similarity-based interpretations:

- Many shape, curve, or object extraction schemes (such as Hough transforms; [Duda and Hart, 1972]) provide only probabilistic guarantees.
- Some topological relationships are more similar to each other than the others (e.g., similarity between two topological relationships may, for example, be computed based on comparisons between nine-intersection matrices).
- Some distances or angles may be relatively insignificant for the given application, and objects may be returned as matches even if they do not satisfy the user-specified distance and/or direction criteria perfectly.

A third alternative is to rely on the properties of the underlying spatial model to develop more specific spatial similarity/distance measures. In this section, we first focus on the case where features of the objects in the space can be represented as points. We then extend the discussion to the cases where the objects are of arbitrary shape.

Without loss of generality,[14] let us consider a 2D space $[0, 1] \times [0, 1]$ and a set, $F = \{\langle f, x, y \rangle \mid f \in features \wedge 0 \leq x, y \leq 1\}$ of feature points, where *features* is a finite set of features of interest.

Spatial Orientation Graph and Similarity Computation

As we have seen in Section 2.3.6.2, the spatial information in a media object, such as an image, can be represented using spatial orientation graphs. Gudivada and Raghavan [1995] provide an algorithm that computes the similarity of two spatial orientation graphs, G_1 and G_2. This algorithm assumes that each feature occurs only once in a given image; that is;

$$((v_i, v_j \in V) \wedge (f_i = f_j)) \rightarrow (v_i = v_j).$$

For each $e_k \in E_1$, the algorithm finds the corresponding edge $e_l \in E_2$ (because each feature occurs only once per image, there is at most one such pairing edge). For

---

[14] The algorithms discussed in this section can be extended to spaces with a higher number of dimensions or to spaces that have different, even discrete, spans.

each such pair of edges in the two spatial orientation graphs, the overall spatial orientation graph similarity value is increased by

$$\left(\frac{1 + cos(e_k, e_l)}{2}\right) \frac{100}{|E_1|},$$

where $cos(e_k, e_l)$ is the cosine of the smaller angle between e_k and e_l. The first term ensures that if the angle between the two edges is 0, then this pair contributes the maximum value $((1 + 1)/2 = 1)$ to the overall similarity score; on the other hand, if the edges are perpendicular to each other, then their contribution is lower $((1 + 0)/2 = 0.5)$. The second term of the foregoing equation ensures that the maximum overall matching score is 100. The total similarity score is then

$$sim(G_1, G_2) = \sum_{e_k \in E_1 \wedge e_l \in E_2 \wedge match(e_k, e_l)} \left(\frac{1 + cos(e_k, e_l)}{2}\right) \frac{100}{|E_1|}.$$

Note that, because of the division by $|E_1|$ in the second term, the overall similarity score is not symmetric. If needed, this measure can be rendered symmetric simply by computing $sim(G_2, G_1)$ by considering the edges in E_2 first, searching each edge in E_1 for pairing, and, finally, averaging the two similarity scores $sim(G_1, G_2)$ and $sim(G_2, G_1)$.

Assuming that given an edge in one graph, the corresponding edge in the other graph can be found in constant time, the complexity of the algorithm is quadratic in the number of features and linear in the number of edges; i.e. $O(|E_1| + |E_2|)$.

2D-String

The preceding scheme has a major shortcoming that makes it less useful in most applications: it assumes that each feature occurs only once. Relaxing the assumption that the features occurs only once, however, significantly increases the complexity of the algorithm. The 2D-string approach [Chang et al., 1987; Chang and Jungert, 1986] to spatial similarity search reduces the complexity of the matching by first mapping the given spatial distribution, $F = \{\langle f, x, y \rangle \mid f \in features \wedge 0 \leq x, y \leq 1\}$, of features in the 2D space into a string. This is achieved by ordering the feature points first in the horizontal direction (i.e., increasing x) and then in the vertical direction (i.e., increasing y). Each ordering is converted into a corresponding string by combining the feature names with symbols "<" and "=" that highlight the pairwise relationships of feature points that are neighboring along the given direction. For example, in Figure 2.40(a), the six features a through f are ordered along the horizontal direction as follows:

$$e < a = c < f < b < d;$$

therefore the horizontal spatial information in this image is represented using the string "e<a=c<f<b<d" (the tie between a and c, which are equal, is broken arbitrarily). In the same example, the six features are ordered vertically as

$$a = b < c < d < e < f;$$

thus the corresponding string "a=b<c<d<e<f" represents this vertical ordering. Once the horizontal and vertical strings are generated, the two strings are combined into

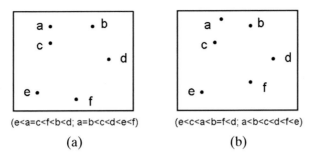

(e<a=c<f<b<d; a=b<c<d<e<f)   (e<c<a<b=f<d; a<b<c<d<f<e)

(a)   (b)

Figure 2.40. (a,b) Two images, each with six features and the corresponding 2D strings.

a single string of the form "(e<a=c<f<b<d;a=b<c<d<e<f)" that represents the spatial relationships of the feature points along both horizontal and vertical directions.

Now let us consider the two images in Figures 2.40(a) and (b), which have the same features, but with slightly different spatial distributions. Chang and Jungert [1986] quantify the degree of matching between these two images by comparing the corresponding 2D strings, "(e<a=c<f<b<d;a=b<c<d<e<f)" and "(e<c<a<b=f<d;a<b<c<d<f<e)". More specifically, Chang and Jungert [1986] propose a similarity matching algorithm that ranks the feature symbols in the two sub-strings based on the number of < symbols that precede each feature symbol and compares these rankings. The algorithm first creates a feature compatibility graph, where feature f_i is connected to feature f_j if there are two corresponding feature instances *similarly* ranked in both strings. Finally, the number of objects in the largest subset of mutually compatible features is returned as the similarity between the two strings.

Identification of a maximal compatible set of objects, however, requires costly maximal clique search in the compatibility graph (this task is known to be NP-complete). A much cheaper alternative to the use of maximal cliques is to compare the given pair of 2D strings directly using the so-called edit-distance measures that are commonly used for approximate string matching (see Section 3.2.2).

2D ⊖R-String

Note that the 2D strings generated using the approach just discussed are highly sensitive to rotations, and this can be a significant shortcoming for many applications. An alternative scheme, suitable to use when the matching needs to be less sensitive to rotations, is the 2D ⊖R-String [Gudivada, 1998]. Given an image, the corresponding 2D ⊖R-String [Gudivada, 1998] is created by imposing a total order of feature points by sweeping a line segment originating from the center of the space and noting the feature points met along the way (and if two points occur along the same angle, breaking the ties based on their distances from the center). For example, for the feature point distribution in Figure 2.41(a), the corresponding 2D ⊖R-String obtained by starting the sweep at $\Theta = 0$ would be "dbacef". For the slightly rotated feature distribution in Figure 2.41(b), on the other hand, the corresponding 2D ⊖R-String obtained by starting the sweep at $\Theta = 0$ is "bacefd".

Note that the two strings created in the preceding example are quite similar, but they are not exactly equal. This highlights the fact that 2D ⊖R-strings obtained by always starting the sweep at $\Theta = 0$ are not completely robust against rotations. This is corrected by first identifying a feature point shared by both images and starting

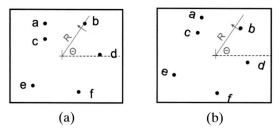

(a)   (b)

Figure 2.41. (a) 2D ΘR-String obtained by starting the sweep at $\Theta = 0$ is "dbacef"; (b) 2D ΘR-String obtained by starting the sweep at $\Theta = 0$ is "bacefd".

the sweep from that point. In the foregoing example, if we pick the feature point a as the starting point of the sweep in both of the example images, then we will obtain the same string, "acefdb", for both images.

The basic 2D ΘR-string scheme is also sensitive to translation: if the features in an image are shifted along some direction, because the center of the image moves relative to the data points, the string would be affected from this shift. Once again, this is corrected by picking the pivot, around which the sweep rotates, relative to the data points (e.g., the center of mass,

$$\left\langle \frac{\sum_{(f_i, x_i, y_i) \in F} x_i}{|F|}, \frac{\sum_{(f_i, x_i, y_i) \in F} y_i}{|F|} \right\rangle,$$

of all data points), instead of picking a pivot centrally located relative to the boundaries of the space.

2D E-String

So far, we have only considered point-based features; if the features are not points but regions in the 2D space (as in Figure 2.39), the preceding techniques cannot be directly applied for computing spatial similarities. The 2D E-string scheme [Jungert, 1988] tries to address this shortcoming.

To create a 2D E-string, we first project each feature region onto the two axes of the 2D space to obtain the corresponding intervals (Figure 2.42(a)). Then, a total order is imposed on each set of intervals projected onto a given dimension of the space (e.g., by using the starting points of the intervals) and a string representing these intervals is created as in the basic 2D-string scheme. Note that unlike a pair of points on a line, which can be compared against each other using only "=" and "<", a pair of intervals requires a larger number of comparison operators (Table 2.3). Thus, the number of symbols used to construct 2D E-strings is larger than the number of symbols used for constructing point-based 2D-strings.

2D G-String, 2D C-String, and 2D C$^+$-String

One major disadvantage of the 2D E-string mechanism is that the resulting strings are more complex because of the existence of new interval-based operators. The 2D G-string approach [Chang et al., 1989] tries to resolve this problem by cutting regions into non-overlapping sub-objects in such a way that each sub-object is either before, after, or equal to the sub-objects of the other regions (Figure 2.42(b)). This eliminates the need for complex interval comparison operators and enables the construction of strings in a way analogous to the basic 2D-string

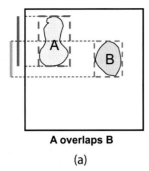
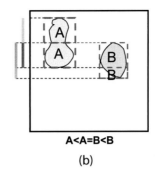

A overlaps B   A<A=B<B

(a)   (b)

Figure 2.42. (a) The 2D E-String projects objects onto the axes of the space to obtain the corresponding intervals; these intervals are then compared using interval comparison operators, (b) the 2D G-string scheme cuts the objects into non-overlapping sub-objects so that the "$<$" and "$=$" operators are sufficient (the figure shows only the vertical strings).

mechanism, with "$<$" and "$=$" symbols (though "$=$" in this case means interval equality).

Despite the resulting simplicity, the 2D G-string approach can be increasingly costly for images with lots of objects: During the construction of the 2D G-string, in the worst case, each object may be partitioned at the begin and end points of the other objects in the image. Thus, if an image contains n objects, each object may be partitioned into as many as $2n$ sub-objects, resulting in $O(n^2)$ sub-objects to be included in the string. This significant increase in the length of the strings can render string comparisons very expensive for practical use. The 2D C-string [Lee and Hsu, 1992] and 2D C$^+$-string [Huang and Jean, 1994] schemes reduce the length of the strings by performing the cuts only at the end points of the overlapping objects, not both start and end points. This reduces the number of cuts needed (each object may be partitioned up to n pieces instead of up to $2n$). However, because certain non-equality overlaps are allowed by the cutting strategy, interval comparison operators other than "$<$" and "$=$" may also be needed during the string construction.

2D B-String, 2D Bϵ-String, and 2D Z-String

The 2D B-String scheme [Lee *et al.*, 1992] avoids cuts entirely and, instead, represents the intervals along the horizontal and vertical axes of the space using only their *start* and *end* points. Thus, each interval is represented using only two points

Table 2.3. Thirteen possible relationships between two intervals A and B^a

Symbol	Relationship	Description
A < B	A before B; B after A	$end(A) < begin(B)$
A = B	A equals B	$(begin(A) = begin(B)) \wedge (end(A) = end(B))$
A ∥ B	A meets B; B met_by A	$end(A) = begin(B)$
A & B	A contains B; B contained_by A	$(begin(A) < begin(B)) \wedge (end(A) > end(B))$
A [B	A started_by B; B starts A	$(begin(A) = begin(B)) \wedge (end(A) > end(B))$
A] B	A finished_by B; B finishes A	$(begin(A) < begin(B)) \wedge (end(A) = end(B))$
A / B	A overlaps B; B overlapped_by A	$begin(A) < begin(B) < end(A) < end(B)$

^{a} See Section 2.3.5.3 for the use of these operators in interval-based temporal data management.

and, once again, "$<$" and "$=$" operators are sufficient for constructing 2D strings. The 2D Bϵ-string scheme [Wang, 2001] also uses an encoding based on the end points of the intervals. However, unlike the 2D B-string scheme, which uses "$<$" and "$=$" operators, the 2D Bϵ-string introduces dummy objects into the space to obtain a total order that eliminates the need for using any explicit operator symbols in the string ("$<$" is implied). Also, unlike the 2D B-string scheme that relies on the original 2D-String scheme for similarity search, Wang [2001] proposes a *longest common subsequence* (LCS)-based similarity function, which has $O(pq)$ time and space cost for matching two strings of length p and q.

The 2D Z-string [Lee and Chiu, 2003] scheme also avoids cuts completely and thus results in strings of length $O(n)$ for spaces containing n regions. Instead of creating cuts, the 2D Z-string combines regions into groups demarcated by "(" and ")" symbols. Along each dimension, the 2D Z-string first finds those regions that are dominating: given a set of regions that have the same end point along the given direction, the one that has the smallest beginning point is the dominating region for the given set. In other words, the dominating region is *finished_by* all the regions it dominates (along the given dimension).

The dominating regions are found by scanning the begin and end points along the chosen dimension starting from the lowest value. If a dominating region is found and there is no other region partially overlapping this region along the chosen dimension, then this dominating region and all the regions dominated by it are combined into a *template region*. If there are any partially overlapping regions, these regions (as well as regions covered by them) are merged with the dominating region (and the regions covered by it) into a single *template region*. The template region combination algorithm presented in Lee and Chiu [2003] operates on the regions being combined into a template in a consistent manner, thus ensuring that there are no ambiguities in the string construction process. Because no region is cut, the length of the resulting string is $O(n)$.

2D-PIR and Topology Neighborhood Graph

2D-PIR [Nabil *et al.*, 1996] combines Allen's interval operators (see Section 2.3.5.3), the 2D-strings discussed previously, and topological relationships (see Section 2.3.6) into a unified representation. As in the case of the 2D E-string, the regions are projected onto the axes of the 2D space and the corresponding x- and y-intervals are noted. A 2D-PIR relationship between two regions is defined as a triple $\langle \delta, \chi, \psi \rangle$, where δ is a topological relationship from the set {*disjoint, meets, contains, inside, overlaps, covers, equals, covered-by*}, whereas χ and ψ are each one of the thirteen interval relationships (see Figure 2.26), along x and y axes, respectively. A 2D-PIR graph is a directed graph, $G(V, E, \lambda)$ where V is the set of regions in the given 2D space and E is the set of edges, labeled by 2D-PIR relationships between the end points of the edges. $\lambda()$ is a function that associates relationship labels to edges.

The degree of similarity between two 2D-PIR graphs is computed based on the degrees of similarity between the corresponding 2D-PIR relationships in both graphs. To support computation of the similarity of a given pair of 2D-PIR relationships, $\langle \delta_i, \chi_i, \psi_i \rangle$ and $\langle \delta_j, \chi_j, \psi_j \rangle$, Nabil *et al.* [1996] propose similarity metrics suitable for comparing the topological and interval relationships. In particular,

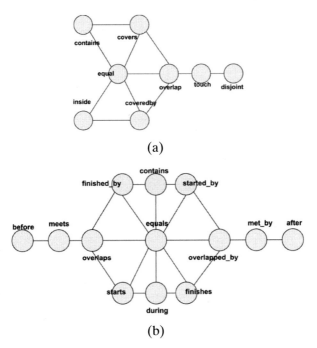

Figure 2.43. Topology and interval neighborhood graphs [Nabil *et al.*, 1996]: (a) Topology neighborhood graph, (b) Interval neighborhood graph.

Nabil *et al.* [1996] introduce a topological neighborhood graph, where two topological relationships are neighbors if they can be *directly* transformed into one another by continuously deforming (scaling, moving, rotating) the corresponding objects. Figure 2.43(a) shows this topological neighborhood graph. For example, the relationships *disjoint* and *touch* are neighbors in this graph, because they can be transformed to each other by moving *disjoint* objects until they *touch* (or by moving apart objects that are *touch*ing to each other to make them *disjoint*). Nabil *et al.* [1996] also define a similar graph for interval relationships (Figure 2.43(b)).

Given a topological or interval neighborhood graph, the distance, Δ, between two relationships is defined as the shortest distance between the corresponding nodes in the graph. The distance between two 2D-PIR relationships, $\langle \delta_i, \chi_i, \psi_i \rangle$ and $\langle \delta_j, \chi_j, \psi_j \rangle$, is computed using the Euclidean distance metric:

$$\Delta(\langle \delta_i, \chi_i, \psi_i \rangle, \langle \delta_j, \chi_j, \psi_j \rangle) = \sqrt{\Delta(\delta_i, \delta_j)^2 + \Delta(\chi_i, \chi_j)^2 + \Delta(\psi_i, \psi_j)^2}.$$

Finally, the distance between two 2D-PIR graphs, $G_1(V_1, E_1)$ and $G_2(V_2, E_2)$, is defined as the sum of the distances between the corresponding 2D-PIR relationships in both graphs. Note that this definition does not associate any penalty to regions that are missing in one or the other space, but penalizes the relationship mismatches for region pairs that occur in both spaces.

The 2D-PIR scheme deals with rotations and reflections by essentially re-rotating one of the spaces until the spatial properties (i.e., x and y intervals) of a selected reference object in both spaces are aligned. The 2D-PIR graphs are revised based on this rotation, and the degree of matching is computed only after the transformation is completed.

SIM_{DTC} and SIM_L

Like 2D-PIR, in order to support similarity assessments under transformations, such as scaling, translation, and rotation, the SIM_{DTC} technique [El-Kwae and Kabuka, 1999] aligns regions (objects) in one space with the matching objects in the other space. To correct for rotations, SIM_{DTC}, introduces a rotation correction angle (RCA) and computes similarity between two spaces as a weighted sum of the number of common regions and the closeness of directional and topological relationships between region pairs in both spaces. In SIM_{DTC}, directional spatial relationships between objects in an image are represented as edges in a spatial orientation graph as in [Gudivada and Raghavan, 1995] (Figure 2.36); directional similarity is computed based on the angular alignments of the corresponding objects in both spaces. Let G_1 and G_2 be two spatial orientation graphs (see Section 2.3.6.4 for the formal definition of a spatial orientation graph). El-Kwae and Kabuka [1999] show that, if G_1 and G_2 are two spatial orientation graphs corresponding to two spaces with the same spatial distribution of objects, but where the objects on G_2 are rotated by some fixed angle, then this rotation angle can be computed as θ_{RCA}:

$$\theta_{RCA} = -tan^{-1}\frac{\sum_{(e_i \in E_1) \wedge (e_j \in E_2) \wedge (e_i \sim e_j)} sin(e_i, e_j)}{\sum_{(e_i \in E_1) \wedge (e_j \in E_2) \wedge (e_i \sim e_j)} cos(e_i, e_j)},$$

where $e_i \sim e_j$ means that the edges correspond to the same object pair in their respective spaces, and $sin(e_i, e_j)$ and $cos(e_i, e_j)$ are the sine and cosine of the (smallest) angle between these two edges.[15]

Like the 2D G-string technique, SIM_{DTC} is applicable to only those images which have only one instance of a given object. SIM_L [Sciascio et al., 2004], on the other hand, removes this assumption. For each image, SIM_L extracts all the angles between the centroids of the objects, and for a given object it computes the maximum error between the corresponding angles. The distance is then defined as the maximum error for all groups of objects.

2.3.7 Audio Models

Audio data are often viewed as 1D continuous or discrete signals. In that sense, many of the feature models, such as histograms or DCT (Section 4.2.9.1), applicable to 2D images have their counterparts for audio data as well. Unlike images, however, audio can also have domain-specific features that one can leverage for indexing, classification, and retrieval. For example, a music audio object can be modeled based on its pitch, chroma, loudness, rhythm, beat/tempo, and timbre features [Jensen, 2007].

Pitch represents the perceived fundamental (or lowest) frequency of the audio data. Whereas frequency can be analyzed and modeled using frequency analysis

---

[15] Note that this is similar to the concept of *reference direction* introduced in Section 2.3.6.3.

(such as DCT) of the audio data, perceived frequency requires psychophysical adjustments. For frequencies lower than about 1 kHZ, the human ear hears tones with a linear scale, whereas for frequencies higher than this, it hears in a logarithmic scale. Mel (or melody) scale [Stevens *et al.*, 1937] is a perceptual scale of pitches that adjusts for this. More specifically, given an audio signal with frequency, f, the corresponding mel scale is computed as [Fant, 1968]

$$m = \frac{1000}{log_{10}2} log_{10}(1 + \frac{f}{1000}).$$

Bark scale [Sekey and Hanson, 1987] is a similar perceptual scale which transforms the audible frequency range from 20 Hz to 15500 Hz into 24 scales (or bands). Most audio (especially music and speech) feature analysis is performed in mel or bark scale rather than the original frequency scale.

Chroma represents how a pitch is perceived (analogous to color for light): pitch perception is periodic; two pitches, p_1 and p_2, where $p_1/p_2 = 2^c$ for some integer c are perceived as having a similar quality or chroma [Bartsch and Wakefield, 2001; Shepard, 1964].

Loudness measures the sound level as a ratio of the power of the audio signal with respect to the power of the lowest sound that the human ear can recognize. In particular, if we denote this lowest audible power as $P_\perp$, then the loudness of the audio signal with P power is measured (in decibels, dB) as $10log_{10}(\frac{P}{P_\perp})$. *Phon* and *sone* are two related psychophysical measures, the first taking into account the frequency response of the human ear in adjusting the loudness level based on the frequency of the signal and the second quantifying the perceived loudness instead of the audio signal power. Experiments with volunteers showed that each 10-dB increase in the sound level is perceived as doubling the loudness; approximately, each 0.25 sone corresponds to one such doubling (i.e., 1 sone $\simeq$ 40 dB).

Beat (or *tempo*) is the perceived periodicity of the audio signal [Ellis, 2007]. Beat analysis can be complicated, because the same audio signal can be periodic at multiple levels and different listeners may identify different levels as the main beat. The analysis is often performed on the onset strength signal, which represents the loudness and time of onsets, that is, the points where the amplitude of the signal rises from zero [Klapuri, 1999]. The tempo (in beats per minute or BPM) can be computed by splitting the signal to its Fourier frequency spectra (Section 4.2.9.1) and picking the frequency(s) with the highest amplitudes [Holzapfel and Stylianou, 2008]. An alternative approach, in lieu of Fourier-based spectral analysis, is to compute the overlapping autocorrelations for blocks of the onset strength signal. Autocorrelation of a signal gives the similarity/correlation[16] of the signal with itself for different amount of temporal shifts (or lags); thus, the size of shift that provides the highest self-similarity corresponds to the period with which the sound repeats itself. Ellis [2007] measures tempo by taking the autocorrelation of the onset strength signal for various lags and finding the lag that leads to the largest autocorrelation value.

---

[16] See Section 3.5.1.2 for a more precise definition of correlation.

Rhythm is the repeated patterns in audio. Thus, while also being related to the periodicity of the audio, it is a more complex measure than pitch and tempo and captures the periodicity of the audio signal as well as its texture [Desain, 1992]. As in beat analysis, the note onsets determine the main characteristics of the rhythm. Jensen [2007] presents a *rhythmogram* feature, which detects the onsets based on the spectral flux of the audio signal which measures how quickly the power spectrum of the signal changes. As in beat detection, the *rhythmogram* is extracted by leveraging autocorrelation. Instead of simply picking the lags that provide largest autocorrelation in the spectral flux, the rhythmogram associates an autocorrelation vector to each time instance describing how correlated the signal is with its vicinity for different lags or rhythm intervals. In general, autocorrelation is thought to be a better indicator of rhythm than the frequency spectra one can obtain by Fourier analysis [Desain, 1992].

Timbre is harder to define as it is essentially a catch-all feature that represents all characteristics of an audio signal, except for pitch and loudness [McAdams and Bregman, 1979]. Jensen [2007] creates a *timbregram* by performing frequency spectrum analysis around each time point and creating an amplitude vector for each frequency band (normalized to bark scale to be aligned with the human auditory system).

2.4 MULTIMEDIA QUERY LANGUAGES

Unlike traditional data models, such as relational and object-oriented, multimedia data models are highly heterogeneous and address the needs of very different applications. Here, we provide a sample of major multimedia query languages and compare and contrast their key functionalities (see Table 2.4 for a more extensive list):

VideoSQL/OVID

Oomoto and Tanaka [1993] propose VideoSQL, one of the earliest query languages for accessing video data, as part of their OVID video-object database system. Being one of the earliest multimedia query languages, it has certain limitations; for example, it does not support spatiotemporal predicates over the video data. The SQL-like language provides a SELECT clause, which helps the user specify the category of the resulting video object as being *continuous* (consisting of a single continuous video frame sequence), *incontinuous*, or *AnyObject*. The FROM clause is used to specify the name of the video database. The WHERE clause allows the user to specify conditions over attribute value pairs of the form [attribute] is [value | video object], [attribute] contains [value | video object], and definedOver [video sequence | video frame]. The last predicate returns video objects that are included in the given video frame sequence.

QBIC

QBIC [Flickner *et al.*, 1995; Niblack *et al.*, 1993] allows for querying of images and videos. Images can be queried based on their *scene* content or based on *objects*, that is, parts of a given image identified to be coherent units. Videos are stored in

Table 2.4. Multimedia query language examples

System/Language/Team	Properties
QPE [Chang and Fu, 1980]	A relational query language for formulating queries on pictorial as well as conventional relations. An early application of the query-by-example idea to image retrieval
PICQUERY [Joseph and Cardenas, 1988] and PICQUERY+ [Cardenas et al., 1993]	An early image querying system. PICQUERY is a high-level query language that also supports a QBE-like interface. PICQUERY+ extends this with abstract data types, imprecise or fuzzy descriptors, temporal and object evolutionary events, image processing operators, and visualization constructs.
OVID/VideoSQL [Oomoto and Tanaka, 1993]	An SQL-like language for describing object containment queries in video sequences.
QBIC [Flickner et al., 1995; Niblack et al., 1993]	An image database, where queries can be posed on image objects, scenes, shots, or their combinations and can include conditions on color, texture, shape, location, camera and object motion, and textual annotations. Queries are formulated in the form of visual examples or sketches.
AV [Gibbs et al., 1993]	An object-oriented model for describing temporal and flow composition of audio and video data.
MQL [Kau and Tseng, 1994]	A multimedia query language that supports complex object queries, version queries, and nested queries. The language supports a *contain* predicate that enables pattern matching on images, voice, or text.
NRK-GM [Hjelsvold and Midtstraum, 1994]	A data model for capturing video content and structure. Video is viewed as a hierarchy of structural elements (shots, scenes).
AVS [Weiss et al., 1994]	An algebraic approach to video content description. The video algebra allows nested temporal and spatial combination of video segments.
OCPN [Day et al., 1995a,b; Iino et al., 1994]	Object Composition Petri-Net (OCPN) is a spatiotemporal synchronization model that allows authoring of multimedia documents and creation of media object hierarchies.
MMSQL [Guo et al., 1994]	An SQL-based query language for multimedia data, including images, videos, and sounds. While most querying is based on metadata, the language also provides mechanisms for combining media for presentation purposes.
SCORE [Aslandogan et al., 1995; Sistla et al., 1995]	A similarity based image retrieval system with an entity-relationship (ER) based representation of image content
Chabot [Ogle and Stonebraker, 1995]	An image retrieval system which allows basic semantic annotations: for example, queries can include pre-defined keywords, such as *Rose Red*, associated to various ranges of the color spectrum.
WS-QBE [Schmitt et al., 2005]	A query language for formulating similarity-based, fuzzy multimedia queries. Visual, declarative queries are interpreted through a similarity domain calculus.

(Continued)

Table 2.4 (*Continued*)

System/Language/Team	Properties
TVQL [Hibino and Rundensteiner, 1995, 1996]	A query language specifically focusing on querying trends in video data (e.g., events of type B frequently follow events of type A).
Virage [Bach *et al.*, 1996]	A commercial image retrieval system. Virage provides an SQL-like query language that can be extended by user-defined data types and functions.
VisualSeek [Smith and Chang, 1996]	An image retrieval system that provides region-based image retrieval: users can specify how color regions will be placed with respect to each other.
SMDS [Marcus and Subrahmanian, 1996]	A formal multimedia data model where each media instance consists of a set of states (e.g., video clips, audio tracks), a set of features, their properties, and relationships. The model supports query relaxation, and the language allows for specification of constraints that allow for synchronized presentation of query results
MMQL [Arisawa *et al.*, 1996]	MMQL models video data in terms of physical and logical *cut*s, which can contain entities. In the underlying AIS data model, entities correspond to real-world objects and relationships are modeled as bidirectional functions.
CVQL [Kuo and Chen, 1996]	A content-based video query language for video databases. A set of functions help the description of the spatial and temporal relationships (such as location and motion) between content objects or between a content object and a frame. Macros help capture complex semantic operations for reuse.
AVIS [Adali *et al.*, 1996]	One of the first video query languages that includes a model, not only based on the visual content but also on semantic structures of the video data. These structures are expressed using a Boolean framework based on semantically meaningful constructs, including real objects, objects' roles, activities, and events.
VIQS [Hwang and Subrahmanian, 1996]	An SQL-like query language that supports searches for segments satisfying a query criterion in a video collection. Query results are composed and visualized in the form of presentations.
VISUAL [Balkir *et al.*, 1996, 2002]	An object-oriented, icon-based query language focusing on scientific data. Graphical objects represent the relationships of the application domain. The language supports relational, nested, and object-oriented models.
SEMCOG/VCSQL [Li and Candan, 1999a; Li *et al.*, 1997b,c]	An image and video data model supporting retrieval using both content and semantics. It supports video retrieval at object, frame, action, and composite action levels. While the user specifies the query visually using IFQ, a corresponding declarative VCSQL query is automatically generated and processed using a fuzzy engine. The system also provides system feedback to the user to help query reformulation and exploration

System/Language/Team	Properties
MOQL [Li *et al.*, 1997a] VisualMOQL [Oria *et al.*, 1999]	An object-oriented multimedia query language based on ODMG's Object Query Language (OQL). The language introduces three predicate expressions: *spatial_expression*, *temporal_expression*, and *contains_predicate*. Spatial and temporal expressions introduce spatiotemporal objects, functions, and predicates. The *contains_predicate* checks whether a media object contains a salient object defined as an interesting physical object. The language also provides presentation primitives, such as spatial, temporal, and scenario layouts.
KEQL [Chu *et al.*, 1998]	A query language focusing on biological media. It is based on a data model with three distinct layers: a representational layer (for low-level features), a semantic layer (for hierarchical, spatial, temporal, and evolutionary semantics), and a knowledge layer (representing metadata about shape, temporal, and evolutionary characteristics of real-world objects). In addition to standard predicates, KEQL supports conditions over approximate and conceptual terms.
GVISUAL [Lee *et al.*, 2001]	A query language specifically focusing on querying multimedia presentations modeled as graphs. Each presentation stream is a node in the presentation graph and edges describe sequential or concurrent playout of media streams. GVISUAL extends VISUAL [Balkir *et al.*, 1996, 2002] with temporal constructs.
CHIMP/VIEW [Candan *et al.*, 2000a]	A system/language focused on visualization of multimedia query results in the form of interactive multimedia presentations. Since, given a multimedia query, the number of relevant results is not known in advance and temporal, spatial, and streaming characteristics of the objects in the results are not known, the presentation language is based on virtual objects that can be instantiated with any number of physical objects and can scale in space and time.
SQL/MM [Melton and Eisenberg, 2001]; [SQL03Images; SQL03Multimedia]	SQL/MM, standardized as ISO/IEC 13249, defines packages of generic data types to enable multimedia data to be stored and manipulated in an SQL database. For example, ISO/IEC 13249-5 introduces user-defined types to describe image characteristics, such as height, width, and format, as well as image features, such as average color, color histogram, positional color, and texture.
MMDOC-QL [Liu *et al.*, 2001]	An XML-based query language for querying MPEG-7 documents. In addition to including support for media and spatiotemporal predicates based on the MPEG-7 descriptors, MMDOC-QL also supports path predicates to support structural queries on the XML document structure itself.
MP7QF [Gruhne *et al.*, 2007]	An effort for providing standardized input and output query interfaces to MPEG-7 databases. The query interface supports conditions based on MPEG-7 descriptors, query by example, and query by relevance feedback.

terms of their visually coherent contiguous frame sequences (referred to as shots), and for each shot a representative frame is extracted and indexed. *Motion objects* are extracted from shots and indexed for motion-based queries. Queries can be posed on image objects, scenes, shots, or their combinations and can include conditions on color, texture, shape, location, camera and object motion, and textual annotations. QBIC queries are formulated through a user interface that lets users provide visual examples or sketches.

SCORE

The SCORE [Aslandogan *et al.*, 1995; Sistla *et al.*, 1995] similarity-based image retrieval system uses a refined entity-relationship (ER) model to represent the contents of images. It calculates similarity between the query and an image in the database based on the query specifications and the ER representation of the images. SCORE does not support direct image matching, but provides an iconic user interface that enables visual query construction.

Virage

Virage [Bach *et al.*, 1996] is one of the earliest commercial image retrieval systems. The query model of Virage is mainly based on visual (such as color, shape, and texture) features. It also allows users to formulate keyword-based queries, but mainly at the whole-image level. Virage provides an SQL-like query language that can be extended by user-defined data types and functions.

VisualSeek

VisualSeek [Smith and Chang, 1996] mainly relies on color information to retrieve images. Although VisualSeek is not directly object-based, it provides region-based image retrieval: users can specify how color regions will be placed with respect to each other. VisualSeek provides mechanisms for image and sketch comparisons. VisualSeek does not support retrieval based on semantics (or other visual features) at the image level or the object level.

VCSQL/SEMCOG

SEMCOG [Li and Candan, 1999a] models images and videos as compound objects each containing a hierarchy of sub-objects. Each sub-object corresponds to image regions that are visually or semantically meaningful (e.g., a car). SEMCOG supports image retrieval at both whole-image and object levels and using semantics as well as visual content. Using a construct called *extent objects*, which can span multiple frames and which can have time-varying visual representations, it extends object-based media modeling to video data. It supports video retrieval at object, frame, action, and composite action levels. It provides a visual query interface, IFQ, for object-based image and video retrieval (Figure 2.44). Query specification for image retrieval consists of three steps: (1) introducing objects in the target image, (2) describing objects, and (3) specifying objects' spatial relationships. Temporal queries are visually formulated through instant- and interval-based predicates. While the user specifies the query visually using IFQ, a corresponding declarative VCSQL query is automatically generated. IFQ and VCSQL support user-defined concepts through combinations of visual examples, terms, predicates, and other

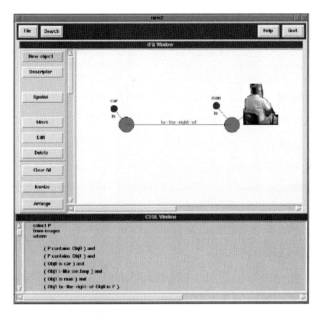

Figure 2.44. The IFQ visual interface of the SEMCOG image and video retrieval system [Li and Candan, 1999a]: the user is able to specify visual, semantic, and spatiotemporal predicates, which are automatically converted into an SQL-like language for fuzzy query processing. See color plates section.

concept definitions [Li *et al.*, 1997c]. The resulting VCSQL query is executed by the underlying fuzzy query processing engine. The degree of relevance of a candidate solution to the user query is calculated based on both object (semantics, color, and shape) matching and image/video structure matching. SEMCOG also provides system feedback to the user to help query reformulation and exploration.

SQL/MM

SQL/MM [Melton and Eisenberg, 2001; SQL03Images; SQL03Multimedia] is an ISO standard that defines data types to enable multimedia data to be manipulated in an SQL database. It standardizes class libraries for full-text and document processing, geographic information systems, data mining, and still images. The *ISO/IEC 13249-5:2001 SQL MM Part5:StillImage* standard is commonly referred to as the SQL/MM Still Image standard. The SI_StillImage type stores collections of pixels representing two-dimensional images and captures metadata, such as image format, dimensions (height and width), and color space. The image processing methods the standard provides include scaling, cropping, rotating, and creating a thumbnail image for quick display. A set of data types describe various features of images. The SI_AverageColor type represents the "average" color of a given image. The SI_ColorHistogram type provides color histograms. The SI_PositionalColor type represents the location of specific colors in an image, and the SI_Texture type represents information, such as coarseness, contrast, and direction of granularity. These data types enable one to formulate SQL queries inspecting image features. Most major commercial DBMS vendors, including Oracle, IBM, and Microsoft, and Informix support the SQL/MM standard in their products.

MP7QF

The work in Gruhne *et al.* [2007] is an effort by the MPEG committee to provide standardized input and output query interfaces to MPEG-7 databases. In addition to supporting queries based on the MPEG-7 feature descriptors and description schemes as well as the XML-based structure of the MPEG-7 documents, the query interface also supports query conditions based on query by example, and query by relevance feedback, which takes into account the results of the previous retrieval. Query by relevance feedback allows user to identify good and bad examples in a previous set of results and include this information in the query.

2.5 SUMMARY

The data and query models introduced in this section highlighted the diversity of information available in multimedia collections. As the list of languages presented in the previous section shows, although there have been many attempts, especially during the 1990s, to develop multimedia query languages, there are currently no universally accepted standards for multimedia querying. This is partly due to the extremely diverse nature of the multimedia data and partly due to the heterogeneity in the way multimedia data can be queried and visualized. For example, while the query by relevance feedback mechanism proposed as part of MP7QF [Gruhne *et al.*, 2007] extends the querying paradigm from one-shot ad hoc queries to iterative browsing-style querying, it also leaves aside many of the functionalities of the earlier languages for the sake of simplicity and usability.

The multitude of facets available for interpreting multimedia data is a challenge not only in the design of query languages, but also for the algorithms and data structures to be used for processing, indexing, and retrieving multimedia data. In the next chapter, however, we see that, although a single multimedia object may have many features that need to be managed, most of these features may be represented using a handful of common representations.

3

Common Representations
of Multimedia Features

Most features can be represented in the form of one (or more) of the four common base models: *vectors*, *strings*, *graphs/trees*, and *fuzzy/probabilistic logic-based representations*.

Many features, such as colors, textures, and shapes, are commonly represented in the form of histograms that quantify the contribution of each individual property (or feature instance) to the media object. Given n different properties of interest, the *vector model* associates an n-dimensional feature vector space, where the ith dimension corresponds to the ith property. Thus, each vector describes the composition of a given multimedia data object in terms of its quantifiable properties.

Strings, on the other hand, are commonly used for representing media of sequential (or temporal) nature, when the ordinal relationships between events are more important than the quantitative differences between their occurrences. As we have seen in Section 2.3.6.4, because of their simplicity, string-based models are also used as less complex representations for more complex features, such as the spatial distributions of points of interest.

Graphs and *trees* are used for representing complex media, composed of other smaller objects/events that cannot be ordered to form sequences. Such media include hierarchical data, such as taxonomies and X3D worlds (which are easily represented as trees), and directed/undirected networks, such as hypermedia and social networks (where the edges of the graph represent explicit or implicit relationships between media objects or individuals).

When vectors, strings, trees, or graphs are not sufficient to represent the underlying imprecision of the data, fuzzy or probabilistic models can be used to deal with this complexity.

In the rest of this chapter, we introduce and discuss these common representations in greater detail.

3.1 VECTOR SPACE MODELS

The vector space model, proposed by Salton *et al.* [1975], for information retrieval is arguably the simplest model for representing multimedia data. In

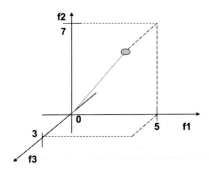

Figure 3.1. Vector space representation of an object, with three features, with values $f_1 = 5$, $f_2 = 7$, and $f_3 = 3$.

this model, a vector space is defined by a set of *linearly independent* basis vectors (i.e., dimensions), and each data object is represented by a vector in this space (Figure 3.1). Intuitively, the vector describes the composition of the multimedia data in terms of its (independent) features. Histograms, for example, are good candidates for being represented in the form of vectors. Given n independent (numeric) features of interest that describe multimedia objects, the vector model associates an n-dimensional vector space, $\mathbb{R}^n$, where the ith dimension corresponds to the ith feature. In this space, each multimedia object, o, is represented as a vector, $\vec{v}_o = \langle w_{1,o}, w_{2,o}, \ldots, w_{n,o} \rangle$, where $w_{i,o}$ is the value of the ith feature for the object.

3.1.1 Vector Space

Formally a vector space, $\mathbb{S}$, is a collection of mathematical objects (called vectors), with addition and scalar multiplication:

> **Definition 3.1.1 (Vector space):** *The set $\mathbb{S}$ is a vector space iff for all $\vec{v}_i$, $\vec{v}_j$, $\vec{v}_k \in \mathbb{S}$ and for all $c, d \in \mathbb{R}$, the following axioms hold:*
>
> - $\vec{v}_i + \vec{v}_j = \vec{v}_j + \vec{v}_i$
> - $(\vec{v}_i + \vec{v}_j) + \vec{v}_k = \vec{v}_j + (\vec{v}_i + \vec{v}_k)$
> - $\vec{v}_i + \vec{0} = \vec{v}_i$ *(for some $\vec{0} \in \mathbb{S}$)*
> - $\vec{v}_i + (-\vec{v}_i) = \vec{0}$ *(for some $-\vec{v}_i \in \mathbb{S}$)*
> - $(c + d)\vec{v}_i = (c\vec{v}_i) + (d\vec{v}_i)$
> - $c(\vec{v}_i + \vec{v}_j) = c\vec{v}_i + c\vec{v}_j$
> - $(cd)\vec{v}_i = c(d\vec{v}_i)$
> - $1.\vec{v}_i = \vec{v}_i$
>
> *The elements of $\mathbb{S}$ are called vectors.*

Although a vector space can be defined by enumerating all its members, especially when the set is infinite, an alternative way to describe the vector space is needed. A vector space is commonly described through its basis:

Definition 3.1.2 (Linear independence and basis): *Let* $V = \{\vec{v}_1, \vec{v}_2, \ldots, \vec{v}_n\}$ *be a set of vectors in a vector space* $\mathbb{S}$. *The vectors in* V *are said to be* linearly independent *if*

$$\left(\sum_{i=1}^{n} c_i \vec{v}_i = \vec{0} \right) \longleftrightarrow \quad c_1 = c_2 = \cdots = c_n = 0.$$

The linearly independent set V *is said to be a basis for* $\mathbb{S}$ *if for every vector,* $\vec{u} \in \mathbb{S}$, *there exist constants* c_1 *through* c_n *such that*

$$\vec{u} = \sum_{i=1}^{n} c_i \vec{v}_i.$$

Intuitively, the basis, V, spans the space $\mathbb{S}$ and is minimal (i.e., you cannot remove any vector from V and still span the space $\mathbb{S}$).

Definition 3.1.3 (Inner product and orthogonality): *The inner product,*[1] *"·", on a vector space* $\mathbb{S}$ *is a function* $\mathbb{S} \times \mathbb{S} \rightarrow \mathbb{R}$ *such that*

- $\vec{u} \cdot \vec{v} = \vec{v} \cdot \vec{u}$,
- $(c_1 \vec{u} + c_2 \vec{v}) \cdot \vec{w} = c_1(\vec{u} \cdot \vec{w}) + c_2(\vec{v} \cdot \vec{w})$, *and*
- $\forall_{\vec{v} \neq \vec{0}} \ \vec{v} \cdot \vec{v} > 0$.

The vectors $\vec{u}$ *and* $\vec{v}$ *are said to be* orthogonal *if*

$$\vec{u} \cdot \vec{v} = 0.$$

An important observation is that a collection, $V = \{\vec{v}_1, \vec{v}_2, \ldots, \vec{v}_n\}$, of mutually orthogonal vectors are linearly independent; thus can be used to define an (orthogonal) basis if they also span the vector space $\mathbb{S}$.

Definition 3.1.4 (Norms and orthonormal basis): *A* norm *(commonly denoted as* $\| \cdot \|$*) is a function that measures the length of vectors. A vector,* $\vec{v}$, *is said to be* normalized *if* $\|\vec{v}\| = 1$. *A basis,* $V = \{\vec{v}_1, \vec{v}_2, \ldots, \vec{v}_n\}$, *of the vector space* $\mathbb{S}$ *is said to be* orthonormal *if*

$$\forall_{\vec{v}_i, \vec{v}_j} \ \vec{v}_i \cdot \vec{v}_j = \delta_{i,j},$$

such that if $i = j$, $\delta_{i,j} = 1$ *and 0 otherwise.*[2]

The most commonly used family of norms are the p-norms. Given a vector $\vec{v} = \langle w_1, \ldots, w_n \rangle$, the p-norm is defined as

$$\|\vec{v}\|_p = \left(\sum_{i=1}^{n} |w_i|^p \right)^{\frac{1}{p}}.$$

At the limit, as p goes to infinity, this gives the max-norm

$$\|\vec{v}\|_\infty = \max_{i=1\ldots n} \{|w_i|\}.$$

---

[1] The *dot product* on $\mathbb{R}^n$ is an inner product function.
[2] This is commonly referred to as the Kronecker delta.

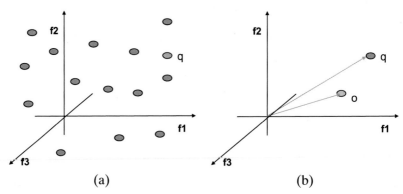

(a)   (b)

Figure 3.2. (a) Query processing in vector spaces involves mapping all the objects in the database and the query, q, onto the same space and (b) evaluating the similarity/difference between the vector corresponding to q and the individual objects in the database.

3.1.2 Linear and Statistical Independence of Features

Within the context of multimedia data, feature independence may mean different things. First of all, two features can be said to be independent if the occurrence of one of the features in the database is not correlated with the occurrence of the other feature. Also, two features may be dependent or independent, based on whether the users are perceiving the two features to be semantically related or not. In a multimedia database, independence of features from each other is important for two major reasons:

- First, the interpretation (or computation) of the similarity or difference between the objects (i.e., vectors in the space) usually relies on the orthogonality of the features mapped onto the basis vectors of the vector space. In fact, many of the multidimensional/spatial index structures (Chapter 7) that are adopted for efficient retrieval of multimedia data assume orthogonality of the basis of the vector space. Also correct interpretation of the user's relevance feedback often requires the feature independence assumption.
- Second, as we discuss in Section 4.2, it is easier to pick the most useful dimensions of the data for indexing if these dimensions are not statistically correlated. In other words, statistical independence (or statistical orthogonality) of the dimensions of the feature space helps with feature selection.

In Section 3.5.1.2, we discuss the effects of the independence assumption and ways to extract independent bases in the presence of features that are not truly independent in the linear, statistical, or semantic sense.

3.1.3 Comparison of Objects in the Vector Space

Given a n-dimensional feature space, $\mathbb{S}$, query processing involves mapping all the objects in the database and the query onto this space and then evaluating the similarity/difference between the vector corresponding to the query and the vectors representing the data objects (Figure 3.2). Thus, given a vector, $\vec{v}_q = \langle q_1, q_2, \ldots, q_n \rangle$,

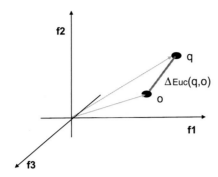

Figure 3.3. Euclidean distance between two points.

representing the user query and a vector $\vec{v}_o = \langle o_1, o_2, \ldots, o_n \rangle$, representing an object in this space, retrieval involves computing a similarity value, $sim(\vec{v}_q, \vec{v}_o)$, or a distance value, $\Delta(\vec{v}_q, \vec{v}_o)$, using these two vectors.

As with the features themselves, the similarity/distance function that needs to be used when comparing two vectors, $\vec{v}_q$ and $\vec{v}_o$, also depends on the characteristics of the application. Next, we list commonly used similarity and distance functions for comparing vectors.

■ *Minkowski distance:* The Minkowski distance of order p (also referred to as p-norm distance or Lp metric distance) is defined as

$$\Delta_{Mink,p}(\vec{v}_q, \vec{v}_o) = \left(\sum_{i=1}^{n} |q_i - o_i|^p \right)^{1/p}.$$

The Euclidean distance (Figures 3.3 and 3.4(b)),

$$\Delta_{Euc}(\vec{v}_q, \vec{v}_o) = \Delta_{Mink,2}(\vec{v}_q, \vec{v}_o) = \left(\sum_{i=1}^{n} |q_i - o_i|^2 \right)^{1/2},$$

commonly used for measuring distances between points in the 3D space we are living in, is in fact the Minkowski distance of order 2. Another special case

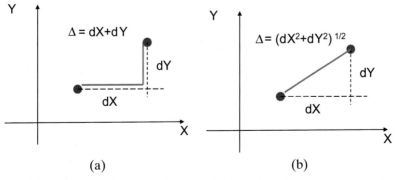

Figure 3.4. (a) Manhattan (1-norm or L1) and (b) Euclidean (2-norm or L2) distances in 2D space.

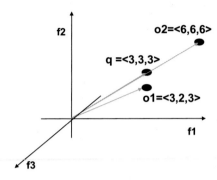

Figure 3.5. Under cosine similarity, q is more similar to o_2 than to o_1, although the Euclidean distance between $\vec{v}_q$ and $\vec{v}_{o_1}$ is smaller than the Euclidean distance between $\vec{v}_q$ and $\vec{v}_{o_2}$.

(preferred in multimedia databases because of its computational efficiency) is the Manhattan (or city block) distance (Figure 3.4(a)):

$$\Delta_{Man}(\vec{v}_q, \vec{v}_o) = \Delta_{Mink,1}(\vec{v}_q, \vec{v}_o) = \sum_{i=1}^{n} |q_i - o_i|.$$

The Manhattan distance is commonly used for certain kinds of similarity evaluation, such as color-based comparisons. Results from computer vision and pattern recognition communities suggest that it may capture human judgment of image similarity better than Euclidean distance [Russell and Sinha, 2001].

At the other extreme, the ∞-norm distance (also known as the Chebyshev distance) is also efficient to compute:

$$\Delta_{Mink,\infty}(\vec{v}_q, \vec{v}_o) = \lim_{p \to \infty} \left(\sum_{i=1}^{n} |q_i - o_i|^p \right)^{1/p} = \max_{i=1...n} \{|q_i - o_i|\}.$$

The Minkowski distance has the advantage of being a metric. Thus, functions in this family make it relatively easy to index data relying on multi-dimensional indexing techniques designed for spatial data (Chapter 7).

- *Cosine similarity:* Cosine similarity is simply defined as the cosine of the angle between the two vectors:

$$sim_{cosine}(\vec{v}_q, \vec{v}_o) = cos(\vec{v}_q, \vec{v}_o).$$

If the angle between two vectors is 0 degrees (in other words, if the two vectors are overlapping in space), then their composition is similar and, thus, the cosine similarity measure returns 1, independent of how far apart the corresponding points are in space (Figure 3.5). Because of this property, the cosine similarity function is commonly used, for example, in text databases, when compositions of the features are more important than the individual contributions of features in the media objects.

- *Dot product similarity:* The dot product (also known as the scalar product) is defined as

$$sim_{dot\_prod}(\vec{v}_q, \vec{v}_o) = \vec{v}_q \cdot \vec{v}_o = \sum_{i=1}^{n} q_i o_i.$$

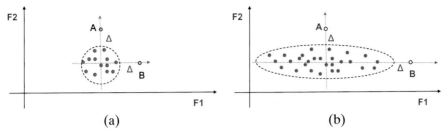

Figure 3.6. Two data sets in a two-dimensional space. In (a) the data are similarly distributed in F_1 and F_2, whereas in (b) the data are distributed differently in F_1 and F_2. In particular, the variance of the data is higher along F_1 than F_2.

The dot product measure is closely related to the cosine similarity:

$$sim_{dot\_prod}(\vec{v}_q, \vec{v}_o) = \vec{v}_q \cdot \vec{v}_o = |\vec{v}_q||\vec{v}_o|cos(\vec{v}_q, \vec{v}_o) = |\vec{v}_q||\vec{v}_o|sim_{cosine}(\vec{v}_q, \vec{v}_o).$$

In other words, the dot product considers both the angle and the lengths of the vectors. It is also commonly used for cheaply computing cosine similarity in applications where the vectors are already prenormalized to unit length.

■ *Intersection similarity:* Intersection similarity is defined as

$$sim_{\cap}(\vec{v}_q, \vec{v}_o) = \frac{\sum_{i=1}^{n} min(q_i, o_i)}{\sum_{i=1}^{n} max(q_i, o_i).}$$

Intersection similarity has its largest value, 1, when all the terms of $\vec{v}_q$ are identical to the corresponding terms of $\vec{v}_o$. Otherwise, the similarity is less than 1. In the extreme case, when q_is are very different from o_is (either o_i very large and q_i very small or q_i very large and o_i very small), then the similarity will be close to 0.

The reason why this measure is referred to as the intersection similarity is because it considers to what degree $\vec{v}_q$ and $\vec{v}_o$ overlap along each dimension. It is commonly used when the dimensions represent counts of a particular feature in the object (as in color and texture histograms).

When applied to comparing sets, the intersection similarity is also known as the *Jaccard similarity* coefficient: given two sets, A and B, the Jaccard similarity coefficient is defined as

$$sim_{jaccard}(A, B) = \frac{|A \cap B|}{|A \cup B|}.$$

A related set comparison measure commonly used for comparing sets is the *Dice similarity* coefficient, computed as

$$sim_{dice}(A, B) = \frac{2|A \cap B|}{|A| + |B|}.$$

■ *Mahalanobis distance:* The Mahalanobis distance extends the Euclidean distance, by taking into account data distribution in the space. Consider the data sets shown in Figure 3.6(a) and (b). Let us assume that we are given two new data objects, A and B, and we are asked to determine whether A or B is a

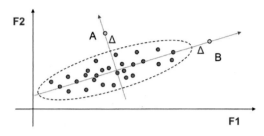

Figure 3.7. A data set in which features F_1 and F_2 are highly correlated and the direction along which the variance is high is not aligned with the feature dimensions.

better candidate to be included in the cluster[3] of objects that make the data set. In the case of Figure 3.6(a), both points are equidistant from the boundary and the data are similarly distributed along F_1 and F_2; thus there is no reason to pick one versus the other. In Figure 3.6(b), on the other hand, the data are distributed differently in F_1 and F_2. In particular, the variance of the data is higher along F_1 than F_2. This implies that the distortion of the cluster boundary along F_1 will have a smaller impact on the shape of the cluster than the same distortion of the cluster boundary along F_2. This can be taken into account by modifying the distance definition in such a way that differences along the direction with higher variance of data receive a smaller weight than differences along the direction with smaller variance.

Given a query and an object vector, the Euclidean distance

$$\Delta_{Euc}(\vec{v}_q, \vec{v}_o) = \left(\sum_{i=1}^{n} |q_i - o_i|^2 \right)^{1/2}$$

between them can be rewritten in vector algebraic form as

$$\Delta_{Euc}(\vec{v}_q, \vec{v}_o) = \sqrt{(\vec{v}_q - \vec{v}_o)^T (\vec{v}_q - \vec{v}_o)} = \sqrt{(\vec{v}_q - \vec{v}_o)^T I (\vec{v}_q - \vec{v}_o)},$$

where I is the identity matrix. One way to assign weights to the dimensions of the space to accommodate the differences in their variances is to replace the identity matrix, I, with a matrix that captures the inverse of these variances.

This can be done, to some degree, by replacing the "1"s in the identity matrix by $1/\sigma_i^2$, where σ_i^2 is the variance along the ith dimension. However, this would not be able to account for large variations in data distribution that are not aligned with the dimensions of the space. Consider, for example, the data set shown in Figure 3.7. Here, features F_1 and F_2 are highly correlated, and the direction along which the variance is high is not aligned with the feature dimensions. Thus, the Mahalanobis distance takes into account correlations in the dimensions of the space by using (the inverse of) the covariance matrix, S, of the space in place of the identity matrix[4]:

$$\Delta_{Mah}(\vec{v}_q, \vec{v}_o) = \sqrt{(\vec{v}_q - \vec{v}_o)^T S^{-1}(\vec{v}_q - \vec{v}_o)}.$$

[3] As introduced in Section 1.3, a cluster is a collection of data objects, which are similar to each other. We discuss different clustering techniques in Chapter 8.
[4] See Section 3.5.1.2 for a detailed discussion of covariance matrices.

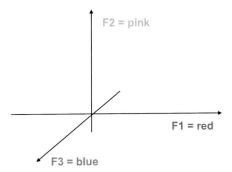

Figure 3.8. A feature space defined by three color features: $F_1 = red$, $F_2 = pink$, and $F_3 = blue$; features F_1 and F_2 are perceptually more similar to each other than they are to F_3.

The values at the diagonal of S are the variances along the corresponding dimensions, whereas the values at off-diagonal positions describe how strongly related the corresponding dimensions are (in terms of how objects are distributed in the feature space).

Note that when the covariance matrix is diagonal (i.e., when the dimensions are mutually independent as in Figure 3.6(b)), as expected, the Mahalanobis distance becomes similar to the Euclidean distance:

$$\Delta_{Mah}(\vec{v}_q, \vec{v}_o) = \left(\sum_{i=1}^{n} \frac{|q_i - o_i|^2}{\sigma_i^2} \right)^{1/2}.$$

Here σ_i^2 is the variance along the ith dimensions over the data set. Consequently, the Mahalanobis distance is less dependent on the scale of feature values. Because the Mahalanobis distance reflects the distribution of the data, it is commonly used when the data are not uniformly distributed. It is particularly useful for data collections where the data distribution varies from cluster to cluster; we can use a different covariance matrix when computing distances to different clusters of objects. It is also commonly used for outlier detection as it takes into account and corrects for the distortion that a given point would cause on the local data distribution.

■ *Quadratic distance:* The definition of quadratic distance [Hafner *et al.*, 1995] is similar to that of the Mahalanobis distance,

$$\Delta_{Mah}(\vec{v}_q, \vec{v}_o) = \sqrt{(\vec{v}_q - \vec{v}_o)^T A (\vec{v}_q - \vec{v}_o)},$$

except that the matrix, A, in this case denotes the *similarity* between the features represented by the dimensions of the vector space as opposed to their statistical correlation. For example, as shown in Figure 3.8, if the dimensions of the feature space correspond to the bins of a color histogram, $[a_{i,j}]$ would correspond to the (perceptual) similarity of the colors represented by the corresponding bins. These similarity values would be computed based on the underlying color model or based on the user feedback.

Essentially, the quadratic distance measure distorts the space in such a way that distances across dimensions that correspond to features that are perceptually similar to each other are shorter than the distances across dimensions that are perceptually different from each other.

- *Kullback-Leibler divergence:* The Kullback-Leibler divergence measure (also known as the KL distance) takes a probabilistic view and measures the so-called *relative entropy* between vectors interpreted as two probability distributions:

$$\Delta_{KL}(\vec{v}_q, \vec{v}_o) = \sum_{i=1}^{n} q_i \, log \frac{q_i}{o_i}.$$

Note that, because the KL distance is defined over probability distributions, $\sum_{i=1}^{n} q_i$ and $\sum_{i=1}^{n} o_i$ must both be equal to 1.0.

The KL distance is not symmetric and, thus, is not a metric measure, though a modified version of the KL distance can be used when symmetricity is required:

$$\Delta_{KL'}(\vec{v}_q, \vec{v}_o) = \frac{1}{2} \left(\sum_{i=1}^{n} q_i \, log \frac{q_i}{o_i} \right) + \frac{1}{2} \left(\sum_{i=1}^{n} o_i \, log \frac{o_i}{q_i} \right).$$

Alternatively, a related distance measure, known as the Jensen-Shannon divergence,

$$\Delta_{JS}(\vec{v}_q, \vec{v}_o) = \Delta_{KL} \left(\vec{v}_q, \frac{\vec{v}_q + \vec{v}_o}{2} \right) + \Delta_{KL} \left(\vec{v}_o, \frac{\vec{v}_q + \vec{v}_o}{2} \right),$$

which is known to be the square of a metric [Endres and Schindelin, 2003], can be used when a metric measure is needed.

- *Pearson's chi-square test:* Like the Kullback-Leibler divergence, the chi-square test also interprets the vector probabilistically and measures the degree of fit between one vector, treated as an observed probability distribution, and the other (treated as the expected distribution). For example, if we treat the query as the expected distribution and the vector of the object we are comparing against the query as the observed frequency distribution, then we can perform the Pearson's chi-square fitness test by computing the following score:

$$\chi^2 = \sum_{i=1}^{n} \frac{o_i - q_i}{q_i}.$$

The resulting χ^2 value is then interpreted by comparing against a chi-square distribution table for $n - 1$ degrees of freedom (n being the number of dimensions of the space). If the corresponding value listed in the table is less than 0.05, the corresponding probability distributions are not statistically related and o_i is not a match for q_i.

- *Signal-to-noise ratio:* The signal-to-noise ratio (SNR) is the ratio of the power of a signal to the power of the noise in the environment. Intuitively, the SNR value measures how noise-free (i.e., close to its intended form) a signal at the receiving end of a communication channel is. Treating the query vector, $\vec{v}_q$, as the intended signal and the difference, $\vec{v}_q - \vec{v}_o$ as the noise signal, the signal-to-noise ratio between them is defined as

$$sim_{SNR}(\vec{v}_q, \vec{v}_o) = 20log_{10} \frac{\sqrt{\sum_{i=1}^{n} q_i^2}}{\sqrt{\sum_{i=1}^{n} (q_i - o_i)^2}}.$$

The SNR is especially useful if the difference between the query and the objects in the database is very small, that is, when we are trying to differentiate between objects using slight differences between them.

In summary, the various similarity and distance measures defined over vector spaces compute the degree of matching between a given query and a given object (or between two given objects) based on different assumptions made about the nature of the data and the interpretation of the feature values that correspond to the dimensions of the space.

3.2 STRINGS AND SEQUENCES

To illustrate the use of sequences in multimedia, let us consider an application where we are interested in capturing and indexing users' navigation *experiences*[5] [Adali *et al.*, 2006; Blustein *et al.*, 2005; D. Dasgupta and F. A. Gonzalez, 2001; Debar *et al.*, 1999; Fischer, 2001; Gemmell *et al.*, 2006; Jain, 2003b; Mayer *et al.*, 2004; Sapino *et al.*, 2006; Sridharan *et al.*, 2003] within a hypermedia document.

3.2.1 Example Application: User Experience Sequences

User experiences can often be represented in the form of sequences of events [Candan *et al.*, 2006]:

Definition 3.2.1 (User experience): *Let $\mathcal{D}$ be a domain of events and $\mathcal{A}$ be a set of events from this domain. A user experience, e_i, is modeled as a finite sequence $e_{i,0} \cdot e_{i,1} \cdot \ldots \cdot e_{i,n}$, where $e_{i,j} \in \mathcal{A}$.*

For example, user experience "navigating in a website" can be modeled as a sequence of Web pages seen by a user:

<www.asu.edu> <www.asu.edu/colleges> <www.fulton.asu.edu/fulton> . . .
. . . <sci.asu.edu>.

The user experience itself does not always have a predefined structure known to the system, although it might implicitly be governed by certain domain-specific rules (such as the hyperlinks forming the website). Capturing the appropriate events that form a particular domain and discovering the relationships between these statements is essential for any human-centric reasoning and recommendation system. In particular, an experience-driven recommendation system needs to capture the past states of the individual and the future states that the individual wishes to reach. Given the history and future goals, the system needs to identify appropriate

---

[5] Modeling user experiences is crucial for enabling the design of effective interaction tools [Fischer, 2001]. Models of expected user or population behavior are also used for enabling prefetching and replication strategies for improved content delivery [Mayer *et al.*, 2004; Sapino *et al.*, 2006]. Recording and indexing individuals' various experiences also carry importance in personal information management [Gemmell *et al.*, 2006], experiential computing [Jain, 2003a,b], desktop information management [Adali and Sapino, 2005], and various arts applications [Sridharan *et al.*, 2003].

propositional statements to provide to the end user as a recommendation. Candan *et al.* [2006] define a popularity query as follows:

Definition 3.2.2 (Popularity query): *Let $\mathcal{D}$ be a domain and $\mathcal{A}$ be a set of propositional statements from this domain. Let $\mathcal{E}$ be an experience collection (possibly representing experiences of a group of individuals). A popularity query is a sequence, q, of propositional statements and wildcard characters from $\mathcal{A} \cup \{``\star", ``//"\}$ executed over the database, $\mathcal{E}$. Here, ``$\star$'' is a wildcard symbol that matches any label in $\mathcal{A}$, and the wildcard ``//'' corresponds to an arbitrary number of ``$\star$''s. The query processor (recommendation engine) returns matches in the order of frequency or popularity.*

For example, in the context of navigation within a website, the wildcard query

$$q := \Big(\langle \text{www.asu.edu} \rangle \ // \ \langle \text{sci.asu.edu} \rangle \Big)$$

is asking about how users of the ASU website are commonly navigating from the ASU main page to the School of Computing and Informatics's home page. The answer to this query will be a list of past user navigations from www.asu.edu to sci.asu.edu, ranked in terms of their popularities.

Note that, when comparing sequences, exact alignment of elements is often not required. For example, when counting navigation sequences for deriving popularity-based recommendations, there may be minor deviations between different users' navigational experiences (maybe because the Web content is dynamically created and personalized for each individual). Whether two experiences are going to be treated as matching or not depends on the amount of difference between them; thus, this difference needs to be quantified. This is commonly done through *edit distance* functions, which quantify the minimum number of symbol *insertions*, *deletions*, and *substitutions* needed to convert one sequence to the other.

3.2.2 Edit Distance Measures

Given two sequences, the distance between them can be defined in different ways depending on the applications requirements. Because they measure the cost of transformations (or edits) required to convert one sequence into the other, the distance measures for sequences are commonly known as the *edit distance* measures.

- *The Hamming distance* [Hamming, 1950], Δ_{Ham}, between two equi-length sequences is defined as the number of positions with different symbols, that is, the number of symbol *substitutions* needed to convert one sequence to the other. The Hamming distance is metric.
- *The episode distance*, $\Delta_{episode}$, only allows insertions, each with cost 1. This distance measure is not symmetric and thus it is not a metric.
- *The longest common subsequence distance*, Δ_{lcs}, allows both insertions and deletions, both costing 1. This is symmetric, but is not guaranteed to satisfy triangular equality; thus it is also not metric.
- *The Kendall tau distance*, Δ_{kt}, (also known as the bubble-sort distance) between two sequences is the number of pairwise disagreements (i.e., the number of swaps) between two sequences. The Kendall tau distance, a metric, is applied mostly when the two sequences are equi-length lists and each symbol occurs at

most once in a sequence. For example, two list objects, each ranked with respect to a different criterion, can be compared using the Kendall tau distance.

■ *The Levenshtein distance*, Δ_{Lev} [Levenshtein, 1966], another metric, is more general: it is defined as the minimum number of symbol *insertions*, *deletions*, and *substitutions* needed to convert one sequence to the other. An even more general definition of Levenshtein distance associates heterogeneous *costs* to insertions, deletions, and substitutions and defines the distance as the minimum cost transition from one sequence to the other. The cost associated with a given edit operation may be a function of (a) the type of operation, (b) the symbols involved in the editing, or (c) the positions of the symbols involved in the edit operation. Other definitions also allow for more complex operations, such as transpositions of adjacent or nearby symbols or entire subsequences [Cormode and Muthukrishnan, 2002; Kurtz, 1996]. The Damerau-Levenshtein distance [Damerau, 1964], Δ_{DL}, is an extension where swaps of pairs of symbols are also allowed as atomic operations. Note that if the only operation allowed is substitution, if the cost of substitution is independent of the characters involved, and if the strings are of equal length, then the Levenshtein distance is equivalent to the Hamming distance.

In Section 5.5, we discuss algorithms and index structures for efficient approximate string and sequence search in greater detail.

3.3 GRAPHS AND TREES

Let D be a set of entities of interest; a graph, $G(V, E)$, defined over $V = D$ describes relationships between pairs of objects in D. The elements in the set V are referred to as the *nodes* or *vertices* of the graph. The elements of the set E are referred to as the *edges*, and they represent the pairwise relationships between the nodes of the graph. Edges can be *directed* or *undirected*, meaning that the relationship can be *nonsymmetric* or *symmetric*, respectively. Nodes and edges of the graph can also be *labeled* or *nonlabeled*. The label of an edge, for example, may denote the name of the relationship between the corresponding pair of nodes or may represent other metadata, such as the certainty of the relationship or the cost of leveraging that relationship within an application.

As we discussed in Section 2.1.5, knowledge models (such as RDF) that produce the greatest representation flexibility reduce the knowledge representation into a set of simple *subject-predicate-object* statements that can easily be captured in the form of relationship graphs (see Figures 2.5 and 2.6). Thus, thanks to this flexibility, the use of graphs in multimedia data modeling and analysis is extensive; for example, graph-based models are often used to represent many diverse aspects of multimedia data and systems, including the following:

■ Spatio-temporal distribution of features in a media object (Figure 2.36)
■ Media composition (e.g., order) of a multimedia document (Figure 2.28)
■ References/citations/links between media objects in a hypermedia system or pages on the Web (Figure 1.9)
■ Semantic relationships among information units extracted from documents in a digital library (Figure 3.9)

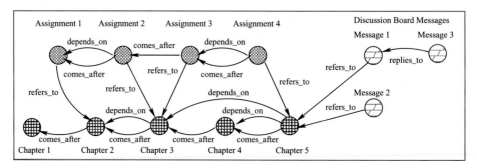

Figure 3.9. An example graph: semantic relationships between information units extracted from a digital library.

■ Explicit (e.g., "friend") or implicit (e.g., common interest) relationships among individuals within a social network (Section 6.3.4)

A tree, $T(V, E)$, is a graph with a special, highly restricted structure: first of all, if the edges are undirected, each pair of vertices of the tree are reachable from each other through one and only one *path* (i.e., a sequence of edges); if the edges are directed, on the other hand, the tree does not contain any cycles (i.e., no vertex is reachable from itself through a non-empty sequence of edges), there is one and only one vertex (called *root*) that is not reachable from any other vertex but that can reach each other vertex (through a corresponding unique edge path). In a *rooted* tree, on any given path, the vertices closer to the root are referred to as the *ancestors* of the nodes that are further away (i.e., descendants). A vertex that does not have a descendant is referred to as a *leaf*, whereas others are referred to as the *internal vertices*. A pair of ancestor-descendant nodes that are connected by a single edge is referred to as a *parent-child* pair, and the children of the same parent vertex are called *siblings* of each other. A tree is called an ordered tree if it is rooted and the order among siblings (nodes under the same parent node) is also given. An unordered tree is simply a rooted tree.

Examples of data types that can be represented using trees include the following:

■ Hierarchical multimedia objects, such as virtual worlds created using the X3D standard (Figure 1.1), where complex objects are constructed by clustering simpler ones

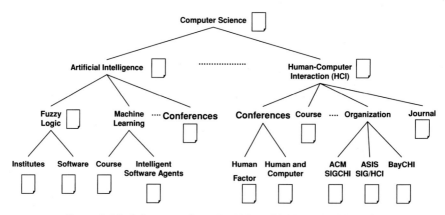

Figure 3.10. A fragment from the Yahoo CS hierarchy [Yahoo].

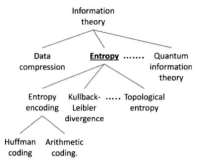

Figure 3.11. A fragment of a concept taxonomy for the domain "information theory."

- Semistructured and hierarchical XML data (without explicit object references; Section 2.1.4)
- Taxonomies that organize concepts into a hierarchy in such a way that more general concepts are found closer to the root (Figures 3.10 and 3.11)
- Navigation hierarchies for content, such as threads in a discussion board (Figure 3.12), that are inherently hierarchical in nature

3.3.1 Operations on Graphs and Trees

Common operations on graph structured data include the following [Cormen *et al.*, 2001]:

- Checking whether a node is reachable from another one
- Checking whether the graph contains a cycle or not
- Searching for the shortest possible paths between a given pair of vertices in the graph
- Extracting the smallest tree-structured subgraphs connecting all vertices (minimum spanning trees) or a given subset of the vertices (Steiner trees)
- Identification of subgraphs where any pair of nodes are reachable from each other (connected components)

buzz proj.	Vander, Ryan	Tue May 25, 2008 9:21 am
Re: buzz proj.	True, Thomas	Thu May 27, 2008 7:53 pm
Re: buzz proj.	Vander, Ryan	Sat May 29, 2008 2:08 pm
Re: buzz proj.	Grain, Robert	Sun May 30, 2008 6:10 pm
Re: buzz proj.	Vander, Ryan	Sun May 30, 2008 10:23 pm
Assignment 4	Rodriguez, Luisa	Thu May 27, 2008 3:04 pm
Report for Assig. 4	True, Thomas	Thu May 27, 2008 7:57 pm
Re: Report for Assig. 4	Candan, Kasim	Mon May 31, 2008 12:07 am
Assignment #4	Atilla, John	Fri May 28, 2008 10:41 pm
Re: Assignment #4	Candan, Kasim	Mon May 31, 2008 12:19 am
Questions on #5	Roosewelt, Daniel	Sat May 29, 2008 11:00 pm
Re: Questions on #5	Candan, Kasim	Mon May 31, 2008 12:23 am
Re: Questions on #5	Ray, Luisa	Mon May 31, 2008 10:34 pm
Re: Questions on #5	Home, Chris	Tue Jun 1, 2008 12:23 am
Report Length	True, Thomas	Tue Jun 1, 2008 11:39 am
Re: Report Length	Candan, Kasim	Wed Jun 2, 2008 1:39 am
Assignment # 6	Bird, Sarah	Tue Jun 1, 2008 9:14 pm

Figure 3.12. A thread hierarchy of messages posted to a discussion board.

- Identification of the largest possible subgraphs such that each vertex in the subgraph is reachable from each other vertex through a single edge (maximal cliques)
- Partitioning of the graph into smaller subgraphs based on various conditions (graph coloring, edge cuts, vertex cuts, and maximal-flow/minimum-cut)

Some of these tasks, such as finding the shortest paths between pairs of vertices, have relatively fast solutions, whereas some others, such as finding maximal cliques or Steiner trees, have no known polynomial time solutions (in fact they are known to be NP-complete problems [Cormen *et al.*, 2001]). Although some of these tasks (such as finding the paths between two nodes or partitioning the tree based on certain criteria) are also applicable in the case of trees, because of their special structures, many of these problems are much easier to compute for trees than for arbitrary graphs. Therefore, tree-based approximations (such as spanning trees) are often used instead of their graph counterparts to develop efficient, but approximate, solutions to costly graph operations.

3.3.2 Graph Similarity and Edit Distance

Let $G_1(V_1, E_1)$ and $G_2(V_2, E_2)$ be two node-labeled graphs.

- *Graph isomorphism:* A *graph isomorphism* from G_1 to G_2 is a bijective (i.e., one-to-one and onto) mapping from the nodes of G_1 to the nodes of G_2 that preserves the structure of the edges. A *subgraph isomorphism* from G_1 to G_2 is similarly defined as an isomorphism of G_1 to a subgraph of G_2. Both approximate graph isomorphism and subgraph isomorphism are known to be NP-complete problems [Yannakakis, 1990].
- *Common subgraphs:* A subgraph common to G_1 and G_2 is said to be *maximal* if it cannot be extended to another common subgraph. The *maximum common subgraph* of $G_1(V_1, E_1)$ and $G_2(V_2, E_2)$ is the largest possible common subgraph of G_1 and G_2. The maximum common subgraph problem is also NP-complete [Ullmann, 1976].

As in the case of symbol sequences, we can define an *edit distance* between two graphs as the least-cost sequence of edit operations that transforms G_1 into G_2. Commonly used graph edit operations include *substitution*, *deletion*, and *insertion* of graph nodes and edges. However, unlike in the case of strings and sequences, the graph edit distance problem is known to be NP-complete. In fact, even approximating the graph edit distance is very costly; the edit-distance problem is known to be APX-hard (i.e., there is no known polynomial time approximation algorithm) [Bunke, 1999]. Bunke [1999] shows that the graph isomorphism, subgraph isomorphism, and maximum common subgraph problems are special instances of the graph edit distance computation problem. For instance, the maximum common subgraph, G_m, of G_1 and G_2 has the property that $\Delta_{gr\_edit}(G_1, G_2) = |G_1| + |G_2| - 2|G_m|$.

We discuss graph edit distances and algorithms to compute them in greater detail in Chapter 6.

3.3.3 Tree Similarity and Edit Distance

Let $T(V, E)$ be a tree, that is, a connected, acyclic, undirected graph. T is called a rooted tree if one of the vertices/nodes is distinguished and called the *root*. T is called a node-labeled tree if each node in V is assigned a symbol from an alphabet Σ. T is called an ordered tree if it is rooted and the order among siblings (nodes under the same parent node) is also given. An unordered tree is simply a rooted tree.

Given two ordered labeled trees, T_1 and T_2, T_1 is said to *match* T_2 if there is a one-to-one mapping from the nodes of T_1 to the nodes of T_2 such that (a) the roots map to each other; (b) if v_i maps to v_j, then the children of v_i and v_j map to each other in left-to-right order; and (c) the label of v_i is equal to the label of v_j. Note that exact matching can be checked in linear time for ordered trees. T_1 is said to *match* T_2 *at node* v if there is a one-to-one mapping from the nodes of T_1 to the nodes of the subtree of T_2 rooted at v. The naive algorithm (which checks for all possible nodes v of T_2) takes $O(nm)$ time where n is the size of T_1 and m is the size of T_2, whereas there are $O(n\sqrt{m})$ algorithms that leverage suffix trees (see Section 5.4.2 for suffix trees) for quick access to subpaths of T_1.

As in the case of strings, given appropriate definitions of insertion, deletion, and swap operations, one can define corresponding edit-distance measures between trees. Unlike the case for strings, however, computing edit distances for trees may be expensive. Although the matching problem is relatively efficient for ordered trees, the problem quickly becomes untractable for unordered trees. In fact, for unordered trees, the matching problem is known to be NP-hard [Kilpelainen and Mannila, 1995]. We discuss tree edit distances and algorithms to compute them in Chapter 6 in greater detail.

3.4 FUZZY MODELS

Vectors, strings, and graphs can be used for multimedia query processing only when the data and query can both be represented as vectors, strings, or graphs. This, however, is not always the case. Especially when the query is not provided as an example object, but formulated using declarative means, such as the logic-based query languages described in Section 2.1, we need an alternative mechanisms to measure the degree of matching between the query and the media objects in the database. Fuzzy and probabilistic models, described in this section, serve this purpose.

3.4.1 Fuzzy Sets and Predicates

Fuzzy data and query models for multimedia querying are based on the fuzzy set theory and fuzzy logic introduced by Zadeh in the mid-1960s [Zadeh, 1965]. A fuzzy set, F, with domain of values D is defined using a membership function, $\mu_F : D \to [0, 1]$. A *crisp* (or conventional) set, C, on the other hand, has a membership function of the form $\mu_C : D \to \{0, 1\}$ (i.e., for any value in the domain, the value is either in the set or out of it). When for an element $d \in D$, $\mu_C(d) = 1$, we say that d is in C ($d \in C$); otherwise we say that d is not in C ($d \notin C$). Note that a crisp set is a special case of fuzzy sets.

A fuzzy predicate corresponds to a fuzzy set: instead of returning Boolean (*true* = 1 or *false* = 0) values as in propositional functions, fuzzy predicates return

---

Table 3.1. *Min* and *products* semantics for fuzzy logical operators

Min semantics	*Product* semantics
$\mu_{P_i \wedge P_j}(x) = min\{\mu_i(x), \mu_j(x)\}$	$\mu_{P_i \wedge P_j}(x) = \dfrac{\mu_i(x) \times \mu_j(x)}{max\{\mu_i(x), \mu_j(x), \alpha\}} \quad \alpha \in [0, 1]$
$\mu_{P_i \vee P_j}(x) = max\{\mu_i(x), \mu_j(x)\}$	$\mu_{P_i \vee P_j}(x) = \dfrac{\mu_i(x) + \mu_j(x) - \mu_i(x) \times \mu_j(x) - min\{\mu_i(x), \mu_j(x), 1 - \alpha\}}{max\{1 - \mu_i(x), 1 - \mu_j(x), \alpha\}}$
$\mu_{\neg P_i}(x) = 1 - \mu_i(x)$	$\mu_{\neg P_i}(x) = 1 - \mu_i(x)$

---

membership values (or scores) corresponding to the members of the fuzzy set. In multimedia databases fuzzy predicates are used for representing the assessments of the imprecisions and imperfections in multimedia data. Such assessments can take different forms [Peng and Candan, 2007]. For example, if the data are generated through a sensor/operator with a quantifiable quality rate (for instance, a function of the available sensor power), then a scalar-valued assessment of imprecision may be applicable. These are referred to as type-1 fuzzy predicates [Zadeh, 1965], which (unlike propositional functions that return true or false) return a membership value to a fuzzy set. In this simplest case, the quality assessment of a given object, o, is modeled as a value $0 \leq qa(o) \leq 1$.

A more general quality assessment model would take into account the uncertainties in the assessments themselves. These types of predicates, where sets have grades of membership that are themselves fuzzy, are referred to as type-2 fuzzy predicates [Zadeh, 1975]. A type-2 primary membership value can be any continuous range in [0, 1]. Corresponding to each primary membership there is a secondary membership function that describes the weights for the instances in the primary membership. For example, the quality assessment of a given object o can be modeled as a normal distribution of qualities, $N(q_{exp}, var)$, where q_{exp} is the expected quality and var is the variance of possible qualities (see Section 3.5). Given this distribution, we can assess the likelihood of possible qualities for the given object based on the given observation (for instance, the quality value q_{exp} is the most likely value). Although the type-2 models can be more general and use different distributions, the specific model using the normal distribution is common because it relies on the well-known central limit theorem. This theorem states that the average of the samples tends to be normally distributed, even when the distribution from which the average is computed is not normally distributed.

3.4.2 Fuzzy Logical Operators

Fuzzy statements about multimedia data combine fuzzy predicates using fuzzy logical operators. Like the predicates, fuzzy statements also have associated scores. Naturally, the meaning of a fuzzy statement (i.e., the score of the whole clause, given the constituent predicate scores) depends on the semantics chosen for the fuzzy logical operators, not ($\neg$), and($\wedge$), and or($\vee$), used for combining the predicates.

3.4.2.1 Min, Product, and Average
Table 3.1 shows popular *min* and *product* fuzzy semantics used in multimedia querying. These two semantics (along with some others) have the property that binary

Table 3.2. Properties of triangular-norm and triangular-conorm functions

	T-norm binary function N (for $\wedge$)	T-conorm binary function C (for $\vee$)
Boundary conditions	$N(0, 0) = 0, N(x, 1) = N(1, x) = x$	$C(1, 1) = 1, C(x, 0) = C(0, x) = x$
Commutativity	$N(x, y) = N(y, x)$	$C(x, y) = C(y, x)$
Monotonicity	$x \leq x', y \leq y' \rightarrow N(x, y) \leq N(x', y')$	$x \leq x', y \leq y' \rightarrow C(x, y) \leq C(x', y')$
Associativity	$N(x, N(y, z)) = N(N(x, y), z)$	$C(x, C(y, z)) = C(C(x, y), z)$

conjunction and disjunction operators are *triangular norms (t-norms)* and *triangular conorms (t-conorms)*. Intuitively, t-norm functions reflect or mimic the (boundary, commutativity, monotonicity, and associativity) properties of the corresponding Boolean operations (Table 3.2). This ensures that fuzzy systems behave like regular crisp systems (based on Boolean logic) when they are fed with precise information.

Although the property of capturing Boolean semantics is desirable in many applications of fuzzy logic, for multimedia querying this is not necessarily the case. For instance, the partial match requirement, whereby an object might be returned as a match even if one of the criteria is not satisfied (e.g., Figure 1.7(a) and (c)) invalidates the boundary conditions: even if a media object does not satisfy one of the conditions in the query, we may still want to consider it as a candidate if it is the best match among all the others in the database. In addition, monotonicity is too weak a condition for multimedia query processing: intuitively, an increase in the score of a given query criterion should result in an increase in the overall score; yet the monotonicity condition in Table 3.2 requires an overall increase only if the scores of all of the query criteria increase.

These imply that the *min* semantics, which gives the highest importance on the lowest scoring predicate, may not be always suitable for multimedia workloads. Other fuzzy semantics commonly used in multimedia systems (as well as other related domains, including information retrieval) include the arithmetic[6] and geometric average semantics shown in Table 3.3. Note that the merge functions in this table are *n*-ary: that is, instead of being considered a pair at a time, more than two criteria can be combined using a single operator.

Average-based semantics do not satisfy the requirements of being a t-norm: in particular, both arithmetic and geometric average fail to satisfy the boundary conditions. Furthermore, neither is associative (a desirable property for query processing and optimization). Yet, both are strictly increasing (i.e., the overall score increases even if only a single component increases). In fact, the *min* semantics is known [Dubois and Prade, 1996; Fagin, 1998; Yager, 1982] to be the only semantics for conjunction and disjunction that preserves logical equivalence (in the absence of negation) and is monotone at the same time. These, and the query processing efficiency it enables because of its simplicity [Fagin, 1996, 1998], make the *min* semantics a popular choice despite its significant semantic shortcomings.

---

[6] Arithmetic average semantics is similar to the *dot product*–based similarity calculation in vector spaces (discussed in Section 3.1.3): intuitively, each predicate is treated as an independent dimension in an *n*-dimensional vector space (where *n* is the number of predicates) and the merged score is defined as the dot-product distance between the complete truth, $\langle 1, 1, \ldots, 1 \rangle$, and the given values of the predicates, $\langle \mu_1(x), \ldots, \mu_n(x) \rangle$.

Table 3.3. N-ary arithmetic average and geometric average semantics

$\mu_{P_1 \wedge \cdots \wedge P_n}(x)$	$\mu_{\neg P_i}(x)$	$\mu_{P_1 \vee \cdots \vee P_n}(x)$
$\dfrac{\mu_1(x) + \cdots + \mu_n(x)}{n}$	$1 - \mu_1(x)$	$1 - \dfrac{(1 - \mu_1(x)) + \cdots + (1 - \mu_n(x))}{n}$
$(\mu_1(x) \times \cdots \times \mu_n(x))^{\frac{1}{n}}$	$1 - \mu_1(x)$	$1 - ((1 - \mu_1(x)) \times \cdots \times (1 - \mu_n(x)))^{\frac{1}{n}}$

Next, we compare various statistical properties of these semantics and evaluate their applicability to multimedia databases. The statistical properties are especially important to judge the effectiveness of thresholds set for media retrieval.

3.4.2.2 Properties of the Common Fuzzy Operators

An understanding of the score distribution of fuzzy algebraic operators is essential in optimization and processing of multimedia queries. Figure 3.13, for example, visualizes the behavior of three commonly used fuzzy conjunction operators under different binary semantics. Figure 3.13 depicts the geometric averaging method, the arithmetic averaging mechanism [Aslandogan et al., 1995], and the minimum function as described by Zadeh [1965] and Fagin [1996, 1998]. As can be seen here, both the arithmetic average and minimum have linear behaviors, whereas the geometric average shows nonlinearity. Moreover, the arithmetic average is the only one among the three that returns zero only when all components are zero. Consequently, the arithmetic average is the only measure among the three that can differentiate among partial matches that have at least one failing subcomponent (Figure 3.14).

The *average score*, or the relative cardinality, of a fuzzy set with respect to its domain is defined as the cardinality of the fuzzy set divided by the cardinality of its domain. For a fuzzy set S with a scoring function $\mu(x)$, where the domain of values for x ranges between 0 and 1 (Figure 3.15), we can compute this as

$$\frac{\int_0^1 \mu(x)dx}{\int_0^1 1\, dx}.$$

Intuitively, average score of a fuzzy operator measures the value output by the operator in the average case. Thus, this value is important in understanding the pruning effects of different thresholds one can use for retrieval. Table 3.4 lists the average score values for alternative conjunction semantics. Note that, if analogously defined,

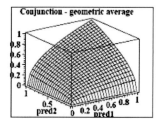 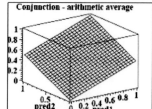 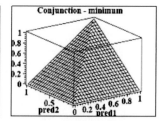

Figure 3.13. Visual representations of various binary fuzzy conjunction semantics: The horizontal axes correspond to the values between 0 and 1 for the two input conjuncts, and the vertical axis represents the resulting scores according to the corresponding function.

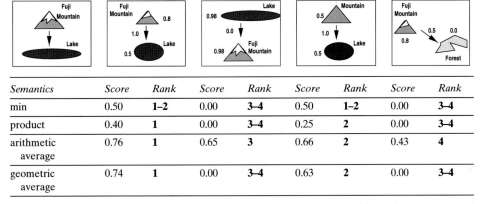

Semantics	Candidate 4 Score	Rank	Candidate 1 Score	Rank	Candidate 2 Score	Rank	Candidate 3 Score	Rank
min	0.50	1–2	0.00	3–4	0.50	1–2	0.00	3–4
product	0.40	1	0.00	3–4	0.25	2	0.00	3–4
arithmetic average	0.76	1	0.65	3	0.66	2	0.43	4
geometric average	0.74	1	0.00	3–4	0.63	2	0.00	3–4

Figure 3.14. Comparison of different conjunction semantics: the table revisits the partial match example provided earlier in Figure 1.7 and illustrates the ranking behavior for different fuzzy conjunction semantics.

the relative cardinality of the crisp conjunction would be

$$\frac{\mu_{(false \wedge false)} + \mu_{(false \wedge true)} + \mu_{(true \wedge false)} + \mu_{(true \wedge true)}}{|\{(false \wedge false), (false \wedge true), (true \wedge false), (true \wedge true)\}|} = \frac{1}{4}.$$

This reconfirms the intuition that the *min* semantics (Figure 3.13(c)) is closer to the crisp conjunction semantics. The arithmetic and geometric average semantics, on the other hand, tend to overestimate scores.

Figure 3.16 visualizes the score distribution of the geometric average and the minimum functions for a statement with conjunction of three fuzzy predicates. As visualized in this figure, higher scores are confined to a smaller region in the *min* function. This implies that, as intuitively expected, given a threshold, the *min* function is most likely to eliminate more candidates than the geometric average.

3.4.3 Relative Importance of Query Criteria

A particular challenge in multimedia querying is that the query processing scheme needs to reflect the specific needs and preferences of individual users. Thanks to its flexibility, the fuzzy model enables various mechanisms of adaptation. First of all, if the user's relevance feedback focuses on a particular attribute in the query, the way

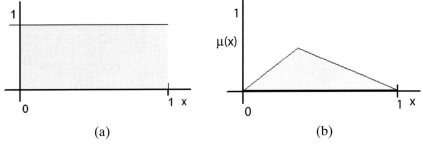

(a)   (b)

Figure 3.15. Example: cardinalities for (a) the continuous domain [0, 1] and (b) the corresponding fuzzy set are computed by measuring the area under the corresponding score curves [Candan and Li, 2001].

Table 3.4. Average scores of various scoring semantics [Candan and Li, 2001]

Arithmetic average	Min	Geometric average
$\dfrac{\int_0^1 \int_0^1 \frac{x+y}{2} dydx}{\int_0^1 \int_0^1 dydx} = \dfrac{1}{2}$	$\dfrac{\int_0^1 \int_0^1 min\{x, y\}dydx}{\int_0^1 \int_0^1 dydx} = \dfrac{1}{3}$	$\dfrac{\int_0^1 \int_0^1 \sqrt{x \times y}\, dydx}{\int_0^1 \int_0^1 dydx} = \dfrac{4}{9}$

the fuzzy score of the corresponding predicate is computed can change based on the feedback. Second, the semantics of the fuzzy logic operator can be adapted based on the feedback of the user. A third mechanism through which the user's feedback can be taken into account is to enrich the merge function, used for merging the fuzzy scores, with weights that regulate the importances of the individual predicates.

3.4.3.1 Measuring Relative Importance

One way to measure the relative importance of criteria in a merge function is to evaluate the size of the impacts any changes in the scores of the individual predicates would have on the overall score. Thus, the relative importance of the predicates in a fuzzy statement can be measured in terms of the corresponding partial derivatives (Figure 3.17 and Table 3.5). Under this interpretation of relative importance, when *product* or *geometric average* semantics is used, the overall score is most impacted by the changes of the component that has the smallest score. This implies that, although the components with high scores have larger contributions to the final score in absolute terms, improving a currently poorly satisfied criterion of the query is the strategy with the most significant impact on the overall score. This makes intuitive sense because improving the lowest matched criterion of the query would cause a significant improvement in the overall degree of *matching*.

Although the *min* semantics has a similar behavior in terms of the relative importance of its constituents (i.e., improvements of the smaller scoring components have larger impacts), in terms of contribution to the overall score the only component that matters is the one with the smallest score. This is rather extreme, in the

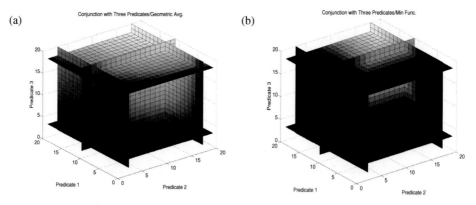

Figure 3.16. (a) Geometric averaging versus (b) minimum with three predicates. Each axis corresponds to an input predicate, and the gray level represents the value of the combined score (the brighter the gray, the higher the score).

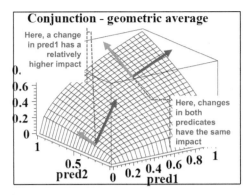

Figure 3.17. The relative impact of the individual criteria in a scoring function can vary based on the scores of the individual predicates.

sense that, given the two configurations $\langle x_1 = 0.1, x_2 = 0.2 \rangle$ and $\langle x_1 = 0.1, x_2 = 0.9 \rangle$, the overall combined score under the $min(x_1, x_2)$ function is identical, 0.1.

When the *arithmetic average* semantics is used for combining scores, on the other hand, the relative importance is constant (and identical) independent of the scores of the individual components. When using the *weighted arithmetic average* ($\mu(x_1, x_2) = w_1 x_1 + w_2 x_2$), the relative importance of the individual components is simply captured by the ratio of their weights.

3.4.3.2 Fagin's Generic Importance Weighting Function

Fagin proposed three intuitive conditions that any function used for capturing relative importance of query criteria should satisfy [Fagin and Maarek, 2000; Fagin and Wimmers, 1997]:

- If all weights are equal, the overall score should be equal to the case where no weights are assigned to any of the query criteria.
- If one of the weights is zero, the subquery can be dropped without affecting the rest.
- The weighted scoring function should increase or decrease continuously as the weights are changed.

Fagin also proposed a generic function that satisfies these three desiderata [Fagin and Maarek, 2000; Fagin and Wimmers, 1997]. Let Q be a query with m criteria and let θ_1 through θ_m denote the weights the user assigns to the individual query criteria. Without loss of generality, let us also assume that $\theta_1 + \cdots + \theta_m = 1$ and $\theta_1 \geq \cdots \geq \theta_m \geq 0$. Finally, let $f()$ be a function (such as min, max, product, or

Table 3.5. Relative importance, $\frac{d\mu(x_1,x_2)}{dx_1} / \frac{d\mu(x_1,x_2)}{dx_2}$, of individual criteria under different scoring semantics					
Arithm. avg.	Weighted Arithm. avg.	**Min**		Product ($\alpha = 1$)	Geometric average
1	$\dfrac{w_1}{w_2}$	$\begin{cases} \infty & \text{if } x_1 \leq x_2 \\ 0 & \text{if } x_1 > x_2 \end{cases}$		$\dfrac{x_2}{x_1}$	$\dfrac{\frac{1}{2}x_1^{-1/2}x_2^{1/2}}{\frac{1}{2}x_1^{1/2}x_2^{-1/2}} = \dfrac{x_2}{x_1}$

average) representing the underlying fuzzy query semantics. Then, Fagin's generic importance weighting function can be written as

$$
\begin{aligned}
f_{(\theta_1,\theta_2,\ldots,\theta_m)}(x_1, x_2, \ldots, x_m) = {} & (\theta_1 - \theta_2)f(x_1) \\
& + 2(\theta_2 - \theta_3)f(x_1, x_2) \\
& + 3(\theta_3 - \theta_4)f(x_1, x_2, x_3) \\
& + \cdots \\
& + (m-1)(\theta_{m-1} - \theta_m)f(x_1, x_2, \ldots, x_{m-1}) \\
& + m\theta_m f(x_1, x_2, \ldots, x_m).
\end{aligned}
$$

To see why $f_{(\theta_1,\theta_2,\ldots,\theta_m)}()$ satisfies the three desiderata, consider the following:

- When all weights are equal, we have $\theta_1 = \theta_2 = \cdots = \theta_m = \frac{1}{m}$. Then,

$$
\begin{aligned}
f_{(\frac{1}{m},\frac{1}{m},\ldots,\frac{1}{m})}(x_1, x_2, \ldots, x_m) = {} & (\frac{1}{m} - \frac{1}{m})f(x_1) \\
& + 2(\frac{1}{m} - \frac{1}{m})f(x_1, x_2) \\
& + \cdots \\
& + (m-1)(\frac{1}{m} - \frac{1}{m})f(x_1, x_2, \ldots, x_{m-1}) \\
& + m\frac{1}{m}f(x_1, x_2, \ldots, x_m) \\
= {} & f(x_1, x_2, \ldots, x_m).
\end{aligned}
$$

  Thus, the overall score is equal to the case where no weights are assigned to any of the query criteria.

- If one of the weights is zero, then $\theta_m = 0$. Thus,

$$
\begin{aligned}
f_{(\theta_1,\theta_2,\ldots,\theta_{m-1},0)}(x_1, x_2, \ldots, x_m) = {} & (\theta_1 - \theta_2)f(x_1) \\
& + 2(\theta_2 - \theta_3)f(x_1, x_2) \\
& + 3(\theta_3 - \theta_4)f(x_1, x_2, x_3) \\
& + \cdots \\
& + (m-1)(\theta_{m-1} - 0)f(x_1, x_2, \ldots, x_{m-1}) \\
& + m\, 0\, f(x_1, x_2, \ldots, x_m) \\
= {} & f_{(\theta_1,\theta_2,\ldots,\theta_{m-1})}(x_1, x_2, \ldots, x_{m-1});
\end{aligned}
$$

  that is, the mth subquery can be dropped without affecting the rest.

- If $f()$ is continuous, then $f_{(\theta_1,\theta_2,\ldots,\theta_m)}$ is a continuous function of the weights, θ_1 through θ_m.

Let us, for example, consider the arithmetic average function, that is, $avg(x_1, x_2) = \frac{x_1+x_2}{2}$. We can write the weighted version of this function as

$$
\begin{aligned}
avg_{(\theta_1,\theta_2)}(x_1, x_2) & = (\theta_1 - \theta_2)avg(x_1) + 2\theta_2 avg(x_1, x_2) \\
& = (\theta_1 - \theta_2)x_1 + 2\theta_2\frac{x_1 + x_2}{2} \\
& = \theta_1 x_1 + \theta_2 x_2;
\end{aligned}
$$

that is, given that $\theta_1 + \theta_2 = 1.0$, $avg_{(\theta_1,\theta_2)}()$ is equal to the weighted average function. Thus, as one would intuitively expect, the importance of the individual query criteria, measured in terms of the partial derivatives of the scoring function, is $\frac{\delta avg(x_1,x_2)}{\delta x_1} = \theta_1$ and $\frac{\delta avg(x_1,x_2)}{\delta x_2} = \theta_2$, respectively.

However, the importance order implied by Fagin's generic scheme and that implied by the partial derivative–based definition of importance are not always consistent. For instance, let us consider the weighted version of the *product* scoring function:

$$product_{(\theta_1,\theta_2)}(x_1, x_2) = (\theta_1 - \theta_2)product(x_1) + 2\theta_2 product(x_1, x_2)$$
$$= (\theta_1 - \theta_2)x_1 + 2\theta_2(x_1 \times x_2).$$

In this case, the importance of the individual query criteria, measured in terms of the partial derivatives of the scoring function, is

$$\frac{\delta product_{(\theta_1,\theta_2)}(x_1, x_2)}{\delta x_1} = (\theta_1 - \theta_2) + 2\theta_2 x_2$$

and

$$\frac{\delta product_{(\theta_1,\theta_2)}(x_1, x_2)}{\delta x_2} = 2\theta_2 x_1,$$

respectively. Note, however, that even if $\theta_1 \geq \theta_2$, we have $\frac{\delta product_{(\theta_1,\theta_2)}(x_1,x_2)}{\delta x_1} \geq \frac{\delta product_{(\theta_1,\theta_2)}(x_1,x_2)}{\delta x_2}$ if and only if

$$(\theta_1 - \theta_2) + 2\theta_2 x_2 \geq 2\theta_2 x_1.$$

In other words, unless

$$x_1 - x_2 \leq \frac{\theta_1 - \theta_2}{2\theta_2},$$

the importance order implied by Fagin's generic scheme and that implied by the partial derivative–based definition of importance are not consistent. Therefore, this generic weighting scheme should be used carefully because its semantics are not always consistent with an intuitive definition of importance.

3.5 PROBABILISTIC MODELS

Unlike fuzzy models, which can capture a large spectrum of application requirements based on the different semantics one can assign to the fuzzy logical operators, probabilistic approaches to data and query modeling are applicable mainly in those cases where the source of imprecision is of a statistical nature. These cases include probabilistic noise in data collection, sampling (over time, space, or population members) during data capture or processing, randomized and probabilistic algorithms (such as Markov chains and Bayesian networks; see Section 3.5.4 and Section 3.5.3) used in media processing and pattern detection, and probabilistic treatment of the relevance feedback [Robertson and Spark-Jones, 1976] (Chapter 12). Thus, in multimedia databases, probabilities can be used for representing, among other things, the likelihood of:

- A feature extraction algorithm having identified a target pattern in a given media object

- An object of interest being contained in a cluster of objects
- A given user finding a given media object relevant to her interests

Whereas the simplest probabilistic models associate a single value between 0 and 1 to each attribute or tuple in the database, more complete models represent the score in the form of an interval of possible values [Lakshmanan *et al.*, 1997] or more generally in terms of a probability distribution describing the possible values for the attribute or the tuple [Pearl, 1985]. Consequently, these models are able to capture more realistic scenarios, where the imprecision in data collection and processing prevents the system from computing the exact precision of the individual media objects, but (based on the domain knowledge) allows it to associate probability distributions to them.

3.5.1 Basic Probability Theory

Given a set, S, of discrete outcomes of a given observation (also referred to as a *random variable*), the *probability distribution* of the observation describes the probabilities with which different outcomes might be observed (Table 3.6). In particular, a probability function (also called the *probability mass function*), $f(x) : S \to [0, 1]$ associates a value of probability to each possible outcome in S. In particular,

$$\sum_{x \in S} f(x) = 1;$$

that is, the sum of all probabilities of all possible outcomes is 1. The probability function $f()$ is also commonly referred to as $P()$ (i.e., $P(x) = f(x)$).

When given a continuous (and thus infinite) space of possible observations, a *cumulative distribution function*, F, is used instead: $F(x)$ returns the probability, $P(X \le x)$, that the observed value will be less than or equal to x. Naturally, as x gets closer to the lower bound of the space, $F(x)$ approaches (in a decreasing fashion) 0, whereas, as x gets closer to the upper bound of the space, $F(x)$ approaches 1 (in an increasing fashion). For cumulative distribution functions that are differentiable, $\frac{dF(x)}{d(x)}$ gives the *probability density function*, which describes how quickly the cumulative distribution function increases at point x.

In discrete spaces, the probability density function is equal to the probability mass function. In continuous spaces, on the other hand, the probability mass function is equal to 0 for any given domain value. Thus, in general, $f()$ is used to denote the probability density function in continuous spaces and the probability density/mass function in discrete spaces.

3.5.1.1 Mean, Variance, and Normal Distribution
Given a space of possible observations and a corresponding probability density function $f(x)$, the *expected value* (or the mean) $E(X)$ of the observation is defined as

$$E(X) = \mu = \int_{lowerbound(S)}^{upperbound(S)} x f(x) dx.$$

Table 3.6. Various common probability distributions and their applications in multimedia systems

Distribution	Definition	Applications
Uniform (discrete)	$f(X, n) = \dfrac{1}{n}$	Estimating the likelihood of a given outcome, when all n outcomes are equally likely.
Bernoulli (discrete)	$f(X, p) = \begin{cases} p & \text{if } X = 1 \\ 1 - p & \text{if } X = 0 \end{cases}$	Estimating the likelihood of success or failure for an observation with a known, constant success rate p.
Binomial (discrete)	$f(X = k, n, p) = \binom{n}{k} p^k (1 - p)^{n-k}$	Estimating the number, k, of successes in a sequence of n independent observations, each with success probability of p.
Multinomial (discrete)	$f(X_1 = k_1, \ldots, X_m = k_m, n, p_1, \ldots, p_m)$ $= \dfrac{n!}{k_1! \cdots k_m!} p_1^{k_1} \cdots p_m^{k_m}, \quad \text{if } \sum_{i=1}^{m} k_m = n; \text{ and}$ $= 0, \qquad\qquad\qquad \text{otherwise}$	Generalization of the binomial distribution to more than two outcomes.
Negative binomial (discrete)	$f(X = \langle k, r \rangle, p) = \binom{k+r-1}{k} \cdot p^r \cdot (1 - p)^k$	Estimating the number of observations, with success probability p, required to get r successes and k failures.
Geometric (discrete)	$f(X = k, p) = p(1 - p)^{k-1}$	Estimating the number, k, of observations needed for one success in a sequence of independent observations, each with success probability p.
Poisson (discrete)	$f(X = k, \lambda) = \dfrac{\lambda^k e^{-\lambda}}{k!}$	Estimating the number, k, of events (with a known average occurrence rate of λ) occurring in a given period.
Zipfian (discrete)	$f(X = k, \alpha) = \dfrac{1/k^\alpha}{\sum_{r=1}^{n} 1/r^\alpha}$	Estimating the frequency for some event as a function of its rank, k, (α is a constant close to 1). Used commonly to model *popularity*.
Uniform (continuous)	$f(X, a, b) = \dfrac{1}{b - a}$	Estimating the likelihood of an outcome for an observation with a continuous range, $[a, b]$, of equally likely outcomes.
Exponential (continuous)	$f(X = t, \lambda) = \begin{cases} \lambda e^{-\lambda t} & t \geq 0, \\ 0 & t < 0. \end{cases}$	Estimating the interarrival times for processes that are themselves Poisson.
Gamma (continuous)	$f(X = t, \alpha, \lambda) = \dfrac{t^{\alpha-1} \lambda^\alpha e^{-\lambda t}}{\int_0^\infty x^{\alpha-1} e^{-x} dx} \text{ for } \alpha, t > 0$	Continuous counterpart of negative binomial dist.
Normal, also known as Gaussian (continuous)	$f(X = t, \mu, \sigma) = \dfrac{1}{\alpha\sqrt{2\pi}} \exp(-\tfrac{1}{2}(\tfrac{t-\mu}{\alpha})^2);$ $-\infty < t < \infty$	(Based on the central limit theorem) The mean of a sample of a set of mutually independent random variables is normally distributed

Given this, the *variance* of the observations, measuring the degree of spread of the observations from the expected value, is defined as

$$Var(X) = E[(X - \mu)^2] = E(X^2) - (E(X))^2.$$

Naturally, the mean and variance can be used to *roughly* describe a given probability distribution. A more complete description, on the other hand, can be achieved by using more *moments* of the random variable X, that is, the powers of $(X - E(X))$. The variance is the second moment of X.

Although there are different probability distributions that describe different phenomena (Table 3.6), the *normal distribution* plays a critical role in many multimedia applications because of the central limit theorem, which states that the average of a large set of samples tends to be normally distributed, even when the distribution from which the average is computed is not normally distributed. Consequently, the average quality assessment of objects picked from a large set can be modeled as a normal distribution of qualities, $N(\mu, \sigma)$, where μ is the expected quality and σ^2 is the variance of the qualities. Thus, the normal distribution is commonly applied when modeling phenomena where many small, independent effects are contributing to a complex observation. The normal distribution is also commonly used for modeling sampling-related imprecision (involving capture devices, feature extraction algorithms, or network devices) because the central limit theorem implies that the sampling distribution (i.e., the probability distribution under repeated sampling from a given population) of the mean is also approximately normally distributed.

In general, such complex statistical assessments of data precision might be hard to obtain. A compromise between lack of detailed statistics and need for a probabilistic model that provides more than the mean is usually found by representing the range of values (e.g., the possible qualities for objects captured by a sensor device) with a lower and an upper bound and assuming a uniform distribution within the range [Cheng *et al.*, 2007].

3.5.1.2 Conditional Probability, Independence, Correlation, and Covariance

Conditional (or a posteriori) probability, $P(X = a | Y = b)$, is the probability of the observation a, given the occurrence of some other observation, b:

$$P(X = a | Y = b) = \frac{P(X = a \wedge Y = b)}{P(Y = b)}.$$

In contrast, the marginal (or prior) probability of an observation is its probability regardless of the outcome of another observation.

A simplifying assumption commonly relied upon in many probabilistic models is that the individual attributes of the data (and the corresponding predicates) are independent of each other:

$$P(X = a \wedge Y = b) = P(X = a)P(Y = b).$$

When the independence assumption holds, the probability of a conjunction can be computed simply as the product of the probabilities of the conjuncts.[7] However, in the real world, the independence assumption does not always hold (in fact, it rarely holds). Relaxing the independence assumption or extending the model to capture nonsingular probability distributions [Pearl, 1985] both necessitate more complex query evaluation algorithms. In fact, as we discuss in the next subsection, when available, knowledge about conditional probability (and other measures of dependencies, such as correlation and covariance) provides strong tools for predicting useful properties of a given system. The correlation coefficient $\rho(X, Y)$, for example, measures the *linearity* of the relationship between two observations represented by the random variables, X and Y, with expected values μ_X and μ_Y, respectively:

$$\rho(X, Y) = \frac{E((X - \mu_X)(Y - \mu_Y))}{\sigma_X \sigma_Y}.$$

It thus can be used to help estimate the dependence between two random variables. Note, however, that correlation is not always a good measure of dependence (because it focuses on linearity): while the correlation coefficient between two variables that are independent is always 0, a 0 correlation does not imply independence in a probabilistic sense.

The nominator of the correlation coefficient, by itself, is referred to as the covariance of the two random variables X and Y,

$$Cov(X, Y) = E((X - \mu_X)(Y - \mu_Y)),$$

and is also used commonly for measuring how X and Y vary together.

3.5.2 Possible-Worlds Interpretation of Uncertainty

As we mentioned earlier, in multimedia databases, a probabilistic "observation" can stand for different aspects of the data in different contexts: for example, the likelihood of a feature extraction algorithm having identified a target pattern in a given media object or a given user finding a given media object relevant to her interests based on her profile both can be represented using probabilistic observations.

Often, databases that contain uncertain or probabilistic data represent such knowledge with *existence* or *truth* probabilities associated with the tuples or attribute values in the database [Green and Tannen, 2006]. Dalvi and Suciu [2004] for example, associate a probability value, between 0 and 1, to each tuple in the database: this value expresses the probability with which the given tuple belongs to the uncertain relation. Sarma *et al.* [2006] compare various models of uncertainty in terms of their expressive power. In the rest of this section, we focus on the probabilistic database model, based on the so called probabilistic or-set-tables (or *p-or-set-tables*).

---

[7] Note that, under these conditions, the probabilistic model is similar to the fuzzy product semantics.

3.5.2.1 Probabilistic Relations

In the simplest case, we can model *uncertain knowledge* in a multimedia database in the form of a probabilistic relation, $R^p(K, A)$, where K is the key attribute, A is the value attribute, and P is the probability associated with the corresponding key-value pair. For example,

Might Enjoy^p		
K	**A**	**(P)**
⟨ Selcuk, "Wax Poetic" ⟩	yes	(0.86)
⟨ Selcuk, "Wax Poetic" ⟩	no	(0.14)
⟨ Selcuk, "Jazzanova" ⟩	yes	(0.72)
⟨ Selcuk, "Jazzanova" ⟩	no	(0.28)
⟨ Maria Luisa, "Wax Poetic" ⟩	yes	(0.35)
⟨ Maria Luisa, "Wax Poetic" ⟩	no	(0.65)
⟨ Maria Luisa, "Jazzanova" ⟩	yes	(0.62)
⟨ Maria Luisa, "Jazzanova" ⟩	no	(0.38)
. . .	. . .	. . .

is an uncertain database, keeping track of the likelihood of users of a music library liking particular musicians.

Because, in the real world, no two tuples in a database can have the same key value (for example, the *"Might Enjoy"* database in the foregoing example cannot contain both ⟨⟨ Selcuk, *"Wax Poetic"*⟩, *yes*⟩ and ⟨⟨*Selcuk*, *"Wax Poetic"*⟩, *no*⟩), each probabilistic relation, R^p, can be treated as a probability space (W, P), where $W = \{I_1, \ldots, I_m\}$ is a set of deterministic relation instances (each a different *possible world* of R^p), and for each key-attribute pair, t, $P(t)$ gives the ratio of the worlds containing t against the total number of possible worlds:

$$P(t) = \frac{|\{(I_i \in W) \wedge (t \in I_i)\}|}{|W|}.$$

A possible tuple is a tuple that occurs in at least one possible world, that is, $P(t) > 0$. Note that, in the probabilistic relation, if for two tuples $t \neq t'$, $K(t) = K(t')$, then the joint probability $P(t, t') = 0$. Moreover, $\sum_{t \in R^p, K(t)=k} P(t) \leq 1$. Green and Tannen [2006] refer to probabilistic relations, where $\sum_{t \in R^p, K(t)=k} P(t) = 1$, as probabilistic or-set-tables (or *p-or-set-tables*).

In a probabilistic relation, the value $\sum_{t \in R^p, K(t)=k} P(t)$ can never be greater than 1; if, on the other hand, $\sum_{t \in R^p, K(t)=k} P(t) < 1$, then such a relation is referred to as an *incomplete probabilistic relation*: for the key value, k, the probability distribution for the corresponding attribute values is not completely known. In such cases, to ensure that the probabilistic relation, R^p, can be treated as a probability space, often a special *"unknown"* value is introduced into the domain of A such that $\sum_{t \in R^p, K(t)=k} P(t) = 1$.

Probabilistic relations can be easily generalized to complex multiattribute relations: a relation R^p with the set of attributes $Attr(R^p)$ and key attributes $Key(R^p) \subseteq Attr(R^p)$ is said to be a probabilistic relation if there is a probability distribution P that leads to different possible worlds. For example, we can also encode the foregoing "*Might Enjoy*" relation in the form of a three-attribute p-or-set, with key attribute pair ⟨*User*, *Band*⟩, as follows:

Might Enjoy^p			
User	**Band**	**Likes**	**(P)**
Selcuk	"Wax Poetic"	yes	(0.86)
		no	(0.14)
Selcuk	"Jazzanova"	yes	(0.72)
		no	(0.28)
Maria Luisa	"Wax Poetic"	yes	(0.35)
		no	(0.65)
Maria Luisa	"Jazzanova"	yes	(0.62)
		no	(0.38)
. . .	. . .	. . .	. . .

3.5.2.2 Probabilistic Databases

We can use this *possible worlds* interpretation of the probabilistic knowledge to generalize the probabilistic databases to more complex multiattribute, multirelational databases [Dalvi and Suciu, 2007]: Let $\mathcal{R} = \{R_1, \ldots, R_k\}$ be a database, where each R_i is a relation with a set of attributes $Attr(R_i)$ and a key $Key(R_i) \subseteq Attr(R_i)$. A probabilistic database, $\mathcal{R}^p$ is a database where the state of the database is not known; instead the database can be in any of the finite number of possible worlds in $\mathcal{W} = \{\mathcal{I}_1, \ldots, \mathcal{I}_m\}$, where each $\mathcal{I}_j$ is a possible-world instance of $\mathcal{R}^p$. Once again, the probabilistic database $\mathcal{R}^p$ can be treated as a probability space $(\mathcal{W}, P)$, such that

$$\sum_{\mathcal{I}_j \in \mathcal{W}} P(\mathcal{I}_j) = 1.$$

Also as before, given two tuples $t \neq t'$ in the same probabilistic relation, if $K(t) = K(t')$, then $P(t, t') = 0$. Moreover, $\sum_{t \in R_{i,j}^p, K(t) = k} P(t) \leq 1$, where $R_{i,j}^p$ is the instance of relation R_i in the world instance $\mathcal{I}_j$.

3.5.2.3 Queries in Probabilistic Databases

A common way to define the semantics of a Boolean statement, s, posed against a probabilistic database, $\mathcal{R}^p = (\mathcal{W}, P)$, is to define it as the event that the statement s is true in the possible worlds of the database [Dalvi and Suciu, 2007]. In other words, if we denote the event that s is true in a database instance $\mathcal{I}$ as $\mathcal{I} \models s$, then

$$P(s) = \sum_{\mathcal{I}_j \in \mathcal{W} \ s.t. \ \mathcal{I}_j \models s} P(\mathcal{I}_j).$$

A probabilistic representation is said to be *closed* under a given database query language if, for any query specified in the language, there is a corresponding probabilistic table *Res^p* [Green and Tannen, 2006; Sarma *et al.*, 2006] that captures the probability of occurrences of the result tuples in the possible worlds of the given probabilistic database.

One way to define the results of a query posed against a probabilistic database is to rely on the probabilistic interpretation specified earlier: Given a query, Q, posed against a probabilistic database, $\mathcal{R}^p = (\mathcal{W}, P)$, the probability that the tuple t is in the result, *Res*, of Q can be computed as

$$P(t \in Res) = \sum_{\mathcal{I}_j \in \mathcal{W} \; s.t. \; \mathcal{I}_j \models (t \in Res)} P(\mathcal{I}_j).$$

Therefore, under this interpretation, *Res*[p] is nothing but the probabilistic table consisting of possible tuples (that are true in the result in at least one instance of the world) and their probability distributions.

Other, *consensus*-based, definitions [Li and Deshpande, 2009] of answers to queries over probabilistic databases take a distance function, Δ (which quantifies the difference between a given pair of results, *Res*[1] and *Res*[2], to a query Q), and define the *most consensus* answer *Res*[*] as a feasible answer to the query such that the expected distance between *Res*[*] and the answer to Q in the possible worlds of the probabilistic database is minimized [Li and Deshpande, 2009]:

$$Res^* = \arg\min_{Res^*} \left\{ \sum_{i=1}^{n} P_i \times \Delta(Res^*, Res_i) \right\},$$

where Res_i is the answer in the possible world $\mathcal{I}_i$ with probability P_i. When *Res*[*] is constrained to belong to one of the possible worlds of the probabilistic database, the consensus answer is referred to as the *median* answer; otherwise, it is referred to as the *mean* answer.

3.5.2.4 Query Evaluation in Probabilistic Databases

Consider probabilistic relations, $\mathcal{R}_1^p, \ldots, \mathcal{R}_n^p$, and an n-ary relational operator Op. Sarma *et al.* [2006] define the result of $Op(\mathcal{R}_1^p, \ldots, \mathcal{R}_n^p)$ as the probabilistic relation $Res^p = (\mathcal{W}, P)$ such that

$$\mathcal{W} = \{\mathcal{I} \mid \mathcal{I} = Op(\mathcal{I}_1, \ldots, \mathcal{I}_n), \mathcal{I}_1 \in \mathcal{W}_1, \ldots, \mathcal{I}_n \in \mathcal{W}_n\}$$

and

$$P = P(\mathcal{I}_1 \in \mathcal{W}_1, \ldots, \mathcal{I}_n \in \mathcal{W}_n).$$

Assuming that the probabilistic relations are independent from each other, we can obtain the probability space of the possible worlds as follows:

$$P = P(\mathcal{I}_1 \in \mathcal{W}_1) \times \cdots \times P(\mathcal{I}_n \in \mathcal{W}_n).$$

Because there are exponentially many possible worlds, in practice, enumeration of all possible worlds to compute P would be prohibitively expensive. Therefore, query processing systems often have to rely on algebraic systems that operate directly on the probabilistically encoded data, without having to enumerate their possible worlds. It is, however, important that algebraic operations on the probabilistic databases lead to results that are consistent with the possible-world interpretation (Figure 3.18). This often requires simplifying assumptions.

Disjoint-Independence

A probabilistic database, $\mathcal{R}^p$, is said to be *disjoint-independent* if any set of possible tuples with distinct keys is independent [Dalvi and Suciu, 2007]; that is,

$$\forall_{t_1, \ldots, t_k \in \mathcal{R}^p, Key(t_i) \neq Key(t_j) \text{ for } i \neq j} \; P(t_1, \ldots, t_k) = P(t_1) \times \cdots \times P(t_k).$$

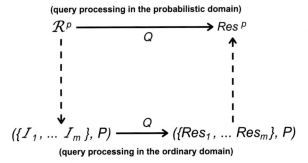

Figure 3.18. Query processing in probabilistic databases.

Disjoint-independence, for example, would imply that, in the probabilistic relation

Might Enjoy^p			
User	**Band**	**Likes**	**(P)**
Selcuk	"Wax Poetic"	yes	(0.86)
		no	(0.14)
Selcuk	"Jazzanova"	yes	(0.72)
		no	(0.28)
. . .	. . .	. . .	. . .

the probabilities associated to the tuples ⟨Selcuk, "Wax Poetic", yes⟩ and ⟨Selcuk, "Jazannova", yes⟩ are independent from each other. Although this assumption can be overly restrictive in many applications,[8] it can also be a very powerful help in reducing the cost of query processing in the presence of uncertainty. For example, this assumption would help simplify the term

$$P(\mathcal{I}_1 \in \mathcal{W}_1, \ldots, \mathcal{I}_n \in \mathcal{W}_n)$$

into a simpler form:

$$P(\mathcal{I}_1 \in \mathcal{W}_1, \ldots, \mathcal{I}_n \in \mathcal{W}_n) = P(\mathcal{I}_1 \in \mathcal{W}_1) \times \cdots \times P(\mathcal{I}_n \in \mathcal{W}_n).$$

In fact, relying on the disjoint-independence assumption, we can further simplify this as

$$P(\mathcal{I}_1 \in \mathcal{W}_1, \ldots, \mathcal{I}_n \in \mathcal{W}_n) = \prod_{t \in \mathcal{I}_1} P(t) \times \cdots \times \prod_{t \in \mathcal{I}_n} P(t) = \prod_{i=1}^{n} \prod_{t \in \mathcal{I}_i} P(t).$$

Note that, although this gives an efficient mechanism for computing the probability of a given possible world, the cost of computing the probability that a tuple is in the result by enumerating all the possible worlds would still be prohibitive. Dalvi and Suciu [2007] showed that for queries without self-joins, computing the result either is #P-hard (i.e., at least as hard as counting the accepting input strings for any polynomial time Turing machine) or can be done very efficiently in polynomial

---

[8] For example, a music recommendation engine that keeps track of users' listening preferences would never make the assumption that likes of a user are independent from each other.

(i) **Select:** when applying a selection predicate to a tuple with probability p, if the tuple satisfies the condition, then assign to it probability p, otherwise eliminate the tuple (i.e., assign the tuple probability 0 in the result)

(ii) **Cross-product:** when putting together two tuples with probabilities p_1 and p_2, set the probability of the resulting tuple to $p_1 \times p_2$.

(iii) **Project:**

  ■ *Disjoint Project:* If the projection operation groups together a set of k disjoint tuples (i.e., tuples that cannot belong to the same world) with probabilities $p_1, \ldots, p_k$, then set the probability of the resulting distinct tuple to $\sum_{i=1}^{k} p_k$.

  ■ *Independent Project:* If the projection operation groups together a set of k independent tuples (i.e., tuples with independent probability distributions) with probabilities $p_1, \ldots, p_k$, then set the probability of the resulting distinct tuple to $1 - \prod_{i=1}^{k}(1 - p_k)$.

(iv) if the required operation is none of the above, then **Fail**.

Figure 3.19. Pseudo-code for a query evaluation algorithm for relational queries, without self-joins, over probabilistic databases (the algorithm terminates successfully in polynomial time for some queries and fails for others).

time in the size of the database. Dalvi and Suciu [2007] and Re *et al.* [2006] give a query evaluation algorithm for relational queries without self-joins that terminates successfully in polynomial time for some queries and fails (again in polynomial time) for some other (harder) queries (Figure 3.19).

Tuple-Independence

An even stronger independence assumption is the *tuple-independence* assumption, where any pairs of tuples in a probabilistic database are assumed to be independent. Obviously, not all *domain-independent* probabilistic relations can be encoded as *tuple-independent* relations. For example, the tuples of the relation

Belongs_to^P		
Object	*Band*	*(P)*
Audio_file$_{15}$	"Wax Poetic"	(0.35)
	"Jazzanova"	(0.6)
	"Seu George"	(0.05)
Audio_file$_{42}$	"Nina Simone"	(0.82)
...	...	...
...		

cannot be independently selected from each other because of the disjointness requirement imposed by the "*Object*" key attribute, without further loss of information. On the other hand, thanks to the binary ("*yes*"/"*no*") domain of the "*Likes*" attribute, the "*Might Enjoy*" relation in the earlier examples can also be encoded as a probabilistic relation, where there are no key constraints to prevent a tuple-independence assumption:

Might Enjoy^p		
User	**Band**	**(P)**
Selcuk	"Wax Poetic"	(0.86)
Selcuk	"Jazzanova"	(0.72)
Maria Luisa	"Wax Poetic"	(0.35)
Maria Luisa	"Jazzanova"	(0.62)
. . .	. . .	. . .

One advantage of the tuple-independence assumption is that Boolean statements can be efficiently evaluated using *ordered binary decision diagrams* (OBDDs), which can compactly represent large Boolean expressions [Meinel and Theobald, 1998]. The OBDD is constructed from a given Boolean statement, s, using a variable elimination process followed by redundancy elimination: Let x be a variable in s; we can rewrite the Boolean statement s as follows:

$$s = (x \land s|_x) \lor (\bar{x} \land s|_{\bar{x}}),$$

where $s|_x$ is the Boolean statement where x is replaced with "*true*" and $s|_{\bar{x}}$ is the statement where x is replaced with "*false*". Visually, this can be represented as in Figure 3.20. The OBDD creation process involves repeated application of this rule to create a *decision tree* (see Section 9.1). As an example, consider the query, Q,

```
SELECT Object
FROM Might_Enjoy m, Belongs_to b
WHERE m.Band = b.Band
```

over the probabilistic relations

Might Enjoy^p		
User	**Band**	**(tuple, P)**
Selcuk	"Wax Poetic"	($t_{1,1}$, 0.86)
Selcuk	"Jazzanova"	($t_{1,2}$, 0.72)
Maria Luisa	"Wax Poetic"	($t_{1,3}$, 0.35)

and

Belongs_to^p		
Object	**Band**	**(tuple, P)**
Audio_file$_{15}$	"Wax Poetic"	($t_{2,1}$, 0.35)
Audio_file$_{42}$	"Jazzanova"	($t_{2,2}$, 0.6)

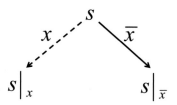

Figure 3.20. Variable elimination.

Note that, here, each tuple is given a tuple ID, which also serves as the tuple variable: if in the result $t_{2,1} = $ "*true*", then the answer is computed in a possible world where the corresponding tuple exists; otherwise the result is computed in a possible world where the tuple does not exist.

Given the foregoing query and the probabilistic relations, we can represent the results of the query Q in the form of a logical statement of the form

$$s = (t_{1,1} \wedge t_{2,1}) \vee (t_{1,2} \wedge t_{2,2}) \vee (t_{1,3} \wedge t_{2,1}).$$

If s is true, then there is at least one tuple in the result. Note that each conjunct $(t_i \wedge t_j)$ corresponds to a possible result in the output. Therefore, statements of this form are also referred to as the *lineage* of the query results.

Given the (arbitrarily selected) tuple order $\pi = [t_{1,1}, t_{2,1}, t_{1,2}, t_{2,2}, t_{1,3}]$, the variable elimination process for this statement would lead to the decision tree shown in Figure 3.21. To evaluate the expression s for a given set of tuple truths/falsehoods, we follow a path from the root to one of the leaves following the solid edge if the tuple is in the possible world and the dashed edge if it is not. The leaf gives the value of the expression in the selected possible world. Note that decision trees can be used to associate confidences to the statements: because paths are pairwise mutually exclusive (or disjoint), this can be done simply by summing up the probabilities of each path leading to 1. This summation can be performed in a bottom-up manner: the probability, $P(n)$, of a node, n, for a tuple variable t and with children n_l for $t = $ "*false*" and n_r for $t = $ "*true*" can be computed as $P(n) = P(n_r)P(t) + P(n_l)P(\bar{t})$.

Note that this decision-tree representation can be redundant and further simplified by determining the cases where truth or falsehood can be established earlier or overlaps between substatements can be determined and leveraged. To see this more clearly, consider for example the case where we are trying to see if the tuple

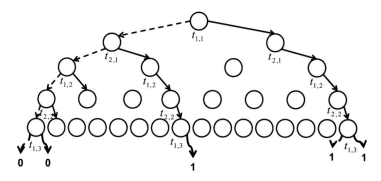

Figure 3.21. Decision tree fragment (only some of the edges are shown).

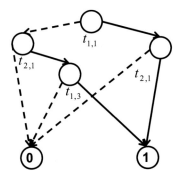

Figure 3.22. OBDD for the statement $s' = (t_{1,1} \wedge t_{2,1}) \vee (t_{1,3} \wedge t_{2,1})$.

$\langle$ "*Audio_file$_{15}$*" $\rangle$ is in the result of the query, Q, or not. We can write the conditions in which this tuple is in the result of Q in the form of the following Boolean statement:

$$s' = (t_{1,1} \wedge t_{2,1}) \vee (t_{1,3} \wedge t_{2,1})$$

Figure 3.22 shows the corresponding OBDD for the same tuple order $\pi = [t_{1,1}, t_{2,1}, t_{1,2}, t_{2,2}, t_{1,3}]$. Note that certain redundancies in the graph have been eliminated; for example, for the right branch of the graph, the truth of $t_{1,3}$ is not being considered at all.

In general, based on the chosen variable order, the size of the OBDD can vary from constant to exponential, and constructing small OBDDs is an NP-hard problem [Meinel and Theobald, 1998]. On the other hand, Olteanu and Huang [2009] showed that for a large class of useful database queries, OBDDs are polynomial size in the number of query variables. Meinel and Theobald [1998] also showed that the OBDD does not need to be materialized in its entirety before computing its probability, helping reduce the cost of confidence calculation process.

3.5.3 Bayesian Models: Bayesian Networks, Language and Generative Models

So far, we have discussed probabilistic models in which different observations are mostly independent from each other. In many real-world situations, however, there are dependencies between observations (such as the color of an image and its likelihood of corresponding to a "bright day"). In multimedia databases, knowledge of such dependencies can be leveraged to make inferences that can be useful in retrieval.

Bayes' rule rewrites the definition of the conditional probability, $P(X = a | Y = b)$, in a way that relates the conditional and marginal probabilities of the observations $X = a$ and $Y = b$:

$$P(X = a | Y = b) = \frac{P(Y = b | X = a) P(X = a)}{P(Y = b)}.$$

The definition for continuous random variables in terms of probability density functions is analogous.

While being simple, the Bayesian rule provides the fundamental basis for statistical inference and belief revision in the presence of new observations. Let H be a random variable denoting available hypotheses and E denote a random variable denoting evidences. Then, the Bayesian rule can be used to revise the hypothesis to account for the new evidence as follows:

$$P(H = h|E = e) = \frac{P(E = e|H = h)P(H = h)}{P(E = e)}.$$

In other words, the likelihood of a given hypothesis is computed based on the prior probability of the hypothesis, the likelihood of the event given the hypothesis, and the marginal probability of the event (under all hypotheses). For example, in multimedia database systems, this form of Bayesian inference is commonly applied to capture the user's relevance feedback (Section 12.4).

3.5.3.1 Bayesian Networks

A Bayesian network is a node-labeled graph, $G(V, E)$, where the nodes in V represent variables, and edges in E between the nodes represent the relationships between the probability distributions of the corresponding variables. Each node $v_i \in V$ is labeled with a conditional probability function

$$P(v_i = y_i \mid v_{in,i,1} = x_{in,i,1} \wedge \cdots \wedge v_{in,i,m} = x_{in,i,m}),$$

where $\{v_{in,i,1}, \ldots, v_{in,i,m}\}$ are nodes from which v_i has incoming edges. Consequently, Bayesian networks can be used for representing probabilistic relationships between variables (e.g., objects, properties of the objects, or beliefs about the properties of the objects) [Pearl, 1985]. In fact, once they are fully specified, Bayesian networks can be used for answering probabilistic queries given certain observations. However, in many cases, both the structure and the parameters of the network have to be learned through iterative and sampling-based heuristics, such as expectation maximization (EM) [Dempster *et al.*, 1977] and Markov chain Monte Carlo (MCMC) [Andrieu *et al.*, 2003] algorithms. We discuss the EM algorithm in detail in Section 9.7.4.3, within the context of learning the structure of a special type of Bayesian networks, called Hidden Markov Models (HMMs).

3.5.3.2 Language Models

Language modeling is an example of the use of the Bayesian approach to retrieval, most successfully applied to (text) information retrieval problems [Lafferty and Zhai, 2001; Ponte and Croft, 1998]. A language model is a probability distribution that captures the statistical regularities of features (e.g., word distribution) of standard collections (e.g., natural language use) [Rosenfeld, 2000]. In language modeling, given a database, D, for each feature f_i and object $o_j \in D$, the probability $p(f_i|o_j)$ is estimated and indexed. Given a query, $q = \langle q_1, \ldots, q_m \rangle$, with m features, for each object $o_j \in D$, the matching likelihood is estimated as

$$p(q|o_j) = \prod_{q_i \in q} p(q_i|o_j).$$

Then, given $p(o_j)$ and using Bayes' theorem, we can estimate the a posteriori probability (i.e., the matching probability) of the object, o_j, as

$$p(o_j|q) = \frac{p(q|o_j)p(o_j)}{p(q)}.$$

Because, given a query q, $p(q)$ is constant, the preceding term is proportional to $p(q|o_j)p(o_j)$. Thus, the term $p(q|o_j)p(o_j)$ can be used to rank objects in the database with respect to the query q.

Smoothing

In order to take into account the distribution of the features in the overall collection, the object language model, $p(f_i|o_j)$, is often *smoothed* using a background collection model, $p(f_i|D)$. This smoothing can be performed using simple linear interpolation,

$$p_\lambda(f_i|o_j) = \lambda p(f_i|o_j) + (1 - \lambda)p(f_i|D),$$

where $0 \leq \lambda \leq 1$ is a parameter estimated empirically or trained using an hidden Markov model (HMM) [Miller *et al.*, 1999].

An alternative smoothing technique is the Dirichlet smoothing [Zhai and Lafferty, 2004], where $p(f_i|o_j)$ is computed as

$$p_\mu(f_i|o_j) = \frac{count(f_i, o_j) + \mu p(f_i|D)}{|o_j| + \mu},$$

where $count(f_i, o_j)$ is the number of occurrences of the feature f_i in object o_j (e.g., count of a term in a document), $|o_j|$ is the size of o_j in terms of the number of features (e.g., number of words in the given document), and μ is the smoothing parameter.

Translation

Berger and Lafferty [1999] extend the model by *semantic smoothing*, where relationships between features are taken into account. In particular, Berger and Lafferty [1999] compute a translation model, $t(f_i|f_k)$ that relates the feature f_k to the feature f_i and, using this model, computes $p(q|o_j)$ as

$$p(q|o_j) = \prod_{q_i \in q} \sum_{f_k} t(q_i|f_k)p(f_k|o_j).$$

For example, Lafferty and Zhai [2001] use Markov chains on features (words) and objects (documents) to estimate the amount of translation needed to obtain the query model. We provide details of this Markov chain–based translation technique in Section 3.5.3.3.

3.5.3.3 Generative Models

Language model–based retrieval is a special case of the more general set of probabilistic schemes, called *generative models*.

Generative Query Models

Generative query models, such as the one presented by Lafferty and Zhai [2001], view the query q as being generated by a probabilistic process corresponding to the user. The query model encodes the user's preferences and the context in which the query is formulated. Similarly, each object in the database is also treated as being generated through a probabilistic process associated with the corresponding source. In other words, the object model encodes information about the document and its source.

More formally, the user, u, generates the query, q, by selecting the parameter values, θ_q, of the query model with probability $p(\theta_q|u)$; the query q is then generated

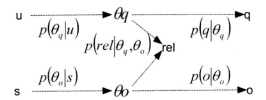

Figure 3.23. Generative model for object relevance assessment.

using this model according to the distribution $p(q|\theta_q)$. The object, o, is also generated through a similar process, where the source, s, selects an object model θ_o according to the distribution $p(\theta_o|s)$ and the object o is generated using these parameter values according to $p(o|\theta_o)$.

Given a database, D, and an object, o_i, Lafferty and Zhai [2001] model the relevance of o_i to the query q through a binary relevance variable, rel_i, which takes the *true* or *false* value based on models θ_q and θ_o, according to $p(rel_i|\theta_q, \theta_o)$ (Figure 3.23).

Given these models, the amount of imprecision $\mathcal{I}$ caused by returning a set R of results is measured as

$$\mathcal{I}(R|u, q, s, D) = \int_{\Theta} L(R, \theta)p(\theta|u, q, s, D)d\theta,$$

where θ is the set of all parameters of the models, Θ is the set of all values these parameters can take, and $L(R, \theta)$ is the information loss associated to the objects in R according to the collective model θ. Given this, the retrieval problem can be reduced [Lafferty and Zhai, 2001] to finding the set, R_{opt}, of objects, such that

$$R_{opt} = \underset{R}{argmin}\, \mathcal{I}(R|u, q, s, D).$$

Within this framework, estimating the relevance of object o_i reduces to the problem of estimating the query and object models, θ_q and θ_o. For example, as we mentioned earlier, Lafferty and Zhai [2001] estimate the query model using Markov chains on features and objects; more specifically, Lafferty and Zhai [2001] focus on the text retrieval problem, where words are the features and documents are the objects. As in PageRank [Brin and Page, 1998; Page *et al.*, 1998] (where the importance of Web pages is found using a random-walk–based connectedness analysis over the Web graph – see Sections 3.5.4 and 6.3.1.2), Lafferty and Zhai [2001] use a random-walk–based analysis to discover the translation probability, $t(q|w)$, from the document word w to query term q. The random walk process starts with picking a word, w_0, with probability, $p(w_0|u)$. After this first step, the process picks a document, d_0 (using distribution $p(d_0|w_0)$) with probability α or stops with probability $1 - \alpha$. Here, the transition probability $p(d_0|w_0)$ is computed as

$$p(d_0|w_0) = \frac{p(w_0|d_0)p(d_0)}{\sum_{d \in D} p(w_0|d)p(d)},$$

where $p(\cdot|d)$ is the likelihood of the word given document d and $p(d)$ is the prior probability of document d. Note that $p(d_i)$ can simply be $\frac{1}{|D|}$ or can reflect some other importance measure for the document d_i in the database. After this, the process picks a word w_1 with probability distribution $p(w_1|d_0)$ and the process continues as before.

This random walk process can be represented using two stochastic matrices: word-to-document transition matrix $\mathcal{A}$, and document-to-word transition matrix $\mathcal{B}$. The generation probability, $p(q_j|u)$, for the query word, q_j, is computed by analyzing these two matrices and finding the probability of the process stopping at word q_j starting from the initial probability distribution, $p(\cdot|u)$.

Dirichlet Models

As we see in Chapters 8 and 9, many retrieval algorithms rely on partitioning of the data into sets or clusters of objects, each with a distinct property. These distinct properties help the user focus on relevant object sets during search.

Generative Dirichlet processes [Ferguson, 1973; Teh *et al.*, 2003] are often used to obtain prior probability distributions when seeking these classes [Veeramachaneni *et al.*, 2005]. A Dirichlet process (*DP*) models a given set, $O = \{x_1, \ldots, x_n\}$, of observations using the set of corresponding parameters, $\{\rho_1, \ldots, \rho_n\}$, that define each class. Each ρ_i is drawn independently and identically from a random distribution G, whose marginal distributions are Dirichlet distributed. More specifically, if $G \sim DP(\alpha, H)$, with a base distribution H and a concentration parameter, α, then for any finite measurable partition P_1 through P_k,

$$\langle G_1, \ldots, G_k \rangle \sim Dir(\alpha H_1, \ldots, \alpha H_k).$$

The Dirichlet process has the property that each G_j is distributed in such a way that

$$E[G_j] = H_j,$$

$$\sigma^2[G_j] = \frac{H_j(1 - H_j)}{\alpha + 1},$$

and

$$\sum G_j = 1.$$

Intuitively the base distribution, H_j gives the mean of the partition and α_j gives the inverse of its variance. Note that G is discrete, and thus multiple ρ_is can take the same value. When this occurs, we say that the corresponding xs with the same ρ belong to the same cluster.

Another important property of the Dirichlet process model is that, given a set of observations, $O = \{x_1, \ldots, x_n\}$, the parameter, ρ_{n+1}, for the next observation can be predicted from the $\{\rho_1, \ldots, \rho_n\}$ as follows:

$$\rho_{n+1}|\rho_1, \ldots, \rho_n \sim \frac{1}{\alpha + n}\left(\alpha H + \sum_{l=1}^{n} \delta_{\rho_l}\right),$$

where δ_ρ is a point mass (i.e., distribution) centered at ρ. This is equivalent to stating that

$$\rho_{n+1}|\rho_1, \ldots, \rho_n \sim \frac{1}{\alpha + n}\left(\alpha H + \sum_{l=1}^{m} n_l\, \delta_{\rho_l^*}\right),$$

where $\rho_1^*, \ldots, \rho_m^*$ are unique parameters observed so far and n_l is the number of repeats for ρ_l^*. Note that the larger the observation count, n_l, is, the higher is the contribution of $\delta_{\rho_l^*}$ to ρ_{n+1}. This is sometimes visualized through a Chinese restaurant process analogy: Consider a restaurant with an infinite number of tables.

- The first customer sits at some table.
- Each new customer decides whether to sit at one of the tables with prior customers or to sit at a new table. The customer sits at a new table with probability proportional to α. If the customer decides to sit at a table with prior customers, on the other hand, she picks a table with probability proportional to the number of customers already sitting in that table.

In other words, the Dirichlet process model is especially suitable for modeling scenarios where the larger clusters attract more new members (this is also referred to as the rich-gets-richer phenomenon).

Note that the Dirichlet process model is an infinite mixture model; that is, when we state that $G \sim DP(\alpha, H)$, we do not need to specify the number of partitions. Consequently, the Dirichlet process model can be used as a generative model for a countably infinite number of clusters of objects. In practice, however, given a set of observations, only a small number of clusters are modeled; in fact, the expected number of components is logarithmic in the number of observations. This is because the Dirichlet process generates clusters in a way that favors already existing clusters. The fact that one does not need to specify the number of clusters as an input parameter makes the Dirichlet processes a more powerful tool than other schemes, such as finite mixture models, that assume a fixed number of clusters. Dirichlet process models are also popular as generative models, because there exists a so called *stick-breaking* construction, which recursively breaks a unit-length stick into pieces, each corresponding to one of the partitions and providing prior probability for the corresponding cluster [Ishwaran and James, 2001; Sethuraman, 1994].

3.5.4 Markovian Models

Probabilistic models can also be used for modeling the dynamic aspects of multimedia data (such as the temporal aspects of audio) and processes.

A process that carries a degree of indeterminacy in its evolution is called a stochastic (or probabilistic) process; the evolution of such a process is described by a probability distribution based on the current and past states of the process (and possibly on external events).

A stochastic process is said to be Markovian if the conditional probability distributions of the future states depend only on the present (and not on the past).

A Markov chain is a discrete-time stochastic process that can be modeled using a transition graph, $G(V, E, p)$, where the vertices, $v_1, \ldots, v_n \in V$, are the various states of the process, the edges are the possible transitions between these states, and $p : E \to [0, 1]$ is a function associating transition probabilities to the edges of the graph (though the edges with 0 probability are often dropped). A random walk on a graph, $G(V, E)$, is simply a Markov chain whose state at any time is described by a vertex of G and the transition probability is distributed equally among all outgoing edges.

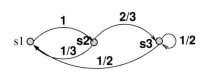

	s1	s2	s3
s1	0	1	0
s2	1/3	0	2/3
s3	1/2	0	1/2

Figure 3.24. A Markov chain and its transition matrix.

Transition Matrix Representation

The transition probabilities for a Markov model can also be represented in a matrix form (Figure 3.24). The (i, j)th element of this matrix, T_{ij}, describes the probability that, given that the current state is $v_i \in V$, the process will be in state $v_j \in V$ next time unit; that is,

$$T_{ij} = p(e_{i,j}) = P(S_{now+1} = v_j | S_{now} = v_i).$$

Because the graph captures all possible transitions, the transition probabilities associated to the edges outgoing from any state $v_i \in V$ add up to 1:

$$\sum_{v_j \in V} T_{ij} = \sum_{v_j \in V} p(e_{i,j}) = 1.$$

Because the state transitions are independent of the past states, given this matrix of one-step transition probabilities, the k-step transition probabilities can be computed by taking the kth power of the transition matrix. Thus, given an initial state modeled as an n-dimensional probability distribution vector, $\vec{\pi}_0$, the probability distribution vector, $\vec{\pi}_k$, representing the k-step can be computed as

$$\vec{\pi}_k = T^k \vec{\pi}_0.$$

If the transition matrix T is irreducible (i.e., each state is accessible from all other states) and aperiodic (i.e., for any state v_i, the greatest common divisor of the set $\{k \geq 1 | T_{ii}^k > 0\}$ is equal to 1), then in the long run, the Markov chain reaches a unique stationary distribution independent of the initial distribution. In such cases, it is possible to study this stationary distribution.

Stationary Distribution and Proximity

When the number of states of the Markov chain is small, it is relatively easy to solve for the stationary distribution. In general, the components of the first eigenvector[9] of the transition matrix of a random walk graph will give the portion of the time spent at each node after an infinite run. The eigenvector corresponding to the second eigenvalue, on the other hand, is known to serve as a *proximity* measure for how long it takes for the walk to reach each vertex [McSherry, 2001]. However, when the state space is large, an iterative method (optimized for quick convergence through appropriate decompositions) is generally preferred [Stewart and Wu, 1992]; for example, Brin and Page [1998] and Page *et al.* [1998] rely on a power iteration method to calculate the dominant eigenvalue (see Section 6.3).

These stationary distributions of Markovian models are used heavily in many multimedia, web, and social network mining applications. For example, popular

---

[9] See Section 4.2.6 for the definitions of the eigenvalue and eigenvector.

Web analysis algorithms, such as HITS [Gibson *et al.*, 1998; Kleinberg, 1999] or PageRank [Brin and Page, 1998; Page *et al.*, 1998], rely on the analysis of the hyperlink structure of the Web and use the stationary distributions of the random walk graphs to measure the importances of the web pages given a user query. Candan and Li [2000] used random-walk–based connectedness analysis to mine implicit associations between web pages. See Section 6.3 for more details of these link analysis applications. Also, see Section 8.2.3 for the use of Markovian models in graph partitioning.

Unfortunately, not all transition matrices can guarantee stationary behavior. Also, in many cases users are not interested in the stationary state behaviors of the system, but for example in how quickly a system converges to the stationary state [Lin and Candan, 2007] or more generally, whether a given condition is true at any (bounded) future time. These problems generally require matrix algebraic solutions that are beyond the scope of this book.

Hidden Markov Models

Hidden Markov models (HMMs), where some of the states are hidden (i.e., unknown), but variables that depend on these states are observable, are commonly used in multimedia pattern recognition. This involves training (i.e., given a sequence of observations, learning the parameters of the underlying HMM) and pattern recognition (i.e., given the parameters of an HMM, finding the most likely sequence of states that would produce a given output). We discuss HMMs and their use in classification in Section 9.7.

3.6 SUMMARY

In this chapter, we have seen that, despite the diversity of features one can use to capture the information of interest in a given media object, most of these can be represented using a handful of common feature representations: vectors, strings/sequences, graphs/trees, and fuzzy or probabilistic based representations. Thus, in Chapters 5 through 10, we present data structures and algorithms that rely on the properties of these representations for efficient and effective retrieval of multimedia data. On the other hand, before a multimedia database system can leverage these data structures and algorithms, it first needs to identify the most relevant and important features and focus the available system resources on those. In the next chapter, we first discuss how to select the best feature set, among the alternative features, for indexing and retrieval of media data.

4

Feature Quality and Independence

Why and How?

For most media types, there are multiple features that one can use for indexing and retrieval. For example, an image can be retrieved based on its color histogram, texture content, or edge distribution, or on the shapes of its segments and their spatial relationships. In fact, even when one considers a single feature type, such as a color histogram, one may be able to choose from multiple alternative sets of base colors to represent images in a given database.

Although it might be argued that storing more features might be better in terms of enabling more ways of accessing the data, in practice indexing more features (or having more feature dimensions to represent the data) is not always an effective way of managing a database:

■ Naturally, more features extracted mean more storage space, more feature extraction time, and higher cost of index management. In fact, as we see in Chapter 7, some of the index structures require exponential storage space in terms of the features that are used for indexing. Having a large number of features also implies that pairwise object similarity/distance computations will be more expensive.

   Although these are valid concerns (for example, storage space and communication bandwidth concerns motivate media compression algorithms), they are not the primary reasons why multimedia databases tend to carefully select the features to be used for indexing and retrieval.

■ More importantly, as we have seen in Section 3.5.1.2, not all features are independent from each other, and this might negatively affect retrieval and relevance feedback.

   Because all features are not equally important (Section 4.2), to support effective retrieval we may want to pick features that are important and mutually independent for indexing, and drop the rest from consideration.

■ A fundamental problem with having to deal with a large number of dimensions is that searches in high-dimensional vector spaces suffer from a *dimensionality curse*: range and nearest neighbor searches in high dimensional spaces fail to

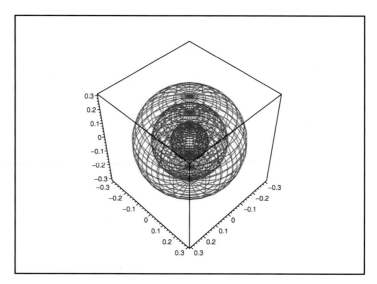

Figure 4.1. Equidistance spheres enveloping a query point in a three-dimensional Euclidean space.

benefit from available index structures, and searches deteriorate to sequential scans of the entire database.

4.1 DIMENSIONALITY CURSE

To understand the dimensionality curse problem, let us consider what happens if we start with a small query range and increase the radius of the query step by step (Figure 4.1).

In two-dimensional Euclidean space, a query with range r forms a circle with area πr^2. In three-dimensional Euclidean space, the same query spans a sphere with volume $\frac{4}{3}\pi r^3$. More generally, in an n-dimensional Euclidean space, the volume covered by a range query with radius r is cr^n, for some constant, c. Consequently, the difference in volume between two queries with the same center, but with radii $(i-1)r$ and ir (for some $r, i > 0$), respectively, can be calculated as

$$vol_\Delta(i-1, i) = c(ir)^n - c((i-1)r)^n = O(i^{n-1}).$$

Hence, if we consider the cases where the data points are uniformly distributed in the vector space, we can see that the ratio of data points that fall into the $(i+1)$th slice (between the spheres of radii $(i+1)r$ and ir) to the points that fall into the previous, ith, slice is $O((\frac{i+1}{i})^{n-1})$. In other words, because for all $i > 0$, $\frac{i+1}{i} > 0$, the number of data points that lie at a distance from the query increases exponentially with each step away from the query point (Figure 4.2). This implies that whereas queries with small ranges are not likely to return any matches, sufficiently large query ranges will return too many matches. Experiments with real data sets indeed have shown that the distributions of the distances between data points are rarely uniform and instead often follow a *power law* [Belussi and Faloutsos, 1998]: in a given d-dimensional space, the number of pairs of elements within a given distance, r, follows the formula

$$pairs(r) = c \times r^d,$$

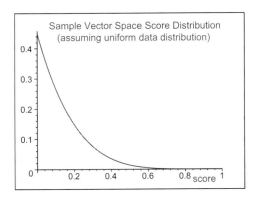

Figure 4.2. Score distribution assuming uniformly distributed data. Here, a score of 1 means that the Euclidean distance between the data point and the query is equal to 0; a score of 0, on the other hand, corresponds to the largest possible distance between any two data points in the vector space. Note that, when the number of dimensions is larger, the curve becomes steeper.

where c is a proportionality constant. More generally, Beyer *et al.* [1999] showed that, if a distance measure Δ_n defined over n-dimensional vector space has the property that, given the data and query distributions,

$$lim_{n \to \infty} \frac{variance(\Delta_n(\vec{v}_q, \vec{v}_o))}{expected(\Delta_n(\vec{v}_q, \vec{v}_o))} = 0,$$

then the nearest and the furthest points from the query converge as n increases. Consequently, the nearest neighbor query looses its meaning and, of course, effectiveness.

4.2 FEATURE SELECTION

Because of the dimensionality curse and the other reasons listed previously, multimedia databases do not use all available features for indexing and retrieval. Instead, the initial step of multimedia database design involves a feature selection (or dimensionality reduction) phase, in which data are transformed and projected in such a way that the selected features (or dimensions) of the data are the important ones (Figure 4.3). A feature might be *important* for indexing and retrieval for various reasons:

- *Application semantics:* The feature might be important for the application domain. For example, the location of the eyes and their spatial separation is important in a mugshot database.
- *Perception impact:* The feature might be what users perceive more than the others. For example, the human eye is more sensitive to some colors than to others. Similarly, the human eye is more sensitive to contrast (changes in colors) and motion (changes in composition).
- *Discrimination power:* The feature might help differentiate objects in the database from each other. For example, in a mugshot database with a diverse population of individuals, hair color might be an important discriminator of faces.

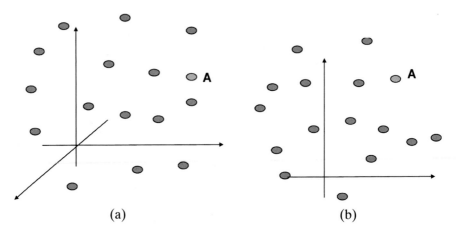

Figure 4.3. Dimensionality reduction involves transforming the original database in such a way that the *important* aspects of the data are emphasized and the less *important* dimensions are eliminated by projecting the data on the remaining ones: in this example, one of the features of the original data has been eliminated from further consideration: (a) Original database, (b) Transformed database.

- *Object description power:* A feature might be important *for a given object*, if it is a good descriptor of it. This would include how dominant the feature is in this object or how well this particular feature differentiates this particular object from the others.
- *Query description power:* A feature might be important for retrieval if it is dominant in the user query. The importance of the query criteria might be user specified or, in QBE systems, might be learned by analyzing the sample provided by the user. This knowledge can be revised explicitly by the user or transparently through relevance feedback, after initial candidates are returned by the system to the user.
- *Query workload:* The feature might be popular as a query criterion. This is related to application semantics; but in some domains, what is *interesting* to the user population might not be static, but evolve over time. For example, in search engines, the set of popular query keywords changes with events in the real world.

Note that some of the criteria (such as application semantics and perception impact) of feature importance just listed might be quantifiable in advance, before the database is designed. In some cases, there may also be studies establishing the discriminatory power of features for the data type from which the data set is drawn. For example, it is observed that the frequency distribution of words in a document collection often follows the so-called Zipf's law[1] [Li, 1992; Zipf, 1949]; that is, they have Zipfian distributions (Section 3.5): if the N words in the dictionary are ranked in nonincreasing order of frequencies, then the probability that the word with rank r occurs is

$$f(X = r, \alpha) = \frac{1/r^{\alpha}}{\sum_{w=1}^{N} 1/w^{\alpha}},$$

---

[1] Many other *popularity* phenomena, such as web requests [Breslau *et al.*, 1999] and query popularity in peer-to-peer (P2P) sites [Sripanidkulchai, 2001], are known to show Zipfian characteristics.

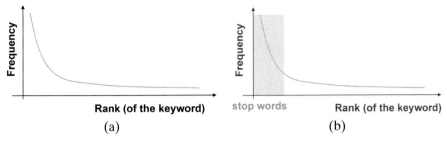

Figure 4.4. (a) The distribution of keywords in a given collection often follows the so-called Zipf's law and, thus, (b) most text retrieval algorithms pre-process the data to eliminate those keywords that occur too frequently (these are often referred to as the "*stop words*").

for some α close to 1. As shown in Figure 4.4(a), this distribution is very skewed, with a handful of words occurring very often. Because most documents in the database will contain one or more instances of these *hot* keywords, they can often be eliminated from consideration before the data are indexed; thus, these words are also referred to as the *stop words* [Francis and Kucera, 1982; Luhn, 1957] (Figure 4.4(b)). Different stop word lists are available for different languages; for example the stop word list for the English language would contain highly common words, such as "a", "an", and "the".

Other criteria, such as discrimination power *specific to a particular data collection*, are available only as the data and query corpus become available.

Example 4.2.1 (TF-IDF weights for text retrieval): In text retrieval, documents are often represented in the form of bags of keywords, where for each document, the corresponding bag contains the keywords (i.e., features used for indexing and retrieval) that the document includes.

Because a good feature (i.e., keyword) needs to represent the content of the corresponding object (i.e., text document) well, the weight of a given keyword k in a given document d is proportional to its frequency in d:

$$tf(k, d) = \frac{count(k, d)}{size(d)}.$$

This is referred to as the *term frequency (TF)* component of the keyword weight.

In addition, a good feature must also help discriminate the object containing it from others in the database, D. This is captured by a term referred to as the *inverse document frequency (IDF)*:

$$idf(k, D) = log\left(\frac{number\_of\_documents(D)}{number\_of\_documents\_containing(k, D)}\right).$$

Thus, the TF-IDF weight of the keyword k for document d in database D combines these two aspects of feature weights (Figure 4.5):

$$tf\_idf(k, d, D) = tf(k, d) \times idf(k, D).$$

An alternative formulation normalizes the TF-IDF weights to a value between 0 and 1, by dividing the inverse document frequency value, $idf(k, D)$, by the maximum

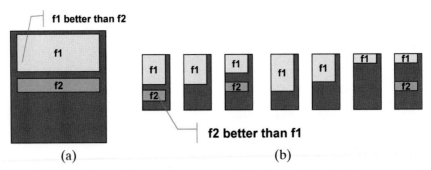

Figure 4.5. TF-IDF weights: (a) term frequency reflects how well the feature represents the object (feature f_1 is better than f_2) and (b) inverse document frequency represents how well it discriminates the corresponding object in the database (feature f_2 discriminates better than f_1).

inverse document frequency value, *max_idf*, for all documents and keywords in the database:

$$normalized\_tf\_idf(k, d, D) = tf(k, d) \times \frac{idf(k, D)}{max\_idf}.$$

Although the foregoing formulas are suitable for setting the weights for keywords in the documents in the database, they may not be suitable for setting the weight of the keywords in the query. In particular, by the simple action of including a keyword in the query (or by selecting a document that contains the keyword as an example), the user is effectively giving more weight to this keyword than other keywords that do not appear in the query. Salton and Buckley [1988b] suggest that the TF formula

$$tf(k, q) = \left(0.5 + \frac{0.5 \times \frac{count(k,q)}{size(q)}}{max\_term\_frequency(q)} \right)$$

should be used for query keywords. Note that, here, the TF value is normalized such that only half of the TF weight is affected by the term frequency value.

Similarly to the corpus-specific discrimination power of the features, the query description power of a feature is also known only immediately before query processing or after the user's relevance feedback; thus it cannot always be taken into account at the database design time. Therefore, whereas some of the feature importance criteria can be considered for selecting features for indexing, others need to be leveraged only for query processing.

4.2.1 False Hits and Misses

Feature selection and dimensionality reduction usually involve some transformation of the data to highlight which features are important features. The features that are not important are then eliminated from consideration (see Figure 4.3). Consequently, the process is inherently lossy.

Let us consider the data space and the range query depicted in Figure 4.6(a). In this figure, three objects are specially highlighted: A is the query object, B is an

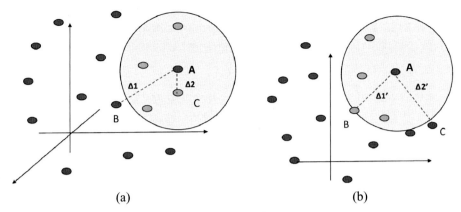

(a)   (b)

Figure 4.6. Transformations and projections that result in overestimations of distances cause misses during query processing; underestimations of distances, on the other hand, cause false hits: (a) Original database; (b) Transformed database, here B is a false hit ($\Delta_1' < \Delta_1$) and C is a miss ($\Delta_2' > \Delta_2$).

object that is outside of the query range (and thus is not a result), and C is an object that falls in the query range, and thus is an answer to this particular query. Figure 4.6(b), on the other hand, shows the same query in a space which is obtained through dimensionality reduction. In this new space, object B falls in the query range, whereas C is now outside of the query range:

- Object B is called a *false hit*. False hits are generally acceptable from a query processing perspective, because they can be eliminated through postprocessing. Thus their major impact is an increase in query processing cost.
- Object C is a *miss*. Misses are unacceptable in many applications: because an object missed due to a transformation is not available for consideration after the query is processed, a miss cannot be corrected by a postprocessing step.

As noted in Figure 4.6(b), false hits are caused by transformations that underestimate the distances in the original data space. Misses, on the other hand, are caused by transformations that overestimate object distances. Thus, in many cases, transformations that overestimate distances are not acceptable for dimensionality reduction.

Example 4.2.2 (Distance bounding): Let D be an image database, indexed based on color histograms: for images $o_i, o_j \in D$,

- $hist_m(o_i)$ denotes an m-dimensional color histogram vector for object o_i and
- $\Delta_{Euc,hist_m}(o_i, o_j)$ denotes the Euclidean distance between histograms of images o_i and o_j.

One way to reduce the number of dimensions used for indexing would be to transform the database by mapping images onto a 3D vector space, where the dimensions correspond to the amounts of green, red, and blue the images have: if $o_i \in D$ has M pixels, then

$$rgb(o_i) = \left\langle \frac{1}{M}\sum_{k=1}^{M} red(pixel(k, o_i)), \frac{1}{M}\sum_{k=1}^{M} green(pixel(k, o_i)), \frac{1}{M}\sum_{k=1}^{M} blue(pixel(k, o_i)) \right\rangle.$$

We can define $\Delta_{Euc,rgb}(o_i, o_j)$ as the Euclidean distance between the images in the new RGB space. Faloutsos *et al.* [1994] showed that the distances in the histogram space and the transformed RGB space are related to each other:

$$\Delta_{Euc,rgb}(o_i, o_j) \leq c(m)\Delta_{Euc,hist_m}(o_i, o_j),$$

where the value of the coefficient $c(m)$ can be computed based on the value of m. This is referred to as the *distance bounding* theorem.

The transformation described in the preceding example distorts the distances. However, the amount of distortion has a predictable upper bound, $c(m)$. Consequently, overestimations of distances can be avoided by taking the query range, δ_q, specified by the user in the original histogram space and using $\frac{\delta_q}{c(m)}$ as a query range in the RGB space. Under these conditions, the distance bounding theorem implies that the RGB space will only underestimate distances, and thus no object will be missed despite the significant amount of information loss during the transformation.

4.2.2 Feature Significance in the Information-Theoretic Sense

In general, a feature that has higher occurrence in the database is less interesting for indexing. This is because it is a poor discriminator of the objects (i.e., too many objects will match the query based on this feature) and thus might not support effective retrieval. In information theory, this is referred to as the *information content* of an event. Given a set of events,

- those that have higher frequencies (i.e., high occurrence rates) carry less information, whereas
- those that have low frequencies carry more information.

Intuitively, a solar eclipse is more interesting (and a better discriminator of days) than a sunset, because solar eclipses occur less often than sunsets. Shannon entropy [Shannon, 1950] measures the information content, in a probabilistic sense, in terms of the uncertainty associated with an event.

> **Definition 4.2.1 (Information Content (Entropy)):** *Let $E = \{e_1, \ldots, e_n\}$ be a set of mutually exclusive possible events, and let $p(e_i)$ be the probability of event e_i occurring. Then, the* information content *(or uncertainty), $I(e_i)$, of event e_i is defined as*
>
> $$I(e_i) = -log_2 p(e_i).$$
>
> *The information content (or uncertainty) of the entire system is, then, defined as the expected information content of the event set:*
>
> $$H(E) = -\sum_{i=1}^{n} p(e_i)log_2 p(e_i).$$

Based on this definition, if an event has a high $p(e_i)log_2\frac{1}{p(e_i)}$ value, then it increases the overall uncertainty in the system. Table 4.1 shows the entropy of a system with two possible events, $E = \{A, B\}$, under different probability distributions.

Table 4.1. Entropy of a system with two events, $E = \{A, B\}$, under different event probability distributions

$p(A)$	$p(B)$	$-log_2\, p(A)$	$-log_2\, p(B)$	$-p(A)log_2\, p(A)$	$-p(B)log_2\, p(B)$	$H(E)$
0.05	0.95	4.322	0.074	0.216	0.07	0.29
0.5	0.5	1	1	0.5	0.5	1
0.95	0.05	0.074	4.322	0.07	0.216	0.29

As it can be seen here, the highest entropy for the system is obtained when neither event is dominating the other in terms of likelihood of occurring; that is, both events are equally and significantly discriminating. In the cases where either one of the events is overly likely (0.95 chance of occurrence) relative to the other, the entropy of the overall system is low: in other words, although the rare event has much higher *relative* information content,

$$\frac{-log_2(0.05)}{-log_2(0.95)} = \frac{4.322}{0.074} = 58.4,$$

these two events together do no provide sufficient discrimination.

In Section 9.1.1, we discuss other information-theoretic measures, including *information gain by entropy* and *Gini impurity*, commonly used for classification tasks.

4.2.3 Feature Significance in Terms of Data Distribution

Consider the 3D vector space representation of a database, shown in Figure 4.7(a). Given a query range along the dimension corresponding to feature F_2, Figure 4.7(b) highlights the matches that the system would return. Figure 4.7(c), on the other hand, highlights the objects that will be picked if the same query range is given somewhere along the dimension corresponding to feature F_1.

As can be seen here, the dimension F_1 (along which the data are distributed with a higher variance) has a greater discriminatory power: fewer objects are picked when the same range is provided along F_1 than along F_2. Thus, variance of the data along a given dimension is an indicator of its quality as a feature.[2] Note that *variance*-based feature significance is related to the *entropy*-based definition of feature importance. Along a dimension which has a higher variance, the values that the feature takes will likely have a more diverse distribution; consequently, no individual value (or particular range of values) will be more likely to occur than the others. In other words, the overall entropy that the feature dimension provides is likely to be high.

Unfortunately, it is not always the case that the direction along which the spread of the data is largest coincides with one of the feature dimensions provided as input to the database. For instance, compare data distributions in Figures 4.8(a)

---

[2] As we see in Section 9.1.1, for classification applications where different classes of objects are given, the reverse is true: a discriminating feature minimizes the overlaps between different object classes by minimizing the variances for the individual classes. *Fisher's discriminant ratio*, a variance based measure for feature selection in classification applications, for example, selects features that have small per-class variances (Figure 9.1).

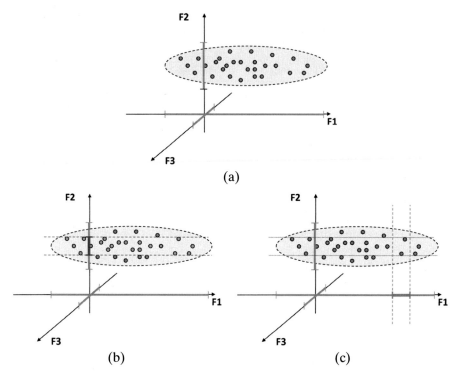

Figure 4.7. (a) 3D vector space representation of a database. (b) Objects that are picked when the query range is specified along dimension F_2. (c) Objects that are picked when the query range is specified along F_1.

and (b). In the case of the data corpus in Figure 4.8(a), the direction along which the data are spread the best coincides with feature F_1. On the other hand, in the data corpus shown in Figure 4.8(b), the data are spread along a direction that is a composition of features F_1 and F_2. This direction is commonly referred to as the principal component of the data.

Intuitively, we can say that it is easier to pick the most discriminating dimensions of the data, if these dimensions are overlapping with the principal, independent

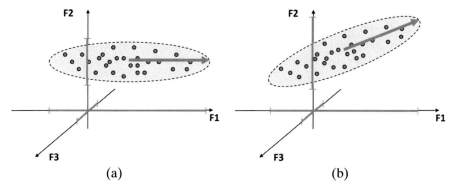

Figure 4.8. (a) The data have largest spread along feature F_1. (b) The largest data spread does not coincide with any of the individual features.

components of the database. In other words, transformations that reduce the correlation between the dimensions should help with dimensionality reduction.

4.2.4 Measuring the Degree of Association between Data Features

As we discussed in Section 3.5.1.2, correlation and covariance are two statistical measures that are commonly used for measuring the relationship between two continuously valued features of the data. However, not all features are valued continuously. In many cases, the features are binary (they either exist in an object or not) and the dependencies between features have to be captured using other measures. He and Chang [2006] and Tan *et al.* [2004] list various measures that can be used to quantify the strength of association between two features based on their co-occurrence (or lack thereof) of features in a given data set (Tables 4.2 and 4.3). In Table 4.2, $P(X)$ corresponds to the probability of selecting a document that has the property X, and $P(X, Y)$ corresponds to the probability of selecting a document that has both properties X and Y. Thus, different measures listed in these tables put different weights to co-occurrence (both features occurring in a given object), co-absence (neither feature occurring in a given object), and cross-presence based evidences (either one or the other feature is occurring in the given object, but not both). Piatetsky-Shapiro [1991] lists three properties that are often useful in measuring feature associations. Let A and B be two features; then

- if A and B are statistically independent, then the measurement should be 0,
- the measurement should monotonically increase with co-occurrence ($P(A, B)$) when $P(A)$ and $P(B)$ remain constant, and
- the measurement of association should monotonically decrease with the overall frequency of a feature ($P(A)$ or $P(B)$) in the data set, when the rest of the parameters stay constant.

Other properties that may be of interest in various applications include *inversion invariance* (or *symmetry*; i.e., the measurement does not change if one flips all feature absences to presences and vice versa) and *null invariance* (i.e., the measurement does not change when one simply adds more objects that do not contain either features to the database). Symmetric measures include ϕ, κ, α, and S. Measures with null invariance (which is useful for applications, such as those with sparse features, where co-presence is more important than co-absence) include cosine and Jaccard similarity [Tan *et al.*, 2004].

4.2.5 Intrinsic Dimensionality of a Data Set

As described earlier, the number of useful dimensions to describe a given data set depends on the distribution of the data and the way the dimensions of the space are correlated with each other. If the dimensions of a given vector space are uniform and independent, then each and every dimension is useful and it is not possible to reduce the dimensionality of the data without loss of information. On the other hand, when there are correlations between the dimensions, the inherent (or intrinsic) dimensionality of the space can be lower than the original number of dimensions.

Table 4.2. Measuring the degree of association between features A and B in a data set of size N [He and Chang, 2006; Tan *et al.*, 2004] ($\overline{A}$ and $\overline{B}$ denote the lack of the corresponding features in a given object)

Measure	Formula
ϕ-coefficient	$\dfrac{P(A,B)-P(A)P(B)}{\sqrt{P(A)P(B)(1-P(A))(1-P(B))}}$
Goodman-Kruskal's (λ) of sets of features	$\dfrac{\sum_i max_j P(A_i,B_j)+\sum_j max_i P(A_i,B_j)-max_i P(A_i)-max_j P(B_j)}{2-max_i P(A_i)-max_j P(B_j)}$
Odds ratio (α, lift)	$\dfrac{P(A,B)P(\overline{A},\overline{B})}{P(A,\overline{B})P(\overline{A},B)}$
Yule's Q	$\dfrac{P(A,B)P(\overline{A},\overline{B})-P(A,\overline{B})P(\overline{A},B)}{P(A,B)P(\overline{A},\overline{B})+P(A,\overline{B})P(\overline{A},B)}=\dfrac{\alpha-1}{\alpha+1}$
Yule's Y	$\dfrac{\sqrt{P(A,B)P(\overline{A},\overline{B})}-\sqrt{P(A,\overline{B})P(\overline{A},B)}}{\sqrt{P(A,B)P(\overline{A},\overline{B})}+\sqrt{P(A,\overline{B})P(\overline{A},B)}}=\dfrac{\sqrt{\alpha}-1}{\sqrt{\alpha}+1}$
Kappa (κ)	$\dfrac{P(A,B)+P(\overline{A},\overline{B})-P(A)P(B)-P(\overline{A})P(\overline{B})}{1-P(A)P(B)-P(\overline{A})P(\overline{B})}$
Mutual information (MI) of sets of features	$\dfrac{\sum_i \sum_j P(A_i,B_j)log\left(\frac{P(A_i,B_j)}{P(A_i)P(B_j)}\right)}{min(-\sum_i P(A_i)log(P(A_i)),-\sum_j P(B_j)log(P(B_j)))}$
J-measure (J)	$max\left(P(A,B)log\left(\frac{P(B|A)}{P(B)}\right)+P(A,\overline{B})log\left(\frac{P(\overline{B}|A)}{P(\overline{B})}\right)\right),$ $\left(P(A,B)log\left(\frac{P(A|B)}{P(A)}\right)+P(\overline{A},B)log\left(\frac{P(\overline{A}|B)}{P(\overline{A})}\right)\right)$
Gini index (G)	$max(P(A)(P(B|A)^2+P(\overline{B}|A)^2)+P(\overline{A})(P(B|\overline{A})^2+P(\overline{B}|\overline{A})^2)$ $-P(B)^2-P(\overline{B})^2,$ $P(B)(P(A|B)^2+P(\overline{A}|B)^2)+P(\overline{B})(P(A|\overline{B})^2+P(\overline{A}|\overline{B})^2)$ $-P(A)^2-P(\overline{A})^2)$
Support (s)	$P(A,B)$
Confidence (c)	$max(P(B|A),P(A|B))$
Laplace (L)	$max\left(\frac{N\,P(A,B)+1}{N\,P(A)+2},\frac{N\,P(A,B)+1}{N\,P(B)+2},\right)$
Conviction (V)	$max\left(\frac{P(A),P(\overline{B})}{P(A,\overline{B})},\frac{P(\overline{A})P(B)}{P(\overline{A},B)}\right)$
Interest (I)	$\dfrac{P(A,B)}{P(A)P(B)}$
cosine	$\dfrac{P(A,B)}{\sqrt{P(A)P(B)}}$
Piatetsky-Shapiro's (PS)	$P(A,B)-P(A)P(B)$
Certainty factor (F)	$max\left(\frac{P(B|A)-P(B)}{1-P(B)},\frac{P(A|B)-P(A)}{1-P(A)}\right)$
Added value (AV)	$max(P(B|A)-P(B),P(A|B)-P(A))$
Collective strength (S)	$\dfrac{P(A,B)+P(\overline{A},\overline{B})}{P(A)P(B)+P(\overline{A})P(\overline{B})}\times\dfrac{1-P(A)P(B)-P(\overline{A})P(\overline{B})}{1-P(A,B)-P(\overline{A},\overline{B})}$
Jaccard (ζ)	$\dfrac{P(A,B)}{P(A)+P(B)-P(A,B)}$
Klosgen (K)	$\sqrt{P(A,B)}max(P(B|A)-P(B),P(A|B)-P(A))$
H-measure (H, negative correlation)	$\dfrac{P(A,\overline{B})P(\overline{A},B)}{P(A)P(B)}$

Table 4.3. Scores corresponding to evidences of relationships between features A and B [He and Chang, 2006; Tan *et al.*, 2004] (rows with three values correspond to measures that can provide evidence for negative association, no association, and positive association; rows with two values correspond to measures that can provide evidence for no association and association)

Measure	Negative assoc.	No assoc.	(Positive) assoc.
ϕ-coefficient	−1	0	1
Goodman-Kruskal's (λ) of sets of features		0	1
Odds ratio (α, lift)	0	1	∞
Yule's Q	−1	0	1
Yule's Y	−1	0	1
Kappa (κ)	−1	0	1
Mutual information (MI) of sets of features		0	1
J-measure (J)		0	1
Gini index (G)		0	1
Support (s)		0	1
Confidence (c)		0	1
Laplace (L)		0	1
Conviction (V)	0.5	1	∞
Interest (I)	0	1	∞
cosine	0	$\sqrt{P(A,B)}$	1
Piatetsky-Shapiro's (PS)	−0.25	0	0.25
Certainty factor (F)	−1	0	1
Added value (AV)	−0.5	0	1
Collective strength (S)	0	1	∞
Jaccard (ζ)		0	1
Klosgen (K)	$\sqrt{\frac{2}{\sqrt{3}}-1}(2-\sqrt{3}-\frac{1}{\sqrt{3}})$	0	$\frac{2}{2\sqrt{3}}$
H-measure (H, negative correlation)	1	$P(\overline{A})P(\overline{B})$	0

As described in Section 4.1, given a set of data points and a distance function, the average number of data points within a given distance is proportional to the distance raised to the number of dimensions of the space; in other words, the number of pairs of elements within a given distance r follows the formula

$$pairs(r) = c \times r^d,$$

where c is a proportionality constant [Belussi and Faloutsos, 1998]. Note that we can also state this formula as

$$log(pairs(r)) = d \times log(c^{1/d}r) = c' + d \times log(r),$$

where c' is a constant. This implies that the intrinsic dimensionality, d, of the data can be estimated by plotting the $log(pairs(r))$ values against $log(r)$ and computing the slope of the line that best fits[3] the resulting plot [Belussi and Faloutsos, 1998; Traina *et al.*, 2000]. Belussi and Faloutsos [1998], leverage this to develop an estimation

---

[3] The fit is especially strong for data that is self-similar at different scales; i.e. is fractal (Section 7.1.1).

method called *box-occupancy counting*: The space is split into grids of different sizes and, for each grid size, the numbers of object pairs in the resulting cells are counted. Given these counts, the *correlation fractal dimension* is defined as the slope of the log-log curve

$$\frac{\delta \log \left(\sum_i count^2_{r,i} \right)}{\delta \log(r)},$$

where r is the length of the sides of the grid cells and $count^2_{r,i}$ is the number of point pairs in the ith cell of the grid.

4.2.6 Principal Component Analysis

Principal component analysis (PCA), also known as the Karhunen-Loeve, KL, transform is a linear transform, which optimally decorrelates the input data. In other words, given a data set described in a vector space, PCA identifies a set of alternative bases for the space along which the spread is maximized.

As we discussed in Section 3.5.1.2, variance and covariance are the two statistical measures that are commonly used for measuring the spread of data. Variance is one-dimensional, in that it measures the data spread along a single dimension, independently of the others. Covariance, on the other hand, measures how much a pair of data dimensions vary from their means with respect to each other. Given a data set, D, in an n-dimensional data space, a covariance matrix, S, can be used to encode pairwise covariance relationships among the dimensions of this space:

$$\forall_{1 \le i,j \le n} \; S[i,j] = Cov(i,j) = E((\vec{o}[i] - \mu_i)(\vec{o}[j] - \mu_j)),$$

where E stands for *expected value* and μ_i and μ_j are the average values of the data vectors along the ith and jth dimensions, respectively. Note that the covariance matrix S can also be written as

$$S = GG^T,$$

where G is an $n \times |D|$ matrix, such that

$$\forall_{1 \le i \le n} \forall_{\vec{o}_h \in D} \; G[i,h] = -\frac{1}{\sqrt{|D|}} (\vec{o}_h[i] - \mu_i).$$

If the dimensions of the space are statistically independent from each other, then for any two distinct dimensions, i and j, $Cov(i,j)$ will be equal to 0; in other words, the covariance matrix S will be diagonal, with the values at the diagonal of the matrix encoding $Cov(i,i) = \sigma_i^2$ (the variance along i) for each dimension i. Otherwise, the covariance matrix S is only symmetric; i.e., $Cov(i,j) = Cov(j,i) = E((\vec{o}[i] - \mu_i)(\vec{o}[j] - \mu_j))$.

The goal of the PCA transform is to identify a set of alternative dimensions for the given data space, such that the covariance matrix of the data along this new set of dimensions is diagonal. This is done through the process of *eigen decomposition*, where the square matrix, S, is split into its eigenvalues and eigenvectors:

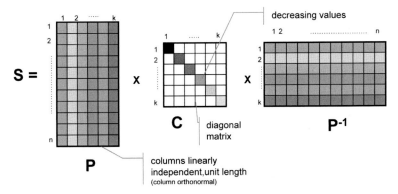

Figure 4.9. Eigen decomposition of a symmetric, square matrix, S.

Definition 4.2.2 (Eigenvector): *Let S be a square matrix. A* right eigenvector *for S is defined as a column vector, $\vec{r}$, such that*

$$S\vec{r} = \lambda_r \vec{r},$$

or equivalently

$$(S - \lambda_r I)\vec{r} = 0.$$

Here I is the identity matrix. The value λ_r is known as the eigenvalue corresponding to the right eigenvector, $\vec{r}$. Similarly, the left eigenvector *for S is defined as a row vector, $\vec{l}$, such that*

$$\vec{l}S = \vec{l}\lambda_l \quad \text{or} \quad \vec{l}(S - \lambda_l I) = 0.$$

When S is symmetric (as in covariance matrices) the left and right eigenvectors are each other's transposes. Furthermore, given an $n \times n$ symmetric square matrix, S, there are $k \leq n$ unique, unit-length right eigenvectors.

Theorem 4.2.1 (Eigen decomposition of a symmetric matrix): *Let S be an $n \times n$ symmetric, square matrix with real values. Then S can always be decomposed into*

$$S = PCP^{-1},$$

where

$$C = \begin{bmatrix} \lambda_1 & 0 & \dots & 0 \\ 0 & \lambda_2 & \dots & 0 \\ \dots & \dots & \dots & \dots \\ 0 & 0 & \dots & \lambda_k \end{bmatrix}$$

is real and diagonal and

$$P = [\vec{r_1}\vec{r_2}\dots\vec{r_k}],$$

where $\vec{r_1}, \dots, \vec{r_k}$ are the unique eigenvectors of S.

Furthermore, the eigenvectors of S are orthogonal to (and thus linearly independent from) each other (see Figure 4.9).

Theorem 4.2.2 (Orthogonality): *Let S be an $n \times n$ square matrix, and let $\vec{r_1}$ and $\vec{r_2}$ be two distinct eigenvectors of S. Then $\vec{r_1} \cdot \vec{r_2} = 0$.*

Note that because the k eigenvectors are orthogonal, they can be used as the orthogonal bases (instead of the original dimensions) to describe the database. Thus, a given database D, of m objects, described in an n-dimensional vector space can be realigned along the eigenvectors by the following linear transformation:

$$D'_{(m,k)} = D_{(m,n)} P_{(n,k)}.$$

This transformation projects each data vector in D onto the k (unit-length) eigenvectors and records the result in a new matrix, D'. Note that because the transformation is orthonormal (i.e., P is such that the columns are orthogonal to each other and are all unit length), all the (Euclidean) object distances as well as the angles between the objects are preserved in the new space.

Moreover, the subspace defined by the eigenvectors $\vec{r_1}, \ldots, \vec{r_k}$ has the largest variance. In fact, the variance is highest along the dimension defined by $\vec{r_i}$ with the largest eigenvalue, λ_i (and so on). To see why, consider the following:

$$S = GG^T$$
$$P^{-1}SP = (P^{-1}G)(G^TP).$$

Because $S = PCP^{-1}$ (or equivalently $P^{-1}SP = C$), we know that the left-hand side is equal to C:

$$C = (P^{-1}G)(G^TP).$$

Furthermore, because P is an orthonormal matrix, $P^{-1} = P^T$, and thus

$$C = (P^TG)(G^TP) = (P^TG)(P^TG)^T.$$

On the other hand, because G is an $n \times |D|$ matrix, such that

$$\forall_{1 \leq i \leq n} \forall_{\vec{o}_j \in D} \quad G[i,j] = \frac{1}{\sqrt{|D|}} (\vec{o}_j[i] - \mu_i),$$

and since P is an orthonormal transformation, we have

$$\forall_{1 \leq h \leq k} \forall_{\vec{o}_j \in D} \quad (P^TG)[h,j] = \frac{1}{\sqrt{|D|}} (\vec{o}_j(h) - \mu_h),$$

where $\vec{o}_j(h)$ is the length of the projection of the vector $\vec{o}_j$ onto the hth eigenvector. In other words, $(P^TG)(P^TG)^T$ is nothing but the covariance matrix of the data on the new $k \times k$ basis defined by the eigenvectors. Because this is equivalent to C, we can also conclude that C is the covariance matrix of the new space. Because C is diagonal, the values at the diagonal (i.e., the eigenvalues) encode the variance along the new basis of the space.

In summary, the eigenvectors of the covariance matrix S define bases such that the pairwise correlations have been eliminated. Moreover, the eigenvectors with the largest eigenvalues also have the greatest discriminatory power and thus are more important for indexing (Figure 4.10). This is performed by keeping only those

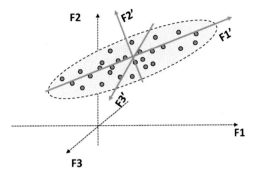

Figure 4.10. The eigenvectors of the covariance matrix S provide an alternative description of the space, such that the directions along which the data spread is maximized can be easily identified.

eigenvectors that have large eigenvalues and discarding those that have small eigen-values (Figure 4.11).

4.2.6.1 Selecting the Number of Dimensions

In Section 4.2.5, we have seen that one way to select the number of dimensions needed to represent a given data set is to compute its so-called intrinsic dimen-sionality. An alternative method for selecting the number of useful dimensions is to pick only those eigenvectors with eigenvalues greater than 1. This is known as the *Kaiser-Guttman* (or simply Kaiser) rule. The *scree test*, on other hand, plots the successive eigenvalues and looks for a point where the plot levels off. The *variance explained criterion* keeps enough dimensions to account for 95% of the variance. The *mean eigenvalue* rule uses only the dimensions whose eigenvalues are greater than or equal to the mean eigenvalue. The *parallel analysis* approach analyzes a random covariance matrix and plots cumulative eigenvalues for both random and intended matrices; the number of dimensions to be used is picked based on where the two curves intersect.

A major advantage of PCA is that, when the number of dimensions is reduced, it keeps most of the original variance intact and optimally minimizes the error under the Euclidean distance measure.

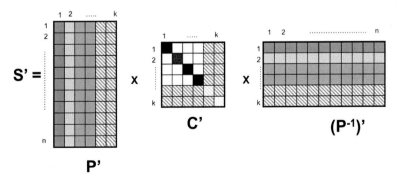

Figure 4.11. The effect of eliminating eigenvectors with small eigenvalues: $S' \neq S$, but the impact on the overall covariance is relatively small.

4.2.6.2 Limitations of PCA

One limitation of the PCA method is that 0 correlation does not always mean statistical independence (although the statistical independence always means 0 correlation). Consequently, while the dimensions of the newly defined space are decorrelated, they may not be statistically independent. However, because uncorrelated Gaussians are statistically independent [Lee and Verleysen, 2007], under the *Gaussian assumption* the dimensions of the bases are also statistically independent. The Gaussian assumption can be validated through the Kolmogorov-Smirnov test [Chakravarti *et al.*, 1967]. Other tests for non-Gaussianity include *negative entropy* and *kurtosis* [Hyvärinen, 1999]. When the Gaussian assumption does not hold, PCA can be extended to find the basis along which the data are statistically independent. This variant is referred to as *independent component analysis (ICA)*.

4.2.7 Common Factor Analysis

PCA is an instance of a class of analysis algorithms, referred to as the *factor analysis* algorithms, which all try to discover the latent structure underlying a given set of observed variables (i.e., the features of the media data). These algorithms assume that the provided dimensions of data can be transformed into linear combinations of a set of unobserved dimensions (or factors).

Common factor analysis (CFA) seeks the least number of *factors* (or dimensions) that can account for the correlation in the given set of dimensions. The input dimensions are treated as linear combinations of the factors, plus certain error terms. In more precise terms, each variable is treated as the sum of common and unique portions, where the common portions are explained by the common factors. The unique portions, on the other hand, are uncorrelated with each other. In contrast, PCA does not consider error terms (i.e., assumes that all variance is common) and finds the set of factors that account for the total variance in the given set of variables.

Let us consider an $n \times n$ covariance matrix, S. Common factor analysis partitions S into two matrices, *common*, C, and *unique*, U:

$$S = C + U,$$

where the matrix C is composed of $k \leq n$ matrices:

$$C = C_1 + C_2 + \cdots + C_k.$$

Each C_i is the outer product of a column vector, containing the correlations with the corresponding common variable and the n input dimensions. Intuitively, each diagonal entry in C_i is the amount of variance in the corresponding dimension explained by the corresponding factor.

Because U is supposed to represent each dimension's unique variability, U is intended to be diagonal. However, in general, if k is too small to account for all the common factors U will have residual errors, that is, off-diagonal nonzero values. In general, the higher k, the better the fit and the smaller the number and sizes of the errors in U.

As in PCA, C_i are derived from the eigenvalues associated to individual eigenvectors. Unlike PCA, on the other hand, in CFA, the proportion of each input dimension's variance, explained by the common factors, is estimated prior to the analysis. This information (also referred to as the communality of the dimension) is leveraged in performing factor analysis: most CFA algorithms initially estimate each dimension's degree of communality as the squared multiple correlation between that dimension and the other dimensions. They then iterate to improve the estimate.

Note that although both PCA and CFA can be used for dimensionality reduction, PCA is commonly preferred over CFA for feature selection because it preserves the total variance better.

4.2.8 Selecting an Independent Subset of the Original Features

Both PCA and CFA aim to find alternative bases for the space that can be used to represent the data corpus more effectively, with fewer dimensions. However, the new dimensions are not always intelligible to the users; for example, in the case of PCA, these dimensions are linear combinations of the input dimensions. In the case of CFA, a postrotation process is commonly used to better explain the new dimensions in terms of the input dimensions; but, nevertheless, the new (latent) dimensions are not always semantically meaningful in terms of application semantics.

In Section 9.6.2, we introduce a probability-driven approach for selecting a subset of the original features by accounting for the interdependencies between the probability distributions of the features in the database. In this section, we discuss an alternative approach, called *database compactness*–based feature selection [Yu and Meng, 1998], which applies dimensionality reduction on the original features of the database based on the underlying object similarity measure.

> **Definition 4.2.3 (Database compactness):** *Let D be a database of objects, let F be the feature set, and let $sim_F()$ be a function that evaluates the similarity between two media objects, based on the feature set, F. The* compactness *of the database is defined as*
>
> $$compactness_F(D) = \sum_{o_i \neq o_j \in D} sim_F(o_i, o_j).$$

As shown in Figures 4.12(a) and (b), a given query range is likely to return a larger number of matches in a compact database. Thus, the compactness of a database is inversely related to how discriminating queries on it will be. Thus, we can measure how good a discriminator a given feature $f \in F$ is by comparing the compactness of the database with and without the feature f considered for similarity evaluation:

> **Definition 4.2.4 (Feature quality based on database compactness):** *Let D be a database of objects, let F be the feature set, and let $sim_F()$ be a function that evaluates the similarity between two media objects, based on the feature set, F. The* quality of feature $f \in F$ based on database compactness *is defined as*
>
> $$quality_{F,D}(f) = compactness_{F \setminus \{f\}}(D) - compactness_F(D).$$

A negative $quality_{F,D}(f)$ indicates that, when f is not considered, the database becomes less compact. In other words, f is making the database compact and, thus,

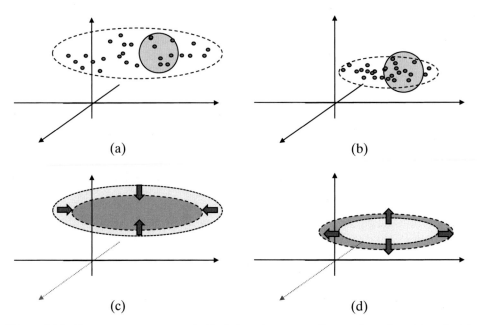

Figure 4.12. The same query range is likely to return a smaller number of matches in (a) a database with large variance than in (b) a compact database. (c) The removal of a *good* feature reduces the overall variance (rendering the queries less discriminating), whereas (d) the removal of a *bad* feature renders the database less compact (eliminating some aspect of the data that is too common in the database).

if there is a need to remove a feature, f should be considered for removal (Figures 4.12(c) and (d)).

Note that database compactness–based dimensionality reduction can be expensive: (a) the number of objects in the database can be very large and (b) removal of one feature may change the quality ordering of the remaining features. The first of these challenges is addressed by computing the feature qualities on a set of samples from the database rather than on the entire database. The second challenge can be addressed through *greedy hill climbing* (which evaluates a candidate subset of features, modifies the subset, evaluates if the modification is an improvement, and iterates until a stopping condition, such as a threshold, is reached) or *branch-and-bound* style search.

4.2.9 Dimensionality Reduction Using Fixed Basis

PCA and CFA, as well as the compactness approach extract the reduced basis for representing the data based on the distribution of the data in the database. Thus, the basis can differ from one database instance to another and may in fact evolve over time for a single data collection that is regularly updated. This, on the other hand, may be costly.

An alternative approach is to use a fixed basis, which does not represent the data distribution but can nevertheless minimize the amount of errors that are caused by dimensionality reduction. As discussed in Section 4.2.1, most transformations

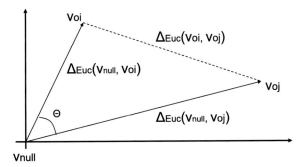

Figure 4.13. Distances among two objects and the origin.

involved in feature selection are lossy, and these losses impact distance function computations. Although transformations that underestimate distances do not cause any misses (i.e., they might be acceptable for media retrieval), they introduce false hits and thus they might require costly postprocessing steps. Consequently, it is naturally important that the error introduced by the dimensionality reduction process be as small as possible.

One approach commonly used for ensuring that the reductions in the dimensionality of the data cause small errors in distance computations is to rely on transformations that concentrate the *energy* of the data in as few dimensions as possible:

Definition 4.2.5 (Energy): *Let $F = \{f_1, f_2, \ldots, f_n\}$ be a set of features and let $\vec{v}_o = \langle w_{1,o}, w_{2,o}, \ldots, w_{n,o}\rangle$ be the feature vector corresponding to object o. The energy of $\vec{v}_o$ is defined as*

$$E(\vec{v}_o) = \sum_{i=1}^{n} w_{i,o}^2.$$

Intuitively, the energy of the vector representing the object is the square of the Euclidean distance of this vector from the hypothetical *null* object, $\vec{v}_{null} = \langle 0, 0, \ldots, 0\rangle$. Given this, we can rewrite the formula for the Euclidean distance between two objects, o_i and o_j, as follows (Figure 4.13):

$$\Delta_{Euc}^2(\vec{v}_{oi}, \vec{v}_{oj}) = \Delta_{Euc}^2(\vec{v}_{null}, \vec{v}_{oi}) + \Delta_{Euc}^2(\vec{v}_{null}, \vec{v}_{oj}) + 2\Delta_{Euc}(\vec{v}_{null}, \vec{v}_{oi})\Delta_{Euc}(\vec{v}_{null}, \vec{v}_{oj})cos\Theta.$$

We can also write this equation in terms of the energies of the feature vectors:

$$\Delta_{Euc}^2(\vec{v}_{oi}, \vec{v}_{oj}) = E(\vec{v}_{oi}) + E(\vec{v}_{oj}) + 2\sqrt{E(\vec{v}_{oi})E(\vec{v}_{oj})}cos\Theta.$$

Thus, transformations that preserve the energies of the vectors representing the media objects as well as the angles between the original vectors also preserve the Euclidean distances in the transformed space.

These include orthonormal transformations. In fact, the goal of PCA was to identify an orthonormal transformation which preserves and concentrates variances in the data. Discrete cosine (DCT) and wavelet (DWT) transforms are two other transforms that are orthonormal. Both of these help concentrate energies of the data vectors at a few dimensions of the data, while preserving both energies as well as the angles between the vectors in the database. The most important difference of these from PCA and CFA is that DCT and DWT each uses a fixed basis, independent of the data corpus available, whereas PCA and CFA extract the corresponding basis to be used considering the nature of the data collection.

4.2.9.1 Discrete Cosine Transform

DCT treats a given vector as a discrete, finite signal in the time domain (the indexes of the feature dimensions are interpreted as the time instances at which the underlying continuous signal is "*sampled*") and transforms this discrete signal into an alternative domain, referred to as the frequency domain. As such, it is most applicable when there is a strong correlation between the indexes of the feature dimensions and the feature values. This, for example, is the case when two equi-length digital audio signals are compared, sample-by-sample, based on their volumes or pitches at corresponding time instances.[4]

Intuitively, the *frequency* of the signal indicates how often the signal changes. DCT measures and represents the changes in the signal values in terms of the cycles of a cosine wave. In other words, it decomposes the given discrete signal into cosine waves with different frequencies, such that when all the decomposed cosine signals are summed up, the original signal is obtained.[5]

Definition 4.2.6 (DCT): *DCT is an invertible function* $dct : \mathbb{R}^n \to \mathbb{R}^n$, *such that given* $\vec{v} = \langle w_1, w_2, \ldots, w_n \rangle$, *the individual components of* $dct(\vec{v}) = \langle w'_1, w'_2, \ldots, w'_n \rangle$, *are computed as follows:*

$$w'_i = a_i \sum_{j=1}^{n} w_j \cos\left(\frac{\pi(i-1)}{n}\left((j-1)+\frac{1}{2}\right)\right),$$

where

$$a_i = \begin{cases} \sqrt{1/n} & \text{for } i = 1 \\ \sqrt{2/n} & \text{for } i > 1. \end{cases}$$

In other words,

$$w'_i = \sum_{j=1}^{n} C[i,j] w_j,$$

where C is an n × n matrix:

$$C[i,j] = a_i \cos\left(\frac{\pi(i-1)}{n}\left((j-1)+\frac{1}{2}\right)\right).$$

Based on the foregoing definition, we can see that DCT is nothing but a linear transform of the input vector:

$$dct(\vec{v}) = C\vec{v}.$$

---

[4] Similarly, images can be compared pixel-by-pixel. Because the corresponding signal is two-dimensional, the corresponding DCT transform also operates on 2D signals (and is referred to as 2D-DCT).

[5] In this sense, it is related to the discrete Fourier transform (DFT). Whereas DCT uses only cosine waves, DFT uses more general sinusoids to achieve the same goal.

This definition implies two things:

- Each component of $\vec{v}$ contributes to each component of $dct(\vec{v})$.
- The contribution of $\vec{v}$ to the ith component of $dct(\vec{v})$ is computed by multiplying the corresponding data signal by the cosine of a signal by the frequency $\sim \frac{\pi(i-1)}{n}$.

In fact, it is possible to show that the row vectors of C are *orthonormal*. In other words, if $\vec{c}_k$ and $\vec{c}_l$ denote two distinct vectors representing two rows of C, then $\vec{c}_k\vec{c}_l = 0$ (i.e., rows are linearly independent) and $\vec{c}_k\vec{c}_k = 1$ (i.e., rows are all unit length). Thus, the row vectors of C form the basis of an n-dimensional space.

Consequently, energies of the individual vectors as well as the angles between pairs of vectors are preserved by the transformation. Thus, Euclidean distances (as well as cosine similarities) of the original vectors are preserved.

Moreover, if the signal is not random (i.e., high-frequency noise), the signal values will be temporally correlated, with neighboring values being similar to each other. This implies that most of the energy of the signal will be confined to the low-frequency components of the signal, resulting in larger w_i' components for small is and small w_i's for large is. This means that most information contained in the vector $\vec{v}$ is captured by the first few components of $dct(\vec{v})$, and replacing the remaining components by 0 (or simply eliminating them for dimensionality reduction) will introduce only small errors (underestimations) in distance computations.[6]

4.2.9.2 Discrete Wavelet Transform

Discrete wavelet transform (DWT) is similar to DCT in that it treats the given vector as a signal in time space and decomposes it into multiple signals using a transformation with orthonormal basis. Unlike DCT, which relies on cosine waves, on the other hand, DWT relies on the so called *wavelet* functions. Furthermore, unlike DCT, which transforms the signal fully into the frequency domain, DWT maintains certain amount of temporal information. Thus, it is most applicable when there is need to maintain temporal information in the transform space.[7]

In the more general, continuous time domain, a wavelet is any continuous function, ψ, which has zero mean:

$$\int_{-\infty}^{+\infty} \psi(t)dt = 0.$$

The *mother* wavelet, which is used for generating a family of wavelet functions, is also generally normalized to 1.0,

$$\|\psi\| = \int_{-\infty}^{\infty} |\psi(t)|^2 \, dt = 1,$$

and centered at $t = 0$. A family of wavelet functions is defined by scaling and translating the mother wavelet at different amounts. More specifically, given a mother

---

[6] Because DCT is an invertible transform, the distorted signal with high-frequency components set to 0 can be brought back to the original domain. Because most of the energy of the signal is preserved in the low-frequency components, the error in the signal will be minimal. This property of DCT is commonly leveraged in lossy compression algorithms, such as JPEG.

[7] This is for example the case for image compression, where the wavelet-transformed image can actually be viewed as a low resolution of the original, without having to decompress it first.

wavelet function, ψ, a family of wavelet functions is defined using a positive scaling parameter, $s > 0$, and a real valued shift parameter, h:

$$\psi_{s,h}(t) = \frac{1}{\sqrt{s}} \, \psi\left(\frac{t-h}{s}\right).$$

Given this family of the wavelet functions, the wavelet transform of a continuous, integrable function $x(t)$, corresponding to the scaling parameter $s > 0$, and the real valued shift parameter h, is as follows:

$$x'(s,h) = \frac{1}{\sqrt{s}} \int_{-\infty}^{\infty} x(t)\psi\left(\frac{t-h}{s}\right) dt.$$

This transform has three useful properties:

- It is linear.
- It is covariant under translations; that is, if $x(t)$ is replaced by $x(t-u)$, then $x'(s,h)$ is replaced with $x'(s, h-u)$.
- It is covariant under dilations; that is, if $x(t)$ is replaced by $x(ct)$, then $x'(s,h)$ is replaced with $\frac{1}{\sqrt{c}}x'(cs, ch)$.

This means that the wavelet transform can be used for zooming into a function and studying it at varying granularities.

In general, discrete wavelets are formed from a continuous mother wavelet, but using scale and shift parameters that take discrete values. We are on the other hand often interested in discrete wavelets that apply on vectors of values (such as rows of pixels). In this case, wavelets are generally defined over $n = 2^m$ dimensional vector spaces. Let $\mathbb{S}^j$ denote the space of vectors with 2^j dimensions, and let Φ^j be a basis for $\mathbb{S}^j$. Let $dbl : \mathbb{S}^j \to \mathbb{S}^{j+1}$ be a *doubling* function, where $dbl(\vec{v}) = \vec{u}$ such that

$$\forall_{1 \le i \le 2^j} \; u_{2i-1} = u_{2i} = v_i.$$

Let $\mathbb{W}^j \subseteq \mathbb{S}^{j+1}$ be a vector space such that $\vec{w} \in \mathbb{W}^j$ iff $\vec{w}$ is orthogonal to $dbl(\vec{v})$ for all $\vec{v} \in \mathbb{S}^j$. The vectors in the basis, Ψ^j, for $\mathbb{W}^j$ are called the (2^{j+1}-dimensional) wavelets.

The 2^{j+1}-dimensional basis vectors for $\mathbb{W}^j$ along with the (*doubled* versions of) the basis vectors in Φ^j define a basis for $\mathbb{S}^{j+1}$. Moreover every basis vector for the vector space $\mathbb{W}^j$ is orthogonal to the (*doubled* versions of) the basis vectors in Φ^j.

Example 4.2.3 (Haar wavelets): Let $\mathbb{S}$ be a space of vectors with 2^n dimensions. Haar basis vectors [Davis, 1995; Haar, 1910] are defined as follows: For $0 \le j \le n$, $\Phi^{j,n} = \{\phi_1^{j,n}, \phi_2^{j,n}, \ldots, \phi_{2^j}^{j,n}\}$, where

$$\forall_{1 \le i \le 2^j} \; \phi_i^{j,n} = dbl(n - j, \; \langle\phi_i(1), \phi_i(2), \ldots, \phi_i(2^j)\rangle),$$

where

$$\phi_i(x) = \begin{cases} 1 & i = x \\ 0 & \text{otherwise.} \end{cases}$$

and where $dbl(k, \vec{v})$ is k times doubling of the vector $\vec{v}$. Similarly, for $0 \le j \le n$, $\Psi^{j,n} = \{\psi_1^{j,n}, \psi_2^{j,n}, \ldots, \psi_{2^j}^{j,n}\}$, where

$$\forall_{1 \le i \le 2^j} \; \psi_i^{j,n}(x) = dbl(n - j - 1, \; \langle\psi_i(1), \psi_i(2), \ldots, \psi_i(2^{j+1})\rangle),$$

Table 4.4. Alternative (not-normalized) Haar wavelet basis for the 4D space of vectors

Basis 1	$\phi_0^{2,2}$	$\phi_1^{2,2}$	$\phi_2^{2,2}$	$\phi_3^{2,2}$
	$\langle 1, 0, 0, 0 \rangle$	$\langle 0, 1, 0, 0 \rangle$	$\langle 0, 0, 1, 0 \rangle$	$\langle 0, 0, 0, 1 \rangle$
Basis 2	$\phi_0^{1,2}$	$\phi_1^{1,2}$	$\psi_0^{1,2}$	$\psi_1^{1,2}$
	$\langle 1, 1, 0, 0 \rangle$	$\langle 0, 0, 1, 1 \rangle$	$\langle 1, -1, 0, 0 \rangle$	$\langle 0, 0, 1, -1 \rangle$
Basis 3	$\phi_0^{0,2}$	$\psi_0^{0,2}$	$\psi_0^{1,2}$	$\psi_1^{1,2}$
	$\langle 1, 1, 1, 1 \rangle$	$\langle 1, 1, -1, -1 \rangle$	$\langle 1, -1, 0, 0 \rangle$	$\langle 0, 0, 1, -1 \rangle$

where

$$
\psi_i(x) = \begin{cases} 1 & x = 2^i - 1 \\ -1 & x = 2^i \\ 0 & \text{otherwise.} \end{cases}
$$

Table 4.4 provides three alternative (not-normalized) Haar basis for 4D vector space. These can be easily normalized by taking into account vector lengths. For example, $\psi_1^{1,2}$ would become $\langle 0, 0, \frac{1}{\sqrt{2}}, \frac{-1}{\sqrt{2}} \rangle$ when normalized to unit length.

Note that vectors in the wavelet basis Ψ extract and represent details. The vectors in the basis Φ, on the other hand, are used for averaging. Thus, the (averaging) basis vectors in Φ are likely to maintain more energy then the (detail) basis vectors in Ψ. As j increases, the basis vectors in Ψ^j represent increasingly finer details (i.e., noise) and thus can be removed from consideration for compression or dimensionality reduction.

4.3 MAPPING FROM DISTANCES TO A MULTIDIMENSIONAL SPACE

Although feature selection algorithms can help pick the appropriate set of dimensions against which the media objects in the database can be indexed, not all database applications can benefit from these directly. In particular, various media (such as those with spatial or hierarchical structures) do not have explicit features to be treated as dimensions of a data space. For example, *distance* between two strings can be evaluated algorithmically using the edit-distance measure as discussed in Section 3.2.2; however, there is no explicit feature space on which these distances can be interpreted.[8]

One way of dealing with these "*featureless*" data types is to exploit the knowledge about distances between the objects to map the data onto a k-dimensional space. Here the dimensions of the space do not correspond to any semantically meaningful feature of the data. Rather, the k dimensions can be interpreted as the *latent* features for the given data set.

---

[8] In Section 5.5.4, we discuss ρ-gram transformation, commonly used to map strings onto a multidimensional space.

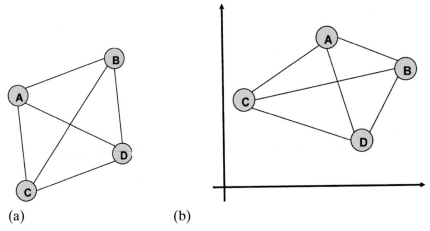

Figure 4.14. MDS mapping of four data objects into points in a two-dimensional space: the original distances are approximately preserved: (a) Distances between the objects, (b) Distances between the objects in the 2D space.

4.3.1 Multidimensional Scaling

Multidimensional scaling (MDS) [Kruskal, 1964a,b] is a family of data analysis methods, all of which discover the underlying structure of the data by embedding them into an appropriate space [Kruskal, 1964a; Kruskal and Myron, 1978; Torgerson, 1952]. More specifically, MDS discovers this embedding of a set of data items from the distance information among them.

MDS works as follows: Given as inputs (1) a set of N objects, (2) a matrix of size $N \times N$ containing pairwise distance values, and (3) the desired dimensionality k, MDS tries to map each object into a point in the k-dimensional space (Figure 4.14). The criterion for the mapping is to minimize a stress value defined as

$$stress = \sqrt{\frac{\sum_{i,j}(d'_{i,j} - d_{i,j})^2}{\sum_{i,j} d^2_{i,j}}},$$

where d_{ij} is the actual distance between two nodes v_i and v_j and d'_{ij} is the distance between the corresponding points p_i and p_j in the k-dimensional space. If, for all such pairs, d_{ij} is equal to d'_{ij}, then the overall stress is 0, that is, minimum. MDS starts with some, possibly random, initial configuration of points in the desired space. It then applies some steepest descent algorithm, which modifies the locations of the points in the space iteratively in a way that minimizes the stress. At each iteration, the algorithm identifies a point location modification that gives rise to a large reduction in stress and moves the point in space accordingly.

In general, the more dimensions (i.e., larger k) that are used, the better is the final fit that can be achieved. On the other hand, because multidimensional index structures do not work well at a high number of dimensions, it is important to keep the dimensionality as low as possible. One method to select the appropriate value of k is known as the *scree* test, where stress is plotted against the dimensionality, and the point in the plot where the stress stops substantially reducing is selected (see Section 4.2.6.1).

(i) *Process* the given N data objects to construct the $N \times N$ distance matrix required as input to MDS.

(ii) Find the configuration (point representation of each document in a k-dimensional space).

(iii) Identify c pivot/representative points (data elements), where each pivot p_i represents r_i many points.

(iv) When a query specification q is provided, map the query into the MDS space using the c pivot points (accounting for r_i for each p_i). Thus the complexity of applying MDS is $O(c)$ instead of $O(N)$.

(v) Once the query is mapped into the k-dimensional place, use the spatial index structure to perform a range search in this space.

Figure 4.15. Extended MDS algorithm.

MDS places objects in the space based on their distances: objects that are closer in the original distance measure are mapped closer to each other in the k-dimensional space; those that have large distance values are mapped away from each other. As a pre-processing step to support indexing, however, MDS suffers from two drawbacks; expensive (1) data-to-space and (2) query-to-space mappings:

■ Because there are $O(N^2)$ pairwise distances to consider, it takes at least $O(N^2)$ time to identify the configuration of N objects in k-d space.

■ Given a query object q, it would take $O(N)$ time to properly map q to a point in the same k-d space as the data objects.

To understand why it takes $O(N)$ to find the spatial representation of q, note that, we need the distance between q and all the objects in the database (N in this case), for MDS to be able to determine the precise spatial representation of q. Although the first drawback may be acceptable, the real disadvantage is that to introduce the query object q into the k-dimensional space requires $O(N)$ time with a large constant. This would imply that relying on MDS for retrieval would be as bad as sequential scan.

Yamuna and Candan [2001] propose an extended MDS algorithm to support more efficient indexing (Figure 4.15). The algorithm works by first mapping the data objects into a multidimensional space through MDS and selecting a set of objects as the pivots. The query object, then, is compared to the pivots and mapped into the same space as the other objects. Naturally, the query mapping is less accurate than the original data mapping, because only the pivots are used for the mapping instead of the entire data set. Note that the quality of the retrieval will depend heavily on the c data points selected for the query-to-space mapping process. Yamuna and Candan [2001] present two approaches for selecting the pivot points: (1) data-driven and (2) space-driven (Figure 4.16). In the *data-driven approach*, the c pivot points are chosen based on the distribution of the data elements. The *space-driven approach* subdivides the space and chooses one data point to represent each space subdivision. The intuition is that the space-driven selection of the points will provide a better coverage of the space itself.

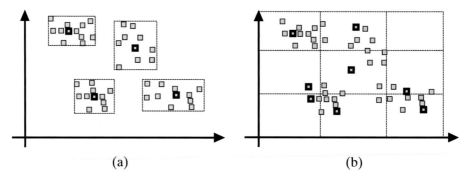

Figure 4.16. (a) Data-driven versus (b) space-driven choice of pivot points.

4.3.2 FastMap

Faloutsos and Lin [1995] propose the *FastMap* algorithm to map objects into points in a k-dimensional space based on just the distance/similarity values between objects. They reason that it is far easier for domain experts to assess the similarity/distance of two objects than it is to identify features and design feature extraction functions.

Their method is conceptually similar to the *multidimensional scaling* approach [Kruskal, 1964a,b]; however, they provide a much more efficient way of mapping the objects into points in space, by assuming that the distance/similarity measure satisfies triangular inequality. In particular, the complexity of their algorithm to map the database to a low-dimensional space is $O(Nk)$, where k is the dimensionality of the target space. Moreover, the algorithm requires $\Theta(k)$ distance computations to map the query to the same space as the data.

The main idea behind the *FastMap* algorithm is to carefully choose *pivot objects* that define mutually orthogonal directions, on which the data are projected. The authors establish the following lemma central to their construction:

> **Lemma 4.3.1:** *Let o_{p_1} and o_{p_2} be two objects in the database selected as pivots. Let $\mathcal{H}$ be the hyperplane perpendicular to the line defined by o_{p_1} and o_{p_2}. Then, the Euclidean distance $\Delta'_{Euc}(o'_i, o'_j)$ between o'_i and o'_j (which are the projections of objects o_i and o_j onto this hyperplane) can be computed based on the original distance, $\Delta_{Euc}(o_i, o_j)$, of o_i and o_j:*
>
> $$(\Delta'_{Euc}(o'_i, o'_j))^2 = (\Delta_{Euc}(o_i, o_j))^2 - (x_i - x_j)^2,$$
>
> *where x_i is the projection of object o_i onto the line defined by the pivots, o_{p_1} and o_{p_2}, computed based on the cosine law:*
>
> $$x_i = \frac{(\Delta_{Euc}(o_i, o_{p_1}))^2 - (\Delta_{Euc}(o_i, o_{p_2}))^2 + (\Delta_{Euc}(o_{p_1}, o_{p_2}))^2}{2\Delta_{Euc}(o_{p_1}, o_{p_2})}.$$
>
> *x_j is also computed similarly.*

Given two pivot objects, this lemma enables *FastMap* to quickly (i.e., in $O(N)$ time) map all N objects onto the line defined by these two pivots (Figure 4.17(a)) and then revise distances of the objects on a hyperplane perpendicular to this line

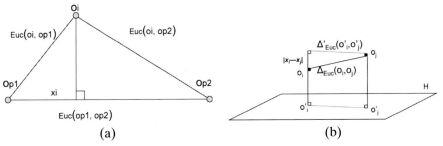

Figure 4.17. (a) The projection of object o_i onto the line defined by the two pivots o_{p_1} and o_{p_2}. (b) Computing the distance between the projections of o_i and o_j on a hyperplane perpendicular to this line between the two pivots.

(Figure 4.17(b)). Thus, the space can be incrementally built, by selecting pivots that define orthogonal dimensions one at a time.

The pivots are chosen from the objects in the database in such a way that the projections of the other objects onto this line are as sparse as possible; that is, the pivots are as far apart from each other as possible. To avoid $O(N^2)$ distance computations, FastMap leverages a linear time heuristic, which

    (i) picks an arbitrary object, o_{temp},
    (ii) chooses the object that is farthest apart from o_{temp} to be o_{p_1}, and
    (iii) chooses the object that is farthest apart from o_{p_1} to be o_{p_2}.

Thus, at each iteration, *FastMap* picks two pivot objects that are (at least heuristically) furthest apart from each other (Figure 4.18(a)). The line between these

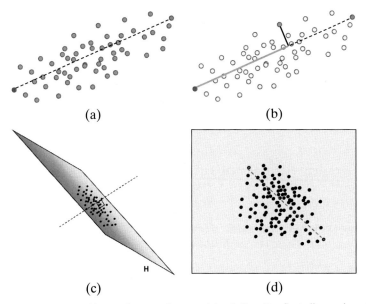

Figure 4.18. (a) Find two objects that are far apart to define the first dimension. (b) Project all the objects onto the line between these two extremes to find out the values along this dimension. (c) Project the objects onto a hyperplane perpendicular to this line. (d) Repeat the process on this reduced hyperspace. See color plates section.

objects becomes the new dimension, and the values of the objects along this dimension are computed by projecting the objects onto line (Figure 4.18(b)). All objects are then (implicitly) projected onto a hyperplane orthogonal to line (Figure 4.18(c)). FastMap incrementally adds more dimensions by repeating this process on the reduced hyperplane, orthogonal to all the dimensions already discovered (Figure 4.18(d)).

4.4 EMBEDDING DATA FROM ONE SPACE INTO ANOTHER

The MDS and FastMap techniques just described both assume that the system is provided only the distances between the objects (possibly computed by a user-defined function) and nothing else. However, in some cases, the system is also provided with a set of feature dimensions, but these are not necessarily orthogonal to each other. In other words, although we have the dimensions of interest, these dimensions are not most appropriate for indexing and retrieval purposes. In such cases, it may be more effective to embed the available data into an alternative (possibly smaller) space, spanned and described by a basis of orthogonal vectors.

One way to achieve this is to use MDS or FastMap. However, these are mainly heuristic approaches that do not necessarily provide a lossless mapping. In this section, we introduce other transformations that perform the embedding in a more principled manner.

4.4.1 Singular Value Decomposition (and Latent Semantic Indexing)

Singular value decomposition (SVD) is a technique for identifying a transformation that can take data described in terms of n feature dimensions and map them into a vector space defined by $k \leq n$ orthogonal basis vectors.

In fact, SVD is a more general form of the eigen decomposition method that underlies the PCA approach to dimensionality reduction: whereas PCA is applied to square symmetric covariance matrix of the database, with the goal of identifying the dimensions along which the variances are maximal, SVD is applied on the object-feature matrix itself. Remember from Section 4.2.6 that given an $n \times n$ symmetric, square matrix, S, with real values, S can be decomposed into

$$S = PCP^{-1},$$

where C is a real and diagonal matrix of eigenvalues, and P is an orthonormal matrix consisting of the eigenvectors of S. SVD generalizes this to matrices that are not symmetric or square:

Theorem 4.4.3 (Singular value decomposition): *Let A be an $m \times n$ matrix with real values. Then, A, can be decomposed into*

$$A = U\Sigma V^{T},$$

where

- *U is a real, column-orthonormal $m \times r$ matrix, such that $UU^{T} = I$*
- *Σ is an $r \times r$ positive valued diagonal matrix, where $r \leq min(m, n)$ is the rank of the matrix A*

■ V^T is the transpose of a real, column-orthonormal $r \times n$ matrix, such that $VV^T = I$

The columns of U, also called the left singular vectors of matrix A, are the eigenvectors of the $m \times m$ square matrix, AA^T. The columns of V, or the right singular vectors of A, are the eigenvectors of the $n \times n$ square matrix, $A^T A$. $\Sigma[i, i] > 0$, for $1 \leq i \leq r$, also known as the singular values of A, are the square roots of the eigenvalues of AA^T and $A^T A$.

Because the columns of U are eigenvectors of an $m \times m$ matrix, they are orthogonal and form an r-dimensional basis. Similarly, the orthogonal columns of V also form an r-dimensional basis.

4.4.1.1 Latent Semantic Analysis (LSA)

Let us consider an $m \times n$ document-term matrix, A, which describes the contribution of a given set of n terms to the m documents in a database.

The $m \times m$ document-document matrix, AA^T, can be considered as a *document similarity* matrix, which describes how similar two documents are in terms of their compositions. Similarly, the $n \times n$ term-term matrix, $A^T A$, can be considered as a *term similarity* matrix, which describes how similar two terms are in terms of their contributions to the documents in the database.

Given the singular value decomposition, $A = U\Sigma V^T$, of the document-term matrix, the r column vectors of U form an r-dimensional basis in which the m documents can be described. Also, the r column vectors of V (or the rows vector of V^T) form an r-dimensional basis in which the n terms can be placed. These r dimensions are referred to as the *latent semantics* of the database [Deerwester *et al.*, 1990]: the orthogonal columns of V (i.e., the eigenvectors of the term-to-term matrix, $A^T A$) can be thought of as independent *concepts*, each of which can be described as a combination of the given terms. In a similar fashion, the columns of U can be thought of as the *eigen documents* of the given document collection, each corresponding to one independent concept.

Furthermore, the r singular values of A can be considered to represent the strength of the corresponding concepts in the database: the ith row of the document-term matrix, corresponding to the ith document in the database, can also be written as

$$\forall_{1 \leq j \leq n} \ A[i, j] = \sum_{k=1}^{r} U[i, k]\Sigma[k, k]V[k, j].$$

Thus, replacing any singular value, $\Sigma[k, k]$ with 0 would result in a total error of

$$error(k) = \Sigma[k, k] \sum_{i=1}^{m} \sum_{j=1}^{n} U[i, k]V[k, j].$$

Thus, the amount of error that would be caused by the removal of a *concept* from the database is proportional to the corresponding singular value. This property of the singular values found during SVD enables further dimensionality reduction: those concepts with small singular values, and the corresponding eigen documents, can be removed and the documents can be indexed against the remaining $c < r$

concepts with high contributions to the database using the truncated U' matrix. Keyword queries are also mapped to the same concept space using truncated Σ' and V' matrices. Because reducing the number of dimensions can save a significant amount of query processing cost ($O(mc + c^2 + cm)$ instead of $O(mn)$, which would be required to compare m vectors of length n each), this process is referred to as *latent semantic analysis* (LSA) or *latent semantic indexing* (LSI) [Berry *et al.*, 1995].

4.4.1.2 Incremental SVD

As illustrated by latent semantic analysis and indexing, SVD can be an effective tool for dimensionality reduction and indexing. However, because it requires $O(m \times n \times min(m, n))$ time for analysis and decomposition of the entire database, its cost can be generally prohibitive. Thus, especially in databases where the content is updated frequently, it is more advantageous to use techniques for incremental updating SVD [Brand, 2006, 2002; O'Brien, 1994; Zha and Simon, 1999].

Folding

One way to implement incremental updates is to simply *fold in* new objects and features to an existing SVD decomposition. New objects (rows) and new features (columns) of the matrix A are represented in terms of their positions in the SVD basis. Let us consider a new object row $\vec{r}^T$ to be inserted into the database. Unless it also introduces new features and assuming that the update did not alter the latent semantics, this insertion will not affect Σ and V^T; thus, $\vec{r}^T$ can be written as

$$\vec{r}^T = \vec{u}^T \Sigma V^T.$$

Based on this, the new row, $\vec{u}^T$, of U can be computed as

$$\vec{u}^T = \vec{r}^T (V^T)^{-1} \Sigma^{-1} = \vec{r}^T V \Sigma^{-1}.$$

A similar process can be used to find the effect of a new feature on the matrix, V^T. Note that, in folding, new objects and features do not change the latent concepts; consequently it is fast but can in the long run negatively affect the orthogonality of the basis vectors identified through SVD. A more effective, albeit slower, approach is to incrementally change the SVD decomposition, including the matrix Σ, as new objects and features are added to the database.

SVD-Update

A particular challenge faced during the incremental updating of SVD is that in many cases, instead of the original A, U, Σ, and V^T matrices, their rank-k approximations (A_k, U_k, Σ_k, and V_k^T, corresponding to the k highest eigenvalues, for some k) are maintained in the database. Thus, the incremental update needs to be performed on an imperfect database. Berry *et al.* [1995] and O'Brien [1994] introduce the SVD-Update algorithm, which deals with this problem by exploiting the existing singular values and singular vectors of the object-feature matrix A. Given a set of p new objects, let us create a new $p \times n$ matrix, N, describing these objects in terms of their feature compositions. Let $A' = \left(\frac{A_k}{N}\right)$ be the object-feature matrix extended with the new objects, and let $U'\Sigma'(V')^T$ be the singular value decomposition of A'. Then

$$U_k^T A_k V_k = \Sigma_k$$

$$\begin{pmatrix} U_k^T & 0 \\ 0 & I_p \end{pmatrix} \begin{pmatrix} A_k \\ N \end{pmatrix} V_k = \begin{pmatrix} \Sigma_k \\ NV_k \end{pmatrix}$$

$$\begin{pmatrix} U_k^T & 0 \\ 0 & I_p \end{pmatrix} \begin{pmatrix} A_k \\ N \end{pmatrix} V_k = U_H \Sigma_H V_H^T,$$

where $U_H \Sigma_H V_H^T$ is the singular value decomposition of $\left(\begin{smallmatrix} \Sigma_k \\ NV_k \end{smallmatrix}\right)$. Thus,

$$\underbrace{\begin{pmatrix} A_k \\ N \end{pmatrix}}_{A'} = \underbrace{\left(\begin{pmatrix} U_k & 0 \\ 0 & I_p \end{pmatrix} U_H \right)}_{U'} \underbrace{\Sigma_H}_{\Sigma'} \underbrace{(V_H^T V_k^T)}_{(V')^T}.$$

A similar process can be used for incorporating new features to the singular value decomposition.

Note, on the other hand, that not all updates to the database involve insertion of new objects and features. In some cases, an existing object may be modified in such a way that the contributions of the features to the object may change. The final correction step of SVD-Update incorporates such updates. Let Δ denote an $m \times n$ matrix describing the changes in term weights, $A'' = A_k + \Delta$ denote the new object-feature matrix, and $U''\Sigma''V''^T$ be the singular value decomposition of A'':

$$U_k^T A_k V_k = \Sigma_k$$

$$U_k^T (A_k + \Delta) V_k = \Sigma_k + U_k^T \Delta V_k$$

$$U_k^T (A_k + \Delta) V_k = U_Q \Sigma_Q V_Q^T,$$

where $U_Q \Sigma_Q V_Q^T$ is the singular value decomposition of $\Sigma_k + U_k^T \Delta V_k$. Thus,

$$\underbrace{(A_k + \Delta)}_{A''} = \underbrace{(U_k U_Q)}_{U''} \underbrace{\Sigma_Q}_{\Sigma''} \underbrace{(V_Q^T V_k^T)}_{(V'')^T}.$$

More General Database Updates

Work on incremental updates to SVD focuses on support for a richer set of modifications, including removal of columns and rows of the database matrix [Gu and Eisenstat, 1995; Witter and Berry, 1998], as well as on improving the complexity of the update procedure [Chandrasekaran *et al.*, 1997; Gu *et al.*, 1993; Levy and Lindenbaum, 2000]. Recently, [Brand, 2006] showed that a number of database updates (including removal of columns) that can all be cast as additive modifications to the original $m \times n$ database matrix, A, can be reflected on the SVD in $O(mnr)$ time as long as the rank, r, of matrix A is such that $r \leq \sqrt{min(m, n)}$. In other words, as long as the latent dimensionality of the database is low, the singular value decomposition can be updated in linear time. Brand further shows that, in fact, the update to the SVD can be computed in a single pass over the database, making the process highly efficient for large databases.

4.4.2 Probabilistic Latent Semantic Analysis

As in LSA, probabilistic latent semantic analysis (PLSA [Hofmann, 1999]) also relies on a matrix decomposition strategy to identify the latent semantics underlying
a data collection. However, PLSA is based on a more solid statistical foundation,
known as the *aspect model* [Saul and Pereira, 1997], based on a generative model of
the data (see Section 3.5.3.3 for generative data and query models).

4.4.2.1 Aspect Model

Given a database, $D = \{o_1, \ldots, o_n\}$, of n objects and a feature set, $F = \{f_1, \ldots, f_m\}$,
the aspect model associates an unobserved class variable, $z \in Z = \{z_1, \ldots, z_k\}$, to
each occurrence of a feature, $f \in F$, in an object, $o \in D$. This can be represented as
a generative model as follows: (a) an object $o \in D$ is selected with probability $p(o)$,
(b) a latent class $z \in Z$ is selected with probability $p(z|o)$, and a feature $f \in F$ is gen-
erated with probability $p(f|z)$. Note that o and f can be observed in the database, but
the latent semantic z is not directly observable and therefore needs to be estimated
based on the observable data (i.e., objects and their features). This can be achieved
using the expectation maximization algorithm, EM [Dempster *et al.*, 1977]; see also
Section 9.7.4.3. EM relies on a likelihood function to tie the parameters whose values are unknown to the available observations and estimates the unknown values
by maximizing this likelihood function. For this purpose, PLSA uses the likelihood
function

$$\prod_{o \in D} \prod_{f \in F} p(o, f)^{count(o,f)}$$

where $count(o, f)$ denotes the frequency of the feature f in the given object o, and
$p(o, f)$ denotes the joint probability of o and f. Note that the joint probability $p(o, f)$
can also be expressed in terms of the unobserved class variables as follows:

$$
\begin{aligned}
p(o, f) &= p(o)p(f|o) \\
&= p(o) \sum_{z \in Z} p(f|z)p(z|o) \\
&= p(o) \sum_{z \in Z} p(f|z) \frac{p(o|z)p(z)}{p(o)} \\
&= \sum_{z \in Z} p(z)p(f|z)p(o|z).
\end{aligned}
$$

Therefore this likelihood function[9] ties observable parameters (joint probabilities of
objects and features and frequencies of the features in the objects in the database)
to unobservable parameters, $p(z), p(o|z)$, and $p(f|z)$, that we wish to discover.

---

[9] Note that often the simpler log-likelihood function,

$$log\left(\prod_{o \in D} \prod_{f \in F} p(o, f)^{count(o,f)}\right) = \sum_{o \in D} \sum_{f \in F} count(o, f) log(p(o, f)),$$

is used instead.

4.4.2.2 Decomposition

Given a database, $D = \{o_1, \ldots, o_n\}$, of n objects, a feature set, $F = \{f_1, \ldots, f_m\}$, and the unobserved class variables, $Z = \{z_1, \ldots, z_k\}$, the PLSA uses the equality

$$p(o, f) = \sum_{z \in Z} p(z)p(f|z)p(o|z)$$

to decompose the $n \times m$ matrix, P, of $p(o_i, f_j)$, as follows:

$$P = U \Sigma V^T,$$

Here,

- U is the $n \times k$ matrix of $p(o_i|z_l)$ entries
- V is the $m \times k$ matrix of $p(f_j|z_l)$ entries
- Σ is the $k \times k$ matrix of $p(z_l)$ entries

Note that despite its structural similarity to SVD, through the use of EM, PLSA is able to search explicitly for a decomposition that has a high predictive power.

4.4.3 CUR Decomposition

Many data management techniques rely on the fact that rows and columns of the object-feature matrix, A, are generally sparse: that is, the number of available features is much larger than the number of features that objects individually have. This is true, for example, for text objects, where the dictionary size of potential terms tends to be significantly large compared to the unique terms in a given document. Such sparseness of a given database matrix usually enables application of more specialized algorithms for its manipulation, from indexing to analysis.

When considered in this context a potential disadvantage of the PCA and SVD techniques is that both take sparse matrices as input, but return two extremely dense left and right matrices. It is true that they also return one extremely sparse (diagonal) central matrix; however, this matrix does not directly relate objects to their compositions and, furthermore, tends to be much smaller than the left and right matrices.

CUR decomposition [Mahoney et al., 2006] tries to avoid destruction of sparsity by giving up the use of eigenvectors for the construction of the left and right matrices and, instead, picking the columns of the left matrix and the rows of the right matrix from the columns and rows of the database matrix, A, itself: given an $m \times n$ matrix, A, and given two integers, $c \leq m$ and $r \leq n$, the CUR decomposition of A is

$$A \sim CUR,$$

where C is an $m \times c$ matrix, with columns picked from columns of A, R is an $r \times n$ matrix, with rows picked from the rows of A, and U is a $c \times r$ matrix, such that $\|A - CUR\|$ is small.

Note that since C and R are picked from the columns and rows of A, they are likely to preserve the sparsity of A. On the other hand, because the constraint of representing the singular values of A is removed from U, it is not necessarily diagonal and instead tends to be much denser than C and R.

CUR decomposition of a given matrix, A, requires three complementary sub-processes: (a) selection of c and r; (b) choice of columns and rows of A for the construction of C and R, respectively; and (c) given these, identification of the matrix U that minimizes the decomposition error. Selection of the values c and r tends to be application dependent. Given c and r, on the other hand, choosing the appropriate *examples* from the database requires care. Although uniform sampling [Williams and Seeger, 2001] is a relatively efficient solution, biased subspace sampling techniques [Drineas *et al.*, 2006a,b] might impose absolute or, at least, relative bounds on the decomposition errors.

One indirect advantage of the CUR decomposition is that the columns of C and the rows of R are in fact *examples* from the original database; thus, they are much easier to interpret than the *composite* singular vectors that are produced by PCA and SVD. However, these columns and rows are no longer orthogonal to each other and, thus, their use of the basis of the vector space is likely to give rise to unintended and undesirable consequences, especially when similarity distance measures that call for orthogonality of the basis are used in retrieval or further analysis.

4.4.4 Tensors and Tensor Decomposition

So far, we have been assuming that the media database can be represented in the form of an object-feature matrix, A. Although in general this representation is sufficient for indexing multimedia databases, there are cases in which the matrix representation falls short. This is, for example, the case when the database changes over time and the patterns of change, themselves, are important: in other words, when the database has a temporal dimension that cannot be captured by a single snapshot.

4.4.4.1 Tensor Basics

Mathematically, a tensor is a generalization of matrices [Kolda and Bader, 2009; Sun *et al.*, 2006]: whereas a matrix is essentially a two-dimensional array, a tensor is an array of arbitrary dimension. Thus, a vector can be thought of as a tensor of first order, an object-feature matrix is a tensor of second order, and a multisensor data stream (i.e., sensors, features of sensed data, and time) can be represented as a tensor of third order. The dimensions of the tensor array are referred to as its *modes*. For example, an $M \times N \times K$ tensor of third order has three modes: M columns (mode 1), N rows (mode 2), and K *tubes* (mode 3). These 1D arrays are collectively referred to as the *fibers* of the given tensor. Similarly, the $M \times N \times K$ tensor can also be considered in terms of its M lateral *slices*, N horizontal slices, and K frontal slices: each slice is a 2D array (or equivalently a matrix, or a tensor of second order).

As matrices can be multiplied with other matrices or vectors, tensors can also be multiplied with other tensors, including matrices and vectors. For example, given an $M \times N \times K$ tensor T and a $P \times N$ matrix A,

$$T' = T \times_2 A$$

is an $M \times P \times K$ matrix where each lateral slice $T[][j][]$ has been matrix multiplied by A^T. In the foregoing example, the tensor-matrix multiplication symbol "$\times_2$" states that the matrix A^T will be multiplied with T over its lateral slices.

Multiplication of a tensor with a vector is defined similarly, but using a different notation: given an M-dimensional vector $\vec{v}$,

$$\mathcal{T}'' = \mathcal{T} \bar{\times}_1 \vec{v}$$

is a $N \times K$ tensor, such that $\vec{v}$ has been multiplied with each column, $\mathcal{T}[][j][k]$. In this example, the tensor-vector multiplication symbol "$\bar{\times}_1$" states that vector $\vec{v}$ and columns of $\mathcal{T}$ will get into the dot product.

4.4.4.2 Tensor Decomposition

Tensors can also be analyzed and mapped into lower dimensional spaces. In fact, because matrices themselves are tensors of second order, we can write the SVD decomposition

$$A_{M \times N} = U_{M \times r} \Sigma_{r \times r} V^T_{r \times N}$$

using tensor notation as follows:

$$A_{M \times N} = \Sigma_{r \times r} \times_1 U_{M \times r} \times_2 V_{N \times r}.$$

Orthonormal Tensor Decompositions

Tucker decomposition [Tucker, 1966] generalizes this to a $M \times N \times K$ tensor, $\mathcal{T}$, as follows:

$$\mathcal{T}_{M \times N \times K} \sim \mathcal{G}_{r \times s \times t} \times_1 U_{M \times r} \times_2 V_{N \times s} \times_3 X_{K \times t}.$$

Like CUR, Tucker decomposition fails to guarantee a unique and perfect decomposition of the input matrix. Instead, most approaches involve searching for orthonormal U, V, X matrices and a $\mathcal{G}$ tensor that collectively minimize the decomposition error. For example the *high-order SVD* approach [Lathauwer *et al.*, 2000; Tucker, 1966] to Tucker decomposition first identifies the left eigenvectors (with the highest eigenvalues) of the lateral, horizontal, and frontal slices to construct U, V, and X.

Because there are multiple lateral (or horizontal, or frontal) slices, these equidirectional slices need to be combined into a single matrix before the corresponding eigenvectors are identified. Once U, V, and X are found, the corresponding optimal tensor, $\mathcal{G}$, is computed as

$$\mathcal{G}_{r \times s \times t} = \mathcal{T}_{M \times N \times K} \times_1 U^T_{r \times M} \times_2 V^T_{s \times N} \times_3 X^T_{t \times K}.$$

This process does not lead into an optimal decomposition. Thus, the initial U, V, and X estimates are iteratively improved using a least-squares approximation scheme before $\mathcal{G}$ is computed [Kroonenberg and Leeuw, 1980; Lathauwer *et al.*, 2000].

Diagonal Tensor Decompositions

CANDECOMP [Caroll and Chang, 1970] and PARAFAC [Harshman, 1970] decompositions take a different approach and, as in SVD, enforce that the core tensor is diagonal:

$$\mathcal{T}_{M \times N \times K} \sim \Lambda_{r \times r \times r} \times_1 U_{M \times r} \times_2 V_{N \times r} \times_3 X_{K \times r}.$$

The diagonal values of the Λ matrix are eigenvalues. The consequence of starting the decomposition process from identifying a central matrix, constrained to be diagonal, however, is that the U, V, and X matrices are not guaranteed to be orthonormal. Thus, this approach may not be applicable when the matrices U, V, and X are to be used as bases that describe and index the different facets of the data.

Dynamic and Incremental Tensor Decompositions

Because tensors are mostly used in domains where data evolve continuously and thus have a temporal aspect, tensors tend to be updated by the addition of new slices (and deletion of the old ones) along the mode that corresponds to time. Consequently, specialized dynamic decomposition algorithms that focus on insertion and deletion of slices can be developed. The *Dynamic Tensor Analysis (DTA)* approach, for example, updates the variance information (used for identifying eigenvalues and eigenvectors to construct the decomposition) incrementally, but rediagonalizes the variance matrix for each new slice [Sun *et al.*, 2006]. The *Window-based Tensor Analysis (WTA)* algorithm builds on this by iteratively improving the decomposition as in Tucker's scheme [Tucker, 1966]. The *Streaming Tensor Analysis (STA)* scheme, on the other hand, takes a different approach and incrementally rotates the columns (representing lines in the space) of the decomposition matrices with each new observed data point [Papadimitriou *et al.*, 2005].

4.5 SUMMARY

In this chapter, we have first introduced the concept of *dimensionality curse*, which essentially means that multimedia database systems cannot manage more than a handful of facets of the multimedia data simultaneously. In Chapter 7 on multidimensional data indexing, Chapter 9 on classification, and Chapter 10 on ranked query processing, we see different instantiations of this very curse. Thus, feature selection algorithms, which operate based on some appropriate definition of significance of features, are critical for multimedia databases. In many cases, in fact, the real challenge in multimedia database design and operation is to identify the appropriate criterion for feature selection. In Chapters 9 and 12, we see that classification and user relevance feedback algorithms, which can leverage user provided labels on the data, are also useful in selecting good features.

In this chapter, we have also seen the importance of managing data using *independent* features. Independence of features not only helps ensure that the few features we select to use do not have wasteful redundancy in them, but also ensures that the media objects can be compared against each other effectively. Once again, we see the importance of having independent features in the upcoming chapters on indexing, classification, and query processing.

5

Indexing, Search, and Retrieval
of Sequences

Sequences, such as text documents or DNA sequences, can be indexed for searching and analysis in different ways depending on whether patterns that the user may want to search for (such as words in a document) are known in advance and on whether exact or approximate matches are needed.

When the sequence data and queries are composed of words (i.e., nonoverlapping subsequences that come from a fixed vocabulary), inverted files built using B+-trees or tries (Section 5.4.1) or signature files (Section 5.2) are often used for indexing. When, on the other hand, the sequence data do not have easily identifiable word boundaries, other index structures, such as suffix trees (Section 5.4.2), or filtering schemes, such as ρ-grams (Section 5.5.4), may be more applicable.

In this section, we first discuss inverted files and signature files that are commonly used for text document retrieval. We then discuss data structures and algorithms for more general exact and approximate sequence matching.

5.1 INVERTED FILES

An inverted file index [Harman *et al.*, 1992] is a search structure containing all the distinct words (subpatterns) that one can use for searching. Figure 5.1(a) shows the outline of the inverted file index structure:

- A *word (or term) directory* keeps track of the words that occur in the database. For each term, a pointer to the corresponding inverted list is maintained. In addition, the directory records the length of the corresponding inverted list. This length is the number of documents containing the term.
- The inverted lists are commonly held in a *postings file* that contains the actual pointers to the documents. To reduce the disk access costs, inverted lists are stored contiguously in the postings file. If the word positions within the document are important for the query, word positions can also be maintained along with the document pointers. Also, if the documents have hierarchical structures, then the inverted lists in the postings file can also reflect a similar structure [Zobel and Moffat, 2006]. For example, if the documents in the database are

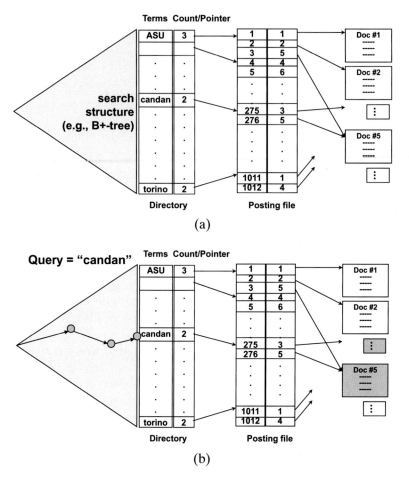

Figure 5.1. (a) Inverted file structure and (b) a search example.

composed of chapters and sections, then the inverted list can also be organized hierarchically to help in answering queries of different granularity (e.g., finding documents based on two words occurring in the same section).

■ A search structure enables quick access to the directory of inverted lists. Different search structures can be used to locate inverted lists matching query words. Hash files can be used for supporting exact searches. Another commonly used search data structure is the B[+]-tree [Bayer and McCreight, 1972]; because of their balanced and high-fanout   organizations, B[+]-trees can help locate inverted lists on disks with only a few disk accesses. Other search structures, such as tries (Section 5.4.1) or suffix automata (Sections 5.4.3), can also be used if prefix-based or approximate matches are needed during retrieval.

Figure 5.1(b) shows the overview of the search process. First the search data structure is consulted to identify whether the word is in the dictionary. If the word is found in the dictionary, then the corresponding inverted list is located in the postings file by following the pointer in the corresponding directory entry. Finally, matching documents are located by following pointers from the inverted list.

5.1.1 Processing Multi-Keyword Queries Using Inverted Files

If the query contains multiple keywords and is conjunctive (i.e., the result must contain all the query keywords), the inverted lists matching the query keywords are retrieved and intersected before the documents are retrieved. If, on the other hand, the query is disjunctive in nature (i.e., finding any query keywords is sufficient to declare a match), then the matching inverted lists need to be unioned.

If the given multikeyword query is fuzzy or similarity-based (for example, when the user would like to find the document that has the highest cosine similarity to the given query vector), finding all matches and then obtaining their rankings during a postprocessing step may be too costly. Instead, by using *similarity accumulators* associated with each document, the matching and ranking processes can be tightly coupled to reduce the retrieval cost [Zobel and Moffat, 2006]:

(i) Initially, each accumulator has a similarity score of zero.

(ii) Each query word or term is processed, one at a time. For each term, the accumulator values for each document in the corresponding inverted index are increased by the contribution of the word to the similarity of the corresponding document. For example, if the cosine similarity measure is used, then the contribution of keyword k to document d for query q can be computed as

$$contrib(k, d, q) = \frac{w(d, k)w(q, k)}{\sqrt{\sum_{k_i \in d} w^2(d, k_i)}\sqrt{\sum_{k_i \in q} w^2(q, k_i)}}.$$

Here $w(d, k)$ is the weight of the keyword k in document d, and $w(q, k)$ is the weight of k in the query.

(iii) Once all query words have been processed, the accumulators for documents with respect to the individual terms are combined into "global" document scores. For example, if the cosine similarity measure is used as described previously, the accumulators are simply added up to obtain document scores. The set of documents with the largest scores is returned as the result.

Note that more efficient ranked query processing algorithms, which may avoid the need for postprocessing and which can prune the unlikely candidates more effectively, are possible. We discuss these ranked query-processing algorithms in more detail in Chapter 10.

5.1.2 Sorting and Compressing Inverted Lists for Efficient Retrieval

A major cost of the inverted file–based query processing involves reading the inverted lists from the disk and performing intersections to identify candidates for conjunctive queries. Keeping the inverted lists in sorted order can help eliminate the need for making multiple passes over the inverted list file, rendering the intersection process for conjunctive queries, as well as the duplicate elimination process for disjunctive queries, more efficient.

One advantage of keeping the documents in the inverted list in sorted order is that, instead of storing the document identifiers explicitly, one may instead store

Text: "Motorola also has a music phone."

Keyword	Signature of word
"Motorola"	0011 0010
"music"	0001 1100
"phone"	0001 0110

Signature of File (bitwiseor)	0011 1110

	User Query	Signature of user query
(a) match :	"Motorola"	0011 0010
(b) no match :	"game"	1000 0011
(c) false match :	"television"	0010 1010

Figure 5.2. Document signature creation and use for keyword search.

the differences (or d-gaps) between consecutive identifiers; for example, instead of storing the sequence of document identifiers

100, 135, 180, 250, 252, 278, 303,

one may store the equivalent d-gap sequence,

100, 35, 45, 70, 2, 26, 25.

The d-gap sequence consists of smaller values, thus potentially requiring fewer bits for encoding than the original sequence. The d-gap values in a sequence are commonly encoded using variable-length code representations, such as Elias and Golomb codes [Zobel and Moffat, 2006], which can adapt the number of bits needed for representing an integer, depending on its value.

5.2 SIGNATURE FILES

Signature files are probabilistic data structures that can help screen out most unqualified documents in a large database quickly [Faloutsos, 1992; Zobel *et al.*, 1998]. In a signature file, each word is assigned a fixed-width bit string, generated by a hash function. As shown in Figure 5.2, the signature of a given document is created by taking the *bitwise-or* of all signatures of all the words appearing in the document. Figure 5.2 also shows the querying process: (a) the document signature is said to match the query if the *bitwise-and* of the query signature and the document signature is identical to the query signature; (b) the document signature is said not to match the query if the *bitwise-and* operation results in a loss of bits.

As shown in Figure 5.2(c), signature files may also return false matches: in this case, signature comparison indicates a match, but in fact there is no keyword match between the document and the query. Because of the possibility of false hits/matches, query processing with document signatures requires three steps: (1) computing the query signature, (2) searching for the query signature in the set of document signatures, and (3) eliminating any false matches.

5.2.1 False Positives

Let us consider a document composed of n distinct words. Let each m-bit word signature be constructed by randomly setting some of the signature bits to 1 in l rounds.

The signature for the entire document is constructed by taking the *bitwise-or* of the m-bit signatures of the words appearing in the document. Hence, the probability of a given bit in the document signature being set to 1 can be computed as follows:

$$1 - \left(\left(1 - \frac{1}{m}\right)^l\right)^n = 1 - \left(1 - \frac{1}{m}\right)^{nl}.$$

Intuitively, this corresponds to the probability of the position corresponding to the selected bit being occupied by a "1" in at least one of the m signatures. The term $\left(1 - \frac{1}{m}\right)^l$ is the probability that in any given word signature the selected bit remains "0", despite l rounds of random selection of bits to be set to "1". Note that it is possible to approximate the preceding equation as follows:

$$1 - \left(1 - \frac{1}{m}\right)^{nl} \approx 1 - e^{-\frac{nl}{m}} = 1 - e^{-n\alpha},$$

where $l = \alpha \times m$.

5.2.1.1 Single Keyword Queries

This implies that, given the m-bit signature of a single keyword query, (where approximately l bits are set to "1"), the probability that all the corresponding "1" bits in the document signature file are also set to "1" is

$$\left(1 - e^{-n\alpha}\right)^l = \left(1 - e^{-n\alpha}\right)^{\alpha m}.$$

In strict terms, this is nothing but the rate of matches and includes both true and false positives. It, however, also approximates the false positive rate, that is, the probability that the bits corresponding to the query in the signature file are all set to "1", although the query word is not in the document. This is because this would be the probability of finding matches even if there is no real match to the query in the database.

Let us refer to the term $(1 - e^{-n\alpha})^{\alpha m}$ as $fp(n, \alpha, m)$. By setting the derivative, $\frac{\delta fp(n,\alpha,m)}{\delta \alpha}$, of the term to 0 (and considering the shape of the curve as a function of α), we can find the value of α that minimizes the rate of false positives. This gives the optimal α value as $\alpha = \frac{ln(2)}{n}$. In other words, given a signature of length m, the optimal number, $l_{optimal}$, of bits to be set to "1" is $\lceil m\frac{ln(2)}{n} \rceil$. Consequently, the false positive rate under this optimal value of l is

$$fp_{opt}(n, m) = fp\left(n, \frac{ln(2)}{n}, m\right) = \left(1 - e^{-n\frac{ln(2)}{n}}\right)^{\lceil \frac{ln(2)}{n}m \rceil} = \left(\frac{1}{2}\right)^{\lceil \frac{ln(2)m}{n} \rceil}.$$

This means that, as shown in Figure 5.3(a), once the signature is sufficiently long, the false positive rate will decrease quickly with increasing signature length.

5.2.1.2 Queries with Multiple Keywords
Conjunctive Queries

If the user query is a conjunction of $k > 1$ keywords, then the query signature is constructed (similarly to the document signature creation) by OR-ing the signatures of the individual query keywords. Thus, by replacing n with k in the corresponding formula for document signatures, we can find that, given a conjunctive query with k

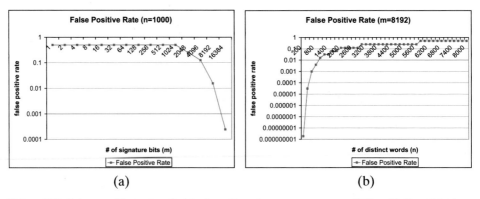

(a)   (b)

Figure 5.3. False positive rate of signature files decreases exponentially with the signature length.

keywords, the likelihood of a given bit being set to "1" in the query signature is $\approx 1 - e^{-\frac{kl}{m}}$. Because there are m bits in each signature, the expected number of bits set to "1" in the query signature can be approximated as

$$\approx \sum_{i=1}^{m} 1 - e^{-\frac{kl}{m}} = m\left(1 - e^{-\frac{kl}{m}}\right).$$

As shown in Figure 5.4, when $m \gg l$, the foregoing equation can be approximated by $k \times l$:

$$\approx \sum_{i=1}^{m} 1 - e^{-\frac{kl}{m}} \approx kl.$$

Using this approximation, for a query with k keywords, the false positive rate can be approximately computed as

$$\approx \left(1 - e^{-\frac{nl}{m}}\right)^{kl} = \left(\left(1 - e^{-\frac{nl}{m}}\right)^{l}\right)^{k}.$$

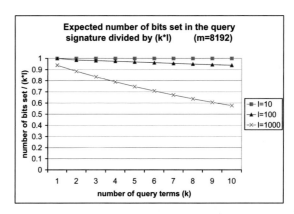

Figure 5.4. Expected number of bits set in the query signature divided by $k \times l$. For $m \gg l$, the ratio is almost 1.0; that is, the expected number of bits set in the query signature can be approximated by $k \times l$.

In other words, for a conjunctive query with more than one keyword, the false positive rate drops exponentially with the number, k, of query words:

$$fp_{conj}(k, n, \alpha, m) \approx \left(\left(1 - e^{-n\alpha} \right)^{\alpha m} \right)^k = fp(n, \alpha, m)^k.$$

Disjunctive Queries

If, on the other hand, the query is disjunctive, then each query keyword is evaluated independently, and if a match is found for any query keyword, then a match is declared for the overall query. Thus, a false positive for any query word will likely result in a false positive for the overall query. Thus, the false positive rate for the query will increase with the number k of words in the disjunctive query:

$$fp_{disj}(k, n, \alpha, m) \approx 1 - (1 - fp(n, \alpha, m))^k.$$

5.2.2 Indexing Based on Signature Files: Bitslice and Blocked Signature Files

In general, checking the signature of a document for a match is faster than scanning the entire document for the query words. Yet, given a database with large number of documents, identifying potential matches may still take too much time. Therefore, especially in databases with large numbers of documents, better organizations of the document signature files may be needed.

Bitslice Signature Files

Given a database with N documents, bitslice signature files organize and store document signatures in the form of "*slices*": the ith bitslice contains bit values of the ith position in all the N document signatures.

Given a query signature where l_{query} bits are set to "1", the corresponding bit-slices are fetched, and all these slices are AND-ed together. This creates a bitmap of potential answers, and only these candidate matches need be verified to find the actual matches.

In practice (if the slices are sufficiently sparse[1]), the false positive rate is acceptably low even if only $s \ll l_{query}$ slices are used for finding candidate documents. According to Kent *et al.* [1990] and Sacks-Davis *et al.* [1987], in practice the number of slices to be processed for conjunctive queries can be fixed around six to eight. For a conjunctive query, if the number of query keywords, k, is greater than this, at least k slices need to be used. If the query is disjunctive, because each query keyword is matched independently, $k \times s$ slices should be fetched.

Blocked Signature Files

In a large database, the bitslices themselves can be very long and costly to fetch. Given that multiple slices need to be fetched per query, having to fetch and process bitslices that are very long might have a negative effect on query processing performance.

Because the bitslices are likely to be sparse, one alternative is to store them in compressed form. Although this may help reduce storage costs, once fetched from

---

[1] According to Kent *et al.* [1990], approximately one bit in eight should be set to "1".

the database, these compressed slices need to be decompressed before the matching process and, overall, this may still be too costly. An alternative to naive compression is to group documents into blocks, where each bit in a slice corresponds to a block of B documents. Although this reduces the sizes of the slices that need to be fetched from the database, block-level aggregation of documents may have two potential disadvantages [Kent *et al.*, 1990]:

- First, the reduction in the slice length may increase the overall slice density. This may then cause an increase in false positives, negatively affecting the retrieval quality. When using blocking, to keep the overall slice density low for the entire database, the signature length (i.e., the total number of slices) needs to be increased. Also, the larger the blocking factor is, the more slices must be fetched to eliminate false matches.
- A second disadvantage of aggregating documents into blocks is that, in the case of a false match, the entire block of documents needs to be verified all together. The degree of block-level false matches needs to be reduced by using different document-to-block mappings for different slices.

When block-based aggregation is used, each bit in the blocked slice corresponds to a set of documents. Consequently, to find the individual matches, the blocked bitslices need to be decoded back to document identifiers. Because blocking may potentially result in a larger number of candidate matches and because more slices would need to be fetched from the database to reduce the false positive rate, identifying candidate matches may require a significant amount of work [Sacks-Davis *et al.*, 1995]. Thus, informed choice of appropriate parameters, based on a cost model (which takes into account the I/O characteristics and the available memory) and a proper understanding of the data characteristics, is crucial.

5.2.3 Data Characteristics and Signature File Performance

As described previously, the likelihood of false positives is a function of the number of distinct words in a given document. Thus, given a database with a heterogeneous collection of documents, setting the appropriate size for the signature is not straightforward: a short signature will result in a large degree of false positives for long documents, whereas a long signature may be redundant if most of the documents in the database are short. Although partitioning the database into sets of roughly equal-sized documents [Kent *et al.*, 1990] or dividing documents into roughly equal-sized fragments might help, in general, signature files are easier to apply when the documents are of similar size.

A related challenge stems from common terms [Zobel *et al.*, 1998] that occur in a large number of documents. Having a significant number of common terms results in bitslices that are unusually dense and thus increases the false positive rate (not only for queries that contain such common terms, but even for other rare terms that share the same bitslices). This problem is often addressed by separating common terms from rare terms in indexing.

5.2.4 Word-Overlap–Based Fuzzy Retrieval Using Signature Files

Although the original signature file data structure was developed for quick-and-dirty lookup for exact keyword matches, it can also be used for identifying fuzzy matches between a query document and the set of documents in the database. Kim *et al.* [2009] extend the basic signature file method, with a range search mechanism to support word-overlap based retrieval.

Let *doc* be a document containing n words and q be a query document that contains the same n words as *doc* plus an additional set of u words.[2] Let Sig_{doc} and Sig_q denote the signatures of these two documents, respectively. As described earlier, document signatures are formed through the *bitwise-OR* of the signatures of the words in the documents. Let us assume that the signature size is m bits and signatures are obtained by setting random bits in $l \leq m$ rounds. As before, the probability of a given bit in the document signature being set to "1" can be computed as follows:

$$1 - \left(\left(1 - \frac{1}{m}\right)^l\right)^n = 1 - \left(1 - \frac{1}{m}\right)^{nl} \approx 1 - e^{-\frac{nl}{m}}.$$

Here, $\left(1 - \frac{1}{m}\right)^l$ is the probability that in any given signature, the selected bit remains "0" despite l rounds in which a randomly selected bit is set to "1". The formula then reflects the probability of the position corresponding to the selected bit being occupied by a "0" in all the contributing n bit-strings.

Let us now consider q. Because q contains u additional words, the bits set to 1 for the query signature, Sig_q, will be a superset of the bits set to 1 in Sig_{doc}. Some of the bits that are 0 in Sig_{doc} will switch to 1 because of the additional u words. The probability of a given bit switching from 0 to 1 as a result of the addition of these u new words can be be computed as follows:

$$P_{bitswitch}(m, l, n, u) = \left(1 - \frac{1}{m}\right)^{nl} \times \left(1 - \left(1 - \frac{1}{m}\right)^{ul}\right) \approx e^{-\frac{nl}{m}} \times \left(1 - e^{-\frac{ul}{m}}\right).$$

Given this, the probability, $P_{exact\_bit\_diff}$, that exactly t bits will differ between *doc* and q due to these u additional words can be formulated as follows:

$$P_{exact\_bit\_diff}(m, l, n, u, t) = \binom{m}{t} P_{bitswitch}(m, l, n, u)^t (1 - P_{bitswitch}(m, l, n, u))^{m-t}.$$

Furthermore, the probability, $P_{max\_bit\_diff}$, that there will be at most d bits differing between signatures, Sig_{doc} and Sig_q, due to u words is

$$P_{max\_bit\_diff}(m, l, n, u, d) = \sum_{1 \leq t \leq d} P_{exact\_bit\_diff}(m, l, n, u, t).$$

Let us assume that the user allows up to u-words flexibility in the detection of word overlaps between the document and the query. Under this condition, *doc* should be returned as a match to q by the index structure with high probability. In other words,

---

[2] Missing words are handled similarly.

under u-words flexibility, for the given values of m, l, n, and u and an acceptable false hit rate ρ_{fp}, we need to pick the largest bit-difference value, d, such that

$$P_{max\_bit\_diff}(m, l, n, u + 1, d) \leq \rho_{fp}.$$

For any document with more than u words difference with the query, the probability of being returned within d bit differences will be at most ρ_{fp}. In other words, given the mismatch upper bound u, d is computed as

$$\underset{d \geq 0}{argmax}\, P_{max\_bit\_diff}(m, l, n, u + 1, d) \leq \rho_{fp}.$$

To leverage this for retrieval, Kim *et al.* [2009] treat the signatures of all the documents in the database as points in an m-dimensional Euclidean space, where each dimension corresponds to one signature bit. Given a query and an upper bound, u, of the number of mismatching words between the query and the returned documents, a search with a range of $\sqrt{d}$ is performed using a multidimensional index structure, such as the Hybrid-tree [Chakrabarti and Mehrotra, 1999] (Section 7.2.4.3), and false positives are eliminated using a postprocessing step.

5.3 SIGNATURE- AND INVERTED-FILE HYBRIDS

Both signature and inverted files have their advantages and disadvantages. Some schemes try combining the inverted file and signature file approaches to get the best of both worlds. Faloutsos and Christodoulakis [1985] argue that if there exist discriminatory terms that are used frequently in user queries but do not appear in data, then significant savings can be achieved in signature files if such high discriminatory terms are treated differently from the others. Based on this observation, Kent *et al.* [1990] propose to index common terms using bitmaps and rare terms using signature files to eliminate the problems signature files face when the distribution of the term frequencies is highly heterogeneous in the database. Chang *et al.* [1989] propose a hybrid method, integrating signature files with postings lists. Similarly, Faloutsos and Jagadish [1992] propose the use of signature files along with variable-length postings lists. The postings file is used only for the highly discriminatory terms, whereas the signature file is built for common, low discriminatory terms. Given a query, a shared index file is used to route the individual query terms to the postings file or the signature file for further matching.

Sacks-Davis [1985] presents a two-level signature file, composed of a block signature file and a record signature file. Given a query, first the block signature file (implemented as a bitslice) is searched to determine matching blocks. Then, the record signatures (implemented as bit strings) of the matching blocks are further searched to identify matching documents. Chang *et al.* [1993] improve the two-level signature method by integrating postings files, for leveraging term discrimination, and block signature files, for document signature clustering. In this scheme, as in the approach by Faloutsos and Jagadish [1992], a shared index file is used to route the individual query terms to the postings or the signature file for further matching. Unlike the approach by Faloutsos and Jagadish [1992], however, both the postings and signature files are implemented as block-based index structures, which cluster multiple documents. Once matching blocks are identified using the postings and

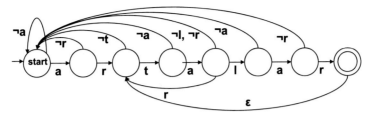

Figure 5.5. The (implicit) KMP state machine corresponding to the query sequence "artalar": each node corresponds to a subsequence already verified, and each edge corresponds to a new symbol seen in the data sequence. When a symbol not matching the query sequence is seen (denoted by "¬"), the state machine jumps back to the longest matching query prefix.

signature files, then the record signatures (implemented as bit strings of the matching blocks) are further searched to identify individual matching documents. Lee and Chang [1994] show experimentally that the hybrid methods tend to outperform the signature files that do not discriminate between terms. More recently, Zobel *et al.* [1998] argue theoretically and experimentally that, because of the postprocessing costs, in general inverted files, supported with sufficient in-memory data structures and compressed postings files, tend to perform better than signature files and hybrid schemes in terms of the disk accesses they require during query processing.

5.4 SEQUENCE MATCHING

In the previous two subsections, we described approaches for addressing the problem of searching long sequences (e.g., documents) based on whether or not they contain predefined subpatterns (e.g., words) picked from a given vocabulary. More generally, the sequence-matching problem (also known as the string-matching problem) involves searching for an occurrence of a given pattern (a substring or a subsequence) in a longer string or a sequence, or to decide that none exists.

The problem can be more formally stated as follows: given two sequences q, of length m, and p, of length n, determine whether there exists a position x such that the query sequence q matches the target sequence p at position x. The query sequence q matches the target sequence p at position x iff $\forall_{0 \leq i \leq m-1} p[x + i] = q[1 + i]$.

A naive approach to the sequence-matching problem would be to slide the query sequence (of size m) over the given data sequence (of size n) and to check matches for each possible alignment of these two sequences. When done naively, this would lead to $O(mn)$ worst-case time. The Knuth-Morris-Pratt (KMP) [Knuth *et al.*, 1977] and Boyer-Moore (BM) [Boyer and Moore, 1977] algorithms improve this by preventing redundant work that the naive approach implies. As in the naive algorithm, KMP slides the data sequence over the query sequence but, using an implicit structure that encodes the overlaps in the given query sequence (Figure 5.5), it skips unpromising alignment positions. Consequently, it is able to achieve linear $O(n)$ worst-case execution time. BM allows linear-time and linear-space pre-processing of the query sequence to achieve *sublinear*, $O(n\log(m)/m)$, *average* search time by eliminating the need to verify all symbols in the sequence. The worst-case

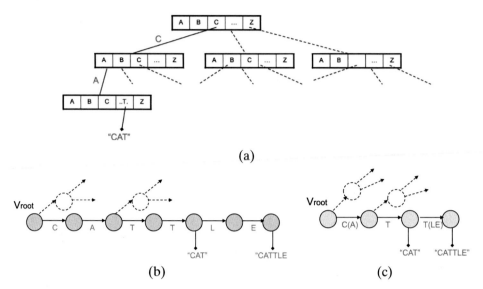

Figure 5.6. (a) Trie data structure. (b) A sample trie for a database containing sequences "cat" and "cattle" among others. (c) The corresponding Patricia trie that compresses the subpaths.

behavior [Cole, 1994] of the BM algorithm, however, is still $O(n)$ and in general is worse than the worst-case behavior of the KMP.

5.4.1 Tries

Tries [Fredkin, 1960] are data structures designed for leveraging the prefix commonalities of a set of sequences stored in the database. Given an alphabet, Σ, and a set, S, of sequences, the corresponding trie is an edge-labeled tree, $T(V, E)$, where each edge, $e_i \in E$, is labeled with a symbol in Σ and each path from the root of T to any node $v_i \in V$ corresponds to a unique prefix in the sequences stored in the database (Figures 5.6(a) and (b)). The leaves of the trie are specialized nodes corresponding to complete sequences in the database. Because each sequence is encoded by a branch, tries are able to provide $O(l)$ search time for a search sequence of length l, independent of the database size. To further reduce the number of nodes that need to be stored in the index structure and, most importantly, traversed during search, Patricia tries [Morrison, 1968] compress subpaths where the nodes do not contain any branching decisions (Figure 5.6(c)).

5.4.2 Suffix Trees and Suffix Arrays

Although benefiting from the prefix commonalities of the sequences in the database may reduce the cost of searches, this also limits the applicability of the basic trie data structure to only those searches that start from the leftmost symbols of the sequences. In other words, given a query sequence q, tries can help only when looking for matches at position $x = 1$.

Suffix trees [McCreight, 1976; Ukkonen, 1992b] support more generalized sequence searches simply by storing all suffixes of the available data: given a

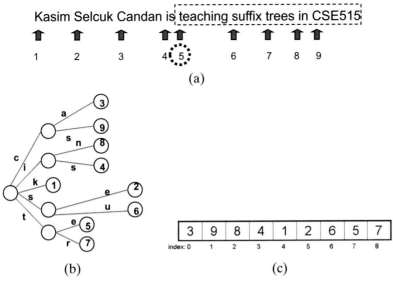

Figure 5.7. (a) Suffixes of a sample string (in this example only those suffixes that start at word boundaries are considered). (b) The corresponding suffix tree and (c) the suffix array.

sequence p, of length n, the corresponding suffix tree indexes each subsequence in $\{p[i, n] \mid 1 \leq i \leq n\}$ in a trie or a Patricia trie (Figure 5.7(a,b)). Thus, in this case, searches can start from any relevant position in p. A potential disadvantage of suffix trees is that, since they store all the suffixes of all data sequences, they may be costly in terms of the memory space they require. *Suffix arrays* [Manber and Myers, 1993] reduce the corresponding space requirement by trading off space with search time: instead of storing the entire trie, a suffix array stores in an array only the leaves of the trie (Figure 5.7(c)). In a database with s unique suffixes, searches can be performed in $log(s)$ time using binary search on this array.

5.4.3 Suffix Automata

As described in Section 5.4.2, suffix trees and suffix arrays are able to look into the stored sequences for matches at positions other than the leftmost symbols. They, on the other hand, assume that the input sequence needs to be matched starting from its leftmost symbol. If the goal, however, is to recognize and trigger matches based on the suffixes of an incoming sequence, these data structures are not immediately applicable.

One way to extend suffix trees to support matches also on the suffixes of the data sequences is to treat the suffix tree as a nondeterministic finite automaton: for each new incoming symbol, search restarts from the root of the trie. When naively performed, however, this may be extremely costly in terms of time as well as memory space needed to maintain all simultaneous executions of the finite automaton.

Directed Acyclic Word Graphs

A *suffix automaton* is a deterministic finite automaton that can recognize all the suffixes of a given sequence [Crochemore and Vrin, 1997; Crochemore *et al.*, 1994]. For example, the *backward directed acyclic word graph matching (BDM)*

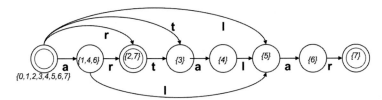

Figure 5.8. A suffix automaton clusters the subsequences of the input sequence (in this case "artalar") to create a directed acyclic graph that serves as a deterministic finite automaton that can recognize all the suffixes of the given sequence.

algorithm [Crochemore *et al.*, 1994] creates a suffix automaton (also referred to as a directed acyclic word graph) for searching the subsequences of a given pattern in a longer sequence. Let p be a given sequence and let u and v be two subsequences of p. These subsequences are said to be equivalent ($\equiv$) to each other for clustering purposes if and only if the set of end positions of u in p is the same as the set of end positions of v in p. For example for the sequence "*artalar*", "*tal*" $\equiv$ "*al*" but "*ar*" $\not\equiv$ "*lar*". The nodes of the suffix automaton are the equivalence classes of $\equiv$, that is, each node is the set of subsequences that are equivalent to each other. There is an edge from one node to another if we can extend the subsequences using a new symbol while keeping the positions that still match (Figure 5.8). The suffix automaton is linear in the size of the given sequence and can be constructed in linear time.

Bit Parallelism

An alternative approach to the deterministic encoding of the automaton, as favored by BDM, is to directly simulate the nondeterministic finite automaton. As described earlier, however, a naive simulation of the nondeterministic finite automaton can be very costly. Thus, this alternative requires an efficient mechanism that does not lead to an exponential growth of the simulation. The *backward nondeterministic directed acyclic word graph matching (BNDM)* algorithm [Navarro and Raffinot, 1998] follows this approach to implement a suffix automaton that simulates the corresponding non-deterministic finite automaton by leveraging the *bit-parallelism* mechanism first introduced in Baeza-Yates and Gonnet [1989, 1992].

In bit parallelism, states are represented as numbers, and each transition step is implemented using arithmetic and logical operations that give new numbers from the old ones. Let m be the length of the query sequence, q, and n be the length of the data sequence, d. Let s_i^j denote whether there is a mismatch between $q[1..i]$ and $d[(j-i+1)..j]$. If $s_m^j = 0$, then the query is matched at the data position j. Let $T[x]$ be a table such that

$$T_i[x] = \begin{cases} 0 & x = q[i] \\ 1 & \text{otherwise.} \end{cases}$$

Then the value of s_i^j can be computed from the value of s_{i-1}^{j-1} as follows:

$$s_i^j = s_{i-1}^{j-1} \vee T_i[d[j]].$$

Here, $s_0^j = 0$ for all j because an empty query sequence does not lead to any mismatches with any data.

Let the global state of the search be represented using a vector of m states: intuitively there are m parallel-running comparators reading the same text position, and the vector represents the current state for each of these comparators. The global state vector, gs_j, after the consumption of the jth data symbol can be represented using a single number that combines the bit representations of all individual m states:

$$gs_j = \sum_{i=0}^{m-1} s_{i+1}^{j} 2^i.$$

For every new symbol in the data, the state machine is transitioned by shifting the vector gs_j left 1 bit to indicate that the search advanced 1 symbol on the data sequence, and the individual states are updated using the table $T[x]$:

$$gs_j = (gs_{j-1} << 1) \vee GT[d[j]],$$

where $GT[x]$ is a generalized version of the table T that matches the bit structure of the global state vector:

$$GT[x] = \sum_{i=0}^{m-1} \left[x \neq q[i+1] \right] 2^i.$$

Because of this, this algorithm is referred to as the *shift-or* algorithm. A match is declared when $gs_j < 2^{m-1}$; that is, there is at least one individual state which finds a match (i.e., $\exists_{1 \leq i \leq m} s_i^j = 0$). Given a computational device with w bit words, the shift-or algorithm achieves a worst-case time of $O(\frac{mn}{w})$.

5.5 APPROXIMATE SEQUENCE MATCHING

Unlike the previous algorithms, which all search for exact matches, approximate string or sequence matching algorithms focus on finding patterns that are *not too different* from the ones provided by the users [Baeza-Yates and Perleberg, 1992; Navarro, 2001; Sellers, 1980].

5.5.1 Finite Automata

One way to approach the approximate sequence matching problem is to represent the query pattern in the form of a nondeterministic finite automaton (NFA). Figure 5.9 shows a nondeterministic finite automaton created for the sequence "SAPINO". Each row of this NFA corresponds to a different number of errors. In the NFA, insertions are denoted as vertical transitions (which consume one extra symbol), substitutions are denoted as diagonal transitions (which consume an alternative symbol), and deletions are denoted as diagonal ϵ (or *null*) transitions (which proceed without consuming any symbols). Note that the NFA-based representation assumes that each error has a cost of 1 and, thus, it cannot be *directly* used when insertions, deletions, and substitutions have different costs.

Ukkonen [1985] proposed a deterministic version of the finite automaton to count the number of errors observed during the matching process. This allows for $O(n)$ worst-case time but requires exponential space complexity. Kurtz [1996] showed that the space requirements for the deterministic automaton can be reduced

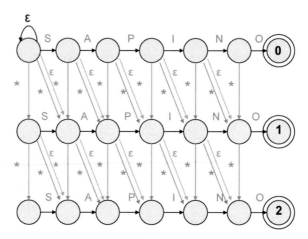

Figure 5.9. The NFA that recognizes the sequence "SAPINO" with a total of up to two insertion, deletion, and substitution errors. See color plates section.

to $O(mn)$ using a lazy construction, which avoids enumerating the states that are not absolutely necessary. More recently, Baeza-Yates and Navarro [1999], Baeza-Yates [1996], and Wu and Manber [1991] proposed bit-parallelism–based efficient simulations of the NFA. These avoid the space explosion caused by NFA-to-DFA conversion by carefully packing the states of the NFA into memory words and executing multiple transitions in parallel through logical and arithmetic operations (Section 5.5.3).

5.5.2 Dynamic Programming–Based Edit Distance Computation

Let q (of size m) and p (of size n) be two sequences. Let $C[i, j]$ denote the edit distance between $p[1..i]$ and $q[1..j]$. The following recursive definition of the number of errors can be easily translated into an $O(mn)$ dynamic programming algorithm for computing edit distance, $C[n, m]$, between p and q:

$$C[i, 0] = i$$
$$C[0, j] = j$$
$$C[i, j] = \begin{cases} \text{if } (p[i] = q[j]) \text{ then} & C[i - 1, j - 1] \\ \text{else} & 1 + min\{C[i - 1, j], C[i, j - 1], C[i - 1, j - 1]\}. \end{cases}$$

Note that the foregoing recursive formulation can also be viewed as a column-based simulation of the NFA, where the active states of the given NFA are iteratively evaluated one column at a time [Baeza-Yates, 1996].

This recursive formulation can easily be generalized to the cases where the edit operations have nonuniform costs associated to them:

$$C[0, 0] = 0$$
$$C[i, j] = min \begin{cases} C[i - 1, j - 1] + substitution\_cost(p[i], q[j]), \\ C[i - 1, j] + deletion\_cost(p[i]), \\ C[i, j - 1] + insertion\_cost(q[j]) \end{cases},$$

where $substitution\_cost(a, a) = 0$ for all symbols, a, in the symbol alphabet and $C[-1, j] = C[i, -1]$ for all i and j.

Landau and Vishkin [1988] improve the execution time of the dynamic programming-based approach to $O(k^2 n)$ time (where k is the maximum number of errors) and $O(m)$ space by considering the diagonals of the NFA as opposed to its columns. Consequently, the recurrence relationship is written in terms of the diagonals and the number of errors, instead of the rows, i, and columns, j. Landau and Vishkin [1989] and Myers [1986] further reduce the complexity to $O(kn)$ time and $O(n)$ space by exploiting a suffix tree that helps maintain the longest prefix common to both suffixes $q[i..m]$ and $p[j..n]$ efficiently.

5.5.3 Bit Parallelism for Direct NFA Simulation

As stated previously, dynamic programming based solutions essentially simulate the automaton by packing its columns into machine words [Baeza-Yates, 1996]. Wu and Manber [1991, 1992], on the other hand, simulate the NFA by packing each row into a machine word and by applying the bit-parallelism approach (which was originally proposed by Baeza-Yates and Gonnet [1989]; see Section 5.4.3). Wu and Manber [1991] maintain $k + 1$ arrays $R^0, R^1, R^2, \ldots, R^k$, such that array R^d stores all possible matches with up to d errors (i.e., R^d corresponds to the dth row).[3] To compute the transition from R^d_j to R^d_{j+1}, Wu and Manber [1991] consider the four possible ways that lead to a match, for the first i characters of the query sequence q, with $\leq d$ errors up to $p[j + 1]$:

- *Matching:* There is a match of the first $i - 1$ characters with $\leq d$ errors up to $p[j]$ and $p[j + 1] = q[i]$.
- *Substituting:* There is a match of the first $i - 1$ characters with $\leq d - 1$ errors up to $p[j]$. This case corresponds to substituting $p[j + 1]$.
- *Deletion:* There is a match of the first $i - 1$ characters with $\leq d - 1$ errors up to $p[j + 1]$. This corresponds to deleting of $q[i]$.
- *Insertion:* There is a match of the first i characters with $\leq d - 1$ errors up to $p[j]$. This corresponds to inserting $d[j + 1]$.

Based on this, Wu and Manber [1991] show that R^d_{j+1} can be computed from R^d_j, R^{d-1}_j, and R^{d-1}_{j+1} using two shifts, one *and*, and three *ors*. Because each step requires a constant number of logical operations, and because there are $k + 1$ arrays, approximate sequence search on a data string of length n takes $O((k + 1)n)$ time.

Wu and Manber [1991] further propose a *partitioning* approach that partitions the query string into r blocks, all of which can be searched simultaneously. If one of the blocks matches, then the whole query pattern is searched directly within a neighborhood of size m from the position of the match. Baeza-Yates and Navarro [1999] further improve the search time of the algorithm to $O(n)$ for small query patterns, where $mk = O(\log n)$, by simulating the automaton *by diagonals* (as opposed to by rows). Baeza-Yates and Navarro [1999] also propose a partition approach that can search for longer query patterns in $O(\sqrt{\frac{mk}{\sigma w}} n)$ time, for a partitioning constant, w, and symbol alphabet size, σ.

---

[3] R^0, that is, the array corresponding to zero matching error, corresponds to the original string.

5.5.4 Filtering, Fingerprinting, and ρ-Grams

Filtering-based schemes rely on the observation that a single matching error cannot affect two widely separated regions of the given sequence. Thus, they split the pattern into pieces and perform exact matching to count the number of pieces that are affected to have a sense of the number of errors there are between the query pattern and the text sequence. For example, given a maximum error rate, k, Wu and Manber [1991] *cut* the pattern into $k + 1$ pieces and verify that at least one piece is matched exactly. This is because k errors cannot affect more than k pieces. Jokinen *et al.* [1996] slide a window of length m over the text sequence and count the number of symbols that are included in the pattern. Relying on the observation that in a subsequence of length m with at most k errors, there must be at least $m - k$ symbols that are belonging to the pattern, they apply a *counting filter* that passes only those window positions that have at least $m - k$ such symbols. These candidate text windows are then verified using any edit-distance algorithm.

ρ-Grams

Holsti and Sutinen [1994], Sutinen and Tarhio [1995], Ukkonen [1992a], Ullmann [1977] and others rely on filtering based on short subsequences, known as ρ-grams, of length ρ.[4] Given a sequence p, its ρ-grams are obtained by sliding a window of length ρ over the symbols of p. To make sure that all ρ-grams are of length ρ, those window positions that extend beyond the boundaries of the sequence are prefixed or suffixed with null symbols. Because two sequences that have a small edit distance are likely to share a large number of ρ-grams, the sets of ρ-grams of the two sequences can be compared to identify and eliminate unpromising matches.

Karp and Rabin [1987] propose a *fingerprinting* technique, referred as KR, for quickly searching for a ρ-length string in a much longer string. Because comparing all ρ-grams of a long string to the given query string is expensive, Karp and Rabin [1987] compare hashes of the ρ-grams to the hash of the query q. Given a query sequence q (of size ρ) and a data sequence p (of size n), KR first computes the hash value, $hash(q)$, of the query sequence. This hash value is then compared to the hash values of all ρ-symbol subsequences of p; that is, only if

$$hash(q) = hash(p[i..(i + \rho - 1)])$$

is the actual ρ-symbol subsequence match at data position i verified. Note that because the hash values need to be computed for all ρ-symbol subsequences of p, unless this is performed efficiently, the cost of the KR algorithm is $O(\rho n)$. Thus, reducing the time complexity requires efficient computation of the hash values for the successive subsequences of p. To speed up the hashing process, Karp and Rabin [1987] introduce a *rolling hash function* that allows the hash for a ρ-gram to be computed from the hash of the previous ρ-gram. The rolling hash function allows computation of $hash(p[i + 1..(i + \rho)])$ from $hash(p[i..(i + \rho - 1)])$ using a constant number of operations independent from ρ. Consider, for example,

$$hash(p[i..(i + \rho - 1)]) = \sum_{k=i}^{i+\rho-1} nv(p[k]) \, lp^{k-i},$$

---

[4] In the literature, these are known as q-grams or n-grams. We are using a different notation to distinguish it from the query pattern, q, and length of the text, n.

where $nv(p[k])$ is the numeric value corresponding to the symbol $p[k]$ and lp is a large prime. We can compute $hash(p[i+1..(i+\rho)])$ as follows:

$$hash(p[i+1..(i+\rho)]) = \frac{hash(p[i..(i+\rho-1)]) - nv(p[i])}{lp}$$
$$+ \left(nv(p[i+\rho])\, lp^{\rho-1}\right).$$

Focusing on the matching performance, as opposed to the hashing performance, Manber [1994] proposes a *modsampling* technique that selects and uses only ρ-gram hashes that are 0 *modulo P*, for some P. On the average, this scheme reduces the number of hashes to be compared to $1/P$ of the original number and is shown to be robust against minor reorderings, insertions, and deletions between the strings. On the other hand, when using modsampling, the exact size of the resulting fingerprint depends on how many ρ-gram hashes are 0 *modulo P*. Heintze [1996] proposes using the n smallest hashes instead. The advantage of this scheme, called *minsampling*, is that (assuming that the original number of ρ-grams is larger than n) it results in fixed-size (i.e., $\rho \times n$) *fingerprints*, and thus the resulting fingerprints are easier to index and use for clustering.

Schleimer *et al.* [2003] extend this with a technique called *winnowing* that takes a guarantee threshold, t, as input; if there is a substring match at least as long as t, then the match is guaranteed to be detected. This is achieved by defining a window size $w = t - \rho + 1$ and, given a sequence of hashes $h_1 h_2 \ldots h_n$ (each hash corresponding to a distinct position on the input sequence of length n), dividing the sequence into nonoverlapping windows of w consecutive hashes. Then, in each window, the minimum hash is selected (if there is more than one hash with the minimum value, the algorithm selects the rightmost ρ-gram in the window). These selected hashes form the signature or fingerprint of the whole string. Schleimer *et al.* [2003] also define a *local* fingerprinting algorithm as an algorithm that, for every window of w consecutive hashes, includes one of these in the fingerprint, and the choice of the hash depends only on the window's contents. By this definition, winnowing is a local fingerprinting scheme. Schleimer *et al.* [2003] show that any local algorithm with a window size $w = t - \rho + 1$ is correct in the sense that any matching pair of substrings of length at least t is found by any local algorithm. Schleimer *et al.* [2003] further establish that any local algorithm with a window size $w = t - \rho + 1$ has a *density* (i.e., expected proportion of hashes included in the fingerprint),

$$d \geq \frac{1.5}{w+1}.$$

In particular, the winnowing scheme has a density of $\frac{2}{w+1}$; that is, it selects only 33% more hashes than the lower bound to be included in the fingerprint.

Ukkonen [1992a] proposes a ρ-*gram* distance measure based on counting the number of ρ-grams common between the given pattern query and the text sequence. A query sequence, q, of length m has $(m - \rho + 1)$ ρ-grams. Each mismatch between the query sequence and the text sequence, p, can affect ρ ρ-grams. Therefore, given k errors, $(m - \rho + 1 - k\rho)$ ρ-grams must be found. Ukkonen [1992a] leverages a suffix tree to keep the counts of the ρ-grams and, thus, implements the filter operation in linear time. To reduce the number of ρ-grams considered, Takaoka [1994] picks nonoverlapping ρ-grams each h symbols of the text. If $h = \lfloor \frac{m-k-\rho+1}{k+1} \rfloor$, at least one ρ-gram will be found and the full match can be verified by examining its neighborhood.

Notes that if, instead of 1, s many ρ-grams of the query pattern are required to identify a candidate match, then the sampling distance needs to be reduced to $h = \lfloor \frac{m-k-\rho+1}{k+s} \rfloor$.

String Kernels

Let $\mathcal{S}$ be an input space, and let $\mathcal{F}$ be a feature space with an inner product (see Section 3.1.1). The function κ is said to be a (positive definite) kernel if and only if there is a map $\phi : \mathcal{S} \rightarrow \mathcal{F}$, such that for all $x, y \in \mathcal{S}$,

$$\kappa(x, y) = \phi(x) \cdot \phi(y).$$

In other words, the binary function κ can be computed by mapping elements of $\mathcal{S}$ into a suitable feature space and computing this inner product in that space. For example, $\mathcal{S}$ could be the space of all text documents, and ϕ could be a mapping from text documents to normalized keyword vectors. Then the inner product would compute the *dot product* similarity between a pair of text documents. String kernels extend this idea to strings. Given an alphabet, Σ, the set, Σ^*, of all finite strings (including the empty string), and the set, Σ^ρ, of all strings of length exactly ρ, the function $\phi_\rho : \Sigma^* \rightarrow 2^{\Sigma^\rho \times \mathbb{Z}^+}$ maps from strings to a feature space consisting of ρ-grams and their counts in the input strings. In other words, given a string s, ϕ_ρ counts the number of times each ρ-gram occurs as a substring in s.

Given this mapping from strings to a feature space of ρ-grams, the ρ-spectrum kernel similarity measure, κ_ρ, is defined as the inner product of the feature vectors in the ρ-gram feature space:

$$\kappa_\rho(s_1, s_2) = \phi_\rho(s_1) \cdot \phi_\rho(s_2).$$

The *weighted all-substrings kernel* similarity (WASK) [Vishwanathan and Smola, 2003] takes into account the contribution of substrings of all lengths, weighted by their lengths:

$$\kappa_{wask}(s_1, s_2) = \sum_{\rho=1}^{\infty} \alpha_\rho \kappa_\rho(s_1, s_2),$$

where α_ρ is often chosen to decay exponentially with ρ.

Martins [2006] shows that both ρ-spectrum kernel and weighted all-substrings kernel similarity measures can be computed in $O(|s_1| + |s_2|)$ time using suffix trees.

Locality Sensitive Hashing

Indyk and Motwani [1998] define a *locality sensitive hash function* as a hash function, h, where given any pair, o_1 and o_2, of objects and a similarity function, $sim()$,

$$prob\,(h(o_1) = h(o_2)) = sim(o_1, o_2).$$

In other words, the probability of collision between hashes of the objects is high for similar objects and low for dissimilar ones.

Conversely, given a set of independent locality-sensitive hash functions, it is possible to build a corresponding similarity estimator [Urvoy *et al.*, 2008]. Consider the *minsampling* scheme [Broder, 1997; Broder *et al.*, 1997; Heintze, 1996] discussed earlier, where a linear ordering $\prec$ is used to order the hashes to pick the smallest

n to form a fingerprint. If the total order $\prec$ is to be picked at random, then for any pair of sequences s_1 and s_2, we have

$$prob(h_\prec(s_1) = h_\prec(s_2)) = \frac{hashes(s_1) \cap hashes(s_2)}{hashes(s_1) \cup hashes(s_2)};$$

that is, the probability that the same n hashes will be selected from both sequences is related to the number of hashes that are shared between s_1 and s_2.

Remember from Section 3.1.3 that this ratio is nothing but the Jaccard similarity,

$$prob(h_\prec(s_1) = h_\prec(s_2)) = sim_{jaccard}(s_1, s_2).$$

Thus, given a set of m total orders picked at random, we can construct a set, $\mathcal{H}$, of independent locality sensitive hash functions, each corresponding to a different order. If we let $sim_{\mathcal{H}}(s_1, s_2)$ be the number of locality-sensitive hash functions in $\mathcal{H}$ that return the same smallest n hashes for both s_1 and s_2, then we can approximately compute the similarity function, $sim_{jaccard}(s_1, s_2)$, as

$$sim_{jaccard}(s_1, s_2) \simeq \frac{sim_{\mathcal{H}}(s_1, s_2)}{m}.$$

In Section 10.1.4.2, we discuss the use of locality-sensitive hashing to support approximate nearest neighbor searches.

5.5.5 Compression-Based Sequence Comparison

The Kolmogorov complexity $K(q)$ of a given object q is the length of the shortest program that outputs q [Burgin, 1982]. Intuitively, complex objects will require longer programs to output them, whereas objects with inherent simplicity will be produced by simple and short programs.

Given this definition of complexity, Bennett *et al.* [1998] define the information distance between two objects, q and p, as

$$\Delta_{Kol}(q, p) = max\{K(q|p), K(p|q)\},$$

where $K(q|p)$ is the length of the shortest program with input p that outputs q. In the extreme case where p and q are identical, the only operation the function that computes q needs to do is to output the input p. Thus, intuitively, $K(q|p)$ measures the amount of work needed to convert p to q and is thus an indication of the difference of q from p.

Similarly, the normalized information distance between the objects can be defined as

$$\Delta_{Norm\_Kol}(q, p) = \frac{\Delta_{Kol}(q, p)}{max\{K(q), K(p)\}}.$$

Because, in the extreme case where p and q have nothing to share, the program can ignore the p (or q) provided as input and create q (or p) from scratch, the denominator corresponds to the maximum amount of work that needs to be done by the system to output p and q independently from the other.

Unfortunately, the Kolmogorov complexity generally is not computable. Therefore, this definition of distance is not directly useful. On the other hand, the length of the maximally compressed version of q can be seen as a form of complexity measure for data object q and thus can be used in place of the Kolmogorov complexity. Based on this observation, Cilibrasi and Vitanyi [2005] introduce a normalized compression distance, Δ_{ncd}, by replacing the Kolmogorov complexity in the definition of the normalized information distance with the length of a compressed version of q obtained using some compression algorithm:

$$\Delta_{ncd}(q, p) = \frac{C(qp) - min\{C(q), C(p)\}}{max\{C(q), C(p)\}}.$$

Here $C(q)$ is the size of the compressed q, and $C(qp)$ is the size of the compressed version of the sequence obtained by concatenating q and p.

5.5.6 Cross-Parsing–Based Sequence Comparison

Ziv and Merhav cross-parsing is a way to measure the relative entropy between sequences [Helmer, 2007; Ziv and Merhav, 1993]. Let q (of size m) and p (of size n) be two sequences. Cross-parsing first finds the longest (possibly empty) prefix of q that appears as a string somewhere in p. Once the prefix is found, the process is restarted from the very next position in q, this continues until the whole document q is parsed. Let $c(q|p)$ be the number of times the process had to start before q is completely parsed. The value

$$\Delta_{cross\_parse}(q, p) = \frac{c(q|p) - 1 + c(p|q) - 1}{2}$$

can be used as a distance measure between strings q and p. Note that each symbol in q is visited only once. In fact, the entire cross-parsing can be performed in linear time if the string p is indexed using a suffix tree (introduced in Section 5.4.2).

5.6 WILDCARD SYMBOLS AND REGULAR EXPRESSIONS

A variant of the non-exact string-matching problem is when wildcard symbols are allowed [Amir et al., 1998; Muthukrishnan and Ramesh, 1995]. For example, a "*" wildcard in the query pattern q can match any symbol in the alphabet and a "//" wildcard can match 0 or more symbols in the text sequence p. When there are wildcard symbols in the query pattern, matches found on p may differ from each other. In general, it is possible to extend edit-distance functions to accommodate these special wildcard symbols. Baeza-Yates and Gonnet [1989] and others have shown that many of the techniques, such as bit parallelism, developed for patterns without wildcard symbols can be adapted to capture patterns with wildcards.

5.6.1 Regular Expressions

Regular-expression–based frameworks further generalize the expressive power of the patterns [Chan et al., 1994]. Each regular expression, R, defines a set, $L(R)$, of strings (symbol sequences). Let Σ be a finite symbol alphabet, and let the regular expression, s, denote the set $L(s) = \{"s"\}$. Also, let ϵ denote the empty string (a sequence without any symbol). We can create more complex regular expressions by combining simpler regular expressions using *concatenation, union,* and *Kleene star* operators. Given two regular expressions R_1 and R_2:

- The concatenation, $R \equiv R_1 R_2$, of R_1 and R_2 denotes the language $L(R_1 R_2) = \{uv \parallel u \in L(R_1) \wedge v \in L(R_2)\}$
- The union, $R \equiv R_1 | R_2$, of R_1 and R_2 defines $L(R_1 | R_2) = \{u \parallel u \in L(R_1) \vee u \in L(R_2)\}$
- The Kleene star, R_1^*, of the regular expression, R_1, denotes the set of all strings that can be obtained by concatenating zero or more strings in $L(R_1)$

For example, the regular expression $R \equiv 1(0|1|...|9)^*$ denotes the set of all strings representing natural numbers having 1 as their more significant digit.

5.6.2 Regular Languages and Finite Automata

Strings in a language described by a regular expression (i.e., a regular language) can be recognized using a finite automaton. Any regular expression can be matched using a nondeterministic finite automaton (NFA) in linear time. However, converting a given NFA into a deterministic finite automaton (DFA) for execution can take $O(m2^m)$ time and space [Hopcroft and Ullman, 1979]. Once again, however, the bit-parallelism approach can be exploited to simulate an NFA efficiently [Baeza-Yates and Ribeiro-Neto, 1999]. Baeza-Yates and Gonnet [1996] use the Patricia tree as a logical model and presents algorithms with sublinear time for matching regular expressions. It also presents a logarithmic time algorithm for a subclass of regular expressions.

5.6.3 RE-Trees

The RE-tree data structure, introduced by Chan *et al.* [1994], enable quick access to regular expressions (REs) matching a given input string. RE-trees are height-balanced, hierarchical index structures. Each leaf node contains a unique identifier for an RE. In addition, the leaf node also contains a finite automaton corresponding to this RE. Each internal node of the RE-tree contains a set of (M, ptr) pairs, where:

- M is a finite automaton
- ptr is pointer to a child node, N, such that the union of the languages recognized by the finite automata in node N is contained in the language recognized by the *bounding* automaton, M

Intuitively, the bounding automaton is used for pruning the search space: if a given sequence q is not contained in M (i.e., is not recognized by the corresponding automaton), then it cannot match any of the regular expressions accessible through the corresponding pointer to node N. Therefore, the closer the language recognized by M is to the union of all the languages recognized by the corresponding node, the more effective will be the pruning. On the other hand, implementing more precise (minimal bounding) automata may require too much space, possibly exceeding the size of the corresponding index node. To reduce the space requirements, the automata stored in the RE-tree nodes are nondeterministic. Furthermore, the number of states used for constructing each automaton is limited by an upper bound, α. For space efficiency, each RE node is also required to contain at least m entries.

Searches proceed top-down along all the relevant paths whose bounding automata accept the input sequence. Insertions of new regular expressions require selection of an optimal insertion node such that the update causes minimal expansions in (the size of the languages recognized by the) bounding automata of the internal nodes. This ensures that the precision is not lost. Furthermore, it minimizes the amount of further updates (in particular splits) that insertions may cause on the path toward the root. Note that estimating the size of a language recognized by an RE is not trivial, in particular since these languages may be infinite in size. Therefore, Chan *et al.* [1994] propose two heuristics. The first heuristic, *max-count*, simply counts the size of the regular language upto some predetermined maximum sequence length. The second heuristic uses the *minimum description length* (MDL) [Rissanen, 1978] instead of the sizes of the language. The MDL is computed by first picking a random set, R, of strings in the language recognized by the automaton, M, and then computing

$$\frac{1}{|R|} \sum_{w \in R} \frac{MDL(M, w)}{|w|},$$

such that for $w = w_1 w_2 w_3 \ldots w_n$ and the corresponding state sequence $s_0 s_1 s_2 s_3 \ldots s_n$,

$$MDL(M, w) = \sum_{i=0}^{n-1} log_2(fanout_i),$$

where $fanout_i$ is the number of outgoing transitions (in a minimal-state DFA representation of M) from state s_i and, thus, $log_2(fanout_i)$ is the number of bits required to encode the transition out of state s_i. This measure is based on the intuition that given two DFAs, M_i and M_j, if $|L(M_i)|$ is larger than $|L(M_j)|$, then the per-symbol cost of a random string in $L(M_i)$ will likely to be higher than the per-symbol cost of a random string in $L(M_j)$. This intuition follows information theoretical observation that, in general, more bits are needed to specify an item that comes from a larger collection of items.

When a node split is not avoidable, the REs in the node need to be partitioned into two disjoint sets such that, after the split, the total sizes of the languages covered by the two sets will be minimum. Furthermore, during insertions, node splits, and node merges (due to deletions), the corresponding bounding automata need to be updated in such a way that the size of the corresponding language is minimal. Chan *et al.* [1994] show that the problems of optimal partitioning and minimal bounding automaton construction are NP-hard and proposes heuristic techniques for implementing these two steps efficiently.

5.7 MULTIPLE SEQUENCE MATCHING AND FILTERING

In many filtering and triggering applications, there are multiple query sequences (also called patterns) that are registered in the system to be checked against incoming data or observation sequences. Although each *filter sequence* can be evaluated separately against the data sequence, this may cause redundant work. Therefore, it

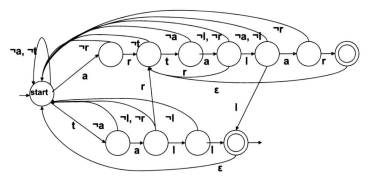

Figure 5.10. Aho-Corasik trie indexes multiple search sequences. Into a single integrated data structure. In this example, sequences "artalar" and "tall" are indexed together.

may be more advantageous to find common aspects of the registered patterns and avoid repeated checks for these common parts.

5.7.1 Trie-Based Multiple Pattern Filtering

Aho-Corasick tries [Aho and Corasick, 1975] eliminate redundant work by extending the KMP algorithm (Section 5.4) with a trie-like data structure that leverages overlaps in input patterns registered in the system (Figure 5.10). Because all overlaps in the registered patterns are accounted for in the integrated index structure, they are able to provide $O(n)$ search with $O(m)$ trie construction time, where n is the length of the data sequence and m is the length of the query sequence. In a similar fashion, the Commentz-Walter algorithm [Commentz-Walter, 1979] extends the BM algorithm with a trie of input patterns to provide simultaneous search for multiple patterns. Unlike Aho-Corasick tries, however, the resulting finite-state machine compares starting from the ends of the registered patterns as in the BM algorithm.

5.7.2 Hash-Based Multiple Pattern Filtering

As described in Section 5.5.4, in contrast to the foregoing algorithms that work on the plain-text or plan-symbol domain, to improve efficiency, the Karp-Rabin (KR) algorithm [Karp and Rabin, 1987] and others rely on sequences' hashes, rather than on the sequences themselves. These techniques can be adapted to the multiple pattern filtering task using a randomized set data structure, such as *Bloom filters* [Bloom, 1970], which can check whether a given data object is in a given set in constant time (but potentially with a certain false positive rate).

Like signature files (introduced in Section 5.2), a Bloom filter is a hash-based data structure, commonly used for checking whether a given element is in a set or not. A Bloom filter consists of an array, A, of m bits and a set, $\mathcal{H}$, of independent hash functions, each returning values between 1 and m. Let us be given a database, D, of objects.

■ To insert the objects in the database into the Bloom filter, for each data object, $o_i \in D$, for each $h_j \in \mathcal{H}$, the bit $A[h_j(o_i)]$ is set to 1.

■ To check whether an object, o_i, is in the database D or not, all bit positions $A[h_j(o_i)]$ are checked, in $O(m)$ time, to see if the corresponding bit is 1 or 0. If any of the bits is "0", then the object o_i cannot be in the database. If all bits are "1", then the object o_i is in the database, D, with false positive probability

$$\left(1 - \left(1 - \frac{1}{m}\right)^{|\mathcal{H}||D|}\right)^{|\mathcal{H}|} \simeq \left(1 - e^{-|\mathcal{H}||D|/m}\right)^{|\mathcal{H}|}.$$

Intuitively, $\left(1 - \frac{1}{m}\right)^{|\mathcal{H}||D|}$ is the probability that a given bit in the array is "0" despite all hash operations for all objects in the database. Then the preceding equation gives the probability for the event that, for the given query and for all $|\mathcal{H}|$ hash functions, the corresponding position will contain "1" (by chance). Thus, given a data sequence of length n, we can use the hashes produced by the KR (or other similar algorithms) as the basis to construct a Bloom filter, which can filter for a set of k registered patterns in $O(n)$ average time, independent of the value of k.

5.7.3 Multiple Approximate String Matching

Navarro [1997] extends the counting filter approach to the multiple pattern matching problem. For each pattern, the algorithm maintains a counter that keeps track of the matching symbols. As the window gets shifted, the counters are updated. Given r query patterns, the multipattern algorithm packs all r counters into a single machine word and maintains this packed set of counters incrementally in a bit-parallel manner. Although the worst-case behavior of this algorithm is $O(rmn)$, if the probability of reverifying (when a potential match is found) is low $(O(1/m^2))$, the algorithm is linear on average.

Baeza-Yates and Navarro [2002] also adapt other single approximate sequence matching algorithms to the multiple matching problem. In particular, it proposes to use a superimposed NFA to perform multiple approximate matching. The proposed scheme simulates the execution of the resulting combined automaton using bit parallelism. Baeza-Yates and Navarro [2002] also propose a multipattern version of the partitioning-based filtering scheme, discussed by Wu and Manber [1991], which *cuts* the pattern into $k + 1$ pieces and verifies that at least one piece is matched exactly. Given r patterns, Baeza-Yates and Navarro [2002] propose to cut each pattern into $k + 1$ partitions, and all $r(k + 1)$ pieces are searched using an exact matching scheme, such as the one adopted by Sunday [1990], in parallel.

5.8 SUMMARY

As we have seen in this chapter, a major challenge in indexing sequences is that, in many cases, the features of interest are not available in advance. Consequently, techniques such as ρ-grams help extract parts of the sequences that can be used as features for filtering and indexing. Still, many operations on sequences, including edit-distance computation or regular expression matching, require very specialized data structures and algorithms that are not very amenable to efficient indexing and require algorithmic approaches. Nevertheless, when the registered data (or query patterns) have significant overlaps, carefully designed index structures can help one leverage these overlaps in eliminating redundant computations.

In the next section, we see that graph- and tree-structured data also show similar characteristics, and many techniques (such as edit distances) applied to sequences can be revised and leveraged when dealing with data with more complex structures.

6

Indexing, Search, and Retrieval of Graphs and Trees

In Chapter 2, we have seen that most high-level multimedia data models (especially those that involve representation of spatiotemporal information, object hierarchies – such as X3D – or links – such as the Web) require tree or graph-based modeling. Therefore, similarity-based retrieval and classification commonly involve matching trees and graphs.

In this chapter, we discuss tree and graph matching. We see that, unlike the case with sequences, computing edit distance for finding matches may be extremely complex (NP-hard) when dealing with graphs and trees. Therefore, filtering techniques that can help prune the set of candidates are especially important when dealing with tree and graph data.

6.1 GRAPH MATCHING

Although, as we discussed in Section 3.3.2, graph matching through edit distance computation is an expensive task, there are various heuristics that have been developed to perform this operation efficiently. In the rest of this section, we consider three heuristics, GraphGrep, graph histograms, and graph probes, for matching graphs.

6.1.1 GraphGrep

Because the graph-matching problem is generally very expensive, there are various heuristics that have been developed for efficient matching and indexing of graphs. GraphGrep [Giugno and Shasha, 2002] is one such technique, relying on a path-based representation of graphs.

GraphGrep takes an undirected, node-labeled graph and, for each node in the graph, finds all paths that start at this node and have length up to a given, small upper bound, l_p. Given a path in the graph, the corresponding *id-path* is defined as the list of the ids of the nodes on the path. The *list-path* is also defined similarly: the list of the labels of the nodes on the path.

Although the id-paths in the database are unique, there can be multiple paths with the same label sequence. Thus, GraphGrep clusters the id-paths corresponding to a single label-path and uses the resulting set of label-paths, where each label-path has a set of id-paths, as the *path representation* of the given graph. The fingerprint of the graph is a hash table, where each row corresponds to a label-path and contains the hash of the label-path (i.e., the key) and the corresponding number of id-paths in the graph.

Given the fingerprint of a query graph and the fingerprints of the graphs in the database, irrelevant graphs are filtered out by comparing the numbers of id-paths for each matching hash key and by discarding those graphs that have at least one value in their fingerprints that is less than the corresponding value in the fingerprint of the query. Among the graphs in the database that have sufficient overlaps with the query, matching subgraphs are found by focusing on the parts of the graph that correspond to the label-paths in the query. After, the relevant id-path sets are selected and overlapping id-paths are found and concatenated to build matching subgraphs.

6.1.2 Graph Histograms and Probes

Let us consider unlabeled graphs and three primitive graph edit operations: vertex insertion, vertex deletion, and vertex update (deletion or insertion of an incident edge). We can define a graph edit distance $\Delta_G()$ based on these primitives. Given a query graph, the goal is then to identify graphs that have small edit distances from this query graph.

6.1.2.1 Graph Histograms

Given an unlabeled undirected graph, $G(V, E)$, let us construct a *graph histogram*, $hist(G)$, by calculating the degree (valence) of each vertex of the graph and assigning the vertex to a histogram bin based on this value. Let us also compute a *sorted graph histogram*, $hist_s(G)$, by sorting the histogram bins in decreasing order. Papadopoulos and Manolopoulos [1999] show that given two graphs, G_1 and G_2,

$$L_1(hist_s(G_1), hist_s(G_2)) = \Delta_G(G_1, G_2),$$

where L_1 is the Manhattan distance between the corresponding histogram vectors (Section 3.1.3). Thus, a sorted graph histogram based multidimensional representation can be used for indexing graphs that are mapped onto a metric vector space, for efficient retrieval.

6.1.2.2 Graph Probes

Graph probes [Lopresti and Wilfong, 2001] are also histogram-based, but they apply to more general graphs. Consider for example two unlabeled, undirected graphs, G_1 and G_2, and a graph distance function, $\Delta_G()$, based on an editing model with four primitive operations: (a) deletion of an edge, (b) insertion of an edge, (c) deletion of an (isolated) vertex, and (d) insertion of an (isolated) vertex. Lopresti and Wilfong [2001] show that the function, $probe(G_1, G_2)$, defined as

$$probe(G_1, G_2) \equiv L_1(PR(G_1), PR(G_2)),$$

where $PR(G)$ is a probe-histogram, obtained by assigning the vertices with the same degree into the same histogram bin, has the following property:

$$probe(G_1, G_2) \leq 4 \cdot \Delta_G(G_1, G_2).$$

Note that, although the $probe()$ function does not provide a bound as tight as the bound provided by the approach based on the sorted graph histogram described earlier, it can still be used as a filter that does not result in any misses. Moreover, under the same graph edit model, the foregoing result can be extended to unlabeled, directed graphs, simply by counting in-degrees and out-degrees of vertices independently while creating the probe-histograms.

Most importantly, for general graph-matching applications, Lopresti and Wilfong [2001] also show that, if the graph edit model is extended with two more operations, (e) changing the label of a node and (f) changing the label of an edge, then a similar result can be obtained for node- and edge-labeled directed graphs as well. In this case, the in- and out-degrees of vertices are counted separately for each edge label. The histogram is also extended with bins that are simply counting the vertices that have a particular vertex label. If α denotes the number of unique edge labels and d is the maximum number of edges incident on any vertex, then the total indexing time for graph $G(V, E)$ is linear in the graph size: $O(\alpha(d + |V|) + |E|)$. Note that, although it is highly efficient when α and d are small constants, this approach does not scale well when the dictionary size of edge labels is high and/or when $d \sim V$.

6.1.3 Graph Alignment

Let us consider two graphs, $G_1(V_1, E_1)$ and $G_2(V_2, E_2)$, with a *partially known* mapping (or correspondence) function, $\mu : V_1 \times V_2 \rightarrow [0, 1] \cup \{\perp\}$, between the nodes in V_1 and V_2, such that if $\mu(v_i, v_j) = \perp$, it is not known whether v_i is related to v_j; that is, v_i and v_j are unmapped. The *graph alignment* problem [Candan et al., 2007] involves *estimation* of the degree of mapping for $v_i \in V_1$ and $v_j \in V_2$, where $\mu(v_i, v_j) = \perp$, using the structural information inherent in G_1 and G_2. Candan et al. [2007] propose a graph alignment algorithm involving the following steps:

    (i) Map the vertices of V_1 and V_2 into multidimensional spaces S_1 and S_2, both with the same number (k) of dimensions.

    (ii) Identify transformations required to align the space S_1 with the space S_2 such that the *common/mapped vertices* of the two graphs are placed as close to each other as possible in the resulting aligned space.

    (iii) Use the same transformations to map the *uncommon vertices* in S_1 onto S_2.

    (iv) Now that the vertices of the two graphs are mapped into the same space, compute their similarities or distances in this space.

6.1.3.1 Step (i): MDS-Based Mapping into a Vector Space

Step (i) is performed using a multidimensional scaling (MDS) algorithm described in Section 4.3.1: for every pair of nodes in a given graph, the shortest distance between them is computed using an all-pairs shortest path algorithm [Cormen et al., 2001], and these distances are used for mapping the vertices onto a k dimensional space using MDS.

6.1.3.2 Step (ii): Procrustes-Based Alignment of Vector Spaces

In step (ii), the algorithm aligns spaces S_1 and S_2, such that related vertices are colocated in the new shared space, using the Procrustes algorithm [Gower, 1975; Kendall, 1984; Schönemann, 1966]. Given two sets of points, the Procrustes algorithm uses linear transformations to map one set of points onto the other set of points. Procrustes has been applied in diverse domains including psychology [Gower, 1975] and photogrammetry [Akca, 2003], where alignment of related but different data sets is required. The orthogonal Procrustes problem [Schönemann, 1966] aims finding an orthogonal transformation of a given matrix into another one in a way that minimizes transformation errors. More specifically, given matrices A and B, both of which are $n \times k$, the solution to the orthogonal Procrustes problem is an orthogonal transformation T, such that the sum of squares of the residual matrix $E = AT - B$ is minimized. In other words, given the $k \times k$ square matrix $S = E^T E$ (note that M^T denotes the transpose of matrix M)

$$trace(S) = \sum_{i=1}^{k} s_{ii} = \sum_{i=1}^{n} \sum_{j=1}^{k} e_{ij}^2 \quad \text{is minimized.}$$

The extended Procrustes algorithm builds on this by redefining the residual matrix as $E = cAT + [11 \ldots 1]^T t^T - B$, where c is a scale factor, T is a $k \times k$ orthogonal transformation matrix, and t is a $k \times 1$ translation vector [Schoenemann and Carroll, 1970]. The general Procrustes problem [Gower, 1975] further extends these by aiming to find a least-squares correspondence (with translation, orthogonal transformation, and scaling) between more than two matrices.

Weighted extended orthogonal Procrustes [Goodall, 1991] is similar to extended orthogonal Procrustes in that it uses an orthogonal transformation, scaling, and translation to map points in one space onto the points in the other. However, unlike the original algorithm, it introduces *weights* between the points in the two spaces. Given two $n \times k$ matrices A and B, while the extended orthogonal Procrustes minimizes the *trace* of the term $E^T E$, where $E = cAT + [11 \ldots 1]^T t^T - B$, the weighted extended orthogonal Procrustes minimizes the trace of the term $S_w = E^T WE$, where W is an $n \times n$ weight matrix: that is;

$$trace(S_w) = \sum_{i=1}^{k} sw_{ii} = \sum_{i=1}^{n} \sum_{h=1}^{n} \sum_{j=1}^{k} w_{ih} e_{ij} e_{hj}$$

is minimum. Note that if the weight matrix, W, is such that $\forall_i \ w_{ii} = 1$ and $\forall_{i,h \neq i} \ w_{ih} = 0$ (i.e., if the mapping is one-to-one and nonfuzzy), then this is equivalent to the nonweighted extended orthogonal Procrustes mapping. On the other hand, when $\forall_i \ w_{ii} \in [0, 1]$ and $\forall_{i,h \neq i} \ w_{ih} = 0$, then we get

$$trace(S_w) = \sum_{i=1}^{k} sw_{ii} = \sum_{i=1}^{n} \sum_{j=1}^{k} w_{ii} e_{ij}^2.$$

In other words, the mapping errors are weighted in the process. Consequently, those points that have large weights (close to 1.0) will be likely to have smaller mapping errors than those points that have lower weights (close to 0.0).

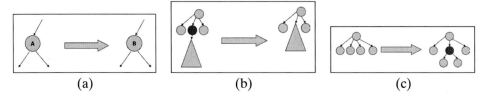

Figure 6.1. (a) Node relabeling, (b) node deletion, and (c) node insertion.

Let us assume that we are given the mapping function, μ, between the nodes of the two input graphs, G_1 and G_2; let us further assume that $\mu(v_i, v_j) \in [0, 1]$ and μ is 1-to-1. Then, μ can be used to construct a weight matrix, W, such that $\forall_i \; w_{ii} \in [0, 1]$ and $\forall_{i,h \neq i} \; w_{ih} = 0$. This weight matrix can then be used to align the matrices A and B, corresponding to the graphs G_1 and G_2, using the weighted extended orthogonal Procrustes technique. When the mapping function μ is not 1-to-1, however, the weighted extended orthogonal Procrustes cannot be directly applied. Candan *et al.* [2007] introduce a further extension to the Procrustes technique to accommodate many-to-many mappings between the vertices of the input graphs.

6.1.3.3 Steps (iii) and (iv): Alignment of Unmapped Vertices and Similarity Computation

Once the transformations needed to align the two spaces, S_1 and S_2, are found, these transformations are used to align unmapped vertices of graphs G_1 and G_2. Similarities or distances of the unmapped vertices are then computed in the resulting aligned space.

6.2 TREE MATCHING

In Section 3.3.3, we have seen that matching unordered trees can be very costly. As in the case of approximate string and graph matching, many approximate tree matching algorithms rely on primitive edit operations that can be used for transforming one tree into another. These primitive operations, *relabeling, node deletion*, and *node insertion*, are shown in Figure 6.1. The following three approximate tree matching problems all are expressed using these primitive edit operations:

- *Tree edit distance:* Let $\gamma()$ be a *metric* cost function associated with primitive tree edit operations. Let T_1 and T_2 be two trees and let S be a sequence of edit operations that transforms T_1 into T_2. The cost of the edit sequence, S, is the sum of the costs of the primitive operations. Given this, the *tree edit distance*, $\Delta_T(T_1, T_2)$ is defined as

$$\Delta_T(T_1, T_2) = \min_{S \; takes \; T_1 \; to \; T_2} \{\gamma(S)\}.$$

- *Tree alignment distance:* The tree alignment distance, $\Delta_{a,T}(T_1, T_2)$, between T_1 and T_2 is defined by considering only those edit sequences where all insertions are performed before deletions.
- *Tree inclusion distance:* The tree inclusion distance, $\Delta_{i,T}(T_1, T_2)$, between T_1 and T_2 is defined by considering only insertions to tree T_1. Conversely, T_1 is included in T_2 if and only if T_1 can be obtained from T_2 by deleting nodes from T_2.

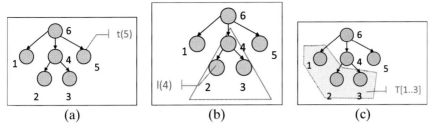

Figure 6.2. (a) Postorder numbering of the tree, (b) leftmost leaf under node $t[4]$, and (c) the substructure induced by the nodes $t[1]$, $t[2]$, and $t[3]$.

Tai [1979] and [Shasha and Zhang, 1990; Zhang and Shasha, 1989] provide postorder traversal-based algorithms for calculating the *editing distance* between ordered, node-labeled trees. Zhang *et al.* [1996] extend their work to edge-labeled trees. They first show that the problem is NP-hard and then provide an algorithm for computing the edit distance between graphs where each node has at most two neighbors. Chawathe *et al.* provide alternative algorithms to calculate the edit distance between ordered node-labeled trees [Chawathe, 1999; Chawathe and Garcia-Molina, 1997]. Other research in tree similarity includes works by Farach and Thorup [1997], Luccio and Pagli [1995], Myers [1986], and Selkow [1977]. In the following subsection, we present Shasha and Zhang's algorithm for tree edit-distance computation [Bille, 2005; Shasha and Zhang, 1995].

6.2.1 Tree Edit Distance

Ordered Trees

Given an ordered tree, T, we number its vertices using a left-to-right postorder traversal: $t[i]$ is the ith node of T during postorder traversal (Figure 6.2(a)).

Given two ordered trees T_1 and T_2, let M be a one-to-one, sibling-order and ancestor-order preserving mapping from the nodes of T_1 to the nodes of T_2. Figure 6.3(a) shows an example mapping. In this example, nodes $t_1[2]$ and $t_1[3]$ in T_1 and nodes $t_2[3]$ and $t_2[4]$ in T_2 are not mapped. Also, the labels of the mapped nodes $t_1[5]$ and $t_2[5]$ are not compatible. This mapping implies a sequence of edit operations

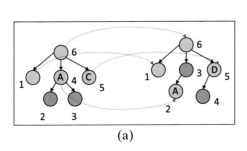

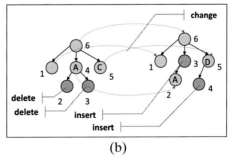

Figure 6.3. (a) A one-to-one, sibling-order and ancestor-order preserving mapping and (b) the corresponding tree edit operations.

(i) $treedist(\emptyset, \emptyset) = 0$;

(ii) For $k = l(i)$ to i
  (a) $forestdist(T_1[l(i)..k], T_2) = forestdist(T_1[l(i)..k-1], T_2) + \gamma(delete(t_1[k]))$

(iii) For $h = l(j)$ to j
  (a) $forestdist(T_1, T_2[l(j)..h]) = forestdist(T_1, T_2[l(j)..h-1]) + \gamma(insert(t_2[h]))$

(iv) For $k = l(i)$ to i
  (a) For $h = l(j)$ to j
    1. if $l(k) = l(i)$ and $l(h) = l(j)$ then
      a. $A = forestdist(T_1[l(i)..k-1], T_2[l(j)..h]) + \gamma(delete(t_1[k]))$
      b. $B = forestdist(T_1[l(i)..k], T_2[l(j)..h-1]) + \gamma(insert(t_2[h]))$
      c. $C = forestdist(T_1[l(i)..k-1], T_2[l(j)..h-1]) + \gamma(change(t_1[k], t_2[h]))$
      d. $forestdist(T_1[l(i)..k], T_2[l(j)..h]) = min\{A, B, C\}$
      e. $treedist(k, h) = forestdist(T_1[l(i)..k], T_2[l(j)..h])$
    2. else
      a. $A = forestdist(T_1[l(i)..k-1], T_2[l(j)..h]) + \gamma(delete(t_1[k]))$
      b. $B = forestdist(T_1[l(i)..k], T_2[l(j)..h-1]) + \gamma(insert(t_2[h]))$
      c. $C = forestdist(T_1[l(i)..l(k)-1], T_2[l(j)..l(h)-1]) + treedist(k, h)$
      d. $forestdist(T_1[l(i)..k], T_2[l(j)..h]) = min\{A, B, C\}$

(v) return($treedist(i,j)$)

Figure 6.4. Pseudocode for computing the edit distance, $treedist(i, j)$, between T_1 and T_2; i and j indicate the roots of T_1 and T_2, respectively.

where $t_1[2]$ and $t_1[3]$ are deleted from T_1 and $t_2[3]$ and $t_2[4]$ are inserted. Furthermore, the sequence of edit operations needs to include a node relabeling operation to accommodate the pair of mapped nodes with mismatched labels (Figure 6.3(b)).

Let us define the cost of the mapping M as the sum of all the addition, deletion, and relabeling operations implied by it. In general, for any given mapping M between two trees T_1 and T_2, there exists a sequence, S, of edit operations with a cost equal to the cost of M. Furthermore, given any S, there exists a mapping M such that $\gamma(M) \leq \gamma(S)$ (the sequence may contain redundant operations). Consequently, the *tree edit distance* $\Delta_T(T_1, T_2)$ can be stated in terms of the mappings between the trees:

$$\Delta_T(T_1, T_2) = \min_{M \text{ from } T_1 \text{ to } T_2} \{\gamma(M)\}.$$

The pseudocode for the tree edit distance computation algorithm is presented in Figure 6.4. In this pseudocode, $l(a)$ denotes the leftmost leaf of the subtree under $t[a]$ (Figure 6.2(b)). Also, given $a \leq b$, $T[a..b]$ denotes the substructure defined by nodes $t[a]$ through $t[b]$ (Figure 6.2(c)). As was the case for string edit-distance computation, this algorithm leverages dynamic programming to eliminate redundant computations. Unlike the string case (where substructures of strings are also strings), however, in the case of trees, the subproblems may need to be described not as other smaller trees, but in terms of sets of trees (or forests). Figure 6.5 provides an overview of the overall process.

- Step (i) initializes the base case, $treedist(\emptyset, \emptyset) = 0$, that is, the edit distance between two empty trees.
- Steps (ii) and (iii) visit the nodes of the two trees in postorder (Figure 6.5(a)). For each visited node, these steps compute the appropriate *forestdist* value (edit

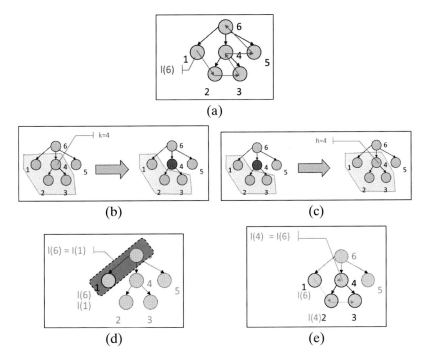

Figure 6.5. Building blocks of the tree edit distance computation process: (a) Post-order traversal of the data; (b) Deletion of a node; (c) Insertion of a node; (d) $l(k) = (i)$; and (e) $l(k) \neq (i)$ $(t[1] \ldots t[4]$ define a forest).

distances between the forest defined by the node and the other tree) using the *forestdist* values computed for the earlier nodes (Figures 6.5(b) and (c)).

■ Step (iv) is the main loop where *treedist* values are computed in a bottom-up fashion. This step involves a double loop that visits the nodes of the two trees in a postorder manner (Figure 6.5(a)). For each pair, $t_1[k]$ and $t_2[h]$, of nodes the *forestdist* and *treedist* values are computed using the values previously computed. There are two possible cases to consider:

– In the first case (step (iv)((a))1), $t_1[k]$ and $t_2[h]$ define complete subtrees (Figure 6.5(d)). Thus, along with a *forestdist* value, a *treedist* value can also be computed for this pair.

– In the other case (step (iv)((a))2), either $t_1[k]$ or $t_2[h]$ defines a forest (Figure 6.5(e)); thus only a *forestdist* value can be computed for this pair.

In both cases, three possible edit operations (corresponding to deletion, insertion, and relabeling of nodes, respectively) are considered, and the operation that results in the smallest edit cost is picked.

The running time of the preceding algorithm is $O(|T_1| \times |T_2| \times depth(T_1) \times depth(T_2))$ (i.e., $O(|T_1|^2 \times |T_2|^2)$ in the worst case), and it requires $O(|T_1| \times |T_2|)$ space. Klein [1998] presents an improvement that requires only $O(|T_1|^2 \times |T_2| \times log(T_2))$ run time.

Unordered Trees

The tree edit-distance problem is NP-hard for unordered trees [Shasha *et al.*, 1994]. More specifically the problem is MAX SNP-hard; that is, unless P = NP; there is no polynomial time approximation solution for the problem. On the other hand, if the number of leaves in T_2 is logarithmic in the size of the tree, then there is an algorithm for solving the problem in polynomial time [Zhang *et al.*, 1992].

6.2.2 Tree Alignment Distance

Because of its restricted nature, the *tree alignment distance* [Jiang *et al.*, 1995] has specialized algorithms that work more efficiently than the tree edit distance algorithms. The algorithm presented by Jiang *et al.* [1995] has $O(|T_1| \times |T_2| \times max\_degree(T_1) \times max\_degree(T_2))$ complexity for ordered trees. Thus, it is more efficient, especially for trees with low degrees.

Unlike the tree edit-distance problem, however, the alignment distance has efficient solutions even for unordered trees. For example, the algorithm presented by Jiang *et al.* [1995] can be modified to run in $O(|T_1| \times |T_2|)$ for unordered, degree-bounded trees. When the trees have arbitrary degree, then the unordered alignment is still NP-hard.

6.2.3 Tree Inclusion Distance

The special case of the problem where we want to decide whether there is an embedding of T_1 in T_2 (known as the *tree inclusion problem* [Kilpelainen and Mannila, 1995]) has a solution with $O(|T_1| \times |T_2|)$ time and space complexities [Kilpelainen and Mannila, 1995]. An alternative solution to the problem, with $O(num\_leaves(T_1) \times |T_2|)$ time and $O(num\_leaves(T_1) \times min\{max\_degree(T_2), num\_leaves(T_2)\})$ space complexities, may work more efficiently for certain types of trees [Chen, 1998]. The problem is NP-complete for unordered trees [Kilpelainen, 1992].

6.2.4 Other Special Cases

There are various other special cases of the ordered tree edit distance problem that often have relatively cheaper solutions.

Top-Down Distance

In the top-down edit distance problem [Nierman and Jagadish, 2002; Yang, 1991], the mapping M from T_1 to T_2 is constrained such that if $t_1[i_1]$ is mapped to $t_2[j_1]$, then the parents of $t_1[i_1]$ and $t_2[j_1]$ are also mapped to each other. In other words, insertions and deletions are not allowed for the parts of the trees that are mapped: any unmapped node (i.e., node insertion or deletion) causes the subtree rooted at this node to be removed from the mapping.

Because, when node insertions and deletions are eliminated, the tree mapping process does not need to consider forests, the top-down edit distance problem has an efficient $O(|T_1| \times |T_2|)$ solution (in the algorithm presented in Figure 6.6, the value of $\gamma(change(t_1[i], t_2[j]))$ is considered only once for each pair of tree nodes). The space complexity of the algorithm is $O(|T_1| + |T_2|)$.

Isolated-Subtree Distance

In the isolated-subtree distance problem [Tai, 1979], the mapping M from T_1 to T_2 is constrained such that if $t_1[i_1]$ is mapped to $t_2[j_1]$ and $t_1[i_2]$ is mapped to $t_2[j_2]$,

(i) Let m denote the number of children of $t_1[i]$;
(ii) Let n denote the number of children of $t_2[j]$;
(iii) For $u = 0$ to m
    (a) $M[u, 0] = 0$

(iv) For $v = 0$ to n
    (a) $M[0, v] = 0$

(v) For $u = 1$ to m
    (a) For $v = 1$ to n

$$1.\ M[u, v] = min \begin{cases} M[u, v - 1], \\ M[u - 1, v], \\ M[u - 1, v - 1] + topdowndist(t_1[i].child(u), t_2[j].child(v)) \end{cases}$$

(vi) $return(M[m, n] + \gamma(change(t_1[i], t_2[j])))$

Figure 6.6. Pseudocode for computing the top-down tree edit distance, $topdowndist(i, j)$, between T_1 and T_2; i and j indicate the roots of T_1 and T_2, respectively.

then the subtree rooted under $t_1[i_1]$ is to the left of $t_1[i_2]$ if and only if the subtree rooted under $t_2[j_1]$ is to the left of $t_2[j_2]$. In other words, isolated-subtree mappings map disjoint subtrees to disjoint subtrees. The isolated-subtree distance problem is known to have an $O(num\_leaves(T_1) \times |T_2|)$ time solution [Tai, 1979].

Note that an isolated-subtree mapping from T_1 to T_2 is also an alignment mapping from T_1 to T_2; moreover, any top-down mapping M is also an isolated-subtree mapping [Wang and Zhang, 2001].

Bottom-Up Distance

A bottom-up mapping is defined as an isolated-subtree mapping in which the children of the mapped nodes are also in the mapping [Valiente, 2001; Vieira *et al.*, 2009]. Consequently, the largest bottom-up mappings between a given pair of trees correspond to the largest common forest, consisting of complete subtrees between these two trees. Valiente [2001] shows that the bottom-up distance between two rooted trees, T_1 and T_2, can be computed very efficiently, in linear time $O(|T_1| + |T_2|)$, for both ordered and unordered trees. Note that the bottom-up distance coincides with the top-down distance only for trees that are isomoporhic [Valiente, 2001].

6.2.5 Tree Filtering

As described earlier, unordered tree matching is an NP-complete problem. Thus, for applications where the order between siblings is not relevant, alternative matching schemes that can handle unordered trees efficiently are needed. One approach to the problem of unordered tree matching is to use specialized versions of the graph-matching heuristics, such as GraphGrep, graph histograms, graph probing, and graph alignment techniques. For example, Candan *et al.* [2007] present a tree alignment technique based on known mappings between nodes of two trees, similar to the one we discussed in Section 6.1.3. In this section, we do not revisit these techniques. Instead, we introduce other techniques that approach the tree-matching problem from different angles.

6.2.5.1 Cousin Set Similarity

Shasha *et al.* [2009] propose to compare unordered trees using a *cousin set similarity* metric. According to this approach *sibling* is defined as a cousin of degree 0, a *nephew* is a cousin of degree 0.5, a *first cousin* is a cousin of degree 1, and so on. Given two trees and the corresponding sets of pairs of cousins up to a fixed degree, the cousin distance metric is computed by comparing the two sets.

6.2.5.2 Path Set Similarity

Rafiei *et al.* [2006] describe the structure of a tree as a set of paths. In particular, it focuses on *root paths*, each of which starts from the root and ends at a leaf. The *path set* of the tree is then defined as the union of its root paths and all subpaths of the root paths. Each path in the path set has an associated frequency, which reports how often the path occurs in the given tree. Two trees are said to be similar if a large fraction of the paths in their path sets are the same. Given a tree with n root paths of maximum length l, there are $\frac{nl(l+1)}{2}$ subpaths in the path set and thus the comparison algorithm runs in $O(nl^2)$.

6.2.5.3 Time Series Encoding

Flesca *et al.* [2005] propose to leverage an alternative encoding of the ordered trees to support comparisons. Each node label, $t \in \Sigma$, in the label alphabet is mapped into a real number, $\phi(t)$, and the nodes of the given tree, T, are considered in a preorder sequence. The resulting sequence of tags of the nodes is then encoded as a series of numbers. Alternative encodings include

$$enq_{value}(T) = \phi(t_1), \phi(t_2), \dots, \phi(t_n)$$

and

$$enc_{prefix\_sum}(T) = \phi(t_1), \phi(t_1) + \phi(t_2), \dots, \sum_{k \leq n} \phi(t_k).$$

Given such an encoding, the distance between the two given trees, T_1 and T_2, is computed as the difference between the discrete Fourier transforms (DFTs) of the corresponding encodings:

$$\Delta(T_1, T_2) = \Delta_{Euclidean}(DFT(enc(T_1)), DFT(enc(T_2))).$$

6.2.5.4 String Encodings

An alternative to time-series encoding of the trees is to encode a labeled tree in the form of a string (i.e., symbol sequence), which can then be used for computing similarities using string comparison algorithms, such as string edit distance (Section 3.2.2), the compression-based sequence comparison scheme introduced in Section 5.5.5, or the Ziv-Merhav cross-parsing [Ziv and Merhav, 1993] algorithm, introduced in Section 5.5.6.

There are many sequence-based encodings of ordered trees. Simplest of these are based on preorder, postorder and in-order traversals of the trees. A common shortcoming of these, on the other hand, is that they are not one-to-one. In particular, the same sequence of labels can correspond to many different trees. Thus, the following encodings are more effective when used in matching algorithms.

Prüfer Encoding

Prüfer [1918] proposed a technique for creating a sequence from a given tree, such that there are no other trees that can lead to the same sequence. Let us be given a tree T of n nodes, where the nodes are labeled with symbols from 1 to n. A Prüfer sequence is constructed by deleting leaves one at a time, always picking the node with the smallest label, and recording the label of the parent of the deleted node. The process is continued until only two nodes are left. Thus, given a tree with n nodes, we obtain a sequence of length $n - 2$ consisting of the labels of the parents of the deleted nodes. Prüfer showed that the original tree T can be reconstructed from this sequence.

Given an ordered tree T where the labels come from the alphabet Σ, a similar process can be used to create a corresponding sequence. In this case, the postorder traversal value of each tree node is associated to that node as a metalabel. The Prüfer node elimination process is followed on these metalabels, but both the actual node labels (from Σ) and the metalabels are used in creating the sequence [Rao and Moon, 2004]; that is, each symbol in the sequence is a pair in $\Sigma \times \{1, \ldots, n\}$.

Note that although this process ensures that a unique sequence is constructed for each labeled tree, the reverse is not true: the sequence contains only non-leaf node labels and, thus, labels of the leaf nodes cannot be recovered from the corresponding sequence. Leaves can be accounted for by separately storing label and postorder number of every leaf node. Alternatively, the Prüfer sequence can be constructed by using as symbols quadruples in $\Sigma \times \{1, \ldots, n\} \times \Sigma \times \{1, \ldots, n\}$, which record information about each deleted node along with the corresponding parent.

Other Encodings

Helmer [2007] proposed to leverage the compression-based sequence comparison scheme introduced in Section 5.5.5 to compute the distance between two ordered trees. More specifically, Helmer [2007] converts each ordered tree into a text document using one of four different mechanisms:

- In the first approach, given an input tree, the labels of the nodes are concatenated in a postorder traversal of the tree.
- In the second approach, parent labels are appended to the node labels during the traversal.
- In the third approach, for each node, the entire path from the root to this node is prepended.
- In the fourth approach, all children of a node are output as one block and thereby all siblings occur next to each other.

The resulting documents are then compressed using Ziv-Lempel encoding [Ziv and Lempel, 1977], and the normalized compression distance between the given trees is computed and used as the tree distance. Alternatively, the Ziv-Merhav cross-parsing [Ziv and Merhav, 1993] algorithm introduced in Section 5.5.6 can also be used to compare the resulting documents.

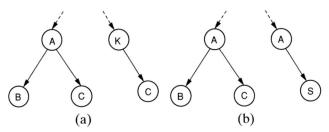

Figure 6.7. (a) Ancestor-supplied context and (b) descendant-supplied context for node differentiation.

6.2.5.5 Propagation Vector-Based Tree Comparison

The *propagation vectors for trees* (PVT) approach [Cherukuri and Candan, 2008] relies on a label propagation process for obtaining tree summaries. It primarily leverages the following observations:

- A node in a given hierarchy clusters all its descendant nodes and acts as a *context* for the descendant nodes (Figure 6.7(a)).
- Similarly, the set of descendants of a given node may also act as a context for the node (Figure 6.7(b)), differentiating the node from others that are similarly labeled.

Consequently, one way to differentiate nodes from each other is to infer the contexts imposed on them by their neighbors, ancestors, and descendants in the given hierarchy, enrich (or annotate) the nodes using vectors representing these contexts, and compare these context vectors along with the label of the node (Figure 6.8).

Mapping a tree node into a vector (representing the node's relationship to all the other nodes in the tree) requires a way to quantify the structural relationship between the given node and the others in the tree. Rada *et al.* [1989], for example, propose that the distance between two nodes can be defined as the number of edges on the path between two nodes in the tree. This approach, however, ignores various structural properties, including variations of the local densities in the tree. To overcome this shortcoming, R. Richardson and Smeaton [1995] associate weights to the edges in the tree: the edge weight is affected both by its depth in the tree and by the local density in the tree. To capture the effect of the depth, Wu and Palmer [1994] estimate the distance between two nodes, c_1 and c_2, in a tree by counting the

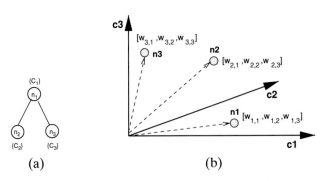

Figure 6.8. Mapping of the nodes of a tree onto a multidimensional space: (a) A sample tree, (b) Vector space defined by the node labels.

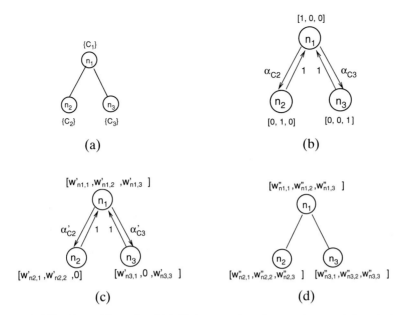

Figure 6.9. (a) The input hierarchy, (b) initial concept vectors and propagation degrees (α), (c) concept vectors and propagation degrees after the first iteration, and (d) status after the second iteration.

number of edges between them, and normalizing this value using the number of edges from the root of the tree to the closest common ancestor of c_1 and c_2.

CP/CV [Kim and Candan, 2006] was originally developed to measure the semantic similarities between terms/concepts in a given taxonomy (concept tree). Given a user-supplied concept tree, $C = \mathcal{H}(N, E)$ with c concepts, it maps each node into a vector in the concept space with c dimensions. These concept vectors are constructed by *propagating* concepts along the concept tree (Figure 6.9). How far and how much concepts are propagated are decided based on the shape of the tree and the structural relationships between the tree nodes. Unlike the original use of CP/CV (which is to compare the concept nodes in a single taxonomy with each other), PVT uses the vectors associated to the nodes of *two* trees to compare the two trees themselves. This difference between the two usages presents a difficulty: whereas the vectors corresponding to the nodes of a single tree all have the same dimensions (i.e., they are all in the same vector space), this is not necessarily the case for vectors corresponding to nodes from different trees. PVT handles the mismatch between the dimensions of the vector spaces corresponding to two different trees being compared by mapping them onto a larger space containing all the dimensions of the given two spaces. A second difficulty that arises when comparing trees is that, unlike a taxonomy where each concept is unique, in trees, multiple tree nodes may have identical labels. To account for this, PVT combines the weights of all nodes with the same label under a single combined weight: let S be a set of tree nodes with the same label; the combined weight, w_S, is computed as $w_S = \sqrt{\sum_{n_i \in S} w_{n_i}^2}$. Note that after the collapse of the dimensions corresponding to the identically labeled nodes in S, the magnitude of the new vector remains the same as that of the original vector. Thus the original vector is transformed from the space of tree nodes to the space of node labels, but keeping its energy (or the distance from the origin, $\mathcal{O}$) the same.

In order to compare two trees using the sets of vectors corresponding to their nodes, one needs to decide which vectors from one tree will be compared to which vectors from the other. In order to reduce the complexity of the process, PVT relies on the special position of the root node in the trees. Because the vector corresponding to the root node represents the context provided to it through all its descendants (i.e., the entire tree), the vector representation for the root node could be considered as a structural summary for the entire tree. Note that, for a given tree, the PVT summary (i.e., the vector corresponding to the root node) consists of only the unique labels in the tree.

The PVT summary vectors, $\vec{v}_1$ and $\vec{v}_2$, of two trees can be compared using different similarity/difference measures: cosine similarity (measuring the angles between the vectors),

$$sim_{cosine}(\vec{v}_1, \vec{v}_2) = cos(\vec{v}_1, \vec{v}_2),$$

average KL divergence (which treats the vectors as probability distributions and measures the so-called relative entropy between them),

$$\frac{\Delta_{KL}(\vec{v}_1, \vec{v}_2) + \Delta_{KL}(\vec{v}_2, \vec{v}_1)}{2} = \frac{1}{2} \sum_{i=1}^{n} v_{1i} log \frac{v_{1i}}{v_{2i}} + v_{2i} log \frac{v_{2i}}{v_{1i}},$$

and intersection similarity (which considers to what degree $\vec{v}_1$ and $\vec{v}_2$ overlap along each dimension),

$$sim_{intersection}(\vec{v}_1, \vec{v}_2) = \frac{\sum_{i=1}^{n} min(v_{1i}, v_{2i})}{\sum_{i=1}^{n} max(v_{1i}, v_{2i})}$$

are candidates. Cherukuri and Candan [2008] showed that, in general, the KL-divergence measure performs best in helping cluster similar trees together.

6.3 LINK/STRUCTURE ANALYSIS

So far, in this chapter, we have concentrated on problems related to the management of graph- and tree-structure data objects. In particular, we have assumed that each data object has a graph or tree structure and that we need to find a way to compare these structures for querying and search. In many other applications of graph- and tree-structured data, however, the main challenge is not comparing two graphs/trees to each other, but to understand the structure of these graphs/trees to support efficient and effective access to their constituent nodes.

As we see in this section, similarly to principal component analysis (PCA, Section 4.2.6) and latent semantic indexing (LSI, Section 4.4.1.1), structural analysis of graphs also relies on eigenvector analysis. The major difference from PCA and LSI is that, instead of the object-feature or document-keyword matrices, for link analysis the adjacency matrices of the underlying graphs are used as input.

6.3.1 Web Search

As mentioned previously in Section 3.5.4, there are many applications requiring such structural analysis of graphs. Consider, for example, the World Wide Web, where the Web can be represented as a (very large) graph, $G(V, E)$, of pages (V) connected to each other through edges (E) representing the hyperlinks. Because each edge in the Web graph is essentially a piece of evidence that the author of the source page found the destination page to be relevant in some context, many systems and techniques have been proposed to utilize links between pages to determine the relative importances of the pages or degrees of page-to-page associations [Brin and Page, 1998; Candan and Li, 2000; Gibson *et al.*, 1998; Kleinberg, 1999; Li and Candan, 1999b; Page *et al.*, 1998].

Given a query q (often described as a set of keywords), web search involves identifying a subset of the nodes that relate to q. Although web search queries can be answered simply by treating each page as a separate document and indexing it using standard IR techniques, such as inverted indexes, early web search systems that relied on this approach failed quickly. The reason for this is that web search queries are often underspecified (users provide only up to two or three keywords), and the Web is very large. Consequently, these systems could not filter out the not-so-relevant pages from important pages and burdened users with the task of sifting through a potentially large number of matches to find the few that are most useful to them.

6.3.1.1 Hubs and Authorities

An edge in the Web graph often indicates that the source page is directing or referring the user to the destination page; thus, each edge between two pages can be used to refer that these two documents are related to each other. *Cocitation* relationship, where two edges point to the same destination, and *social filtering*, where two pages are linked by a common page, indicate topical relationships between sources and destinations, respectively. More generally, an $m : n$ bipartite core of the Web graph consists of two disjoint sets, V_i and V_j, of vertices such that there is an edge from each vertex in V_i to each vertex in V_j, $|V_i| = m$, and $|V_j| = n$. Such bipartite cores indicate close relationships between groups of pages. We discuss properties of bipartite cores of graphs in Section 6.3.5.

One of the earlier link-analysis algorithms, HITS [Gibson *et al.*, 1998; Kleinberg, 1999], recognized two properties of web pages that can be useful in the context of web search:

■ *Hubness:* A hub is essentially a web page that can be used as a *source* from which one can locate many good web pages on a given topic.
■ *Authoritativeness:* An authority, on the other hand, is simply a web page that contains good content on a topic.

A web page can be a good hub, a good authority, or neither. Given a web search query, the HITS algorithm tries to locate good authorities related to the query to help prevent poor pages from being returned as results to the user. HITS achieves this by further recognizing that

■ a good hub must be pointing to a lot of good authorities, and
■ a good authority must be pointed to by a lot of good hubs.

This observation leads to an algorithm that leverages mutual reinforcement between hubs and authorities in the Web. In particular, given a keyword query, q,

    (i) HITS first uses standard keyword search to identify a set of candidate web pages relevant for the query.

(ii) It then creates a web graph, $G_q(V_q, E_q)$ consisting of these core pages as well as other pages that link and are linked by this core set.

(iii) Next, in order to measure the degrees of hubness and authoritativeness of the pages on the Web, HITS associates a hubness score, $h(p)$, and an authority score, $a(p)$, to each page, p. Note that, based on the earlier observation that hubs and authorities are mutually enforcing, HITS mathematically relates these two scores as follows: given a page, $p \in V_q$, let $in(p) \subseteq V_q$ denote the pages that link to p and $out(p) \subseteq V_q$ denote the set of pages that are linked by p; then we have

$$\forall p_i \in V_q \left(a(p_i) = \sum_{p_j \in in(p_i)} h(p_j) \right) \quad \text{and} \quad \left(h(p_i) = \sum_{p_j \in out(p_i)} a(p_j) \right).$$

(iv) Finally, HITS solves these mathematical equations to identify hubs and authority scores of the pages in V_q and selects those pages with high authority scores to be presented to the user as answers to the query, q.

Bharat and Henzinger [1998] refer to this process as *topic distillation*.

One way to solve the foregoing set of equations is to rewrite them in matrix form. Let m denote the number of pages in v_q and E be an $m \times m$ adjacency matrix, where $E[i, j] = 1$ if there is an edge $\langle p_i, p_j \rangle \in E_q$ and $E[i, j] = 0$ otherwise. Let $\vec{h}$ be the vector of hub scores and $\vec{a}$ be the vector of authority scores. Then, we have

$$\vec{a} = E^T \vec{h} \quad \text{and} \quad \vec{h} = E\vec{a}.$$

Moreover, we can further state that

$$\vec{a} = E^T E\vec{a} \quad \text{and} \quad \vec{h} = EE^T \vec{h}.$$

In other words, $\vec{a}$ is the eigenvector of $E^T E$ with the eigenvalue 1, and $\vec{h}$ is the eigenvector of EE^T with the eigenvalue 1 (see Section 4.2.6 for eigenvectors and eigenvalues).

As discussed in Section 3.5.4, when the number of pages is small, it is relatively easy to solve for these eigenvectors. When the number of pages is large, however, approximations may need to be used. One solution, which is often effective in practice, is to assign random initial hub and authority scores to each page and iteratively apply the foregoing equations to compute new hub and authority scores (from the old ones). This iterative process is repeated until the scores converge (the differences between old and new values become sufficiently small). In order to prevent iterations from resulting in ever-increasing authority and hub scores, HITS maintains an invariant that ensures that, before each iteration, the scores of each type are normalized such that $\sum_{p \in V_q} h^2(p) = 1$ and $\sum_{p \in V_q} a^2(p) = 1$. If the process is repeated infinitely many times, the hub and authority scores will converge to the corresponding values in the hub and authority eigenvectors, respectively. In practice, however, about twenty iterations are sufficient for the largest scores in the eigenvectors to become stable [Gibson et al., 1998; Kleinberg, 1999].

Note that a potential problem with the direct application of the foregoing technique for web search is that, although the relevant web neighborhood (G_q) is identified using the query, q, the neighborhood also contains pages that are not necessarily relevant to the query, and it is possible that one of these pages will be identified as the highest authority in the neighborhood. This problem, where authoritative pages are returned as results even if they are not directly relevant to the query, is referred to as *topic drift*. Such topic drift can be avoided by considering the content of the pages in addition to the links in the definition of hubs and authorities:

$$\forall p_i \in V_q \left(a(p_i) = \sum_{p_j \in in(p_i)} w_{j,i} h(p_j) \right) \quad \text{and} \quad \left(h(p_i) = \sum_{p_j \in out(p_i)} w_{i,j} a(p_j) \right),$$

where $w_{i,j}$ is a weight associated to the edge between p_i and p_j (based on content analysis) within the context of the query q.

6.3.1.2 PageRank

A second problem with the preceding approach to web search is that, even for relatively small neighborhoods, the iterative approach to computing hub and authority scores in query time can be too costly for real-time applications.

In order to avoid query-time link analysis, the PageRank [Brin and Page, 1998; Page *et al.*, 1998] algorithm performs the link analysis as an offline process independently of the query. Thus, the entire web is analyzed and each web page is assigned a *pagerank* score denoting how important the page is based on structural evidence. At the query time, the keyword scores of the pages are combined with the pagerank scores to identify the best matches by content and structure.

The PageRank algorithm models the behavior of a random surfer. Let $G(V, E)$ be the graph representing the entire web at a given instance. The random surfer is assumed to navigate over this graph as follows:

- At page p with probability β the random surfer follows one of the available links:
  - If there is at least one outgoing hyperlink, then the surfer jumps from p to one of the pages linked by p with uniform probability.
  - If there is no outgoing hyperlink, then the random surfer jumps from p to a random page.
- Occasionally, with probability $1 - \beta$, the surfer decides to jump to a random web page.

Let the number of web pages be N (i.e., $|V| = N$). This random walk (see Section 3.5.4) over G can be represented with a transition matrix

$$T = \beta M + (1 - \beta) \left[\frac{1}{N} \right]_{N \times N},$$

where $\left[\frac{1}{N} \right]_{N \times N}$ is an N-by-N matrix where all entries are $\frac{1}{N}$ and M is an N-by-N matrix, where

$$M[i, j] = \begin{cases} \frac{1}{|out(p_i)|}, & \text{if there is an edge from } p_i \text{ to } p_j, \\ \frac{1}{N}, & \text{if } |out(p_i)| = 0, \\ 0, & \text{if } |out(p_i)| \neq 0 \text{ but there is no edge from } p_i \text{ to } p_j. \end{cases}$$

Given the transition matrix, T, the pagerank score of each page, p, is defined as the percentage of the time the random surfer spends on visiting p. As described in

Section 3.5.4, the components of the first eigenvector of T will give the portion of the time spent at each node after an infinite run; that is, (similarly to HITS) the components of this eigenvector can be used as the pagerank scores of the pages (denoting how important the page is based on link evidence).

6.3.1.3 Discovering Page Associations with Respect to a Given Set of Seed Pages

Let us assume that we are given a set, S, of (seed) pages and asked to create a summary of the Web graph with respect to the pages in S. In other words, we need to identify pages in the Web that are structurally critical with respect to S. Candan and Li [2000] observe that, given a set, S, of seed pages,

- a structurally critical page must be close to the pages in S, and
- it must also be highly connected to the pages in S.

A page with high overall connectivity (i.e., more incoming links and outgoing links) is more likely to be included in more paths. Consequently, such a page is more likely to be ranked higher according to the foregoing criteria. This is consistent with the principle of topic distillation discussed earlier. On the other hand, a page with a high connectivity but far away from the seed pages may be less significant for reasoning about the associations than a page with low connectivity but close to the seed pages. A page that satisfies both of the foregoing criteria (i.e., near seed URLs and with high connectivity) would be a critical page with respect to the seeds in S.

Based on the preceding observation, Candan and Li [2000] first calculate for each page a penalty that reflects the page's overall distance from the seed pages. Because a page with high penalty is less likely to be critical with respect to S, each outgoing link from page p is associated with a weight inversely proportional to the destination page's penalty score. By constraining the sum of all weights of the outgoing links from p to be equal to 1.0, Candan and Li [2000] create a random walk graph and show that the primary eigenvector of the transition matrix corresponding to this graph can be used to pick the structurally critical pages that can then be used to construct a map connecting the pages in S [Candan and Li, 2002].

6.3.2 Associative Retrieval and Spreading Activation

As we have seen, given a data collection modeled as a graph, understanding associations between the nodes of this graph can be highly useful in creating summaries of these graphs with respect to a given set of seed nodes. Researchers have also noticed that such associations can also be used to improve retrieval, especially when the features of the objects are not sufficient for purely feature-based (or content-based) retrieval [Huang *et al.*, 2004; Kim and Candan, 2006; Salton and Buckley, 1988a]. Intuitively, in these associative retrieval schemes, given a graph representation of the data (where the nodes represent objects and edges represent certain – transitive – relationships between these objects), first pairwise associations between the nodes in the graph are discovered; and then these discovered associations are used for sharing features among highly associated data nodes. Consequently, whereas originally the features of the nodes may be too sparse to support effective retrieval, after the feature propagation the nodes may be more effectively queried.

For example, in Section 6.2.5.5, we have seen a use of the feature-sharing approach in improving retrieval of tree-structured data: whereas originally the label of the root of the tree is not sufficient for similarity-based search, after label propagation in the tree using the CP/CV propagation technique [Kim and Candan, 2006], the root of the tree is sufficiently enriched in terms of labels to support efficient and effective tree-similarity search.

Most of the existing associative-retrieval techniques are based on the spreading activation theory of the semantic memory [Collins and Loftus, 1975], where the memory is modeled as a graph: when some of the nodes in the graph are activated (for example, as a result of an observation), spreading activation follows the links of the graph to iteratively activate other nodes that can be reached from these nodes. These activated nodes are *remembered* based on the initial observations.

Note that, when the iterative activation process is unconstrained, all nodes reachable from the initial nodes will eventually be activated. Different spreading activation algorithms regulate and constrain the amount of spreading in the graph in different ways. Kim and Candan [2006], for example, regulate the degree of propagation based on the depth and density of the nodes in a given hierarchy. Candan and Li [2000], which we discussed in Section 6.3.1.3, on the other hand, regulate the degree of activation based on distance from the seeds as well as the degree of connectivity of the Web pages. In addition, the spreading activation process is repeated until certain predetermined criteria are met. For example, because its goal is to inform all nodes in a given hierarchy of the content of all other nodes, in theory the CP/CV [Kim and Candan, 2006] algorithm continues the process until all nodes in the given hierarchy have had chance to affect all other nodes. In practice, however, the number of iterations required to achieve a stable distribution is relatively small. Most algorithms, thus, constrain the activation process in each step in such a way that only a small subset of the nodes in the graph are eventually activated.

Note that the algorithms previously mentioned [Candan and Li, 2000; Kim and Candan, 2006] leverage certain domain-specific properties of the application domains in which they are applied to improve the effectiveness of the spreading process. In the rest of this section, we discuss three more generic spreading activation techniques: (a) the constrained leaky capacitor model [Anderson, 1983b], (b) the branch-and-bound [Chen and Ng, 1995], and the Hopfield net approach [Chen and Ng, 1995].

6.3.2.1 Constrained Leaky Capacitor Model

Let $G(V, E)$ be a graph, and let S be the set of starting nodes. At the initialization step of the constrained leaky capacitor model for spreading activation [Anderson, 1983b], two vectors are created:

- A seed vector, $\vec{s}$, where each entry corresponds to a node in the graph G and all entries of the vector, except for those that correspond to the starting nodes are set to 0; those entries that are corresponding to the starting nodes in S are set to 1.
- An initial activation vector, $\vec{d}_0$, which captures the initial activation levels of all the nodes in G: since no node has been activated yet, all entries of the vector are initialized to 0.

The algorithm also creates an adjacency matrix, G, corresponding to the graph G and a corresponding activation control matrix, M, such that

$$M = (1 - \lambda)I + \alpha G.$$

Here, λ is the amount of decay of the activation of the nodes at each iteration, and α is the efficiency with which the activations are transmitted between neighboring nodes. Given M, at each iteration, the algorithm computes a new activation vector using a linear transformation:

$$\vec{d_t} = \vec{s} + M\vec{d}_{t-1}.$$

Often, only a fixed number of nodes with the highest activation levels keep their activation levels; activation levels of all others are set back to 0. The algorithm terminates after a fixed number of iterations or when the difference between $\vec{d_t}$ and $\vec{d}_{t-1}$ becomes sufficiently small. The threshold can be constant, or to speed up convergence, it can be further tightened with increasing iterations.

6.3.2.2 Hopfield Net Spreading Activation

Structurally, the Hopfield net based spreading activation algorithm [Chen and Ng, 1995] is very similar to the constrained leaky capacitor model just described. However, instead of a spreading strategy based on linear transformations, the Hopfield net uses sigmoid transformations. In this scheme, at the initialization step only one vector is created:

- An initial activation vector, $\vec{d_0}$, where only those entries that are corresponding to the starting nodes in S are set to 1 and all others are set to 0.

Once again, the algorithm creates an activation control matrix, M, where the entry $M[i, j]$ is the weight of the link connecting node v_i of the graph to node v_j. At each iteration, the activation levels are computed based on the neighbors' activation levels as follows:

$$\vec{d_t}[j] = f\left(\sum_{v_i \in V} M[i, j]\, \vec{d}_{t-1}[i]\right),$$

where $f()$ is the following nonlinear transformation function:

$$f(x) = \frac{1}{1 + e^{\frac{\theta_1 - x}{\theta_2}}}.$$

Here θ_1 and θ_2 are two control parameters that are often emprically set.

Once again, after each iteration, often only a fixed number of nodes with the highest activation levels keep their activation levels. Also, the algorithm terminates after a fixed number of iterations or when the difference between $\vec{d_t}$ and $\vec{d}_{t-1}$ becomes sufficiently small.

6.3.2.3 Branch-and-Bound Spreading Activation

The branch-and-bound algorithm [Chen and Ng, 1995] is essentially an alternative implementation of the matrix multiplication approach used by the constrained leaky capacitor model. In this case, instead of relying on repeated matrix multiplications which do not distinguish between highly activated and lowly activated nodes in computations, the activated nodes are placed into a priority queue based on their activation levels, and only the high-priority nodes are allowed to activate their neighbors. This way, most of the overall computation is focused on highly activated nodes that have high spreading impact. In this algorithm, first

- an activation vector, $\vec{d}_0$, where only those entries that are corresponding to the starting nodes in S are set to 1 and all others set to 0, is created; and
- then, each node $v_i \in V$ is inserted into a priority queue based on the corresponding activation level, $\vec{d}_0[i]$.

The algorithm also creates an activation control matrix, M.

At each iteration, the algorithm first sets $\vec{d}_t = \vec{d}_{t-1}$. Then, the algorithm picks a node, v_i, with the highest current activation level from the priority queue, and for each neighbor, v_j, of v_i, it computes a new activation level:

$$\vec{d}_t[j] = \vec{d}_{t-1}[j] + \mathsf{M}[i, j]\vec{d}_{t-1}[i].$$

All the nodes whose activation scores changed in the iteration are removed from the priority queue and are reinserted with their new weights.

In many implementations, the algorithm often terminated after a fixed number of iterations.

6.3.3 Collaborative Filtering

Another common use of link analysis is the *collaborative filtering* application [Brand, 2005; Goldberg *et al.*, 1992], where analysis of similarities between individuals' preferences is used for predicting whether a given user will prefer to see or purchase a given object or not. Although the collaborative filtering approach to recommendations dates from the early 1990s [Goldberg *et al.*, 1992], its use and impact greatly increased with the widespread use of online social networking systems and e-commerce applications, such as Amazon [Amazon] and Netflix [Netflix].

In collaborative filtering, we are given a bipartite graph, $G(V_u, V_o, E)$, where

- V_u is a set of individuals in the system.
- V_o is the set objects in the data collection.
- E is the set of edges between users in V_u and objects in V_o denoting past access/purchase actions or ratings provided by the users. In other words, the edge $\langle u_i, o_j \rangle \in E$ indicates that the user u_i declared his preference for object o_j through some action, such as purchasing the object o_j.

In addition, each user $u_i \in V_u$ may be associated with a vector $\vec{u}_i$ denoting any metadata (e.g., age, profession) known about the user u_i. Similarly, each object $o_j \in V_o$ may be associated with a vector $\vec{o}_j$ describing the content and metadata (e.g., title, genre, tags) of the object o_j.

Generating recommendations through collaborative filtering is essentially a classification problem (see Chapter 9 for classification algorithms): we are given a set of preference observations (the edges in E) and we are trying to associate a "preferred" or "not preferred" label or a rating to each of the remaining user-object pairs (i.e., $(V_u \times V_o) - E$). Relying on the assumption that similar users tend to like similar objects, collaborative filtering systems leverage the graph $G(V_u, V_o, E)$ and the available user and object vectors to discover unknown preference relationships among users and objects. Here, similarity of two users, u_i and u_k, may mean similarity of the metadata vectors, $\vec{u}_i$ and $\vec{u}_k$, as well as the similarity of their object preferences (captured by the overlap between the destinations, $out(u_i)$ and $out(u_k)$, of the outgoing edges from u_i and u_k in the graph). In a parallel manner, similarity of the objects, o_j and o_l, may be measured through the similarity of content/metadata vectors, $\vec{o}_j$ and $\vec{o}_l$, as well as the similarity of the sets of users accessing these objects (i.e., sources, $in(o_j)$ and $in(o_l)$, of incoming edges to o_j and o_l).

We discuss the collaborative filtering–based recommendation techniques in more detail in Section 12.8.

6.3.4 Social Networking

Online social networking gained recent popularity with the emergence of web-based applications, such as Facebook [Facebook] and LinkedIn [LinkedIn], that help bring together individuals with similar backgrounds and interests. These social networking applications are empowering for their users, not only because they can help users maintain their real-world connections in a convenient form online, but also because social networks can be used to discover new, previously unknown individuals with shared interests. The knowledge of individuals with common interests (declared explicitly by the users themselves or discovered implicitly by the system through social network analysis) can also be used to improve collaborative feedback based recommendations: similarities between two individuals' preferences can be used for predicting whether an object liked by one will also be liked by the other or not. Moreover, if we can analyze the network to identify prominent or high-prestige users who tend to affect (or at least reflect) the preferences of a group of users, we may be able to fine-tune the recommendations systems to leverage knowledge about these individuals [Shardanand and Maes, 1995].

A social network is essentially a graph, $G(V, E)$, where V is a set of individuals in the social network and E is the set of social relationships (e.g., friends) between these individuals [Wasserman *et al.*, 1994].

Because their creation processes are often subject to the *preferential-attachment* effect, where those users with already large numbers of relationships are more likely to acquire new ones, most social networks are inherently scale-free (Section 6.3.5). This essentially means that, as in the case of the Web graphs, social network graphs can be analyzed for key individuals (who act as hubs or authorities) in a given context. More generally though, social networks can also be analyzed for various social properties of the individuals or groups of individuals, such as *prestige* and *prominence* (often measured using the authority scores obtained through eigen analysis), *betweenness* (whether deleting the node or the group of nodes would disconnect social network graph), and centrality/cohesion (quantified using the clustering coefficient that measures how close to a clique a given node and its neighbors are; see Section 6.3.5). The social network graph can also be analyzed for locating strongly connected subgroups and cliques of individuals (Section 8.2). As in the case of web graphs, given a group of (seed) individuals in this network, one can also search for other individuals that might be structurally related to this group. An extreme version of this analysis is searching for individuals that are structurally equivalent to each other; this is especially useful in finding very similar (or sometimes duplicate) individuals in the network [Herschel and Naumann, 2008; Yin *et al.*, 2006, 2007].

6.3.5 The Power Law and Other Laws That Govern Graphs

In the rest of this section, we see that there are certain laws and patterns that seem to govern the shape of graphs in different domains. Understanding of these patterns is important, because these can be used not only for searching for similar graphs, but also for reducing the sizes of large graphs for more efficient processing and indexing. Graph data reduction approaches exploit inherent redundancies in the data to find reduction strategies that preserve statistical and structural properties of the graphs [Candan and Li, 2002; Leskoec *et al.*, 2008; Leskovec and Faloutsos, 2006]. Common approaches involve either node or edge sampling on the graph or graph partitioning and clustering (see Section 8.2) to develop summary views.

6.3.5.1 Power Law and the Scale-Free Networks

In the late 1990s, with the increasing research on the analysis of the Web and the Internet, several researchers [Barabasi and Albert, 1999; Kleinberg, 1999] observed that the graphs underlying these network have a special structure, where some *hub* nodes have significantly more connections than the others. The degrees of the vertices in these graphs, termed *scale-free* or *Barabási-Albert* networks, obey a power law distribution, where the number, *count(d)*, of nodes with degree d is $O(d^{-\alpha})$, for some positive α. Consequently, the resulting frequency histograms tend to be heavy-tailed, where there are many vertices with small degrees and a few vertices with a lot of connections. In other words, the graph degree frequency distributions in these graphs show the Zipfian-like behaviors we have seen for keyword distributions in document collections (Sections 3.5 and 4.2) and the inverse exponential distribution we have seen for the number of objects within a given distance from a point in a high-dimensional feature space (Sections 4.1, 4.2.5, and 10.4.1). The term "scale-free" implies that these graphs show fractal-like structures, where low-degree nodes are connected to hubs to form a dense graphs, which are then connected to other higher-degree hubs to form bigger graphs, and so on. The scale-free structure emerges due to *preferential-attachment* effect, where vertices with high degrees/relationships with others are more likely to acquire new relationships. As we have seen in Sections 6.3.1 through 6.3.4, this strongly impacts the analysis of web and social-network structures for indexing and query processing.

6.3.5.2 Triangle and Bipartite Core Laws

Degrees of the vertices are not the only key characteristic that can be leveraged in characterizing a graph. The number and distribution of triangles (for example, highlighting friends of friends who are also friends in social networks [Faloutsos and Tong, 2009]) can also help distinguish or cluster graphs.

Tsourakakis [2008] showed that for many real-world graphs, including social networks, coauthorship networks for scientific publications, blog networks, and Web and Internet graphs, the distribution of the number of triangles the nodes of the graphs participate in, obeys the power law. Moreover, the number of triangles also obeys the power law with respect to the degree of the nodes (i.e., the number of triangles increases exponentially with the degree of the vertices). Tsourakakis [2008] also showed that the number of triangles in a graph is exactly one sixth of the sum of cubes of eigenvalues and proposes a triangle counting algorithm based on eigen analysis of graphs.

Not all social communities are undirected. Many others, such as citation networks, are directed. In these cases, the number and distribution of bipartite cores can also be used to characterize (index and compare) graphs. An $m : n$ bipartite core consists of two disjoint sets, V_i and V_j, of vertices such that there is an edge from each vertex in V_i to each vertex in V_j, $|V_i| = m$, and $|V_j| = n$. Similar to the triangles in (undirected) social networks, bipartite cores can indicate a close relationship between groups of individuals (for example members of V_i being fans of members of V_j). Kumar *et al.* [1999] showed that in many networks, bipartite cores also show power-law distributions. In particular, the number of $m : n$ bipartite cores is $O(m^{-\alpha} \times 10^{\beta - \gamma n})$, for some positive α, β, and γ.

6.3.5.3 Diameter, Shortest Paths, Clustering Coefficients, and the Small-Worlds Law

Other properties of graphs that one can use for comparing one to another include diameter, distribution of shortest-path lengths, and cluster coefficients. The small-worlds law observes that in many real-world graphs, the diameter of the graph (i.e., the largest distance between any pair of vertices) is small [Erdos and Renyi, 1959]. Moreover, many of these graphs also have large clustering coefficients in addition to small average shortest path lengths [Watts and Strogatz, 1998]. It has also been observed that in most real-world graphs (such as social networks) the networks are becoming denser over time and the graph diameter is shrinking as the graph grows [Leskoec *et al.*, 2008; Leskovec *et al.*, 2007]. The clustering coefficient of a vertex measures how close to a clique the vertex and its neighbors are. In directed graphs, the clustering coefficient of vertex, v_i, is defined as $\frac{|E_i|}{degree(v_i)(degree(v_i) - 1)}$, where E_i is the number of edges in the neighborhood of v_i (i.e., among v_i's immediately connected neighbors); in undirected graphs, the coefficient is defined as $\frac{2|E_i|}{degree(v_i)(degree(v_i) - 1)}$.

6.3.6 Proximity Search Queries in Graphs

As mentioned earlier, in many multimedia applications, the underlying data can be seen as a graph, often enriched with weights, associated with the nodes and edges of the graph. These weights denote application specific desirability/penalty assessments, such as *popularity*, *quality*, or *access cost*.

Let us be given a graph structured data, $G(V, E)$, where V is the set of atomic data objects and E is the links connecting these. Given a set of features, let $\pi : V \to 2^F$ denote the node-to-feature mapping. Also, let $\delta : E \to \mathbb{R}$ be a function that associates cost or distance to each edge of the graph. Given a set of features, $Q = \{f_1, \ldots, f_n\}$, each answer to the corresponding *proximity query* is a set, $\{v_1, \ldots, v_m\} \subseteq V$ of nodes that covers all the features in the query [Li *et al.*, 2001a]:

$$\pi(v_1) \cup \ldots \cup \pi(v_m) \supseteq Q.$$

For example, if the graph G corresponds to the Web and Q is a set of keywords, an answer to this proximity query would be a set of web pages that collectively covers

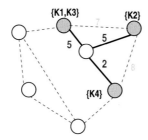

Figure 6.10. A graph fragment and a minimal-cost answer to the proximity query $Q = \{K_1, K_2, K_3, K_4\}$, with cost 12.

all the keywords in the query. A *minimal answer* to the proximity query, Q, is a set of pages, V_Q, such that no proper subset of V_Q is also an answer to Q. Let $\mathcal{V}_Q$ be the set of all minimal answers to Q and V_Q be a minimal answer in $\mathcal{V}_Q$. The cost, $\delta(V_Q)$ of this answer to Q is the sum of the edge costs of the tree with minimal cost in G that connects all the nodes in V_Q. Figure 6.10 shows an example: in the given graph fragment, there are at least two ways to connect all three vertices that make up the answer to the query. One of these ways is shown with solid edges; the sum of the corresponding edge costs is 12. Another possible way to connect all three nodes would be to use the dashed edges with costs 7 and 8. Note that if we were to use this second option, the total edge costs would be 15; that is, greater than 12, which we can achieve using the first option. Consequently, the cost of the answer is 12, not 15.

Li *et al.* [2001a] called the answers to such proximity queries on graphs *information units* and showed that the problem of finding minimum-cost information units (i.e., the minimum weighted connected subtree, T, of the given graph, G, such that T includes the minimum cost answer to the proximity query Q) can be formulated in the form of a *group Steiner tree* problem, which is known to be NP-hard [Reich and Widmayer, 1991]. Thus, the proximity search problem does not have known polynomial time solutions except for certain special cases, such as when vertex degrees are bounded by 2 [Ihler, 1991] or the number of groups is less than or equal to 2 (in which case the problem can be posed as a shortest path problem). However, there are a multitude of polynomial time approximation algorithms that can produce solutions with bounded errors [Garg *et al.*, 1998]. In addition, there are also various heuristics proposed for the group Steiner tree problem. Some of these heuristics also provide performance guarantees, but these guarantees are not as tight. Such heuristics include the minimum spanning tree heuristic [Reich and Widmayer, 1991], shortest path heuristic [Reich and Widmayer, 1991], and shortest path with origin heuristic [Ihler, 1991]. However, because users are usually interested in top-k best only, proximity query processing algorithms that have practical use, such as RIU [Li *et al.*, 2001a], BANKS-I [Bhalotia *et al.*, 2002], BANKS-II [Kacholia *et al.*, 2005], and DPBF [Ding *et al.*, 2007], rely on efficient heuristics and approximations for progressively identifying the small (not necessarily smallest) k trees covering the given features.

6.4 SUMMARY

Graph- and tree-structured data are becoming more ubiquitous as more and more applications rely on the higher-level (spatial, temporal, hierarchical) structures of the media as opposed to lower level features, such as colors and textures. Analysis and understanding of graphs is critical because most large-scale data, such as collections of media objects in a multimedia database or even user communities, can be represented as graphs (in the former case, based on the object similarities and in the second case, based on explicit relationships or implicit similarities between individual users). In Chapter 8, we discuss how the structure of graphs can be used for clustering and/or partitioning data for more efficient and effective search. Later, in Chapter 12, we discuss collaborative filtering, one of the applications of social graph analysis, in greater detail.

7

Indexing, Search, and Retrieval of Vectors

As we have seen in the previous chapters, it is common to map the relevant features of the objects in a database onto the dimensions of a vector space and perform nearest neighbor or range search queries in this space (Figure 7.1). The nearest neighbor query returns a predetermined number of database objects that are *closest* to the query object in the feature space. The range query, on the other hand, identifies and returns those objects whose distance from the query object is less than a provided threshold.

A naive way of executing these queries is to have a lookup file containing the vector representations of all the objects in the database and scan this file for the required matches, pruning those objects that do not satisfy the search condition. Although this approach might be feasible for small databases where all objects fit into the main memory, for large databases, a full scan of the database quickly becomes infeasible. Instead, multimedia database systems use specialized indexing techniques to help speed up search by pruning the irrelevant portions of the space and focusing on the parts that are likely to satisfy the search predicate (Figure 7.2).

Index structures that support range or nearest neighbor searches in general lay the data out on disk in sorted order (Figure 7.3(a)). Given a pointer to a data element on disk, this enables constraining further reads on the disk to only those disk pages that are in immediate neighborhood of this data element (Figure 7.3(b)). Search structures also leverage the sorted layout by dividing the space in a hierarchical manner and using this hierarchical organization to prune irrelevant portions of the data space. For example, consider the data layout in Figure 7.3(c) and consider the search range [6, 10]:

(i) The root of the hierarchical search structure divides the data space into two: those elements that are ≤ 14.8 and those that are > 14.8. Because the search range falls below 14.8, the portion of the data space > 14.8 (and the corresponding portions of the disk) are pruned.

(ii) In this example, the next element in the search structure divides the space into the data regions ≤ 4.2 and > 4.2 (and ≤ 14.8); because the search range

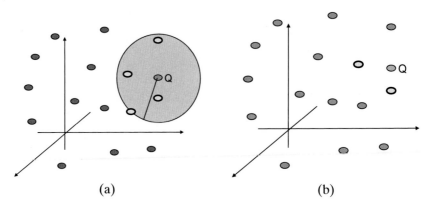

(a)   (b)

Figure 7.1. (a) δ-Range query, (b) Nearest-2 (or top-2) query on a vector space; matching objects are highlighted.

       falls above 4.2, the portion of the data space ≤ 4.2 (and the corresponding portions of the disk) are eliminated from the search.

(iii) The process continues by pruning the irrelevant portions of the space at each step, until the data elements corresponding to the search region are identified.

This basic idea of hierarchical space subdivision led to many efficient index structures, such as B-trees and B^+-trees [Bayer and McCreight, 2002], that are used today in all database management systems for efficient data access and query processing.

    Note that the underlying fundamental principle behind the space subdivision mechanism just described is a sorted representation of data. Such a sorted representation ensures the following:

- *Desideratum I:* Data objects closer to each other in the value space are also closer to each other on the disk.
- *Desideratum II:* Data objects further away from each other in the value space are also further away from each other on the storage space.

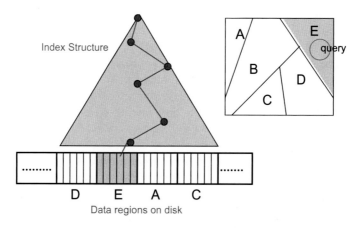

Figure 7.2. A multidimensional index structure helps prune the search space and limit the lookup process only to those regions of the space that are likely to contain a match. The parts of the disk that correspond to regions that are further away from the query are never accessed.

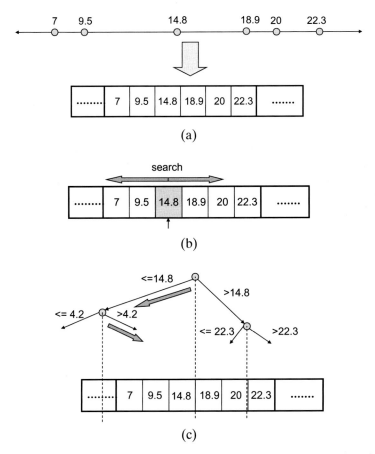

Figure 7.3. (a) Data are usually laid out on disk in a sorted order to enable (b,c) processing of range searches and nearest neighbor searches with few disk accesses.

The sorted representation of data, on the other hand, requires a totally ordered value space; that is, there must exist some function, $\prec$, which imposes a total order[1] on the data values. A particular challenge faced when dealing with multidimensional vector spaces, on the other hand, is that usually an intuitive total order does not exist. For example, given a two-dimensional space and three vectors $\vec{v}_a = \langle 1, 3 \rangle$, $\vec{v}_b = \langle 3, 1 \rangle$, and $\vec{v}_c = \langle 2.8, 2.8 \rangle$, even though there exist total orders for the individual dimensions (e.g., $1 \prec 2.8 \prec 3$), these total orders do not help us define a similar $\prec_{vec}$ order for the vectors, $\langle 1, 3 \rangle$, $\langle 3, 1 \rangle$, and $\langle 2.8, 2.8 \rangle$:

- If we consider the first dimension, then the order is

  $$\langle 1, 3 \rangle \prec_{vec} \langle 2.8, 2.8 \rangle \prec_{vec} \langle 3, 1 \rangle.$$

- If, on the other hand, we consider the second dimension, the order should be

  $$\langle 3, 1 \rangle \prec_{vec} \langle 2.8, 2.8 \rangle \prec_{vec} \langle 1, 3 \rangle.$$

---

[1] The binary relation $\prec$ is said to be a *total* order if *reflexivity*, *antisymmetry*, *transitivity*, and *comparability* properties hold.

Although one can pick these or any other arbitrary total order to layout the data on the disk, such orders will not necessarily satisfy the desiderata I or II listed here. For example, if we are given the query point $\vec{v}_c = \langle 0, 0 \rangle$ and asked to identify the closest two points based on Euclidean distance, the result should contain vectors, $\langle 1, 3 \rangle$ and $\langle 3, 1 \rangle$, which are both $\sqrt{10}$ unit away (as opposed to the vector $\langle 2.8, 2.8 \rangle$, which is $\sqrt{15.68}$ away from $\langle 0, 0 \rangle$). However, neither of the foregoing orders place the vectors, $\langle 1, 3 \rangle$ and $\langle 3, 1 \rangle$, together so that they can be picked without having to read $\langle 2.8, 2.8 \rangle$. Consequently, multidimensional index structures require some form of postprocessing to eliminate false hits (or false positives) that the given data layout on the disk implies.

In this chapter, we cover two main approaches to multidimensional data organization: *space-filling curves* and *multidimensional space subdivision techniques*. The first approach tries to impose a total order on the multidimensional data in such a way that the two desiderata listed earlier are satisfied as well as possible. The second approach, on the other hand, tries to impose some subdivision structure on the data such that, although it is not based on a total order, it still helps prune the data space during searches as effectively as possible.

7.1 SPACE-FILLING CURVES

As their names imply *space-filling curves* are curves that visit all possible points in a multidimensional space [Hilbert, 1891; Peano, 1890]. Although multidimensional curves can also be defined over real-valued vector spaces, for simplicity we will first consider an n-dimensional nonnegative integer-valued vector space $S = \mathbb{Z}^n_{\geq 0}$, where each dimension extends from 0 to $2^m - 1$ for some $m > 0$. Let π be a permutation of the dimensions of this space. A π-order traversal, $C_{\pi\_order} : \mathbb{Z}^n_{\geq 0} \to \mathbb{Z}_{\geq 0}$, of this space is defined as follows:

$$C_{\pi\_order}(\vec{v}) = \sum_{i=1}^{n} \vec{v}[\pi(i)] \times (2^m)^{n-i}.$$

Figure 7.4 shows two possible traversals,[2] row-order and column-order, of an 8×8 2D space. In column-order traversal, for example, $\pi(1)$ corresponds to the x dimension and $\pi(2)$ corresponds to the y dimension. Thus, the value that the $C_{columnorder}$ takes for the input point $\langle 1, 2 \rangle$ can be computed as

$$C_{columnorder}(\langle 1, 2 \rangle) = \left(1 \times 8^1\right) + \left(2 \times 8^0\right) = 10.$$

It is easy to show that $C_{columnorder}(\langle 1, 1 \rangle) = 9$ and $C_{columnorder}(\langle 1, 3 \rangle) = 11$. In other words, if the points in the space are neighbors along the y-axis, the column-order traversal is able to place them on the traversal in such a way that they will be neighbors to each other. On the other hand, the same cannot be said about points that are neighbors to each other along the other dimensions. For example, if we again consider the column-order traversal shown in Figure 7.4(b), we can see that while $C_{columnorder}(\langle 0, 1 \rangle) = 1$, $C_{columnorder}(\langle 1, 1 \rangle) = 9$; that is, for two points neighboring along the x-axis, desideratum I fails significantly. A quick study of Figure 7.4(b) shows that desideratum II also fails: while $C_{columnorder}(\langle 0, 7 \rangle) = 7$ and

---

[2] Note that these are not curves in the strict sense because of their noncontinuous nature.

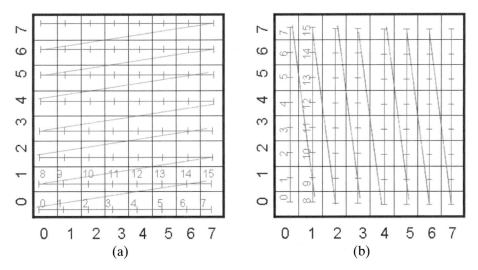

Figure 7.4. (a) Row- and (b) column-order traversals of 2D space. See color plates section.

$C_{columnorder}(\langle 1, 0\rangle) = 8$, these two points that are far from each other in the 2D space are mapped onto neighboring positions on the $C_{columnorder}$ traversal.

It is easy to see that the reason why both desiderata I and II fail are the long jumps that these two row-order and column-order filling traversals are making. Therefore, errors that space-filling traversals introduce can be reduced by reducing the length and frequency of the jumps that the traversal has to make to fill the space. Row-prime-order and Cantor-diagonal-order traversals[3] of the space are two such attempts (Figure 7.5(a) and (b), respectively). For example, whereas in the row-order traversal, $C_{roworder}(\langle 7, 0\rangle) = 7$ and $C_{roworder}(\langle 7, 1\rangle) = 15$, in the row-prime-order traversal, this problem has been solved: $C_{rowprimeorder}(\langle 7, 0\rangle) = 7$ and $C_{rowprimeorder}(\langle 7, 1\rangle) = 8$. On the other hand, the row-prime-order traversal is actually increasing the degree of error in other parts of the space. For example, whereas

$$|C_{roworder}(\langle 0, 0\rangle) - C_{roworder}(\langle 0, 1\rangle)| = |0 - 8| = 8,$$

for the same pair of points neighboring in the 2D space, the amount of error is larger in the row-prime-order traversal:

$$|C_{rowprimeorder}(\langle 0, 0\rangle) - C_{rowprimeorder}(\langle 0, 1\rangle)| = |0 - 15| = 15.$$

In general, given an n-dimensional nonnegative integer valued vector space $\mathcal{S} = \mathbb{Z}_{\geq 0}^n$, where each dimension extends from 0 to $2^m - 1$ for some $m > 0$, and a traversal (or a curve), C, filling this space, the error measure, $\varepsilon(\mathcal{S}, C)$ can be used for assessing the degree of deviation from desiderata I and II:

$$\varepsilon(\mathcal{S}, C) = \sum_{\vec{v}_i \in \mathcal{S}} \sum_{\vec{v}_j \in \mathcal{S}} \left| \Delta(\vec{v}_i, \vec{v}_j) - \left| C(\vec{v}_i) - C(\vec{v}_j) \right| \right|,$$

where Δ is the distance metric (e.g., Euclidean, Manhattan) in the original vector space $\mathcal{S}$. Intuitively, the smaller the deviation is, the better the curve

---

[3] Note that these traversals lead to curves in that they are continuous.

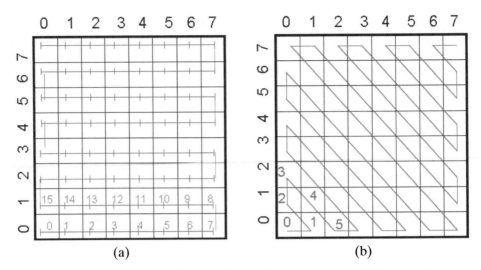

Figure 7.5. (a) Row-prime- and (b) Cantor-diagonal-order traversals of 2D space. See color plates section.

approximates the characteristics of the space it fills. Although any curve that fills the space approximates these characteristics to some degree, a special class of curves, called *fractals*, are known to be especially good in terms of capturing the characteristics of the space they fill.

7.1.1 Fractals

A fractal is a structure that shows self-similarity; that is, it is composed of similar structures at multiple scales. A fractal curve, thus, is a curve that looks similar when one zooms in or zooms out in the space that contains it. Fractals are commonly generated through *iterated function systems* that perform contraction mappings [Hutchinson, 1981]: Let $F \subset \mathbb{R}$ be the set of points in n-dimensional real valued space corresponding to a fractal. Then, there exists a set of mappings $\mathcal{F}$, where

- $f_i \in \mathcal{F}$ are contraction mappings; that is, $f_i : \mathbb{R}^n \to \mathbb{R}^n$ and

$$\exists_{0 < k < 1} \forall_{x,y \in \mathbb{R}^n} \quad \Delta(f_i(x), f_i(y)) \leq k \, \Delta(x, y)$$

such that F is the fixed set of $\mathcal{F}$:

$$F = \bigcup_{f_i \in \mathcal{F}} f_i(F).$$

Because of the recursive nature of the definition, many fractals are created by picking an initial fractal set, F_0, and iterating the contraction mappings until sufficient detail is obtained. (Figure 7.6 shows the iterative construction of the fractal known as the Hilbert curve; we discuss this curve in greater detail in the next subsection.)

How well a fractal covers the space can be quantified by a measure called the *Hausdorff dimension*. Traditionally, the dimension of a set is defined as the number of independent parameters needed to uniquely identify an element of the set. For example, a point has dimension 0, a line 1, a plane 2, and so on. Although the *Hausdorff dimension* generalizes this definition (e.g., Hausdorff dimension of a

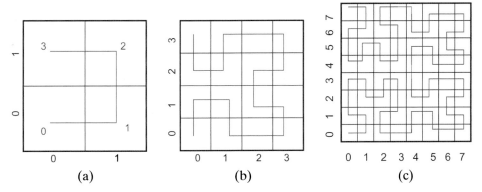

Figure 7.6. Hilbert curve: (a) First order, (b) Second order, (c) Third order. See color plates section.

plane is still 2), its definition also takes into account the metric used for defining the space. Let F be a fractal and let $N(F, \epsilon)$ be the number of balls of radius at most ϵ needed to cover F. The Hausdorff dimension of F is defined as

$$d = \frac{ln(N(F, \epsilon))}{ln(1/\epsilon)}.$$

In other words, the Hausdorff dimension of a fractal is the exponential rate, d, at which the number of balls needed to cover the fractal grows as the radius is reduced ($N(F, \epsilon) = \frac{1}{\epsilon}^d$). Fractals that are space-filling, such as the Hilbert curve and Z-order curve (both of which we discuss next), have the same Hausdorff dimension as the space they fill.

7.1.2 Hilbert Curve

The Hilbert curve is one of the first continuous fractal space-filling curves described. It was introduced in 1891 by Hilbert [1891] as a follow-up on Peano's first paper on space-filling curves in 1890 [Peano, 1890]. For that reason, this curve is also know as the Peano-Hilbert curve.

Figure 7.6 shows the first three orders of the Hilbert curve in 2D space. Figure 7.6(a) shows the base curve, which spans a space split into four quadrants. The numbers along the "U"-shaped curve give the corresponding mapping from the 2D coordinate space to the 1D space. Figure 7.6(b) shows the second-order curve in which each quadrant is further subdivided into four subquadrants to obtain a space with a total of 16 regions. During the process, the line segments in each quadrant are replaced with "U"-shaped curve segments in a way that preserves the adjacency property (i.e., avoiding discontinuity – which would require undesirable jumps). To obtain the third-order Hilbert curve, the same process is repeated once again: each cell is split into four cells and these cells are covered with "U"-shaped curve-segments in a way that ensures continuity of the curve.

Note that however many times the region is split into smaller cells, the resulting curve is everywhere continuous and nowhere differentiable; furthermore, it passes through every cell in the square once and only once. If this division process is continued to infinity, then every single point in the space will have a corresponding position on the curve; that is, all 2D vectors will be mapped onto a 1D value and vice

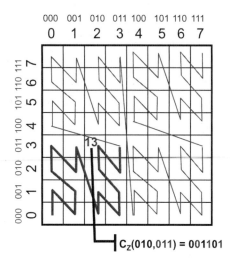

Figure 7.7. *Z*-order traversal of 2D space. See color plates section.

versa. Thus, since the Hilbert curve is filling the 2D space, its *Hausdorff dimension* is 2 (i.e., equal to the number of dimensions that it fills).

The Hilbert curve fills the space more effectively than the row-prime- and Cantor-diagonal-order traversals of the space. In particular, its continuity ensures that any two nearby points on the curve are also nearby in space. Furthermore, its fractal nature ensures that each "U" *clusters* four neighboring spatial regions, implying that points nearby in space also tend to be nearby on the curve. This means that the Hilbert curve is a good candidate to be used as a way to map multidimensional vector data to 1D for indexing.

However, to be useful in indexing and querying of multidimensional data, a space-filling curve has to be efficient to compute, in addition to filling the space effectively. A *generating state-diagram*–based algorithm, which leverages structural self-similarities when computing Hilbert mappings from multidimensional space to 1D space, is given by Faloutsos and Roseman [1989]. For spaces with a large number of dimensions, even this algorithm is impractical because it requires large state space representations in the memory. Other algorithms for computing Hilbert mappings back and forth between multidimensional and 1D spaces are given by Butz [1971] and Lawder [1999]. None of the existing algorithms, however, is practical for spaces with large numbers (tens or hundreds) of dimensions. Therefore, in practice, other space filling curves, such as the *Z*-order curve (or *Z*-curve), which have very efficient mapping implementations, are preferred over Hilbert curves.

7.1.3 Z-Order Curve

Because it allows for jumps from one part of the space to a distant part (i.e., because it is discontinuous), the *Z*-order (or Morton-order [Morton, 1966]) curve, shown in Figure 7.7, is not a curve in the strict sense. Nevertheless, like the Hilbert curve, it is a fractal; it covers the entire space and is composed of repeated applications of the same base pattern, a *Z* as opposed to a *U* in this case. Thus, despite the jumps that it makes in space, like the Hilbert curve, it clusters neighboring regions in the space and, except for the points where continuity breaks, points nearby in space are nearby on the curve.

Because of the existence of points of discontinuity, the Z-order curve provides a somewhat less effective mapping for indexing than the Hilbert mapping. Yet, because of the existence of extremely efficient implementations, Z-order mapping is usually the space-filling curve of choice when indexing vector spaces with large numbers of dimensions.

Let us consider an n-dimensional nonnegative integer-valued vector space $S = \mathbb{Z}_{\geq 0}^n$, where each dimension extends from 0 to $2^m - 1$ for some $m > 0$. Let $\vec{v} = \langle v[1], v[2], \ldots, v[n] \rangle$ be a point in this n-dimensional space. Given an integer a $(0 \leq a \leq 2^m - 1)$, let $a.\mathsf{base2}(k) \in \{0, 1\}$ denote the value of the kth least significant bit of the integer a. Then,

$$\forall_{1 \leq j \leq n} \forall_{1 \leq k \leq m} \ \mathcal{C}_{Z\_order}(\vec{v}).\mathsf{base2}((m - k)n + j) = v[j].\mathsf{base2}(k).$$

Because of the way it operates on the bit representation of the components of the vector provided as input, this mapping process is commonly referred to as the *bit-shuffling* algorithm. The bit-shuffling process is visualized in Figure 7.7: Given the input vector $\langle 2, 3 \rangle$, the corresponding Z-order value, 001101_2 $(= 13_{10})$, is obtained by shuffling the bits of the inputs, 010_2 $(= 2_{10})$ and 011_2 $(= 3_{10})$. Given an n-dimensional vector space with 2^m resolution along all its dimensions, the *bit-shuffling* algorithm takes only $O(nm)$ time; that is, it is linear in the number of dimensions and logarithmic in the resolution of the space.

7.1.4 Executing Range Queries Using Hilbert and Z-order Curves

As we have discussed, space-filling curves can be used for mapping points (or vectors) in multidimensional spaces onto a 1D curve to support indexing of multidimensional data using data structures designed for 1D data. However, because the point-to-point mapping does not satisfy desiderata I and II, mapping multidimensional query ranges onto a single 1D query range is generally not possible. Because a space-filling mapping can result in both over-estimations and under-estimations of distances, range searches may result in false hits and misses. Since in many applications misses are not acceptable (but false hits can be cleaned through a post-processing phase) one solution is to pick 1D search ranges that are sufficiently large to cover all the data points in the original search range. This, however, can be prohibitively expensive.

An alternative solution is to partition a given search range into smaller ranges such that each can be processed perfectly in the 1D space. Figure 7.8 illustrates this with an example: The query range shown in Figure 7.8(a) corresponds to two separate ranges on the Z-curve: $[48, 51]$ and $[56, 57]$. These ranges can be considered under their binary representations (*"don't care"* symbol "*" denoting both 0 and 1) as "$1100**$" and "$11100*$", respectively. When ranges are represented this way, each range corresponds to a prefix of a string of binary symbols and, thus, range queries can be processed using a prefix-based index structure, such as the tries introduced in Section 5.4.1.

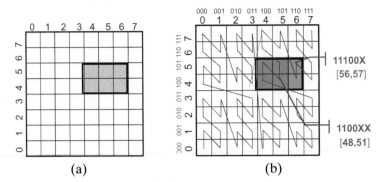

Figure 7.8. (a) A range query in the original space is partitioned into (b) two regions for Z-order curve based processing on a 1D index structure. See color plates section.

7.2 MULTIDIMENSIONAL INDEX STRUCTURES

As discussed previously, when the multidimensional data is mapped to a one-dimensional space for storage using traditional index structures, such as B+-trees, there is an inherent degree of information loss that may result in misses or false positives. An alternative to multidimensional to one-dimensional mapping is to keep the dimensions of the original data space intact and to apply subdivision process directly in this multidimensional space.

Multidimensional space subdivision based indexing, however, poses new challenges. In the case of 1D space subdivision, the main task is to find where the subdivision boundaries should be and how to store these boundaries in the form of a search data structure to support efficient retrieval. In the case of multidimensional spaces, on the other hand, there are new issues to consider and new questions to answer. For example, one critical parameter that has a significant impact on choosing the appropriate strategy for dividing a multidimensional space is the distance measure/metric underlying the multidimensional space. In other words, to be able to pick the right subdivision strategy, we need to know how the different dimensions affect the distance between a pair of objects in the space.

A multidimensional space introduces new degrees of freedom, which can be leveraged differently by different subdivision strategies. When we decide to place a boundary on a point on a one-dimensional space, the boundary simply splits the space into two (before and after the boundary). In a two-dimensional space, however, once we decide that a boundary (a line) is to be placed such that it passes over a given point in the space, we further have to decide what the slope of this line should be (Figure 7.9). This provides new opportunities for more informed subdivision, but it also increases the complexity of the decision-making process. In fact, as we see next, to ensure that the index creation and updating can be done efficiently, most index structures simply rely on rectilinear boundaries, where the boundaries are aligned with the dimensions of the space; this reduces the degrees of freedom, but consequently reduces the overall index management cost as well.

Space subdivision decision strategies can be categorized into two: *open* (Figure 7.10(a)) and *closed* (Figure 7.10(b,c,d)) approaches. In the former case, the space is divided into two open halves, whereas in the latter cases, one of the

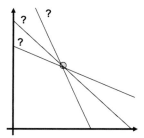

Figure 7.9. Multidimensional spaces introduce degrees of freedom in space sub-division.

subdivisions created by the boundary is a closed region of the space. As shown in Figures 7.10(b) through (d), there can be different ways to carve out closed subdivisions of the space, and we discuss the advantages and disadvantages of these schemes in the rest of this section.

7.2.1 Grid Files

As its name implies, a grid file is a data structure where the multidimensional space is divided into cells in such a way that the cells form a grid [Nievergelt *et al.*, 1981]. Commonly, each cell of the grid corresponds to a single disk page (i.e., the set of data records in a given cell can all be fetched from the disk using a single disk access). Consequently, the sizes of the grid cells must be such that the number of data points contained in each cell is not more than what a disk page can accommodate. Conversely, the cells of the grid should not be too small, because if there are many cells that contain only few data elements, then

- The pages of the disk are mostly empty and consequently the data structure wastes a lot of storage space
- Because there are many grid cells, the lookup directory for the grid as well as the cost of finding the relevant cell entry in the directory are large, and
- Because query ranges may cover or touch a lot of cells, all the corresponding disk pages need to be fetched from disk, increasing the search cost substantially.

Therefore, most grid files adaptively divide the space in such a way that the sizes of the grid cells are only large enough to cover as many data points as a data page can contain (Figure 7.11(a)). However, because boundaries in a grid cut the space from one end to the other, when the data distribution in the space is very skewed, this

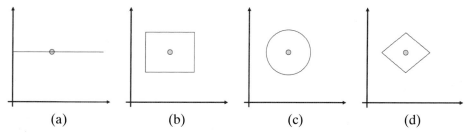

Figure 7.10. (a) An open subdivision strategy and (b,c,d) three closed subdivision strategies.

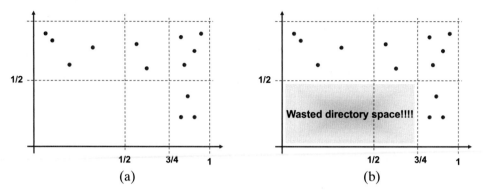

Figure 7.11. (a) A grid file where the cell boundaries are placed in such a way as to adapt to the data distribution (in this example, each cell contains at most four data points). (b) Nevertheless, when the data are not uniformy distributed, grid files can result in significant wastages of directory and disk space.

can result in significant imbalance in utilization of the disk pages (Figure 7.11(b)). More advanced grid file schemes, such as [Hinrichs, 1985], allow for the combination of adjacent, under-utilized cells in the form of supercells whose data points can all be stored together in a single disk page. This, however, requires complicated directory management schemes that may introduce large directory management overheads.

7.2.2 Quadtrees

While relying on a gridlike subdivision of space, *quadtrees* are better able to adapt to the distribution of the data [Finkel and Bentley, 1974]. The reason for this is that, instead of cutting through the entire space, the boundaries creating the partitions of the space have more *localized* extents. Thanks to this property, while subdividing a dense region of the space finely using a large number of partitions, the boundaries created in the process do not necessarily affect distant regions of the space that may have much thinner distributions of points.

7.2.2.1 Point Quadtrees
A *point quadtree* [Finkel and Bentley, 1974] is a hierarchical partitioning of the space where, in an m-dimensional space, each node in the tree is labeled with a *point* at which the *corresponding* region of the space is subdivided into 2^m smaller partitions. Consequently, in two-dimensional space, each node subdivides the space into $2^2 = 4$ partitions (or quadrants); in three-dimensional space, each node subdivides the space into $2^3 = 8$ partitions (or octants); and so on. The root node of the tree represents the whole region, is labeled with a point in the space, and has 2^m pointers corresponding to each one of the 2^m partitions this point implies (Figure 7.12(a)). Similarly, each of the descendants of the root node corresponds to a partition of the space and contains 2^m pointers representing the subpartitions the point corresponding to the node implies (Figure 7.12(b,c,d)).

Insertion
As shown in Figure 7.12, in the case of the simple *point quadtree*, each new data point is inserted into the tree by comparing it to the nodes of the tree starting from

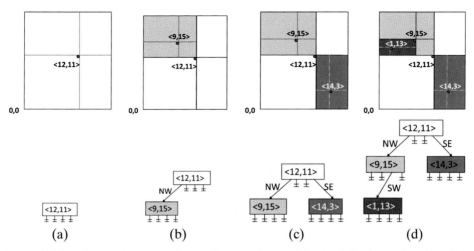

Figure 7.12. Point quadtree creation: points are inserted in the following order: $\langle 12, 11 \rangle$, $\langle 9, 15 \rangle$, $\langle 14, 3 \rangle$, $\langle 1, 13 \rangle$.

the root and following the appropriate pointers based on the relative position of the new data point with respect to the points labeling the tree nodes visited during the process. For example, in order to insert the data point $\langle 1, 13 \rangle$, the data point is first compared to the point $\langle 12, 11 \rangle$ corresponding to the root of the quadtree. Because the new point falls to the *northwest* of the root, the insertion process follows the pointer corresponding to the northwest direction. The data point $\langle 1, 13 \rangle$ is then compared against the next data point, $\langle 9, 15 \rangle$, found along the traversal. Because $\langle 1, 13 \rangle$ falls to the *southwest* of $\langle 9, 15 \rangle$, the insertion process follows the southwest pointer of this node. Because there is no child node along that direction (i.e., the pointer is empty), the insertion process creates a new node and attaches that node to the tree by pointing the southwest pointer of the node with label $\langle 9, 15 \rangle$ to the new data node. Note that, as shown in this example, the structure of the tree depends on the order in which the points are inserted into the tree. In fact, given n data points, the worst-case height of a point quadtree can be n (Figure 7.13). This implies that, in the worst case, insertions can take $O(n)$ time. The expected insertion time for the

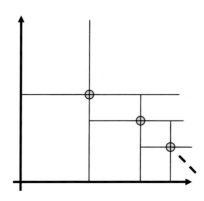

Figure 7.13. In the worst case, a point quadtree with n data points creates a tree of height n.

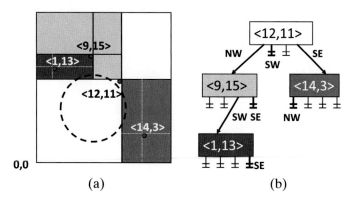

Figure 7.14. (a) A search range and (b) the pointers that are inspected during the search process.

nth node in a random point quadtree in an m-dimensional space is known to be $O(\frac{\log(n)}{m})$ [Devroye and Laforest, 1990].

Range Searches

Range searches on a point quadtree are performed similarly to the insertions: relevant pointers (i.e., pointers to the partitions of the space that intersect with the query range) are followed until no more relevant nodes are found. Unlike the case of insertions, however, a range search may need to follow more than one pointer from a given node. For example, in Figure 7.14, the search region touches *southwest*, *southeast*, and *northwest* quadrants of the root node. Thus all the corresponding pointers need to be examined. Because there is no child along the southwest pointer, the range search proceeds along southeast and northwest directions. Along the southeast direction, the search range touches only the *northwest* quadrant of $\langle 14, 3 \rangle$; thus only one pointer needs to be inspected. In the northwest quadrant of the root, however, the search region touches both southeast and southwest quadrants of $\langle 9, 15 \rangle$, and thus both of the corresponding pointers need to be inspected to look for matches. The southeast pointer of $\langle 9, 15 \rangle$ is empty; however, there is a child node, $\langle 1, 13 \rangle$, along the southwest direction. The search region touches only the *southeast* quadrant of $\langle 1, 13 \rangle$ and the corresponding pointer is empty. Thus, the range search stops as there are no more pointers to follow.

Nearest Neighbor Searches

A common strategy for performing nearest neighbor searches on point quadtrees is referred to as the *depth-first k-nearest neighbor algorithm*. The basic algorithm visits elements in the tree (in a depth-first manner), while continuously updating a candidate list consisting of k closest points seen so far. If we can determine that a partition corresponding to a node being visited cannot contain any points closer to the query point than the k candidates found so far, the node as well as all of its descendants (which are all contained in this partition) are pruned. We discuss nearest neighbor searches in Section 10.1 in more detail.

Deletions

Deletions in point quadtrees can be complex. Consider the example shown in Figure 7.15(a). Here, we want to delete the point corresponding to the root node;

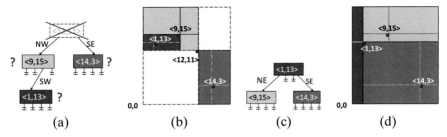

Figure 7.15. (a) When ⟨12, 11⟩ is deleted, (b) some regions of the space are not searchable by any of the remaining nodes; thus, (c,d) one of the remaining nodes must replace this deleted node, and the tree must be updated in such a way that the entire space is properly covered.

however, if we simply remove that point from the tree, portions of the original space are not indexable by any of the remaining nodes (Figure 7.15(b)). Thus, we need to restructure the point quadtree by selecting one of the remaining nodes to replace the deleted node. Such replacements may require significant restructurings of the tree. Consider Figure 7.15(c), where the node ⟨1, 13⟩ is picked to replace the deleted node. After this change, the node ⟨9, 15⟩ that used to be to the *northwest* of the old root has moved to the *northeast* of the new root.

Because such restructurings may be costly, the replacement node needs to be selected in a way that will minimize the likelihood that nodes will need to move from one side of the partition to the other. As illustrated in Figure 7.16(a), the nodes that are affected (i.e., need to move in the tree) are located in the region between the original partition boundaries and the new ones. Therefore, when choosing among the replacement candidates in each partition (as shown in Figure 7.16(b)), only the leaves in each partition are considered; this eliminates the need for cascaded replacement operations), the candidate node with the smallest affected area is picked for replacing the deleted node. In the example shown in Figure 7.16, the affected area due to node C is smaller than the affected area due to node B; thus (unless one of the nodes D and E provides a smaller affected area), the node C will replace deleted node A.

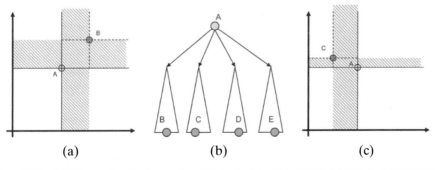

Figure 7.16. (a) The nodes that may be affected when the deleted node A is replaced by node B are located in the shaded region; thus, (b,c) when choosing among replacement candidates in all quadrants, we need to consider the size of the affected area for each replacement scenario.

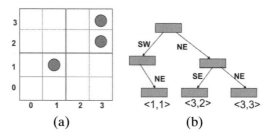

Figure 7.17. Three points in a $2^2 \times 2^2$ space and the corresponding MX-quadtree.

Shortcomings of Point Quadtrees

As we have discussed, deletions in point quadtrees can be very costly because of restructurings. Although restructurings are not required during range and nearest neighbor searches, those operations can also be costly. For example, even though the range search in the example shown in Figure 7.14 did not return any matches, a total of seven pointers had to be inspected. The cost is especially large when the number of dimensions of the space is large: because for a given m-dimensional space, each quadtree node splits the space into 2^m partitions, the number of pointers that the range search algorithm needs to inspect and follow can be up to 2^m per node. This means that, for point quadtrees, the cost of the range search may increase exponentially with the number of dimensions of the space. This, coupled with the fact that the tree can be highly unbalanced, implies that range and nearest neighbor queries can be highly unpredictable and expensive.

7.2.2.2 MX Quadtrees

In point quadtrees, the space is treated as being real-valued and is split by drawing rectilinear partitions through the data points. In MX-quadtrees (for *matrix* quadtrees), on the other hand, the space is treated as being discrete and finite [Samet, 1984]. In particular, each dimension of the space is taken to have integer values from 0 to $2^d - 1$. Thus, a given m-dimensional space potentially contains 2^{dm} distinct points.

Unlike the point quadtree, where the space is split at the data points, in MX-quadtrees, the space is always split at the center of the partitions. Because the space is discrete and because the range of values along each dimension of the space is from 0 to $2^d - 1$, the maximum depth of the tree (i.e., the number of times any given dimension can be halved) is d.

In a point quadtree, because they also act as criteria for space partitioning, the data points are stored in the internal nodes of the data structure. In MX-quadtrees, on the other hand, the partitions are always halved at the center; thus, there is no need to keep data points in the internal nodes to help with navigation. Consequently, as shown in Figure 7.17, in MX-quadtrees, data points are kept only at the leaves of the data structure. This ensures that deletions are easy and no restructuring needs be done as a result of a deletion: when a data point is deleted from the database, the corresponding leaf node is simply eliminated from the MX-quadtree data structure and the nodes that do not have any remaining children are collapsed. Note that the shape of the tree is independent of the order in which data points are inserted to the data structure.

Figure 7.18. PR-quadtree based partitioning of the space.

Another major difference between point quadtrees and MX-quadtrees is that, in MX-quadtrees, the leaves of the tree are all at the same, dth, level. For example, in Figure 7.17, the point $\langle 1, 1 \rangle$, is stored at a leaf at depth 2, even though this leaf is the only child of its parent. Although this may introduce some redundancy in data structure (i.e., more nodes and pointers than are strictly needed to store all the data points), it ensures that the search, insertion, and deletion processes all have the same, highly predictable cost.

In case the data points are not integers, but real numbers, then such data can be stored in MX-quadtrees after a *discretization* process: each cell of the MX-quadtree is treated as a unit-sized region, and all the data points that fall into this unit-sized region are kept in an overflow list associated with the corresponding cell. This may, however, increase the search time if the data distribution is very skewed and there are cells that contain a large number of data points that need to be sifted through. An alternative to this is to use PR-quadtrees as described next.

7.2.2.3 PR Quadtree

A *point-region (PR)-quadtree* [Samet, 1984] (also referred to as a uniform quadtree [Anderson, 1983a]) is a cross between a point quadtree and an MX-quadtree (Figure 7.18). As in point quadtrees, the space is treated as being real-valued. On the other hand, as in MX-quadtrees, the space is always split at the center of the partitions and data are stored at the leaves. Consequently, the structure of the tree is independent of the insertion order and deletion is, as in MX-quadtrees, easy. One difference from the MX-quadtrees is that, in most implementations of PR-quadtrees, all leaves are not maintained at the same level.

7.2.2.4 Summary of Quadtrees

Quadtrees and their variants are, in a sense, similar to the binary search tree: At each node, the binary search tree divides the 1D-space into 2 ($= 2^1$) halves (or partitions). Similarly, at each node, the quadtree divides the given m-dimensional space into 2^m partitions. In other words, quadtrees can be seen as a generalization of binary search idea to multidimensional spaces. While extending from 1D to multidimensional space, however, the quadtree data structure introduces a potentially significant disadvantage: having 2^m partition per node implies that, as the number of dimensions of the space gets larger,

- ■ The storage space needed for each node grows very quickly
- ■ More critically, range searches may be negatively affected because of the increased numbers of pointers that need to be investigated and partitions of the space that need to be examined.

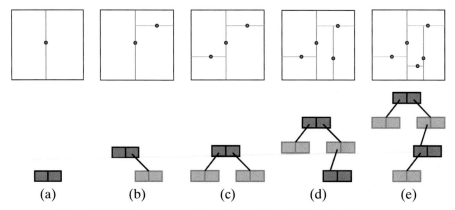

Figure 7.19. A sequence of insertions into a KD-tree in 2D space.

We next consider a different space subdivision scheme, called *KD-tree*, which, as in binary search trees, always divides a given partition into two (independent of the number of dimensions of the space).

7.2.3 KD-Trees

A *KD-tree* is a binary space subdivision scheme, where whatever the number of dimensions of the space is, the fanout (i.e., the number of pointers) of each tree node is never more than two [Bentley, 1975]. This is achieved by dividing the space along only a single dimension at a time. In order to give a chance for each dimension of the space to contribute to the discrimination of the data points, the space is split along a different dimension at each level of the tree. The order of split directions is usually assigned to the levels of the KD-tree in a round-robin fashion. For example, in the KD-tree shown in Figure 7.19, the first and third splits along any branch of the tree are vertical, whereas the second and fourth splits are horizontal.

Figure 7.20 shows the point quadtree that one would obtain through the same sequence of data point insertions. Comparing Figures 7.19 and 7.20, it is easy to see that the KD-tree partitioning results in more compact tree nodes, thus

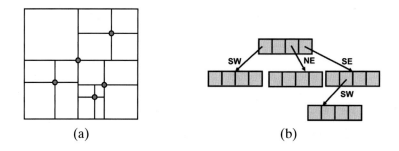

Figure 7.20. (a) The point quadtree that one would obtain through the sequence of data point insertions in Figure 7.19. (b) The corresponding data structure.

providing savings in both storage and the number of comparisons to be performed per node. Conversely, though, because the fanout of the KD-tree nodes is small (i.e., always 2), the resulting tree is likely to be deeper than the corresponding quadtree. A quick comparison of Figures 7.19 and 7.20 verifies this. In fact, the problem with the quadtree data structure is not that the fanout is large, but that the required fanout grows exponentially with the number of dimensions of the space. As we see in Section 7.2.4, bucketing techniques can be used for increasing the fanout of KD-trees in a *controlled* manner, without giving rise to exponential growth (as in quadtrees) with the number of dimensions.

Because, aside from picking the dimensions for the splits in a round-robin manner, the KD-tree is quite similar to the quadtree data structure, most versions of the quadtree (e.g., point quadtree, MX-quadtree, PR-quadtree) have KD-tree counterparts (e.g., point KD-tree, MX-KD-tree, PR-KD-tree).

7.2.3.1 Point KD-Trees

As in point quadtrees, the *point KD-tree* data structure partitions the space at the data points. The resulting tree depends on the order of insertions, and the tree is not necessarily balanced.

The insertion and search processes also mimic those of the point quadtrees, except that the partitions considered for insertion and search are chosen based on a single dimension at each node. The data deletion process, on the other hand, is substantially different from that of point quadtrees. The reason for this is that, because of the use of different dimensions for splitting the space at each level, finding a suitable node that will minimize the restructuring is not a straightforward task. In particular, this *most suitable* node needs not be located at the leaves of the tree, and thus the deletion process may need to be performed iteratively by (a) finding a most suitable descendant to be the replacement for the deleted node, (b) removing the selected node from its current location to replace the node to be deleted, and (c) repeating the same process to replace the node that has just been removed from its current position. For selecting the *most suitable* descendant node to replace the one being deleted, one has to consider how much the partition boundary will shift because of the node replacement. It is easy to see that the node that will cause the smallest shift is the descendant node that is closest to the boundary along the dimension corresponding to the node being deleted. In fact, because there will be no nodes between the one deleted and the one selected for replacement along the split axis, unlike the case in quadtrees, no single node will need to move between partitions (Figure 7.21). Thus, in KD-trees the cost of moving the data points across partitions is replaced with the cost of repeated searches for the *most suitable* replacement nodes. Bentley [1975] showed that average insertion and deletion times for a random point are both $O(log(n))$. Naturally, deleting nodes closer to the root has a considerably higher cost, as the process could involve multiple searches for *most suitable* replacement nodes.

7.2.3.2 Adaptive KD-Trees

The *adaptive KD-tree* data structure is a variant of the KD-tree, where the requirement that the partition boundaries pass over the data points is relaxed. Instead, as

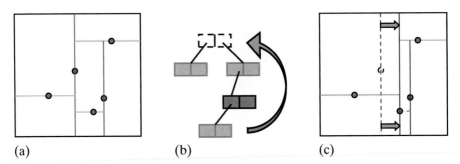

(a)   (b)   (c)

Figure 7.21. Deletion in KD-trees: (a) Original tree, (b) The root is deleted and replaced by a descendant, (c) The resulting configuration.

in PR-quadtrees, all data points are stored at the leaves and split points are chosen in a way that maximizes the data spread:

- In *data-dependent split strategies*, the split position is chosen based on the points in the region: a typical approach is to split a given partition at the average or median of points along the split dimension.
- In *space-dependent strategies*, the split position is picked independently of the actual points. An example strategy is to split a given region into two subregions of equal areas.

The basic adaptive KD-tree picks the median value along the given dimension to locate the partition boundary [Friedman *et al.*, 1977]. This helps ensure that the data points have equal probability of being on either side of the partition. The VAM-Split adaptation technique considers the discrimination power of the dimensions and at each level picks the dimension with the maximum variance as the split dimension [Sproull, 1991; White and Jain, 1996b]. The *fair-split* technique [Callahan and Kosaraju, 1995] is based on a similar strategy: at each iteration, the algorithm picks the longest dimension and divides the current partition into two geometrically equal halves along it. Consequently, it allows for $O(nlog(n))$ construction of the KD-tree. *The binary space partitioning* tree (or BSP-tree) [Fuchs *et al.*, 1980] is a further generalization where the partition boundaries are not necessarily aligned with the dimensions of the space, but are hyperplanes that are selected in a way that splits the data points in a manner that best separates them (Figure 7.22).

Note that in order to create an adaptive KD-tree, we need to have the data points available in advance. Because insertions and deletions could cause changes

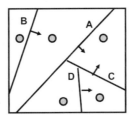

Figure 7.22. A sample BSP-tree.

in the location of the median point, performing these operations on an adaptive KD-tree is not cheap.

7.2.4 Bucket-Based Quadtree and KD-Tree Variants

The quadtree and KD-tree variants discussed so far all take data points as the units of data access and, thus, associate at most one data point per tree node. In reality, however, disks are accessed one disk page at a time, and each page may have sufficient space to contain more than one data point. Consequently, when the multidimensional search data structures are implemented over secondary storage devices, it is more advantageous to aggregate multiple data points into *buckets* that are mapped onto disk pages.

7.2.4.1 k-d-B-Tree

A *k-d-B-tree* is a cross between an adaptive KD-tree and a B-tree [Robinson, 1981]. Each node of a *k-d-B-tree* corresponds to a region of space. As in B-trees, the leaves contain more than one data entry (the number of data entries is determined based on the size of the disk page and storage requirement of each data point). K-d-B-trees are balanced like B-trees and, also like B-trees, nodes can contain more than two pointers. Each nonleaf node of the tree is referred to as a *region page* and represents a KD-tree partitioning of the corresponding region of the space. For each subregion, the nonleaf node contains a pointer to another tree node: if that node is a leaf, then it will simply contain the data points in the corresponding subregion; if the node is not a leaf, on the other hand, it will in turn represent a KD-tree partitioning of the corresponding subregion into smaller sub-subregions.

Maintaining the k-d-B-tree in the presence of insertions and deletions is not straightforward. When insertions cause a leaf node to overflow, the corresponding region needs to be partitioned into two, and this needs to be reflected into the parent node, potentially resulting in cascading splits. Most importantly, though, the hyperplane that repartitions the region must be selected in such a way that the resulting subregions themselves do not overflow.

Point deletions may cause leaf pages to become underutilized and when the utilization of the pages goes beyond a certain level, underutilized pages may need to be merged. However, not all leaf pages are compatible with each other, because they may result in irregularly shaped regions when combined. Thus, merging pages may require shifting some of the existing partition boundaries to render the merged region regular. This may, in turn, require some of the points to move across partitions (and thus across the corresponding disk pages), increasing the cost of the whole process.

7.2.4.2 LSD-Tree

The *local split decision tree* (or LSD-tree) [Henrich *et al.*, 1989] structure partitions the space into disjoint regions such that each region is associated with a bucket of fixed size (corresponding to a disk page). The LSD partitioning directory is maintained in a binary tree as in KD-trees. Each node represents one split decision, described using a split dimension and a split position. Each split decision is made purely based on local information (as opposed to, for example, assigning split

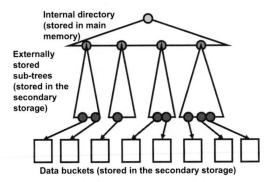

Figure 7.23. LSD-tree organization: when the main memory is not sufficient to keep the directory structure (which is essentially an adaptive KD-tree), some subtrees are pushed onto secondary storage.

dimensions in a round-robin fashion); hence, the resulting tree is referred to as a local split decision tree.

The most significant difference between the LSD-tree and other adaptive KD-tree variants is that the LSD-tree insertion and deletion algorithms preserve an *external balancing property* [Henrich *et al.*, 1989]: "*The number of external directory pages which are traversed on any two paths from the directory root to a bucket differs by at most 1.*" The tree is kept at the main memory as much as possible. When the tree grows to a size where it can no longer be maintained in the main memory in its entirety, then a *paging algorithm* determines the parts of the tree that will be paged on (i.e., stored at) secondary storage (Figure 7.23). The paging process ensures that the external balancing property is preserved by selecting a subtree that has the following properties: (a) the paths from the root of the subtree down to data buckets contain minimal number of external directory pages (across the entire LSD-tree) and (b) the selected in-memory subtree fits into a single disk page (Figure 7.24).

7.2.4.3 Hybrid-Tree

As in k-d-B-trees and LSD-trees, the *hybrid-tree* data structure [Chakrabarti and Mehrotra, 1999] splits a given node along a single dimension. Also as in the k-d-B-trees, the space partitioning within each internal node is represented using a KD-tree. However, the hybrid-tree scheme avoids cascading splits by relaxing the requirement that the partitions created in the process are always mutually disjoint:

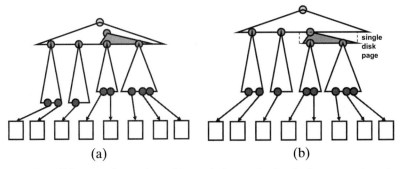

(a)   (b)

Figure 7.24. The LSD-tree selects the subtrees to be pushed onto the secondary storage in such a way that the external balancing property is preserved.

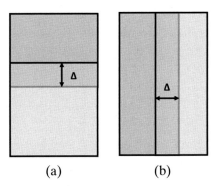

Figure 7.25. When splitting data nodes, the hybrid tree chooses the dimension along which the corresponding bounding region has the largest extent: the scenario (a) results in a smaller area of overlap for the same length, Δ, of overlap along the selected dimension.

overlaps are allowed (only) when a split will cause cascading splits. In order to accommodate overlaps, internal nodes of the *hybrid tree* maintain two split positions instead of a single one. When the two split positions are equal, this corresponds to the standard KD-tree partitioning. Overlaps occur when the two split positions are different from each other.

The split dimension is chosen in a way that minimizes the expected number of disk accesses per query. Because when two partitions overlap (i.e., cover the same region of the space) a query for the shared region may need to inspect both partitions, the split dimension is selected in a way that minimizes the likelihood of an overlap: in particular, the hybrid tree chooses the dimension along which the bounding region has the largest extent for splitting data nodes, because this is likely to result in the least volume of overlap (Figure 7.25). Note that this choice also implies that less discriminating dimensions are never used for partitioning the space and, thus, the hybrid tree implicitly eliminates nondiscriminating features. Furthermore, unlike the earlier KD-tree schemes that either perform round-robin assignment of split dimensions or rely on the variance of the data distribution, the hybrid-tree data structure also takes into account the distribution of the query sizes.

For the leaves, where the data points are stored, the split position is chosen as close to the middle as possible, as this results in more cube-like partitions with small surface areas, thus reducing the probability that range queries will unnecessarily overlap with the resulting partitions. For the internal nodes, the split positions are chosen in such a way that the overlaps between the partitions are minimized, yet the utilizations of the resulting partitions are sufficiently high.

The hybrid tree tries to reduce the number of disk accesses during search by further eliminating the dead space (i.e., space that does not contain any data points) in the partitions through a *live space encoding* scheme [Henrich, 1998]. In live space encoding, a grid is placed on each KD-tree partition and the *live space* (i.e., the bounding box that contains all the corresponding data points) is encoded using few bits per dimension (Figure 7.26).

7.2.5 R-Trees and Their Variants

As the live space discussion illustrates, top-down space subdivision techniques, such as quadtrees and KD-trees, commonly result in dead space simply because, at all

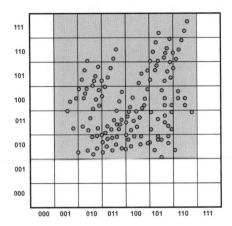

Figure 7.26. Live space encoding with 3-bit precision: $\langle 001, 010; 110, 111 \rangle$.

levels of the tree, the entire space (even the parts that do not contain any data points) needs to be covered. This means that, even though a search range may not contain any data points, the search process would still need to continue all the way to the leaves. The live space encoding somewhat alleviates this, but in an ad hoc manner.

R-trees [Guttman, 1984] address the dead space problem directly by building the index structure using a bottom-up *data partitioning* strategy as opposed to a top-down *space partitioning strategy*. In particular, the data buckets (i.e., the leaves) of the R-tree directory structure simply correspond to the minimum bounding regions (MBRs) that cluster nearby data items. Consequently, the leaves represent only the portions of the space needed to cover the data points. Similarly, the nodes at the higher levels of the R-tree cluster close-by lower-level minimum bounding regions to form ever-larger minimum bounding regions. The only node in the R-tree that is guaranteed to cover the entire space is the root.

A distinctive feature of the R-tree data insertion and deletion processes is that the resulting trees are always balanced. The R-tree achieves this by generalizing the B-tree mechanism [Bayer and McCreight, 1972] from one dimension to multiple dimensions:

- In B-trees, each node corresponds to an interval of values; in R-trees, each node is a minimum bounding region of data points contained within.
- As in B-trees, each node in an R-tree (except for the root) must contain *at least* $\frac{M}{2}$ children (where M is the fanout capacity of the node).
- Also as in B-trees, all the leaves are at the same level and the root has at least two children unless it itself is a leaf.
- The data point insertion and deletion processes also follow the B-tree scheme (Figure 7.27): (a) when a node becomes full, it is split (Figure 7.28) and the resulting regions are pushed up the hierarchy, and (b) when a node becomes unacceptably empty, exchanges between neighboring nodes help keep all nodes sufficiently full.

In R-trees, each node represents a region and each child node represents a subregion. As stated previously, the parent node is the MBR of its children. Each region is

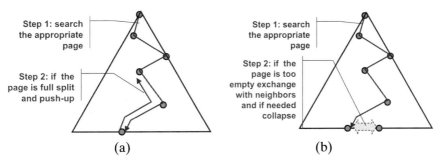

Figure 7.27. Overview of the R-tree insertion and deletion processes: (a) insertion, (b) deletion.

described using the two end points of a diagonal; therefore, given an m-dimensional space, each MBR requires $2m$ values to describe the corresponding region.

A significant difference between R-trees and B-trees (as well as the quadtree and KD-tree variants – except for the hybrid tree) is that in R-trees the regions corresponding to sibling nodes may overlap. Consequently, R-tree variants employ different heuristics to minimize the likelihood of overlaps. One such heuristic is to split an overful node in such a way that the MBRs of the two resulting nodes have a minimum overlap (Figure 7.29(a,b)). Although this strategy helps attack the problem of overlaps directly, it may result in dead space that may overlap with future queries and MBRs. An alternative heuristic is to minimize the total area covered by the resulting nodes (Figure 7.29(a,c)). This scheme does not explicitly target or prevent overlaps; instead, the idea is that by minimizing the total area (even if it causes overlaps) now, one may save a lot in the future because the dead areas generated in the process are smaller.

Another major difference between R-trees and B-trees is that, whereas in B-trees the node to which a new entry will go is deterministic, because R-trees do not cover the entire space or may multiply cover a given region of the space, there may be multiple candidate nodes to store a newly inserted entry (Figure 7.30). Once again, R-tree variants employ different heuristics to select the suitable node among the candidates.

7.2.5.1 Hilbert R-Tree
A successfully applied heuristic for selecting the appropriate node for inserting a new entry is to compare the Hilbert value (see Section 7.1.2) of the center of the new

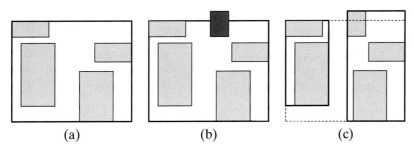

Figure 7.28. A node that can hold at most four MBRs would need to be split if it receives a new MBR to keep: (a) Before insertion, (b) New entry, (c) After split.

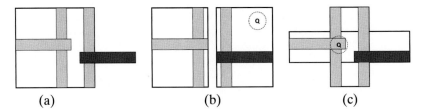

Figure 7.29. (a) A node that can hold at most three entries receives a new entry, and thus it needs to be split. (b) One possible heuristic is to minimize the overlaps of the resulting MBRs (but this may cause dead space that may unnecessarily overlap with a future query, Q). (c) Another heuristic is to minimize the total area (but this does not explicitly minimize current overlaps between the MBRs; thus a query, Q, may require access to both resulting nodes).

entry with the *largest Hilbert values* (LHVs) of the MBRs contained in the candidate nodes. Among all the candidates, this heuristic picks the node with the smallest LHV that is greater than the Hilbert value of the new entry. In other words, the *Hilbert R-tree* [Kamel and Faloutsos, 1994] imposes a linear order on all the candidate MBRs based on Hilbert values and uses this order to select among the candidate nodes.

7.2.5.2 R+-Tree

R+-trees [Sellis *et al.*, 1987] avoid overlaps of MBRs altogether by allowing entries to be replicated in multiple data nodes (Figure 7.31). This helps reduce search time as only one single path in the tree corresponds to any single point in space. On the other hand, because entries are replicated, the resulting index structure may be significantly larger than the equivalent R-tree. Furthermore, insertions and deletions are costlier because more than one leaf may need to be accessed to maintain the tree.

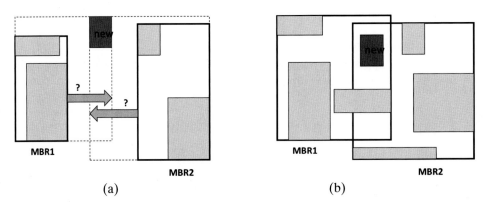

(a)   (b)

Figure 7.30. (a) The new region is not covered by any existing MBR, so one of the MBRs needs to be extended to include the new entry. (b) In this case, the new entry is covered by more than one MBR; thus one of these candidates must be selected to contain the new entry.

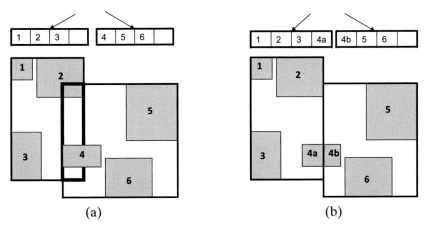

Figure 7.31. The R+-tree prevents overlaps of MBRs by replicating entries in multiple nodes.

7.2.5.3 R*-Tree

The *R*-tree* data structure [Beckmann *et al.*, 1990] explicitly optimizes parameters that correspond to the following three criteria when choosing the subtree for point insertion and for selecting the split strategy when a node is full:

- The volumes of the MBRs must be small to ensure that the size of the dead space in each node is minimized.
- The overlap between the MBRs should be minimized.
- The margins of the MBRs must be minimized. This means that given two MBRs of equal size, the one that has a more balanced shape will be preferred. Because such shapes are easier to pack, this helps reduce the volumes of the higher level MBRs that will contain them.

The R*-tree also employs a *forced re-insertion* strategy that generally results in trees with better structures: when a node overflows, some of its children are chosen to be deleted and re-inserted. The use of such forced insertions, as opposed to blind localized splits, gives an opportunity to the tree to re-adjust its structure in a more globally meaningful manner.

7.2.5.4 Trees with Spherical Bounding Regions

The *SS-tree* [White and Jain, 1996a], *M-tree* [Ciaccia *et al.*, 1997], and *sphere/rectangle-tree (SR-tree)* [Katayama and Satoh, 1997] all use spherical bounding regions along with or instead of the rectangular ones.

Rectangular regions tend to result in long diagonals, which implies that two objects that are not necessarily close to each other can be placed into the same region if they are along the diagonal. In order to avoid long diagonals, the SS-tree employs bounding spheres instead of bounding rectangles. A second advantage of using spheres is that they require less storage space to describe: in an m-dimensional space, the MBR of a region requires $2m$ values to describe two diagonal corners; in the same space, the sphere requires $m + 1$ values to describe the center point and the radius.

Given a set of entries, the center of the sphere containing them is the centroid of all the points included in the region. During insertion, the SS-tree algorithm determines the most suitable subtree by choosing the one with the centroid closest to the new entry. When a sphere is full, the algorithm calculates the variance (of the centroids of its children of the point entries contained in the region) along each dimension and uses the dimension with the highest variance for splitting the sphere.

When inserting points, the M-tree data structure tries to pick the node that will result in the least enlargement of the radius. If there are multiple such nodes, the closest one is chosen. When a node is full, like other R-tree variants, M-tree tries to pick a split that minimizes the total volume, while also minimizing the overlap.

Although bounding spheres help divide points into short diameter regions, as shown by Katayama and Satoh [1997], given a fixed diameter, bounding spheres occupy much larger volumes than bounding rectangles (especially when the number of dimensions is high). As stated earlier, regions with larger volumes tend to create more overlaps. The SR tree brings together advantages of spherical and rectangular regions by specifying the regions as the intersections of bounding spheres and bounding rectangles. This helps reduce the volumes of the regions and, while requiring more storage space, helps eliminate dead space and minimize overlaps.

7.2.5.5 VAMSplit R-Tree

The *VAMSplit R-tree* [White and Jain, 1996b] leverages the VAMSplit adaptation technique (discussed in Section 7.2.3.2), which considers the discrimination powers of the dimensions when selecting the split point. This helps the data structure adapt to varying data distributions and outperform R*-trees for databases where points are not uniformly distributed.

7.2.5.6 X-Tree

The *eXtended node tree (X-tree)* [Berchtold *et al.*, 1996] data structure is an R-tree variant that tries to avoid splits. R-tree splits (commonly performed using only local information) can result in inefficient directory structures whose MBRs are prone to high degrees of overlap, especially when the dimensionality of the space increases. To avoid splits, the X-tree introduces the concept of *supernodes*, which are essentially R-tree nodes consisting of multiple consecutive disk pages. Because they can hold more entries, supernodes help reduce the need for splits and protect the structure of the R-tree from deformations due to frequent splits.

In X-trees, supernodes are created only if there is no other possibility to avoid overlap. First, the X-tree tries to choose an overlap-free (or at least overlap-minimal) split axis. When an overlap-minimal split will result in underfilled nodes, however, the split algorithm terminates without executing the split. Only in that case is the current (super-)node extended with an additional disk page.

A positive side effect of the supernode strategy is the increase in the fanout of the tree: a supernode of k pages will have k times more children than a regular node. Of course, supernodes do not come for free: a supernode consisting of multiple disk pages may require multiple disk accesses (or at least one disk seek operation followed by multiple rotations) and, thus, when a given query does not cover the entire MBR of the supernode, the extra disk accesses result in unnecessary overhead. Furthermore, as the supernode grows (i.e., as k gets larger), the process may in fact deteriorate to a sequential scan of a large file: consider, for example, the extreme case where the entire database is a single supernode consisting of an MBR that covers all the data points. Clearly, this data structure would be inefficient in that each query would require scanning of the entire database.

7.2.5.7 Packed R-Trees

So far, we have discussed R-trees designed to support dynamic updates, insertions, and deletions. In many cases, however, the data are static and, once they are created, the R-tree will be used only for searching. In these cases, it is better to *pack* the R-tree in such a way that the utilization of the pages is maximized. This is usually achieved by picking an order in which the space will be visited during insertion and building the R-tree bottom-up following this order.

There are different heuristics to build the R-tree in a packed fashion. Roussopoulos and Leifker [1985] proposed sorting the data along a single dimension. The sorted list of entries is scanned, and each entry is assigned to a leaf node until this leaf node is full. When the leaf node is full, a new leaf node is created, and this process is continued until the data are all inserted into the leaves. Once the leaf nodes are created, the same process is repeated with (selected corners of) their MBRs to obtain the next level of the R-tree, and so on. Once this bottom-up process is over, the resulting packed R-tree is almost 100% full. Experiments showed that the resulting packed R-tree is better than linear- and quadratic-split R-trees and R*-tree. The *Hilbert packed R-tree* [Kamel and Faloutsos, 1993] improves the query performance significantly by relying on the clustering properties of the Hilbert curves during packing.

The *sort-tile-recursive (STR) packed R-tree* [Leutenegger *et al.*, 1997] first sorts all n entries in a given m-dimensional space according to the first coordinate of their centers. Then, given disk pages that can hold b entries, the set of entries is divided into $\lceil \left(\frac{n}{b}\right)^{\frac{1}{m}} \rceil$ groups, each with $\sim \frac{n}{\left(\frac{n}{b}\right)^{\frac{1}{m}}} = b^{\frac{1}{m}} n^{\frac{m-1}{m}}$ data entries. Then, each of these sorted groups of entries goes through the same process recursively using the remaining $m-1$ dimensions. When the process is over (i.e., all the dimensions are considered), the resulting *sorted tiles* are packed into the leaves of the R-tree, and the process is repeated recursively in a bottom-up manner to obtain the higher levels of the tree. Experiments showed that this scheme requires about 50% fewer disk accesses for uniformly distributed or mildly skewed data sets.

7.2.6 TV-Trees

Although essentially being a variant of R-trees, the *telescoping vector tree (TV-tree)* [Lin *et al.*, 1994] data structure fights the dimensionality curse in a way that is quite different from other R-trees.

As we have discussed in Section 4.1, range and nearest neighbor searches in high-dimensional spaces fail to benefit from available index structures, and searches deteriorate to sequential scans of the entire database. This is primarily for three reasons:

- As the number of dimensions increases, the nearest and the furthest points from the query converge, and nearest neighbor and range queries lose their meanings.

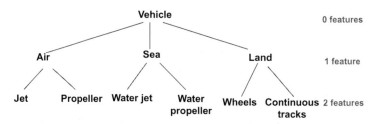

Figure 7.32. A class hierarchy may use a higher number of features at the lower levels to better discriminate the objects.

■ In R-trees and their variants, the dead space and the degrees of overlaps between the MBRs of various nodes increase as the number of dimensions becomes larger.

■ Because of the fixed sizes of the disk pages, the fanouts of the directory nodes get smaller as the number of dimensions and thus the number of values needed to describe the MBRs increase. Consequently, the depth of the tree and the number of pages that one needs to access to reach the appropriate leaf nodes also increase.

One solution to this problem is to apply a feature selection algorithm (see Section 4.2) to reduce the number of relevant dimensions before attempting to index the data points. It is, however, not always possible to pick the right number of dimensions to represent the entire data set. In fact, different subsets of the data may require different numbers of dimensions for effective representation and indexing.

TV-trees use a *vector telescoping* scheme to help pick the appropriate number of dimensions needed to represent different MBRs in the data structure. In particular, Lin *et al.* [1994] observe that not all features are equally important, and in many cases it is possible to order features based on some importance criterion (i.e., discrimination power). The telescoping technique helps *contract* and *extend* feature vectors based on need and, thus, use as little features as possible to avoid the dimensionality curse. In some sense, the idea is similar to those of class or concept hierarchies, which tend to use more features at the lower levels of the hierarchy to better discriminate the objects (Figure 7.32). Similar to this, the telescoping scheme used by the TV-trees uses a smaller number of features at the higher levels of the tree and a larger number of features at the lower levels, where finer discrimination between points is needed.

As in SS- and M-trees, TV-trees also rely on spherical MBRs that are defined using center/radius pairs. However, TV-trees do not use all the available dimensions to define the MBRs. Instead, only a few dimensions, sufficient to discriminate the points covered by the MBR, are used. The center and the radius of an MBR are defined along different dimensions. Let us consider an m-dimensional vector space. An MBR, mbr_i is a pair $\langle center_i, r_i \rangle$, where $center_i$ is defined using the first c dimensions and the radius, r_i, is defined using the next k dimensions of the space; note that $c + k \leq m$ (Figure 7.33). Given a c-dimensional center description, $\langle w_1, w_2, \ldots, w_c \rangle$, this corresponds to the point

$$\langle w_1, w_2, \ldots, w_c, \underbrace{0, 0, \ldots, 0}_{(m-c)\ zeros} \rangle$$

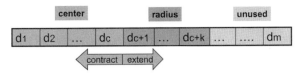

Figure 7.33. In TV-trees, only the first few dimensions, sufficient to discriminate the points covered by the region, are used to describe a given MBR.

in the m-dimensional space. Given the foregoing center and a radius, r, defined in k dimensions, all the points that lie in the corresponding region are of the form

$$\langle w_1, w_2, \ldots, w_c, \underbrace{w_{c+1}, w_{c+2}, \ldots, w_{c+k}}_{k\ \text{weights}}, w_{c+k+1}, \ldots, w_m \rangle,$$

such that

$$\Delta(\langle w_{c+1}, w_{c+2}, \ldots, w_{c+k} \rangle, \underbrace{\langle 0, 0, \ldots, 0 \rangle}_{k\ \text{zeros}}) \leq r.$$

The last $m - c - k$ weights are left unused.

The value of k (i.e., the number of dimensions used for defining the radius) determines the dimensionality of the bounding region. The value is picked at design time and is kept constant throughout the evolution of the data structure. Thus, TV-trees are usually specified with the corresponding k values (e.g., TV-2 trees, for $k = 2$, and TV-3 trees, for $k = 3$). At design time, one can also choose between different metrics for computing the distance between the points in the space: for example, if the L1-metric (or the Manhattan distance) is used, then the bounding regions are diamond shaped; when the L2-metric (or the Euclidean distance) is picked to compute the distance between the points, then the bounding regions are spherical, and so on (Figure 7.34).

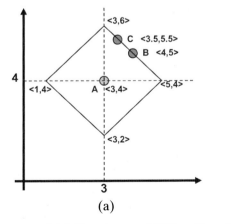
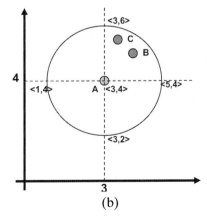

(a)   (b)

Figure 7.34. The shapes of MBRs with radius $r = 2$, defined in 2D space ($k = 2$), and centered at the point $\langle 3, 4 \rangle$, when the distance measure is (a) L1 and (b) L2. Note that the positions of the points B and C with respect to the boundary of the region differ based on the metric used to descibe the radius.

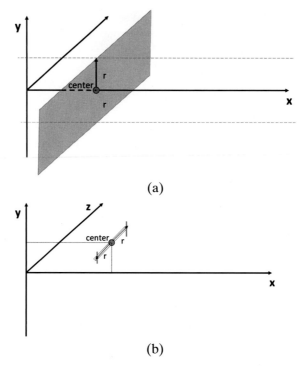

(a)

(b)

Figure 7.35. The shapes of the MBRs for a TV-1 tree in a three-dimensional space for different values of c. (a) When $c = 1$, the center is described using x, the radius using y, and the z dimension is left unused; consequently, the MBRs are planar stripes along the z dimension. (b) When $c = 2$, on the other hand, the resulting MBRs are line segments of length r along z. In a sense, telescoping from $c = 1$ to $c = 2$ involves shredding the given stripe into its fibers.

While the value k is kept constant, the TV-tree is able to adapt itself to the inherent dimensionality of the data by dynamically telescoping (*extending* and *contracting*) the number, c, of dimensions used for describing the centers of the individual MBRs (Figures 7.33 and 7.35).

For a new data point, the TV-tree insertion algorithm traverses the tree choosing the most suitable branch to hold the new point. For this purpose it uses the following criteria in descending priority: (a) minimum increase in overlapping regions within the selected node; (b) minimum decrease in the dimensionality (of the value c) needed to accommodate the point in the MBR; (c) minimum increase in the radius; and (d) minimum distance from the center of the MBR.

When a node becomes full, it is split to redistribute the entries into two groups. One way to perform the split operation is to apply a *clustering* scheme that will group similar vectors. In this scheme, the algorithm picks two branches that have the smallest common prefix in their centers, and the other branches are clustered around these two based on the four criteria listed earlier. An alternative scheme is to *order* the centers of the entries (using, for example, Hilbert ordering) and find a partition such that (a) the sum of the radii of the two new MBRs is minimized and (b) the value (the sum of the radii of the two new MBRs minus the distance between centers) is minimized. The first of these tries to minimize the area that the MBRs cover, and the second minimizes their overlaps.

Deletion is performed by removing the remaining branches of any node that becomes underutilized and re-inserting them into the tree.

Extensions of the dimensionality occur during splits and deletions. In either case, if the remaining entries all agree in more dimensions, the definition of the center can be extended to describe the MBR more precisely. The *contraction* occurs during insertions. When a new point is inserted into an MBR such that the center of the MBR does not agree with the corresponding dimensions of the new point, then some dimensions will need to be contracted to ensure that the center of the MBR and the corresponding dimensions of the point agree. Note that these imply that, in most cases, the nodes closer to the root will have lower dimensionality (i.e., high fanout). This helps prune the database more effectively and thus reduces the number of disk accesses required to perform searches using TV-trees.

7.2.7 Pyramid Trees

Pyramid trees [Berchtold *et al.*, 1998] attack the dimensionality curse by taking a radically different approach from hierarchical space subdivision. Remember from Section 4.1 and the previous discussion of TV-trees that, because the nearest and the furthest points from the query start converging, clustering in high-dimensional spaces fails to provide any benefits in supporting range and nearest neighbor searches. This is mainly because the space becomes extremely sparse and the number of data points that lie at a distance from any given point increases exponentially with each step away from the point (Figure 7.36). Consequently, the amount of dead space grows exponentially and, thus, the resulting cluster boundaries (MBRs) overlap significantly.

The pyramid technique completely avoids overlaps by discarding the use of distance-based clusters. Instead, it maps the multidimensional space onto a 1D space as in space-filling curves; the data points mapped onto the 1D space are then partitioned in a nonoverlapping fashion, as in B-trees.

Unlike the space-filling curves, however, the pyramid technique does not try to fill the space in a way that brings the closer points together, essentially rejecting the desiderata listed near the beginning of this chapter. Instead, as shown in Figure 7.37, the pyramid technique splits the space into pyramids (such that each pyramid has its peak at the center of the space and its base at one of the bounding hyperplanes) and numbers each pyramid uniquely. For each point, then, the pyramid ID and the distance between the center of the space and the hyperplane passing through the point and parallel to the base of the pyramid are combined to obtain its key.

Once the keys are obtained, the data are then simply stored in a 1D data structure, such as a B+-tree, which partitions the data and maps them onto disk pages in a nonoverlapping manner. Note that, unlike space-filling curves, in this scheme the mapping from the multidimensional space to the 1D space is not one-to-one. In fact, any two points that are in the same pyramid and on the same plane with respect to the corresponding base have the same key, and thus are likely to be stored together, irrespective of how far apart they are. Because each disk page can hold a fixed number of points, and because, when the data are uniformly distributed in the space, the

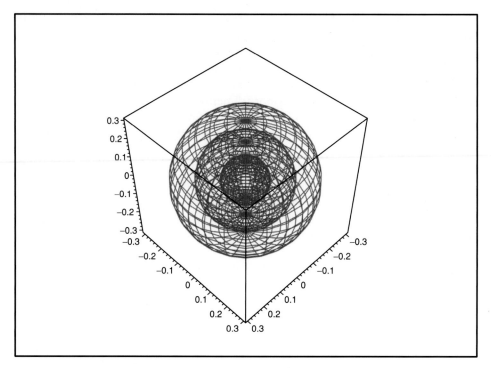

Figure 7.36. The dimensionality curse: The volume between the slices between equidistance spheres enveloping a query point increases exponentially.

number of points increases exponentially as one gets further away from the center (the dimensionality curse!), this results in partitions that get progressively thinner as one gets away from the tip of the pyramid (Figure 7.38(a)). Consequently, queries that are closer to the center of the space and away from the boundaries result in fewer disk accesses.

Queries that are closer to the boundary, on the other hand, may need to read a larger number of pages that need to be filtered out later (Figure 7.38(b)). Berchtold *et al.* [1998] showed analytically that when the queries are uniformly distributed, on average, the number of pages that need to be fetched using the pyramid technique

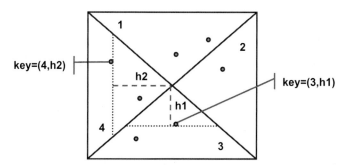

Figure 7.37. The keys of each point are computed by combining the ID of the pyramid containing the point and the point's height.

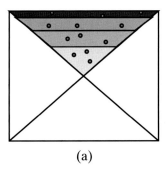
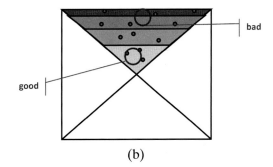

(a) (b)

Figure 7.38. (a) Partitions get thinner as one gets further away from the center. (b) Queries that are closer to the center result in smaller numbers of page accesses.

is significantly smaller than the number of pages that clustering-based hierarchical solutions would require. In a sense, the pyramid techniques turns the key contributor to the dimensionality curse (the fact that *most points lie further away than any selected point*) into a weapon to attack the curse itself. Berchtold *et al.* [1998] also show how to form and use pyramids whose centers are not at the center when the data and queries are not uniformly distributed.

7.2.8 VA-Files

As we have mentioned, almost all hierarchical data structures become ineffective as the number of dimensions of the space increases. In many cases, searches through index structures become as costly as simple sequential scans of the entire database. The *vector-approximation files (VA-files)* [Weber and Blott, 1998] simply take this observation to its natural conclusion: They eliminate the entire hierarchical structure altogether and optimize the sequential access instead.

As in grid files, the VA-file technique divides the space into 2^b rectangular cells, where b is a user-specified number of bits. Each cell essentially approximates all the points that fall in it. Unlike the grid files (or any hierarchical organization schemes) the VA-file is simply an array of these compact representations and a search is performed simply by scanning the entire VA-file. Experiments reported by Weber and Blott [1998] showed that VA-file approach scales better than R*- and X-tree data structures as the number of dimensions increases.

Ferhatosmanoglu *et al.* [2000] build on the VA-file approach to develop a *VA+-file* data structure that performs better for data sets where the data points are not uniformly distributed. In particular, before the approximation is carried out, the VA+-file first applies the Karhunen-Loeve transform (see Section 4.2.6) to identify the principal components of the data that can support more effective approximations. Given these principal dimensions, the VA+-file assigns appropriate number of bits to different dimensions. In particular, those dimensions along which data require more precision are allocated a higher number of bits than the dimensions along which data can be compressed without losing much of the discriminatory power of the VA+-file. Finally, once the algorithm knows how many bits are allocated to a given principal component, the data along this dimension are quantized (i.e., approximated) nonuniformly [Lloyd, 1982], based on the local density of the points along this dimension. This last phase is similar to K-means, a popular clustering algorithm that we discuss in the next chapter.

7.3 SUMMARY

Vectors play an important role in representing and managing multimedia data. Once relevant features are identified and quantified, most media data can be mapped onto a multidimensional feature space, and queries can be formulated as range searches or nearest neighbor searches in this space. As we have seen in this chapter, when the underlying distance/similarity measure is metric, this helps significantly with efficient indexing of multidimensional data. In Chapter 10, we revisit the problem of performing nearest neighbor searches, this time in the more general context of ranked query processing (not necessarily in metric spaces) and skyline queries.

Unfortunately, most multidimensional data indexing schemes fail to scale with the number of dimensions necessary to describe the multimedia data. We have seen that a number of schemes, such as TV-trees, X-trees, pyramid trees, and VA-files, attempt to address this shortcoming. When the data cannot be mapped onto multi-dimensional space or when the space onto which the data are mapped is not suitable for efficient indexing, other techniques, such as *clustering*, can be used for pruning the irrelevant data during query processing. We cover this next.

8

Clustering Techniques

In the previous chapter, we described mechanisms for indexing multimedia data for quick access. The indexing process, in general, is based on establishing some order between the data objects so that queries can be routed toward the ones that are likely to be matches for the query and prune away those objects that are non-matches. Thus, most indexing techniques are based on some form of data clustering. In fact, hierarchical multidimensional index structures are sometimes referred to as *self-clustering* techniques.

Naturally, establishing an order on the given set of data objects requires an understanding of the fundamental characteristics and features of the media and the use of data structures appropriate for these features. We have seen that the index structures applicable for different media (e.g., sequences, graphs, trees, and vectors) are based on different principles and operate differently from each other.

In many multimedia databases, however, we may not have prior knowledge about the explicit features of data. This is the case, for example, when we have "black-box programs" that can compare two objects or when the similarity of the pair is simply evaluated subjectively by users. In both cases, we can obtain information about distances and/or similarities between pairs of objects, but there are no explicit features that one can use as a basis for an index structure. As we have seen in Section 4.3, one possible solution in these cases is to map or *embed* the objects into a multidimensional space (using MDS or FastMap) using the available distance values. Once the data are mapped into a multidimensional space, queries can be supported using appropriate index structures, such as R-trees.

Such embeddings, however, are not always desirable. First, any embedding comes with some information loss, and this may be undesirable. Second, queries also need to be mapped onto the same space as the data objects and, as we have seen in Section 4.3, this may be very costly.

An alternative strategy is to rely on *clustering techniques* that do not need explicit features to operate. In this section, we cover such clustering techniques. Although different clustering schemes operate differently, most first group related objects together and then select a single representative for the entire cluster (Figure 8.1(a)).

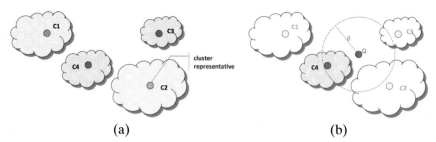

Figure 8.1. (a) Data are grouped into four clusters, and a representative is selected for each cluster. (b) Only the representative of the fourth cluster matches the query; thus, all the other clusters are pruned away (even though they may contain a few matches).

The query is then compared against the cluster representatives, and only those clusters whose representatives match the query are further investigated (Figure 8.1(b)). Although this often saves time by reducing the number of comparisons one would need to make with a naive scan of the entire database, it may result in *misses* if there are matching objects in clusters whose representatives are not a sufficiently good match to the query. Thus, in general, clusters need to be *compact*, and the representatives must be selected carefully.

8.1 QUALITY OF A CLUSTERING SCHEME

The quality of a clustering scheme can be quantified in various ways, some of which may conflict with each other. The appropriate quality measures are application dependent.

Let $C = \{C_1, C_2, \ldots, C_k\}$ be the set of clusters obtained by processing the objects in a given set, S. The following are some commonly used cluster quality measures.

Cluster Diameter

The diameter of a cluster is the maximum distance (or dissimilarity) of objects included in the cluster. The problem of partitioning a given set of entities into k clusters, such that the sum of the diameters of the clusters is minimum, is known to be NP-complete for $k \geq 3$ [Brucker, 1977].

Cluster Homogeneity/Compactness

One can quantify the homogeneity (or *compactness*) of a cluster by computing the sum or average of all similarities of object pairs in the cluster:

$$compactness(C_i) = \sum_{o_k \neq o_l; o_k, o_l \in C_i} sim(o_k, o_l).$$

A method that is more efficient to compute, and thus often used, is the *sum-of-squares*, which is the sum of squared distances of all objects in the cluster from the corresponding cluster centroid (or representative). The *minimum sum-of-squares clustering* problem of partitioning a given set of entities into k clusters in such a way that the sum of squared distances is minimized is known to be NP-hard [Aloise *et al.*, 2008] in the Euclidean space.

A related quality measure is the root-mean-square-error (RMSE) measure, which is the average of the squared distances from the objects to the cluster centroid. Given a clustering scheme $\mathcal{C} = \{C_1, C_2, \ldots, C_k\}$, the root-mean-squared error is computed as

$$RMSE(\mathcal{C}) = \frac{1}{k} \sum_{1 \leq i \leq k} \sqrt{\frac{1}{|C_i|} \sum_{o_j \in C_i} (|o_j - \mu_i|^2)},$$

where μ_is are the cluster centroids.[1] Essentially, RMSE normalizes the sum-of-squares cluster measure with respect to the size of the cluster.

Cluster Sizes

Many applications, especially the ones that go through the clustering process to improve mapping of media objects to resources, require clusters to be evenly sized. If some cluster contains too few items, this may result in resources that are wasted; clusters that are overly crowded may not fit into resources allocated on a per-cluster basis. A commonly used measure of clustering balance is the *clustering entropy*. Assuming that the clusters are nonoverlapping, maximizing the clustering entropy, defined as

$$entropy(\mathcal{C}) = \sum_{1 \leq i \leq k} P(C_i) log \left(\frac{1}{P(C_i)} \right),$$

where $P(C_i)$ is the probability that a randomly selected object in S will be in cluster C_i, will encourage more balanced clusters (see Section 4.2.2 for a discussion of entropy). If the clusters are overlapping, $\rho = \sum_{1 \leq i \leq k} P(C_i)$ is not equal to 1; however, a similar measure can be defined by normalizing the probabilities by ρ so that $\sum_{1 \leq i \leq k} P'(C_i) = \sum_{1 \leq i \leq k} \frac{P(C_i)}{\rho} = 1$.

Cluster Separation

As stated earlier, objects in a given cluster should be highly connected (or similar) with each other. Conversely, a good cluster should be as separated from other clusters as possible. One way to define this is as follows:

$$min\_separation(C_i) = \underset{o_l \in C_i, o_h \notin C_i}{MIN} (dist(o_h, o_l)).$$

A good cluster would have a high *min_separation* value.

Let $cut(C_i, C_j)$ be defined as the number of pairs in $C_i \times C_j$ that have similarities above a given threshold. Then, the separation quality of the clustering scheme, $\mathcal{C}$, can also be based on how small the total cut value,

$$\sum_{C_i \neq C_j; C_i, C_j \in \mathcal{C}} cut(C_i, C_j),$$

is. One way to quantify the impact of a cut is through the use of *Cheeger's ratio*. Given a cluster C_i its *Cheeger's ratio* is defined as

$$ratio_{Cheeger}(C_i) = \frac{\sum_{C_i \neq C_j; C_i, C_j \in \mathcal{C}} cut(C_i, C_j)}{min\{\sum_{o_h \in C_i} degree(o_h), \sum_{o_h \notin C_i} degree(o_h)\}},$$

---

[1] If the objects are not in the vector space, μ_i would correspond to C_i's cluster representative, and $|o_j - \mu_i|$ would be the distance between the object, o_j, and the cluster representative, μ_i, under the corresponding distance model.

where $degree(o_h)$ measures how connected o_h is with the other objects. Cheeger's ratio normalizes the size of the cut as a function of the density of the connection edges inside and outside the cluster. Because a small cluster with a lot of objects similar to those that are external to the cluster is worse than a larger cluster with the same number of connections to the outside, Kannan *et al.* [2000] normalize the cuts with the sizes of the corresponding clusters:

$$expansion(C_i, C_j) = \frac{cut(C_i, C_j)}{min\{|C_i|, |C_j|\}}.$$

The quality of the clustering scheme, C, can then be based on how small the sum of all the expansions is. Alternatively, one can also define the separation quality of a clustering scheme as how small the following value is:

$$\underset{C_i \in C}{MAX} \; expansion(C_i, S - C_i);$$

in other words, the quality of the clustering scheme is based on how well the objects in any of the clusters are separated from the rest of the objects in S.

Note that cut- and expansion-based schemes ignore the actual similarity and distance values, but it is possible to generalize these definitions by weighting the cut and expansion sizes with the similarity weights of the object pairs involved. Conductance is a measure that gives greater importance to vertices that have many similar neighbors.

Cluster Integrity

Although previously we have used the *cut* and *expansion* concepts to define intercluster separation measures, we can also use them to define intracluster *integrity* measures. Based on the observation that if there is a cut of small weight that divides a given cluster into two comparable pieces, then the cluster has lots of dissimilar object pairs and, thus, is of low quality, Kannan *et al.* [2000] define the expansion of a cluster, $C_i \in C$, as the minimum expansion over all the cuts of C_i. The cluster integrity of the clustering scheme, C, is then defined in terms of the cluster with the smallest expansion.

Cut- and expansion-based quality measures, in general, result in clustering problems that are NP-hard.

Clustering Modularity

Newman and Girvan [2004] introduce the following *modularity* quality measure to assess a given clustering scheme $C = \{C_1, C_2, \ldots, C_k\}$:

$$modularity(C) = \sum_{C_i \in C} \left[\frac{cut(C_i, C_i)}{|E|} - \left(\frac{\sum_{C_j \in C} cut(C_i, C_j)}{|E|} \right)^2 \right],$$

where $cut(C_i, C_i)$ is simply the number of connections among the objects in cluster C_i, and E is the set of all connections among all objects in the database. Maximization of the first term of the modularity measure implies that many connections should be contained within individual clusters (i.e., edges in the cuts must be small in number). Maximizing only this term, however, can give rise to clusters that are too big; in the extreme case, for example, putting all the objects into a single cluster would maximize this term. To account for this, modularity measure introduces a second term that ensures that each cluster accounts for only a small portion of the connections in the database. Thus, the modularity measure captures both of these conflicting criteria simultaneously. Brandes *et al.* [2008] show that, in general, maximizing modularity is an NP-complete problem.

8.2 GRAPH-BASED CLUSTERING

As in multidimensional scaling (MDS, Section 4.3.1), which embeds a given set of objects into a metric vector space using the a priori knowledge about the distances among them, graph-based clustering techniques also embed the objects into another platform for clustering. Unlike MDS, however, these techniques embed the data into a graph (instead of a vector space), which is then analyzed for identifying clusters. The general outline of the graph-based clustering methods is as follows:

 (i) Compute the similarity/distance between all object pairs.
 (ii) Compute a threshold if not already given.
 (iii) Create a graph that represents each object with a node and each pair whose similarity is above the threshold (or distance less than the threshold) with an edge.[2]
 (iv) Analyze the resulting graph to identify clusters.

In the rest of the section, we assume that we are given an undirected graph, $G(V, E)$, where each vertex corresponds to a media object and each edge corresponds to a pair of objects whose distances from each other are less than a given upper bound. The adjacency matrix, $A(G)$, of this graph is a $|V| \times |V|$ matrix, such that if two nodes have an edge between them in the graph, the adjacency matrix has a 1 in the corresponding entry and has 0 otherwise. The Laplacian matrix, $L(G)$, of the graph, on the other hand, is a $|V| \times |V|$ matrix, such that

 ■ If $i = j$, then $L(G)[i, j]$ is equal to the degree of the node i,
 ■ If nodes i and j are connected with an edge, then $L(G)[i, j] = -1$, and
 ■ $L(G)[i, j] = 0$ otherwise.

8.2.1 Connected Components

The *connected components* based clustering scheme works on the premise that if two objects are to be put into the same cluster, there must be some (direct or indirect) linkage between these two objects; otherwise, if two objects do not have any path between them, then they must belong to different clusters. Based on this premise this clustering method searches for the groups of nodes that are pairwise reachable and labels each group as a different cluster (Figure 8.2). Note that this method generates *nonoverlapping clusters*.

---

[2] In the rest of this section, unless otherwise specified, we treat the graph as being undirected. In case the distance measure is not symmetric, then we can take the smallest or largest value, depending on whether we want optimistic or pessimistic clustering.

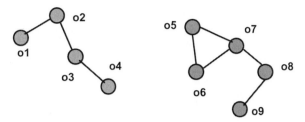

Figure 8.2. Connected components clustering: there are two connected components (hence two clusters) in this example graph.

A major advantage of connected components–based clustering is the efficiency of the process: starting from an arbitrary node, one can follow all the adjacent edges until no more adjacent edges can be found; this gives a cluster; the process then can be repeated starting from any of the remaining nodes until no unvisited nodes/edges remain. The cost of the process is $O(|V| + |E|)$, that is, linear in the graph size.

A major disadvantage of this approach, on the other hand, is that the resulting clusters may contain objects that are quite dissimilar from each other. For example, objects o_1 and o_4 in Figure 8.2 are in the same cluster, although they are not neighbors. Furthermore, they are not even in each other's two-edge neighborhood. When connected components contain such long chains, the objects at the remote ends of these chains may be very different from each other.

Also, the resulting clusters are heterogeneous in size, and this may not be appropriate in some applications where clusters are needed to be bounded (for example, to be packed as a unit into fixed-size disk pages).

8.2.2 Maximal Clique Clustering

The critical shortcoming of the connected component scheme is that it does not enforce any *tightness* of the resulting clusters. As we have seen, a connected component may consist of a long chain of nodes, thus including very dissimilar objects in the same cluster. A cluster, on the other hand, is a group of objects that are all similar to each other; thus, for clustering, it may be more effective to look for graphs that consist of nodes where all edges are neighbors of each other. This would mean that all pairs of nodes in the cluster have similarity greater than the given threshold.

Graphs where all nodes are neighbors of each other are called *cliques*. Given a graph, a subset of the nodes that forms a clique and where one cannot add any other nodes to obtain a bigger clique is called a *maximal clique* of this graph (Figure 8.3). A cluster, composed of mutually similar objects, then forms a maximal clique in the object similarity graph.

The number of cliques in a given graph can be exponential in the number of vertices [Moon and Moser, 1965]. For example, there are as many as $3^{|V|}$ cliques in the socalled Moon-Moser's graphs [Moon and Moser, 1965]. Although there are polynomial time delay algorithms for enumeration of cliques (i.e., if the graph of size n contains C cliques, the time to output all cliques is bounded by $O(n^a C)$ for some constant a) [Johnson and Papadimitriou, 1988], because in general graphs $C = O(2^n)$, one cannot efficiently search for maximal cliques by enumerating all the cliques of the graph. The number of maximal cliques in a graph, on the other hand, is

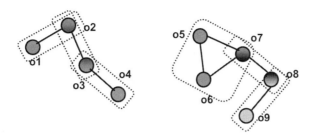

Figure 8.3. Maximal clique clustering: there are 6 (overlapping) maximal cliques in this graph.

polynomial in the size of the graph. Yet, finding a maximal clique in a given graph is known to be an NP-complete problem [Boppana and Halldórsson, 1992]. Thus, in general, clique-based clustering is expensive for use with large data sets.

8.2.3 Spectral Graph Partitioning

As we have discussed, the problem of partitioning a graph into clusters using cliques is an NP-hard problem. An alternative is to rely on *spectral clustering*, where the eigenvectors of the adjacency matrix (describing the pairwise similarities of the nodes) or the Laplacian matrix (describing the second-order connectivity) of the graph are used for identifying clusters [Boppana, 1987; Fiedler, 1973; Kannan *et al.*, 2000; McSherry, 2001; Pothen *et al.*, 1990; Schaeffer, 2007; Spielman and Hua Teng, 1996]. In the former case, the eigenvalues indicate the path capacity of the graph [Harary and Schwenk, 1979]; in the latter case, they indicate its algebraic connectivity [Chung, 1997; Fiedler, 1973].

An advantage of the spectral clustering algorithms over clique-based approaches is that, using randomized algorithms, such as [Drineas *et al.*, 1999] and [Frieze *et al.*, 1998], spectral clustering can be implemented in nearly linear time.

8.2.3.1 Angular Clustering
Similar to the latent semantic indexing (LSI) approach discussed in Section 4.4.1.1, an angular spectral clustering algorithm first finds the k left singular vectors, $\vec{u}_1, \ldots, \vec{u}_k$ with the highest singular values, $\lambda_1, \ldots, \lambda_k$. Each of these k singular vectors corresponds to a cluster. Let the *clustering* matrix, C, be such that the jth column (corresponding to the jth cluster) is equal to $\lambda_j \vec{u}_j$. Then, the node n_i of the graph is placed in cluster j if the largest entry in the ith row is $C[i, j]$ [Kannan *et al.*, 2000]. Note that, essentially, one assigns each node to the cluster whose singular vector has the smallest angle from the adjacency vector of the node.

8.2.3.2 Random Walk–Based (or Markovian) Clustering
An alternative approach relies on the idea of random walks over Markov chains. As described in Section 3.5.4, random walk on a graph, $G(V, E)$, is simply a stochastic process whose state at any time is described by a vertex of G and whose transition probability is distributed equally among all outgoing edges. The transition probability distribution for the random walk can be represented as a matrix. The (i, j)th element of this matrix, T_{ij}, describes the probability that, given that the current state is node i, the process will be in node j in the next time unit; that is,

$T_{ij} = P(S_{now+1} = j | S_{now} = i)$. The components of the first singular vector of the adjacency matrix of a random walk on a graph will give the portion of the time spent at each node after an infinite run. The singular vector corresponding to the second eigenvalue, on the other hand, is known to serve as a *proximity* measure for how long it takes for the walk to reach each vertex [McSherry, 2001]. Thus, based on the premise that the points in the same cluster should be more connected to each other than to points in other clusters (and that two vertices in the same cluster should be quickly reachable from each other), one can argue that if two nodes are in the same cluster, then the corresponding values in the second eigenvector must be close to each other. Consequently, the *closeness* of the value in the second eigenvector of the graph can be used as a measure of being in the same cluster, and the graph can be partitioned by looking for significant jumps in the (sorted) values of entries.

Focusing on the Laplacian matrix as opposed to the adjacency matrix, Fiedler [1975] showed that the second smallest eigenvalue of the Laplacian matrix is equal to 0 if and only if the graph is connected. Furthermore, the corresponding eigenvector can be used to partition the graph into two connected subgraphs [Fiedler, 1975] simply by putting those nodes that have negative weights in the eigenvector into one group and the others into another: the resulting "negative" group is connected; the resulting "nonnegative" group is also connected, as long as no member of this group has a 0 value in the second smallest eigenvector (i.e., all values are positive). Thus, the second eigenvector of the Laplacian is commonly referred to as the *algebraic connectivity* of the graph. In fact, Fiedler [1975] also showed that given two graphs $G_1(V, E_1)$ and $G_2(V, E_2)$, such that $E_1 \subset E_2$, then the second eigenvector of G_1 cannot be larger than that of G_2. It has also been argued that the smaller the second smallest eigenvector of the Laplacian is, the more likely is that the data set contains a clustering with a small cut.

8.2.4 Minimum Cut–Based Clustering

Let $G(V, E)$ be a connected graph and let C_1 and C_2 be two subsets of V such that $C_1 \cap C_2 = \emptyset$. As described in Section 8.1, the number (or sum of weights) of edges that cross between C_1 and C_2 is the value of cut of the pair (C_1, C_2) and a good clustering scheme has a low cut value.

Flake *et al.* [2004, 2000] and Kannan *et al.* [2000] present schemes that create clusters that have small intercluster cuts and large intracluster cuts. Because minimum cut–based cluster selection, in general, is NP-hard, these provide heuristics and approximation algorithms. The technique used by Kannan *et al.* [2000] is spectral in nature. In this section, we review the graph-theoretical *cut-clustering* approach presented by Flake *et al.* [2004, 2000].

Given a graph, G, let the spanning tree, T_G, where the minimum cut between any two nodes v_i and v_j in G is through the edge with the minimum weight on the path that connects v_i and v_j in T_G, be called the minimum cut (or *min-cut*) tree. Gomory and Hu [1961] show that for every undirected graph, there is a min-cut tree. The *cut-clustering* algorithm described by Flake *et al.* [2004, 2000] leverage this min-cut tree by (a) introducing an artificial node, t, connected to all nodes in V with some weight α and (b) calculating the minimum cut tree, T', of the expanded graph. To obtain the clusters, the algorithm (c) removes the artificial node, t, from T', and (d) the remaining connected components of T' form the clusters of G.

The correctness of the foregoing algorithm is based on the following property proven by Flake *et al.* [2004]: Let T_G be a min-cut tree of a graph $G(V, E)$, and let $\langle u, w \rangle$ be an edge of T_G. Consider any cut (U, W) in G over the edge $\langle u, w \rangle$, such that $u \in U$ and $w \in W$. If we take any cut (U_1, U_2) of U, so that U_1 and U_2 are nonempty, $u \in U_1$, $U_1 \cup U_2 = U$, and $U_1 \cap U_2 = \varnothing$, then

$$cut(W, U_2) \leq cut(U_1, U_2).$$

Using the foregoing *triangular equality-like* property, Flake *et al.* [2004] showed that each of the clusters formed by elimination of edges of weight α incident on the artificial node t will have intracluster expansion values (i.e., integrity) of at least α. Using the same property, Flake *et al.* [2004] also showed that the intercluster expansion value (i.e., opposite of the separation) for any of these clusters with respect to the rest of the graph is at most α. In other words, α puts lower bounds on the intercluster integrity values as well as the intracluster separation values. Consequently, α can be used to control the trade-off between the two criteria of cluster separation and cluster integrity.

This implies, though, that the quality of the resulting clustering scheme heavily depends on the value of α, yet there is no analytical mechanism to pick the α value to obtain the best clustering. Flake *et al.* [2004, 2000] propose the use of a binary-search–like scheme to pick the best value for α.

8.2.5 Adaptive Thresholding

One of the reasons why the cheap connected components–based schemes do not work effectively in practice is that, in general, it is hard to fix a single threshold that will work effectively in the entire database. In most cases, different data localities may require different similarity lower bounds. One way to resolve this problem is to rely on *adaptive thresholding* techniques that pick locally meaningful thresholds.

The most commonly used adaptive thresholding technique relies on the *minimum-distance spanning tree* of the complete graph. Given a graph $G(V, E)$, a minimum spanning tree of G is a tree T that spans the graph (i.e., includes every node in the graph), and the sum of edge weights (i.e., object distances) is the smallest among all such spanning trees [Cormen *et al.*, 2001]. The time cost of finding a minimum spanning tree of G in an undirected graph is $O(|V| + |E|)$.

The adaptive thresholding algorithm starts with a complete graph containing all nodes and all edges, where each edge is weighted with the dissimilarity/distance between the objects corresponding to the end points. Thus, the graph has $O(|V|^2)$ edges. The first step of the process involves finding a minimum spanning tree of this complete graph. This process takes $O(|V|^2)$ time and results in a tree with $|V| - 1$ edges.

As shown in Figure 8.4(a), each edge on the minimum spanning tree partitions the nodes in the graph into two sets. Let us consider the edge a in this figure. Because the tree is minimal, any other edge in E that connects these two partitions but not included in the tree must have a distance weight greater than or equal to the weight of a. In other words, the distance weight of a is the shortest distance between these two partitions. Similarly, the weight of each of the edges on the tree describes the shortest distance between the partitions that would be created if that edge is removed.

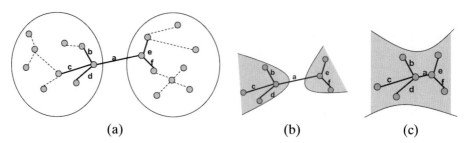

Figure 8.4. (a) Each edge on the minimum spanning tree partitions the nodes in the graph into two sets. (b,c) The length of an edge relative to the average length of the edges in its neighborhood determines whether the edge is kept or removed from the tree (the shaded area denotes the *inside* of the cluster).

Once the minimum spanning tree is created, the adaptive thresholding algorithm proceeds by investigating each of the edges in the tree and comparing its weight to the average of the weights of the edges that are incident on its end points. For example, in Figure 8.4, the distance weight $\Delta(a)$ is compared to the average distance weight $\frac{\Delta(b)+\cdots+\Delta(f)}{5}$. If the weight of the edge is greater than the neighborhood average, this is interpreted as the corresponding two partitions being too far apart from each other relative to the corresponding local neighborhoods, and the edge is removed (Figure 8.4(b)). If the weight of the edge is smaller than the neighborhood average, on the other hand, it is not a good candidate for being used for partitioning the corresponding nodes into two different clusters (Figure 8.4(c)).

8.3 ITERATIVE METHODS

The graph-based clustering algorithms we discussed in the previous section all have at least $O(N^2)$ initial cost, where N is the number of objects in the database, because they require distance or similarity values to be computed for all pairs of objects. For large databases, computing pairwise scores may simply be infeasible. A second category of clustering methods, commonly referred to as the *iterative clustering methods*, try to avoid the quadratic time complexity and reduce the execution time to $O(N)$.

8.3.1 Single-Pass Iterative Clustering

The general outline of the single-pass iterative clustering methods is as follows:

(i) *choose* an object and create a cluster that contains that object;
(ii) **while** there are more unprocessed objects **do**
    (a) *choose* a new object, o;
    (b) find the *most suitable* cluster, c, to include o;
    (c) **if** a *suitable* cluster, c, to insert o is found, then add o into c;
    (d) **else** create a new cluster containing only o

It is easy to see that the cost of iterative algorithms is in general $O(kN)$, where k is the number of resulting clusters: the main loop goes over each object once and compares this object to all clusters created so far to pick the most suitable cluster. Thus, the total amount of work performed per object is at most $O(k)$, and the cost of the algorithm is linear in the number, N, of objects.

Naturally, the foregoing single-pass iterative algorithm can be implemented in many different ways.

Scan Order

The first design criterion includes the order in which the objects are *chosen* to be processed. Because the very first object found to not match any of the existing clusters creates a new cluster, the order in which the objects are scanned has an impact on the quality of the clusters created.

Cluster Quality

A second criterion is needed to pick the most suitable cluster among the ones identified so far. If we are provided a threshold in advance, one solution is to pick the very first cluster found to satisfy this threshold. Although fast, this may not always result in high-quality clusters (see Section 8.1). An alternative is to pick the smallest cluster among those that satisfy the threshold. This would *spread the wealth* and promote more balanced (and high-entropy) clusterings. A third alternative is to find the closest cluster among all clusters identified so far. Obviously, this would promote the creation of compact and homogeneous clusters.

Leader Selection

A third design criterion enables the computation of the distance between an object and a cluster. In the *fixed leader* approach, the first object included in the cluster becomes the *leader* (or the representative) of the cluster, and the distances between new objects to this cluster are computed by comparing those objects to this leader. In *adaptive leader* schemes, the leader or the representative of the cluster is continuously updated as new objects are included in the cluster. This ensures that the first leader, which may eventually migrate to a perimeter of the cluster as new objects are included and lose its representative quality, is not unnecessarily forced to act as the representative for the whole cluster. This adaptation can be performed in an incremental manner if the objects are represented as vectors and the representative point is the centroid of the objects in the cluster (which may or may not correspond to an actual object in the cluster). However, adaptation may be costly if it cannot be performed in an incremental manner. This is the case, for example, when the objects are not represented in a vector space and a search has to be performed to identify the object that is closest to all others to represent the cluster.

If the target number of clusters are known in advance, then one can use an alternative leader selection scheme, called *max-a-min*, which picks all the leaders before the single-pass clustering process starts (Figure 8.5). Based on the premise that the cluster representatives (i.e., the leaders) should well separate the data in different clusters from each other, the max-a-min scheme picks objects that are further away from each other as leaders.[3] Although this process can be implemented in different ways, the most basic scheme first picks a random object (Figure 8.5(b)) as the first leader, then picks the objects furthest from the first leader as the second leader (Figure 8.5(c)), then picks the objects furthest from both leaders as the third leader, and so on (Figure 8.5(d,e)). The single-pass iterative clustering is then performed with

---

[3] Note the similarity between max-a-min and the FastMap pivot selection technique discussed in Section 4.3.2.

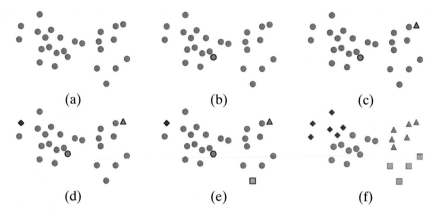

Figure 8.5. Max-a-min approach: (a) given a number of clusters, first (b,c,d,e) leaders that are sufficiently far apart from each other are selected, and then (f) the clustering is performed using the single-pass scheme.

the remaining objects (Figure 8.5(f)), except that in this case, all objects are mapped to the clusters corresponding to one of the preselected leaders (i.e., no threshold is needed to decide whether to create a new cluster).

Threshold Value

A fourth criterion needed to execute the single-pass clustering algorithm is an upper bound on the acceptable distance between the object and the cluster. This threshold can be fixed globally or can be computed locally; for example, it can be set as a function of the diameter of the cluster being considered. Once again any adaptive scheme would increase the complexity of the algorithm, as the threshold has to be readjusted for each cluster as new objects arrive. If the objects are in a vector space, an alternative is to use the Mahalonobis distance (Section 3.1.3), which adapts the distance function itself to each cluster.

8.3.2 Agglomerative Clustering

An alternative approach to clustering, which may involve more than one passes over the data, is the agglomerative clustering scheme, which builds up clusters in a bottom-up, hierarchical fashion.

The *agglomerative clustering* approach starts by assigning each object in the database to an individual cluster. In other words, each object is a cluster by itself. Then these clusters are iteratively merged until some quality threshold (see Section 8.1) is met or a target number of clusters is reached. Alternatively, the entire hierarchy is created (i.e., clusters are merged until only one single cluster remains) and, then, an appropriate clustering strategy is picked by navigating down the hierarchy to find the appropriate depth (i.e., degree of clustering) along each branch.

8.3.3 K-Means and Iterative Improvement

Although the *k-means* algorithm is commonly described as a clustering algorithm, it is in fact a name for a family of algorithms for iteratively improving a given clustering scheme [Lloyd, 1982, 1957; Steinhaus, 1956].

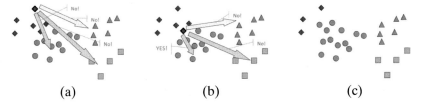

Figure 8.6. K-means iterative improvement: (a) No change, (b) One object changes cluster, (c) Final status.

8.3.3.1 K-Means and Related Algorithms

Given N objects preclustered into k clusters, a k-means algorithm goes repeatedly over the objects and checks whether the quality (described through a global quality function based on any suitable combination of the measures introduced in Section 8.1) of the clustering scheme can be improved by moving the object into another cluster (Figures 8.6(a) and (b)). The scan over the database is repeated either for a fixed number of times or until no more improvements can be obtained. The reason why the technique is referred to as the k-means algorithm is that, in most popular implementations of the technique (such as [Lloyd, 1982, 1957]), the objects are assumed to be represented in a vector space and the quality of a clustering scheme, $\mathcal{C} = \{C_1, C_2, \ldots, C_k\}$, is evaluated using the root-mean-square error,

$$quality_{rmse}(\mathcal{C}) = \frac{1}{k} \sum_{1 \le i \le k} \sqrt{\frac{1}{|C_i|} \sum_{\vec{v}_j \in C_i} (|\vec{v}_j - \vec{\mu}_i|^2)},$$

or the squared error,

$$quality_{se}(\mathcal{C}) = \sum_{1 \le i \le k} \sum_{\vec{v}_j \in C_i} (|\vec{v}_j - \vec{\mu}_i|^2),$$

measures, both of which consider the cluster centroids (i.e., cluster means, $\vec{\mu}_i$) as cluster representatives.

Although the preceding formulation is based on centroids or representatives of the clusters, there are versions of the algorithm more specific to cut-based partitioning of graphs, where the cluster quality is not measured relative to a centroid or a representative, but is based on the size of the edge cuts. The KL algorithm [Kernighan and Lin, 1970] incrementally swaps nodes among partitions of a graph to reduce the edge-cut of the partitioning, until a local minimum is reached. The FM algorithm [Fiduccia and Mattheyses, 1988] computes, for each node of the graph, the gain achieved by moving the node to each other partition. These vertices are inserted into max-priority queues, one for each partition, based on their corresponding gain values. The algorithm selects a node v with the largest gain from the heavier partition and moves it to the other partition corresponding to this gain. This node is locked (i.e., it cannot move anymore in this iteration), and the gain values of the other neighboring nodes are updated. After each step, the FM algorithm records the size of the cut. After all the nodes have been processed and there are no more unlocked nodes, the step where the minimum cut was observed is found, and all nodes that changed partitions after that step are moved back to their original partitions. Once again, the process is repeated until a local minimum is reached.

Note that, in k-means, as well as other iterative algorithms, the initial k clusters can be provided by another clustering algorithm or can, in fact, be a random grouping of the objects in the database. When a k-means algorithm is executed over a random initial grouping, the iterative improvement process essentially behaves as a clustering algorithm. For this reason, the k-means technique is commonly used alone as the sole clustering algorithm, instead of being used as a companion to another clustering technique.

8.3.4 Estimating the Number of Clusters in the Database

As we have seen, some clustering algorithms such as max-a-min and k-means require the number of clusters, k, to be provided as an input parameter.

In general, estimating the number of clusters is not an easy task. In some cases, the number of clusters is determined by the application's needs; for example, objects may be split into k pieces, each of which will be processed by a separate processor in a parallel computing environment. In these cases, k is determined by external factors. In many other cases, however, the number of clusters needs to reflect the characteristics of the data. Because what one expects from the clustering scheme (such as the quality measures described in Section 8.1) would vary from application to application, the characteristic number of clusters of a data set is also application dependent.

8.3.4.1 Probabilistic Estimation

When one specifically focuses on the vector data, it is possible to establish a relationship between the cluster centroids and the principal components of the corresponding vector space [Ding and He, 2004]. Thus the problem of finding the number of clusters is analogous to finding the number of principal components of the space.

An alternative estimation model for k in vector data is based on a probabilistic model, especially suitable to be used along with other probabilistic information retrieval tools such as TF and IDF. Given a database of N objects and d feature dimensions, let us define pairwise covering of objects o_i and o_j as

$$covering(o_i, o_j) = \sum_{1 \le l \le d} p(feature_l | o_i) p(o_j | feature_l),$$

where $p(feature_l | o)$ describes the prominence of $feature_l$ in object o, and $p(o | feature_l)$ is the likelihood of picking the object o among all the objects that contain $feature_l$. Suppose now that the database is a perfect single cluster, in the sense that all the features are uniformly distributed in all the objects and all the objects are equally likely to be selected for all given features. In this case, we can see that all the pairwise coverings would be equal to $\frac{1}{N}$:

$$covering(o_i, o_j) = \sum_{1 \le l \le d} p(feature_l | o_i) p(o_j | feature_l) = \sum_{1 \le l \le d} \frac{1}{d} \frac{1}{N} = \frac{1}{N}.$$

Thus, if we add up the self-coverings of all the objects in this one perfect cluster, we get 1:

$$\sum_{1 \leq i \leq N} covering(o_i, o_i) = \sum_{1 \leq i \leq N} \frac{1}{N} = 1.$$

It is easy to see that the result generalizes to multiple perfect clusters as well. For example, let us assume that the database contains two perfect clusters, C_1 and C_2, where the first one has N objects with d_1 uniform feature dimensions and the second one has M objects with d_2 uniform feature dimensions. Because the clusters are perfect, let us further assume that there are no shared features between the clusters. Then

$$\sum_{o_i \in C_1 \cup C_2} covering(o_i, o_i) = \sum_{o_i \in C_1} covering(o_i, o_i) + \sum_{o_i \in C_2} covering(o_i, o_i)$$

$$= \sum_{o_i \in C_1} \sum_{1 \leq l \leq d_1} \frac{1}{d_1} \frac{1}{N} + \sum_{o_i \in C_2} \sum_{1 \leq l \leq d_2} \frac{1}{d_2} \frac{1}{M}$$

$$= N \frac{1}{N} + M \frac{1}{M} = 2.$$

In other words, given a database of objects, if we compute the *total self-covering* value for the entire database, this value can be considered as an approximation of the number of *perfect clusters*; of course, because the clusters are in general not perfect, the number of clusters in the database is likely to be different than the total self-covering value implies.

8.3.4.2 Incremental Selection of the Number of Clusters

As we discussed in Section 4.3.1, while embedding a given set of distances onto a metric space, the multidimensional scaling (MDS) scheme picks the number of dimensions of the resulting space incrementally, as needed to improve the structure of the space, instead of picking the number in advance. In this section, we see that it is possible to use a similar incremental selection process in determining the appropriate number of clusters as well.

An example of this approach is shown in [Pelleg, 2000], which introduces the X-means scheme that exploits the available data statistics to estimate the value of k as well as for selecting the most promising clusters to be processed in run-time during k-means iterative improvement process. The X-means scheme requires from the user only the range in which k lies. The algorithm starts with the lower bound of the range and adds centroids as needed, until the upper bound is reached. An improve-structure operation finds out when new clusters need to be inserted and which clusters need to be split into two new clusters. For each split candidate, the algorithm performs a model selection test that asks whether the children after the split will model the data distribution well or, before the split, the parent was a better model for the distribution of the points. To choose between the parent and its children, X-means uses *BIC* scores [Kass and Wasserman, 1995] for evaluating the models the clusters represent. The BIC score for a given model (cluster), M, of data, D, approximates the posterior probability, $prob(M|D)$. Thus, it describes how well a given cluster matches the points it covers. For more details on BIC (and other criteria that can be used for selecting the appropriate complexity of a model for representing the data), see Section 9.8.

Another significant example of this scheme is the G-means algorithm [Hamerly and Elkan, 2003], which performs statistical tests for the clustered data, under the assumption that a properly clustered data would have a Gaussian distribution (see Section 3.5). Based on this assumption, G-means runs k-means clustering with increasing k until a *Gaussian fit* test accepts all the resulting clusters. If the test determines that the data around the center of the cluster are not sampled from a Gaussian distribution, then the corresponding cluster is split and the test is repeated on the children until all the resulting clusters are Gaussian. Given a cluster C with a center c, the Gaussian fit test is performed as follows:

(i) The algorithm runs k-means for the data points in C for $k = 2$.
(ii) Let c_1 and c_2 be the centers of the clusters of the two children. The vector $v = c_1 - c_2$ gives the direction which k-means believes to be important for separating the data. As in FastMap (Section 4.3.2), G-means projects all the data in the given cluster, C, onto this vector v.
(iii) Once all the points are mapped onto the most significant one-dimensional space and after all the values are normalized such that the mean is 0 and the variance is 1, G-means performs the Anderson-Darling test [Stephens, 1974] on the resulting one-dimensional list of values, which checks whether the set of values is Gaussian. At this stage, the algorithm uses the statistical significance level, α, provided by the user to determine whether there is statistically significant evidence that the data form a Gaussian.

The test essentially checks whether the given list of values have a Gaussian distribution or not under the given statistical significance bounds. Projecting the data in the cluster onto a one-dimensional space allows the algorithm to consider the data along the direction that k-means considers important for separating the data. Thus, if the test fails, we can argue that the cluster C is not Gaussian along this significant dimension, and we can split the cluster into two.

8.4 MULTICONSTRAINT PARTITIONING

As we have seen in Section 8.1, there can be multiple, even conflicting criteria one may want to use when partitioning data. Karypis and Kumar [1998] propose to treat the task of minimizing the edge cuts as the objective function to a constraint program that can take an arbitrary number of balancing constraints (e.g., the requirement that the partitions are of the same size). In particular, Karypis and Kumar [1998] assign a vector of weights (considering various constraints) to each vertex and formulate a constraint program whose goal is to produce an edge-cut minimal partitioning of the underlying graph in such a way that a balancing constraint associated with each weight is satisfied.

Let $G = (V, E)$, be a graph such that each vertex $v \in V$ has a weight vector $\vec{w}_v$[4] of size m associated with it, and each edge e has a scalar weight w_e. Given a k-way partitioning, P, of vectors, where $P[v]$ is the partition number of the vertex v,

---

[4] Without loss of generality, Karypis and Kumar [1998] assume that $\forall_i \sum_{v \in V} w_v[i] = 1$.

Karypis and Kumar [1998] define the load imbalance with respect to the ith weight as

$$l_i = k \times \underset{j}{MAX} \left(\sum_{v \ s.t. \ P[v]=j} \vec{w}_v[i] \right).$$

Given this definition of load imbalance, one can formulate two different multiconstraint partitioning problems [Karypis and Kumar, 1998]:

- *Horizontal formulation:* Find an edge-cut minimizing partitioning such that, given an upper bound-vector $\vec{u}$ of size m, each weight i is balanced within the limits specified by the corresponding entry in $\vec{u}$:

  $$\forall_i \ l_i \leq \vec{u}[i].$$

- *Vertical formulation:* Find an edge-cut minimizing partitioning such that, given a total upper bound value, $u \leq 1.0$, and a *relative importance* vector, $\vec{r}$,

  $$\sum_{i=1}^{m} l_i \vec{r}[i] \leq u.$$

Karypis and Kumar [1998] show that given a set S of objects, where each object n_i has two weights, $\vec{w}_i[1]$ and $\vec{w}_i[2]$, one can partition these objects into two clusters A and B such that

$$\left| \sum_{n_i \in A} \vec{w}_i[1] - \sum_{n_i \in B} \vec{w}_i[1] \right| \leq 2\mu \quad and \quad \left| \sum_{n_i \in A} \vec{w}_i[2] - \sum_{n_i \in B} \vec{w}_i[2] \right| \leq 2\mu,$$

where μ is the maximum of all weights. If the number of weights is more than two, then the algorithm first puts all the objects in A and then iteratively moves objects from A to B, considering the relative weight orders of the objects in A. The result is a partitioning where for m weights, the partition imbalance is bounded by $(m-1)\mu$. However, when $m > 2$, the algorithm presented by Karypis and Kumar [1998] may fail to find appropriate objects to move from A to B. Karypis and Kumar [1998] argue that for sufficiently large and diverse data sets, there often are suitable partitioning solutions. Finally, Karypis and Kumar [1998] show that these bounds are sufficient to implement iterative refinement–based k-way partitioning algorithms that can iteratively improve the edge cuts while also balancing the partitions to solve the horizontal and vertical constraint formulations presented earlier.

8.5 MIXTURE MODEL BASED CLUSTERING

As we have seen in Section 3.5.3.3, considering the data sets as being generated by model-driven random processes can help in developing algorithms to discover various properties of the data. Mixture model based clustering algorithms apply this idea to data clustering [McLachlan and Basford, 1988]: in particular, each cluster is treated as a data generator and each point in the input data set is treated as being generated by one of these clusters. Thus, given a set of input objects, a target number of clusters, a statistical model, such as Gaussian [Permuter *et al.*, 2006; Roberts *et al.*, 1998; Rudzkis and Radavicius, 1995], which drives data generation by the clusters, and a known or assumed prior probability for each of the clusters, the parameters best describing each cluster and the cluster membership for each input object are discovered using expectation maximization (EM [Dempster *et al.*, 1977], see Section 9.7.4.3). Intuitively, this process is similar to the probabilistic latent semantic analysis (PLSA) discussed in 4.4.2, except that advanced knowledge about the statistical properties of the clusters are also leveraged during the clustering process.

8.6 ONLINE CLUSTERING WITH DYNAMIC EVIDENCE

The clustering schemes we have discussed so far all assume that all the distance/similarity values required for clustering are either available before the process starts or, at least, available on an on-demand basis. In many scenarios, however, these values may not be known a priori or on demand. For example, if the similarity value is based on user feedback or users' use and access patterns to data, this information will be available only when the user has occasion to provide feedback or access the data. Furthermore, a given user's assessment or use patterns may evolve over time. Thus, clustering schemes that assume static distance/similarity values are not suitable for use in these cases.

8.6.1 Confidence Clustering

A commonly used approach to clustering with dynamic information is to assign a confidence score for each object/cluster pair and revise this confidence score as new evidence becomes available.

Let $O = \{o_1, \ldots, o_N\}$ be a set of objects and $C = \{C_1, \ldots, C_k\}$ be a clustering. Let initially each object, o_i, be assigned to a cluster C_j, and let $0 < conf(o_i, C_j) \leq \theta$ denote how confident we are that o_i belongs to C_j. The initial assignment can be random or may reflect an initial clustering performed using some static properties of the objects in O. Similarly, initial confidence values can be assigned randomly or may reflect how close each object is to the corresponding cluster representative, based on the static data properties.

As new evidence based on user access or direct feedback becomes available, the confidence values are revised. Let us assume that at some point, the user either explicitly (through feedback) or implicitly (through simultaneous access) provided the evidence that object o_h and o_i are *related*:

- If o_h and o_i are already in the same cluster, C_j, this provides further support for the fact that both belong to that cluster; thus $conf(o_h, C_j)$ and $conf(o_i, C_j)$ are incremented (of course as long as they are less than the upper bound, Θ).
- If o_h is in cluster C_j and o_i is in cluster C_l, then this is evidence against the current clustering; the clustering and the confidence values need to be revised:
    - If both $conf(o_h, C_j)$ and $conf(o_i, C_l)$ are larger than 1, then these confidence values are decremented;
    - If $conf(o_h, C_j) = 1$ and $conf(o_i, C_l)$ is larger than 1, then
        - □ if there is at least one object, o_v in cluster C_l such that $conf(o_v, C_l) = 1$, objects o_h and o_v are swapped and their confidences in their new clusters are set to the lowest possible value, that is, 1;
        - □ if there is no such object, then $conf(o_i, C_l)$ is decremented.

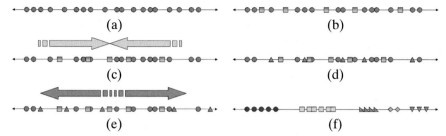

Figure 8.7. Adaptive clustering based on user access patterns: (a) Initial mapping, (b) A set of objects are accessed together, (c) Objects moved together, (d) A random set of objects are selected, (e) Objects moved away, (f) Final mapping.

> The case where $conf(o_i, C_l) = 1$ and $conf(o_h, C_j)$ is larger than 1 is similarly handled.
> – If both $conf(o_h, C_j) = 1$ and $conf(o_i, C_l) = 1$, then
>   □ If there is at least one object, o_v in cluster C_l such that $conf(o_v, C_l) = 1$, then objects o_h and o_v are swapped and their confidences in their new clusters are set to the lowest possible value, that is, 1;
>   □ else if there is at least one object, o_v in cluster C_j such that $conf(o_v, C_j) = 1$, then objects o_i and o_v are swapped and their confidences in their new clusters are set to the lowest possible value, that is, 1;
>   □ else no adjustments are performed.

The threshold value Θ has a significant impact one how adaptive the system is. When Θ is large, the system may take more time to move an object to another cluster when the user's behavior changes. When Θ is small, on the other hand, the clustering can undesirably fluctuate because of temporally localized variations in the usage pattern. Therefore, the value of Θ must be set with care.

8.6.2 Perturbation-Based Clustering

The confidence clustering scheme just described assumes that an initial clustering (or at least the number of clusters) is known in advance. In many cases, however, such information may not be available a priori either.

An alternative dynamic evidence-based clustering scheme starts with a random mapping of objects onto a one-dimensional space (Figure 8.7(a)) and *perturbs* (or moves) the objects on this space as new evidence is collected. When there is evidence that a set of objects are related (Figure 8.7(b)), these objects are moved toward their centroid (Figure 8.7(c)). Because at every iteration related objects are forced together, all these objects will eventually form a cluster on the one-dimensional space. On the other hand, there is a risk that the resulting clusters will overlap in space and thus different clusters will not be separable from each other. Thus, there is also a need for a second force that separates unrelated objects. This is realized by picking a random set of objects (Figure 8.7(d)) and moving these away from their centroid (Figure 8.7(e)). Of course, this random separation may also affect clusters that are being formed; however, the *centripetal* force that brings the related objects closer to cluster centroids is likely to be more consistent than the *centrifugal* force that separates random related objects. Consistently, the tendency to form clusters will not be significantly affected. Yet, when aggregated over all the unrelated pairs of objects, the weak *centrifugal* force will cause the different clusters to form elsewhere along the 1D space, ensuring the separability of the resulting clusters (Figure 8.7(f)).

The time at which this clustering scheme converges on separable clusters depends on the number of objects, the number of objects that are accessed together at each iteration, the consistency of the feedback, and the relative strengths of the centripetal and centrifugal forces. Note also that the output of this scheme is not the clusters, but a mapping from objects to the 1D space. Thus, there is a need for a separate clustering algorithm to use these mappings and separate the clusters of objects from each other.

8.7 SELF-ORGANIZING MAPS

A self-organizing map (SOM) is a neural network model that simulates the topographic mappings of the sensory data (from the retina) to the cerebral cortex in the human brain [Kohonen, 1988]. Because it simulates the way the brain readjusts (i.e., self-organizes) to learn patterns within the sensory data set, it is also used in other clustering and classification contexts.

8.7.1 Neural Networks

Neural networks emulate the way brains perform cognitive tasks. In particular, a neural network consists of *neurons* that are interconnected, and the learning process involves modification and reconfiguration of these synaptic connections and their weights. When presented with a set of examples (e.g., labeled observations), neural networks adjust the weights of the synaptic connections in a way that best represents the most intrinsic properties of the underlying patterns. More specifically, given an input stimulus, neurons in the network *compete* for ownership; the winners of this competition strengthen their weights with respect to this input under the so called Hebbian learning rule [Hebb, 1949]: *"When cell A excites cell B repeatedly and persistently, some changes take place in such a way that improves A's efficiency in firing B."* In other words, if A and B are fired together, the connection between them should be strengthened, whereas if their firings are not coherent, then the weight should be weakened:

$$\frac{\delta w_{AB}(t)}{\delta t} = \alpha A(t) B(t),$$

where w_{AB} is the weight of the link between A and B, $A(t)$ is the firing status of A at time t, $B(t)$ is the firing status of B at time t, and $\alpha \in (0, 1)$ is a learning rate. After the training phase, where the weights between the cells in the network are learned, when presented with unknown data, the neural network can now be used for performing recognition by tracking which cells are fired for the given input.

8.7.2 Clustering Using Self-Organizing Maps

A self-organizing map (SOM) is a special type of neural network, consisting of neurons arranged into a 2D rectangular grid. Given a set, X, of data points in

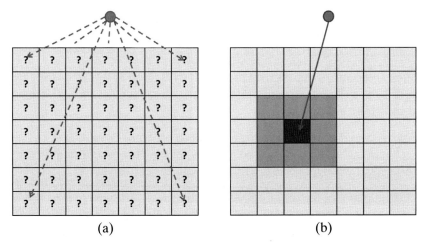

Figure 8.8. Self-organizing maps: Given a new data instance, (a) first a winner neuron (i.e., grid cell) is selected, and then (b) the weights of the winning neuron and the neurons nearby are adjusted.

n-dimensional space, the neurons in the SOM fight for the ownership of each data point. This is performed as follows:

Let S be a SOM in the shape of a $k \times l$ grid, and let $S[i, j]$ denote the neuron at row i, column j. Each neuron $S[i, j]$ has an associated small random weight $\vec{w}_{i,j}$ that itself is a vector in the same n-dimensional space as the input data. At each time instant, t, an input from X is taken as the current input, $\vec{x}(t)$, and a winner neuron closest to $\vec{x}(t)$ is selected:

$$v(t) = \underset{i \leq k, j \leq l}{argmin} \; \Delta(\vec{x}(t), \vec{w}_{i,j}(t)).$$

Here, $v(t)$, is the index of the winner neuron (Figure 8.8(a)). Once the winner is selected, the weights of the winner and its neighbors in the grid are updated (Figure 8.8(b)); intuitively, the winning neuron and the neurons nearby are rewarded by becoming more like the input vector $\vec{x}(t)$:

$$\forall_{i \leq k, j \leq l} \; \delta \vec{w}_{i,j} = \alpha(t) n(v, i, j, t)(\vec{x}(t) - \vec{w}_{i,j}(t)),$$

where

- $\delta \vec{w}_{i,j}$ is the resulting change in the weight of neuron $S[i, j]$,
- $\alpha(t)$ is the current learning rate, and
- $n(v, i, j, t) \in [0, 1]$ is a neighborhood function, which gives 1 for the winning neuron, close to 1 for nearby neurons, and close to 0 for neurons far away. (A commonly used neighborhood function is

$$e^{-\frac{\|v - (i,j)\|^2}{2\sigma^2}},$$

where σ^2 is the variance describing how far the neighborhood extends from the winning neuron.)

The process is repeated until the map converges or until all the data in X have been consumed. In order to prevent weights from becoming saturated or unlimited, the learning rate $\alpha(t) \in (0, 1)$ needs to satisfy

$$\lim_{t \to \infty} \sum \alpha(t) \to \infty \quad \text{and} \quad \lim_{t \to \infty} \alpha(t) \to 0.$$

Note that at the end of this training process, the resulting SOM can be used to cluster points in X (as well as data points not seen yet): we expect that (if X is large enough), at the end of the training phase,

- Similar-valued neurons will be close to each other in the grid;
- Yet there will also be cluster boundaries on the grid, where despite the spatial closeness, the weight vectors will have significant differences.

Such boundaries can be found using segmentation algorithms, such as the ones we have discussed in Section 2.3.3. Once the cluster boundaries are discovered, each point can be placed into a cluster based on the location of the winning neuron.

8.7.3 Distance-Preserving Self-Organizing Maps

In addition to clustering, self-organizing maps can also be used for other nonsupervised learning tasks, such as distance-preserving dimensionality reduction, as in multidimensional scaling (Section 4.3.1) and PCA (Section 4.2.6).

To achieve this, in addition to cluster topology (nearby neurons having similar weights), the mapping should also preserve distances (similar vectors mapped to nearby neurons). Yin [2002] and Yin [2007] achieve this by decomposing the weight update term $\vec{x}(t) - \vec{w}_{i,j}(t)$ into

$$(\vec{x}(t) - \vec{w}_v(t)) + (\vec{w}_v(t) - \vec{w}_{i,j}(t)).$$

The first term represents the correction due to the winner ($\vec{w}_v(t)$ is the weight of the winning neuron); the second term is a *lateral* force that essentially brings neighboring neuron at position (i, j) closer to the winner at position v. In order to help preserve the distances, the weight update term, $\delta \vec{w}_{i,j}$, is revised as follows:

$$\forall_{i \leq k, j \leq l} \ \delta \vec{w}_{i,j} = \alpha(t) n(v, i, j, t)((\vec{x}(t) - \vec{w}_v(t)) + \beta(\vec{w}_v(t) - \vec{w}_{i,j}(t))),$$

where $\beta = \frac{\Delta(\vec{w}_v(t), \vec{w}_{i,j}(t))}{\lambda \|v - (i,j)\|} - 1$ regularizes this lateral contraction force in such a way that interneuron distances on the resulting SOM are in proportion to the distances in the data space (that is , $\lambda \|v - (i, j)\| \sim \Delta(\vec{w}_v(t), \vec{w}_{i,j}(t))$ for the given constant λ). In other words, as in MDS, the distances between the points onto which data are mapped reflect the corresponding distances in the original data space.

8.8 CO-CLUSTERING

The various clustering techniques we have introduced earlier in this chapter all take a matrix describing *object-to-object* or *object-to-feature* mappings and analyze this mapping to obtain clusters of objects. In other words, while the mapping provides bidirectional information (for instance, a matrix describing objects in terms of features simultaneously describes features in terms of objects), the clustering algorithms return only object clusters.

8.8.1 **SVD and LSI as Co-clustering Schemes**

As we have seen in Section 4.4.1.1, on the other hand, it is possible to operate on both aspects of the database matrix simultaneously: the latent semantic indexing (LSI) scheme, based on the singular-valued decomposition (SVD) technique, takes a document-term matrix A and decomposes it into three matrices U, V, and Σ, such that

$$A = U\Sigma V^T,$$

where the columns of U can be thought of as the *eigen documents* of the given document collection, each corresponding to one independent concept, and the columns of V can be thought of as the *eigen terms* of the collection, each, once again, corresponding to a concept in the database. The Σ matrix gives the strength of the corresponding concepts in the database. In other words, the LSI technique leverages the inherently symmetric nature of the SVD to extract *concepts* that can be used for clustering both documents and terms simultaneously. This is commonly referred to as *co-clustering*.

8.8.2 **Information-Theoretical Co-clustering**

Dhillon *et al.* [2003] introduced an alternative, *information-theoretical* co-clustering technique for simultaneously clustering the rows and the columns of the input matrix. The algorithm views the database matrix as a joint probability distribution of two discrete random variables and poses the problem of optimal co-clustering as maximizing the *mutual information* between the *clustered* random variables[5]:

> **Definition 8.8.1 (Mutual information):** *Let U and V be two sets of events (or random variables). Let $P_1(u)$ denote the probability of event $u \in U$. Let $P_2(v)$ denote the probability of event $v \in V$. The mutual information of P_1 and P_2 is then defined as*
>
> $$MI(U; V) = \sum_{u \in U, v \in V} P(u \wedge v) \, log \frac{P(u \wedge v)}{P_1(u)P_2(v)},$$
>
> *where $P(u \wedge v)$ is the joint probability of events u and v.*

To understand the definition of mutual information and why it can represent the dependency between two random variables, remember from Section 3.1.3 that relative entropy (or the Kullback-Leibler divergence) can be used for measuring the similarity between two probability distributions, P_a and P_b, both defined over a set of events E:

$$RE(P_a, P_b) = \sum_{e \in E} P_a(e) \, log \frac{P_a(e)}{P_b(e)}.$$

We also know that if two random variables X and Y are independent from each other, then

$$\forall_{u \in U, v \in V} P(u \wedge v) = P_1(u)P_2(v).$$

---

[5] Also see Table 4.2 in Section 4.2.4.

Thus, if U and V are independent, we would expect that $RE(P(u \wedge v), P_1(u)P_2(v)) = 0$; furthermore, the more U and V are related (i.e., the more similarly they are distributed), the higher will be $RE(P(u \wedge v), P_1(u)P_2(v))$. Thus, $MI(U; V)$, which is in fact equal to $RE(P(u \wedge v), P_1(u)P_2(v))$, measures the dependence between the two random variables. Thus, because mutual information reflects the dependency between the row and column variables (e.g., documents and terms), Dhillon *et al.* [2003] define the optimal co-clustering as the clustering that minimizes the difference in mutual information between the original random variables and the mutual information between the clustered ones.

The co-clustering algorithm operates in stages and mixes row clustering and column clustering: row clustering is performed by measuring the similarity of each row distribution to a *row-cluster prototype* in terms of relative entropy (i.e., the Kullback-Leibler divergence); similarly for column clustering. The row- and column-clustering stages are iterated, incrementally improving the co-clustering quality, until a locally optimal clustering is found. Let X be a random variable denoting the rows and Y be a random variable denoting the columns; let also $\hat{X}$ and $\hat{Y}$ denote the clustered row and column random variables. Dhillon *et al.* [2003] define the objective function as

$$minimize \quad MI(X; Y) - MI(\hat{X}; \hat{Y}).$$

In other words, an optimal co-clustering minimizes the information loss between the mutual information of the original matrix and the co-clustered matrix. The outline of the co-clustering algorithm is as follows:

(i) Start with an initial row (column) clustering, such that the row-cluster (column-cluster) distributions are maximally apart from each other.

(ii) REPEAT
   (a) Given the current column clusters, compute *row-cluster prototypes*, which act similar to *centroids* of the row-clusters.
   (b) Reassign each row to a new row cluster whose row-cluster prototype is closest in terms of Kullback-Leibler divergence.
   (c) Given the new row clusters, compute *column-cluster prototypes*, which act similar to *centroids* of the column clusters.
   (d) Reassign each column to a new column cluster whose column cluster prototype is closest in terms of Kullback-Leibler divergence.
   UNTIL the drop in mutual information loss between consecutive iterations of the algorithm is smaller than a given threshold.

The foregoing co-clustering algorithm has a complexity of $O(num\_nonzeros \times num\_iter \times (k + l))$, where *num_nonzeros* is the number of nonzeros in the input matrix, k is the desired number of row clusters, and l is the desired number of column clusters. The value of *num_iter* is the number of iterations required to converge on a local optimum. Although this number depends on the data, Dhillon *et al.* [2003] report that empirically, 20 iterations seem to suffice. Note that because the complexity of the algorithm does not depend on the size of the database matrix, but depends on the number of nonzero entries in it, the algorithm is especially suitable for clustering sparse matrices.

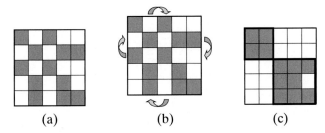

Figure 8.9. Discovering *cross-associates*: the resulting matrix has a simpler form. Note that one of the resulting cross-associates (i.e., rectangular regions of the matrix dense with 1s) is imperfect: (a) Original matrix, (b) row/cluster permutations, and (c) the final matrix.

8.8.3 Cross-Association

Although it is highly efficient, especially for sparse matrices, a shortcoming of the co-clustering scheme presented in the previous subsection is that as input parameters it requires the target numbers of row and column clusters. As we have discussed earlier, however, picking the target number of clusters is not always straightforward. Thus, instead of relying on user-supplied values, Chakrabarti *et al.* [2004] present an information-theoretic scheme for choosing the number of row and column clusters and computing *cross-associations* between these groups in a fully automated manner.

Unlike the algorithm of Dhillon *et al.* [2003], which performs a lossy transformation that gets less and less lossy as the numbers of row and column clusters increase, the cross-association scheme aims to losslessly represent the input matrix in terms of a set of *cross-associates* (Figure 8.9). The main idea behind the cross-association algorithm is that a matrix describing cross-associations of a given input matrix should have a simpler form than the original matrix (Figure 8.9), and thus it must be cheaper to describe than the input matrix. Based on this observation, Chakrabarti *et al.* [2004] rely on the *minimum description length* principle [Rissanen, 1978] to pick the appropriate numbers of rows and columns. Let D be an $M \times N$ binary data matrix.[6] Chakrabarti *et al.* [2004] describe the problem of finding an optimal cross-association as finding

- a number, k, of row groups,
- a number, l, of column groups,
- a mapping, $\Psi : \{1, 2, \ldots, M\} \rightarrow \{1, 2, \ldots, k\}$, from rows to row groups, and
- a mapping $\Phi : \{1, 2, \ldots, N\} \rightarrow \{1, 2, \ldots, l\}$, from columns to column groups,

such that the number of bits required for encoding all the information in sufficient detail that the original matrix can be constructed is minimized. This involves encoding (a) the matrix dimensions M and N, (b) the row and column permutations used in simplifying the matrix, (c) the values of k and l, (d) the number of rows and columns in each row group and column group, and (e) lossless compressions of the resulting binary matrices using a compression algorithm, such as arithmetic coding [Howard and Vitter, 1991].

---

[6] Note that unlike the other schemes we discussed earlier, cross-associations assume that the input matrix is binary, each "1" describing an *association* between a row and a column.

The algorithm starts with small values of k and l and increases them as needed while rearranging rows and columns of the input matrix. At each iteration, as in [Dhillon *et al.*, 2003], the algorithm first keeps the columns fixed and operates on the rows. For each row, x, the algorithm reassigns the row into the row group such that the resulting description length will be the smallest. Then, the algorithm keeps the rows fixed and similarly operates on the columns. After each iteration, the algorithm recomputes the best k and l values based on the current arrangement. For this purpose, at each iteration, the algorithm first picks the row group with the maximum entropy per row and splits it into two such that the overall entropy of the group decreases.[7] Then, the algorithm tries to obtain *cheaper-to-describe* cross-associations with the new group. If such a cross-association is found, the new grouping is kept; otherwise, the original row groups are maintained. After this, before the next iteration starts, the algorithm also tries to increase the number of columns to see if such an increase would help reduce the description length. Only if the description length drops is the number of column groups increased.

8.9 SUMMARY

Clustering is a fundamental operation in multimedia databases: it serves many roles, from helping reduce query processing costs by pruning parts of the database that is not likely to contribute to the query result to helping identify strongly related components of a data object to help summarize its content. Many of the techniques we have covered here are also fundamental in summarizing videos, long text documents, or the Web into their respective information units.

Clustering, however, is rarely perfect. In many cases, there are conflicting criteria that need to be taken into account simultaneously. Furthermore, many times, there is not sufficient evidence to properly treat objects at the cluster boundaries effectively and map them to the most appropriate cluster. In Chapter 11, we discuss how to evaluate retrieval quality when such imperfections cause false hits or misses.

---

[7] Remember from Section 4.2.2 that reducing the entropy means reducing the uncertainty and randomness in the data.

9

Classification

Unlike indexing and clustering processes which aim to place similar media objects together for efficient access and pruning, the classification process aims to associate media objects into known semantically meaningful categories. A classifier learns how to recognize, from a given set of media objects preclassified into a set of categories, what the critical features of these categories of interest are and, based on these, associates new media objects to these categories.

In a classification algorithm, the input data (i.e., the *training set*) are objects with multiple attributes or features, and each training object is labeled with a class label. The goal of the classification process is to analyze the input data and develop a description, or a model, for each class using the characteristics of the corresponding training data. Thus, the classification algorithms detect patterns, or sets of features, which define categories. Because the input training data have been labeled, this set of algorithms are also called *supervised learning* algorithms. In contrast, the clustering algorithms covered in the previous chapter are often referred to as *unsupervised learning* techniques.

9.1 DECISION TREE CLASSIFICATION

Decision tree based classification is a simple, efficient, and often effective scheme for partitioning a given set of observations into homogeneously labeled classes.

Let us be given a set of observations, O, where each observation is a pair, $\langle \vec{x}, y \rangle$, where $\vec{x} \in \mathbb{R}^n$ is a vector in an n-dimensional vector space and $y \in Y$ is the label associated with the observation. A corresponding decision tree, $T(V, E)$, is such that

- leaf nodes in V are sets of observations with the same label,
- internal nodes in V are tests on one or more dimensions of $\vec{x}$, and
- each edge in E corresponds to a test outcome.

In a decision tree, a given path from the root of the tree is interpreted as a conjunction of all the tests associated to the internal nodes of this path.

Decision trees are commonly created by partitioning the available observations into subsets based on tests on the features (i.e., $\vec{x}$) of the observations until each partition of observations is homogeneously labeled. The simplest decision tree classifier operates a single feature at a time and builds the tree in a top-down fashion. Initially, it creates a root node $v_0 \in V$ and a single leaf node and assigns all available observations (i.e., training data) to this node. If this set of observations are heterogeneous in terms of their labels, then it iterates over the following steps until all leaf nodes correspond to observation sets with homogeneous labels:

(i) It picks a leaf node with a set, L, of heterogeneous class labels and removes the leaf node from the tree.

(ii) It picks a feature dimension, f_i, and associates this as the decision attribute to the parent, v_{par}, of the eliminated leaf.

(iii) For each distinct value, a_j, of the selected feature dimension, f_i,[1]

    (a) it creates a new child node, v, under the node v_{par},

    (b) it associates the test outcome, "$f_i = a_j$" to the edge between v_{par} and v,

    (c) it creates a new leaf node under v and associates the set, $L_{f_i=a_j} \subset L$, of observations such that the feature attribute f_i of each observation has the value a_j.

The algorithm stops when all leaf nodes are homogeneous.

Decision tree classification algorithms differ from each other in the way they choose the decision test corresponding to the internal nodes of the tree and the way they build the tree (bottom-up or top-down).

9.1.1 Selecting the Feature Dimension for Partitioning a Given Set of Observations

Selecting a feature dimension, f_i, for splitting a given observation set, L, into subsets requires a way to compare the benefits (or gains) of using different feature dimensions. One approach to formulating a measure for benefit analysis is to note that the ultimate goal in classification is to reduce the *uncertainty* in the class labels. Picking the features in such a way that the label uncertainties are lower closer to the root is likely to result in shallower decision trees. This would also mean that classification of new data would require fewer tests. Thus, a measure of "reduction in uncertainty" can be used as a suitable measure for judging which feature dimension is likely to contribute better to the classification of the available observations.

Remembering from Section 4.2.2 that entropy *is* a measure of uncertainty, we can formulate $gain(L, f_i)$ in terms of the expected reduction in entropy due to the partitioning of the set L based on the values of the feature dimension f_i:

Definition 9.1.1 (Information gain by entropy): *Let L be a set of observations and f_i be a feature dimension. Information gain by entropy, $gain_{entropy}(L, f_i)$, is defined as follows:*

$$gain_{entropy}(L, f_i) = entropy(L) - \sum_{a_j \in domain(f_i)} \frac{|L_{f_i=a_j}|}{|L|} entropy(L_{f_i=a_j}),$$

where given an observation set $O = \{\langle \vec{x}_1, y_1 \rangle, \ldots, \langle \vec{x}_o, y_o \rangle\}$,

---

[1] Continuous valued features are usually *discretized* by setting test boundaries.

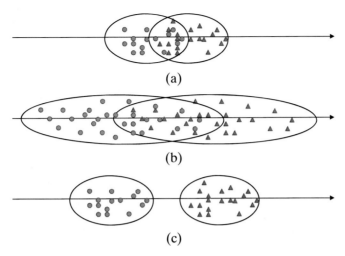

Figure 9.1. A feature is most discriminant with respect to two classes when the means of these classes are far apart and the variances of the classes are low along the corresponding feature dimension (i.e., case (c)): (a) Low variance, but close means; (b) far means, but also high variance; (c) low variance and far means.

$$entropy(O) = \sum_{y \in Y} \frac{|\{\langle \vec{x}_l, y_l \rangle \in O \text{ s.t. } y_l = y\}|}{|O|} \, log \left(\frac{|\{\langle \vec{x}_l, y_l \rangle \in O \text{ s.t. } y_l = y\}|}{|O|} \right),$$

and

$$O_{f_i = a_j} = \{\langle \vec{x}_l, y_l \rangle \in O \text{ s.t. } \vec{x}_l[i] = a_j\}.$$

Commonly used algorithms, ID3 [Quinlan, 1975], C4.5 [Quinlan, 1996, 1993], and C5.0 [Quinlan, 2008] all rely on this definition of information gain. An alternative measure of gain, commonly referred to as the Gini impurity, is used by another commonly used scheme called Classification And Regression Tree (CART [Breiman *et al.*, 1984]):

Definition 9.1.2 (Information gain by impurity): *Let L be a set of observations and f_i be a feature dimension. Information gain by impurity, $gain_{impurity}(L, f_i)$, is defined as follows:*

$$gain_{impurity}(L, f_i) = impurity(L) - \sum_{a_j \in domain(f_i)} \frac{|L_{f_i = a_j}|}{L} impurity(L_{f_i = a_j}),$$

where, given $O = \{\langle \vec{x}_1, y_1 \rangle, \dots, \langle \vec{x}_o, y_o \rangle\}$, the observation set is said to be impure if the chance of seeing two different labels in the set is high:

$$impurity(O) = \sum_{y_a \neq y_b \in Y} \frac{|\{\langle \vec{x}_l, y_l \rangle \in O \text{ s.t. } y_l = y_a\}|}{|O|} \frac{|\{\langle \vec{x}_l, y_l \rangle \in O \text{ s.t. } y_l = y_b\}|}{|O|}.$$

Intuitively, the impurity of a set of observations, O, is low if all observations have the same label.

Fisher's discriminant ratio is another measure commonly used for selecting features based on their discrimination power (Figure 9.1).

> **Definition 9.1.3 (Fisher's discriminant ratio):** *Let y_1 and y_2 be two class labels. For a given feature, f_i, Fisher's discriminant ratio for these two class labels is defined as*
>
> $$\frac{(\mu_{i,1} - \mu_{i,2})^2}{\sigma_{i,1}^2 + \sigma_{i,2}^2},$$
>
> *where $\mu_{i,*}$ are the means and $\sigma_{i,*}^2$ are the variances of the corresponding class labels along the given dimension, f_i.*

A feature dimension with a high ratio is likely to separate the two classes from each other better.[2] Fisher's discriminant ratio can be extended to handle cases with more than two class labels by computing ratios for pairs of feature dimensions and combining these using a suitable merge function, such as *average* or *min*.

9.1.2 Overfitting

Decision tree classifiers are simple to implement and usually highly efficient. The simplicity and the efficiency, however, come with the risk of *overfitting* trees to the observations. Especially when the observations are noisy, that is, there are entries that have similar feature vectors but different labels, the greedy nature of the basic decision tree construction may result in trees having a single or a few observations per leaf node. This would mean that each observation becomes its own class, possibly deteriorating the effectiveness of the decision tree classifier.

One method for eliminating overfitting of the tree to the observations is to allow leaves that are not perfectly homogeneous; in other words, the tests associated with the branches *almost* partition the observations to homogeneously labeled sets, but *not quite*. This can be achieved by either changing the stopping condition of the tree construction algorithm such that the partitioning stops before homogeneous partitions are obtained, or pruning the decision tree based on further evidence. This second approach is usually achieved by using a separate validation set of observations to evaluate classification effectiveness and pruning those branches of the tree that do not classify the validation observations well.

Although overfitting elimination is now widely used in improving the effectiveness of decision tree classifiers, it has also been argued that any overfitting avoidance strategy may, in fact, degrade performance instead of improving it, and the appropriate strategy must be based on an understanding of the data and application [Schaffer, 1993].

9.1.3 Random Forests

Random forests aim at improving the classification performance by relying on an *ensemble* of decision trees [Breiman, 2001; Ho, 1995] instead of a single one. A given not-yet-classified data object is classified separately by each tree, and the class label with the highest support is picked as the class label of this data object.

---

[2] Fisher's discriminant ratio measures separability along a given feature dimension. Having low ratios for all available dimensions does not necessarily mean that the classes are not separable, but may mean that the separation boundary is not parallel to any of the feature dimensions.

In the *bagging* approach [Breiman, 1996], for example, each decision tree in the random forest is constructed by using a random subset of the observations in O. In *random split selection* approach [Dietterich, 2000], on the other hand, all observations are used, but the feature used for partitioning the available observations is selected randomly among the best partitioning candidates. The *random subspace method* [Ho, 1998] picks in advance a random subspace (i.e., a set of dimensions) for constructing each decision tree in the random forest.

Naturally, the accuracy of a random forest depends on the strength of the individual tree classifiers and their independence from each other [Amit and Geman, 1997]. However, random forests with large numbers of trees are shown to converge in way that eliminates overfitting [Breiman, 2001; Ho, 2000].

9.2 *k*-NEAREST NEIGHBOR CLASSIFIERS

The k-nearest neighbor (k-NN) classification scheme is voting-based, where an object is classified based on the majority vote of its k most similar already-classified objects. k-NN classifiers differ from each other in the *similarity/distance* measure they use and in the way they choose the order in which they consider the unclassified objects. The efficiency of the k-NN classifier depends on the value of k and the dimensionality of the vector space, as well as the index structure used to identify the k nearest neighbors (Section 10.1). The value of k also affects the quality of the classification. Although having larger k values ensures that the class selection is not distorted by a few unrepresentative neighbors, very large k values may cause distant but large classes to overvote nearby smaller classes.

9.3 SUPPORT VECTOR MACHINES

As we discussed in Section 7.2, one way to keep related data objects together is to rely on space-partitioning techniques. For efficiency purposes, most multidimensional index structures partition the space along the dimensions of the given vector space. We have also seen, however, that it is not always the case that the most discriminant features are properly aligned with the given dimensions. Although this may be somewhat corrected by techniques such as principal component analysis, when a similarly labeled set of observations cover differently shaped regions of space, such global techniques, which treat the given set of vectors as a uniform collection, cannot work effectively.

While introducing decision trees in Section 9.1, we have seen that the discriminatory power of a feature dimension with respect to a given set of class labels can be measured using *information gain* and *Fisher's discriminant ratio*. However, we have also seen that these discrimination-based feature selection techniques can fall short when the most discriminating hyperplane is not aligned with the dimensions of the space.

9.3.1 Linear Discriminant Analysis

In Section 4.3.2, we learned the FastMap approach for finding the direction along which the data are best separated. The method was designed specifically for efficiency. Another common approach for discovering a hyperplane that best

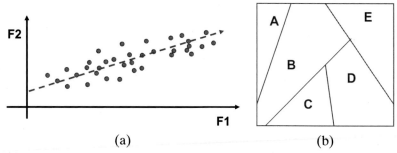

Figure 9.2. (a) Linear regression to find a hyperplane that best distributes the data and (b) partitioning the space using linear discriminants.

distributes the data is the *linear regression* analysis. In this approach, given a collection of vectors, $X \subset \mathbb{R}^n$, one looks for a hyperplane, $H : \vec{w} \cdot \vec{x} + b = 0$, which best fits the data (Figure 9.2). Although FastMap and *linear regression* work well for identifying most discriminant directions of a given set of vectors, they do not explicitly consider class labels.

An alternative formulation of the problem takes into account the class labels as well: given a set of observations, O, where each observation is a pair, $\langle \vec{x}, y \rangle$ and $y \in Y$ is the (numeric) label associated with the observation, we look for a family of hyperplanes, such that

$$\forall_{y \in Y} \forall_{\langle \vec{x}_i, y_i \rangle \in O \; s.t. \; y_i = y} \; H_{y_i} : \; \vec{w} \cdot \vec{x}_i + b = y_i.$$

In other words, each hyperplane is a predictor for a given class label and, thus, separates the observations with different class labels from each other. This task is usually formulated as a least-squares minimization problem,

$$min \; \sum_{\langle \vec{x}_i, y_i \rangle \in O} (\vec{w} \cdot \vec{x}_i + b - y_i)^2,$$

which minimizes the L2 norm. Alternatively, one can minimize the L1 norm instead:

$$min \; \sum_{\langle \vec{x}_i, y_i \rangle \in O} |\vec{w} \cdot \vec{x}_i + b - y_i|.$$

This is referred to as the least absolute regression deviation (LAD).

9.3.2 Overfitting and Regularization

One frequently observed problem with linear learners and other classification and machine learning algorithms is that it is possible to create complex models and predictors that *overfit* the observations well, while being ineffective in classifying unlabeled data. This often occurs when the number of unknown parameters of the model is more than what can be determined given the number of observations.

In order to avoid overfitting, most classification techniques introduce additional constraints that reduce the degrees of freedom (i.e., complexity) of the models. In linear learning algorithms, such as linear regression, the constraints that can be introduced to reduce overfitting include the *least absolute shrinkage and selection operator (LASSO)*, *L1-*, and *L2*-regularization strategies.

As we mentioned in Section 9.3.1, given a collection of vectors, $X \subset \mathbb{R}^n$, linear regression analysis involves searching for a hyperplane, $H : \vec{w} \cdot \vec{x} + b = 0$, that best fits the data, by solving the least-squares minimization problem,

$$min \sum_{\langle \vec{x}_i, y_i \rangle \in O} (\vec{w} \cdot \vec{x}_i + b - y_i)^2.$$

The LASSO method [Tibshirani, 1996] constrains the hyperplane by putting a limit on $\vec{w}$; in particular a solution to the minimization problem is subjected to the following additional constraint:

$$\sum_j |\vec{w}[j]| \le t,$$

where $t \ge 0$ is the tuning parameter. Imposing this constraint on $\vec{w}$ results in some coefficients of $\vec{w}$ shrinking exactly to 0; thus, in a sense LASSO uses the t parameter to implement and control an automatic feature selection process. Because this constraint can be seen as the length of the $\vec{w}$ in L1 metric space, this approach is also referred to as the L1-regularization. In contrast, *ridge regression* uses the constraint

$$\sum_j (\vec{w}[j])^2 \le t$$

to constrain the length of the vector in the L2 metric space and is also known as L2-regularization.

9.3.3 Max-Margin Classification and SVMs

Support vector machines (SVMs) [Bennett and Campbell, 2000; Burges, 1998; Vapnik, 1979] also perform linear discriminant analysis; but, unlike the linear regression approach (which tries to find linear predictors for class labels), SVMs looks for linear boundaries that best separate given classes from each other. Thus, SVMs are in the class of algorithms often referred to as *max-margin learning algorithms* [Guo *et al.*, 2007].

Let us be given a set of observations, O, where each observation is a pair, $\langle \vec{x}, y \rangle$, where $\vec{x} \in \mathbb{R}^n$ is a vector in a given *n*-dimensional vector space and y is the label associated with the observation. The goal of the SVMs is to partition the space using these observations (i.e., the training data) into regions, such that each region contains observations with a single label (Figure 9.2). Assuming that the data and observations on the data have the same distribution, this would mean that the regions would partition the data into single-label classes. SVMs are becoming increasingly popular supervised learning tools because of their many desirable properties: they always find global optima and there are usually only a few parameters (called kernel parameters) to be picked in advance.

Let us initially assume that each observation label has only one of the two values, -1 or 1. Let us also assume that the observations are *linearly separable*; that is, there exists at least one plane in the given *n*-dimensional space that can separate the two sets of observations from each other. When two sets of observations are linearly separable, it is possible that there may actually be more than one such plane that can

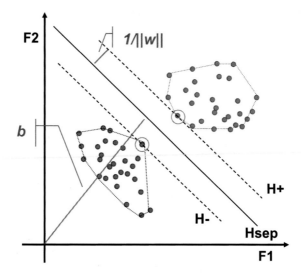

Figure 9.3. Linear SVM partitioning with a hyperplane with the largest margin (the two support vectors are highlighted); the hyperplane also bisects the line defined by the two closest points on the convex hulls.

separate these sets. The SVM method tries to find a plane that is as far from *both* sets of observations as possible: this ensures that the effect of any observations, at the boundary of the two sets, missing due to sampling will be less likely to introduce classification errors.

Let H be some hyperplane separating the two sets of observations. We can describe the points lying on this hyperplane using the equation $\vec{w} \cdot \vec{x} + b = 0$, where $\vec{w} = \langle w_1, w_2, \ldots, w_n \rangle$ is normal (i.e., perpendicular) to the hyperplane and $b/\|\vec{w}\|$ is the perpendicular distance from the hyperplane to the origin (Figure 9.3). Let δ_+ be the shortest distance from this hyperplane to any observation with label 1, and let δ_- be the shortest distance to any observation with label -1. SVM looks for the hyperplane, H_{sep}, with the largest margin, $\Delta = \delta_+ + \delta_-$ (Figure 9.3).

Because so far we assume that the observations are separable, the observation vectors will fall onto either side of the plane. Let us pick $\|\vec{w}\|$ and b such that all the observations with label 1 satisfy

$$\vec{w} \cdot \vec{x}_i + b \geq 1,$$

with at least one observation point on the hyperplane $H_+ : \vec{w} \cdot \vec{x}_i + b = 1$. Let also $\|\vec{w}\|$ and b such that all observations with label -1 satisfy

$$\vec{w} \cdot \vec{x}_i + b \leq -1,$$

with at least one observation point on the hyperplane $H_- : \vec{w} \cdot \vec{x}_i + b = -1$. Note that H_{sep}, H_+, and H_- are all parallel to each other. It can also be shown that the distance between H_{sep} and H_+ in the direction of the normal is $1/\|\vec{w}\|$. Similarly, under these conditions, the perpendicular distance between H_{sep} and H_- can be shown to be equal to $1/\|\vec{w}\|$. Thus, the two hyperplanes with the largest margin, $\Delta = \delta_+ + \delta_- = 2/\|\vec{w}\|$, can be found by minimizing $\|\vec{w}\|/2$ subject to linear separation constraints implied by the observations; that is,

$$y_i(\vec{w} \cdot \vec{x}_i + b) \geq 1,$$

for all observations $\langle \vec{x}_i, y_i \rangle \in O$. This can be formulated as a quadratic optimization problem[3] by rephrasing the minimization function as

$$min\|\vec{w}\|^2/2 \quad \text{or as} \quad min \sum_{j=1}^{n} \frac{w_j{}^2}{2}.$$

Note that the result is determined by those observation points (also called *support vectors*) that lie on the hyperplanes H_+ and H_-; if these points are removed from the set of observations, the solution would change. These points also lie on the convex hulls of the two sets of observations. Thus, as a solution strategy, we can consider the *convex hulls* of each set of observations, find the closest points on the two convex hulls, and find a plane that bisects these points (i.e., perpendicular to the line defined by the two closest points on the convex hulls and equidistant to both of these points).

9.3.4 Lagrangian Formulation

Although the preceding quadratic optimization problem can be solved directly, most systems rely on an alternative Lagrangian formulation, which enables simpler constraints and more efficient solutions. The Lagrangian method introduces a new scalar, α_i, for each constraint, C_i, of the optimization problem and combines all in the form of a single function, L, referred to as the Lagrangian function. The optimal solution to the optimization problem is then found by minimizing the Lagrangian function subject to the constraint that $\delta L/\delta \alpha_i = 0$ for all constraints. In other words, once the optimal points are found, there would not remain any reason to change or tweak the Lagrangian scalars.

The dual Lagrangian formulation for the SVM optimization problem is obtained by introducing Lagrangian multipliers, $\alpha_i \geq 0$, for each of the observations. The result is the Lagrangian,

$$L = \frac{1}{2}\|\vec{w}\|^2 + \sum_{\langle \vec{x}_i, y_i \rangle \in O} \alpha_i y_i (\vec{x}_i \cdot \vec{w} + b) + \sum_{\langle \vec{x}_i, y_i \rangle \in O} \alpha_i,$$

to be minimized subject to the constraints $\alpha_i \geq 0$ and $\frac{\delta L}{\delta \alpha_i} = 0$ for all $\langle \vec{x}_i, y_i \rangle \in O$. An alternative formulation of this is to minimize the Lagrangian,

$$L' = \frac{1}{2}\left(\sum_{\langle \vec{x}_i, y_i \rangle \in O} \sum_{\langle \vec{x}_j, y_j \rangle \in O} \alpha_i \alpha_j y_i y_j (\vec{x}_i \cdot \vec{x}_j) \right) - \sum_{\langle \vec{x}_i, y_i \rangle \in O} \alpha_i,$$

subject to the constraints, $\alpha_i \geq 0$ and

$$\sum_{\langle \vec{x}_i, y_i \rangle \in O} y_i \alpha_i = 0.$$

---

[3] Note that the problem is quadratic only if the Euclidean definition of space is used. Computing the length of $\vec{w}$ using the L1 norm as opposed to the Euclidean (L2 norm) would render the optimization problem linear,

$$min \sum_{j=1}^{n} w_j,$$

and thus more efficient to solve. Also as it is the case for linear regression (Section 9.3.1), using the L1 norm instead of L2 norm to define SVMs also has the affect of setting many of the coefficients to zero, thus helping SVMs act as feature selectors [Bradley and Mangasarian, 1998].

An advantage of this alternative formulation is that the input observations (i.e., training data) appear only in dot products with each other. This means that it might be possible to precompute and reuse these dot products. Bennett and Bredensteiner [2000] show that this representation, in fact, corresponds to the convex hull–based formulation of the linear separation problem described earlier.

9.3.5 Classification with Non–"Linearly Separable" Observations

Not all observations will be linearly separable. Some observations will have so much noise that the observation sets will intermingle in space to some degree. Some others will be separable, but not by planar surfaces.

Let us first focus on the case where the observations are separable, but a hyperplane is not sufficient as a boundary between observations. The naive approach in this case is to formulate the optimization problem explicitly using a hypersurface of higher degree instead of a hyperplane. This, however, would complicate the formulation of the problem significantly. Fortunately, this problem can be surmounted by leveraging a side effect of the Lagrangian formulation: in the Lagrangian form of the optimization problem, the input observations (i.e., training data) appear only in dot products with each other. Thus, nonlinear classification can be achieved simply by replacing the dot product with an appropriate nonlinear kernel function that, indirectly, distorts the space in such a way that each hyperplane on the distorted space corresponds to a hypersurface of a higher degree in the original space.[4] Nonlinear kernels commonly used for this purpose include the following:

- Polynomial, $K(\vec{u}, \vec{v}) = (\vec{u}.\vec{v} + c)^p$, for some p and c
- Gaussian radial basis, $K(\vec{u}, \vec{v}) = e^{-\gamma \|\vec{u} - \vec{v}\|^2 / 2\sigma^2}$, for some γ and σ
- Sigmoid, $K(\vec{u}, \vec{v}) = tanh(\kappa \vec{u}.\vec{v} + c)$ for some κ and c

The effect is that the underlying vector space is distorted, and although the same maximum-margin based hyperplane selection algorithm is used for classification in the distorted space, the resulting boundary is nonlinear.

Soft-margin SVM optimization handles nonseparable observations: soft-margin formulation of the problem does not require picking a nonlinear kernel but simply allows for a few observations to fall on the wrong side of the H_+ and H_- surfaces. Thus, this approach can handle the cases where there is no appropriate distortion of the space that can separate the sets of observations. The approach introduces a nonnegative error variable, e_i, to the constraints that enforce observations falling only on the required side of the H_+ and H_- surfaces. Naturally, to ensure that the number of errors is not high, it also modifies the objective term to minimize the total amount of error in the solution:

$$min \frac{\|\vec{w}\|^2}{2} + C \sum_{\langle \vec{x}_i, y_i \rangle \in O} e_i,$$

such that

$$y_i(\vec{w} \cdot \vec{x}_i + b) + e_i \geq 1$$

---

[4] This kernel trick can be applied in other domains where dot products are used. Schölkopf *et al.* [1998] develop a nonlinear version of PCA with a similar use of nonlinear kernels.

and $e_i \geq 0$ for all observations $\langle \vec{x}_i, y_i \rangle \in O$. Here C is a constant for trading off the size of the margin against the degree of errors allowed in classification.

9.3.6 *N*-ary Classification

The SVM classifier as just discussed is binary: there are only two possible labels for the observations, $+1$ and -1. In many cases however, we have more than two classes of observations. Thus, we need to extend the basic binary SVM to handle cases where there are multiple classes.

A common and simple solution to the problem is to use multiple binary SVM classifiers, each trained for one class against all the others. For each point, then, the best matching class (highest distance from the separating hyperplane) is used [Boser *et al.*, 1992]. A slightly different non-binary classification problem involves observations with ordinal (i.e., rank) as opposed to nominal (i.e., arbitrary class) labels. An ordinal regression SVM [Herbrich *et al.*, 2000] searches for a linear function $h()$ such that

$$h(\vec{x}_i) > h(\vec{x}_j) \longleftrightarrow y_i > y_j$$

by formulating a soft-margin SVM that minimizes the number of pairs of observations that are out of their specified order. Waegeman and Boullart [2006] formulate the same problem as an ensemble of $N - 1$ binary weak classifiers, where N is the number of different ordinals (ranks) used as labels. Joachims [2006], on the other hand, proposes a solution which uses a single SVM.

9.3.7 SVM versus Other Classifiers

As discussed earlier, SVM has many advantages against other classifiers, including always having a global optimum and the lack of parameters to be set for good performance. Compare this, for example, with neural networks, where local minima can render classification erroneous [Burges, 1998]. Fortunately, this simplicity does not come with performance degradations. In fact, many studies showed that linear SVMs perform very well for text classification tasks.

9.3.8 Complexity of SVMs

The quadratic programming problem is, in its most general form, NP-hard in terms of its input variables and constraints [Pardalos and Vavasis, 1991]. In practice, however, many existing algorithms handle large number of dimensions efficiently, but have super-linear training behavior in terms of the number, $o = |O|$, of observations. The training time of SVMs is shown to be polynomial, o^p, with p ranging between 1.7 and 2.1 [Chakrabarti, 2002]. Joachims [2006] presents a cutting plane–based SVM that has training time $O(so)$ for classification problems and $O(s\, o\, log(o))$ for ordinal regression problems. Here, s is the maximum number of nonzero dimensions the input observations have. Thus the nominal classification algorithm performs in linear time if the number of features each training data has is bounded by a constant. For applications with a dense feature space and large number of feature dimensions, this algorithm is not efficiently applicable.

9.3.9 Voted Perceptron Classification

Freund and Schapire [1998] present a simpler algorithm, called *voted-perceptron*, for linear max-margin classification. Taking advantage of data that are linearly separable with large margins, this algorithm builds on the iterative perceptron algorithm [Rosenblatt, 1958] rather than solving quadratic programming problems.

Let us again be given a set of observations, O, where each observation is a pair, $\langle \vec{x}, y \rangle$, where $\vec{x} \in \mathbb{R}^n$ is a vector in a given n-dimensional vector space and y is the label associated with the observation. Let us also assume that the observation labels can have only one of the two values, -1 or 1. The perceptron algorithm (commonly used in online learning scenarios where only a single pass over the data is allowed) starts with an initial prediction vector, $\vec{v} = 0$, and predicts the label of the first observation instance $\vec{x}_1$ to be $Q = sign(\vec{v}\vec{x}_1)$. If this prediction is different from y_1, it updates the prediction vector to $\vec{v} = \vec{v} + y_1\vec{x}_1$. If the prediction is correct, then $\vec{v}$ is not changed. The process then repeats with the next example. It has been shown that if the observations are linearly separable, then the perceptron algorithm will make a finite number of mistakes [Novikoff, 1963] (upper bounded by a function of the gap between positive and negative observations); therefore, if provided a sufficiently large data set, the algorithm will eventually converge to a correct classifier.

Freund and Schapire [1998] convert this online algorithm into a batch setup, where the data might not be separable or the user might not want to wait till convergence is achieved. In this case, given the various prediction vectors (i.e., classifiers) the algorithm generates, we need to pick one as the best prediction rule. One approach is to test the prediction rules on a second observation set [Littlestone, 1989]. A second alternative is to pick the prediction rule that has survived for a long time [Gallant, 1986]. Freund and Schapire [1998] leverage the *leave-one-out* method for weak learning [Helmbold and Warmuth, 1995]: given the set, O, of labeled observations and given an unlabeled data object, $\vec{x}$, for all $0 \leq r \leq |O|$, the voting-based algorithm picks the first r observations from O and appends the unlabeled data to the end to obtain a sequence of length $r + 1$. Then the online perceptron algorithm is run for each resulting sequence, to obtain a total of $|O| + 1$ predictions for $\vec{x}$. Finally, the majority label is used as the class label for this unlabeled data object. Freund and Schapire [1998] show that if E is the expected number of mistakes the online perceptron algorithm would make on a sequence of $|O| + 1$ randomly generated (independent and identically distributed) observations, then the expected probability that the voted perceptron makes a mistake is only $\frac{2E}{|O|+1}$.

9.4 RULE-BASED CLASSIFICATION

Rule-based systems are very convenient as a knowledge representation and reasoning paradigm, for many different reasons. Such systems are a plausible model of human reasoning, because it is quite natural to model the heuristic nature of human expertise in terms of rules. Moreover, the paradigm separates the knowledge component (i.e., the state of the system and the set of rules) from the control component (the interpreter, or "inferential engine"). Rule-based systems also allow tracking and explanation of the adopted resolution process. A rule-based system for classification has the following three major components:

- A set of *assertions* collectively form the *working memory* and represent the knowledge on which the classification is based.
- A set of *rules* specify how to use the assertion set for classification. Rules can be seen as if-then statements that encode the knowledge of a (hypothetical) domain expert and reproduce the reasoning that the expert would apply during classification based on the available data. The *production rules*, or simply *productions*, are of the form *antecedent → consequent*, where
  - the *antecedent* is a schema (or pattern) expressing the *firing* condition for the rule (determining the conditions under which the rule is applicable) and
  - the *consequent* determines the action to be taken when the antecedent is satisfied. For example, the action can ask for the addition to or the removal from the knowledge base of some fact.

  The rules may have priority values that play a role when multiple (possibly conflicting) production rules can be fired at the same time.
- A *termination condition* determines that the classification has been finalized or that no classification is possible with the present knowledge.

The activity of a rule-based system can be described as a loop, which ends when the termination condition is reached. Every iteration of the loop acts through the following steps. (i) First, all the antecedent conditions of the rule are checked to isolate the set of conditions that are satisfied in the current working memory. If the identified set is empty, the system stops (even if the specified termination condition is not yet reached). Otherwise, from the set of applicable rules (referred to as the conflict set), one candidate will be chosen to be fired. The choice of the rule to be triggered, among all the candidates in the conflict set, depends on the conflict resolution strategy associated to the system. One commonly used conflict resolution strategy is the *best rule* strategy: each rule is given a *salience*, which specifies its priority over the alternatives, and the candidate rule with the highest salience is chosen. When the selected rule is fired, all the actions specified in its consequent clause are carried out. These actions can have multiple effects, on different targets. In some cases, they simply modify the working memory. In other cases, they also update the rule base or execute any actions coded by the system programmer in the consequent clause.

For a rule-based system to be used for classification, assertions and rules have to be properly specified. This can be either performed by a human domain expert or automatically extracted from another pattern learning tool that extracts classification rules from a given training set. Candidates for this process include neural networks [Nauck and Kruse, 1999], genetic algorithms [Ishibuchi *et al.*, 1999], clustering [Setnes and Roubos, 2000], and decision trees [Han and Kamber, 2001]. In the rest of this section, we focus on the use of decision trees for the identification of (crisp as well as fuzzy) rules for classification.

9.4.1 From Decision Trees to Rule-Based Classifiers

As described in Section 9.1, *decision trees* are one of the simplest and most widely used classification tools. A decision tree (also called a *classification tree*) is a tree structure whose leaf nodes correspond to class labels, while branches denote the sets of properties that lead to classification of objects under these labels. Each internal node of the decision tree can be thought of as a macro-class, that is, the union of all the classes represented by its descendants. Moreover, each internal node has a corresponding predicate, called *a splitting condition*, which determines how the data corresponding to the class labels under this node are partitioned among this node's children. Thus, the set of production rules needed for classification can be generated from a given decision tree.

Let O be a set of observations and let $T(V, E)$ be a decision tree created from these observations. Each path from the root of this tree to any leaf v_k can be read as a rule of the form

$$if \ (\Theta_a \wedge \Theta_b \wedge \ldots \wedge \Theta_z) \ then \ c_k,$$

where c_k denotes the class label corresponding to leaf v_k, while $v_a, v_b, \ldots, v_z$ are the nodes along the path from the root to v_k. Each node, v_i, on this path, expresses a condition of the form "feature dimension f_i satisfies $\theta_i(f_i)$"; thus, $\Theta_a, \Theta_b, \ldots, \Theta_z$ are Boolean variables expressing conditions of the form $\Theta_i = \theta_i(f_i)$.

9.4.2 Simplifying Rule-Based Classifiers

A decision tree with ϕ leaves corresponds to ϕ distinct production rules. If there are different leaves of the decision tree corresponding to the same class label, then this corresponds to a set of rules, all of which infer the same label based on the different aspects of this label. While being distinct from each other, the set of rules for the same label may be redundant. The logical formalism in which the rules are formulated enables simplification of these rule sets, using logical equivalences, thus resulting in classifiers that are more compact than the original decision trees. Heuristics can also help eliminate conditions and rules that are less needed than the others, further reducing the complexity of the classifier [Han and Kamber, 2001]:

(i) *Condition pruning based on estimated accuracy:* After generating all the possible rules (one per leaf), the rules are simplified by removing from every rule those conditions whose presence does not increase the estimated accuracy of the rule. Note that this is a lossy process and, after the elimination, there is no guarantee that all of the original classes are reproduced.

(ii) *Rule elimination based on estimated accuracy:* Rules are grouped based on their class labels, and for each class only the rules with the highest estimated accuracy are kept. Once again, this is a lossy step.

(iii) *Rule set ordering and elimination based on actual accuracy:* Rule groups are ordered according to each group's ability to accurately classify the training set, and those groups whose overall accuracies are low are eliminated.

(iv) *Rule elimination based on actual accuracy:* The contribution of each remaining rule to the accuracy is computed using the training set. Those rules that give a low contribution to the overall accuracy of the corresponding rule set are removed.

The preceding four steps are iterated until the set of rules stabilizes, that is, until the set of rules cannot be reduced and compacted any further.

9.5 FUZZY RULE-BASED CLASSIFICATION

Fuzzy extensions of rule-based systems are useful when dealing with classification of multimedia objects whose characterizing properties (i.e., features) are partial, incomplete, or imprecise. In fuzzy rule-based classification systems, the if-then rules that define the pattern used for classifying media objects are of the form:

$$if \ (\Theta_a \wedge \Theta_b \wedge \ldots \wedge \Theta_z) \ then \ c_k,$$

where c_k is a class label and Θ_a through Θ_z are fuzzy predicates. For example, in the sample fuzzy classification rule,

$$if \ (HIGH(obj.motion) \wedge SHORT(obj.length)) \ then \ is\_commercial,$$

HIGH and SHORT are linguistic terms expressed as fuzzy predicates.

Note that in the foregoing rule, the satisfaction of the antecedent is inherently fuzzy, while the rule itself is inherently crisp; that is, this rule specifies a certain correlation between the antecedent and the consequent, which are themselves fuzzy. A different type of rule-based system associates "certainty degrees" to the rules:

$$if \ (\Theta_a \wedge \Theta_b \wedge \ldots \wedge \Theta_z) \ then \ c_k \ with \ w_k.$$

Here w_k is the weight or confidence associated with the inference stated by the rule. For example,

$$if \ (HIGH(obj.motion) \wedge SHORT(obj.length)) \ then \ is\_commercial \ with \ 0.7$$

indicates that if a media object has high degrees of motion and is short, the system can be 0.7 confident that the object can be classified as a commercial. In this case, fuzziness is not limited to the tests that are combined to form the antecedent of the rule, but applies to the implication stated by the rule as well.

Let Y be the set of class labels and R be a fuzzy rule base. Given an object, obj, to be classified, the fuzzy rule base will return a set, $\{\langle y_i, S_i \rangle \mid y_i \in Y\}$, where S_i is the set of confidence scores of rules that fired for label y_i. Which class label will be associated with object obj depends on how the scores in sets S_i are interpreted and combined to obtain a single value (Section 3.4.1). Alternative combination functions include minimum, maximum, and average. Once the scores corresponding to each class label are combined to obtain a single score, these scores can be compared to select the unique class label for the observation. Note that the weights (i.e., the certainty degrees) associated to the rules affect the overall classification result when there are multiple rules firing for the same object. Thus, the weights must reflect the confidence associated with the underlying patterns learned from the training set used as input.

9.5.1 Fuzzy Decision Trees for Fuzzy Classification

Fuzzy rules are composed of fuzzy predicates and (optionally) confidence weights associated with the rules. In general, the confidence weight corresponds to the classification accuracy associated with the path in the decision tree corresponding to the rule. On the other hand, the predicates associated with the internal nodes of a regular decision tree are crisp and, thus, associating fuzzy predicates to the internal nodes of a decision tree requires a different decision tree construction mechanism.

Han and Kamber [2001] present a fuzzy decision tree construction algorithm that "fuzzifies" the decision predicates. In this approach, each fuzzy predicate is described using a value interval and a membership function. The construction of the decision tree takes into account the fact that a given value can fit – with possibly different memberships degrees – in more than one such interval.

The fact that an attribute value can fit, at the same time, in several different intervals (each corresponding to a different fuzzy predicate) has an impact on the definitions of measures, such as information gain relied upon during the decision tree construction (Section 9.1). In particular, the definitions of information content and entropy need to be revised to accommodate the fact that an observation (i.e., attribute value) may satisfy not only one, but multiple predicates.[5] Remember from Section 9.1.1 that given a *crisp* observation set, $O = \{\langle \vec{x}_1, y_1 \rangle, \ldots, \langle \vec{x}_o, y_o \rangle\}$ where $\vec{x}_i$ are training data and y_i are the corresponding class labels, the corresponding entropy is defined as

$$entropy(O) = \sum_{y \in Y} \frac{|\{\langle \vec{x}_l, y_l \rangle \in O \text{ s.t. } y_l = y\}|}{|O|} log \left(\frac{|\{\langle \vec{x}_l, y_l \rangle \in O \text{ s.t. } y_l = y\}|}{|O|} \right).$$

In the case of a *fuzzy* observation set $O = \{\langle \vec{x}_1, Y_1 \rangle, \ldots, \langle \vec{x}_o, Y_o \rangle\}$, where Y_i is a set of $\langle y_{i,j}, w_{i,j} \rangle$ pairs, each corresponding to an observation label and its weight, the definition of entropy is revised as follows:

$$weighted\_entropy(O) = \sum_{y \in Y} \frac{total\_weight(y, O)}{total\_weight(O)} log \left(\frac{total\_weight(y, O)}{total\_weight(O)} \right),$$

where $total\_weight(y, O)$ is the total weight of all observations labeled y,

$$total\_weight(y, O) = \sum \{w_{l,k} \mid \langle \vec{x}_l, Y_l \rangle \in O \wedge \langle y_{l,k}, w_{l,k} \rangle \in Y_l \wedge y_{l,k} = y\},$$

and $total\_weight(O)$ is the total weight of all observations,

$$total\_weight(O) = \sum_{y \in Y} total\_weight(y, O).$$

Given this revision, the definition of the information gain is also revised by using *weighted_entropy* as opposed to *entropy* and, similarly to crisp decision trees, the choice of the feature on which the subdivision will be based is made by maximizing this refined information gain measure.

9.5.2 Learning Fuzzy Classification Rules Directly from Observations

As stated earlier, there are many different approaches to learning classification rules. Examples for fuzzy classification include neuro-fuzzy methods [Nauck and Kruse, 1999], genetic algorithms [Ishibuchi *et al.*, 1999], combinations of fuzzy clustering and genetic algorithms [Berlanga *et al.*, 2006; Setnes and Roubos, 2000], and other data mining techniques [Hu *et al.*, 2003].

Roubos *et al.* [2003] propose an approach for the construction of rule-based fuzzy classifiers from a training set without having to generate a decision tree as a prior step. In this approach, each rule, $rule_j$, is of the form

$$if \ (\theta_{j,1}(\vec{x}[1]) \wedge \theta_{j,2}(\vec{x}[2]) \wedge \ldots \wedge \theta_{j,n}(\vec{x}[n])) \ then \ c_j,$$

---

[5] This is similar to the normalization performed in Section 8.1 for computing cluster entropies when clusters are overlapping.

where $\theta_{j,1}$ through $\theta_{j,n}$ are fuzzy predicates, $\vec{x}[l]$ is the value of the lth dimension of the n-dimensional vector $\vec{x}$, and c_j is the class label corresponding to $rule_j$. Given an observation set $O = \{\langle \vec{x}_1, y_1 \rangle, \ldots, \langle \vec{x}_o, y_o \rangle\}$, the initial rule set is determined through a three-step process that relies on clustering techniques that partition the training data around class labels:

(i) The first step identifies regions in the feature space that can be approximated by a single fuzzy rule. This initial partitioning of the feature space can be performed using various clustering algorithms that would identify the regions that correspond to each class label.

Under the hypothesis that the shape of the obtained sets can be approximated by ellipsoids, Roubos *et al.* [2003] represent each class region by a center and its covariance matrix (see Sections 3.1.3, 3.5.1.2, and 4.2.6). If the hypothesis supporting this first step (i.e., each class can be described by a single compact construct in the feature space) does not hold, one can create multiple clusters, each corresponding to a different fuzzy rule for the same class label. In the rest of this section, we assume that each class has one single corresponding cluster.

(ii) The second step of the algorithm computes the Mahalanobis distance between each observation vector and the centers of all clusters (remember from Section 3.1.3 that the Mahalanobis distance reflects the distribution of the data and, thus, is particularly useful when different clusters have different data distributions). The membership value, $\mu(\vec{x}_i, y_j)$, of an observation (i.e., training data object) $\vec{x}_i$ to class y_j is then computed as a function of the Mahalanobis distance between $\vec{x}_i$ and the cluster center of class y_j. For example, Roubos *et al.* [2003] compute the membership degree $\mu(\vec{x}_i, y_j)$ as follows:

$$\mu(\vec{x}_i, y_j) = \frac{1}{\sum_{\langle \vec{x}_k, y_k \rangle \in O} \left(\frac{D_{i,j}}{D_{k,j}} \right)^\alpha},$$

where α is an empirical constant and $D_{k,j}$ is the distance between vector $\vec{x}_k$ and the center of the cluster corresponding to class label y_j.

(iii) The third step of the algorithm computes the fuzzy scoring functions corresponding to the predicates $\theta_{j,l}$ in the rule base. Remember that each rule, $rule_j$, is of the form

if $(\theta_{j,1}(\vec{x}[1]) \wedge \theta_{j,2}(\vec{x}[2]) \wedge \ldots \wedge \theta_{j,n}(\vec{x}[n]))$ *then* c_j,

where $\vec{x}[l]$ is the value of the lth dimension of the n-dimensional vector $\vec{x}$. The fuzzy scoring function for the predicate $\theta_{j,l}$ in the rule, $rule_j$, corresponding to class label y_j is computed by considering pairs,

$\langle \vec{x}_i[l], \mu(\vec{x}_i, y_j) \rangle$,

for all training data vectors $\vec{x}_i$ and approximating this set of pairs with a suitable parametric function.

This initial rule set is then improved iteratively through feature selection based on class separability and rule simplification methods, similar to the ones discussed in Section 9.4.2.

Once the rules are computed, given an object $\vec{x}_i$, the overall score, w, of the rule is computed based on the scores of the individual predicates. In particular, the logic connective $\wedge$ is modeled through the "product" semantics (Section 3.4.1):

$$\theta_1(\vec{x}_i[1]) \times \theta_2(\vec{x}_i[2]) \times \ldots \times \theta_n(\vec{x}_i[n]).$$

The output of the classifier is, then, determined by the rule with the highest score.

9.6 BAYESIAN CLASSIFIERS

Once again let us consider a set of observations, O, where each observation is a pair, $\langle \vec{x}, y \rangle$ such that $\vec{x} \in \mathbb{R}^n$ is a vector in an n-dimensional vector space and $y \in Y$ is the label associated with the observation.

Bayesian classifiers start with the assumption that each class label $y \in Y$ has a prior probability $P(y)$. Furthermore, given a class label, the corresponding vectors are generated with probability $P(\vec{x}|y)$, conditioned on the class label. Given these, Bayes' rule can be used to formulate the conditional probability of a given vector $\vec{x}$ having label $y \in Y$ as follows:

$$P(y|\vec{x}) = \frac{P(y)P(\vec{x}|y)}{\sum_{y_i \in Y} P(y_i)P(\vec{x}|y_i)}.$$

Note that to use this formulation to find the most likely label for $\vec{x}$, we need to leverage the available observations, O, to compute the values $P(y_i)$ and $P(\vec{x}|y_i)$ for all $y_i \in Y$. Computing $P(y_i)$ using O is relatively easy: one can simply count the number of observations with class label y_i and divide this by $|O|$.

Computing the probability of $P(\vec{x}|y_i)$ is not as easy. In particular, because $\vec{x}$ has not been seen before, counting vectors and dividing them by the size of the class of observations labeled y_i does not help. Instead, we need to formulate this in terms of things that we can count more easily.

9.6.1 Independence Assumption

The problem can be significantly simplified if one can assume that the dimensions of the vector space are statistically independent from each other. In that case,

$$P(\vec{x}|y_i) = \prod_{j=1}^{n} P(\vec{x}[j] \mid y_i),$$

where $\vec{x}[j]$ is the value of $\vec{x}$ along the jth dimension. Thus, it is sufficient to be able to estimate the probability of having value $\vec{x}[j]$ given class label y_i. This is usually achieved using *maximum likelihood estimation (MLE)*, a statistical technique for finding the best fit between the parameters of a model and given data. For example, if one assumes that the values along the jth dimension have a normal distribution, then one can first estimate the parameters (mean and variance) of the underlying distribution (by studying the values along the jth dimension of all the observations with label y_i) and use this distribution to compute $P(\vec{x}[j] \mid y_i)$.

A particular risk with this approach is that if a feature value does not occur at all in the given set of observations, then the corresponding probability estimate will be

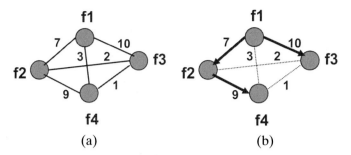

Figure 9.4. (a) A 4-feature *PD* graph and (b) its maximum spanning tree (rooted at f_1).

zero. This will then result in $P(\vec{x}|y_i) = 0$ irrespective of what the other probabilities are. Of course, if the statistical model used for MLE is accurate, this problem is less severe. However, when, for example, the MLE is implemented simply by counting how many times a feature value is observed in the given set and dividing by the set size, any feature value that is missing in the observation set will cause errors in estimation. This situation is usually prevented by the help of a smoothing (or *small-sample correction*) technique, such as the *Laplace law of succession*: "if of m observations, s have the feature value a, then the probability that the feature value is observed in the next observation is approximately $\frac{s+1}{m+2}$." When the observation set is empty, the prior distribution of the feature value is assumed to be $1/2$. If $s = 0$, then the likelihood, $\frac{1}{m+2}$, of a decreases with the number of observations, but never reaches 0; in other words, the probability of the unseen feature has been smoothed to a value larger than 0.

9.6.2 Relaxing the Independence Assumption

Bayesian classifiers that rely on the independence assumption are also referred to as *naive* Bayesian classifiers. The name highlights the fact that it is rare that the dimensions of the vector space are statistically independent from each other.

One way to relax the independence assumption is to account for the dependence between the probability distributions of different features. This is done by measuring the *mutual information* between two distributions (Section 8.8.2) and computing the dependence between the jth and kth features, given a class label y_i, as $MI(P(\vec{x}[j] \mid y_i), P(\vec{x}[k] \mid y_i))$. Thus, if we consider all pairs of features, we can create a complete *pairwise dependence* graph, $PD(V, E, mi)$, where each node in V is a feature dimension and E contains an edge between all pairs of nodes (Figure 9.4(a)). Also, for each edge, $e = \langle j, k \rangle \in E$, $mi(j, k) = MI(P(\vec{x}[j] \mid y_i), P(\vec{x}[k] \mid y_i))$ is the weight of the edge.

Although $PD(V, E, mi)$ captures the feature dependence between all pairs of features, it is not easy to leverage PD for computing the joint feature distribution $P(\vec{x}|y_i)$ directly. The lack of reliable joint distributions, however, is the very reason why $P(\vec{x}|y_i)$ cannot be computed directly relying on MLE (i.e., by counting the matching observations in O). Instead, the common approach (see, for example, [van Rijsbergen *et al.*, 1981]) to leveraging the knowledge about the available feature dependencies is to extract a directed, tree-structured Bayesian network, PD_{tree} from

PD using a rooted maximum spanning tree [Cormen *et al.*, 2001]. This keeps those edges denoting the highest dependencies, but eliminates edges that correspond to pairs of features that are almost independent (Figure 9.4(b)). The advantage of the tree representation is that the joint distribution can be written in such a way that for each feature, its dependence on only one other feature needs to be considered. For example, the *PD* graph in Figure 9.4(a) and its maximum spanning tree in Figure 9.4(b) can be used for computing the joint distribution of features, f_1, f_2, f_3 and f_4 as follows:

$$P(f_1 \wedge f_2 \wedge f_3 \wedge f_4) = P(f_1) \, P(f_2|f_1) \, P(f_3|f_1) \, P(f_4|f_2).$$

Note that in formulating the product for joint distribution, only the dependencies of the children features in PD_{tree} to their parents are considered. Thus, this formulation is imperfect; but, most significant dependencies are captured.

Given the foregoing approach to joint probability computations, based on the tree-structured Bayesian networks, we can write $P(\vec{x}|y_i)$ as

$$P(\vec{x}|y_i) = \prod_{j=1}^{n} P(\vec{x}[j] \mid \vec{x}[parent(\,j)], y_i),$$

where *parent*(*j*) denotes the parent of the *j*th feature dimension in the corresponding PD_{tree}.[6] Thus, the only probabilities that need to be computed from the available observations (by counting feature occurrences) are of the form $P(\vec{x}[j] \mid \vec{x}[k], y_i)$ for pairs of dimensions, *j* and *k* = *parent*(*j*).

9.7 HIDDEN MARKOV MODELS

Hidden Markov models (HMMs) are a type of Bayesian graph, commonly used in machine-learning–based multimedia pattern recognition, especially when the corresponding classification task has a temporal or sequence-based nature. Underlying an HMM there is a finite-state machine with probabilistic state transitions. As the name implies, some of these states are hidden (i.e., they are not directly observable), but some variables, whose values depend on these hidden states, are in the open (and thus observable).

Example 9.7.1: For example, consider the task of extracting portions of a long text document relevant to a given query [Jiang and Zhai, 2006; Li *et al.*, 2008; Rabiner, 1990]. This task can be modeled using HMMs by treating the document as an observable symbol (word) chain and assuming that there is a state chain revealing whether a given word in the document falls in the relevant portion or not (Figure 9.5(a)). Before the relevant and irrelevant parts of the given document are identified, we do not know when the switch between the underlying generative models occurs. In other words, the process that governs the switching between the two models is hidden.

HMM-based classification involves two complementary tasks: given a sequence of observations, *training* involves learning the parameters of the underlying HMM. Then, given the learned parameters of a specific HMM, *classification/pattern*

---

[6] The feature at the root of the PD_{tree} does not have a parent; thus it depends only on the class label y_i.

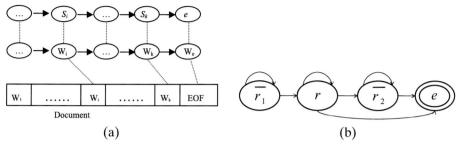

(a)   (b)

Figure 9.5. (a) Representation of a document as an HMM (S_j is the hidden state of the corresponding word, w_j, in the document) and (b) the underlying hidden state transition probability graph (r means relevant and $\bar{r}$ not relevant).

recognition finds the most likely sequence of states that would produce a particular output.

Example 9.7.2: For the previous example, let us assume that each document has only one relevant part. Thus the underlying process that governs the hidden states of the HMM can be modeled as the state transition probability graph shown in Figure 9.5(b). r means that the current word falls into the relevant portion of the document. The irrelevance states are split into two: $\bar{r}_1$ denotes the irrelevance state before the relevant portion is met and $\bar{r}_2$ denotes the irrelevance state after the relevant portion of the document has been consumed. In this model, e is the end state matching the special end-of-file (EOF) character.

In the training phase, the parameters (i.e., the transition probabilities) of the graph in Figure 9.5(b) will be discovered. In the classification phase, using the learned model, the words of the document will be classified into states, "*before the relevant portion*" ($\bar{r}_1$), "*in the relevant portion*" (r), and "*after the relevant portion*" ($\bar{r}_2$).

In a standard Markov chain, all the states of the underlying state machine are observable; thus, the state transition probabilities can be learned directly from the available observations, including the input sequence and the corresponding state changes (Section 3.5.4). In the case of HMMs, on the other hand, the states are not directly observable. Instead, we can observe output symbols produced by the hidden states. Thus, we first have to discover the probability of a given hidden state resulting in a particular output.

9.7.1 Markov Models with Hidden States: Formal Definition

Unlike in the regular Markov models (Section 3.5.4), where the states themselves are observable and only state transitions are stochastic, in Markov models with hidden states, the model is doubly stochastic: the current state of the model cannot be observed directly, and the variables that are observable are governed by a second set of stochastic processes that determine their values. A hidden Markov model, $H(V, E, O, p_\tau, p_o, \vec{\pi}_0)$, is a discrete-time stochastic process, such that

- $V = \{v_1, \ldots, v_n\}$ is the set of hidden states of the process,
- edges in E are the possible transitions between these states,
- $O = \{o_1, \ldots, o_n\}$ is the set of observation symbols,

- $p_\tau : E \rightarrow [0, 1]$ is a function associating transition probabilities to the edges of the graph,
- $p_o : V \times O \rightarrow [0, 1]$ is a function associating observation symbol probabilities to each state, and
- $\vec{\pi}_0$ is the probability distribution in the initial state.

9.7.2 Computing the Probability of an Observation Sequence from an HMM

Let us first focus on the task of computing the likelihood of a particular observation sequence. Although this problem is not directly related to the classification task, it serves as a stepping stone for the steps of the HMM classification procedures.

A given HMM, H, can be thought of as a generator of observation sequences, where each sequence is generated with a probability governed by the three distributions, $p_\tau, p_o,$ and $\vec{\pi}_0$, of H. Given an observation sequence, $seq = o(0) : o(1) : \ldots : o(k-1)$, where $o(i) \in O$ is the value observed at state S_i at time $t = i$, the probability of H generating this observation sequence can be computed as

$$P(seq) = \sum_{S_0:S_1:\ldots:S_{k-1}} P(o(i)|S_i)P(S_i) = \sum_{S_0:S_1:\ldots:S_{k-1}} p_o(S_i, o(i))P(S_i).$$

This can also be written as

$$P(seq) = \sum_{S_0:S_1:\ldots:S_{k-1}} \pi_0(S_0)p_o(S_0, o(0)) \left(\prod_{j=1}^{k-1} p_\tau(S_{j-1}, S_j)p_o(S_j, o(j)) \right).$$

The naive computation of this by enumerating all possible state sequences would require $O(kn^k)$ time. The *forward-backward* procedure [Baum and Sell, 1968; Baum and Eagon, 1967], a dynamic programming algorithm which exploits the overlaps in the set of all possible state sequences to reduce the time complexity of the computation, solves this in $O(kn^2)$ time. Forward-backward has two components:

(i) Computation of the *forward* probability, $\alpha(seq_{0,t}, v_i)$, of a partial observation sequence, $seq_{0,t} = o(0) : o(1) : \ldots : o(t)$ (from time 0 until some time $t \leq k - 1$) with the final state being $S_t = v_i$

(ii) Computation of the *backward* probability, $\beta(seq_{t+1,k-1}, v_i)$, of a remaining partial observation sequence, $seq_{t+1,k-1} = o(t+1) : \ldots : o(k-1)$ (from time $t+1$ until time $k-1$) given that at time t, the state is $S_t = v_i$

Note that the computation of $P(seq)$ requires only the *forward* component of the forward-backward procedure. The backward component, on the other hand, comes handy in other HMM tasks (Section 9.7.4).

9.7.2.1 Forward Algorithm
The forward probabilities, $\alpha(seq_{0,t}, v_i)$, for all t and v_i are computed simultaneously using dynamic programming based on an indicative formulation. For the base case, $t = 0$, forward probabilities are set based on the parameters of the given HMM as follows:

$$\forall_{1 \leq i \leq n} \; \alpha(seq_{0,0}, v_i) = \vec{\pi}_0[i]p_o(v_i, o(0)).$$

The inductive step reuses the forward probabilities computed during the earlier steps:

$$\forall_{1 \le j \le n} \forall_{0 \le t \le k-2} \; \alpha(seq_{0,t+1}, v_j) = \left(\sum_{1 \le i \le n} \alpha(seq_{0,t}, v_i) p_\tau(v_i, v_j) \right) p_o(v_j, o(t+1)).$$

Note that this is where the power of dynamic programming lies. Once $\alpha(seq_{0,t}, v_i)$ is computed for some t and state v_i, it is repeatedly used to compute $\alpha(seq_{0,t+1}, v_j)$ for different states v_j at time $t+1$. There are overall $O(kn)$ forward probabilities to compute, with each computation requiring n inductive summations. Thus, the cost is $O(kn^2)$. Finally, the forward component is completed by computing $P(seq)$:

$$P(seq) = P(seq_{0,k-1}) = \sum_{1 \le i \le n} \alpha(seq_{0,k-1}, v_i).$$

We discuss the solution to the backward component of the forward-backward procedure in Section 9.7.4.

9.7.3 Classification by Predicting the Sequence of Hidden States

Given an HMM, H, the classification problem can be formulated as predicting the underlying hidden state sequence $S_0 : S_1 : \ldots : S_{k-1}$ from an observation sequence $seq = o(0) : o(1) : \ldots : o(k-1)$. In other words, the classification problem is equivalent to the problem of identifying the hidden state sequence that *best* explains the given observation sequence. This problem is commonly solved by finding the state sequence that maximizes $P(S_0 : S_1 : \ldots : S_{k-1}, o(0) : o(1) : \ldots : o(k-1))$. This probability can be computed efficiently using a dynamic programming–based method called the *Viterbi* algorithm [Forney, 1973; Viterbi, 1967].

The Viterbi algorithm computes the probability of the most likely state sequence ending at state v_i at time t; that is,

$$\delta(seq_{0,t}, v_i) = \max_{S_0:S_1:\ldots:S_{t-1}} \{P(S_0 : S_1 : \ldots : S_t = v_i, o(0) : o(1) : \ldots : o(t))\},$$

where the base case can be stated as

$$\delta(seq_{0,0}, v_i) = \vec{\pi}_0[i] p_o(v_i, o(0)).$$

These together give rise to the following inductive formulation:

$$\delta(seq_{0,t+1}, v_j) = \left(\max_{1 \le i \le n} \{\delta(seq_{0,t}, v_i) p_\tau(v_i, v_j)\} \right) p_o(v_j, o(t+1)).$$

Given this formulation, the probability, P_{max}, of the most likely state sequence, $S_{max,0} : S_{max,1} : \ldots : S_{max,k-1}$, can be computed as

$$P_{max} = \max_{0 \le i \le n} \{\delta(seq_{0,k-1}, v_i)\}.$$

Note, however, that P_{max} is not sufficient for the classification task. We instead need the state sequence that corresponds to this maximum probability. The Viterbi algorithm identifies this most likely state sequence by using a separate array,

$\psi(seq_{0,t}, v_i)$, which keeps track of the contributing state for each time t and state v_i:

$$\forall_{1 \le i \le n} \ \psi(seq_{0,0}, v_i) = 0,$$

$$\forall_{1 \le j \le n} \forall_{1 \le t \le k-1} \ \psi(seq_{0,t}, v_j) = \underset{1 \le i \le n}{argmax}\{\delta(seq_{0,t-1}, v_i)p_\tau(v_i, v_j)\},$$

$$S_{max,k-1} = \underset{1 \le i \le n}{argmax}\{\delta(seq_{0,k-1}, v_i)\}.$$

The intermediary states can then be enumerated by backtracking on the ψ array:

$$\forall_{0 \le t \le k-2} \ S_{max,t} = \psi(seq_{0,t+1}, S_{max,t+1}).$$

In order to apply Viterbi for a classification problem, in many cases, we first need to find the parameters of the HMM; that is, we need to identify the initial state distribution (π_0), and the output (p_o) and transition (p_τ) probability distributions using the available set of observations.

9.7.4 Learning the Parameters of a Hidden Markov Model

The major challenge with learning the HMM that best describes a given set of input sequences is that there is no optimal way of estimating the parameters $\vec{\pi}_0$, p_o, and p_τ, of an HMM, $H(V, E, O, p_\tau, p_o, \vec{\pi}_0)$, with a given structure. Thus, this problem is commonly solved in a locally optimal manner, using the Baum-Welch method [Baum et al., 1970]. This method builds on the forward-backward algorithm to compute initial estimates and then iteratively improves the probability estimates in a *hill-climbing* fashion.

9.7.4.1 Backward Algorithm
Given HMM, $H(V, E, O, p_\tau, p_o, \vec{\pi}_0)$ (with known structure and probabilities) and an observation sequence, $seq = o(O) : o(1) : \ldots : o(k-1)$, the backward algorithm computes the *backward* probability, $\beta(seq_{t+1,k-1}, v_i)$, of a remaining partial observation sequence, $seq_{t+1,k-1} = o(t+1) : \ldots : o(k-1)$ (from time $t+1$ until time $k-1$) given that at time t, the state is $S_t = v_i$.

As in the forward algorithm, the backward probabilities are computed simultaneously for all t and v_i in a bottom-up fashion using dynamic programming, based on an inductive formulation of β:

$$\forall_{1 \le i \le n} \ \beta(seq_{k,k-1}, v_i) = 1,$$

$$\forall_{1 \le j \le n} \forall_{0 \le t \le k-2} \ \beta(seq_{t+1,k-1}, v_j) = \sum_{1 \le i \le n} p_\tau(v_j, v_i)p_o(v_i, o(t+1))\beta(seq_{t+2,k-1}, v_i).$$

Note that $seq_{k,k-1}$ is an empty sequence. Like the forward algorithm, the backward algorithm also requires $O(kn^2)$ time to compute the β values for all $v_i \in V$ and $0 \le t \le k-2$.

9.7.4.2 Baum-Welch Method
Given an HMM, H, and an observation sequence, $seq : o(0) : o(1) : \ldots : o(k-1)$ of length k, let $\xi(seq, t, v_i, v_j) = P(S_t = v_i, S_{t+1} = v_j | seq)$ be the probability of being at state v_i at time t and at state v_j at the next time unit, $t+1$. Using the forward, α, and

backward, β, probabilities for time t and $t+1$ respectively, we can write $\xi(seq, t, v_i, v_j)$ as follows:

$$\xi(seq, t, v_i, v_j) = \frac{\alpha(seq_{0,t}, v_i)p_\tau(v_i, v_j)p_o(v_j, o(t+1))\beta(seq_{t+2,k-1}, v_j)}{P(seq)},$$

where

$$P(seq) = \sum_{1 \leq i, j \leq n} \alpha(seq_{0,t}, v_i)p_\tau(v_i, v_j)p_o(v_j, o(t+1))\beta(seq_{t+2,k-1}, v_j).$$

Given the observation sequence, seq, let us denote the probability of being at state v_i at time t with the term, $\gamma(seq, t, v_i)$:

$$\gamma(seq, t, v_i) = P(S_t = v_i | seq) = \frac{\alpha(seq_{0,t}, v_i)\beta(seq_{t+1,k-1}, v_i)}{\sum_{1 \leq i \leq n} \alpha(seq_{0,t}, v_i)\beta(seq_{t+1,k-1}, v_i)}.$$

Given a new observation sequence, seq, the Baum-Welch method uses the current estimates for the parameters, π_0, p_o, and p_τ, of H, to compute ξ and γ values based on seq. These are then used for updating the estimates for the three HMM parameters in light of the new evidence:

$$\pi_0'[v_i] = \gamma(seq, 0, v_i).$$

$$p_\tau'(v_i, v_j) = \frac{\sum_{0 \leq t \leq k-2} \xi(seq, t, v_i, v_j)}{\sum_{0 \leq t \leq k-2} \gamma(seq, t, v_i)}.$$

$$p_o'(v_i, o) = \frac{\sum_{0 \leq t \leq k-1 \, s.t. \, o(t)=o} \gamma(seq, t, v_i)}{\sum_{0 \leq t \leq k-1} \gamma(seq, t, v_i)}.$$

Baum and Eagon [1967] showed that π_0', p_o', and p_τ' are at least as likely as π_0, p_o, and p_τ; more specifically, the a posteriori estimate of probabilities increases the likelihood of the given input observation. Thus, the repeated execution of these steps based on the new evidence leads to improved estimates of the HMM parameters. Of course, this greedy, hill-climbing–based approach is not guaranteed to reach the *best* (globally optimal) solution. Rather, the Baum-Welch method leads to a local maximum.

9.7.4.3 Expectation Maximization (EM)

The Baum-Welch method is an instance of a class of algorithms, called *expectation maximization* (EM) algorithms [Dempster *et al.*, 1977; Welch, 2003], for finding maximally likely parameter estimates for models with variables hidden from the observer. As in the Baum-Welch method, the EM algorithms have two distinct phases. The *expectation* phase (E) formulates a function that links the current estimates, λ, of the hidden parameters to their revised estimates, λ'. The *maximization* step (M) maximizes over possible values of λ'.

More formally, EM algorithms maximize $P(y, \lambda)$, where y denotes the incomplete observation, which is linked to a larger hidden model, x. There is an underlying mapping function, $F(x) = y$, which relates the observed data values to the values of the hidden data. Given this function, the distribution, q, of incomplete observations is linked to the distribution of the hidden data as follows:

$$q(y, \lambda) = \sum_{x \, s.t. \, F(x)=y} p(x, \lambda).$$

Thus, the conditional distribution of the hidden data given the observed data, y, can be computed as follows:

$$\forall_{F(x)=y} \ p(x|y, \lambda) = \frac{p(x, \lambda)}{q(y, \lambda)}.$$

Using this conditional probability, the expectation phase of EM formulates the function, $Q(\lambda, \lambda')$, to link the current estimate, λ, to the next estimate, λ'. More specifically, $Q(\lambda, \lambda')$ is the *expected* value of $log(p(x, \lambda'))$[7] given the current estimate, λ, and the observation, y:

$$Q(\lambda, \lambda') = \sum_{x \ s.t. \ F(x)=y} p(x|y, \lambda) log(p(x, y|\lambda')).$$

The maximization step then maximizes Q by varying over λ'.

In the case of the Baum-Welch method for learning the parameters of the hidden Markov model, H,

- the computation of $p(x|y, \lambda)$ corresponds to finding the likelihood of the sequence, x, of hidden states, given the current estimates of the model, $\lambda = \langle \pi_0, p_\tau, p_o \rangle$, and the current observations, y, and
- the computation of $p(x, y|\lambda') = p(x|y, \lambda')p(y|\lambda')$ corresponds to
  - estimating the likelihood of the sequence of hidden states, x, based on observation, y, and HMM parameters, $\lambda' = \langle \pi_0', p_\tau', p_o' \rangle$, and
  - estimating the likelihood of the sequence of observations, y, given the HMM parameters λ'.

Note, however, that the Baum-Welch method does not explicitly formulate $Q(\lambda, \lambda')$ in one phase and maximize this by enumerating all possible λ' in a second one. Instead, it computes the gradients for the HMM parameters and climbs along the direction of these gradients. Dempster *et al.* [1977] and Welch [2003] showed that this is equivalent to the EM formulation of the problem.

9.8 MODEL SELECTION: OVERFITTING REVISITED

As discussed in Sections 9.1.2 and 9.3.2, for many classification algorithms, overfitting of the models to the provided set of observations (or training data) is a serious problem. Especially when using classification schemes where one can pick among different models with varying complexities (or free parameters), it is often more desirable to pick classification models that are simpler and thus less prone to overfitting, even if they are not able to provide the best available fits to the input observations.

In order to reduce the risk of overfitting, *model selection techniques* quantify

- the *degree of complexity* of the given model and
- the *degree of fit* of the model to the observations

---

[7] Remember from Section 4.2.2 that $-log(p(e))$ is the information content of event, e, which measures the uncertainty of e, that is, how rare the event is. Thus, $log(p(x, \lambda'))$ measures how certain the pair $\langle x, \lambda' \rangle$ is.

and pick models that provide a reasonable trade-offs between these two measures. The LASSO technique we discussed in Section 9.1.2 was an example where a constraint on the complexity was introduced in the linear regression process, along with a measure capturing the degree of fit of the hyperplane to the data, in order to prevent overfitting.

More general criteria, which can be used in any model selection scenario, include the Bayesian information criterion (BIC), Akaike's information criterion (AIC), and the minimum description length (MDL).

9.8.1 Bayesian Information Criterion (BIC)

As introduced in Section 3.5.3, the Bayes' rule relates the conditional and marginal probabilities of two events a and b:

$$P(a|b) = \frac{P(b|a)P(a)}{P(b)}.$$

Consequently, given an observation $\vec{x}$ and two models M_0 and M_1 and the user's prior judgements, $P(M_0)$ and $P(M_1)$, of the two models, the ratio

$$\frac{P(M_0|\vec{x})}{P(M_1|\vec{x})} = \frac{P(\vec{x}|M_0)P(M_0)}{P(\vec{x}|M_1)P(M_1)}$$

can be used to judge whether M_0 or M_1 fits the observation $\vec{x}$ better. In other words, the (relative) likelihood of a model, M, is proportional to $P(\vec{x}|M)P(M)$. For a parametric model, $M(\mathcal{R})$, we can generalize this using the weighted average of the likelihoods at all possible values of the set, $\mathcal{R}$, of parameters; that is, the likelihood of the model M is proportional to $\int_{\vec{r} \in \mathcal{R}} P(\vec{x}|M(\vec{r}))P(\vec{r}, M)d\vec{r}$, where $P(\vec{r}, M)$ is the prior probability distribution for the parameters of the model M.

For a model with k parameters and a set O of N samples over which the likelihood of the model is computed, the Bayesian Information Criterion or BIC [Raftery, 1986, 1999; Schwarz, 1978; Weakliem, 1999] approximates the negative log likelihood as

$$-2ln(P(O|M(\vec{r}\,^*))) + kln(N),$$

where $\vec{r}\,^*$ is the vector of maximum likelihood estimates of the parameters of the model. Note that, intuitively, in the definition of BIC, the first term measures the degree of fit, whereas the second term penalizes for the complexity of the model. Often, this is further simplified as

$$-2ln(L) + kln(N),$$

where L is the maximized value of likelihood of the observations for the given model. Since the likelihood terms are negated in the definition of BIC, given two models, the model with small BIC value is more desirable.

9.8.2 Akaike's Information Criterion (AIC)

Akaike's Information Criterion or AIC [Akaike, 1974] is defined very similarly to BIC:

$$-2ln(P(O|M(\vec{r}\,^*))) + 2k.$$

Once again, k is the number of parameters of the model, and $P(O|M(\vec{r}^*))$ is the maximized value of the likelihood of the set, O, of the observations for the given model. Note that, unlike BIC, the penalty for the complexity is not multiplied by $ln(N) = ln(|O|)$, but multiplied only by the constant 2; thus AIC tends to penalize the complexity of the model less strongly than BIC does.

9.8.3 Minimum Description Length (MDL)

The concept of minimum description length (MDL) is related to the Kolmogorov complexity we discussed in Section 5.5.5. The Kolmogorov complexity $K(q)$ of a given object q is the length of the shortest program that outputs q [Burgin, 1982]. Because the Kolmogorov complexity is generally not computable, often approximations, such as compressed code length [Cilibrasi and Vitanyi, 2005], are used instead of the Kolmogorov complexity.

Compression algorithms, such as Huffman coding [Huffman, 1952], are based on the observation that given a set of events with a probability distribution, P, it is possible to minimize the code length needed to represent this set of events by associating to each event e a code of length $-log_2 P(e)$. That is, there is a strong relationship between the probability distribution of a given set of observations and the minimum code length needed for representing them. The MDL principle for model selection argues that, given two models M_0 and M_1, the model whose corresponding probability distribution results in the shortest encoding of these observations plus the model itself should be preferred [Hansen and Yu, 2001]. It has been shown that, under Bayesian statistics, the MDL principle leads to BIC as the valid code length, whereas under other interpretations of the available statistics, the MDL principle may lead to other measures of complexity.

9.9 BOOSTING

As we have seen in this chapter, there are many different ways one can solve the classification problem, each with different assumptions, advantages, and disadvantages. Sometimes, it may be possible to merge results from multiple classifiers to obtain better and stronger classification results. In Section 9.1.3, for example, we learned the random forests technique, which improves the classification performance by relying on an *ensemble* of decision trees instead of a single one: the object to be classified is considered by multiple decision trees and the class label with the highest support is assigned as the class label of this data object. Another example is the voted perceptron classifier (Section 9.3.9), where, given a set of prediction vectors (i.e., classifiers), the majority label is selected as the class label for a given unlabeled data object.

Boosting is the name of the general approach where a *stronger* classification is obtained by combining multiple, *weak* classification results. The weak classification results that are being combined often correspond to the results obtained using different parameter settings of a single weak classifier. In fact, the simplest way to achieve the boosting effect is to vary the parameters of a given classifier and take weighted average of the corresponding classification results. Of course, the real

Inputs: A set, O, of observations

(i) $\forall o_i \in O \; D_1(i) = \frac{1}{|O|}$; here D_1 is the initial distribution, intuitively indicating the importance of each observation instance

(ii) for $t = 1 \ldots T$ do

    (a) train the weak learner using distribution D_t to obtain a hypothesis function, $h_t()$

    (b) compute the weight, α_t, of this iteration,

    (c) compute the importance distribution, D_{t+1}, for the next iteration:

$$\forall o_i \in O \; D_{t+1}(i) = \frac{D_t(i)e^{-\alpha_t h_t(x_i) y_i}}{Z_t},$$

    where Z_t is a normalization factor to ensure that D_{t+1} is a probability distribution; i.e.,

$$\sum_{o_i \in O} D_{t+1}(i) = 1.$$

(iii) $h^*(x) = sign\left(\sum_{t=1}^{T} \alpha_t h_t(x)\right).$

Figure 9.6. AdaBoost algorithm.

challenge is choosing the weights for different parameter settings. Uniformly assigning the same weight to all alternatives may not give the best results. AdaBoost algorithm [Freund and Schapire, 1995, 1997] solves the weight assignment problem iteratively and tries to reduce the cumulative loss (with respect to the best combination strategy) progressively.

The basic AdaBoost algorithm applies boosting to binary classification problems. More recently, AdaBoost has also been extended to multilabel classification problems. Schapire and Singer [1999] also describe how to assign confidence ratings to the predictions of the strong classifier obtained through AdaBoost. In Section 12.8.4.1 we see an application of the boosting technique to collaborative filtering problems.

In this section, we present a slightly generalized version of the AdaBoost algorithm, presented by Schapire and Singer [1999]. Let us be given a set of observations, O, where each observation is a pair, $\langle x, y \rangle$, where x is an instance of some domain X and $y \in \{-1, +1\}$ is the classification label associated with the observation (i.e., we focus on the binary classification problems). Let us also assume that we are given a weak classifier producing a hypothesis given an instance of the domain X. The hypothesis $h(x)$ is real-valued, where the sign of $h(x)$ denotes the predicted label and the magnitude, $|h(x)|$, gives the confidence of this weak hypothesis.

The outline of the AdaBoost algorithm is presented in Figure 9.6; the output of the algorithm is the final strong hypothesis function $h^*()$. Note that, instead of averaging many randomly selected classifiers, the algorithm in Figure 9.6 uses the *importance distribution*, D, associated with the objects in the given observation set, to train the weak classifier in such a way that the predictions are more precise with respect to the observations that are more critical. In fact, it is this importance distribution that is iteratively computed based on the current importance distribution and the matches and mismatches between the results of the corresponding weak classifier and the input training observations. This enables AdaBoost to help focus the training of the weak classifier on the critical parts of the observation space. Freund and Schapire [1997] showed that using the iteration weight

$$\alpha_t = \frac{1}{2} \ln \left(\frac{1+r_t}{1-r_t} \right),$$

where $r_t = \sum_i D_t(i)h_t(x_i)y_i$ is sufficient to bound the training errors. Once the iterations are over, the final strong classifier is constructed by combining the weak classifiers obtained during the iterations of the algorithm using the iteration weights discovered through the process.

9.10 SUMMARY

In this chapter, we have introduced the most commonly used techniques for classifying media data into predetermined categories, based on prior knowledge, available in the form of training data. Most of these techniques are based on identifying features or feature sets that can help discriminate objects in different categories. As such, the measures used in assessing features to support the classification process show a strong resemblance to the feature quality measures discussed in Chapter 4. The major difference is that the measures we covered in Chapter 4 did not have prior knowledge about the semantic labels attached to the media objects, whereas classifiers have the distinct advantage of being able to analyze training data for more informed discrimination-power analysis.

In a multimedia database, classification is not only used for attaching semantic tags onto media objects, but also leveraged in assessing the relevance (or irrelevance) of media and features to a user, based on his or her past feedback. In fact, the relevance feedback and recommendation processes we cover in Chapter 12 can be considered as biclassification: the given set of objects is partitioned into relevant and irrelevant subsets, based on the prior evidence and the user's current context and feedbacks.

10

Ranked Retrieval

Ranked query processing is important in many application domains, including information retrieval and multimedia, where results presented to the user need to be ordered based on their scores of matching.

As discussed in earlier chapters, fuzziness is inherent in multimedia retrieval for many reasons, including similarity of features, imperfections in the feature extraction algorithms, imperfections in the query formulation methods, partial match requirements, and imperfections in the available index structures. Data (whether captured in real time through sensory measurements or processed, materialized, and stored for later use) are many times accurate only within a margin of error. Also, in many cases the importance of a feature depends on how dominant it is in a particular data object and how discriminatory/rare the feature is in the entire data collection. The popular term frequency/inverse document frequency (TF-IDF) keyword weights (Section 4.2) used in text retrieval rely on this principle. The importance of the feature can also reflect the retrieval context. For example, a keyword, say, "entropy," may carry different meanings and relevance and imply different semantic similarity relationships when used within a computer science context versus within its physics context. Thus, in many applications, the utility of a data element to a particular retrieval task depends on the user's query and the usage context. Consequently, users are usually not interested in obtaining all possible matches to a query, but only the k best results, where k is application specific or provided by the user.

Because the number of candidate matches is usually large (potentially each object in the database is a match to the user's query, but most of these objects have very low scores), the retrieval system often cannot rely on processing strategies that would require it to touch or enumerate all candidate objects. Instead, multimedia systems prefer to use data structures and algorithms that can prune unpromising data objects from consideration without having to evaluate them at all. This is often referred to as ranked or top-k query processing.

10.1 k-NEAREST OBJECTS SEARCH

A commonly used ranked query processing strategy is the k-nearest neighbor search [Broder, 1990; Fukunaga and Narendra, 1975; Hjaltason and Samet, 1999; Kamgar-Parsi and Kanal, 1985; Larsen and Kanal, 1986; Roussopoulos et al., 1995; Samet, 1990], often applied when the data and queries are all in a multidimensional vector or metric space. Given a set of data points (or vectors) in the space, and a query vector, the goal of k-nearest neighbor queries is to identify those k data points that are closest to the query point, based on the underlying distance measure (see Figure 7.1(b)).

10.1.1 Branch and Bound–Based Nearest Neighbor Search

As also briefly mentioned in Section 7.2.2.1, a common strategy for performing nearest neighbor searches is to rely on an existing hierarchical partitioning of the data, such as multidimensional search trees, and perform *branch and bound* search on this structure until k objects are found [Fukunaga and Narendra, 1975]: The basic algorithm visits elements in the hierarchy (in a depth first manner), while continuously updating a candidate list consisting of the k closest points seen so far. If the system can determine that a visited partition cannot contain any points closer to the query point than the k candidates found so far, the node and all of its descendants are eliminated from further consideration.

Let us be given a database, D, with $|D| = n$ objects and a hierarchical search hierarchy, T, which partitions the database into subsets (or partitions), such that each node in T is a subset of D and children of any given node cover the set corresponding to the parent. Given a query object q, the basic branch-and-bound technique is as follows:

- First pick a (random) object $o \in D$ and compute the distance $dist(q, o)$; this is the first nearest neighbor candidate.
- Start a range search on the hierarchy using the range, $r = dist(q, o)$.

  Usually, the range search involves a depth-first traversal of the hierarchy, where at every node the distance lower bound for the subtree is computed and those subtrees with lower bounds greater than the search range are pruned.

  However, for nearest neighbor search, whenever we find a data object o' such that the distance $dist(q, o') < r$, where r is the current nearest-neighbor range, o' is picked as the new nearest neighbor candidate and r is set to $dist(q, o')$.

The time savings in this branch-and-bound search process is due to the tightening of the pruning range as better nearest neighbor candidates are discovered. The *best-first* or *best-bin-first* branch-and-bound search modifies this basic strategy slightly to promote more effective pruning. In particular, instead of using a depth-first traversal of the hierarchy (where the data partitions are met in the order implied by the hierarchy), a *priority queue* is maintained for the *active* partitions that have been met, but not yet further explored. At each iteration, the priority queue is used to pick the partition with the smallest *lower-bound* distance to the query for further exploration: (a) the lower bounds are computed for the children of the selected partition, (b) those children whose lower bounds are above the current range are eliminated, and (c) those that are not eliminated are placed into the priority queue for further exploration.

There are various algorithms for nearest neighbor searches for different data structures. For example, Friedman *et al.* [1977] and Sproull [1991] propose algorithms for KD-trees, and Samet [1981] and Samet and Shaffer [1985] for quadtrees, and Roussopoulos *et al.* [1995] present a branch-and-bound–based search algorithm for R-trees. The common aspect of all these algorithms is their reliance on the underlying distance measure (commonly metric, or more often Euclidean) to identify appropriate pruning (or *bounding*) strategies that help decide whether a partition may contain a promising candidate or whether any point in the partition is likely to be worse than the points already discovered. These algorithms also rely on different criteria for deciding the order in which the subpartitions will be visited (*branching*).

The efficiency of a *k*-nearest neighbor search algorithm depends on its effectiveness in selecting the most promising branches to visit so that a higher degree of bounding can be achieved earlier in the search. While performing a depth-first, branch-and-bound search for *k* nearest neighbors, the optimal visit ordering of the partitions depends on the distance from the query point to partitions as well as on their sizes and layouts in space. However, considering all relevant factors to identify an optimal ordering can be too costly. Therefore, often heuristics that rely on a few cheap-to-compute measures are used to give ordering and pruning decisions.

10.1.1.1 Nearest Neighbor Searches in Euclidean Vector Spaces

Roussopoulos *et al.* [1995] present two distance-based measures for ordering and pruning minimum bounding regions (MBRs) to be used with hierarchical search data structures that form rectangular minimum bounding regions with boundaries aligned with the axes of the space (e.g., R-trees):

- *MINDIST:* Given a query point, $\vec{q}$ and MBR, m, the MINDIST measure estimates the minimum possible distance between the query and the objects contained within the MBR. In particular, Roussopoulos *et al.* [1995] observe that each face of the MBR must contain at least one data object (otherwise, a smaller MBR could have been created); consequently, given a query point, $\vec{q}$, and an MBR, m, the smallest possible distance of any object in the MBR and $\vec{q}$ is the minimum distance, MINDIST, between $\vec{q}$ and any of the faces of m. In other words, MINDIST is an optimistic lower bound on the distances of the objects in m and the query point $\vec{q}$. Roussopoulos *et al.* [1995] show that MINDIST can be computed in $O(d)$ time, where d is the number of dimensions of the space.
- *MINMAXDIST:* Unlike MINDIST, which is a lower bound on the distances, the MINMAXDIST forms an upper bound. Given a query point, $\vec{q}$, and an MBR, m, MINMAXDIST is the minimum of all the maximum distances between the query point, $\vec{q}$, and points on each of the axes of the vector space: For each axis of the space, the algorithm selects the MBR face that is closest to the query point and orthogonal to this axis and picks the furthest vertex from the query point on this face. MINMAXDIST is the minimum of the distances to each of these points. Roussopoulos *et al.* [1995] show that there is at least one object within the MBR at a distance less than or equal to MINMAXDIST; in other words, a search distance larger than or equal to MINMAXDIST would always find some object inside this MBR, but a smaller distance would miss at least one object. Roussopoulos *et al.* [1995] also show that MINMAXDIST can be computed in $O(d)$ time, where d is the number of dimensions of the vector space.

Roussopoulos *et al.* [1995] experimentally show that, although optimistic and not necessarily the theoretically optimal ordering, (at least in R-trees with minimal dead-space, constructed with data that were spatially pre-sorted) MINDIST ordering of the partitions provides good pruning opportunities. Roussopoulos *et al.* [1995] present three pruning strategies:

- *Downward pruning:* An MBR, *m*, with MINDIST greater than the MINMAXDIST of another MBR, *m′*, cannot contain the nearest neighbor.
- *Object pruning:* An already discovered object $\vec{o}$ whose distance from the query point, $\vec{q}$ is greater than the MINMAXDIST of an MBR, *m*, can be discarded, because the MBR contains at least one object that is better than $\vec{o}$.
- *Upward pruning:* An MBR, *m*, with MINDIST greater than the distance of an already discovered object, $\vec{o}$, to the query point can be discarded because it cannot contain an object closer than $\vec{o}$.

In general, the search algorithm maintains a sorted buffer of *k* current nearest objects and prunes active MBRs (those that have been discovered, but not yet explored) according to the distance of the furthest nearest neighbor in this buffer.

10.1.1.2 Search Data Structures in Metric Spaces

As mentioned before, the foregoing pruning and ordering heuristics are applicable for hierarchical search data structures that form rectangular minimum bounding regions with boundaries aligned with the axes of the space. Furthermore, in many cases, the hierarchical partitioning may be in a metric space, but not in a vector space: that is, the distances between the objects satisfy the conditions of being metric, but there are no explicit dimensions of the space [Chavez *et al.*, 1999; Hjaltason and Samet, 2003; Wang and Shasha, 1990]. Hierarchical metric-space data structures that do not assume knowledge about the axes of the space include the vantage-point tree (VP-tree) [Yianilos, 1993], Burkhard-Keller tree [Burkhard and Keller, 1973], MVP-tree [Bozkaya and Ozsoyoglu, 1999], post-office tree [Knuth, 1998], M-trees [Ciaccia *et al.*, 1997], generalized-hyperplane tree (GH-tree) [Uhlmann, 1991], and geometric near-neighbor access tree (GNAT) [Brin, 1995]. For these and other metric-space data structures, the pruning strategies specified previously cannot be used, and more general pruning strategies that do not rely on the availability of axes of the space are needed.

Fukunaga and Narendra [1975], Kamgar-Parsi and Kanal [1985], and Larsen and Kanal [1986] propose four general pruning rules for branch-and-bound search in hierarchically partitioned metric spaces: Let $dist_k$ be the distance from the query point, *q*, to the currently known *k*th nearest object.

- An active MBR,[1] *m*, with mean $center_m$ and distance MAX_m from $center_m$ to the farthest object in *m* cannot contain the *k*th nearest neighbor if

$$dist_k + MAX_m < dist(q, center_m).$$

Intuitively, this implies that the two hyperspheres, one (S_q) centered around the query and extending until the current *k*th nearest neighbor and the other

---

[1] Because these heuristics also apply for the special case of Euclidean-based data structures, here we use MBR, commonly used in the context of Euclidean-based structures, to refer to the partition of objects and the minimum space covering these objects.

($S_{m,outer}$) centered around $center_m$ and extending until the outermost object in m, are nonintersecting. Consequently, there cannot be any object in m that is closer to q than its current kth nearest neighbor.

■ An MBR, m, with mean $center_m$ and distance MIN_m from $center_m$ to the closest object in m cannot contain the kth nearest neighbor if

$$dist_k + dist(q, center_m) < MIN_m.$$

This implies that q and the kth nearest neighbor are both spatially contained within the boundaries of m (but not in the partition – or set – of data associated to m); moreover, the hypersphere S_q centered around the query and extending until the current kth nearest neighbor falls into the dead space, $S_{m,inner}$, between the center point $center_m$ and the closest point to it in the data partition m.

■ An object o in MBR m, with mean $center_m$ cannot be the kth nearest neighbor if

$$dist_k + dist(o, center_m) < dist(q, center_m).$$

This rule is similar to the first one above, but it can be used in cases where, while MAX_m is not tight enough to enable the pruning of the entire MBR, a specific object discovered in the data partition of m can be pruned because of its closeness to $center_m$.

■ An object o in MBR m, with mean $center_m$ cannot be the kth nearest neighbor if

$$dist_k + dist(q, center_m) < dist(o, center_m).$$

This rule is similar to the second one just given, but it can be used in cases where, although MIN_m is not lax enough to contain the entire hypersphere S_q centered around the query and extending until the current kth nearest neighbor, a specific object discovered in the data partition of m is far enough from $center_m$ to define a hypersphere that contains S_q.

For the special case where $k = 1$, Larsen and Kanal [1986] propose that given an MBR m, with mean $center_m$ and distance MIN_m from $center_m$ to the closest object in m, the distance, $dist_1$, between q and its nearest object cannot be larger than $dist(q, center_m) + MIN_m$. Thus, even before MBR, m, is explored, the upper bound on the distance from q to its nearest object can be updated, leading to further pruning opportunities. This is similar to the MINMAXDIST pruning described earlier: the maximum distance (MINMAXDIST) from q to its nearest neighbor in m is calculated and is checked as to whether this is closer to q than its current nearest neighbor. Samet [2005] shows that this can also be extended to the cases where $k > 1$.

During search, child MBRs can be considered in the order of MINDIST, MINMAXDIST, or simply based on the distance from the query point to the means of the regions. Hjaltason and Samet [1999] show that, as was the case for search data structures with rectangular bounding regions, in general, MINDIST order is the most effective solution.

10.1.2 Nearest Neighbor Search without Hierarchical Partioning

Not all nearest neighbor search algorithms assume the existence of a vector space or even a hierarchical partitioning of the objects that can help guide and prune the search process. One approach to handle nearest neighbor searches in this case is to map (or embed) the database objects into a multidimensional vector space (see Section 4.3) and create an index structure on the database objects in this space. Because the mapping from the distances to the vector space is generally imperfect, the index serves as a *filter* and the retrieved objects have to pass through a *refinement* process for correctness [Korn *et al.*, 1996; Orenstein, 1989; Seidl and Kriegel, 1998]. In the rest of this section, we focus on algorithms and data structures that do not rely on such vector-space embeddings.

10.1.2.1 Delaunay Graphs

The most traditional nonhierarchical approach to the nearest neighbor search involves the creation and use of Voronoi decomposition and/or *Delaunay graphs* [Navarro, 2002, 1999]. Given a set of data objects in a d-dimensional metric space, the Voronoi decomposition splits the space into cells, each containing one single data object: Let o_i be a data object and *cell_i* be the corresponding Voronoi cell; the partitioning is such that, for any point v in *cell_i*, the distance between v and o_i is less than or equal to the distances between v and other data objects in the space. Given n points in space, the complexity of the process is known to be $O(n^{d+\epsilon})$, for $\epsilon > 0$ [Sharir, 1994]. The Delaunay graph is then obtained by connecting data points in neighboring cells to each other. Because of the way the space is split, on this graph, if q is closer to o than to any of the neighbors of o, then o is the object closest to q. Based on this observation, the nearest neighbor search starts with a random data point and continues by checking all the neighbors of this data point on the Delaunay graph. If any of the neighbors is closer to the query, q, then the search moves to that point. The search continues until there are no closer neighbors. The GH-tree [Uhlmann, 1991] and geometric near-neighbor access tree (GNAT) [Brin, 1995] data structures, mentioned earlier, try to split the space hierarchically into cells that have the foregoing *Voronoi property*. Unfortunately, Navarro [1999] showed that given only the distances between the pairs of objects, there can be multiple Delaunay graphs corresponding to different metric spaces. In fact, the only superset of the Delaunay graph that works for any arbitrary metric space is the complete graph of the data. Therefore in an unknown metric space, Delaunay graph-based data structures cease to be effective. The SA-tree [Navarro, 1999], on the other hand, creates a spanning tree of the data points in a way that approximates the Delaunay graph to help guide the search, without having to consider too many edges.

10.1.2.2 Orchard's Algorithm

Given a set of objects in metric space, the Orchard's algorithm [Orchard, 1991] starts with picking a random object $o \in D$ and declaring it as the current nearest neighbor. It then inspects all the other objects in D in the order of their distances to the current nearest neighbor. Whenever an object closer to the query than the current nearest neighbor is found, this new object is declared as the new nearest neighbor and the remaining objects are visited by their distances to the new object. The search stops when an object o', whose distance to q is twice the distance of the current nearest neighbor to the query object, is found.

An alternative approach, which tends to converge more quickly on the nearest neighbor, first randomly organizes the data, D, into l sets, such that $D_1 \subset D_2 \subset \cdots \subset D_{l-1} \subset D_l$ and $\frac{|D_i|}{|D_{i-1}|} \simeq \alpha > 1$. The algorithm starts from D_1 and identifies the nearest neighbor in this set. The process is repeated incrementally for all the remaining layers by using the result obtained in the previous layer as the starting point.

10.1.2.3 **AESA, LAESA, and TLAESA**

The *approximating and eliminating search* algorithm (AESA [Vidal, 1994; Vilar, 1995]) computes and stores all $O(n^2)$ distances between object pairs in the database. Given a nearest neighbor search query, the algorithm first computes the distance from the query, q, to an arbitrary object, p, in the database. This establishes a lower bound that can be used to prune objects whose lower-bound distances from the query are larger than this distance, thus reducing the total number of distance computations. This relies on the following observation: Let q be a query and p and o be two objects in the database; then, in metric spaces, triangular inequality implies that

$$dist(q, o) + dist(p, o) \geq dist(q, p) \quad \text{and} \quad dist(q, o) + dist(q, p) \geq dist(p, o)$$

and, thus,

$$|dist(q, p) - dist(p, o)| \leq dist(q, o).$$

Consequently, if P is the set of objects whose distances from q have already been computed, the lower bound on the distance between $o \notin P$ and q is simply

$$dist_\perp(q, o) = \max_{p \in P}\{|dist(q, p) - dist(p, o)|\}.$$

This implies that, given P, any object in the database whose distance lower bound computed as just shown is greater than the known kth nearest neighbor candidate can be eliminated. At each step, after the unpromising objects are eliminated, the next object in the data set such that $dist_\perp(q, o)$ is the smallest is selected and its distance to the query object is computed. This helps tighten the distance lower bound to promote the potential for more effective pruning.

Experiment results reported in [Vidal, 1994] showed that AESA is at least an order faster (in terms of run-time distance calculations) than other methods. The main shortcoming of the technique, however, is the $O(n^2)$ pre-processing and storage costs associated with it. The methods proposed by Shapiro [1977], Wang and Shasha [1990], and the *linear AESA (LAESA)* [Micó *et al.*, 1994] methods pick c maximally separated *pivot* objects in advance and compute the distance between all objects in the database and these c pivots, resulting in $O(cn)$ pre-processing and storage costs. Although this approach reduces the preprocessing and storage, it potentially results in inefficiencies during the run time. In particular, not all distance computations in run time can be used to tighten the lower bound and, thus, help prune more data. This is because only the pivot objects' distances to all objects in the database are known, and hence only they can help tighten distance lower bounds. Consequently, it is better to select, whenever possible, pivot objects over others for distance computations and to avoid early pruning of pivots, which may be needed to help tighten the distance lower bounds. To further reduce the run-time costs, Vilar [1995] partitions the set of unvisited objects into two, *alive* and *not-alive*, and limits the lower-bound distance updates to only those objects that are in the alive set: in the first round, the lower-bound distances are computed between all objects in the database and the initially picked object; then, in the following iterations, objects are made alive only if their currently known distance lower bounds are less than both the current nearest neighbor candidate and the minimum lower bound of the currently alive objects.

The TLAESA [Micó *et al.*, 1996] method combines distance lower bounding and hierarchical partitioning–based methods and leverages the distance lower bounds computed through the LAESA process to reduce the number of distance computations needed during the branch-and-bound–based nearest neighbor search.

10.1.3 Incremental Nearest Neighbor Search

The depth-first search with branch-and-bound technique, presented previously, will stop when there are no MBRs left that were not either explored or pruned. At the end of the process, the k objects that are nearest the query point will be available to be returned to the user. However, during the search process itself, there are no guarantees that these k objects will have been identified progressively, from the closest object to the furthest one: for example, although the MINDIST ordering scheme tries to order the MBRs in a way that those that have the closest object to the query are visited first, the depth-first nature of the traversal prevents the k nearest objects from being discovered incrementally, in a ranked manner.

Intuitively, processing nearest neighbor search in an incremental manner requires the search range to grow progressively from being close to 0 to being $\geq \Delta_k$, where Δ_k is the distance of the kth nearest neighbor of the query. This can be, for example, done by finding the first-nearest neighbor, removing the found element, and repeating the process k times, until k nearest objects are found. If different iterations start from scratch, this of course will be wasteful, as the same MBRs will be visited again and again for each iteration. Thus, instead, it will be more effective to use data structures that will enable continuing with a search to the $(i + 1)$th nearest neighbor, after the ith nearest neighbor is identified. This can be done by maintaining data structures that remember the pruned MBRs when looking for the ith nearest neighbor when the $(i + 1)$th nearest neighbor is searched and consider only the relevant ones. Hjaltason and Samet [2000][2] present a generalized *best-first* search strategy, where at each step, the algorithm explores the active MBR with the smallest distance from the query, q. This is achieved by putting all active MBRs into a priority queue based on their MINDIST values and visiting them in the order implied by the priority queue as opposed to a depth-first manner. Using two priority queues, one for the current candidates and another for the MBRs, the algorithm presented by Hjaltason and Samet [2000] is able to leverage the distance of the kth current nearest neighbor candidate to reduce the number of operations on the priority queue of MBRs: those MBRs whose distances are larger than the distance of the kth current nearest neighbor candidate do not need to be enqueued. Samet [2005] shows that the priority queue of MBRs can also be leveraged to help speed up the convergence, by leveraging the MINMAXDIST-based estimates to prune unpromising objects from the priority queue of the current candidates.

---

[2] Hjaltason and Samet [2000] also present an extension of the generalized best-first strategy that can return the farthest neighbors instead of the nearest neighbors.

Hjaltason and Samet [2000] show that other, originally nonhierarchical schemes, such as AESA and LAESA, can also benefit from this best-first strategy in identifying *k* nearest neighbors in an incremental manner.

10.1.4 Approximate Nearest Neighbor Searches

As is the case for range searches in multidimensional spaces, nearest neighbor search also suffers performance degradations as the number of dimensions of the space increases. The lack of efficient solutions for spaces with a large number of dimensions implies that it may be more effective to accept *approximate* nearest neighbor solutions that can be identified quickly, as opposed to waiting for *exact* ones [Ciaccia and Patella, 2000].

10.1.4.1 Branch and Bround based Approximate Nearest Neighbors

Arya *et al.* [1994, 1998], Clarkson [1994], and Kleinberg [1997] define the $(1 + \epsilon)$-*approximate* *i*th *nearest neighbor* as a data point, *p*, such that

$$dist(p, q) \leq (1 + \epsilon)dist(p_i, q),$$

where p_i is the true *i*th nearest neighbor.

Arya *et al.* [1994] present an algorithm that, given *n* data points in a *d*-dimensional Minkowski space, constructs an index structure in $O(dn \log n)$ time and, given $\epsilon > 0$, identifies $k (1 + \epsilon)$-approximate nearest neighbors in $O((c_{d,\epsilon} + kd)\log n)$ time, where $c_{d,\epsilon}$ is a constant such that $c_{d,\epsilon} \leq d\lceil 1 + 6d/\epsilon\rceil^d$. The algorithm first locates, in $O(\log n)$ time, the leaf partition containing the query point using a simple root-to-leaf point search. Starting from this leaf node, the remaining leaf cells (each containing a single point by construction) are enumerated in increasing distance from the query point. When the distance from *q* to the current leaf cell exceeds $\frac{dist(q,p)}{1+\epsilon}$, where *p* denotes the closest point seen so far, the search terminates: any point in the remaining nodes cannot be close enough to *q* to be the approximate neighbor instead of *p*. This *priority search* process is performed in $O(d \log n)$ time using a heap-based priority queue. The algorithm is generalized to *k* nearest neighbors by maintaining the *k* closest data points to *q*, met during priority search. The search terminates when the distance from the current cell to *q* exceeds $\frac{dist_k}{1+\epsilon}$, where $dist_k$ is the distance from the query point to the currently known k^{th} nearest point.

Hjaltason and Samet [2000] also present an approximate version of their best-first based algorithm. In the approximate version, the key values for MBRs are multiplied by $(1 + \epsilon)$ before they are inserted into the priority queue. Consequently, if an object *p* is returned as the *i*th nearest neighbor instead of the true *i*th nearest neighbor, p_i, then

$$dist(q, p) \leq (1 + \epsilon)dist(q, p_i).$$

10.1.4.2 Locality Sensitive Hashing

As described earlier in Section 5.5.4, Indyk and Motwani [1998] define a *locality-sensitive hash (LSH) function* as a hash function, *h*, where given any pair, o_1 and o_2, of objects and a similarity function, *sim*(), the probability of collision between hashes of the objects is high for similar objects. Approximate nearest neighbor search algorithms that rely on LSH [Andoni and Indyk, 2006b, 2008; Indyk and Motwani, 1998] hash the data points using multiple independent locality-sensitive hash functions. Then, given a nearest neighbor query, matches can be determined by hashing the query point and retrieving those elements that are stored in the corresponding hash buckets. Recently, Tao *et al.* [2009] proposed a *locality sensitive B-tree (LSB-tree)* data structure for processing approximate nearest neighbor queries more efficiently.

More formally [Andoni and Indyk, 2006b], an LSH family,[3] $\mathcal{H}$, is said to be (r, cr, P_1, P_2)-sensitive if it consists of a set of hash functions, such that for any hash function $h \in \mathcal{H}$ and two objects o_i and o_j,

- if $dist(o_i, o_j) \leq r$ then $prob(h(o_i) = h(o_j)) \geq P_1$,
- if $dist(o_i, o_j) \geq cr$ then $prob(h(o_i) = h(o_j)) \leq P_2$, and
- $P_1 > P_2$.

Given a (r, cr, P_1, P_2)-sensitive hash family, $\mathcal{H}$, L composite hash functions[4] $g_j(o) = (h_{1,j}(o), \ldots, h_{k,j}(o))$, for $1 \leq j \leq L$, are constructed by picking $L \times k$ hash functions, $h_{i,j} \in \mathcal{H}$, independently and uniformly at random from $\mathcal{H}$. Once the L composite hash functions are constructed, the objects in D are hashed against $g_j()$, for $1 \leq j \leq L$, and placed into the corresponding hash buckets. Because the probability of collision is much larger for objects that are closer to each other than for those that are further, given a query, q, the contents of hash buckets $g_1(q)$ through $g_L(q)$ are collected and the distances from the objects in these buckets to q are computed.

Andoni and Indyk [2006b] showed that if L is chosen such that $L = log_{1-(P_1{}^k)}\delta$, then, any object within range[5] r is found in these buckets with probability at least $1 - \delta$. Moreover, if the search stops after finding the first $3L$ objects, where $L = \Theta(n^\rho)$ and $\rho = \frac{ln(1/P_1)}{ln(1/P_2)}$, then the algorithm returns objects within range cr with probability at least $1 - \delta$ (i.e., for any given $\delta < 1$ it is possible to select L and k in such a way that the condition is satisfied). In this second case, the algorithm is shown to run in sublinear time (proportional to n^ρ, where $\rho < 1$).

10.1.5 Nearest Neighbor Search with Batch-Oriented Data Sources

Most of the nearest neighbor search algorithms described previously assume that all the necessary data and/or index structures are available locally for query processing. This, however, may not always be true. In cases where data are stored remotely, data sources may not provide fine-grained access to the data or, even if the data are stored locally, index structures may not be available a priori. Moreover, there may be multiple remote data sources (or local algorithms) that may be available, and one has to choose among these the most promising ones to answer the nearest neighbor query.

Yu *et al.* [2003] propose a two-step method to execute nearest neighbor queries under these conditions. In the first step, the algorithm ranks the available candidate

---

[3] Several LSH families exist for different types of data representations [Andoni and Indyk, 2006a,b; Broder, 1997; Broder *et al.*, 1997; Charikar, 2002; Datar *et al.*, 2004; Indyk and Motwani, 1998; Terasawa and Tanaka, 2007].

[4] The goal of creating these composite hash functions is to *amplify* the effect of the difference between P_1 and P_2 if P_1 and P_2 are close to each other.

[5] Andoni and Indyk [2006b] refer to these as the *r*-near neighbors of *q*.

data sources based on their likelihood of containing the nearest neighbors to the given query object. Yu *et al.* [2003] argue that given a set of data sources $\mathcal{D}, D_i \in \mathcal{D}$ are optimally ranked with respect to a given query, q, as $D_1, D_2, \ldots, D_n$, if for every user-specified k, there exists a threshold, t, such that $D_1, D_2, \ldots, D_t$ collectively contain all the k nearest neighbors of q and each D_i, $1 \leq i \leq t$, contains at least one of the k nearest neighbors. This implies that, for a given query, q, if the available data sources are ranked in ascending order of their distances of their closest objects to q, then they are ranked optimally. This can be achieved either by requesting the best match from all the sources and ranking the sources based on the distances of their best matches from the query point or by using histograms that can help estimate the distances of the best matching objects.

In the second step, a subset of the data sources are accessed and the results are merged to obtain the nearest neighbors. Yu *et al.* [2003] provide two algorithms to help select tuples from the databases ranked in the first step. The *merge-1* algorithm accesses the databases in the order in which they are ranked, one at a time. For each new database accessed, the algorithm first receives and stores the top-k tuples. Consider the case where the jth database, D_j, is accessed and d_j is the distance of the best match in the database D_j to the query q. *Merge-1* considers all objects in the databases D_1 through D_j and all the objects in those databases closer to the query than d_j units. If k objects are found, then the algorithm stops ($t = j$); otherwise, the algorithm continues with the next database, D_{j+1}.

The *min-2* algorithm first accesses D_1 and D_2, finds the closest of the two best matched tuples (one from each source), sets $d = min\{d_1, d_2\}$, and identifies those objects in $D_1 \cup D_2$ whose distances to the query are $\leq d$ units. If at least k objects are found, the process stops; otherwise, a new database is accessed. When the database, D_j, is accessed, the algorithm computes $d = min\{d_{j-1}, d_j\}$ and retrieves all objects in $D_1 \cup D_2 \cup \ldots \cup D_j$ whose distances to the query are $\leq d$ units. The process stops when k objects are found in this manner. A slightly modified version of the algorithm runs both *merge-1* and *min-2* and maintains only those that have lower distances.

Note that, if only estimates are available to rank the databases, then the resulting top-k results may not be the actual top-k objects. Yu *et al.* [2003] show that *Merge-1* requires fewer database accesses per query, but *min-2* is likely to retrieve more of the actual top-k objects.

10.2 TOP-*k* QUERIES

All nearest neighbor algorithms described in the previous section assume that there is an explicitly provided target object, which enables the definition of *nearness* along with a suitable distance measure. Moreover, most of the algorithms also assume that the objects in the database can be mapped to *points* in a multidimensional space that can then be indexed by a suitable multidimensional index structure. Both of these assumptions, however, may fail in many real-world applications:

■ It is, for example, possible that the user does not have a target object (or an example) in mind, but simply wants to order the objects available in the database based on some criterion.

■ It is also possible that the various features of the objects are extracted and separately indexed by different subunits of a multimedia processing environment. In other words, although the objects can still be considered as points in a multidimensional space, these points are never explicitly materialized; instead, projections of the points along each dimension of the space are available independently from each other.

Consider for example, the following SQL-like query (see also Example 1.2.1 in Section 1.2):

```
select image P, imageobject object1, object2 where
        contains(P, object1) and contains(P, object2) and
        (semantically_similar(P.semanticannotation, "Fuji Mountain") and
        visually_similar(object1.imageproperties, "Fujimountain.jpg")) and
        (semantically_similar(P.semanticannotation, "Lake") and
        visually_similar(object2.imageproperties, "Lake.jpg")) and
        above(object1, object2).
```

This query is asking for images that best satisfy a given set of criteria, some of which are visual in nature, some others are semantic, and still others are spatial. Each of these features is indexed and searched using algorithms and data structures especially designed for it. For example, whereas visual match may require indexes built on color and shape features, finding semantic matches may be best performed using available taxonomies. Consequently, although we can consider each image in the database as a point in a multidimensional space, where different dimensions represent visual, semantic, and spatial aspects of the data (with respect to the given criteria), these points can never be materialized without doing an exhaustive pass over the entire database. Instead, what we need is algorithms and data structures that can efficiently and progressively *join* data from these different dimensions to identify the best matches to the query in the database.

Let us consider a simple query with two criteria, formulated as a *fuzzy* statement (see Section 3.4):

$$q(X) \leftarrow p_1(X) \wedge p_2(X),$$

where p_1 is the semantic match predicate and p_2 is the visual match predicate. Let us also assume that the merge function corresponding to the fuzzy logical operator $\wedge$ is *average*: that is, if there is an image that has a semantic annotation with a matching score μ_{p_1} and a visual match of μ_{p_2}, then the combined score of this image will be $\frac{\mu_{p_1}+\mu_{p_2}}{2}$. Let us also consider six images, o_1 through o_6, in the database, with the following scores:

■ *semantic* (p_1): $\langle o_1, 0.5 \rangle$, $\langle o_2, 0.9 \rangle$, $\langle o_3, 0.4 \rangle$, $\langle o_4, 0.6 \rangle$, $\langle o_5, 0.8 \rangle$, and $\langle o_6, 0.7 \rangle$;
■ *visual* (p_2): $\langle o_1, 0.74 \rangle$, $\langle o_2, 0.75 \rangle$, $\langle o_3, 0.85 \rangle$, $\langle o_4, 0.7 \rangle$, $\langle o_5, 0.8 \rangle$, and $\langle o_6, 0.74 \rangle$.

Let us also assume that the user is interested in identifying the top three matches to the query. The naive way of executing this query would be to *join* the sets of semantic and visual scores, based on the object IDs, to obtain the combined scores for the images:

- *combined scores:* $\langle o_1, 0.62 \rangle$, $\langle o_2, 0.825 \rangle$, $\langle o_3, 0.625 \rangle$, $\langle o_4, 0.65 \rangle$, $\langle o_5, 0.8 \rangle$, and $\langle o_6, 0.72 \rangle$.

Out of these six combined scores, the best three (corresponding to images o_2, o_5, and o_6) can then be selected easily. The problem with this naive approach, however, is that it requires each and every object in the database to be accessed at least once for each of the two dimensions. In fact, if the two data sets are not each sorted along the object IDs, processing this query could take as much as $O(|D|^2)$ time for a database, D. Naturally, the cost would grow exponentially with the number of independent query criteria (or predicates) one has to join to obtain the combined scores. Therefore, it is more desirable to develop algorithms that will support progressive, top-k query processing, where only those objects that are likely to be in the top-k are considered.

As introduced in Section 3.4.2, the meaning of a fuzzy query (i.e., the score of the whole clause, given the constituent predicate scores) depends on the semantics associated to the fuzzy logical operators used for combining the constituting predicates. As we also discussed in that section, these semantics are usually represented in terms of functions that are used for combining the scores returned by the individual predicates. For example, *min*, *product*, and *average* are three of the commonly used semantics associated to the fuzzy- and operation.

A key property of many commonly used combination or merge functions (including *min*, *product*, and *average*) is that these functions are *monotonic*: if μ is an *m*-way merge function, which combines m scores, then monotonicity implies that

$$\forall_{1 \leq i \leq m} \ s_i \leq s_i' \to \mu(s_1, \ldots, s_m) \leq \mu(s_1', \ldots, s_m').$$

In other words, an object that is as good as another one in all aspects should not have a combined score lower than that object. This property is critical in the design of efficient *ranked join* algorithms.

10.2.1 Fagin's Algorithm (FA)

Fagin [1996, 1998] proposed an efficient top-k query execution algorithm (commonly known as *Fagin's algorithm* or *FA*) for ranked, top-k processing for monotonic, fuzzy queries. Let us consider a query

$$q(x) \leftarrow \Theta(p_1(x), p_2(x), \ldots, p_m(x)),$$

where Θ is a fuzzy clause with a monotonic merge function, μ_Θ. Let us also assume that each of these predicates is indexed in such a way that two access strategies are possible:

- *Sorted access:* for all p_is, the system is able to return objects in D in the non-increasing order of the predicate scores; i.e., if $\mu_{p_i}(o) > \mu_{p_i}(o')$, then o is enumerated before o'.
- *Random access:* for any p_i and given any $o \in D$, the system is able to quickly identify the corresponding score $\mu_{p_i}(o)$.

(i) $M = \emptyset$; $C = \emptyset$;

(ii) repeat

    (a) perform sorted access on one of the m predicates in an interleaved fashion (let o be the object met)

    (b) check if you have already seen o in all of the remaining $m - 1$ predicates sorted object streams

    (c) if o has already been met in all m predicates then

        1. remove o from M

        2. insert $\langle o, \mu_\Theta(o) \rangle$ into C

    (d) else if o is met for the first time, then

        1. put o into M

    until $|C| = k$.

(iii) for each object $o \in M$

    (a) perform random access to all remaining predicates to obtain all missing scores and compute $\mu_\Theta(o)$

    (b) insert $\langle o, \mu_\Theta(o) \rangle$ into C

(iv) pick and return the highest scoring k objects from C.

Figure 10.1. Fagin's top-k ranked join algorithm.

Fagin's algorithm operates as described in Figure 10.1. To see how this algorithm works, let us reconsider the query

$$q(X) \leftarrow p_1(X) \wedge p_2(X),$$

and the six objects with the corresponding scores for predicates p_1 and p_2:

- *semantic (p_1):* $\langle o_1, 0.5 \rangle$, $\langle o_2, 0.9 \rangle$, $\langle o_3, 0.4 \rangle$, $\langle o_4, 0.6 \rangle$, $\langle o_5, 0.8 \rangle$, and $\langle o_6, 0.7 \rangle$;
- *visual (p_2):* $\langle o_1, 0.74 \rangle$, $\langle o_2, 0.75 \rangle$, $\langle o_3, 0.85 \rangle$, $\langle o_4, 0.7 \rangle$, $\langle o_5, 0.8 \rangle$, and $\langle o_6, 0.74 \rangle$.

    Let us assume once again that the user is interested in finding the best three objects under the *average* merge function. As shown in Figure 10.2(a), the FA algorithm first accesses objects in the database in nonincreasing order of scores for both p_1 and p_2 until three candidate objects ($C = \{o_2, o_5, o_6\}$, with combined scores 0.825, 0.8, and 0.72, respectively) are found. Monotonicity of the average merge function implies that any object not met yet during the decreasing order of the visit cannot have a higher score than the lowest score found so far, that is, 0.72. On the other hand, there is a chance that $o_3 \in M$, which was met in p_2, but not yet in p_1,

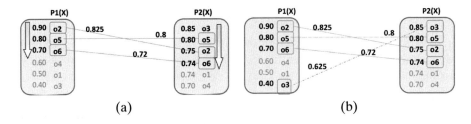

(a)   (b)

Figure 10.2. Sorted and random access phases of Fagin's algorithm: (a) Sorted access, (b) Random access.

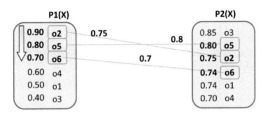

Figure 10.3. Top-*k* processing with the *min* merge function.

may have a higher combined score than 0.72. Therefore, in its second stage, the FA algorithm performs a random access to obtain the score of o_3 for predicate p_1 and, using this, computes the combined score, 0.625. Because this score is less than 0.72, o_3 is not in the top three; and the top three results for this query are o_2, o_5, and o_6.

Note that, taking advantage of the monotonicity of the underlying merge function, *FA* found these three best objects *without* having to consider objects o_1 and o_4 at all. Fagin [1996] showed that, given a query with m predicates, the cost of the algorithm (in terms of the number of objects visited), with a very high probability, is $O(k^{\frac{1}{m}}|D|^{1-\frac{1}{m}})$. Note that when $m = 2$, the query processing cost, $O(\sqrt{k|D|})$, is much smaller than the full scan of the database; on the other hand, as the number of predicates increases, the cost of top-*k* query processing using the FA algorithm approaches the cost, $O(|D|)$, of the full scan of the database. This is another instance of the dimensionality curse problem (Section 4.1).

10.2.2 Threshold Algorithm (TA)

FA has special cases, for instance when the *min* is used as the underlying merge function. In this case, one of the predicates can be chosen for the sorted access and the others used only for random access. First, the top-*k* objects for the predicate that provides sorted access are considered. The combined *min* scores for these objects are computed through random accesses on the remaining predicates (Figure 10.3). Let the score of the *k*th candidate be τ. The object enumeration process continues until the next value in the sorted list is less than τ. For example, in Figure 10.3, the lower-bound threshold, τ, is equal to 0.7, and the next element in the sorted list is 0.6. Therefore, the process stops right away: under the *min* merge semantics, the top three objects in the database are o_2, o_5 and o_6, and objects o_1, o_3, and o_4 have not been considered at all during the process.

The *threshold algorithm (TA)* [Fagin *et al.*, 2001; Güntzer *et al.*, 2000; Nepal and Ramakrishna, 1999] generalize this approach to more general merge functions. Like FA, TA assumes that we are given m sorted lists, where each object has a single score in each list and a monotone merge function that will be used to combine objects' scores from each list. The TA algorithm is similar to FA in its structure, but it incorporates the use of an explicit threshold to minimize unnecessary object enumerations. It is also similar to the *min* variant of the FA algorithm in its eager use of random accesses to calculate and maintain the threshold value, τ, which establishes a lower bound of the possible scores of the elements in the top-*k* result (Figure 10.4).

(i) $C = \emptyset; \tau = 0;$
(ii) repeat
    (a) perform sorted access on one of the m predicates in an interleaved fashion (let o be the object met)
        1. perform random access to all remaining predicates to obtain all missing scores and compute the combined score, $\mu_\Theta(o)$
        2. if $|C| < k$
           A. insert $\langle o, \mu_\Theta(o) \rangle$ into C
           B. $minscore_k = min\{\mu_\Theta(o_i) \mid o_i \in C\}$
        3. else if $minscore_k < \mu_\Theta(o)$
           A. remove the object with the smallest score from C
           B. insert $\langle o, \mu_\Theta(o) \rangle$ into C
           C. $minscore_k = min\{\mu_\Theta(o_i) \mid o_i \in C\}$
        4. if at least one object has been seen for each predicate
           A. Let τ_i be the score of the last object seen under sorted access for predicate p_i
           B. $\tau = \mu_\Theta(\tau_1, \ldots, \tau_m)$
        until at least k objects have been seen with grade at least τ.
(iii) return C

Figure 10.4. Threshold algorithm (TA).

To establish the optimality of the TA algorithm, Fagin *et al.* [2001] introduced the notion of *instance optimality*. Let $\mathcal{A}$ be a class of algorithms and let $\mathcal{D}$ be a class of databases. Let $cost(A, D)$ be the total I/O accesses incurred when executing $A \in \mathcal{A}$ on $D \in \mathcal{D}$. A is said to be instance optimal over $\mathcal{A}$ and $\mathcal{D}$ if for every $B \in \mathcal{A}$ and $D \in \mathcal{D}$, there exist two constants $c, c' > 0$ such that

$$cost(A, D) \leq c \times cost(B, D) + c'.$$

In other words, $cost(A, D) = O(cost(B, D))$. Fagin *et al.* [2001] showed that, whereas FA is optimal only for certain cases, TA is always optimal with regard to the total number of accesses. In addition, TA uses much less buffer space as it does not need to maintain objects seen earlier for a late random-access phase. The cost of the algorithm can, however, still be high because of the potentially large number of random accesses that the algorithm may need to perform. Lang *et al.* [2004] present a variant of the TA algorithm that selects the next predicate for which the random access will be performed based on a cost-estimation strategy, instead of relying on a simple round-robin–based interleaving. Other cost-aware algorithms that aim to minimize the cost of random accesses for top-k query processing include [Chang and Hwang, 2002; Marian *et al.*, 2004; Yu *et al.*, 2001].

Fagin *et al.* [2001] also proposed an *approximation* version of the TA algorithm that stops the accesses early: given a $\phi > 1$, the ϕ-*approximation* to a top-k query is defined as the set, C, of k objects such that for each $o \in C$ and each $o' \notin C$, $\phi \mu_\Theta(o) \geq \mu_\Theta(o')$. In other words, the objects returned in the results set are only a constant factor away from the actual top-k objects. This is achieved simply by changing the stopping condition of the algorithm presented in Figure 10.4 from "*until at least k objects have been seen with grade at least τ*" to "*until at least k objects have been seen with grade at least τ/φ*". Other variants of the TA algorithm include [Arai *et al.*, 2007;

Let τ_i^d denote the score of the object at depth d (i.e., object with rank d) for predicate p_i

Let $w^d(o)$ denote the worst-case estimate for the score of object o when the sorted access is at depth d;

Let $b^d(o)$ denote the best-case estimate for the score of object o when the sorted access is at depth d;

(i) repeat
   (a) perform sorted access on one of the m predicates in an interleaved fashion (let o be the object met)
      1. compute the worst case combined score, $w^d(o)$, for o by replacing missing scores with 0
      2. compute the best case combined score, $b^d(o)$, for o by replacing each missing score with the corresponding τ_i^d
      3. let C^d be the current set of top-k objects at depth d based on their worst-case scores (if two objects have the same worst case scores, then the one with the better best-case score is used)
      4. let $minscore_k$ be the smallest worst-case score in C^d

until
   ■ at least k objects have been seen ($|C^d| = k$) and
   ■ $\mu_\Theta(\tau_1^d, \ldots, \tau_m^d) \leq minscore_k$ (i.e., there are no viable objects left outside of C^d).

(ii) return C^d

Figure 10.5. No random access algorithm (NRA).

Bansal *et al.*, 2008; Chakrabarti *et al.*, 2006; Ilyas *et al.*, 2003; Theobald *et al.*, 2004; Tsaparas *et al.*, 2003].

10.2.3 No Random Access Algorithm (NRA)

Although both FA and TA algorithms rely on random accesses to compute the combined score of the objects obtained through sorted accesses, such random accesses may not always be available [Fagin *et al.*, 2001; Güntzer *et al.*, 2001; Marian *et al.*, 2004].

The *no random access algorithm (NRA)* and *stream-combine* [Güntzer *et al.*, 2001] both avoid random accesses completely by maintaining worst- and best-score bounds for objects based on available partial knowledge. The stopping condition of the top-k ranked join algorithm is modified to compare the *worst score* of the kth result with the best possible score of all other candidate objects. Figure 10.5 shows the pseudocode of the NRA algorithm presented by Fagin *et al.* [2001, 2003]. Note that NRA identifies top-k results, but does not compute output scores since the process stops as soon as it is decided based on the current upper- and lower-bounds that there are no unseen viable objects in the database.

Ilyas *et al.* [2003] propose an NRA-like algorithm, called *RANK-JOIN*. For each new retrieved object from one of the streams, the algorithm first generates all new valid join combinations with all the objects seen so far from other streams, and for each resulting combination the algorithm computes a score. Then, the algorithm computes an upper bound, T, of the scores of join combinations not seen so far:

$$T = max\{ \quad \mu_\Theta(\tau_1^{d_1}, \tau_2^1, \ldots, \tau_m^1),$$
$$\mu_\Theta(\tau_1^1, \tau_2^{d_2}, \ldots, \tau_m^1),$$
$$\ldots$$
$$\mu_\Theta(\tau_1^1, \tau_2^1, \ldots, \tau_m^{d_m}) \quad \},$$

where $\mu_\Theta()$ is the score combination function, τ_i^d denotes the score of the object at depth d (i.e., object with rank d) for predicate p_i, and d_i denotes the number of objects retrieved for p_i at a given point in time. The algorithm stops when the lowest score of the best k results seen so far is greater than T. Ilyas *et al.* [2003] show that *RANK-JOIN* is instance optimal.

Fagin *et al.* [2001] present a *combined algorithm (CA)* that merges TA and NRA in such a way that the random access costs (relative to the cost of the sorted accesses) are taken into account. In particular, the algorithm considers a random access periodicity parameter, h. In the extreme case, if $h > |D|$, the algorithm works as NRA, because no random accesses are allowed. On the other extreme if $h = 1$, the algorithms works similar to TA and performs random accesses for all of the missing predicates of a subset[6] of the objects seen during sorted access.

Probabilistic versions of the NRA algorithm, which rely on probabilistic estimations to decide when it is safe to prune candidates, are presented by Arai *et al.* [2007] and Theobald *et al.* [2004]. These probabilistic algorithms take different score distributions (such as uniform or Poisson) or histograms for the predicates to predict the score of an object, for which some of the predicate scores are known, without having to wait to obtain all m predicate scores. More recently, various researchers [Gurský and Vojtáš, 2008; Mamoulis *et al.*, 2006; Xin *et al.*, 2007] refined the NRA top-k algorithm to improve its computational costs in terms of sorted and random accesses as well as the memory requirement. Arai *et al.* [2007] present *anytime* versions of the TA and NRA algorithms, which start with imperfect top-k results and improve the quality of the results as more computation time is allocated to the process. At any point during the top-k query execution, these algorithms are able to assess the current set of answers and provide guarantees in terms of the following:

- *Confidence:* The probability that the current set of top-k objects are indeed true top-k tuples.
- *Precision:* The ratio of the current top-k objects that belong to the true top-k objects (see Section 11.1 for more details on this measure).
- *Rank distance:* The sum of the absolute differences between the current ranks and real ranks of the objects that are currently in the top-k list (see Section 11.1 for more details on this rank correlation).
- *Score distance:* A probabilistic upper bound on the difference between the lowest score of the true top-k objects and the current set of top-k objects.

---

[6] Remember from Section 10.2.2 that TA algorithm performs random accesses for all of the missing predicates of *all* of the objects seen in sorted access. Consequently, TA never makes more sorted accesses than CA, but CA is more selective about random accesses.

Arai *et al.* [2007] show that these measures are monotone for TA and probabilistically (in expectation) monotone for NRA, enabling implementation of anytime versions of these algorithms that are able to provide appropriate guarantees.

10.2.4 Partial Sorted Access Algorithm (PSA) and Minimization of Random Accesses

In contrast to NRA, which tackles the problem of predicates for which there is no random access, the *partial sorted access (PSA)* [Candan *et al.*, 2000b] algorithm focuses on situations where one or more of the predicates are nonprogressive; that is, do not have sorted access facilities.

As described in Section 10.2.2, a special variant of the FA algorithm under the *min* merge function can limit the sorted access to only one of the predicates and use random accesses for all the remaining ones. This, however, does not generalize to arbitrary monotonic merge functions. Relying on the available statistics about the score distributions, PSA is able to compute an *approximate* result to the top-*k* query; in particular, PSA takes a probability, ρ, and identifies *k* objects such that each of these objects is in the actual top-*k* result with probability greater than $1 - \rho$. The PSA query evaluation algorithm is similar FA, but, for each object, based on the partial scores available and the score distributions for the predicates, the algorithm computes the probability of seeing a better scoring object in the future. The algorithm stops when *k* objects that are likely to be in the top-*k* list are identified.

As in PSA, Chang and Hwang [2002] also focus on situations where some of the predicates (e.g., those that have precomputed indexes on the score attributes) are available for sorted access, while others require potentially expensive per-object random accesses (or *probes*) to evaluate object scores. Because in multimedia databases, such *probe predicates* may often necessitate costly media processing and matching functions, reducing the number of probes is critical for the efficiency of top-*k* processing. This means that if one can avoid probing for those objects that are not promising or stop probing as soon as one can determine that an object cannot be in the top-*k*, this will help reduce the overall top-*k* execution cost. Thus, as in the NRA algorithm, Chang and Hwang [2002] limit the execution to only those probes that are necessary for the computation of the top-*k* results, regardless of the algorithm or the results of other probes. This is achieved by maintaining a *ceiling score* for each object by substituting the unknown predicate scores with their maximal-possible value. Objects are ranked based on their current ceiling scores, and probes are executed only for those objects that are currently in top-*k*. When there are multiple probe predicates to be executed for a given object, probes are scheduled in the order implied by a predicate *rank* metric, which puts those predicates with high filtering rates and low costs before the others (also see Section 10.4).

Chakrabarti *et al.* [2006] and Marian *et al.* [2004] present other NRA-like algorithms that maintain upper- and lower-bound scores of partially seen objects. Relying on the observation that any object whose upper-bound score is lower than the lower bounds for at least *k* objects cannot be in the top-*k*, such objects are pruned right away. Moreover, as observed by Marian *et al.* [2004], if *o* is the object with the highest upper-bound score, then one of the following is true for this object:

- If the score of this object is completely known, then none of the other objects can have a better score, so this object can be returned right away, without having to wait for the whole top-*k* set to be identified.
- If the score of this object is partial, then
  - If *o* is in the top-*k* set, then the system needs to probe all of its attributes to identify its score (note that NRA does not identify final scores);
  - On the other hand, if *o* is not actually in the top-*k* result set, then *o* requires further probes to reduce its upper bound before the top-*k* set is identified.

  In short, the object with the highest upper bound will have to be probed before the set of objects in the solution to the top-*k* query and their scores are identified.

Marian *et al.* [2004] refer to this as the *upper* strategy. To select which of the available predicates to probe, as in [Chang and Hwang, 2002], Marian *et al.* [2004] use a *predicate rank* measure that ranks those predicates that are expected to have high impacts on the score range, while being also fast. Marian *et al.* [2004] also present a *pick* strategy that tries to measure the distance between the current state of the top-*k* set and the final state, where all the top-*k* objects and their scores are known. Let *M* be the set of objects that have already been identified through sorted access. Marian *et al.* [2004] compute the following to measure the distance of the current state from the final state:

$$B = \sum_{o \in M} max\{0, upper\_bound(o) - max\{lower\_bound(o), expected(o')\}\},$$

where *o'* is the object with the *k*th highest expected score in *M*. Intuitively, when the algorithm reaches its final state, *o'* will be the object with the actual *k*th highest score, and all objects in *M* that are not in top-*k* will be known not to have scores above that of *o'*. This means that *B* will be 0:

- For an object in top-*k*, the upper bound will be equal to the lower bound, and this lower bound will be greater than the score of *o'*; thus the contribution of such an object to *B* will be zero.
- For an object not in top-*k*, the upper bound will be lower than the score of *o'*; thus the contribution of such an object to *B* will also be zero.

Because the goal is to help *B* reach 0 as quickly as possible, unlike in the case of *upper*, the *pick* strategy selects the probe that is likely to decrease *B* the fastest. Also unlike the *upper* strategy, *pick* needs to retrieve all objects that might belong to the top-*k* answer (based on the upper and lower bound scores) during an initial sorted access phase, but this might in fact result in all objects from the database being retrieved.

10.2.5 Pre-Processing for Layer Ordering

Layer ordering methods evaluate top-*k* queries in terms of precomputed layers of objects: the first layer consists of a set of data objects that is guaranteed to

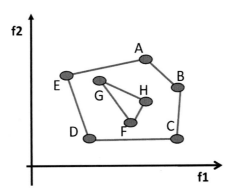

Figure 10.6. Layers of convex hulls.

contain the top data element; the first two layers together make up of a set of objects that is guaranteed to contain the top two objects, and so on. Thus, starting from the first layer, the top-*k* query is answered by touching at most *k* layers of data objects. Especially for cases where the data objects can be represented as vectors in a multidimensional space, where each dimension corresponds to a different query predicate, a common approach to identify these layers a priori to the top-*k* query processing is to leverage the layout of the data points in the space to partition the data into *dominance* sets.

10.2.5.1 Onion Technique

Some algorithms focus on linear combination functions, which help them partition the space using certain geometrical characteristics of the underlying vector space [Chang *et al.*, 2000b; Dantzig, 1963]. In particular, given a set of points in a multidimensional space and a linear maximization (or minimization) criterion, the maximum (or minimum) objective value is known to be located at one or more vertices of the *convex hull* of the data points (Figure 10.6). Relying on this observation, the *Onion* technique, presented by Chang *et al.* [2000b], create layers of objects in such a way that the convex hull corresponding to the outer layers encloses the convex hull corresponding to inner layers (Figure 10.6). Each data object is indexed by the corresponding layer number (e.g., 1 for object *A* and 2 for object *G* in Figure 10.6). The objects in the database are considered from outer layers to inner layers. An optimal object at a given layer is always better than any object from inner layers. However, given $k > 1$ there may be objects in the inner layers dominating some objects in the outer layers. Therefore, to ensure that no object is missed, the algorithm selects the best object from the outer convex hull, the second best object from the outer two convex hulls, the third best object from the outer three convex hulls, and so on.

10.2.5.2 Robust Indexing

Xin *et al.* [2006] observe that it is beneficial to create the layers in such a way that nonpromising objects appear in the deeper layers so that they have less chance to be considered during query evaluation. Thus, for minimizing the worst-case performance for the layered top-*k* processing, for any *l*, the number of objects in the top *l* layers should be minimal in comparison with all other layering alternatives.

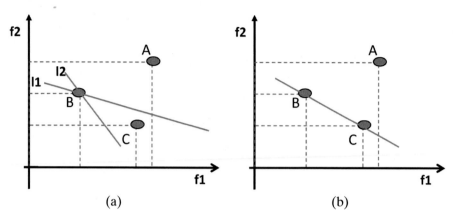

Figure 10.7. (a) Object *A* ranks first for any linear, monotone combination function, if the combination function corresponds to l_1, then *B* ranks second, whereas for the combination function corresponding to l_2, then *C* ranks second instead. (b) the line corresponding to the critical combination function where *B* and *C* are equi-ranked: any change in the slope would cause either *B* or *C* to become the second-ranked object in the database.

Intuitively, this requires the computation of the minimum ranking for all objects in the database for all possible linear combinations, which would be prohibitively expensive. Fortunately, the ranking of a given object does not change with each combination function. In fact, when the combination functions are linear, the rank of each object can be determined by considering the (hyper)planes combining the objects. Consider the three-object database shown in Figure 10.7:

- The object *A* has higher f_1 and f_2 values with respect to objects *B* and *C*; thus it ranks 1 for all linear (in fact monotone) combination functions.
- The rank of the object *B* can be determined by comparing the angle of the line connecting it to the object *C* against the angle implied by the linear combination function.

To compute the minimum ranking of a given object, Xin *et al.* [2006] leverage the foregoing property to limit the evaluation to such boundaries formed by the other objects in the space: the algorithm sorts these boundary hyperplanes by their angles relative to the hyperplane implied by the combination function and then traverses them in this order to obtain the minimum ranking of the object. Xin *et al.* [2006] also present an approximation algorithm that reduces the number of boundaries to consider for a given object by partitioning the space into only a fixed number of boundaries around this object and counting the number of objects in each region implied by these boundaries. The numbers of objects in the subregions of the space are then used for finding the lower bound on the layer corresponding to this object.

10.2.6 Relaxing the Monotonicity Requirement

Unlike most earlier work in ranked joins, which all require that the combination function be monotonic, Zhang *et al.* [2006] focus on supporting arbitrary ranking functions. The authors achieve this by handling top-*k* query processing fundamentally different from the various methods we have seen so far. In particular, they formulate top-*k* retrieval as an optimization task: the optimization function captures the Boolean expression underlying the join condition (it returns zero for those tuples that do not satisfy the join criterion) as well as the ranking function that ranks the tuples. The optimization problem is stated such that the optimization function has the maximum value when the *k* tuples with the highest scores are selected. The problem is solved using a search algorithm based on A^* [Hart *et al.*, 1972], which explores the solution state space based on a heuristic function that guides state-to-state transitions. Xin *et al.* [2007] also handle nonmonotonic score functions, as long as they are lower bounded. Once again, the proposed ranked join algorithm is very different from the algorithms described so far: instead of considering data as sorted input streams, the authors propose an *INDEX-MERGE* approach, where the input data are assumed to have been indexed using B-trees or R-trees (depending on the type of data). Instead of directly joining the tuples, the algorithm merges the index nodes and prunes those that are guaranteed not to have any tuples that will be in top-*k* as descendants. The lower bounds on the scores are used for deciding the order in which the index nodes will be merged and the state space will be explored.

Qi *et al.* [2007] and Kim and Candan [2009] recognize that specialized versions of the ranked join algorithms can also be implemented in various situations where the combination function is not monotonic in the strict sense, but exhibits properties that are partly monotonic. Next we discuss these two algorithms, *horizon-based ranked join (HR-Join)* and *skip-and-prune join (SnP-Join)*, which leverage special properties of commonly used, yet nonmonotonic, score merge functions.

10.2.6.1 Sum-Max Monotonicity

Qi *et al.* [2007] focus on top-*k* query evaluation in applications where the underlying data (the Web, an XML document, or a relational database) can be seen as a weighted graph.

Top-*K* Tree Pattern Query Evaluation in Weighted Graphs

As described in Section 6.3.6, the weights associated to the edges of the graph can denote various application-specific desirability/penalty assessments, such as *popularity*, *trust*, or *cost*. Let $G(V, E)$, denote a node- and edge-labeled directed graph. Furthermore, let *tag(v)* denote the data label corresponding to the data node $v \in V$ and *cost(e)* denote the cost label for edge $e \in E$. The type of queries Qi *et al.* [2007] consider on this graph are referred to as twig or tree pattern queries: tree patterns can be visualized as trees, where nodes correspond to tag-predicates and edges correspond to "/" or "//" axes (Figure 10.8(a)). More formally, a given query, *q*, can be represented in the form of a node- and edge-labeled tree, $T_q(V_q, E_q)$, where *tag_pred(qv)* denotes the tag predicate corresponding to the vertex $qv \in V_q$ and *axis_pred(qe)* denotes the axis predicate ("/" or "//") associated with the edge $qe \in E_q$. An answer to query $q = T_q(V_q, E_q)$ over the data graph $G(V, E)$ is a pair, $r = \langle \mu_{node}, \mu_{edge} \rangle$, of mappings:

- μ_{node} is a mapping from the nodes of the query tree to the nodes of the data graph, such that given $qv \in V_q$ and the corresponding data node, $\mu_{node}(qv)$, $tag(\mu_{node}(qv))$ satisfies *tag_pred(qv)*.
- μ_{edge} is a mapping from the edges of the query tree to *simple paths* in the data graph, such that given $qe = \langle qv_i, qv_j \rangle \in E_q$, the path μ_{qe}, from $\mu_{node}(qv_i)$

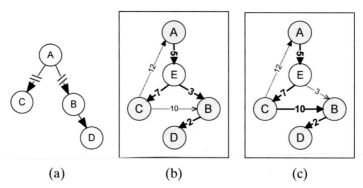

(a)   (b)   (c)

Figure 10.8. An example query twig and two matches on a weighted graph, where the weighs denote *cost*: the first match with weight 17 is more desirable and should be enumerated and ranked before the second result. (b) cost $= 17$, (c) cost $= 24$.

to $\mu_{node}(qv_j)$, satisfies *edge_pred(e)*: a path consisting of a single edge can satisfy both "/" and "//" axes, whereas a multiedge path can satisfy only "//" axes.

Let $\mathcal{E}$ denote the set of edges used in the answer to q:

$$\mathcal{E} = \{e \parallel e \in \mu_{edge}(qe) \text{ for a query edge } qe \in E_q\}.$$

$\mathcal{E}$ does not define a cycle.

Moreover, given an answer $r = \langle \mu_{node}, \mu_{edge} \rangle$ to query $q = T_q(V_q, E_q)$ over the data graph $G(V, E)$, Qi *et al.* [2007] define the cost, *cost(r)*, of the answer[7] as the sum of the costs of the relevant edges in the graph. When there are overlaps among paths matching query edges, the cost of the shared edges needs to be counted only once (Figures 10.8(b) and (c)). Qi *et al.* [2007] refer to this as the *nonredundancy* property of the results. As a consequence, as illustrated in Figures 10.8(b) and (c), the cost of an answer is not necessarily equal to, but is bounded by, the sum of the path costs. Thus, the cost order of the data paths matching query edges may not correspond to the cost order of the query results. In other words, two costly sub results (i.e., paths) with large overlaps may provide a combined result cheaper than two other individually less costly, but non-edge overlapping sub-results: in short, the cost function, or its inverse that one can use for ranking the results, is not monotonic.

Sum-Max Monotonicity

Although the monotonicity condition does not hold, Qi *et al.* [2007] show that one can establish a range for the costs of query results in terms of the costs of their subresults; in particular, if we let $q = T_q(V_q, E_q)$ be a twig query, $r = \langle \mu_{node}, \mu_{edge} \rangle$ be a corresponding answer, and let $SR = \{sr_1, sr_2, \ldots, sr_m\}$ be a set of subresults that give r, then per Qi *et al.* [2007], the following is true:

$$\max_{sr_i \in SR} (cost(sr_i)) \leq cost(r) \leq \sum_{sr_i \in SR} cost(sr_i).$$

This observation enables Qi *et al.* [2007] to introduce a *sum-max monotonicity prop-erty* for twig results: Let $q = T_q(V_q, E_q)$ be a twig query and let r_1 and r_2 be two

---

[7] Note that, because edge weights are *costs*, in this case, the top-k results are those that have the smallest costs.

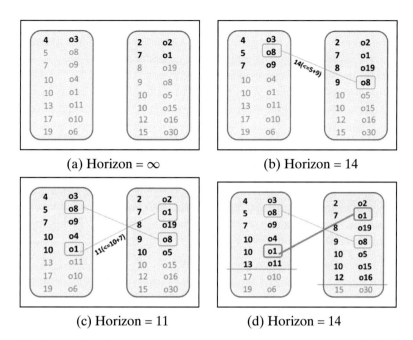

Figure 10.9. Ranked join by the *sum-max monotonicity*: (a) no results yet; (b) the first candidate with cost 14 is found; (c) a second candidate with lower cost of 11 is found; and (d) the stopping *sum-max* condition is reached for returning the current best candidate.

answers. Let also R_1 and R_2 be the corresponding sets of subresults that give r_1 and r_2, respectively. Then, the following is true:

$$\left(\sum_{sr_i \in R_1} cost(sr_i) \leq \max_{sr_j \in R_2}\left(cost(sr_j)\right)\right) \rightarrow cost(r_1) \leq cost(r_2).$$

Horizon-Based Ranked Join (HR-Join)

Qi *et al.* [2007] leverage this property of twig queries to implement a ranked join algorithm for cost-ordered inputs. The *sum-max monotonicity* property of answers enables the algorithm to leverage the cost evaluations of initial, *candidate*, matches as *horizons* that limit the candidates that need to be explored before a *confirmed* result can be produced. Let us consider a twig query, q, which consists of two path subqueries, m_1 and m_2, that join on a query node. Let us also assume that m_1 and m_2 can return paths in cost order, progressively. Figures 10.9(a)–(d) show the various stages of the two path streams matching m_1 and m_2, respectively. The individual paths are shown as rectangles, each containing the ID of the data vertex (matching the query vertex common in m_1 and m_2) and the total cost of the path. Each stream grows with subresults arriving in ascending order of cost. The stages of the process are as follows:

(i) In Figure 10.9(a), we are seeing a state where none of the subresults, matching m_1 and m_2, can be joined. At this stage, because there is no join, the upper bound on the cost of the first result is ∞.

(ii) In Figure 10.9(b), a match is found. The cost of the combined match is 14. Note that, although this is the first discovered match, it is not necessarily the best one. Per the *sum-max monotonicity* property, this first match sets the *horizon* for the *best* match to 14. Thus, the process has to continue until all the subresults of cost up to 14 are considered.

(iii) In Figure 10.9(c), a second match, with cost 11, is found. Per the *sum-max monotonicity* property, this match lowers the *horizon* from 14 to 11. Thus, the process now has to continue only until all the subresults of cost up to 11 are considered.

(iv) In Figure 10.9(d), the stopping condition is reached: in both subresult streams, all the paths of cost less than or equal to 11 have been considered. Thus, among the two matches found so far, the best (with cost 11) can be returned as the top-1 result.

(v) When further results are required, the process continues by setting a new horizon. In this example, because there is a known candidate match, the cost (14) of this candidate will be used as the new horizon value.

Note that, unlike the ranked join algorithms, which stop the sorted-access process as soon as a prescribed number of candidates are found, the stopping condition of the foregoing process is based not on the cardinality of initial candidates but on their *costs*.

10.2.6.2 Skip-and-Prune: Cosine-Based Top-K Query Processing

As we introduced in Section 3.1.3, in most text retrieval systems, given a query vector $\vec{q}$ and a document vector $\vec{d}$, the match between the vectors is computed using the *cosine similarity*:

$$sim_{cos}(\vec{d}, \vec{q}) = cos(\vec{d}, \vec{q}) = \frac{\vec{d} \cdot \vec{q}}{\|\vec{d}\| \, \|\vec{q}\|},$$

where "·" denotes the *dot product* operator. Intuitively, $sim_{cos}(\vec{d}, \vec{q})$ measures the degree of alignment between the interests of the user and the characteristics of the document: in the best case, when the vectors are identical, the similarity score is 1. In fact, to get a perfect match, the vectors do not need to be identical; as long as the angle between the vectors is 0 degrees (i.e., their relative keyword compositions are equal), then the document and query vectors are said to match perfectly ($sim_{cos}(\vec{d}, \vec{q}) = 1$). Naturally, as the angle between the two vectors grows, the difference between the query and the document also gets larger.

The key obstacle in query processing with cosine similarity function is that most top-k ranked query processing schemes assume that the underlying scoring function is monotonic (e.g., *max*, *min*, *product*, and *average*). These scoring functions guarantee that a candidate dominating (or equal to) the other one in its subscores will have a combined score better than (or as good as) the other one. This, however, is not the case for a scoring function based on *cosine* similarity. For example, given two pairs, $\langle 0.2; 0.2 \rangle$ and $\langle 0.2; 0.8 \rangle$, the second pair is dominating the first one, yet we have

$$cos(\langle 1; 1 \rangle, \langle 0.2; 0.2 \rangle) = 1 \; > \; 0.857 = cos(\langle 1; 1 \rangle, \langle 0.2; 0.8 \rangle).$$

Thus, a scoring function of the form $score(x) = cos(\langle 1; 1 \rangle, x)$ would not be monotonic. We can easily generalize this and state that, in general, a cosine-based

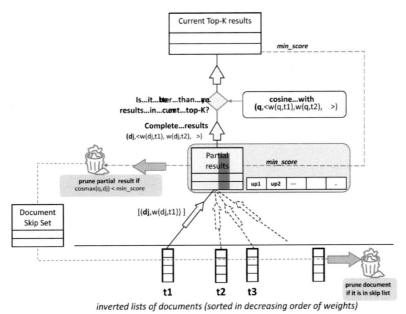

Figure 10.10. Skip-and-prune: partially observed candidate documents are pruned based on their maximum possible scores.

scoring function, which compares documents in the database to the user's query, is not monotonic. Because a cosine-based scoring function is not monotonic, the use of existing top-*k* algorithms would lead to errors in the ranked results.

Kim and Candan [2009] present an efficient query processing algorithm, *skip-and-prune (SnP)*, to process top-*k* queries with cosine-based scoring functions. Let $w(d, t)$ be the weight of the keyword or term t in document d and $w(q, t)$ be the weight of t in the query. The outline of the algorithm is shown in Figure 10.10. The algorithm relies on inverted lists, maintained in the database in decreasing order of document-keyword weights. These inverted lists are consumed as input streams. The SnP algorithm maintains partial vectors of the candidate results, based on the keyword scores seen so far in the input document/keyword streams. A cutoff score, *min_score*, corresponding to the lowest score in the current top-*k* candidate list, is also maintained. Given the user's query, $\vec{q}$, and the *min_score*,

- For any candidate document, d_i, whose keyword scores are fully available, SnP computes the matching score between d_i and $\vec{q}$ and updates the current list of top-*k* documents if d_i's score is better than *min_score*.
- Any document, d_j, whose term vector is only partially available is pruned from consideration if the maximum possible score, up_j, it can eventually have (based on the current knowledge) is less than *min_score*.

If d_j is eliminated from consideration, there is no need to enumerate the remaining term scores of d_j. Thus, the algorithm maintains a skip set, which consists of the IDs of the documents pruned from further consideration. Note that unlike the TA family of the algorithms, the foregoing process cannot end before the sorted inverted files are completely consumed. In that sense, SnP is similar to the inverted-file based scheme discussed in Section 5.1. The major difference is that the *skip set* mechanism ensures that documents are pruned early from the input streams; thus the total processing needed by the algorithm is much less than that of the inverted files. The key to the efficiency, therefore, is data structures for efficient pruning of documents in the skip list from further consideration.

Under the vector model, each document, d_i, corresponds to a point (or vector) in the keyword space. Kim and Candan [2009] observe that if one of the weights is not known, the possible vectors will define a line in the space; if two weights are not known, then the possible vectors will define a plane, and so on. Thus, given a query vector, $\vec{q}$, and a partially observed document, d_i, computing the maximum possible score $sim_{cos}^{max}(d_i, \vec{q})$ involves measuring the minimum possible angle between the $\vec{q}$ and the hyperplane corresponding to d_i. Given a document only partially observed during the top-k processing, the corresponding line, plane, or hyperplane is bounded by the current upper bounds on the scores of its missing keywords. As the streams corresponding to these keywords are consumed, these upper bounds will also get increasingly tight.

10.2.7 Top-*K* Query Processing within Traditional Databases

Because of the increasing demand for top-k query processing, many relational DBMSs,[8] including Microsoft SQL Server, MySQL, PostgreSQL, Oracle, and Sybase, provide mechanisms to limit the number of tuples returned as a result of a query. Although the language constructs provided by different DBMS suppliers to express top-k queries vary (e.g., "SELECT TOP k..." in SQL Server versus "SELECT..FROM... LIMIT k..." in MySQL), they are functionally similar to each other, and the recent ISO SQL:2008 standard [SQL-08] aims to unify these different SQL dialects under one standard convention. In particular, the standard uses a new "FETCH FIRST k" clause along with the existing "ORDER BY" clause to express top-k queries. Most importantly, though, both "FETCH FIRST" and "ORDER BY" clauses can be used not only in top-level query expressions, but also in subqueries and views enabling the expression of rich top-k queries.

10.2.7.1 Filter-Based Implementation of Ranking Expressions

The work of Chaudhuri and Gravano [1999] was one of the first attempts for expressing and processing top-k queries within traditional databases. In the framework proposed by Chaudhuri and Gravano [1999], and later extended by Gravano *et al.* [2004], a top-k query is formulated as

```
SELECT oid
FROM Repository
WHERE Filter_condition
ORDER[k] by Ranking_expression
```

where the filter condition specifies thresholds on the grade of match of the admissible objects, whereas the ranking expression describes how the results should be

---

[8] See Section 2.1.2 for an overview of relational databases.

ranked. Attribute handling differs significantly from traditional systems; in particular, attribute values can be compared using a *Grade* function that evaluates the degree of match between the input values. For example, the following is a top-10 query in the proposed language:

```
SELECT oid
FROM Repository
WHERE (Grade(color_histogram,"yellow")>= 0.5 and
        Grade(shape,"circle")>=0.9)
ORDER[10] by max (Grade(color_histogram,"blue"),
                  Grade(annotation,"sunny"))
```

The combination function in this example is *max* applied over color histogram and annotation features of the objects in the repository. To execute query plans for this type of query, Chaudhuri and Gravano [1999] rely on three index-supported access methods:

■ *GradeSearch(attribute, value, min_grade)* returns objects whose match to the given attribute/value pair is higher than the given *min_grade* threshold.
■ *TopSearch(attribute, value, count)* returns *count* many highest scoring objects for the given attribute/value pair.
■ *Probe(attribute, value, {oid})* gets the grade of an object for a given attribute/value pair.

The query execution algorithm presented by Chaudhuri and Gravano [1999] selects a cost-optimal subset of the filter conditions for searching for candidate objects, and the residual filter condition is used for probing the grades to verify admissibility. Because the underlying DB engine does not have a ranked query processor, the ranking expressions are also processed as filter conditions; however, the algorithm uses knowledge about the grade distribution (e.g., selectivity estimates) to convert each ranking expression into a filter condition (i.e., a range query). In other words, based on the available knowledge about how the grades are distributed, the algorithm picks a lower bound of the grades for each atomic filter expression, processes the new filter condition, and outputs the top objects. If there are not sufficient tuples because of the selected cutoff threshold, then a smaller cutoff is selected and the process is repeated. On the average, the algorithm searches no more objects than the FA algorithm.

10.2.7.2 *Stop* and *Restart*
Carey and Kossmann [1997a] also extend SQL with support for limiting the cardinality of the results. The proposed SQL extension relies on a STOP AFTER clause to declare the number of tuples the result should contain:

```
SELECT ... FROM ... WHERE ...
GROUP BY ... HAVING ...
ORDER BY (sort specification)
STOP AFTER (value expression)
```

The value expression, which specifies the maximum number of tuples desired, can be an integer constant or a subquery that evaluates to a constant. The ranking condition is specified using SQL's ORDER BY clause, but unlike the earlier SQL standards, the ORDER BY columns do not need to appear in the SELECT clause and ORDER BY clauses can be used in sub-queries. Carey and Kossmann [1997a,b] also propose an extension to the relational database engine. In particular, the extension involves a new *stop* operator that produces, in order, the top or bottom k tuples of the input stream data. The operator takes three parameters: k; a *sort directive* that states whether the data will be sorted in increasing or decreasing order; and a *sort expression* that corresponds to the ordering expression associated to the ORDER BY clause. Carey and Kossmann [1997a,b] also propose policies to insert the stop operators into the traditional relational query plans. A *conservative* policy avoids the insertion of *stop* operators at points in the query plan where it can cause tuples to be discarded that may be required to obtain the requested k tuples. The *aggressive* policy, on the other hand, inserts *stop* operators wherever they can provide savings and relies on a *restart* operator that restarts the query if the result stream is exhausted before k tuples are produced. Carey and Kossmann [1998] present range partitioning-based strategies to reduce the cost of executing STOP AFTER clauses. To avoid sorting a large collection of data and then discarding a significant portion of it to obtain the top-k results, Carey and Kossmann [1998] present "range-based braking" algorithms that divide data into buckets based on attribute values and prune unpromising ranges.

Note that the *stop* operator requires at least a partial sorting of the input data stream. Donjerkovic and Ramakrishnan [1999] avoid sorting of the data except for the outputs. Recognizing that every top-k query is in fact equivalent to a selection query with a specific cutoff value on the output scores, Donjerkovic and Ramakrishnan [1999] focus on identifying the appropriate cutoff parameters using the available statistics about data distributions. The main challenge is that a lax cutoff will result in unnecessary processing, whereas a tight cutoff will cause multiple restarts due to having fewer than k results in the outputs. Given a cutoff threshold, τ, the expected cost of a query execution plan with restart is

$$E(cost) \simeq E(initial\_cost(\tau)) + E(restart\_cost(\tau))P_{restart,\tau},$$

where $E(initial\_cost(\tau))$ is the expected cost of the initial query with cutoff threshold τ, $E(restart\_cost(\tau))$ is the cost of the restart that would complete the query,[9] and $P_{restart,\tau}$ is the probability that fewer than k results have been generated with cutoff τ. Given a τ value, each of the foregoing terms can be estimated using a traditional query optimizer. The value of the τ itself is estimated by using a *golden section search* technique, which repeatedly tries different τ values until the expected cost converges to a fixed, minimum value [Kiefer, 1953; Press *et al.*, 1988].

Hristidis *et al.* [2001] recognize that different users may ask the same query, using different ranking expressions to express different preference criteria. To leverage past computations, instead of executing the query from scratch and reranking query results each time according to the new ranking criterion, Hristidis *et al.* [2001]

---

[9] Note that this is a worst-case assumption. In reality, instead of searching for the complete answer to the query, the restart operation will repeatedly relax τ until k matches are identified. Therefore, there is a chance that the complete answer to the query will never be needed.

recompute top-*k* queries using the old results (or *views*) for queries that have "similar" preference criteria to the current one. Given two *linear* preference criteria (μ_q, for the query and μ_v, for the available view), Hristidis *et al.* [2001] compute a watermark threshold as the maximum score, τ, such that

$$\forall_t \ (\mu_v(t) < \tau) \ \rightarrow \ (\mu_q(t) < \mu_q(t')),$$

for the top result t' in the view. Intuitively, if the score of a tuple t in the view is below the watermark, τ, then t cannot be the top result of the query, because there is at least one other tuple t' in the view better than t. Consequently, the top result according to the query preference criterion μ_q must also be above the watermark in the view. The algorithm reorders (according to μ_q) all the tuples in the view above the watermark and picks the set of tuples until t' in the new order. Hristidis *et al.* [2001] show that the tuples in this set are the highest ranking answers to the query according to μ_q. If the size of the set is less than k, the process is repeated by identifying a new, lower, threshold.

10.2.7.3 Specialized Top-*K* Join Operators
Unlike the foregoing algorithms that emulate top-*k* joins using existing relational operators, a number of other works attempt to inject specialized versions of the TA and NRA top-*k* operators within more traditional (e.g. relational) databases.

Natsev *et al.* [2001], for example, introduce a pull-based, no-random-access, J^* join operator that performs an A^* type search in the join space. A^* type of search algorithms estimate the *gain* of candidate solutions and use these estimates to guide the search; as long as the gain estimate never underestimates the true gain, A^* search will find the optimal solution in the fewest number of steps [Hart *et al.*, 1972; Russell and Norvig, 1995]. J^* estimates an upper bound of the combination score for each partial result and maintains a priority queue of partial join combinations ordered on these upper bounds. Thus, partial joins are processed in the order of these estimates. At each step, J^* considers the combination at the top of the priority queue and selects the next stream from which to pull the next tuple to join to the partial result in a way to complete this top combination. The top-1 retrieval process terminates when the join combination at the head of the queue is complete; the next top results are found incrementally by repeating the process until k results are obtained. In order to reduce the database access cost (i.e., the number of tuples considered from each stream) and to reduce the space requirements, Natsev *et al.* [2001] propose an *iterative deepening* heuristic which divides the computation into successive rounds. In particular, J^* defines the ith round to include all computation from depth $i \times s$ to depth $i \times s + s - 1$, for some constant $s \geq 1$. Solution correctness and optimality are still guaranteed because solutions in earlier rounds are better than the ones in later rounds. To leverage indexes when they are available, Natsev *et al.* [2001] also present a random-access variation, J^*_{PA}, which (when processing an incomplete result at the top of the priority queue) first checks whether the result is instantiated sufficiently to allow completion by predicate access. Similar to the CA algorithm discussed in Section 10.2.3, the threshold is determined dynamically by balancing the sorted access and random access costs.

Ilyas *et al.* [2002] introduce another NRA-like join operator, NRA-RJ, to be used in current database engines for key-equality conditions. Unlike NRA, which does not associate scores to the results in the output stream, NRA-RJ associates a score range for each output object. To enable composability of multiple NRA-RJ operators within a single query plan, NRA-RJ also allows ranges of scores associated to the objects in the input stream. The algorithm maintains best and worst possible scores for each partial object; as new objects are observed from the input streams, these best and worst possible scores are updated. If, at any point, an object whose worst possible score is greater than the highest scores of all other objects is found, then this object is returned. Also, as in iterative deepening J^*, which layers the input objects, NRA-RJ also proceeds in stages, where only some of the inputs are considered at each stage.

Ilyas *et al.* [2004a] propose a pipelined rank join operator, HRJN, which is able to perform join operation under general join conditions (as opposed to being limited to equality joins as in NRA-RJ). HRJN implements the NRA-like *RANK-JOIN* algorithm presented in Section 10.2.3. The instance optimality of the underlying *RANK-JOIN* algorithm plays an important role in the optimization of the I/O cost. Remember from Section 10.2.3 that, for each new retrieved object from one of the streams, the basic *RANK-JOIN* algorithm generates all new valid join combinations with all the objects seen so far from other streams, and for each resulting combination the algorithm computes a score. The physical implementation of HRJN is similar to those of symmetric hash joins [Hong and Stonebraker, 1993; Mokbel *et al.*, 2004] or hash ripple-joins [Haas and Hellerstein, 1999]: in the binary version of the HRJN operator, internally, two hash tables hold input tuples seen so far, and a priority queue holds the valid join combinations ordered on their combined scores. Implementing an N-ary ranked join operator involves staging multiple binary HRJN operators in a pipelined manner; the order of the binary HRJN operators is selected in a way that minimizes the number of intermediary results that need to be considered. When the score distributions are heterogeneous (such as large values in one input and much smaller ones in the other), the rates at which objects from different input streams are consumed are selected in such a way that the value of the *RANK-JOIN* threshold is reduced faster, potentially leading to faster completion of the ranked join operation: let μ_Θ be the score merge function, L_{top} and L_{bottom} be the best and worst known scores for the left input, respectively, and R_{top} and R_{bottom} be the corresponding scores for the right input; because in the binary version of the *RANK-JOIN* algorithm we had discussed in Section 10.2.3, the threshold would be computed as $max(\mu_\Theta(L_{top}, R_{bottom}), \mu_\Theta(L_{bottom}, R_{top}))$, more inputs are fetched from the input which would reduce this threshold the most; for example, if the first merged term is larger than the second one, it is better to fetch results from R to reduce the first merged score.

10.2.7.4 Extended Algebraic Formulations

Extending traditional databases with top-k or ranked query processing functionality may require significant revisions of the underlying database engines. A particular requirement is being able to generate query plans that include ranking operators along with the more traditional algebraic operators, such as select, project, and join. Adali *et al.* [2004, 2007] and Li *et al.* [2005] extend the relational algebra, which is the basis of query planning and optimization in relational databases, to support ranking as a first-class construct.

With the goal of supporting multimedia database applications, Adali *et al.* [2004, 2007] consider ranks as properties of media objects that can be queried and compared with each other. In particular, the data schema is assumed be composed of two types of attributes: *property attributes* and *order attributes*. The property attributes describe information about the features of the objects, whereas each *order attribute* describes the ordering of objects in the relation with respect to a given criterion. Adali *et al.* [2007] also introduce *order distance functions*, which are used to compute the distance between two order attributes based on the object rankings that they imply,[10] and *order functions*, which are essentially rank aggregation functions [Dwork *et al.*, 2001] that can be used to obtain a new ranking based on existing object rankings. Given these, Adali *et al.* [2007] extend the relational algebra with the following operators that operate on ordered relations:

■ The *order* operator adds a new order column to an order relation by evaluating a given order function on the relation.

■ The *merge* operator puts together the same objects in two ordered relations and their corresponding ranks into a single ordered relation (if an object in one relation is missing in the other, similarly to the behavior of traditional outer join operator, the missing rank is set to a special *null-rank,* ⊤).

■ The *order group by* operator is analogous to the *group by* operator used in relational algebra for partitioning the data to support aggregate computations (such as *max*, *min*, and *count*). In the case of ordered relations, the operator also takes an order distance function and a pair of order attributes and, for each *group by* partition, computes and returns the distance between the corresponding rankings in the partition.

As an example, consider two ordered relations *TVRankings₁*(*ShowName*, *Network*, *Rank*) and *TVRankings₂*(*ShowName*, *Network*, *Rank*) storing TV ratings for two subsequent weeks. For finding how much the rankings for TV channels changed over time, we need to first *merge* the two ordered relations based on show names and then apply *group by* on the resulting ordered relation with respect to the channel name attribute. Finally, an order distance function is applied to each individual partition [Adali *et al.*, 2007].

Note that, under the algebraic formulation proposed by Adali *et al.* [2007], a ranked join operation is represented by a *merge* operator that pulls together data from different sources and a following *order* operator that associates a new, combined ranking to the objects in the resulting ordered relation. For instance, if, in the foregoing example, we wanted to compute the average ratings of the shows, we would *merge* the two ordered relations based on show names and then apply the *order* operator with the *avg*() function on the two rank attributes. RankSQL, proposed by Li *et al.* [2005], on the other hand, treats ranked operation in an atomic fashion, instead of splitting this operation into two suboperations as in [Adali *et al.*, 2007]. Similarly to Adali *et al.* [2007], Li *et al.* [2005] also define a *rank-relation* as a relation with its tuples scored by some scoring function. However, unlike in [Adali *et al.*, 2007] (where the ranking attribute is materialized, yet the order of the objects is only implicit), in rank-relations, scores of the tuples are implicit, whereas the tuples are physically ordered according to the underlying scoring function. The algebraic framework underlying RankSQL builds upon the relational algebra by introducing a new operator, *rank*, and extending the various existing operators to be

---

[10] See Section 11.5 for more details on rank comparison functions.

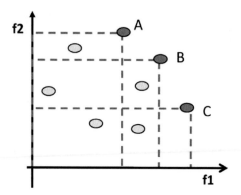

Figure 10.11. The skyline of the data set in this figure consists of three objects: $\{A, B, C\}$; all other objects are dominated by one of these three.

rank aware. The *rank* operator takes as input a ranked relation R (already ordered based on a set of ranking predicates, $\mathcal{P}$) and a new ranking predicate p and reorders the objects in R based on $\mathcal{P} \cup p$.

The traditional relational algebraic operators, select (σ), project (π), union ($\cup$), intersection ($\cap$), difference ($-$), and join ($\bowtie$), are all redefined to both determine membership (based on the associated Boolean predicate) and order (based on the ranking predicate). Unary operators, such as select, process the tuples in the input relation as in their relational counterparts, but simply maintaining the input tuple orders. Binary operators (except for difference) also perform similarly to their Boolean counterparts, but they reorder output tuples using ranking predicates from both operands; the difference operator outputs tuples in the order of the outer relation, because the tuples from the inner one are eliminated by the operation. The *rank* operator enables a complex ranking predicate to be split and evaluated in stages, predicate by predicate; thus, ranking can be interleaved with other operators and pushed down joins if required for query optimization.

10.3 SKYLINES

A nearest neighbor query locates a *predetermined* number of objects that are the closest to a *given* query object based on a *given* distance measure. Similarly, a top-k query identifies a *predetermined* number of objects that are the best according to a *given* scoring function. A *skyline* operation, on the other hand, simply searches for a set of objects that are not dominated by other objects in the database [Borzsonyi et al., 2001]. Consider a database, D, of objects, each represented as a vector in a d-dimensional space. Object o_i in the database D is said to *dominate* object $o_j \in D$ (denoted as *dominating*(o_i, o_j)) iff

$$(\vec{o}_i \neq \vec{o}_j) \ \wedge \ (\forall_{1 \leq l \leq d} \ \vec{o}_i[l] \geq \vec{o}_j[l]).$$

The skyline of the data set, D, consists of objects that are not dominated by any other object in D (Figure 10.11):

$$skyline(D) = \{o_j \mid (o_j \in D) \wedge (\not\exists_{o_i \in D} \ dominating(o_i, o_j))\}.$$

Intuitively, the skyline is the set of maximal vectors in the space [Kung *et al.*, 1975; Preparata and Shamos, 1985]. In other words, given a set D, the set of objects in *skyline*(D) consists of the set of *interesting* objects, where:

- No object in the skyline is *better (or more interesting)* than any other one in the skyline set with respect to all the dimensions of the space.
- No object in the data set, D, is in the skyline if there is at least one other object that is *better (or more interesting)* in all dimensions.

This is also known as the *Pareto frontier* (or Pareto curve), where for any object in this frontier, it is not possible to improve any of its features (by picking some other object in the database) without worsening some other feature [Papadimitriou and Yannakakis, 2001]. Note that, unlike the top-k queries, for skyline queries, there is no scoring function that combines the weights of the different features of the objects: the domination relationship between objects is simply defined in terms of a $\geq$ relationship on the values of the data features. Moreover, the number of objects in the skyline set is not known in advance. Yet the set of skyline objects is very much related to top-k query results [Borzsonyi *et al.*, 2001]:

- For any monotone scoring (or preference) function, if the object o maximizes the scoring function (i.e., o is the result to the top-1 query), then o is in the skyline.
- Moreover, each object in the skyline is the top object for some monotone scoring function.

The first of these properties implies that, whenever available, the skyline set can potentially be used to prune irrelevant objects for top-k query processing. The second property, on the other hand, states that the skyline represents the closure over the highest scoring objects with respect to all monotone scoring functions, and thus the skyline set is minimal (it does not contain any objects that are not top according to somebody's preference). A more tightly coupled combination of top-k and skyline queries, called the *top-k dominating query*, is introduced and studied by Yiu and Mamoulis [2007] (see Section 10.3.4).

10.3.1 Skylines without Indexes

Skyline queries can be executed over indexed or nonindexed data sets. Often, when the set of dominating objects of an ad-hoc data set (such as results of a user query) is needed, a suitable index may not be available to help speed up the skyline computation.

10.3.1.1 Nested-Loops–Based Skylines
In its simplest implementation, computing a skyline of a given data set, D, involves comparing all possible pairs of objects in the database to identify and eliminate those that are dominated by others. This can be represented as a self-join operation on the data set D,

$$skyline(D) = D - \Pi_{o_j}\left(D_1 \underset{o_i \in D_1, o_j \in D_2 \ dominating(o_i, o_j)}{\bowtie} D_2\right),$$

(i) *window* = Ø
(ii) *in_temp_file* = D; *out_temp_file* = Ø
(iii) *in_count* = 0; *limit* = ∞
(iv) repeat until *in_temp_file* = Ø
    (a) repeat until *in_temp_file* = Ø
        1. get an o_i ∈ *in_temp_file*
        2. o_i.*timestamp* = *in_count*
        3. *in_count* = *in_count* + 1
        4. if there exists o_j ∈ *window* such that *dominating*(o_j, o_i) is true, then drop o_i
        5. else if there exists o_j ∈ *window* such that *dominating*(o_i, o_j) is true,
           A. drop all o_j ∈ *window* such that *dominating*(o_i, o_j) is true from *window*
           B. insert o_i into *window*
        6. else (o_i is incomparable with all tuples in *window*)
           A. if *window* is not full, insert o_i into *window*
           B. else (if *window* is full),
              ■ insert o_i into *out_temp_file*
              ■ if *limit* == ∞ then *limit* = o_i.*timestamp*
    (b) for all o_i ∈ *window*
        1. if o_i.*timestamp* < *limit* then output o_i
        2. else o_i.*timestamp* = 0
    (c) *in_temp_file* = *out_temp_file*; *out_temp_file* = Ø
    (d) *in_count* = 0
(v) for all o_i ∈ *window*
    (a) output o_i

Figure 10.12. Block-nested-loop based skyline computation.

where $D_1 = D_2 = D$, and can easily be implemented using a nested-loop algorithm consisting of two for-loops, where

  (i) the outer-loop scans the data set, D, one object at a time and for each object, o_i, encountered
    (a) the inner-loop scans all objects, o_j, in D;
        1. for each object pair, $\langle o_i, o_j \rangle$, if o_i is found to be dominating o_j, then o_j is dropped from the set, D.

The remaining set of objects will be those that are not dominated by any object in D and can be returned as the skyline set.

Although this algorithm is very easy to implement, it has a high, $O(|D|^2)$ cost. A more efficient alternative, which still relies on nested loops but uses the main memory more efficiently, was presented by Borzsonyi *et al.* [2001]. This algorithm, which the authors refer to as the *block-nested-loops skylines*, is reminiscent of the block-nested-loop joins commonly used by DBMSs to implement joins when no index structures are available. Unlike the naive algorithm described earlier, the *block-nested-loops skylines* algorithm keeps the set of incomparable pairs (those that are not dominated by each other) in the main memory.

The algorithm, presented in Figure 10.12, keeps as many of the skyline candidates in the main memory (in a set called *window*) as possible to ensure that comparing other objects to these candidates is as efficient as possible. If the skyline is small and fits into the main memory (allocated to hold the *window* data structure), then the algorithm makes only one full pass of the data, resulting in only

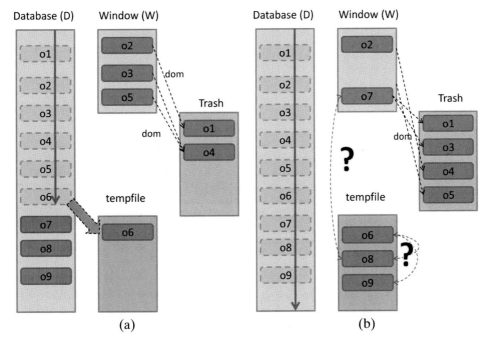

Figure 10.13. (a) During this iteration, object o_6 in the database is checked against all the objects in the *window* and found to be not dominated by any one; however the *window* is currently full, so o_6 is written into a temporary file. (b) When the iteration is over, some objects in the window moved to trash because they were dominated by o_7, which is not in the *window*. At the end of this iteration we know that all objects in the trash are dominated by at least one object in the window, and we also know that there are no object pairs in the window that dominate each other; however, we do not know if those objects in the temporary file dominate each other or not. Moreover, we also do not know if any of the objects (such as o_7) that were put into the window after o_6 are dominated by any other object in the temporary file. In this example, only o_2 can be included in the skyline at the end of this iteration.

$O(|D|)$ disk accesses. On the other hand, if the skyline does not fit into the main memory, then those objects that do not fit need to be written into a temporary file (Figure 10.13(a)). At the end of each iteration, the algorithm considers the current objects in the window (Figure 10.13(b)):

■ Those objects that have been inserted into the *window* set before any object is pushed to the temporary file have been vetted against all the objects considered in the iteration; therefore they are guaranteed to be in the skyline and can be included in the output.

■ Those objects that have been inserted into the *window* after some objects have been pushed into the temporary file have not been compared against those objects in the temporary file; therefore, there is a chance that they are not in the skyline and, thus, cannot be provided to the user yet.

Each subsequent iteration considers those objects that were not committed yet and compares them to objects remaining in the temporary file.

Improvements of the algorithm described by Borzsonyi *et al.* [2001] include (a) ordering the candidates in the *window* set in such a way that those objects in the window that are more likely to prune others are considered first so that the number

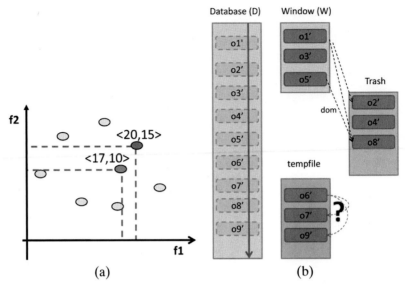

Figure 10.14. (a) $\langle 20, 15 \rangle$ dominates $\langle 17, 10 \rangle$; thus if f is a monotonic function, then $f(20, 15) > f(17, 10)$; for example $20 + 15 > 17 + 10$. (b) This implies that, if the data are sorted using a monotonic function (such as "+") before the iteration starts, then later objects cannot unseat objects that are already in the window; moreover, at the end of the iteration, we can be sure that no objects in the temporary file can dominate any object in the window and, thus, all objects (o'_1, o'_2, and o'_3) in the window can be provided to the user as part of the skyline before the next iteration starts (compare this with the situation in Figure 10.13(b), where data are not presorted).

of in-memory comparisons is reduced; and (b) instead of pushing to the disk simply those tuples that are considered later than the others, using a *replacement policy* that keeps in the *window* those objects with higher pruning power (likely to cover more objects[11]), while pushing to the disk those that have less. The worst-case complexity of the window-driven algorithm is $O(|D|^2)$ like the naive algorithm, but the window-driven algorithm tends to be more efficient because of the use of main memory as buffer, which limits the input/output (I/O) activity.

10.3.1.2 Presorting-Based Skylines

The disadvantages of block-nested loop–based skylines include heavy reliance on the availability of the main memory and the fact that it has to scan the entire data file before it can provide any single skyline object. To reduce the cost of skyline computations, the *sort-filter-skyline* algorithm [Chomicki *et al.*, 2003, 2005] first sorts D based on a monotone function. Any total order of the objects in the database with respect to any given monotone scoring function is a topological sort with respect to the skyline dominance partial relation; in other words, no object can dominate another object that comes before it in the sorted order (Figure 10.14(a)). Consequently, sorting ensures that an object o dominating an object o' is included in the list before o', and this helps improve the pruning effectiveness of the overall process,

---

[11] In [Borzsonyi *et al.*, 2001], this is measured by the volume of space defined by the origin and the vector corresponding to the objects: the higher the volume, the more likely that it will cover other objects.

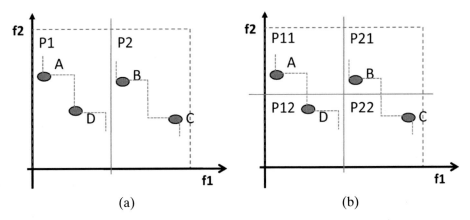

Figure 10.15. (a) Space partitioning results in two seperate partial skylines. (b) Merging of these two skylines into one (i.e., removing of nonskyline objects from these two partial skylines) may involve further partitioning of the two partial skylines to be compared until they fit into memory.

ensuring that, at each iteration, a large number of objects can be output as part of the skyline (Figure 10.14(b)).

The foregoing algorithm requires an external (i.e., disk-based) sort process which potentially performs multiple passes over the entire data set to obtain the initial sorted data. The *linear elimination sort skylines* algorithm [Godfrey *et al.*, 2005] improves on the sort-filter-skyline by using these sorting related passes in a way that they also contribute to the elimination of nonskyline objects: (a) the first pass of the external sort algorithm is modified with an elimination-filter window that identifies and eliminates some of the dominated objects; (b) the final pass of the external sort is combined with the first pass of the skyline filtering process.

A similar sorting-based approach is also used by Tan *et al.* [2001], who map the multidimensional data points onto a single dimensional space. Unlike the foregoing algorithms, however, Tan *et al.* [2001] insert objects into a B+-trees: the leaves of the B+-tree are then scanned to access the objects in sorted order (see Section 10.3.2.1).

10.3.1.3 Divide-and-Conquer–Based Skylines

In order to reduce the cost of the skyline query processing, the divide-and-conquer schemes break up D recursively into smaller and smaller partitions, until each small partition fits into main memory. Individual skylines are computed for each partition, and these skylines are combined to identify those points that are not dominated by any others [Borzsonyi *et al.*, 2001; Kung *et al.*, 1975].

The merging of the partial skylines has to be performed carefully, because skylines themselves may not fit into the main memory, resulting in a significant amount of I/O. Consider, for example, the two partitions and the corresponding two skylines, $\{A, D\}$ and $\{B, C\}$, shown in Figure 10.15(a). If neither of these partitions fits into the main memory, then merging of these two skylines involves repartitioning the skylines across a new dimension as shown in Figure 10.15(b). In this figure, it is easy to see that any skyline object in partition P_{11} (say A) will be incomparable with any skyline object (say C) in partition P_{22}. Therefore, skyline objects in these partitions do not need to be compared against each other. Merges of the remaining three pairs of skylines are performed by recursively applying the foregoing merge operation, until either there are no more dimensions left for partitioning or one of the pairing partitions fits into the memory.

The cost of this algorithm is $O(|D|(log|D|)^{d-2}) + O(|D|log|D|)$. Improvements, such as using multi-way partitioning strategies for obtaining smaller partitions early on or block-based schemes that load as many objects into main memory as possible to eliminate objects that are dominated by others earlier, provide gains of only constant factor.

10.3.2 Skylines over Indexed Data

The skyline algorithms just described (except for [Tan *et al.*, 2001]) did not leverage any preconstructed index structures. Naturally, when available (and if properly used) index structures can help improve skyline execution performance.

10.3.2.1 B-trees
Borzsonyi *et al.* [2001] provide a *B*-tree–based method for computing skylines efficiently. Assuming that all d dimensions have B-tree indexes on them, the skyline is processed by scanning all indexes simultaneously (in decreasing order of value) to find a first match:

- Because this object is not dominated by any other, it is definitely in the skyline set and can be included in the output without further investigation.
- Any object that has not been seen yet in any of the dimensions is dominated by this first object and thus cannot be in the result.
- Any object that has been seen during the initial scan is a candidate. The remaining skyline objects can be picked among these using any other skyline algorithm.

Note that this scheme is using the B-tree simply to access each dimension in a (decreasing) sorted order of values; thus it is reminiscent of the top-k join algorithms we discussed in the previous subsection. The hierarchical nature of the B-tree indexes is not leveraged.

An alternative to using multiple B-trees for skyline computation is to rely on a transformation that maps the multidimensional data points onto a single dimensional space so that they can be indexed [Tan *et al.*, 2001]. A suitable transformation is presented by Ooi *et al.* [2000] and Tan *et al.* [2001]. This transformation organizes the data in such a way that the resulting B+-tree orders (and thus implicitly partitions) the data based on the dimension that has the largest value. Moreover, in each partition, data are sorted based on the values along this dimension. For example, consider the following points in a three-dimensional space:

$$\{\langle 1, 4, \mathbf{5}\rangle, \langle \mathbf{5}, 1, 3\rangle, \langle 6, \mathbf{8}, 7\rangle, \langle 7, \mathbf{9}, 6\rangle, \langle \mathbf{8}, 5, 1\rangle, \langle 2, 3, \mathbf{4}\rangle\}.$$

For each point, the dimension in bold corresponds to the dimension that has the largest value among all dimensions. The transformation would sort the data based on these highlighted values as follows:

$$\langle \mathbf{8}, 5, 1\rangle\langle \mathbf{5}, 1, 3\rangle \quad \langle 7, \mathbf{9}, 6\rangle\langle 6, \mathbf{8}, 7\rangle \quad \langle 1, 4, \mathbf{5}\rangle\langle 2, 3, \mathbf{4}\rangle.$$

Here the gaps correspond to the boundaries between the logical partitions of the sorted list of points. Note that the sort order in each partition allows the algorithm to examine points that are likely to be skyline points first. Second, the algorithm is able to prune some of the points without having to consider them explicitly: if the minimum value among all dimensions for object o_1 is larger than the maximum value among all dimensions for object o_2, then the o_1 dominates o_2 and o_2 can be eliminated. Because each partition of the structure is organized in sorted order based on the maximum value, this means that once an object is found to be eliminated, all subsequent objects in the partition can be eliminated.

10.3.2.2 Bitmap Skylines

Tan *et al.* [2001] present a bitmap-based method to compute skylines, progressively. Let $1 \le l \le d$ be one of the d dimensions of the space and let $p_{l1} > p_{l2} > \cdots > p_{lu_l}$ be the u_l unique values along this dimension. Each data vector, $\vec{o}$, corresponding to object $o \in D$ is represented in the form of an m-bit vector as follows:

- The lth dimension of the space is represented using u_l bits, where u_l is the number of unique values along this dimension. Consequently, the length of the bitmap signature for an object in the database is $m = \sum_{l=1}^{d} u_l$.
- Let $\vec{o}[l]$ (i.e., the value of the lth feature dimension for object o) be the qth distinct largest value. The u_l bit signature segment corresponding to this dimension is constructed by setting bits 1 to $q - 1$ to 0 and bit q to u_l to 1.

Consequently, given two objects, o_1 and o_2, it is possible to look at their bit representations for any given dimension and quickly tell which of these objects has a higher value along that dimension. For example, if the bit representation for o_1 along the lth feature dimension is "0111" and for o_2 the corresponding bit representation is "0001", it is clear that o_1 has a higher value along dimension l than o_2.

Given the foregoing representation, the resulting set of signature vectors are transposed and indexed in the form of bitslices,[12] where a unique bitslice signature of length d is associated to each signature position. Let $BS_{l,q}$ denote the bitslice corresponding to the qth bit position along the lth dimension. Intuitively, this bitslice will tell for each object in the database whether the value of the object's lth feature dimension is greater than or equal to the qth largest (distinct) value along the dimension. Given these bitslices and a data object o, where $\vec{o}[l]$ is the q_lth largest distinct value along the lth dimension, let $A(o)$, $B(o)$, and $C(o)$ be bit-strings such that

- $A(o) = BS_{l,q_1} \ \& \ BS_{2,q_2} \ \& \ \cdots \ \& \ BS_{d,q_d}$,
- $B(o) = BS_{l,(q_1-1)} \ | \ BS_{2,(q_2-1)} \ | \ \cdots \ | \ BS_{d,(q_d-1)}$, and
- $C(o) = A(o) \ \& \ B(o)$,

where "&" is the bitwise *and* operation and "|" is the bitwise *or* operation. $A(o)$'s nth bit is 1 if and only if the nth object in the database has value greater than or equal to the corresponding value of o in *each of the d dimensions*. On the other hand, $B(o)$'s nth bit is 1 if and only if the nth object in the database has value greater than the corresponding value of o in *at least one of the d dimensions*. Thus, if $C(o)$ has

---

[12] This is similar to the bitslices used for keyword-based document search in signature files (Section 5.2.2).

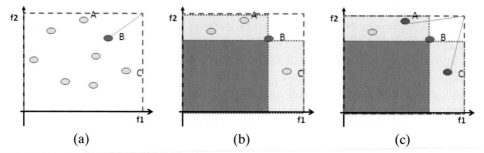

Figure 10.16. Repeated use of nearest neighbor queries to identify the skyline objects: (a) nearest neighbor query, (b) elimination of all dominated objects and partitioning of the space, and (c) execution of nearest neighbor queries (and potentially repeating this process recursively) in each partition to identify the remaining skyline objects.

any single nonzero bit, then o is dominated by at least one object in the database; therefore it cannot be in the skyline and can be eliminated from consideration.

10.3.2.3 Nearest-Neighbor Based Skylines

Kossmann *et al.* [2002] observe that there is a very close relationship between nearest neighbor queries and skylines and uses this observation to develop an index-supported *divide-and-conquer* style algorithm for skyline computation. Consider a point, represented by a d-dimensional vector $\vec{p}_{max}$, which dominates all points in the database. Kossmann *et al.* [2002] observe that

- if the point $\vec{o}$ (corresponding to an object, $o \in O$) is the nearest object to $\vec{p}_{max}$ according to some monotonic distance function, then o is in the skyline; moreover,
- if $Dom(m)$ is a region of the space containing all the points dominating some $\vec{m}$ and if the point $\vec{o}$, in the region $Dom(m)$, is the nearest object to $\vec{p}_{max}$ according to some monotonic distance function, then $\vec{o}$ is in the skyline of O.

The first observation implies that a nearest neighbor query can be used for identifying the first element of the skyline quickly (Figure 10.16(a)) and the portion of the space dominated by this object can be eliminated from further consideration (Figure 10.16(b)). The second observation implies that the skyline objects found so far can be used to partition the space in such a way that the new skyline objects can be found by executing nearest neighbor queries (and repeating this process recursively) in each partition (Figure 10.16(c)).

Kossmann *et al.* [2002] show that, although the foregoing algorithm is correct, for $d > 2$ the partitioning process may lead to overlapping partitions and, hence, to duplicate objects (identified once for each partition containing it) in the skyline. This problem can be addressed by a postprocessing phase in which the duplicate skyline objects are found and eliminated, by progressively removing points that are discovered from all not-yet-visited partitions, or by repeatedly modifying (repartitioning or merging) the space partitions based on the skyline objects that are discovered.

10.3.2.4 Branch-and-Bound Skylines

Borzsonyi *et al.* [2001] also propose a scheme that leverages R-tree index structures for skyline queries when they are available. In particular, Borzsonyi *et al.* [2001] use a branch-and-bound technique, similar to the ones considered for executing nearest neighbor queries, to eliminate unpromising branches of the tree. The scheme traverses the R-tree in a depth-first manner, and for every skyline object found in the process, it eliminates the branches of the R-tree that are guaranteed to contain only objects that are dominated by this object.

Papadias *et al.* [2005] also leverage R-trees for supporting progressive, branch-and-bound–based skyline computation. However, unlike the work of Borzsonyi *et al.* [2001], the proposed branch-and-bound algorithm also leverages the nearest neighbor search described earlier. Thus, in addition to the R-tree that supports branch-and-bound search, Papadias *et al.* [2005] also construct a priority queue (heap) to arrange objects based on their distances from $\vec{p}_{max}$.[13] The branch-and-bound process is similar to the best-first nearest neighbor algorithm discussed in Section 10.1.1: The process starts from the root node and inserts all its children into the heap. Then, the node with the minimum distance is picked from the heap and expanded and its children are inserted back into the heap. As in [Borzsonyi *et al.*, 2001], the process continues examining the remaining nodes one by one, while recording any skyline objects found in the process and pruning those nodes that are dominated by these skyline objects. Unlike the work of Borzsonyi *et al.* [2001], however, the order in which nodes are visited is not depth-first, but based on their distances to $\vec{p}_{max}$, as enforced by the priority queue.

10.3.3 Skylines with Partially Ordered Data

The skyline algorithms described so far all assume that the individual dimensions of the objects are all totally ordered. However, there are many cases in which the values taken by the relevant features do not come from a totally ordered domain (such as integers or real numbers), but a partially ordered domain (such as intervals, sets, and probability distributions; see Section 3.4). A partially ordered set (or *poset*), denoted as $(S, \preceq)$ is such that $\preceq$ has the following properties: for all $s_1, s_2, s_3 \in S$,

- *reflexivity:* $s_1 \preceq s_1$,
- *antisymmetry:* $(s_1 \preceq s_2) \wedge (s_2 \preceq s_1) \rightarrow (s_1 = s_2)$,
- *transitivity:* $(s_1 \preceq s_2) \wedge (s_2 \preceq s_3) \rightarrow (s_1 \preceq s_3)$.

For example, let Q be a set of normally distributed quality assessments: that is, for all $qa_i \in Q$, we have $qa_i = N(q_i, \xi_i)$, where q_i represents the expected quality of an observation, whereas ξ_i represents the variance: Then [Peng *et al.*, 2010],

- the ordered set $(Q, \preceq_c)$ defined as

$$(qa_i \preceq_c qa_j) \equiv_{def} \left(\int_c^\infty qa_i(q)\, dq \right) \leq \left(\int_c^\infty qa_j(q)\, dq \right)$$

  is totally ordered, because qa_i is mapped to a single scalar value belonging to a totally ordered domain; on the other hand,
- the ordered set $(Q, \preceq_p)$ defined as

$$(qa_i \preceq_p qa_j) \equiv_{def} (q_j \geq q_i) \wedge (\xi_j \leq \xi_i)$$

---

[13] Papadias *et al.* [2005] use L1-norm; also, the distance an MBR to $\vec{p}_{max}$ is computed using its top-right corner point.

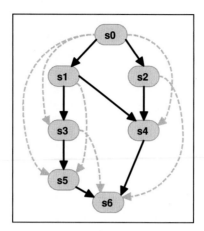

Figure 10.17. A partially ordered data set: the dashed edges show the dominance relation-ships that are implied by transitivity; the graph consisting of the solid edges is also referred to as a lattice or a *Hasse* diagram.

is partially ordered. For example, $qa_i = (0.8, 0.1)$ and $qa_j = (0.9, 0.05)$ are com-parable by the definition of $\preceq_p$, but $qa_i = (0.8, 0.05)$ and $qa_j = (0.9, 0.1)$ are not.

Partially ordered data sets form lattices that can be visualized using Hasse diagrams as shown in Figure 10.17.

10.3.3.1 Interval Mapping–Based Branch-and-Bound
Chan *et al.* [2005a,b] argue that, although it is possible to evaluate skylines over par-tially ordered value domains by modifying the block nested-loop algorithms, this will be likely to produce inefficient solutions. Chan *et al.* [2005b] also argue that, although partitioning the partially ordered data onto multiple totally ordered do-mains (in such a way that the original partial order is preserved[14]) might be possi-ble, the increase in the number of dimensions would be very costly. Instead, Chan *et al.* [2005b] map partially ordered data onto an interval domain in such a way that the original partial order is preserved in the transformed domain. In other words, the domain mapping f is such that, for any pair of distinct values v_1 and v_2, if $f(v_1)$ contains $f(v_2)$, then $v_1 > v_2$ in the original space [Agrawal *et al.*, 1989].

Furthermore, to account for the partially ordered nature of the interval domain itself, the definition of dominance is extended as follows: Given two objects o_1 and o_2, o_1 m-dominates o_2 if

- for any totally ordered dimension, the value of o_1 along that dimension is greater than or equal to that of o_2,
- for any partially ordered dimension, the *interval transformation* of the value of o_1 along that dimension is equal to or contains that of o_2, and
- there exists at least one totally (or partially) ordered dimension, where the value (or interval transformation of the value) of o_1 along that dimension is greater than (or contains) that of o_2.

---

[14] Once the total orders are obtained, objects are indexed and skyline objects are found using an index-based scheme.

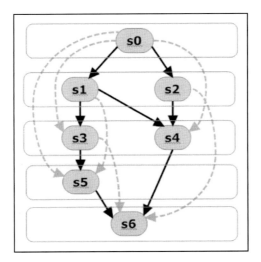

Figure 10.18. Levels of a partially ordered value domain.

Because the mapping is not precise, however, skyline processing in this interval space may result in false positives that need to be cleaned before returning skylines. Therefore, Chan *et al.* [2005b] modify branch-and-bound–based skyline search in such a way that false positives are found and eliminated as skyline objects are identified.

10.3.3.2 Weak Pareto Dominance and *I*-cuts

An alternative approach to the problem is proposed by Balke and Güntzer [2005] and Chomicki [2003]. These authors replace the Pareto dominance condition (one object having better or equal values with respect to all dimensions and being strictly better in at least one) between objects with that of *weak Pareto dominance* as follows: object o_1 weakly dominates object o_2 with respect to partially ordered dimensions if and only if there is at least one dimension along which o_1's value dominates the corresponding value of o_2 and there exists no dimension along which o_2's value dominates the corresponding value of o_1. The set of all non–weakly dominated objects in O is referred to as the *restricted skyline*. Balke and Güntzer [2005] show that restricted skylines are part of the Pareto set (or skyline) and that restricted skylines can be computed more efficiently than the full Pareto skyline.

The algorithm assumes that data along each dimension are sorted in such a way that high values are returned on smaller ranks. This is achieved by associating a *level* to each value in the domain representing this value's distance from the maximum value in the underlying lattice (Figure 10.18). These levels have the property that, given a partially ordered set, $(S, \preceq)$, and two distinct values s_1 and s_2 in this set, the following is true:

$$(s_2 \preceq s_1) \quad \rightarrow \quad (level(s_1) > level(s_2)).$$

The values in each partially ordered domain are sorted in their levels by performing a breadth-first topological sort on the lattice. Note that this is analogous to the

(i) Perform sorted access along each subdimension
    (a) Consider all minimum l-cuts among the objects accessed so far
    (b) When all objects of some cut have been accessed along all dimensions
        1. Prune all objects on lower levels
        2. For the remaining objects, perform random accesses and compare the objects for pairwise Pareto dominance
        3. Remove all weakly dominated objects and return the remaining set as the restricted skyline

Figure 10.19. l-Cuts–based skyline computation over partially ordered value domains.

distance based sorting in nearest neighbor–based skyline algorithms described in Section 10.3.2.3.

Let l-cut denote a set of values that dominate all values below the lth level. Although the set of all values at level l would trivially form an l-cut, there may be a subset of values at level l that may dominate all values below the lth level as well. Balke and Güntzer [2005] prove that if a set, $O \subset D$, of objects form an l_i cut for each dimension i, then no object that occurs on a higher level than l_i for all i can be part of the *restricted skyline* under weak Pareto dominance. This gives rise to a sort and merge based algorithm for computing restricted skylines (Figure 10.19). Balke and Güntzer [2005] achieve efficiency by focusing the skyline processing to only the minimum l-cuts of the domains of the dimensions.

Balke *et al.* [2006] further extend this level-based processing approach by considering additional (possibly user-provided) equivalence relationships between values in the partial domain, for example to represent indifference of a user: under this model, an object o_1 is said to dominate o_2 if and only if it explicitly dominates o_2 with respect to at least one dimension and either it also dominates o_2 with respect to all remaining dimensions or can be considered equal based on the explicit equivalence relationships. Other models and algorithms for considering explicitly provided equivalence and preference relationships include works by Chomicki [2003], Kiessling [2002, 2005], and Wong *et al.* [2008].

10.3.4 Top-K Dominating Queries

Papadias *et al.* [2005] and Yiu and Mamoulis [2007] focus on a special case of skylines, where the user is not interested in obtaining all skyline objects, but only the k *most dominating* ones in terms of the number of data objects they dominate. Note that, unlike the skyline objects, the top-k most dominating objects are not necessarily mutually nondominating; it is, for example, possible that the second most dominating object in the database is covered (or dominated) by the first object, and so on. Papadias *et al.* [2005] extend existing progressive skyline schemes for top-k dominating queries as follows: first, a skyline is computed for the given data set; then the most dominating object in the skyline is found and removed from the data; and the process is repeated until top-k dominating objects are located.

Yiu and Mamoulis [2007] propose branch-and-bound–based schemes that rely on a specialized R-tree, called the aggregate R-tree (or aR-tree [Lazaridis and Mehrotra, 2001]), where each nonleaf node is annotated with the number of data

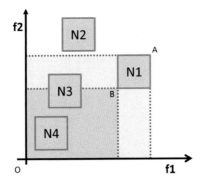

Figure 10.20. Let N_1 through N_4 denote four different MBRs in the aR-tree: it is easy to see that no point in N_1 dominates any point in N_2, some points in N_1 may dominate some points in N_3, and any point in N_1 is dominating all points in N_2. In other words, the number of points in the region defined by the origin O and the point A is an upper bound, whereas the number of points in the region defined by O and B is a lower bound on the number of points dominated by the aR-tree node N_1.

points contained with the corresponding minimum bounded region. These counts are used in developing *counting-guided* and *priority-based* tree traversal schemes. The counting-guided scheme is a *best-first* approach, where for each aR-tree node encountered, a tight upper score on the number of data points dominated by this node (Figure 10.20) is computed in an *eager* fashion by using the aggregate values whenever possible, and these bounds are used to determine the order in which the nodes are visited. The alternative, priority-based scheme, on the other hand, avoids eager computation of tight upper bounds and instead maintains upper and lower bounds that become gradually refined as more tree nodes are accessed. The nodes of the aR-tree are visited based on a priority order, and those nodes whose upper bounds are worse than the lower bounds of other nodes are pruned. The effectiveness of the pruning process depends on the tightness of the lower bounds. Thus, in order to minimize the likelihood of partially dominating entry pairs (such as N_1 and N_3 in Figure 10.20), the priority-based scheme proposed by Yiu and Mamoulis [2007] prioritize the visited nodes based on their levels in the tree. Moreover, among the nodes at the highest level, the priority scheme chooses those nodes with highest upper bound to promote the early discovery of points with the highest domination scores.

10.4 OPTIMIZATION OF RANKING QUERIES

As we discussed in Sections 1.3 and 2.1.2, the role of a query optimizer is to take a user-provided (often declarative) query specification and create an execution plan for it that is not likely to require unnecessary disk accesses or run-time processing. For example, it is the job of the query optimizer to pick between the two query plans shown in Figure 10.21. The query optimizer achieves this by employing various heuristics (such as processing predicates that can eliminate irrelevant objects earlier to eliminate costly joins – as we discuss later) and leveraging statistics about relations, tuples, and disk characteristics. Also taking into account statistical

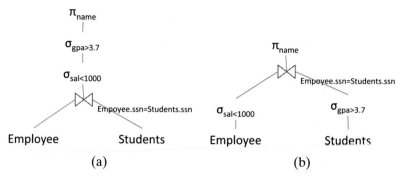

Figure 10.21. Two equivalent query plans; in terms of efficiency, though, the second plan is likely to be more efficient because the restriction predicates are pushed down.

knowledge about available indexes, the query optimizer estimates the query execution cost for different query plans and chooses a plan that is relatively cheap according to some suitable cost model. The reasons why, most of the time, the plan returned by a query optimizer will not be the best possible plan are that (a) the cost models are often imperfect, (b) the statistics are often rough, and (c) the number of alternative plans is too large to be completely enumerated. Instead, most optimization algorithms aim to avoid costly query plans rather than trying to find the cheapest plan possible.

As we see in this section, the process of optimizing and executing queries that contain top-k clauses and expensive predicates (such as those involving media processing) is fundamentally different from optimizing relational queries.

10.4.1 Cost Estimation for Multidimensional Queries and Power Law

Query optimizers have to estimate the cost of query plans (often in terms of the I/O they will require) to be able to select a low-cost plan. This often requires estimation of the selectivity of the query in terms of the number of database objects that will satisfy the query criterion. For nearest neighbor and top-k queries where the number of output objects is fixed, however, the system needs to estimate the number of database objects that need to be considered before those that are in the query result are identified.

Selectivities can be estimated either globally, that is, one selectivity for the complete data set (e.g., [Belussi and Faloutsos, 1995]), or locally, that is, different selectivities for the different regions in the data space. Spatial histograms [Acharya *et al.*, 1999; Theodoridis *et al.*, 2000], which divide the data space into regions (referred to as buckets) and record the number of objects in each region, can be used to obtain location-sensitive estimates for query selectivities. Unfortunately, because histograms often assume that points in small regions of the space are uniformly distributed, they are not effective for most real data. The primary reason behind this is that, as we have seen in Section 4.1 on the dimensionality curse, the density of the space changes significantly with the distance from any given point in the space.

In order to deal with the deficiency of histograms in estimating the costs of multimedia queries, Tao *et al.* [2003] propose a *power law* based selectivity estimation technique, which leverages the knowledge about the exponential behavior of the data-distance distribution to obtain more accurate predictions. The power law states that, given a point, $\vec{p}$, and a radius, r, the number, n, of points within r distance from $\vec{p}$ can be computed as

$$n(\vec{p}, r) = c_{\vec{p}} \times r^{m_{\vec{p}}},$$

where $c_{\vec{p}}$ is the local constant and $m_{\vec{p}}$ is the local exponent. Because, as described in Section 4.1, the exponent depends on the number of dimensions of the space, $m_{\vec{p}}$ captures the intrinsic dimension of the region $\vec{p}$ lies in. The constant $c_{\vec{p}}$ on the other hand, reflects the density of points in the vicinity of $\vec{p}$. Given a ρ-neighborhood (a hypersphere, centered around $\vec{p}$ with ρ radius), this constant can be computed by dividing the number of points in the neighborhood by $\rho^{m_{\vec{p}}}$.

Let us be given a data set with N elements and power-law behavior. Tao *et al.* [2003] estimate the selectivity for a range search with query point, $\vec{q}$, and radius, r, as follows:

$$sel_{range}(\vec{q}, r) = \frac{1}{N} \times c_{\vec{q}} \times r^{m_{\vec{q}}}.$$

Based on this selectivity, and assuming R-tree data structure to support searches, Tao *et al.* [2003] estimate the cost (number of leaf accesses) of the preceding range search as follows:

$$cost_{range}(\vec{q}, r) = \frac{c_{\vec{q}}}{f} \times \left[\left(\frac{f}{c_{\vec{q}}} \right)^{\frac{1}{m_{\vec{q}}}} + r \right]^{m_{\vec{q}}},$$

where f is the average fanout of the R-tree. Using the same model, Tao *et al.* [2003] also estimate the cost of k nearest neighbor searches as follows:

$$cost_{knn}(\vec{q}, k) = \frac{1}{f} \times \left[f^{\frac{1}{m_{\vec{q}}}} + k^{\frac{1}{m_{\vec{q}}}} \right]^{m_{\vec{q}}}.$$

10.4.2 Dealing with Expensive Filtering Predicates

Another major difference between relational and multimedia query processing is that, in relational databases, verifying whether a given object/tuple satisfies a given selection predicate is cheap: usually, the whole tuple fits into the main memory, and verifying whether the tuple satisfies the given numeric or alphanumeric condition can be done extremely fast. So these *restriction* predicates, which can be used to identify unpromising tuples, are often pushed down in the query plan as much as possible (i.e., they are processed as early as possible to eliminate nonproductive tuples). Consider, for example, the two equivalent relational algebraic statements

$$\pi_{name}(\sigma_{gpa>3.7}(\sigma_{sal<1000}(Employee \bowtie_{Employee.ssn=Students.ssn} Students)))$$

and

$$\pi_{name}((\sigma_{gpa>3.7}(Students)) \bowtie_{Students.ssn=Employee.ssn} (\sigma_{sal<1000}(Employee))).$$

Because, the second plan processes restriction predicates earlier than the join operation that will need to combine data from two different relations (and thus will potentially have a cost quadratic in the number of input tuples), it is often preferred to the first one.

Because multimedia processing can be costly, however, performing restriction predicates that involve media processing early might in fact be counterproductive in terms of overall query processing cost. Consider, for example, the two foregoing statements, but with image matching predicates instead of GPA and salary restrictions. In that case, it might in fact be more efficient to perform the join predicates (checking SSN match) earlier to reduce the number of tuples that will be passed to image match operators (see Figure 10.21). Hellerstein [1998] focuses on the placement of these restriction predicates within a query plan. In particular, it proposes a *predicate migration* algorithm, which assigns a rank to each predicate, p,

$$rank(p) = \frac{selectivity(p) - 1}{cost\_per\_input\_tuple(p)},$$

where the *selectivity* term corresponds to the ratio of the database that satisfies the restriction predicate and shows that applying the restriction predicates in an ascending order of ranks (i.e., the more negative the rank is, the earlier it is applied) provides an optimal query plan for single table queries. For multitable queries, first the join plan is created using a traditional query optimizer, such as the ones described in [Chaudhuri, 1998], and then the restriction predicates are appropriately placed (or *migrated*) in the plan. For this purpose, the definition of the predicate rank is expanded to reflect the global cost of the restriction predicate $p(x_1, x_2, \ldots, x_k)$ with respect to the entire query $q(x_1, x_2, \ldots, x_n)$:

$$rank(p) = \frac{selectivity(p) - 1}{global\_cost(p)},$$

where $global\_cost(p)$

$$= \frac{cost\_per\_input\_tuple(p) \times cardinality(x_1) \times \ldots \times cardinality(x_k)}{cardinality(x_1) \times \ldots \times cardinality(x_n)}$$

$$= \frac{cost\_per\_input\_tuple(p)}{cardinality(x_{k+1}) \times \ldots \times cardinality(x_n)}$$

reflects the total expected execution cost of the predicate p within the context of the query q, normalized with respect to the database size. The placements of the restrictive predicates within an optimal join query plan need to conform to these (modified definitions of) ranks as well as the order implied by the join operations: in particular, it is not possible to apply a filtering predicate that requires two attributes that are originally in two different sources, without combining these two sources (or predicates) using a join operation first. Thus, Hellerstein [1998]

(i) first optimizes the query plan consisting of only the join operations to obtain a join tree describing the order in which data from different sources will be combined; and

(ii) pushes all predicates as far down in the tree as possible:

■ For any two predicates p_1 and p_2 such that p_1 needs to precede p_2 due to the data constraints but $rank(p_1) > rank(p_2)$, then, p_1 is put before p_2, with no other unconstrainted predicates in between.

This is achieved by repeatedly applying the *series-parallel algorithm using parallel chains* [Monma and Sidney, 1979] to each leaf-to-root branch in the tree, until no more progress can be made.

The result is a plan such that, along each branch of the query-plan tree, any set of operations that have the same data constraint relationship with all the operations outside of the set has an optimal rank ordering.

10.4.3 Dealing with Expensive Join Predicates

Unlike Hellerstein [1998], Mahalingam and Candan [2004] treat both restriction and join predicates in a similar manner and recognize that media-related predicates can be implemented using multiple user-defined functions or indexes, each corresponding to different ways the same predicate can be invoked. For instance, a query predicate, extract_pattern(image,pattern), can have three different implementations that can be picked by the query planner:

■ Given an image, one implementation extracts a predetermined number of patterns using a pattern extraction function.
■ Given a pair of an image and a pattern, another implementation searches for the pattern in the image using a pattern-matching algorithm.
■ Given a pattern, a third implementation may retrieve all matching images using a cache of preextracted pattern/image pairs maintained in a multidimensional index structure.

Moreover, each implementation may return different sets of results reflecting the particular implementation of the algorithm: For example, whereas the first alternative above limits the matches to a predetermined number of pairs per image, the second alternative may be able to identify any match without a predetermined bound. From the accuracy perspective, on the other hand, both the first and third alternatives may result in candidate objects that are not identified because of limitations of the data structures. Therefore, optimization algorithms have to consider (a) the variations in the expected query result sizes as a function of the query execution plan and (b) the expected result qualities of the different execution orders.

Mahalingam and Candan [2004] present *cost*, *fanout*, and *quality* models to help in optimizing such queries. The *cost* model predicts the cost of a query execution plan, *fanout* predicts the number of output objects, and the *quality* model predicts the expected quality of the query plan. In particular, the authors show that the traditional query optimization schemes, which assume that the number of resulting tuples for a query or a subquery will not vary for different query plans, are not suitable for optimizing queries that use user-provided predicates that may return different number of tuples for different execution orders. Based on this observation, Mahalingam and Candan [2004] introduce different cost- and fanout-based query plan desirability criteria, including *min_cost*, *min_unit_cost*, and *min_fanout*, and shows that *min_unit_cost* and *min_fanout* schemes lend themselves to the traditional *dynamic programming*-based query optimization schemes commonly used in relational databases. *Min-cost*, however, cannot be implemented using dynamic programming, because optimal *min_cost* plans may not have optimal *min_cost* subplans and, thus, we cannot use any recursively structured algorithm, such as dynamic programming, for optimization. To address this problem, Mahalingam and Candan [2004] use the *min_unit_cost* as a heuristic to reduce the search space at every level of a dynamic programming algorithm. In other words, at each level of dynamic programming, the algorithm (1) ranks subplans based on their unit costs and (2) considers only those plans with small unit costs. The amount of pruning is controlled to achieve different levels of optimization speed and optimality. Mahalingam and Candan [2004] also integrate the expected result quality with cost and fanout to obtain criteria that reflect all three aspects of media queries.

10.4.4 Rank-Aware Query Optimization

Traditional query optimizers often assume that the subplans of an optimal plan must be optimal themselves. This assumption enables the development of relatively efficient dynamic programming-based optimization algorithms that can leverage this recursive optimality property to prune the large solution space [Chaudhuri, 1998]. However, even these systems recognize that there are exceptional cases in which the subplan optimality may not hold. This, for example, is true when the final result needs to be sorted: a costlier subplan that is able to provide ordered intermediate results may be better in the long run than a cheaper subplan that fails to provide ordered intermediate results and thus necessitates a much costlier postprocessing step to sort the final results. Thus, in addition to maintaining cheap subplans, query optimizers also maintain additional subplans that (though they are not the cheapest subplans available) may be useful in the future steps of the optimization to help obtain *interesting orders* of the data cheaply.

Ilyas *et al.* [2004b] leverage the idea of interesting orders to extend the capabilities of traditional query optimizers to handle ranked join operators along with the more traditional join operators. For example, because for top-k ranked joins it is useful to have input data sorted, the optimizer can be told to generate subplans that will provide intermediate results sorted in the corresponding score attributes. In addition to this, though, the query optimizer also needs new costing mechanisms that will enable the optimizer to prune plans that are both higher cost and weaker in terms of the interesting orders they satisfy. A traditional join operator consumes all its inputs and therefore has a relatively predictable processing cost; a top-k ranked join operator, however, does not need to consume all its inputs and can stop processing as soon as the first k results are found. Therefore, the cost of the top-k ranked-join operator can be estimated based on k, the distribution of the input data, and the selectivity of the join operator (i.e., the likelihood of data from different input streams to join with each other).

As in Mahalingam and Candan [2004], RankSQL [Li *et al.*, 2005] also extends bottom-up dynamic programming style optimization with rank-aware features. Remember from Section 10.2.7.4 that rank relations possess two properties: membership to the relation and a ranking order implied by a given set of ranking predicates; moreover, new ranking predicates are only introduced using the *rank* operators (all other operators operate on ranking predicates that have been introduced earlier). Each subplan $(\mathcal{R}, \mathcal{P})$ is defined based on the set, $\mathcal{R}$, of relations and the set, $\mathcal{P}$, of ranking predicates in the subplan; subplans with the same pairs of sets result in the same rank relation. The plan $(\mathcal{R}, \mathcal{P})$ is obtained by

- joining two plans $(\mathcal{R}_1, \mathcal{P}_1)$ and $(\mathcal{R}_2, \mathcal{P}_2)$, such that $\mathcal{R} = \mathcal{R}_1 \cup \mathcal{R}_2$ and $\mathcal{P} = \mathcal{P}_1 \cup \mathcal{P}_2$,
- adding a new ranking predicate to an existing subplan, or
- using a scan that reads the ranked relations from secondary storage.

Because, unlike the approach proposed by Ilyas *et al.* [2004b], RankSQL does not consider top-k predicates, but only ranking predicates (with score lower bounds), it is possible to show that no suboptimal subplan can be part of the optimal execution strategy; hence, for all the different ways a subplan $(\mathcal{R}, \mathcal{P})$ can be obtained, only the best plan is maintained and the others are discarded. Because the cardinality of the results depends on the score distribution, during plan enumeration the optimizer estimates the output cardinality and the cost of each considered subplan by executing it on a small set of samples and extrapolating the costs to the full database.

10.5 SUMMARY

In this chapter, we have seen that the fuzziness and imprecision inherent in multimedia data necessitate various types of ranked query processing techniques, each suitable for different data models and retrieval scenarios. The k-nearest neighbor search algorithms mostly assume that the data objects can be mapped into a multidimensional feature space and that there exists an explicit distance function to measure how similar or different the objects are. Furthermore, these algorithms are generally applicable when the query itself is (or can be described) within the same feature space as the objects in the database. Top-k ranked join algorithms, on the other hand, assume that the query can be described in the form of a fuzzy logical statement, which in turn can be represented as a monotonic score merge function. This function is used for combining the various scores the multimedia object has with respect to the individual query predicates into a single score representing how well the object matches the query. Skyline algorithms, however, focus on identifying the minimal yet complete set of objects in the database that are all desirable for a different reason. Consequently, unlike the nearest neighbor or ranked join algorithms, which both require an input, k, that specifies the number of objects in the result, the number of skyline objects is determined simply by the distribution of the data within the feature space.

11

Evaluation of Retrieval

In the previous chapters, we have covered various feature extraction, indexing, clustering, and classification techniques, all of which transform the raw data collected through various capture devices into models and data structures that support efficient and effective matching and retrieval. Many of these techniques are, however, lossy in nature:

- Feature extraction algorithms need to map a potentially infinite, continuous feature space into a finite feature model that can be represented using a finite data structure.
- Feature selection (to avoid the dimensionality curse) for indexing and query processing usually involves some transformation of the data to highlight important features and to eliminate others that are not as important from consideration.
- Indexing, clustering, and classification algorithms often trade efficiency against effectiveness. Therefore, they can introduce both false hits and misses.

As we briefly discussed in Section 4.2.1, all forms of information loss may not have the same impact on the retrieval effectiveness. For example, false hits (which can be eliminated through postprocessing) are often acceptable, whereas misses (which cannot be eliminated) are not. On the other hand, in many other applications (especially in those cases where user queries are not precise and, thus, there are large numbers of matches), completeness of the result set is less important than the precise ranking of the few initial results: a ranking that can help the user pick a promising result from the first few is better than a ranking that is complete but puts the most promising results in the bottom of a long list.

Thus, evaluating the effectiveness of a particular multimedia retrieval process (or a particular feature extraction, feature selection, indexing, clustering, or classification algorithm) requires an understanding of the characteristics of the particular application and a measure that can reflect how well this process or algorithm bridges the underlying semantic gap between the user and the system (Section 1.1.2). Thus, effectiveness measures have to rely on ground truth collected from the users of the application.

11.1 PRECISION AND RECALL

Consider a database, D, of multimedia objects and a user query, Q, on this database. Let $R_s \subseteq D$ be the set of objects identified by the system as being a match for Q. Let $R_u \subseteq D$ be the set of objects identified by the user (after considering all the objects in the entire database) as matches to this query. The *precision* of the retrieval process for this query is defined as the ratio of the system-returned objects that are also identified as a match by the user:

$$precision_{Q,D}(R_s, R_u) = \frac{|R_s \cap R_u|}{|R_s|}.$$

Essentially, precision measures the impact of false hits and thus needs to be used when false hits are detrimental for the retrieval effectiveness. The precision values are often reported as averages of the precision rates for multiple queries.

For the same situation as before, the *recall* of the retrieval process is defined as the ratio of the user-identified matches that are also identified as a result by the system:

$$recall_{Q,D}(R_s, R_u) = \frac{|R_s \cap R_u|}{|R_u|}.$$

Thus, recall measures the impact of misses and thus needs to be used when completeness of the result set is critical for the application. The recall values are also reported as averages of the recall rates for multiple queries.

11.2 SINGLE-VALUED SUMMARIES OF PRECISION AND RECALL

Given two systems, their precision and recall values can be compared to get an idea about which of these two is more effective in retrieval. If a system has both better precision and better recall than the other, then this system is clearly the better one. However, when one of the systems has a better precision and the other has a better recall, comparing the effectiveness of these two systems requires a combination function that can aggregate the precision-recall behaviors of each of these systems into a single score; the resulting two scores then can be compared against each other to choose between the two systems.

11.2.1 Arithmetic and Harmonic Means

A straightforward way to create a single-valued summary to evaluate a system is to use the *arithmetic average (or mean)* of the precision and recall rates. Let us consider two systems, A and B, with average precisions, p_A and p_B, and average recalls, r_A and r_B; if $\frac{p_A+r_A}{2} > \frac{p_B+r_B}{2}$, then it is possible to argue that the system A is more effective than the system B. Based on this, the arithmetic average, $avg(p,r)$, measure for assessing the effectiveness of retrieval is defined as $avg(p,r) = \frac{p+r}{2}$.

Using the arithmetic average as a summary of the precision/recall behavior of a system, however, has a significant disadvantage. Let us consider three systems, A, B, and C, where

- $p_A = 0.1, r_A = 0.9$
- $p_B = 0.5, r_B = 0.5$
- $p_C = 0.9, r_C = 0.1$

All these three systems have the same average precision/recall value of 0.5, yet systems A and C fail significantly in one or the other aspect of retrieval effectiveness. Therefore, arguably, B is more desirable than another system that is able to provide either very high precision or very high recall, but fails significantly in the other. The arithmetic average, however, is not able to distinguish among the systems A, B, and C.

The *harmonic mean $H(p, r)$ (also known as the F-measure)* of the precision and recall is defined as

$$H(p, r) = \frac{2pr}{p + r}.$$

Unlike arithmetic average, which cannot differentiate between systems if the sums of their precision and recall values are identical, the harmonic mean tends to return high values only in cases where *both* precision and recall are high. For example, for the foregoing three systems, we have $H(p_A, r_A) = \frac{2(0.1 \times 0.9)}{0.1 + 0.9} = 0.18$, $H(p_C, r_C) = \frac{2(0.9 \times 0.1)}{0.9 + 0.1} = 0.18$, and $H(p_B, r_B) = \frac{2(0.5 \times 0.5)}{0.5 + 0.5} = 0.5$. Thus, the harmonic mean measure would pick the system B over the other two.

11.2.2 Weighted Arithmetic and Harmonic Means and the Effectiveness Measure

As we mentioned earlier, different applications may associate different degrees of importance to precision and recall. The arithmetic and harmonic mean measures described earlier are *balanced* in that they do not assign a preference to precision or recall. Therefore, in applications where either precision or recall is more preferred, we need to use single-valued measures that can take this preference into account.

Let w_p and w_r (where $0 \leq w_p, 0 \leq w_r$, and $w_p + w_r = 1.0$) denote the user's preference of precision and recall, respectively. The *weighted arithmetic average (or weighted arithmetic mean)*, $w\_avg(p, r)$, measure for assessing the effectiveness of retrieval is simply defined as $w\_avg(p, r) = w_p \times p + w_r \times r$. When $w_r = w_p = 0.5$, this measure naturally reduces to the balanced arithmetic mean measure given earlier.

Let β denote how much the user prefers recall in retrieval against precision. Given β, the *weighted harmonic mean* of precision and recall is defined as

$$H_\beta(p, r) = \frac{(1 + \beta^2)(pr)}{\beta^2 p + r}.$$

$H_\beta(p, r)$ has the property that when $\frac{r}{p} = \beta$, we also have $\frac{\delta H_\beta}{\delta p} = \frac{\delta H_\beta}{\delta r}$. In other words, when $r = \beta p$, the contributions of precision and recall to the effectiveness measure

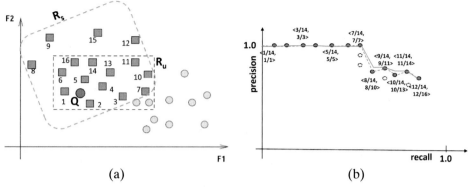

Figure 11.1. (a) A query Q, the set, R_s, of results returned by the system, and the set, R_u, of objects identified as correct matches by the user (note that $|R_s| = 16$, $|R_u| = 14$, and $|R_s \cap R_u| = 12$). (b) As k increases from 1 to 16, the recall-precision value pairs vary as follows: $\langle \frac{1}{14}, \frac{1}{1} \rangle$; $\langle \frac{2}{14}, \frac{2}{2} \rangle$; $\langle \frac{3}{14}, \frac{3}{3} \rangle$; $\langle \frac{4}{14}, \frac{4}{4} \rangle$; $\langle \frac{5}{14}, \frac{5}{5} \rangle$; $\langle \frac{6}{14}, \frac{6}{6} \rangle$; $\langle \frac{7}{14}, \frac{7}{7} \rangle$; $\langle \frac{7}{14}, \frac{7}{8} \rangle$; $\langle \frac{7}{14}, \frac{7}{9} \rangle$; $\langle \frac{8}{14}, \frac{8}{10} \rangle$; $\langle \frac{9}{14}, \frac{9}{11} \rangle$; $\langle \frac{9}{14}, \frac{9}{12} \rangle$; $\langle \frac{10}{14}, \frac{10}{13} \rangle$; $\langle \frac{11}{14}, \frac{11}{14} \rangle$; $\langle \frac{11}{14}, \frac{11}{15} \rangle$; and $\langle \frac{12}{14}, \frac{12}{16} \rangle$.

are identical; that is, H_β is balanced with respect to the changes in precision and recall exactly at the point where recall is β times the precision. Note also that, when β is equal to 1, the weighted harmonic mean measure is identical to the balanced harmonic mean measure given earlier. The H_β measure (also known as the F_β-function) is a simplified version of the *effectiveness, E, function* introduced by van Rijsbergen [1979]:

$$E(p, r) = \frac{1}{\frac{\alpha}{p} + \frac{1-\alpha}{r}}, \quad \text{where } E(p, r) = 1 - F_\beta(p, r) \text{ and } \alpha = \frac{1}{\beta^2 + 1}.$$

11.3 SYSTEMS WITH RANKED RESULTS

In many retrieval systems, such as when the underlying retrieval algorithm is based on range (or nearest neighbor) search, it is possible to trade precision with recall by choosing tighter or lax query ranges (or small or large numbers of neighboring objects to be returned by the system). In effect, in these cases, the objects in the result set, $R_s \subseteq D$, have an implicit order (Figure 11.1(a)). Thus, potentially, the user can control the number, $1 \le k \le |R_s|$, of the objects in R_s that are returned by the system.

Let $R_s(k)$ denote the first k objects in the result set. The k-precision (also known as the precision at k) of the retrieval process is defined as the ratio of the first k system-returned objects that are also identified as a match by the user:

$$precision_{Q,D}(R_s, R_u, k) = \frac{|R_s(k) \cap R_u|}{|R_s(k)|} = \frac{|R_s(k) \cap R_u|}{k}.$$

Similarly, the k-recall of the retrieval process (also known as the recall at k) for this query is the ratio of the user-identified matches that are also included in the first k results returned by the system:

$$recall_{Q,D}(R_s, R_u, k) = \frac{|R_s(k) \cap R_u|}{|R_u|}.$$

11.3.1 Precision-Recall Curve

The precision-recall curve of the retrieval system is obtained by plotting and interpolating the $recall_{Q,D}(R_s, R_u, k)$ and the corresponding $precision_{Q,D}(R_s, R_u, k)$ values on a two-dimensional plot.

Note that as the value of k increases, the recall rate either increases or stays the same, but it never decreases. The precision values, on the other hand, tend to start high, but they decrease as objects that are not identified by the user as matches are returned by the system (Figure 11.1(b)). Therefore, when plotting precision-recall curves, the x axis is often used for representing the (monotonically increasing) recall values, whereas the y axis represents the corresponding precision values. Because the precision values are not monotonic, the resulting curve can have a *saw* shape, where the precision values can drop and rise; this behavior is often avoided by plotting an *interpolated* curve, where for each recall point, r, the highest precision corresponding to all recalls higher than r is used instead of the original precision value. Consequently, as shown in Figure 11.1(b), the precision values reported by a given precision-recall curve monotonically decrease as recall increases.

The precision-recall curves are often reported as averages of the precision-recall curves for multiple queries. In order to simplify the process of averaging precision-recall curves for multiple queries, the precision-recall curves are often reported by using an *11-point interpolated average precision* mechanism, where the precision values at the recall levels 0.0, 0.1, 0.2, ..., 1.0 are computed through interpolation and the corresponding eleven recall-precision pairs are reported instead of the original recall-precision pairs.

11.3.2 Receiver Operator Characteristic (RoC) Curve

A commonly used alternative to the precision-curve is the *receiver operator characteristic* (RoC) curve [Davis and Goadrich, 2006; Provost *et al.*, 1998]. Whereas the precision-recall curve is generated by plotting recall on the x-axis with respect to precision on the y-axis, the RoC curve is created by plotting the *false positive rate* (i.e., the fraction of objects that should not be in the result but have been included in the result) on the x-axis with respect to the *true positive rate* (the fraction of all the relevant objects that are included in the result) on the y-axis. Note that, whereas the true positive rate is analogous to recall, the false positive rate does not directly measure precision; thus the precision-recall curve and the RoC curve visualize different characteristics of the retrieval system.

When dealing with a highly skewed system (where the false positive rate grows much faster than the true positive rate), precision-recall curves are known to give a more accurate indication of the retrieval performance [Davis and Goadrich, 2006].

11.4 SINGLE-VALUED SUMMARIES OF THE PRECISION-RECALL CURVE

Given two systems, their precision-recall curves can be compared to get an idea about which of these two systems is more effective in retrieval. As shown in Figure 11.2(a), if the curve of one of these systems provides a better precision rate for each recall value, then the corresponding system is the best of the two. If,

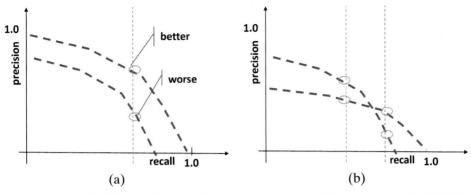

Figure 11.2. (a) Precision-recall curves for two systems: one of the systems is clearly better than the other because it is able to provide a higher precision rate for each degree of recall (or, equivalently, a higher recall for each precision value). (b) Two systems whose precision-recall curves intersect: these two systems are harder to compare.

on the other hand, the precision-recall curves intersect as in Figure 11.2(b), then comparing the effectiveness of these two systems requires a more careful study of the corresponding curves. This is commonly done by computing single-value summaries of the precision-recall behaviors of the two systems and comparing these summaries instead of the curves themselves.

11.4.1 Area under the Precision-Recall Curve

Remember from Figure 11.2(a) that the curve that provides the highest precision for each recall rate is preferable to the others. Thus, the area under the curve can be used as an indicator of the overall effectiveness of a system. Given a precision-recall curve c (where $p = c(r)$), let $area(c) = \int_0^1 c(r)\delta r$; then, given two precision-recall curves c_A and c_B, if $area(c_A) > area(c_B)$, then we can argue that the system corresponding to the precision-recall curve, c_A, is more effective than the system corresponding to c_B.

11.4.2 R-Precision

An alternative measure that can be used to compare two systems, both of which return results in a ranked manner, is the *ranked precision (or R-precision)* measure. R-precision does not rely explicitly on the precision-recall curve; instead, it indirectly relates the precision of a given system to the number of relevant objects it identifies.

Let ϱ to be the number of relevant objects in the database; that is, $\varrho = |R_u|$. R-precision deems the given system effective if it is able to return all of the ϱ relevant objects in the database as its first ϱ matches:

$$R\text{-}precision_{Q,D}(R_s, R_u) = \frac{|R_s(\varrho) \cap R_u|}{\varrho}, \quad \text{where } \varrho = |R_u|.$$

Note that (assuming that $|R_s| \geq \varrho$) we have

$$precision_{Q,D}(R_s, R_u, \varrho) = \frac{|R_s(\varrho) \cap R_u|}{|R_s(\varrho)|} = \frac{|R_s(\varrho) \cap R_u|}{\varrho}$$

and

$$recall_{Q,D}(R_s, R_u, \varrho) = \frac{|R_s(\varrho) \cap R_u|}{|R_u|} = \frac{|R_s(\varrho) \cap R_u|}{\varrho}.$$

Thus, in a sense, R-precision reflects both recall and precision of the system at rank ρ:

$$R-precision_{Q,D}(R_s, R_u) = precision_{Q,D}(R_s, R_u, \varrho) = recall_{Q,D}(R_s, R_u, \varrho).$$

In Figure 11.1, the total number of relevant objects in the database is $\varrho = |R_u| = 14$. The number of relevant objects among the first 14 returned by the system is 11. Therefore, the $R-precision_{Q,D}(R_s, R_u)$ for this example is $\frac{11}{14} = 0.786$.

11.4.3 (Noninterpolated) Average Precision

The *(noninterpolated)* average-precision *(NIAP)* measure [Manning and Schtze, 1999], commonly used by the TREC community for assessing the effectiveness of text document retrieval systems [TREC], reports the average of the precision values obtained for the retrieved documents after each relevant document:

$$NIAP_{Q,D}(R_s, R_u) = \frac{1}{|R_s \cap R_u|} \sum_{o_i \in R_s \cap R_u} precision_{Q,D}(R_s, R_u, rank_s(o_i)).$$

11.4.4 Recall at Θ Precision

Unlike the R-precision and average-precision measures, which report the precision as a function of the ranks of the relevant documents, the *recall at Θ precision* measure reports the recall at the rank where precision drops below Θ. As such, it measures what portion of the relevant documents the system will be able to identify (without having to eliminate irrelevant results through a post-processing step) if the application has a lower-bound on precision.

11.4.5 Rank First Relevant

In some applications, the user is interested in finding a relevant match quickly. In other words, it is important that at least one relevant match is ranked close to 1, but it is not as important that all the relevant documents are ranked close to 1. In these cases, a *rank first relevant* measure, which reports the rank of the highest-ranked relevant document, might be appropriate. Note that the closer this measure is to 1, the better the retrieval effectiveness.

11.5 EVALUATING SYSTEMS USING RANKED AND GRADED GROUND TRUTHS

So far, we have assumed that the system is able to rank the objects in the database according to their degrees of matching to the given query, whereas the user who is providing the ground truth only separates the results into relevant and nonrelevant sets. Naturally, a more precise way to assess the system's ranking performance would be to collect a preferred ranking from the user as the ground truth and evaluate the degree of matching between system's and user's rankings.

Given an object $o \in D$, let $rank_u(o)$ be the user's ranking of the object, whereas $rank_s(o)$ is the system's ranking for the same object. In general, given two objects, $o_i, o_j \in D$, an effective retrieval system would ensure that

$$(rank_u(o_i) > rank_u(o_j)) \longleftrightarrow (rank_s(o_i) > rank_s(o_j)).$$

Therefore, one can compare the user's ranking assessment with the system's ranking by counting the number of violations of the foregoing condition:

$$\frac{\left| \left\{ \langle o_i, o_j \rangle \mid (o_i \neq o_j \in D) \wedge \left(\frac{rank_u(o_i) - rank_u(o_j)}{rank_s(o_i) - rank_s(o_j)} < 0 \right) \right\} \right|}{|\{ \langle o_i, o_j \rangle \mid (o_i \neq o_j \in D) \}|}.$$

This measure, however, would fail to capture the difference between the impacts of errors at different ranking levels: in many retrieval applications, because the users are only interested in the best few matches, it is more critical to ensure that the preceding condition is satisfied for user and system rankings close to 1, whereas violations of the condition for cases where ranks are very large are not as important. Thus, a more precise generic measure of ranking effectiveness would be

$$\frac{\sum_{\langle o_x, o_y \rangle \in \left\{ \langle o_i, o_j \rangle \mid (o_i \neq o_j \in D) \wedge \left(\frac{rank_u(o_i) - rank_u(o_j)}{rank_s(o_i) - rank_s(o_j)} < 0 \right) \right\}} sig\_ranks(o_x, o_y)}{\sum_{\langle o_x, o_y \rangle \in \{ \langle o_i, o_j \rangle \mid (o_i \neq o_j \in D) \}} sig\_ranks(o_x, o_y)},$$

where $sig\_ranks(o_x, o_y)$ represents the application dependent significance of the user and system rankings ($rank_s(o_x), rank_s(o_y), rank_u(o_x)$, and $rank_u(o_y)$) for a given pair of objects, o_x and o_y.

In addition to system and user rankings, in some cases, the scores ($score_s$ and $score_u$) that the system and the user associate to the objects in the database may also be available. In the rest of this section, we introduce various measures used in the literature to assess the alignment between user- and system-provided rankings and/or scores.

11.5.1 Pearson's Correlation, Spearman's Rank Correlation Coefficient, and the Kendall-Tau Rank Coefficient

Given a result object, o, we expect that its system-assigned score, $score_s(o)$, will be positively correlated with its user-supplied score $score_u(o)$. The *Pearson's correlation coefficient* (ρ), discussed in Section 3.5.1.2, is the standard measure to assess the linear correlation between two variables, in this case the system- and user-assigned scores of the objects in the database. When only the ranking information is available, the correlation coefficient can be computed using object ranks instead of the object scores as the input variables. Alternatively, when there are no ties in the rankings, *Spearman's rank correlation coefficient* [Spearman, 1904] can be used instead of the more complex Pearson correlation coefficient:

$$SRCC_{Q,D} = 1 - \frac{6 \sum_{o_i \in D} (diff_i)^2}{|D| \times (|D|^2 - 1)},$$

where D is the database and $diff_i = |rank_u(o_i) - rank_s(o_i)|$ is the difference between the user- and system-provided ranks for object o_i.

However, both Pearson's and Spearman's correlation measures assume that the relationship between the two variables being compared is linear; thus, they are not necessarily suitable to assess the alignment between system- and user-supplied scores which may have nonlinear relationships. In such cases, the *Kendall-tau rank coefficient*, which does not make the assumption of linearity can be used [Candan *et al.*, 2008; Joachims, 2002; Kendall, 1938]. Let D be a database and Q be a query. Let n denote the total number of object pairs, n_c denote the number of *concordant* object pairs where the ranking agreement condition is satisfied, and n_d denote the number of *discordant* object pairs, where the ranking agreement condition is violated. The *Kendall-tau rank coefficient* is defined as

$$\tau_{Q,D} = \frac{n_c - n_d}{n}.$$

Note the similarity between this and the general definition of rank assessment measures presented earlier.

11.5.2 Maximum and Minimum F-Measure Scores

In general, a result presented to the user is *good* if it has a high user score (ranking) as well as a high system score (ranking). In some applications, however, the user expects only that the best matching result will be in the candidate list with a high score (ranking), but does not care about the rest of the candidates in the result set (this is especially the case when there are only a few real matches to a user query, but the system identifies a predetermined number anyhow). In such cases, a retrieval system is good if the best user result is in the result list with a high score (ranking). As we introduced in Section 11.2.1, given two values $0 \le x, y \le 1$, the F-measure (defined as $\frac{2xy}{x+y}$) is known to give a high score only if both x and y are large. Therefore, given a set of results, R_s, and their scores or rankings, we can quantify an F-measure value, F_i, for each object $o_i \in R_s$. Given the F-measures of the results, the *maximum F-measure* value would show whether the result set contains any result matching the user's ground truth with a very high score [Candan *et al.*, 2008]. Note that this is similar to the *rank first relevant* measure introduced in Section 11.4.5.

In other applications, the user may require that *all* results presented to her be good. In those cases, the *minimum F-measure* value would show whether the result set consists only of results matching the user's ground truth with very high scores.

11.5.3 Normalized Discounted Cumulative Gain

Unlike the foregoing measures, which consider either the results' scores or their ranks in assessing the retrieval effectiveness, the *discounted cumulative gain* measure considers both simultaneously. Let Q be a query and R_s be a set of results. As before, for each object $o_i \in R_s$, let $score_u(o_i)$ denote the relevance score associated the o_i by the user. In addition, for $1 \le r \le |R_s|$, let $oid[r]$ denote the index (or the ID) of the object at rank r in the result. Then, the *discounted cumulative gain* measure *at rank r* is defined as

$$DCG_{Q,D}(R_s, R_u, r) = score_u(o_{oid[1]}) + \sum_{i=2}^{|r|} \frac{score_u(o_{oid[i]})}{log_2 i},$$

or, alternatively as

$$DCG_{Q,D}(R_s, R_u, r) = \sum_{i=1}^{|r|} \frac{2^{score_u(o_{oid[i]})} - 1}{log_2(1 + i)}.$$

Intuitively, these measures associate a cumulative gain score for each position in the result; the gains, however, are discounted by the (logarithm of the) position, because gains at ranks closer to 1 are generally assumed to be more important than the gains at ranks that are larger.

The *normalized* discounted cumulative gain (NDCG) measure, on the other hand, associates an ideal discounted cumulative gain value, $idcg_i$ to each rank position, i, based on the score expected at that position. The *normalized discounted cumulative gain* of the result set is then computed as

$$NDCG_{Q,D}(R_s, R_u) = \frac{1}{|R_s|} \sum_{i=1}^{|R_s|} \frac{DCG_{Q,D}(R_s, R_u, i)}{idcg_i}.$$

Note that the normalized discounted cumulative gain measure is close to 1 only if the discounted cumulative gain at each position is close to the corresponding ideal (or expected) cumulative gain. In a sense, unlike the previous measure, the normalized discounted cumulative gain measure takes into direct account the expected score-rank relationship when assessing the retrieval effectiveness.

11.5.4 Normalized Modified Retrieval Rank

The *normalized modified retrieval rank* measure is defined as part of the MPEG-7 standard [MPEG-7xm] to measure the effectiveness of retrieval algorithms. Similar to R-precision, the *normalized modified retrieval rank (NMRR)* measure also picks a particular result size, k, to focus on; however, in this case, k is selected based on the number of ground truth objects available. In particular, given a query Q, NMRR examines the first $k = 4 \times |R_u|$ results, where R_u is the set of (ground truth) objects identified by the user for Q.[1] For any object $o_i \in R_s$, NMRR defines $rank(o_i)$ as follows:

$$rank(o_i) = \begin{cases} rank_s(o_i), & if\ o_i \in R_u \\ k+1, & otherwise. \end{cases}$$

Given this, the *modified retrieval rank (MRR)* for the query, Q, is defined as

$$MRR_{Q,D}(R_s, R_u) = \left(\sum_{o_i \in |R_u|} \frac{rank(o_i)}{|R_u|} \right) - 0.5 - \frac{|R_u|}{2}.$$

---

[1] When NMRRs of multiple queries are averaged to obtain a single average normalized modified retrieval rank, $k = min(4 \times |R_u|, 4 \times gtm)$, where gtm is the maximum number of ground truth objects for all queries.

This MRR measure has the property that, if the objects in R_u are the top retrievals in R_s, then its value is equal to 0. The *normalized modified retrieval rank* normalizes this measure in such a way that the scores are always in the range of $[0, 1]$:

$$NMRR_{Q,D}(R_s, R_u) = \frac{MRR_{Q,D}(R_s, R_u)}{k + 0.5 - \frac{|R_u|}{2}}.$$

Note that, unlike most other measures we presented in the chapter, the smaller the NMRR value, the better the effectiveness of retrieval.

11.6 NOVELTY AND COVERAGE

The effectiveness measures described so far treat retrieval as a one-shot process and assume that the user has no prior knowledge of the data in the database. In many cases (including when relevance feedback, which we discuss in detail in Chapter 12, is used), however, retrieval is an interactive process by which the user approaches the desired result set incrementally, one request at a time. Consequently, the effectiveness measures have to take into account how fast the user discovers the relevant objects and what she already knows about the database.

As before, given a query, Q, over the database, D, let us assume that the system returns the set, R_s, of results, whereas the set of correct matches to Q is R_u. In addition, let us assume that before the query is posed, the user already knows that $R'_u \subseteq R_u$ is relevant to her query. The *novelty* measure aims to assess how many new results the system is able to identify beyond the ones already known by the user before query processing:

$$novelty_{Q,D,R'_u}(R_s, R_u) = \frac{|R_s \cap (R_u - R'_u)|}{|R_s \cap R_u|}.$$

The *coverage* measure, on the other hand, aims to assess whether the system is able to identify at least those objects that are already known by the user to be relevant:

$$coverage_{Q,D,R'_u}(R_s, R_u) = \frac{|R_s \cap R'_u|}{|R'_u|}.$$

Note that, given a fixed number of results to be returned by the system, novelty and coverage are potential conflicting goals: if a result contains more unknown but relevant results, it may not be able to cover those that are already known by the user; conversely, if the system covers the results that are already known by the user (and its precision is already high), it may not be able to return any unknown but relevant results. In many cases, the most desirable situation is when an iterative process trades irrelevant results in one iteration with relevant and unknown results in the following one.

11.7 STATISTICAL SIGNIFICANCE OF ASSESSMENTS

As discussed in previous sections, virtually all effectiveness measures for assessing retrieval systems require collection of ground truth from a set of users (preferably for multiple queries) and comparing retrieval results against this ground truth. It is important, however, to recognize that given a query, different human assessors may have different relevance judgments. Similarly, some queries may be easier to process than the others. Thus, the number of assessors and the queries used for assessing a system need to be selected in such a way that the results will be statistically significant. This requires precise formulation of the *hypotheses* that are being tested for statistical significance and the use of appropriate statistical measures for verifying or refuting these hypotheses.

11.7.1 T-Test

Let us consider an assessor comparing two systems X and Y, where given a set of questions X has an average precision larger than Y. Before publishing these results, however, the assessor may want to check whether, based on the available assessment points, she can in fact state that the system X is better than Y in a *statistically significant manner*. In other words, the assessor needs to provide evidence that the observed difference in the average precision is not due to chance. To verify the statistical significance of her results, this assessor can formulate the (null) hypothesis

■ "there is no significant difference between systems X and Y,"

and see if she can refute this hypothesis based on the available experimental data. If she is able to refute this null hypothesis, then she can state, with confidence, that the average precision of X is larger than the average precision of Y in a statistically significant manner. Otherwise, she cannot make any statistically meaningful claims and may decide to run more experiments.

The statistical test that is commonly used to assess whether the means of the data sets are statistically different from each other or not is known as the *t-test*. The t-test assumes that the per-query scores are distributed normally (an assumption that itself may need to be verified) and each result is a random sample from a broader population (of queries that the user could have used if she ran the same experiment using a larger collection of queries). Based on these assumptions, the t-test determines whether two sets of samples (i.e., sets of results) are from the same population (i.e., there is no statistical difference between them) or from different populations (i.e., the results are statistically different from each other). In particular, the t-test judges the difference between the means of two sets of samples relative to the spread of their corresponding scores. A small difference between means will be hard to detect if the spread is high, whereas a large difference will be easy to detect if the variability (or the noise) in the observations is low. Thus, the t-test discounts for the size of the variances of the samples.

The t-test is applied differently if the observations in the two sets are *paired* (e.g., when the same set of queries are used for assessing the two systems) or *independent* (e.g., when the queries used to assess the two systems are possibly different from each other).

■ *Independent t-test:* Let us be given two sets, X and Y, with means μ_X and μ_Y and variances σ_X^2 and σ_Y^2, respectively. Let $|X|$ be M and $|Y|$ be N. The formula for the independent t-test[2] is

$$t = \frac{\mu_X - \mu_Y}{\sqrt{\frac{\sigma_X^2}{M} + \frac{\sigma_Y^2}{N}}}.$$

---

[2] Note the similarity of this formula to Fisher's discriminant ratio discussed in Section 9.1.1.

- *Paired t-test:* Let us be given two sets, X and Y, with means μ_X and μ_Y and variances σ_X^2 and σ_Y^2, respectively. Let also $|X| = |Y| = N$, and let the samples be paired. The formula for the paired t-test is

$$t = \frac{\mu_{X-Y} - \mu_0}{\sigma_{X-Y}/\sqrt{N}},$$

  where μ_{X-Y} and σ_{X-Y}^2 are mean and variance of the *differences of the pairs*, respectively, and μ_0 is the expected average difference between the means of X and Y; for example, if we are testing for equivalence of the means of X and Y, we set μ_0 to 0.

Once the t-value is computed, the significance of the difference between the groups can be assessed by first picking a level, $0 \le s \le 1$, of statistical significance (or, equally, a *risk level*, $\alpha = 1 - s$) and checking whether the number of data points in the samples is sufficient to match this level of statistical significance. A degree of freedom, df, parameter is used to keep track of the number of samples. The value of df is $M + N - 2$ for independent t-tests and $N - 1$ for paired t-tests. Statistical tables that list lower bounds on the α for given t and df values are commonly available. This lower bound (i.e., the probability that a variate takes a value greater than or equal to the observed value by chance) is also known as the p-value. Statistical significance of results depends on the selected risk level α. The common practice is to seek 95% significance (or aim for $\alpha \le 0.05$).

11.7.2 Wilcoxon Signed-Rank Test

A commonly used alternative to the *paired* t-test is the Wilcoxon signed-rank test. Unlike the t-test, the Wilcoxon signed-rank test [Wilcoxon, 1945] does not assume that the data are normally distributed; thus it can be applied in more general cases.

Let us be given two sets of values, X and Y, where $|X| = |Y| = N$, and let the samples be paired (values X_i and Y_i refer to the values corresponding to the related – paired – observations; e.g., the performance assessment for the same query for two different systems). Once again, let us assume that the evaluator formulates the (null) hypothesis

- "there is no significant difference between X and Y,"

and tries to see if she can refute this hypothesis based on the available experimental data. More specifically, she defines the set $Z_i = Y_i - X_i$ and tests whether the median of the values in Z is equal to 0.

Let R_i denote the rank of $|Z_i|$ among all absolute values (omitting those cases where $Z_i = 0$ and using average ranks where ties are observed), $|Z_1|$ through $|Z_N|$. The Wilcoxon signed rank parameter is defined as

$$W = \sum_{i=1}^{N} \phi_i R_i,$$

where $\phi_i = 1$ if $Z_i > 0$ and $\phi_i = 0$ otherwise. Let N' be the number of Z_i, where $Z_i \ne 0$. Assuming that the median difference really is zero, the probability that the random sampling would result in a median difference as far from zero as observed (i.e., the p-value) is found using a statistical table for values W and N'. If the p-value is small, then the difference from 0 is not by coincidence, and the null hypothesis can be rejected. If the p-value is large, on the other hand, there is no compelling evidence to conclude that there is a significant difference between X and Y.

The Mann-Whitney U test extends the Wilcoxon test for nonpaired independent sample sets with potentially different sample sizes.

11.7.3 Analysis of Variance (ANOVA) Test

The *analysis of variance (ANOVA) test* also examines whether the differences between means of different (normally distributed) groups are significant or not. This test, however, is useful when the evaluator is comparing the means of more than two sample sets. Consider, for example, a researcher who has collected performance results for a set of alternative retrieval algorithms and wants to check whether there is a statistically significant difference between the average behaviors of these algorithms before further investigating these differences. Instead of comparing the algorithms one pair at a time using the t-test, this evaluator can use the (so called one-way) ANOVA test to compare all of the algorithms, collectively, for statistically significant differences.

11.7.3.1 One-Way ANOVA

The (null) hypothesis the evaluator aims to reject in a one-way ANOVA test is

- "there is no significant difference between the means of the underlying populations."

Consider a set, $\{X_1, \ldots, X_k\}$, of experiments, where each experiment, X_i, consists of N_i observations. Let $X_{i,j}$ denote the value of the jth observation in the ith experiment (or system). One-way ANOVA treats $X_{i,j}$ as

$$X_{i,j} = \mu + \tau_i + \epsilon_{i,j},$$

where μ is the common mean for all observations, τ_i represents the difference from the mean in the ith experiment, and $\epsilon_{i,j}$ is the difference in the jth observation of the ith experiment. In one-way ANOVA, $\epsilon_{i,j}$ are assumed to be normally and independently distributed. On the other hand, the effects of individual experiments, that is, τ_i, either can be fixed such that $\sum \tau_i = 0$ or can themselves be normally distributed with a mean of 0.

The main idea in ANOVA is that if the null hypothesis is true, then the variance due to different experiments (or treatments) and due to different observations (or errors) should be approximately equal in magnitude. This is tested by computing two values, mean square treatments (MST) and mean square errors (MSE), where

$$MST = \frac{\sum_{i=1}^{k}(\mu_i - \mu)^2}{k - 1}$$

and

$$MSE = \frac{\sum_{i=1}^{k} \sum_{j=1}^{N_i}(X_{ij} - \mu_i)^2}{(\sum_{i}^{k} N_i) - k}.$$

If the null hypothesis is false, then we should be able to argue in a statistically significant manner that MST is larger than MSE. Thus, the so called F-value

$$F = \frac{MST}{MSE}$$

is used to test the equality of experiments. However, simply comparing the F-value against 1.0 is not sufficient to reject the null hypothesis in a statistically significant manner. Instead, the F-value obtained from the experiments needs to be compared against the minimum F-value sufficient to reject the null hypothesis for the user-provided risk level, α, and the degrees of freedom, $k - 1$ and $(\sum_i^k N_i) - k$. If the F-value obtained through the experiment is larger than this *critical* F-value, then there is sufficient evidence to reject the null hypothesis in a statistically significant manner (i.e., there is a significant difference in the experiments). Otherwise (i.e., the F-value is less than the *critical* F-value), there is not sufficient evidence to reject the null hypothesis claim.

The one-away ANOVA test between two samples and the t-test are essentially identical ($t^2 = F$). Other tests that are commonly used to assess differences across multiple sets of values include Friedman's analysis of variance by ranks test, the Cochran test for binary outcomes, and the Kruskal-Wallis one-way analysis of variance by ranks (which does not assume normality of the input groups).

11.7.3.2 Two-Way ANOVA
Unlike one-way ANOVA, where there is only one independent variable (different experiments) accounting for the variance, in two-way ANOVA there are two variables, also referred to as the factors, affecting the dependent variable being observed. Consequently, unlike the one-way ANOVA, where the only null hypothesis is

- "there is no significant difference between the means of the underlying populations,"

in two-way ANOVA, there are three different null hypotheses:

- "there is no significant difference between the means of the populations for the first factor,"
- "there is no significant difference between the means of the populations for the second factor," and
- "there is no significant interaction between the two factors."

To understand the meaning of these null hypotheses, let us organize all the observations in the form of the following table:

	$F_{2,1}$	$F_{2,2}$	...	$F_{2,n}$	AVG(1)
$F_{1,1}$	$o_{1,1}$	$o_{1,2}$	...	$o_{1,n}$	$avg_{1,1}$
$F_{1,2}$	$o_{2,1}$	$o_{2,2}$	...	$o_{2,n,}$	$avg_{1,2}$
...	...	...	...	...	...
$F_{1,m}$	$o_{m,1}$	$o_{m,2}$	...	$o_{m,n}$	$avg_{1,m}$
AVG(2)	$avg_{2,1}$	$avg_{2,2}$	...	$avg_{2,n}$	

where

- the row $F_{1,i}$ corresponds to the ith unique value of the first factor,
- the column $F_{2,j}$ corresponds to the jth value of the second factor, and
- the entry $o_{i,j}$ corresponds to the observed value given $F_{1,i}$ and $F_{2,j}$.

Given these observations, the first two null hypotheses in two-way ANOVA state the following:

- "there is no significant difference among $avg_{1,i}$ for different values of i (i.e., different values of the first factor have no impact on the observed results)" and
- "there is no significant difference among $avg_{2,j}$ for different values of j (i.e., different values of the second factor have no impact on the observed results)."

The final null hypothesis argues that the two factors are independent. In two-way ANOVA, there is a separate F-test for each of these three null hypotheses.

11.7.3.3 ANOVA with Repeated Measures

Let us revisit the notation we used when introducing the standard one-way ANOVA (in Section 11.7.3.1): we have a set $\{X_1, \ldots, X_k\}$ of experiments, where each experiment, X_i, consists of N_i observations; $X_{i,j}$ denotes the value of the jth observation in the ith experiment.

Now, let us consider the jth observations of two different experiments, X_i and X_l. In the standard one-way ANOVA, there is nothing that ties these two observations ($X_{i,j}$ and $X_{l,j}$) to each other. In some experiment designs, however, jth observations of two different experiments are paired to each other by some common factor, F_j (e.g., both corresponding to the evaluation of the system by the same jth user or both corresponding to the measurement on the same jth data set):

	X_1	X_2	$\ldots$	X_k	AVG
F_1	$X_{1,1}$	$X_{1,2}$	$\ldots$	$X_{1,k}$	avg_{F_1}
F_2	$X_{2,1}$	$X_{2,2}$	$\ldots$	$X_{2,k,}$	avg_{F_2}
$\ldots$	$\ldots$	$\ldots$	$\ldots$	$\ldots$	$\ldots$
F_m	$X_{m,1}$	$X_{m,2}$	$\ldots$	$X_{m,k}$	avg_{F_m}
AVG	avg_{X_1}	avg_{X_2}	$\ldots$	avg_{X_k}	

In this case, using standard one-way ANOVA to analyze the results would not be appropriate because this would fail to account for the correlation between the repeated measures for the same pairing factor. In contrast to one-way ANOVA (where there is only one null hypothesis), in ANOVA with repeated measures, one formulates and verifies (or rejects) multiple null hypotheses:

- "there is no significant difference among avg_{X_i} for different values of i (i.e., there is no difference between the experiments results),"
- "there is no significant difference among avg_{F_j} for different values of j (i.e., there is no difference between the pairing factor – e.g., users of the system)," and

- "there is no significant interaction between the experiments and the pairing factors."

11.7.4 Confidence Intervals and Two-Step Sampling

The number of experiment samples (assessors and queries) is important for the accuracy of the estimates obtained from the sampling data. Naturally, few samples will not provide a close approximation of the actual distribution. As more samples are collected (by adding assessors and/or queries) to the evaluation, the performance of the overall evaluation will likely improve because the samples will more closely reflect the actual distribution.

However, as more and more samples are collected (and, thus, the sample mean approaches the real mean of the data), the benefits of the additional samples will get smaller and smaller. Unfortunately, it is usually impossible to specify in advance how many samples will be sufficient for reaching conclusions that are statistically significant. In such cases, a *two-step* sampling technique can be used [Brewer and McCann, 1997]. In two-step sampling, an initial small set of samples is leveraged to predict how many additional samples will be needed to achieve the target level of statistical reliability.

Let X be a set of M samples, with mean μ_X and variance σ_X^2. Let also the t-value $t_{\alpha,df}$ denote the t-value corresponding to the risk level α and degree of freedom df. The *confidence interval* corresponding to the set X at the risk level α and degree of freedom $df_X = M - 1$ is defined as

$$\left[\mu_X - t_{\alpha/2,df_X}\left(\frac{\sigma_X}{\sqrt{M}}\right), \quad \mu_X + t_{\alpha/2,df_X}\left(\frac{\sigma_X}{\sqrt{M}}\right)\right].$$

Intuitively, given X, we can be certain that the true mean of X is within the foregoing confidence interval with $1 - \alpha$ certainty. Obviously, for a given standard deviation, an increase in the sample size will make the confidence interval tighter, leading to more accurate conclusions from the sample set. The two-step sampling process uses the mean and variance values obtained during the first sampling process to determine how many additional samples are needed to obtain a confidence interval with the required size. Once again, let X be a set of M values (initial samples) with mean μ_X and variance σ_X^2. Let us assume that the experimenter wants to be $1 - \alpha$ certain that the results are within $\pm c$ of the true mean. To achieve this, the experimenter needs a set, $Y(\supseteq X)$, of observations with $N(\geq M)$ samples such that

$$t_{\alpha,df_Y}\left(\frac{\sigma_Y}{\sqrt{N}}\right) \leq c, \quad \text{or equivalently} \quad N \geq \frac{t_{\alpha,df_Y}^2 \times \sigma_Y^2}{c^2}.$$

To solve for N using this inequality, we need the values of the t_{α,df_Y} and σ_Y parameters. However, these are unknown; thus, they need to be approximated based on the information collected during the initial, small sampling phase. In particular, the standard deviation, σ_X, of the initial set of samples can be used as an *approximation* of the unknown σ_Y. The value of t_{α,df_Y} can also be approximated using t_{α,df_X} (if $M \leq N$, t_{α,df_X} is likely to be larger than t_{α,df_Y}; therefore this will provide a relatively pessimistic estimate of the number of additional samples needed).

11.8 SUMMARY

Given that for various reasons multimedia retrieval is imperfect, it is important to assess the effectiveness of various candidate retrieval algorithms, before selecting a particular one for implementation. The choice of effectiveness measure for assessing retrieval algorithms depends on the characteristics of the application (e.g., are misses or false positives more important? Are we interested in a one-shot execution of the algorithm, or are we interested in a sequence of executions where the user discovers more about the data at each iteration?), as well as the availability and the type of the ground truth (e.g., is the ground truth available for assessment simply a set of relevant objects in the database identified by the users, or have the assessors provided more detail – such as ranks and/or relevance grades – for the assessed objects?). Moreover, because the comparison of candidate systems generally requires comparing the average behaviors of these systems, assessed based on multiple queries with ground truth provided by multiple users, it is important that these comparisons be made in a statistically significant manner. The statistical significance of the statements made about the systems being evaluated can be (and should be) validated using appropriate statistical tests.

12

User Relevance Feedback and Collaborative Filtering

As we discussed in Section 1.2, retrieval in multimedia databases is inherently imprecise and subjective. Consequently, multimedia query processing usually involves answering ill-posed questions: there may be multiple ways to interpret the query and data, and the appropriate query processing strategy may be user- and use context-dependent.

Imprecisions in retrieval can be due to many factors, including feature extraction algorithms that are imprecise, partial matching requirements in the query, and the imperfections in the underlying indexing, clustering, and classification algorithms. Moreover, in the absence of precise knowledge about the objects in the database, users' initial queries may be too vague. The set of results provided by the system in response to such imprecisely formulated queries, however, may contain hints to help users make their (initially vague) specifications iteratively more precise. Especially when users are not sufficiently informed about the data (or sometimes of their interests) to formulate a precise initial query, feedback-based data exploration plays a critical role in helping users find the relevant information.

Given a query (say, an image example provided for similarity search), which features of the query object are relevant (and how much so) for the user's query may not be known in advance. Consequently, it is almost impossible to expect that a multimedia database will be able to provide perfect answers to a user's query in its first attempt. Furthermore, most of the (large number of) candidate matches are only marginally relevant to the user's query and must be eliminated from consideration.

Thus, multimedia data management systems often complement the query processing engine with a user relevance feedback process that can help the user explore the result alternatives: (1) Given a query, using the available index structures, the system (2) identifies an initial set of candidate results; because the number of candidates may be large, the system presents a small number of samples to the user. (3) This initial set of samples and (4) the user's relevance/irrelevance inputs are used for (5) learning the user's interests (in terms of relevant features), and this information is provided as an input to the next cycle for (6) having the retrieval

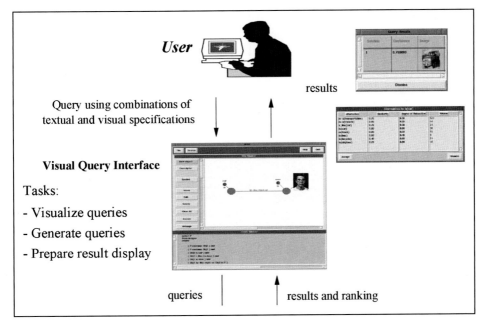

Figure 12.1. User relevance feedback process. See color plates section.

algorithm suitably update the query or the retrieval/ranking scheme (Figure 12.1). Steps 2–6 are then repeated until the user is satisfied with the results returned by the system. This process helps the system reduce the underlying imprecision and bridge the semantic gap between the system and the user. Cao *et al.* [2010] differentiate between hard and soft user feedback:

- After observing the initial set of results returned by the system, the user may identify certain aspects of the objects or features that are critical to her interests, but not included in the original query. These explicit assertions of additional requirements are referred to as the *hard feedback*. Often, hard feedback is suitable for expert users who know what they are looking for but do not know the data to formulate "accurate" queries in advance.
- When the user does not have well-defined query criteria in mind yet, she may want the system to rank the results in the next iteration according to the statements of desirability or undesirability she provides on the current results. This is referred to as *soft feedback*.

In many applications, the user is not an expert to formulate explicit assertions and, thus, the soft user feedback is most suited for improving retrieval effectiveness. In fact, when the database is large and dynamically growing, the user may not even be able to provide sufficient feedback to identify the relevant objects in the database. In such cases, *collaborative filtering*, where analysis of similarities between different users' preferences are used for predicting whether a given user will find a given object relevant or not, may be more appropriate. In this chapter, we first focus on the

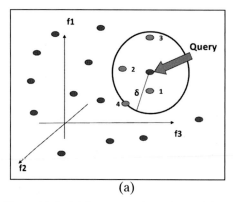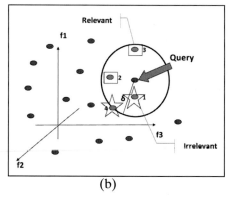

(a)   (b)

Figure 12.2. (a) A query and results and (b) the user's relevance feedback. See color plates section.

single user relevance feedback process. In Section 12.8, we then discuss techniques for implementing collaborative filtering-based recommendation systems.

12.1 CHALLENGES IN INTERPRETING THE USER FEEDBACK

Consider the basic relevance feedback process:

(i) User submits a query, Q (Figure 12.2(a))
(ii) System retrieves and ranks a set, S, of objects (Figure 12.2(a))
(iii) User selects sets of relevant, R, and irrelevant, I, objects from S or provides a preferred ranking (Figure 12.2(b))

Given the feedback, the system has to decide how to improve the retrieval results. In its simplest form, the relevance feedback process can be thought of as a "classification" task: Given a query, Q, and the corresponding set of results, S, the user marks some of the results in S as relevant and some others as irrelevant; with this knowledge, the system has to classify the rest of the database into *relevant* and *irrelevant* objects. In this process, the interpretation of the user's feedback by the system may be complicated by a multitude of factors:

- *Feature granularity:* There are a multitude of features that can be used to describe a given media object. Therefore, understanding which features are affecting the relevance/irrelevance of objects requires a *feature selection* process. Available features can be of different granularities (e.g., "color" feature versus "blue" feature). The knowledge "color is more important than shapes" will imply a different adaptation mechanism from "blue is more important than red"; thus, the system has to determine at what granularity the feedback has to be analyzed and processed.
- *Little evidence:* During relevance feedback, the number of objects labeled by the user is often very small. Moreover, most often users find it easier to express *relevance* than *irrelevance* (possibly because there are many more ways an object can be irrelevant to the query). Therefore, the relevance feedback process has to be performed with only a small set of relevance/irrelevance labels.

■ *Small and biased sample set:* Very often, the number of objects in S available for the user to provide relevance feedback does not exceed 10 or 20. This is simply because most users do not prefer to go over hundreds of objects to provide relevance feedback. Moreover, this small set of objects made available to the user are *biased* by the initial user query and the previous user feedback. Consequently, the objects in this set are related to the query and, thus, the set is not necessarily a good representative of the objects in the entire database.

Especially during negative feedback, when the user marks objects that are irrelevant to the query, this bias can be detrimental: because most objects marked irrelevant will contain query-related features, if the bias is not taken into account, the system may incorrectly identify that these query-related features are the causes of irrelevance.

■ *Early errors and the user drift:* Because the initial sample set and the set of objects labeled by the user tend to be small, the feedback process often requires multiple iterations. Assuming that the user always provides consistent feedback, this iterative process can help direct the user to the relevant objects in the database. However, the user's feedback over time may not be consistent. First of all, especially in earlier iterations, the user (who does not know the database well) may provide poorly selected feedback. Even if the user is able to provide good feedback, because of the small size of the initial sample set, the system may not be able to properly interpret this feedback. Moreover, during subsequent iterations, the user may change her mind about what is most relevant. Thus, the feedback process must be able to lower the contributions of old feedback statements relative to the newer ones.

12.2 ALTERNATIVE WAYS OF USING THE COLLECTED FEEDBACK IN QUERY PROCESSING

Once the user's relevance feedback is interpreted, this knowledge can be leveraged in query processing in various ways:

■ *Modification of the query:* Assuming that the user's initial query was poorly phrased, the feedback can be used to modify the user's query in a way that eliminates irrelevant results (Figure 12.3(a)).

■ *Modification of the range:* If the system recognizes that the initial query range is too tight (missing a lot of potentially relevant results) or too lax (returning a lot of false positives), the query range can be appropriately modified (Figure 12.3(b)).

■ *Modification of the distance/similarity function:* In the previous chapters, we have seen that for many types of media objects, different distance or similarity measures may be used for supporting retrieval. Relevance feedback may be used to identify whether the measure currently being used by the system for indexing the media objects is the most suitable one or not and for modifying the distance measure accordingly [Yu *et al.*, 2008] (Figure 12.3(c)).

■ *Modification of the feature importance/significance:* One of the ways subjectivity affects retrieval is through the importances users associate to the different features of the media objects. For example, in image retrieval, while one

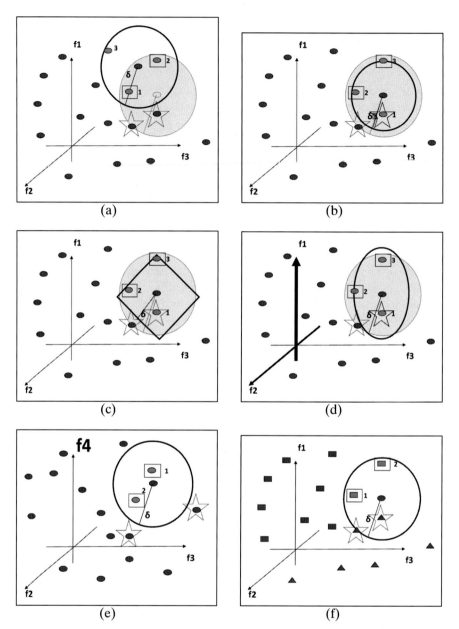

Figure 12.3. Alternative mechanisms for relevance feedback based adaptation: (a) Query rewriting, (b) query range modification, (c) modification of the distance function, (d) feature reweighting, (e) feature insertion/removal, and (f) reclassification (the numbers next to the matching data objects indicate their ranks in the result). See color plates section.

user may place more importance on color features, for another user the shape features might be more critical. The relevance feedback process may be used to learn the significance of different features for different users and queries (Figure 12.3(d)).

Note that feature importance may mean different things in different contexts: (a) the user might be interested in seeing more (or less) of one particular feature in the results (e.g., a user looking for images that contain a higher percentage of "red" pixels) or (b) the user might want the retrieval to be more precise about one of the features (e.g., a user wanting the retrieved objects to be more faithful to the shades and amount of red in the query).

Obviously, these two different semantics require different mechanisms for reflecting the feature significance learned through the relevance feedback process. The first interpretation can be handled by modifying the query itself as in the first item earlier. Depending on the feature model and the underlying query processing scheme, the second interpretation can be implemented by

- modifying the similarity/distance function in a way that amplifies differences along the more important features, or
- reweighting the combination function used for combining different feature scores (see Section 3.4.3).

■ *Modification of the feature set:* This is a special case of the previous item. Because of the dimensionality curse in retrieval (Section 4.1), most indexing algorithms use only a subset of the available features for indexing media objects. Based on the relevance feedback, the constituents of the feature set used for retrieval can be altered (by removing a less important feature and including a more important one, Figure 12.3(e)). In other words, in this approach, the feature significance learned through the relevance feedback process is used for supporting the feature selection process we had discussed earlier in Section 4.2.

■ *Reclustering/reclassification:* In most cases, media objects are preclustered (Chapter 8) or classified (Chapter 9) to prune the database and, thus, improve efficiency. The results of the relevance feedback process can be used to improve the underlying clustering or classification scheme (Figure 12.3(f)). Examples of such adaptive clustering schemes were discussed in Section 8.6.

Obviously, costs of these different feedback handling schemes are not equivalent. Changes in the distance measure, feature set and clustering/classification scheme (Figures 12.3(c),(e), and (f)) require changes in the organization of the data. Thus, these three alternatives cannot be applied for each query; because they involve the redesign of the database, they need to be applied only after sufficient feedback evidence is collected after many user queries. Modifications of the query, query range, or feature significance (Figures 12.3(a),(b), and (d)), on the other hand, do not involve redesign of the database. Thus, they are relatively cheaper to execute and can be applied for each new query.

It is also important to note that, given a query Q and the corresponding set of results S, user feedback can be used either to reprocess the (modified) query on the database to obtain a completely new set of results or to filter or rerank the existing result set, S. Because it involves processing of the whole query, the first alternative is costlier than the second one, which only involves reevaluation of the media objects already in the result set. However, because this second approach cannot help discover previously unseen relevant objects, it can only be applied when the initial result set, S, is thought to contain all the relevant results.

12.3 QUERY REWRITING IN VECTOR SPACE MODELS

One of the oldest, and arguably simplest (yet often quite effective), relevance feedback mechanisms in information retrieval is the *query rewriting* (or *query adjustment*) in the vector space (Figure 12.3(a)).

Let D be a data set consisting of media objects represented as vectors. Let $R \subseteq D$ be the set of all relevant items and $D - R$ be the set of nonrelevant items. Rocchio [1971] showed that, if R is known, under the dot product similarity measure, the optimal query can be described in terms of the elements in R:

$$\vec{q} = \frac{1}{|R|} \sum_{o_i \in R} \frac{\vec{o}_i}{|\vec{o}_i|} - \frac{1}{|D - R|} \sum_{o_i \in (D-R)} \frac{\vec{o}_i}{|\vec{o}_i|}.$$

The foregoing equation assumes that all the relevant objects are already known; however, it can also be generalized for supporting the relevance feedback process [Ide and Salton, 1971b]: Let $\vec{q}_j$ be the query at the start of the jth iteration of the relevance feedback process, R be the set of relevant objects, and I be the set of irrelevant objects; then, the query can be rewritten as follows:

$$\vec{q}_{j+1} = \alpha \vec{q}_j + \frac{\beta}{|R|} \sum_{o_i \in R} \frac{\vec{o}_i}{|\vec{o}_i|} - \frac{\gamma}{|I|} \sum_{o_i \in I} \frac{\vec{o}_i}{|\vec{o}_i|}.$$

Here, α, β, and γ are weights that control how much emphasis is placed on the query, positive (relevance) feedback, and negative (irrelevance) feedback, respectively. Note that, in general, appropriate values for α, β, and γ themselves can vary from user to user and query to query; thus, learning the appropriate values for a given user and query itself can be a challenge [Yu *et al.*, 1976].

When $\alpha = \beta = \gamma = 1$, this is often referred to as the standard *Rocchio* scheme. A special case of the general formulation, where the set R contains all relevant items retrieved in the previous iterations, whereas I contains only the top-most nonrelevant items, is referred to as the *Ide Dec-Hi* scheme [Ide and Salton, 1971a].

12.4 RELEVANCE FEEDBACK IN PROBABILISTIC MODELS

An alternative formulation of the relevance feedback problem can be stated as follows [Robertson and Jones, 1976; Robertson and Sparck Jones, 1988; van Rijsbergen, 1979]: Let D be a set of objects in the database, R be the set of objects known to be relevant, and I be the set of objects known to be irrelevant; then the goal of the relevance feedback process is to estimate the probability $p(rel|o_i)$; that is, the probability that an object $o_i \in D$ is relevant to the user query. If this probability is correctly estimated, the only thing the system has to do is to order the objects in the database such that

$$p(rel|o_i) > p(rel|o_j) \quad \leftrightarrow \quad rank(o_i) < rank(o_j);$$

in other words, those objects that are predicted to be more relevant will be ranked closer to top, whereas objects that are not as likely to be relevant will have worse ranks.

The probability, $p(rel|o_i)$, is often rewritten in terms of $p(o_i|rel)$ and $p(o_i|\overline{rel})$ (i.e., the probabilities that a relevant or nonrelevant item, respectively, looks like o_i) using the Bayesian theorem, which relates the conditional and marginal probabilities of the available observations (Section 3.5.3):

$$p(rel|o_i) = \frac{p(o_i|rel)p(rel)}{p(o_i)} = \frac{p(o_i|rel)p(rel)}{p(o_i|rel)p(rel) + p(o_i|\overline{rel})p(\overline{rel})},$$

where $p(rel)$ is the probability that a randomly picked object in D is relevant and $p(\overline{rel})$ is the probability that the object is irrelevant. Because $p(rel)$ and $p(\overline{rel})$ are not always known in advance, even if one can compute $p(o_i|rel)$ and $p(o_i|\overline{rel})$, it may not be possible to directly arrive at $p(rel|o_i)$. However, using the foregoing Bayesian formulation, the inequality $p(rel|o_i) > p(rel|o_j)$ can first be rewritten as

$$\frac{p(o_i|rel)p(rel)}{p(o_i|rel)p(rel) + p(o_i|\overline{rel})p(\overline{rel})} > \frac{p(o_j|rel)p(rel)}{p(o_j|rel)p(rel) + p(o_j|\overline{rel})p(\overline{rel})}$$

and then can be further simplified as

$$\frac{p(o_i|rel)}{p(o_i|\overline{rel})} > \frac{p(o_j|rel)}{p(o_j|\overline{rel})}.$$

In other words, the larger the ratio $\frac{p(o_i|rel)}{p(o_i|\overline{rel})}$ is, the better the rank of the object o_i must be. The relevance feedback task, therefore, is reduced to the problem of estimating $p(o_i|rel)$ and $p(o_i|\overline{rel})$ for each object, o_i.

12.4.1 Estimating $p(o_i|rel)$ and $p(o_i|\overline{rel})$

Once again, let D be the set of objects in the database, R be the set of objects known to be relevant, and I be the set of objects known to be irrelevant. Estimating $p(o_i|rel)$ and $p(o_i|\overline{rel})$ using these requires the analysis of distributions (in D, R, and I) of the features that constitute the object o_i:

- If a feature dominant in R is also dominant in o_i, then $p(o_i|rel)$ is likely to be high.
- If a feature dominant in R is not dominant in o_i, then $p(o_i|rel)$ is likely to be low.
- If a feature dominant in I is also dominant in o_i, then $p(o_i|rel)$ is likely to be low.
- If a feature dominant in I is not dominant in o_i, then $p(o_i|rel)$ has greater chance of being high.

Similar observations can also be used to relate $p(o_i|\overline{rel})$ to the distributions of the features in o_i, R, and I. Using these to compute $p(o_i|rel)$ and $p(o_i|\overline{rel})$, however, requires an appropriate object model.[1]

---

[1] Note that probabilistic relevance feedback is especially suitable for systems with Boolean features; that is, a given feature either exists in the media object or does not. If the feature model is not Boolean, then when computing probabilities, a threshold is often used to decide whether a given feature is sufficiently dominant in a given object or not.

Let us model each object, o_i, in the form of a binary vector, $\vec{o}_i$, where if feature f_j is dominant in o_i, $\vec{o}_i[j] = 1$, and otherwise, $\vec{o}_i[j] = 0$. If features are independently distributed[2] in the data set, then we can write

$$p(o_i|rel) = \left(\prod_{\vec{o}_i[j]=1} p(f_j = 1 \mid rel) \right) \left(\prod_{\vec{o}_i[j]=0} p(f_j = 0 \mid rel) \right).$$

Similarly,

$$p(o_i|\overline{rel}) = \left(\prod_{\vec{o}_i[j]=1} p(f_j = 1 \mid \overline{rel}) \right) \left(\prod_{\vec{o}_i[j]=0} p(f_j = 0 \mid \overline{rel}) \right).$$

Therefore, the problem reduces to estimating the terms $p(f_j = 1 \mid rel)$, $p(f_j = 0 \mid rel)$, $p(f_j = 1 \mid \overline{rel})$, and $p(f_j = 0 \mid \overline{rel})$.

12.4.2 Estimating the Probabilities of Feature Occurrences in Relevant and Nonrelevant Objects

As before, let D be a set of objects in the database. Let $\vec{q}$ be the vector representation of the user query. Let R be the set of objects known to be relevant and I be the set of objects known to be irrelevant. Also, let f_j be an object feature. If the distribution of f_j in R is similar to the distribution of f_j in all relevant documents in D, then we can simply write

$$p(f_j = 1 \mid rel) = p(f_j = 1 \mid R) = \frac{|\{o_i \| (o_i \in R) \wedge (\vec{o}_i[j] = 1)\}|}{|R|}.$$

This is often assumed to be the case when f_j is not dominant in the query. In contrast, when f_j is dominant in the query, then f_j is more likely to occur in the result set S than it is likely to occur in the database, D. Consequently, the distribution of f_j in R (which is the set of result objects that are marked relevant by the user) is *biased* and dissimilar to the distribution of f_j in D.

When this is the case (i.e., f_j is dominant in the query), then we first need to eliminate the bias on the feature by considering (instead of q) the query $q_{(-j)}$, where $\forall f_k \neq f_j \ \vec{q}_{(-j)}[k] = \vec{q}[k]$ and $\vec{q}_{(-j)}[j] = 0$. Let $S_{(-j)}$ be the set of answers to this modified query. Then we can write

$$p(f_j = 1 \mid rel) = \frac{|\{o_i \| (o_i \in S_{(-j)} \cap R) \wedge (\vec{o}_i[j] = 1)\}|}{|S_{(-j)} \cap R|}.$$

The other terms, $p(f_j = 0 \mid rel)$, $p(f_j = 1 \mid \overline{rel})$, and $p(f_j = 0 \mid \overline{rel})$, are also similarly computed using R and I.

When relevance information is not available or is insufficient to assess a given feature, then $p(f_j = 1 \mid rel)$ and $p(f_j = 0 \mid rel)$ are replaced by constants, often 0.5. The two probabilities, $p(f_j = 1 \mid \overline{rel})$, and $p(f_j = 0 \mid \overline{rel})$, on the other hand, are often approximated using the distribution of f_j in the whole data set, D [Croft and Harper, 1979; Salton and Buckley, 1990]. Also, when R is available but I is not

---

[2] See Section 9.6.2 for algorithms for relaxing the independence assumption when the features are not independently distributed.

(i.e., when the user provides only positive relevance feedback), I is often approximated by $D - R$.

12.4.3 Query Adjustment

As a corollary of the observation

$$\left(\frac{p(o_i|rel)}{p(o_i|\overline{rel})} > \frac{p(o_j|rel)}{p(o_j|\overline{rel})} \right) \leftrightarrow rank(o_i) < rank(o_j),$$

we can argue that the best query, q_{opt}, that the system can formulate based on user feedback should be such that

$$\left(\frac{p(o_i|rel)}{p(o_i|\overline{rel})} > \frac{p(o_j|rel)}{p(o_j|\overline{rel})} \right) \leftrightarrow sim(q_{opt}, o_i) > sim(q_{opt}, o_j).$$

Relying on the observations that

- if a feature dominant in R is also dominant in o_i, then $p(o_i|rel)$ is likely to be high,
- if a feature not dominant in I is dominant in o_i, then $p(o_i|rel)$ has a higher chance of being high,
- if a feature not dominant in R is dominant in o_i, then $p(o_i|\overline{rel})$ has a higher chance of being high, and
- if a feature dominant in I is also dominant in o_i, then $p(o_i|\overline{rel})$ is likely to be high,

the term on the right-hand side can be further expanded and rewritten as

$$\prod_{f_k} \left(\vec{o}_i[k] \frac{p(f_k|R)(1 - p(f_k|I))}{p(f_k|I)(1 - p(f_k|R))} \right) > \prod_{f_k} \left(\vec{o}_j[k] \frac{p(f_k|R)(1 - p(f_k|I))}{p(f_k|I)(1 - p(f_k|R))} \right).$$

If we take the logarithm of both sides, we have[3]

$$sim(q_{opt}, o_i) \sim log \left(\prod_{f_k} \left(\vec{o}_i[k] \frac{p(f_k|R)(1 - p(f_k|I))}{p(f_k|I)(1 - p(f_k|R))} \right) \right),$$

and, thus, assuming the use of the dot product similarity function, we obtain

$$q_{opt} \sim \left\langle log \left(\frac{p(f_1|R)(1 - p(f_1|I))}{p(f_1|I)(1 - p(f_1|R))} \right), \ log \left(\frac{p(f_2|R)(1 - p(f_2|I))}{p(f_2|I)(1 - p(f_2|R))} \right), \ldots \right\rangle.$$

It has indeed been shown empirically that

$$\vec{q}_{opt}[k] = log \left(\frac{p(f_k|R)(1 - p(f_k|I))}{p(f_k|I)(1 - p(f_k|R))} \right)$$

performs well in capturing the significance of the features; thus, it is often used as the feedback-adjusted term weight in modified queries [Robertson and Jones, 1976; Ruthven and Lalmas, 2003; Salton and Buckley, 1990]. Robertson [1990], on the other hand, suggests that, although the preceding term can indeed be used for query

---

[3] Here, we are using $p(f|X)$ as a shorthand for $p(f = 1|X)$.

adjustment, for feature significance ranking, the term

$$log\left(\frac{p(f_k|R)(1-p(f_k|I))}{p(f_k|I)(1-p(f_k|R))}\right) \times (p(f_k|rel) - p(f_k|\overline{rel}))$$

is more suitable. Note that, when $I = D - R$, this term can be computed as

$$log\left(\frac{r_k(|D-R|-(d_k-r_k))}{(d_k-r_k)(|R|-r_k)}\right) \times \left|\frac{r_k}{|R|} - \frac{d_k - r_k}{|D-R|}\right|,$$

where r_k is the number of objects in R such that f_k exists and d_k is the number of objects in D with f_k.

12.4.4 Dealing with the Boundary Cases

Let us consider the simplified formulation

$$\vec{q}'[k] = log\left(\frac{r_k(|D-R|-(d_k-r_k))}{(d_k-r_k)(|R|-r_k)}\right)$$

for the weight of the feature f_k in the adjusted query, q'. This formula can be problematic for small values of $|R|$ and r_k. In the extreme case, where

- the number of objects marked as relevant by the user is 1 (i.e., $|R| = 1$) and
- the feature f_k does not occur or is not sufficiently dominant in this single relevant object (i.e., $r_k = 0$),

the term becomes $log(0) = -\infty$. To prevent this, $p(f_k|R)$ and $p(f_k|I)$ are often approximated as

$$p(f_k|R) = \frac{r_k + 0.5}{|R| + 1} \quad \text{and} \quad p(f_k|I) = \frac{(d_k - r_k) + 0.5}{|D-R| + 1},$$

instead of $\frac{r_k}{|R|}$ and $\frac{d_k-r_k}{|D-R|}$, respectively. The fixed correction (0.5), however, is not necessarily effective in all cases. Based on the observation that when $|R| = 0$ (and hence $r_k = 0$) the best estimate for $p(f_k|R)$ is the probability of the feature f_k in the whole database, Salton and Buckley [1990] suggest the use of the following variation:

$$p(f_k|R) = \frac{r_k + \frac{d_k}{|D|}}{|R| + 1} \quad \text{and} \quad p(f_k|I) = \frac{(d_k - r_k) + \frac{d_k}{|D|}}{|D-R| + 1}.$$

12.5 RELEVANCE FEEDBACK IN PROBABILISTIC LANGUAGE MODELING

Remember from Section 3.5.3.2 that language modeling is a special case of the Bayesian probabilistic models often applied in text retrieval [Lafferty and Zhai, 2001; Ponte and Croft, 1998]. Lafferty and Zhai [2001] (as was also discussed in detail in Section 3.5.3.3), for example, reduce the problem of estimating the relevance of object o_i to the problem of estimating probabilistic query and object models, θ_q and θ_o, where

- the query model encodes user's preferences as well as the context in which the query is formulated, and
- the object model encodes information about the document and the data source.

Using these models, Lafferty and Zhai [2001] seek to find a set, R, of result objects that minimizes the amount of imprecision, $\mathcal{I} = L(R, \theta_q \cup \theta_o)$, where L is an information loss function measuring the distance between the returned objects and the theoretically optimal objects given the query and object models. For example, the KL-distance (Section 3.1.3) can be used to measure the *relative entropy* between the query and the document probability distributions [Zhai and Lafferty, 2001]. Note that user preferences (which are often represented in the form of $P(f|u)$, where u is a user and f is a feature) are inherently captured by the query model, θ_q. Therefore, this and other language models are very suitable for the application of probabilistic relevance feedback techniques.

12.5.1 Feedback using a Generative Model

Zhai and Lafferty [2001] rewrite the query model θ_q as

$$\theta'_q = (1 - \alpha)\theta_q + \alpha\theta_+,$$

where θ_q is the query model based on the original assumptions, θ_+ is the feedback model, and α is a mixture parameter that controls the impact of feedback. θ_+ is estimated assuming that the (positive) feedback objects are generated by a probabilistic model, $p(F_+|\theta)$, which generates each feature in the set, F_+, of feedback objects independently; in other words,

$$p(F_+|\theta) = \prod_{o_j \in D} \prod_{f_i \in o_j} p(f_i|\theta)^{count(f_i, o_j)},$$

where $count(f_i, o_j)$ is the amount of the feature f_i in object o_j and $p(f_i|\theta)$ is the probability of the feature f_i given the user feedback. The probability $p(f_i|\theta)$ is often smoothed using a background collection language model $p(f_i|D)$ to reduce the impact of the non-critical background content in the objects marked as feedback by the user:

$$p(F_+|\theta) = \prod_{o_j \in D} \prod_{f_i \in o_j} ((1 - \lambda)p(f_i|\theta) + \lambda p(f_i|D))^{count(f_i, o_j)}.$$

Intuitively the query model will be based on features that are common in the feedback objects, but not very common according to the collection language model. The mixture parameter, λ, can be estimated or set empirically. The feedback model θ_+ is estimated by selecting the appropriate θ based on the maximum likelihood criterion using an expectation maximization process (EM, see Section 9.7.4.3).

12.5.2 Feedback using Divergence Minimization

Zhai and Lafferty [2001] also propose an alternative feedback scheme that, unlike the preceding method (which assumes that the feedback objects are generated by a mixture of feedback and background models and estimates the underlying feedback model using the maximum likelihood criterion), chooses the query model that has the smallest average KL-distance from the smoothed feature distribution of the feedback objects:

$$\Delta_{KL,avg}(\theta, F_+) = \frac{1}{|F_+|} \sum_{o_j \in D} \Delta_{KL}(\theta, \theta_{o_j}),$$

where θ_{o_j} is the feature distribution in object o_j and Δ_{KL} is the KL-distance function (Section 3.1.3). Once again, this is smoothed by incorporating the background model in a way that reduces the impact of the background content:

$$\Delta_{KL,smooth}(\theta, F_+) = \frac{1}{|F_+|} \sum_{o_j \in D} \Delta_{KL}(\theta, \theta_{o_j}) - \lambda \Delta_{KL}(\theta, p(.|D)),$$

where $0 \leq \lambda < 1$ is a mixture parameter and $p(.|D)$ is the collection language model. Given this θ_+ is estimated by minimizing the KL-distance:

$$\theta_+ = \underset{\theta}{argmin} \, \Delta_{KL,smooth}(\theta, F_+).$$

12.5.3 Negative Feedback

Note that both of the foregoing schemes use only positive feedback in adapting the query model based on the user feedback. Consequently, they cannot leverage the user's irrelevance feedback. Wang et al. [2007] propose an extension to the language modeling approach to deal with negative feedback. In particular, similarly to the Rocchio scheme discussed in Section 12.3, Wang et al. [2007] first estimate a negative topic model based on the negative example documents and then penalizes objects whose models are similar to the negative topic model. Given a set, F_-, of negative feedback objects, one possible way to achieve this is to create a negative feedback model, θ_-, through an approach similar to the ones discussed in the previous two subsections (but using F_- instead of F_+).

One complication that needs to be taken into account, however, is the bias in the sample set used for negative feedback: as discussed in Section 12.1, most objects marked irrelevant by the user will contain query-related features; hence, if this bias is not corrected, the system may incorrectly identify that these features cause the irrelevance. Wang et al. [2007] eliminate the query features from the negative model by setting their probabilities to zero.

Another complication that is specific to negative feedback is that, whereas usually there is one (or only a few) reasons why an object might be relevant, there are often a multitude of reasons why it might be irrelevant; thus, while a single feedback model is often sufficient for capturing the positive feedback, multiple models might be needed to capture the negative feedback. Wang et al. [2007] handle this by learning subtopics from the objects marked as negative feedback using probabilistic latent semantic indexing (Section 4.4.2) and using each individual subtopic to learn a different negative model. Then, given this set of negative models, the minimum of the corresponding KL distances is used as the combined divergence. Wang *et al.* [2008] show that modeling multiple negative models is more effective than a single negative model; the authors also argue that (especially when considering negative feedback) language model–based approaches are more effective than vector space model–based approaches.

12.6 PSEUDORELEVANCE FEEDBACK

Several researchers [Buckley *et al.*, 1995; Croft and Harper, 1997; Mitra *et al.*, 1998] suggested that one can leverage relevance feedback techniques even when user relevance feedback is not available. This pseudo-relevance feedback is performed by picking top-ranked matches to the user query as being relevant and using the features of these in a positive feedback cycle (Figure 12.4). Although experiments showed that pseudo-relevance feedback can be useful in improving the relevance of the results to the user's query, there is the risk that (especially when the initial query results are very poor) the pseudo-relevance feedback process will actually hurt the results more than it helps. Buckland and Gey [1994] propose an alternative two-stage retrieval process where first a high-recall strategy is used to retrieve results to the user's query and, then, a high-precision strategy is used to pick the best answers within this initial result set. Essentially, the first (high-recall) stage helps remove noise (without by mistake removing any of the real results); the second (high-precision) stage, then, focuses on getting a more complete and precise set of results.

12.7 FEEDBACK DECAY

As discussed in Section 12.1, a particular challenge in relevance feedback is the drift in the user's feedback across multiple iterations: in general, there is no guarantee that the user's feedback across multiple iterations will be consistent. Such inconsistencies may be due to the user focusing on different aspects of the query or simply changing her mind about what is relevant to her as she explores the available media objects. To prevent old feedback from unnecessarily constraining the exploration and to help the feedback process focus on the most recent feedback statements, *ostensive relevance* techniques lower the contributions of old feedback statements relative to the newer ones [Campbell, 2000a, 1995; Ruthven *et al.*, 2002]. This is also referred to as *feedback decay* or *aging of user feedback*.

The decay or aging factor can be inserted into the feedback models in different ways. Campbell [2000b], for example, incorporates decay into the probabilistic model by changing the definitions of $p(f_j = 1 \mid rel)$, $p(f_j = 0 \mid rel)$, $p(f_j = 1 \mid \overline{rel})$, and $p(f_j = 0 \mid \overline{rel})$ in a way that accounts for feedback aging. Remember from Section 12.4.2 that, given a feature f_j (if the distribution of f_j in R is similar to the distribution of f_j in all relevant documents in D), we can write

$$p(f_j = 1 \mid rel) = p(f_j = 1 \mid R) = \frac{|\{o_i \| (o_i \in R) \wedge (\vec{o}_i[j] = 1)\}|}{|R|}.$$

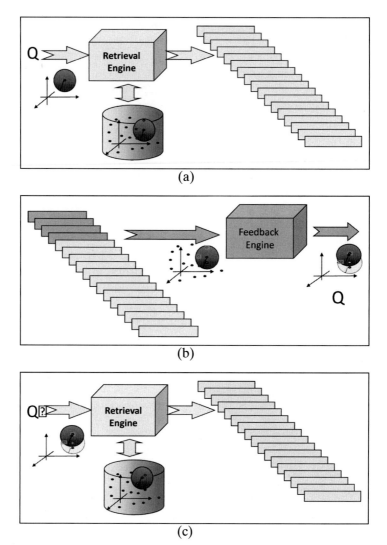

Figure 12.4. Psudo-feedback process. (a) The user's initial query is used to receive a set of results; (b) the top-most few results are used as positive feedback to obtain a new query; and (c) this new query is used to get a new set of results.

To account for feedback aging, we can rewrite the foregoing equation as

$$p(f_j = 1 \mid rel) = \frac{\sum_{o_i \in R} contrib(o_i) \times x_{i,j}}{\sum_{o_i \in R} contrib(o_i)},$$

where

- $x_{i,j} = 1$ if o_i contains feature f_j and $x_{i,j} = 0$ otherwise; and
- $contrib(o_i) \in [0, 1]$ is the probability that o_i can still be accounted in the set, R, of relevant objects (given the chosen decay behavior).

For example, when the user feedback does not decay, $contrib(o_i)$ is simply 1 for all objects in R and 0 otherwise. A contribution function, $contrib(o_i) = 2^{-age(o_i)}$, on the other hand, will quickly reduce the contribution of objects in R that have been marked as relevant in the past.

The other terms, $p(f_j = 0 \mid rel)$, $p(f_j = 1 \mid \overline{rel})$, and $p(f_j = 0 \mid \overline{rel})$, are also similarly aged.

12.8 COLLABORATIVE FILTERING

As we have briefly discussed in Section 6.3.3, *collaborative filtering* [Brand, 2005; Goldberg *et al.*, 1992; Sarwar *et al.*, 2000; Zunjarwad *et al.*, 2007] is a recommendation generation approach where the analysis of similarities between objects and/or individuals' preferences is used for predicting whether a user will prefer to see/purchase a given media object or not. As such, collaborative filtering can be thought of as an indirect and transparent mechanism for relevance feedback: instead of the user providing explicit feedback, similar users' past behaviors are used as an implicit feedback to improve retrieval.

As formalized earlier in Section 6.3.3, in collaborative filtering analysis, the input is a bipartite graph, $G(V_u, V_o, E)$, where

- V_u is a set of $N (= |V_u|)$ individuals in the system.
- V_o is the set of $M (= |V_o|)$ objects in the data collection.
- E is the set of edges between users in V_u and objects in V_o denoting past access/purchase actions or ratings provided by the users. In other words, the edge $\langle u_i, o_j \rangle \in E$ indicates that the user u_i declared his preference for object o_j through some action, such as purchasing the object o_j. Moreover, each edge $\langle u_i, o_j \rangle \in E$ may have an associated vote or rating label, $vote_{i,j}$ describing the degree of preference expressed by the user for this object.

This graph can alternatively be represented in the form of an $N \times M$ user-object voting matrix, $\mathcal{V}$, where

- if $\langle u_i, o_j \rangle \in E$, then $\mathcal{V}[i, j] = vote_{i,j}$ and takes values within the domain of possible user ratings, and
- if $\langle u_i, o_j \rangle \notin E$, then $\mathcal{V}[i, j] = vote_{i,j} = \perp$.

Note that, in addition to this graph/matrix that provides information about which users prefer/access which objects, we can also have additional information about users and objects to support more informed recommendations:

- Each user $u_i \in V_u$ may be associated with a vector $\vec{u}_i$ denoting any metadata (e.g., age, profession) known about the user u_i.
- Each object $o_j \in V_o$ may be associated with a vector $\vec{o}_j$ describing the content and metadata (e.g., title, genre, tags) of the object o_j.

Relying on the assumption that similar users will prefer similar objects, collaborative filtering systems leverage the graph $G(V_u, V_o, E)$ and the available user and object metadata vectors to generate recommendations.

Collaborative Filtering as a Classification Task

The collaborative filtering process can be thought of as a classification problem where, given a set of preference observations (the edges in E), the system is aiming to associate a recommendation label or rating to each of the remaining user-object pairs (i.e., $(V_u \times V_o) - E$). For example, Breese *et al.* [1998] present a decision tree–based algorithm to predict scores for unrated movies in a movie database.

Collaborative Filtering as a Top-k Retrieval Task

Alternatively, given a user u_i and a query, q, collaborative filtering can be thought of as a top-k object retrieval process, where the best k objects are selected within the context of query q using the similarities of the users (in terms of metadata and prior histories) and the objects they access (again in terms of metadata/content and access histories). Given a user u_i, let $out(u_i)$ denote the set of objects rated by/accessed by u_i (i.e., destinations of outgoing edges from u_i); similarly, given an object o_j, let $in(o_j)$ denote the set of users who have accessed/rated o_j (i.e., sources of incoming edges to o_j). Here,

- The similarity of two users, u_i and u_k, may be quantified using the similarity of the metadata vectors, $\vec{u}_i$ and $\vec{u}_k$, as well as the similarity of the users' object preferences (captured by the overlap between the sets, $out(u_i)$ and $out(u_k)$, of outgoing edges in the graph).
- The similarity of two objects, o_j and o_l, may be measured through the similarity of their content/metadata vectors, $\vec{o}_j$ and $\vec{o}_l$, as well as the similarity of the sets of users who have accessed these objects (i.e., $in(o_j)$ and $in(o_l)$, of incoming edges in E).

Types of Collaborative Filtering Schemes

Breese *et al.* [1998] partition collaborating filtering algorithms into two broad categories: in *memory-based* schemes the user/object database is directly used to make predictions; in *model-based* approaches, on the other hand, first relevant models (such as properties of a preferred genre or features of a user group interested on a particular topic) are learned and these models are used to support predictions.

Alternatively, collaborative filtering schemes can be classified into two categories based on whether object similarities are used in the collaborative filtering process or not. If only the user metadata vectors are used to evaluate similarities between the users, these are called *user-based collaborative filtering* schemes. When the user-object graph or the corresponding user-object matrix is used for generating recommendations, these are referred to as *item-based* approaches to collaborative filtering [Deshpande and Karypis, 2004; Sarwar *et al.*, 2001]. Because the relationships between objects are relatively static (whereas relationships between the users can evolve and be highly context-sensitive), in order to reduce the complexity of the problem, item-based algorithms first focus on the relationships between objects and then generate recommendations by finding items that are similar to other items the user has liked.

Mooney and Roy [2000], for example, take the item-based approach to the extreme and provide recommendations solely based on contents of the objects, rather than attempting to leverage other users' preferences. Although such content-based approaches have the advantage of being able to recommend previously unrated objects and to also provide explanations (in terms of object features) for their suggested ratings, in most recommendation systems (e.g., [Basu *et al.*, 1998]), object information is used to complement the user preferences, rather than being treated as the only information source to support recommendations.

12.8.1 Memory-Based Algorithms

In memory-based algorithms, the user-object graph, $G(V_u, V_o, E)$, or the (equivalent) voting matrix, V, is used directly for estimating the rating of a particular item for a given user who has not already rated that item, based on the ratings of other users on the same or similar objects.

12.8.1.1 Voting-Based CF

Breese *et al.* [1998] propose a voting-based approach to collaborative filtering. In this scheme, the user-object database is represented as a voting matrix, V, where the entry $V[i, j]$ consists of the vote of user u_i for object o_j (or "$\perp$" if there is no voting information). Given a user u_i and object o_j, where $V[i, j] = \perp$, the predicted vote for user the u_i on object o_j is computed as

$$vote_{avg,i} + \sum_{l=1}^{n}(\kappa \times sim(i, l))(vote_{l,j} - vote_{avg,l}),$$

where

- $vote_{avg,i}$ is the average vote for user u_i for all objects in the database,
- $sim(i, l)$ is the similarity between users u_i and u_l, and
- κ is a normalizer such that the absolute values of user similarities sum up to unity,

As mentioned previously, $sim(i, l)$ can be computed either based on available metadata about the objects or by leveraging the user-object database. For example, Resnick *et al.* [1994] use the Pearson correlation coefficient of votes (see Section 3.5.1.2) to measure the similarity between the users (who have at least one matching item). However, because in general the number of objects that are voted by both users u_i and u_l can be very low, Breese *et al.* [1998] propose a default voting strategy, where some number of additional nonvoted items are treated as being voted by both users with a neutral or slightly negative vote. Intuitively, this has the effect of assuming that there are some additional unspecified items on which neither of the users has voted, but on which they would nonetheless agree.

Alternatively, Breese *et al.* [1998] propose to use the cosine similarity between the voting vectors of the users to measure $sim(i, l)$. As in the case of inverse document frequency mechanism (see Section 4.2) used in text databases for reducing the weights of commonly used terms, Breese *et al.* [1998] also suggest that reducing the weights of the universally liked items (which are not as informative in capturing similarity as less commonly liked items) can improve the recommendation qualities. In particular, the term $log\frac{N}{N_j}$, where N is the total number of users of the system and N_j is the number of users who have voted for object o_j, is used to adjust the ratings.

Note that, in this scheme, if everyone has voted for object o_j, then the contribution of o_j to the user similarity score is 0.

12.8.1.2 Nearest Neighbor–Based CF

Hill *et al.* [1995] look for correlations between the target user's ratings and ratings of known users. However, to reduce the number of correlations to be computed, instead of using the entire user base for each prediction, Hill *et al.* [1995] use only a small random subsample of the users. Among these the most similar users are found and are used as variables in a multiple-regression equation to predict the new user's ratings. Such algorithms where only the few most similar users are used for prediction are commonly referred to as "nearest neighbor"–based collaborating filtering schemes.

One difficulty with the memory-based approaches is that, in general, only very few truly similar users will exist in the system to support predictions. Recognizing that simple correlation or nearest neighbor–based approaches will not be able to overcome this *data sparsity* problem, Aggarwal *et al.* [1999] differentiate between the concepts of *horting* (i.e., users being comparable in terms of their rating behavior) and *predictability* (i.e., a pair of users whose ratings are genuinely close or opposite – but nevertheless predictive). Given a user u_i, let $out(u_i)$ denote the set of objects rated by/accessed by u_i (i.e., destinations of outgoing edges from u_i); similarly, given an object o_j, let $in(o_j)$ denote the set of users who have accessed/rated o_j (i.e., sources of incoming edges to o_j). Aggarwal *et al.* [1999] define *horting* as follows: user u_i *horts* user u_k if there is sufficient overlap between the sets of objects they have accessed or rated: that is, if

$$\frac{|out(u_i) \cap out(u_k)|}{|out(u_i)|} \geq F \quad \text{or} \quad |out(u_i) \cap out(u_k)| \geq G,$$

where $F \leq 1$ and G are predetermined constants. Note that horting does not imply predictability, because the definition of horting does not consider the values of the ratings. A user u_i is said to predict another user u_k if

- u_k horts u_i (i.e., there is sufficient commonality among the jointly accessed or rated objects to decide – from the perspective of u_k – if u_i predicts u_k or not) and
- one can construct a linear transformation that translates u_i's ratings into u_k's ratings. More specifically, u_i's ratings translate to u_k's ratings if there exist $s \in \{-1, 1\}$ and t such that

$$\sum_{o_j \in (out(u_i) \cap out(u_k))} \frac{|vote_{i,j} - (s \times vote_{k,j} + t)|}{|out(u_i) \cap out(u_k)|} < U,$$

for a given threshold U.

Let $s_{i,k}$ and $t_{i,k}$ be the s and v values that minimize the foregoing term:

- If $s_{i,k} \sim 1$ and $t_{i,k} \sim 0$, user u_i behaves like user u_k.
- If $s_{i,k} \sim 1$ and $t_{i,k} > 0$, user u_k tends to give more positive ratings than u_i.
- If $s_{i,k} \sim 1$ and $t_{i,k} < 0$, user u_k tends to give more negative ratings than u_i.
- If $s_{i,k} \sim -1$, user u_i behaves in a manner opposite of u_k, but still predicts her.

Aggarwal *et al.* [1999] create and maintain a directed graph whose nodes are the users and whose directed edges correspond to the predictability relationships identified in the user-object database. To predict the rating of object o_j for user u_i, the algorithm first identifies a set of prediction paths from the set, U_j, of users who have rated object o_j to user u_i. Because the goal of these paths is to propagate predictions from the source users to the destination user, u_i, paths along which there already are users who have rated o_j are pruned. For each remaining path, the overall rating is computed by considering all edges from the source and composing the linear transformations corresponding to the edges on the path. The final rating is computed by taking an average of the ratings predicted by all such paths.

12.8.1.3 Associative Retrieval–Based CF

Associative retrieval–based collaborative filtering techniques, such as the one proposed by Huang *et al.* [2004], which build graph-based model of users and objects to explore the transitive associations among them, further generalize the nearest neighbor techniques. As we have already discussed in the context of web-summarization in Section 6.3.1.3, intuitively, the higher the number of paths on the graph connecting two nodes (such as an object and a user), the higher the association between them. When we find that an object is strongly associated with a user, we can interpret this as an indication that the object should be recommended to this user [Brand, 2005; Huang *et al.*, 2004; Soboroff and Nicholas, 2000].

As we have seen in Section 6.3.2, associative retrieval algorithms are often implemented through some form of graph-based spreading activation technique: when some of the nodes in the graph are activated, spreading activation follows the links of the graph iteratively to activate other nodes that can be reached from these initial nodes. Once the iterations of the spreading process are completed, the final degrees of activation of the nodes of the graph are treated as the degrees of association of these nodes to the starting nodes. Huang *et al.* [2004] reduce the collaborative filtering task into associative retrieval as follows: Given the bipartite user-object rating graph, $G(V_u, V_o, E)$, where

- V_u is a set of $N (= |V_u|)$ individuals in the system,
- V_o is the set of $M (= |V_o|)$ objects in the data collection, and
- E is the set of edges between users in V_u and objects in V_o denoting past access/purchase actions or ratings provided by the users,

we create a single directed graph, $G'(V', E')$, where

- $V' = V_u \cup V_o$,
- for edge $\langle u_i, o_j \rangle \in E$, there are two edges, $\langle u_i, o_j \rangle$ and $\langle o_j, u_i \rangle$ in E', and
- for all $v_i \in V'$ there is an edge $\langle v_i, v_i \rangle$ in E'.

Given G' and a user u_i, the spreading activation process is applied starting from $u_i \in V'$. Here the amount of spreading can be regulated based on the ratings associated with edges: users spread their activation levels more to the objects that they rate higher; similarly objects spread their activations levels more to the users who rated them higher. Finally, when the process stops, the object nodes (that are not already in $out(u_i)$) with the highest associations are recommended to the user u_i.

12.8.2 Model-Based Algorithms

Memory-based schemes work reasonably well when the user for whom the prediction is being made has rated a significant number of objects [Breese *et al.*, 1998]. To help where this is not the case, the model-based approaches aim to create semantically richer models. Unlike the memory-based approaches, where the recommendation is directly computed from the underlying user-object database, in the model-based schemes, first an intermediary model is extracted and this model is used to support predictions.

12.8.2.1 Classification-Based CF

One model-based approach is to see the collaborative filtering problem as a classification problem (where recommendation labels are attached to unlabeled objects based on the discovered dependencies between the observed object ratings). Under this formulation, many of the classification schemes presented in Chapter 9 can be applied to solve collaborative filtering problem. Breese *et al.* [1998], for example, create a Bayesian network where each node corresponds to an object in the database and the states of the nodes correspond to the possible votes (including no vote or "$\perp$"). The Bayesian network is trained using the available votes (including "$\perp$"); in the resulting Bayesian network each object will have a set of predictor objects (which are the best predictors of the votes of this object). In particular, Breese *et al.* [1998] use the learning algorithm presented by Chickering *et al.* [1997] to create, for each object, a decision tree (see Section 9.1) that determines the probability of this object being relevant for a given user, based on a set of other objects' having been preferred/accessed by the user.

Note that the predictability-based scheme we discussed in Section 12.8.1.2 is similar to the scheme described above, except that the predictability is measured among users (instead of among objects) and a linear model is used to quantify predictability instead of a Bayesian probabilistic model as in Breese *et al.* [1998].

12.8.2.2 Clustering-Based CF

One problem with memory-based schemes is that the size of the user-object rating database tends to be very large for run-time predictions. Moreover, the rating matrix tends to be sparse, making predictive analysis less effective [Billsus and Pazzani, 1998]. Clustering-based collaborative filtering schemes deal with these problems by recognizing that instead of treating individual users, it may be possible to identify a set, $\mathcal{T}$, of types of users that capture a common set of preferences or tastes [Breese *et al.*, 1998]. Similarly, the set of objects can also be clustered into a set, $\mathcal{G}$, of genres, representing different content or topic types. Given such clusters, then, the probability $p(vote_{i,j} = k)$ can be formulated as

$$p(vote_{i,j} = k) = \sum_{t \in \mathcal{T}} \sum_{g \in \mathcal{G}} p(vote_{i,j} = k \mid (u_i \in t) \wedge (o_j \in g)) p(u_i \in t) p(o_j \in g).$$

Note that, for reducing the impact of the sparsity problem, metadata about the users and the objects can be represented by additional random variables, and the preceding model can be extended with prior and conditional probability distributions of these variables. The foregoing model, where users are assumed to fall into certain latent classes and object ratings are conditionally independent of the user given the user's class, is often referred to as the mixture of multinomials model (or as the aspect model).

Breese *et al.* [1998] use expectation-maximization (EM, see Section 9.7.4.3) to cluster users into m types based on their votes. Hofmann [2001] also relies on EM to identify to what extent a user participates in a common interest pattern, that is, which fraction of a given user's ratings are explained by a latent (hidden) reason. In general many of the dimensionality reduction (such as PCA – see Section 4.2.6) and clustering schemes covered in Chapter 8 can be used to put together users based on preference types or objects based on access patterns. For example, the $N \times M$ user-object rating matrix, V, can be analyzed through the latent semantic analysis process to identify meta-users, meta-products, and their latent associations. Remember from Section 4.4.1.1 that the singular value decomposition can be used to eigen-decompose the matrix V into three matrices, $V = U\Sigma O^T$, such that

- the r column vectors of the $N \times r$ matrix U would form an r-dimensional basis in which the N users can be described (i.e., the columns of U can be thought of as the *meta-users* of the given system, each corresponding to a different *taste* group);
- The r column vectors of the $M \times r$ matrix O (or the rows vector of O^T) would form an r-dimensional basis in which the M objects can be placed (i.e., the orthogonal columns of O can be thought of as independent *genres*, each of which described as a combination of the objects in the database); and
- the values of the diagonal $r \times r$ matrix Σ can be used for representing the strengths of the corresponding genre-tastes in the database.

Knowledge of such high-level user tastes, corresponding genres, and their strengths in the database can be used in supporting cluster-based recommendations [Billsus and Pazzani, 1998; Nati and Jaakkola, 2003]. Other alternative techniques one can use for identifying user and object clusters include

- co-clustering applied on the user-object rating matrix, V (see Section 8.7), and
- graph clustering/partitioning techniques (see Section 8.2) applied on the $N \times N$ user-similarity matrix $\mathcal{U}$ and $M \times M$ object-similarity matrix $\mathcal{O}$. These matrices can be generated based on user-user and object-object correlation or cosine similarities, as is done in the voting-based collaborative filtering schemes (Section 12.8.1.1).

12.8.3 Combining Model- and Memory-Based Approaches

Note that there are many different ways one can approach the collaborative filtering problem, each with different assumptions. Experimental results showed that often the predictions made by different collaborative filtering algorithms do not agree with each other. One way to reduce the bias due to the use of a priori selection of model- and memory-based approaches is to combine them into hybrid schemes. Pennock *et al.* [2000], for example, present a probabilistic approach that combines model- and memory-based schemes. In particular, instead of modeling taste groups by clustering multiple users based on their preferences, the rating vector of each user is treated as an individual predictor as in the memory-based schemes. On the other hand, differently from the purely memory-based schemes, the ratings in the database are not treated as users' ideal ratings, but only as noisy approximations of users' true ratings. More specifically, Pennock *et al.* [2000] model user u_i's personality as an unknown vector, $\hat{\vec{u}}_i$, of *true* ratings of the user for all the objects in the database. Pennock *et al.* [2000] also assume that users' reporting of their ratings is subject to noise (thus the same user may report different ratings on different occasions); in particular user u_i's observed rating, $vote_{i,j}$, for object o_j is drawn from an independent normal distribution with mean $\hat{\vec{u}}_i[j]$. In other words,

$$p(vote_{i,j} = k \mid \vec{\hat{u}}_i[j] = l) \sim e^{\frac{(k-l)^2}{2\sigma^2}}.$$

Let us assume that there are N users of the system and M objects in the database. Assuming that given a user's personality type his or her ratings are independent and assuming that the distribution of ratings vectors in the database is representative of the distribution of personalities in the population of users (in a sense, each user u_i corresponds a different type t_i), the probability that the user u_i would rate an (unrated) object o_j with rating k can be modeled as

$$p(vote_{i,j} = k \mid vote_{i,1}, \ldots, vote_{i,M})$$

$$= \sum_{l=1}^{N} p(vote_{i,j} = k \mid \vec{\hat{u}}_i = \vec{t}_l) \, p(\vec{\hat{u}}_i = \vec{t}_l \mid vote_{i,1}, \ldots, vote_{i,M}).$$

Here, the term $p(vote_{i,j} = k \mid \vec{\hat{u}}_i = \vec{t}_l)$ can be computed using the Gaussian distribution assumption stated earlier. In order to compute the second multiplier, we need to apply Bayes' theorem:

$$p(\vec{\hat{u}}_i = \vec{t}_l \mid vote_{i,1}, \ldots, vote_{i,M})$$

$$\sim \left(\prod_{j=1}^{M} p(vote_{i,j} \mid \vec{\hat{u}}_i[j] = \vec{t}_l[j]) \right) p(\vec{\hat{u}}_i = \vec{t}_l).$$

Once again, the term $p(vote_{i,j} \mid \vec{\hat{u}}_i[j] = \vec{t}_l[j])$ can be computed using the Gaussian noise assumption. Finally, relying on the aforementioned assumption that the distribution of ratings vectors in the database is representative of the distribution of personalities in the target population of users, we can set the second term, $p(\vec{\hat{u}}_i = \vec{t}_l)$, to $\frac{1}{N}$ to complete the computation.

12.8.4 Ensemble (or Boosting) Style CF

Another approach to reduce the bias in the recommendations due to the a priori selection of the collaborative filtering technique is to use multiple predictors and pick the recommendations agreed by most.

12.8.4.1 Combining Ratings

Nakamura and Abe [1998], for example, present an ensemble-style[4] weighted majority scheme, where given a user u_i and object o_j, a large number of simple recommendation strategies (or *weak recommenders*, each one essentially modeling an expert for predicting ratings for some subset of objects and users[5]) are used to predict the corresponding ratings. Each *expert* is given a weight based on its past correct and incorrect predictions. Finally, a single combined rating is computed by taking the weighted average of all the *expert* ratings.

One problem with this approach to combining recommendations is that using absolute values of the ratings of individual objects (instead of the rankings of the objects with respect to each other) is likely to be prone to errors: in general, the rankings implied by the weak recommenders are likely to be more accurate than the absolute ratings they associate to the objects. Therefore, an alternative approach to combining recommendation evidence from multiple weak recommenders into a single recommendation is to combine the rankings in a way that minimizes the number of disagreements [Cohen *et al.*, 1998; Freund *et al.*, 2003].

12.8.4.2 Combining Rankings using AdaBoost

Cohen *et al.* [1998] present a two-stage approach to combining rankings. In stage 1, the algorithm learns a preference function, $pref(o_j, o_l) : V_o \times V_o \rightarrow [0, 1]$, which represents how certain the system is (based on the individual rankings provided by the weak recommenders) that o_j should be ranked before o_l. In particular,

- if $pref(o_j, o_l) \sim 1$ then o_j should be ranked before o_l;
- if $pref(o_j, o_l) \sim 0.5$ then there is no sufficient evidence to rank o_j before o_l (or vice versa); and
- if $pref(o_j, o_l) \sim 0$ then o_l should be ranked before o_j.

In the second stage, this preference function is evaluated over all pairs of objects in the database and an ordering that agrees best with this preference function is selected.

Let $R = \{r_1, \ldots, r_h\}$ be the set of weak recommenders (or experts). Let $rank_i : V_o \times V_o \rightarrow [0, 1]$ be the ranking returned by r_i, such that for all object pairs o_j and o_l,

- $rank_i(o_j, o_l) = 1$, if the weak recommender ranks o_j before o_l;
- $rank_i(o_j, o_l) = 0$, if the weak recommender ranks o_l before o_j; and
- $rank_i(o_j, o_l) = 0.5$, if either o_j or o_l is unranked by the weak recommender.

Note that the *rank()* function ignores the absolute values of the ratings but focuses solely on the recommendation ranking of the objects.

---

[4] See Section 9.1.3 for other examples of ensemble-based classification process.
[5] Note that, in the extreme case, each weak recommender corresponds to a single individual user of the system; in this case, the boosting schemes generalize the voting-based collaborative filtering techniques discussed in Section 12.8.1.1.

Given a set, R, of weak recommenders and their rankings, Cohen *et al.* [1998] first learn a preference function of the form

$$pref(o_j, o_l) = \sum_{r_i \in R} w_i \ rank_i(o_j, o_l),$$

where w_i is the weight for the weak recommender r_i. These weights are learned incrementally through user feedback using an AdaBoost-based strategy [Freund and Schapire, 1997; Schapire and Singer, 1999] (see Section 9.9): the algorithm assumes that the user feedback is a set of statements of the form "o_j should be ranked before o_l"; those weak recommenders whose rankings agree with the feedback are given higher weights than the weak recommenders whose rankings disagree with the user statements.

Once the $pref()$ function is learned, the next step is to find an optimal total ordering, $>_{opt}$ (where $o_j >_{opt} o_l$ iff o_j is ranked before o_l in the total ordering), that agrees with this preference function; that is,

$$agree(>_{opt}, pref) = \sum_{o_j, o_l \ s.t. \ o_j >_{opt} o_l} pref(o_j, o_l),$$

is maximized. Cohen *et al.* [1998] show that finding a total order that maximizes this agreement term is NP-complete. Thus, instead of an optimal algorithm, it provides an approximate algorithm that can find a solution within a factor of 0.5 of the optimal agreement; that is, if $>_{apx}$ is the total order returned by the approximation algorithm, then

$$agree(>_{apx}, pref) \geq \frac{1}{2} agree(>_{opt}, pref).$$

This approximation algorithm proceeds, in a greedy fashion, as follows. Let V_r be initially an empty set (i.e., $V_r = \emptyset$);

(i) The algorithm computes a weight $\pi(o_j)$ for each unranked object:

$$\forall_{o_j \in (V_o - V_r)} \ \pi(o_j) = \sum_{o_l \in (V_o - V_r)} pref(o_j, o_l) - \sum_{o_l \in (V_o - V_r)} pref(o_l, o_j).$$

Intuitively, the weight of the object o_j corresponds to the amount of evidence suggesting that o_j should be ranked early relative to the other objects in the database against the amount of evidence indicating that o_j should be ranked late relative to the other objects.

(ii) Next, the algorithm picks the highest weighted unranked object (i.e., the object with the best evidence to be ranked early relative to the other unranked objects); let this object be o^*:

   (a) First, the object is included in the total order, $>_{apx}$, such that
- $\forall_{o_j \in V_r} \ (o_j >_{apx} o^*)$, and
- $\forall_{o_j \in (V_o - (V_r \cup \{o^*\}))} \ (o^* >_{apx} o_j)$.

   (b) Then, the object is included in the set of objects that have already been ranked; that is, $V_r = V_r \cup \{o^*\}$.

The foregoing process is repeated until $V_r = V_o$. Intuitively, at each iteration, the weights of the objects are updated based on the ranking evidence relative to the remaining, not-yet-ranked objects. Based on this evidence, at the end of the iteration, a winning object is selected and returned to be recommended to the user.

12.8.4.3 Combining Rankings using RankBoost

One problem with the preceding approach is that, because of the inherent computational complexity of the total order extraction process, the system has to rely on a heuristic that can have, in the worst case, only half of the optimal agreement between the evidence provided by the individual rankings. RankBoost [Freund *et al.*, 2003] uses a similar problem formulation and solution framework, but avoids this intractability problem. Once again, let $R = \{r_1, \ldots, r_h\}$ be the set of weak recommenders (or simply users of the system who provide their own preference rankings for the objects in the database). This time, however, the ranking function of weak recommender, r_i, is defined slightly differently:

- For objects o_j, $rank_i(o_j) = \bot$ means o_j has not been ranked by r_i.
- For all object pairs, o_j and o_l, such that $rank_i(o_j) \neq \bot$ and $rank_i(o_l) \neq \bot$,
  - $rank_i(o_j) > rank_i(o_l)$, if the weak recommender ranks o_j before o_l; and
  - $rank_i(o_j) = rank_i(o_l)$, if the weak recommender ranks o_j and o_l the same.

RankBoost first finds a combined ranking, $rank' : V_o \rightarrow \{0, 1\}$ with a similar interpretation, but without any $\bot$; that is, all objects (even those that have not been ranked by the weak recommenders) will be ranked by this combined recommender. This initial combination, however, is still *weak* in the sense that it has not been verified (and boosted) based on further user feedback. Thus, RankBoost uses additional user feedback to improve the combined ranking into a final ranking function $rank^* : V_o \rightarrow \mathbb{R}$. In RankBoost, the feedback used for boosting the rankings is modeled as a set of statements of the form "o_j should be ranked before o_l." More specifically, feedback is represented as a function $f : V_o \rightarrow \{0, 1\}$ such that

- $f(o_j, o_l) > 0$ means o_j should be ranked before o_l,
- $f(o_j, o_l) < 0$ means o_j should be ranked after o_l, and
- $f(o_j, o_l) = 0$ means that there is no preference between o_j and o_l.

Given a set $R = \{r_1, \ldots, r_h\}$ of weak recommenders, a threshold, $\theta \in \mathbb{R}$, a default value, $\alpha \in \{0, 1\}$, and a weak recommender $r_i \in R$, let us define $rank_{\theta,\alpha,i} : V_o \rightarrow \mathbb{R}$ as follows: for all $o_j \in V_o$,

- $rank_{\theta,\alpha,i}(o_j) = 1$, if $rank_i(o_j) > \theta$,
- $rank_{\theta,\alpha,i}(o_j) = 0$, if $rank_i(o_j) \leq \theta$,
- $rank_{\theta,\alpha,i}(o_j) = \alpha$, if $rank_i(o_j) = \bot$.

Given a feedback function $f()$, RankBoost computes a weak-ranking function, $rank' : V_o \rightarrow \mathbb{R}$ by selecting θ, α, and r_i in such a way that maximizes the term $|match(\theta, \alpha, r_i)|$, where

$$match(\theta, \alpha, r_i) = \sum_{f(o_j, o_l) > 0} \mathcal{I}(o_j, o_l) \, (rank_{\theta,\alpha,i}(o_j) - rank_{\theta,\alpha,i}(o_l)),$$

and setting $rank' = rank_{\theta,\alpha,i}$. Here, $\mathcal{I}(o_j, o_l)$ is a probability distribution denoting how critical it is to maintain o_j ranked before o_l (if o_j does not need to be ranked before o_l, then $\mathcal{I}(o_j, o_l) = 0$). Initially, $\mathcal{I}(o_j, o_l)$ is set to $c \times max(0, f(o_j, o_l))$ and, to ensure that $\mathcal{I}$ is a probability distribution, the constant c is selected in such a way that

$$\sum_{o_j,o_l} \mathcal{I}(o_j, o_l) = 1.$$

Note that, unlike in the greedy algorithm described earlier, RankBoost does not treat each and every pair of objects equivalently: while maintaining the correct relative order may be very critical for one pair of objects in the database, it may be less so for another pair. In fact, it is this importance function, $\mathcal{I}()$ that is boosted iteratively by focusing the precision of the ranking on the most important object pairs.

Given the pair importance function $\mathcal{I}()$, the term $match(\theta, \alpha, r_i)$ can be simplified as follows:

$$= \sum_{f(o_j,o_l)>0} \mathcal{I}(o_j, o_l)\,(rank_{\theta,\alpha,i}(o_j) - rank_{\theta,\alpha,i}(o_l))$$

$$= \sum_{o_j,o_l} \mathcal{I}(o_j, o_l)\,(rank_{\theta,\alpha,i}(o_j) - rank_{\theta,\alpha,i}(o_l))$$

$$= \sum_{o_j,o_l} \mathcal{I}(o_j, o_l)\,rank_{\theta,\alpha,i}(o_j) - \sum_{o_j,o_l} \mathcal{I}(o_j, o_l)\,rank_{\theta,\alpha,i}(o_l)$$

$$= \sum_{o_j,o_l} \mathcal{I}(o_j, o_l)\,rank_{\theta,\alpha,i}(o_j) - \sum_{o_l,o_j} \mathcal{I}(o_l, o_j)\,rank_{\theta,\alpha,i}(o_j)$$

$$= \sum_{o_j} rank_{\theta,\alpha,i}(o_j) \left(\sum_{o_l} \mathcal{I}(o_j, o_l) - \sum_{o_l} \mathcal{I}(o_l, o_j) \right)$$

$$= \sum_{o_j} rank_{\theta,\alpha,i}(o_j) \sum_{o_l} (\mathcal{I}(o_j, o_l) - \mathcal{I}(o_l, o_j)).$$

$$= \sum_{o_j} rank_{\theta,\alpha,i}(o_j)\,\pi(o_j).$$

Note that the *object potential* function,

$$\pi(o_j) = \sum_{o_l} (\mathcal{I}(o_j, o_l) - \mathcal{I}(o_l, o_j)),$$

can be computed once for the given $\mathcal{I}()$ and used repeatedly when scanning alternative values of θ, α, and r_i to search for the triple that will maximize the term $|match(\theta, \alpha, r_i)|$. Once the appropriate θ, α, and r_i are found, the ranker, $rank_{\theta,\alpha,i}$, is selected as the weak ranker, $rank'$, corresponding to $\mathcal{I}()$.

Starting from the initial distribution, $\mathcal{I}(o_j, o_l) = c \times max(0, f(o_j, o_l))$, RankBoost iteratively adjusts the importance function $\mathcal{I}()$ (and the corresponding weak ranker $rank'$) to compute the final ranking function $rank^*$ as follows:

(i) $\forall_{o_j,o_l}\ \mathcal{I}_1(o_j, o_l) = c \times max(0, f(o_j, o_l))$.
(ii) Starting from $t = 1$ until $t = T$, the algorithm iteratively computes new weak rankers and the associated weights:
    (a) It first finds the weak ranker, $rank'_t$, corresponding to $\mathcal{I}_t()$ as described earlier.

(b) Let $m_t = match(\theta, \alpha, r_i)$ be the degree of match corresponding to $rank'_t$;
RankBoost defines the weight corresponding to the weak ranker $rank'_t$
as $w_t = \frac{1}{2}ln\left(\frac{1+m_t}{1-m_t}\right)$.

(c) Next, the algorithm computes the next pair-importance function, $\mathcal{I}_{t+1}()$,
as follows:

$$\forall_{o_j, o_l}\ \mathcal{I}_{t+1}(o_j, o_l) = c_t\ \mathcal{I}_t(o_j, o_l)\ e^{w_t(rank'_t(o_l)-rank'_t(o_j))},$$

where c_t is selected in such a way that

$$\sum_{o_j, o_l} \mathcal{I}_{t+1}(o_j, o_l) = 1.$$

(iii) Finally, RankBoost computes the boosted ranking function $rank^*$ as a
weighted combination of all the weak rankers computed so far:

$$\forall_{o_j}\ rank^*(o_j) = \sum_{t=1}^{T} w_t\ rank'_t(o_j).$$

This boosted ranking function (computed based on the recommendations provided
by the available weak recommenders and taking into account the user feedback)
can now be used for selecting and recommending the best objects to the user.

12.9 SUMMARY

In this chapter, we have discussed user relevance feedback and collaborative filtering techniques, both designed to improve the relevance of the objects presented to
the users. The user relevance feedback process leverages an iterative framework,
where the semantic gap between what the user wants and what the system interprets as what the user wants is incrementally bridged. The collaborative filtering
technique, on the other hand, takes a more proactive approach and (assuming that
there were in the past other users of the system who have made similar queries
and obtained results that they deemed relevant) relies on the relevance judgment of
other users to improve the quality of the results. In the extreme case, recommendation and social-networking systems completely avoid querying and, simply based on
similarities between the profiles of the users and based on their declared relationships (such as "friend"), identify and present relevant objects even before the user
may think about searching for new objects. Achieving this in a most effective and
efficient manner is, in a sense, the *holy grail* of multimedia retrieval.

Bibliography

Swarup Acharya, Viswanath Poosala, and Sridhar Ramaswamy. Selectivity estimation in spatial databases. In *SIGMOD '99: Proceedings of the 1999 ACM SIGMOD International Conference on Management of Data*, pages 13–24, 1999.

S. Adali and M. L. Sapino. An activity based data model for desktop querying. In *Proceedings of the Semantic Desktop Workshop*, 2005.

S. Adali, M. L. Sapino, and V. S. Subrahmanian. A multimedia presentation algebra. *SIGMOD Rec.*, 28(2):121–132, 1999.

S. Adali, B. Bouqata, A. Marcus, F. Spear, and B. Szymanski. A day in the life of a metamorphic petrologist. In *Proc. ICDE Workshop on Semantic Web and Databases*, 2006.

Sibel Adali, K. Selçuk Candan, Su-Shing Chen, Kutluhan Erol, and V. S. Subrahmanian. The advanced video information system: data structures and query processing. *Multimedia Syst.*, 4(4):172–186, 1996.

Sibel Adali, Corey Bufi, and Maria Luisa Sapino. Ranked relations: Query languages and query processing methods for multimedia. *Multimedia Tools Appl.*, 24(3):197–214, 2004.

Sibel Adali, Maria Luisa Sapino, and Brandeis Marshall. A rank algebra to support multimedia mining applications. In *MDM '07: Proceedings of the 8th International Workshop on Multimedia Data Mining*, pages 1–9, 2007.

R. Adams and L. Bischof. Seeded region growing. *IEEE Trans. Pattern Anal. Mach. Intell.*, 16(6):641–647, 1994.

Charu C. Aggarwal, Joel L. Wolf, Kun-Lung Wu, and Philip S. Yu. Horting hatches an egg: a new graph-theoretic approach to collaborative filtering. In *KDD '99: Proceedings of the Fifth ACM SIGKDD International Conference on Knowledge Discovery and Data Mining*, pages 201–212, 1999.

R. Agrawal, A. Borgida, and H. V. Jagadish. Efficient management of transitive relationships in large data and knowledge bases. In *SIGMOD '89: Proceedings of the 1989 ACM SIGMOD International Conference on Management of Data*, pages 253–262, 1989.

A. V. Aho and M. J. Corasick. Efficient string matching: An aid to bibliographic search. *Communications of the ACM*, 18(6):333–340, June 1975.

H. Akaike. A new look at the statistical model identification. *IEEE Trans. Automat. Contr.* 19(6):716–723, 1974.

D. Akca. Generalized Procrustes analysis and its applications in photogrammetry. In *Internal Colloquium at Photogrammetry and Remote Sensing Group of IGP – ETH Zurich, Zurich, Switzerland*, 2003.

James F. Allen. Maintaining knowledge about temporal intervals. *Commun. ACM*, 26(11):832–843, 1983.

James F. Allen. Towards a general theory of action and time. *Artif. Intell.*, 23(2): 123–154, 1984.

D. Aloise, A. Deshpande, P. Hansen, and P. Popat. NP-hardness of Euclidean sum-of- squares clustering. *Cahiers du GERAD, G-2008-33*, 2008.

Rajeev Alur and David L. Dill. A theory of timed automata. *Theor. Comput. Sci.*, 126:183–235, 1994.

A. Amir, G. M. Landau, M. Lewenstein, and N. Lewenstein. Efficient special cases of pattern matching with swaps. *Inf. Proc. Lett.*, 68(3):125–132, 1998.

Yali Amit and Donald Geman. Shape quantization and recognition with randomized trees. *Neural Comput.*, 9(7):1545–1588, 1997.

D. P. Anderson. Techniques for reducing pen plotting time. *ACM Trans. Graph.*, 2(3):197–212, 1983a.

John R. Anderson. A spreading activation theory of memory. *J. Verbal Learn. Verbal Behav.*, 22:261–295, 1983b.

Alexandr Andoni and Piotr Indyk. Efficient algorithms for substring near neighbor problem. In *SODA '06: Proceedings of the Seventeenth Annual ACM-SIAM Symposium on Discrete Algorithms*, pages 1203–1212, 2006a.

Alexandr Andoni and Piotr Indyk. Near-optimal hashing algorithms for approximate nearest neighbor in high dimensions. In *FOCS '06: Proceedings of the 47th Annual IEEE Symposium on Foundations of Computer Science*, pages 459–468, 2006b.

Alexandr Andoni and Piotr Indyk. Near-optimal hashing algorithms for approximate nearest neighbor in high dimensions. *Commun. ACM*, 51(1):117–122, 2008.

Christophe Andrieu, Nando de Freitas, Arnaud Doucet, and Michael I. Jordan. An introduction to mcmc for machine learning. *Mach. Learn.*, 50(1–2):5–43, 2003.

Benjamin Arai, Gautam Das, Dimitrios Gunopulos, and Nick Koudas. Anytime measures for top-k algorithms. In *VLDB*, pages 914–925, 2007.

Hiroshi Arisawa, Takashi Tomii, and Kiril Salev. Design of multimedia database and a query language for video image data. In *ICMCS*, 1996.

Sunil Arya, David M. Mount, Nathan S. Netanyahu, Ruth Silverman, and Angela Y. Wu. An optimal algorithm for approximate nearest neighbor searching in fixed dimensions. In *ACM-SIAM Symposium on Discrete Algorithms*, pages 573–582, 1994.

Sunil Arya, David M. Mount, Nathan S. Netanyahu, Ruth Silverman, and Angela Y. Wu. An optimal algorithm for approximate nearest neighbor searching fixed dimensions. *J. ACM*, 45(6):891–923, 1998.

Y. Alp Aslandogan, Chuck Thier, Clement T. Yu, Chengwen Liu, and Krishnakumar R. Nair. Design, implementation and evaluation of score (a system for content based retrieval of pictures). In *ICDE '95: Proceedings of the Eleventh International Conference on Data Engineering*, pages 280–287, Washington, DC, USA, 1995. IEEE Computer Society.

Bengt Aspvall and Yossi Shiloach. A polynomial time algorithm for solving systems of linear inequalities with two variables per inequality. *SIAM J. Comput.*, 9(4): 827–845, 1980.

M. P. Atkinson, F. Bancillon, D. De-Witt, K. Dittrich, D. Maier, and S. Zdonik. The object-oriented database system manifesto. In *Proceedings of the First Deductive and Object-oriented Database Conference*, pages 40–57, Kyoto, 1989.

Jeffrey R. Bach, Charles Fuller, Amarnath Gupta, Arun Hampapur, Bradley Horowitz, Rich Humphrey, Ramesh C. Jain, and Chiao-Fe Shu. *Virage Image Search Engine: an Open Framework for Image Management*, Volume 2670, pages 76–87. SPIE, 1996.

R. Baeza-Yates and G. H. Gonnet. Fast text searching for regular expressions or automaton searching on tries. *J. ACM (JACM)*, 43(6):915–936, 1996.

R. A. Baeza-Yates and G. H. Gonnet. A new approach to text searching. In *SIGIR '89: Proceedings of the 12th annual international ACM SIGIR conference on Research and development in information retrieval*, pages 168–175, 1989.

Ricardo Baeza-Yates and Gaston H. Gonnet. A new approach to text searching. *Commun. ACM*, 35(10):74–82, 1992.

Ricardo Baeza-Yates and Gonzalo Navarro. New and faster filters for multiple approximate string matching. *Random Struct. Algorithms*, 20(1):23–49, 2002.

Ricardo Baeza-Yates and Gonzalo Navarro. Faster approximate string matching. *Algorithmica*, 23:174–184, 1999.

Ricardo A. Baeza-Yates. A unified view to string matching algorithms. In *SOFSEM '96: Proceedings of the 23rd Seminar on Current Trends in Theory and Practice of Informatics*, pages 1–15, 1996.

Ricardo A. Baeza-Yates and Chris H. Perleberg. Fast and practical approximate string matching. In *CPM '92: Proceedings of the Third Annual Symposium on Combinatorial Pattern Matching*, pages 185–192, 1992.

Ricardo A. Baeza-Yates and Berthier A. Ribeiro-Neto. *Modern Information Retrieval*. ACM Press/Addison-Wesley, 1999.

Gianfranco Balbo. Introduction to Stochastic Petri Nets, pages 84–155, 2002.

W.-T. Balke and U. Güntzer. Efficient skyline queries under weak Pareto dominance. In *Proc. of the IJCAI-05 Multidisciplinary Workshop on Advances in Preference Handling (PREFERENCE)*, pages 1–7, 2005.

Wolf-Tilo Balke, Ulrich Guntzer, and Wolf Siberski. Exploiting indifference for customization of partial order skylines. In *IDEAS '06: Proceedings of the 10th International Database Engineering and Applications Symposium*, pages 80–88, 2006.

Nevzat Hurkan Balkir, Eser Sükan, Gultekin Özsoyoglu, and Z. Meral Özsoyoglu. Visual: A graphical icon-based query language. In Stanley Y. W. Su, editor, *Proceedings of the Twelfth International Conference on Data Engineering, February 26–March 1, 1996, New Orleans, Louisiana*, pages 524–533, 1996.

Nevzat Hurkan Balkir, Gultekin Ozsoyoglu, and Z. Meral Ozsoyoglu. A graphical query language: Visual and its query processing. *IEEE Trans. Knowl. Data Eng.*, 14(5):955–978, 2002.

L. Balmelli and A. Mojsilovic. Wavelet domain features for texture description, classification and replicability analysis. In *ICIP99*, pages IV:440–444, 1999.

Nilesh Bansal, Sudipto Guha, and Nick Koudas. Ad-hoc aggregations of ranked lists in the presence of hierarchies. In *SIGMOD Conference*, pages 67–78, 2008.

A. L. Barabasi and R. Albert. Emergence of scaling in random networks. *Science*, 286:509–512, October 1999.

Chitta Baral, Graciela Gonzalez, and Tran Cao Son. Design and implementation of display specification for multimedia answers. In *ICDE '98: Proceedings of the Fourteenth International Conference on Data Engineering*, pages 558–565. IEEE Computer Society, 1998.

Mark A. Bartsch and Gregory H. Wakefield. To catch a chorus: Using chroma-based representations for audio thumbnailing. In *Proceedings of the 2001 IEEE Workshop on Applications of Signal Processing to Audio and Acoustics*, pages 15–18, 2001.

Chumki Basu, Haym Hirsh, and William Cohen. Recommendation as classification: using social and content-based information in recommendation. In *AAAI '98/IAAI '98: Proceedings of the Fifteenth National/Tenth Conference on Artificial Intelligence/Innovative Applications of Artificial Intelligence*, pages 714–720, 1998.

L. E. Baum and G. R. Sell. Growth transformations for functions on manifolds. *Pacific J. Math.*, 27:211–227, 1968.

L. E. Baum and J. A. Eagon. An inequality with applications to statistical estimation for probabilistic functions of Markov processes and to a model for ecology. *Bull. Am. Math. Soc.*, 73:360–363, 1967.

Leonard E. Baum, Ted Petrie, George Soules, and Norman Weiss. A maximization technique occurring in the statistical analysis of probabilistic functions of markov chains. *Ann. Mathemat. Statist.*, 41(1):164–171, 1970.

Herbert Bay, Tinne Tuytelaars, and Luc Van Gool. Surf: Speeded up robust features. In *ECCV*, pages 404–417, 2006.

Rudolf Bayer and E. McCreight. Organization and Maintenance of Large Ordered Indexes, pages 245–262, 2002.

Rudolf Bayer and Edward M. McCreight. Organization and maintenance of large ordered indices. *Acta Inform.*, 1:173–189, 1972.

Norbert Beckmann, Hans-Peter Kriegel, Ralf Schneider, and Bernhard Seeger. The r*-tree: an efficient and robust access method for points and rectangles. In *Proceedings of the 1990 ACM SIGMOD International Conference on Management of Data*, pages 322–331, 1990.

Serge Belongie, Jitendra Malik, and Jan Puzicha. Shape matching and object recognition using shape contexts. *IEEE Trans. Pattern Anal. Mach. Intellig.*, 24:509–522, 2002.

Alberto Belussi and Christos Faloutsos. Estimating the selectivity of spatial queries using the "correlation" fractal dimension. In *VLDB '95: Proceedings of the 21th International Conference on Very Large Data Bases*, pages 299–310, 1995.

Alberto Belussi and Christos Faloutsos. Self-spatial join selectivity estimation using fractal concepts. *ACM Trans. Inf. Syst.*, 16(2):161–201, 1998.

Charles H. Bennett, Pter Gcs, Senior Member, Ming Li, Paul M. B. Vitnyi, and Wojciech H. Zurek. Information distance. *IEEE Trans. Inform. Theory*, 44:1407–1423, 1998.

Kristin P. Bennett and Erin J. Bredensteiner. Duality and geometry in svm classifiers. In *ICML '00: Proceedings of the Seventeenth International Conference on Machine Learning*, pages 57–64, 2000.

Kristin P. Bennett and Colin Campbell. Support vector machines: hype or hallelujah? *SIGKDD Explor. Newsl.*, 2(2):1–13, 2000.

J. L. Bentley. Algorithms for klee's rectangle problems. Dept. of Computer Science, Carnegie Mellon University, 1977.

Jon Louis Bentley. Multidimensional binary search trees used for associative searching. *Commun. ACM*, 18(9):509–517, 1975.

Stefan Berchtold, Daniel A. Keim, and Hans-Peter Kriegel. The x-tree: an index structure for high-dimensional data. In *VLDB '96: Proceedings of the 22th International Conference on Very Large Data Bases*, pages 28–39, 1996.

Stefan Berchtold, Christian Böhm, and Hans-Peter Kriegel. The pyramid-tree: Breaking the curse of dimensionality. In *SIGMOD 1998. Proceedings ACM SIGMOD International Conference on Management of Data*, pages 142–153, 1998.

Adam Berger and John Lafferty. Information retrieval as statistical translation. In *Proceedings of the 1999 ACM SIGIR Conference on Research and Development in Information Retrieval*, pages 222–229, 1999.

Francisco José Berlanga, María José del Jesús, María José Gacto, and Francisco Herrera. A genetic-programming-based approach for the learning of compact fuzzy rule-based classification systems. In *ICAISC*, pages 182–191, 2006.

Michael W. Berry, Susan T. Dumais, and Todd A. Letsche. Computational methods for intelligent information access. In *Proceedings of the 1995 ACM/IEEE Supercomputing Conference*, 1995.

S. Beucher. Watersheds of functions and picture segmentation. In *Proceedings of the IEEE International Conference on Acoustics, Speech, and Signal Processing*, pages 1928–1931, 1982.

S. Beucher and C. Lantuejoul. Use of watersheds in contour detection. In *Proceedings of the International Workshop on Image Processing, Real-Time Edge and Motion Detection/Estimation*, 1979.

S. Beucher and F. Meyer. The morphological approach of segmentation: The watershed transformation. chapter 12. pages 1928–1931. 1992.

Kevin S. Beyer, Jonathan Goldstein, Raghu Ramakrishnan, and Uri Shaft. When is "nearest neighbor" meaningful? In *ICDT '99: Proceedings of the 7th International Conference on Database Theory*, pages 217–235. Springer-Verlag, 1999.

Gaurav Bhalotia, Charuta Nakhe, Arvind Hulgeri, Soumen Chakrabarti, and S. Sudarshan. Keyword searching and browsing in databases using BANKS. In *ICDE*, 2002.

Krishna Bharat and Monika R. Henzinger. Improved algorithms for topic distillation in a hyperlinked environment. In *SIGIR '98: Proceedings of the 21st Annual International ACM SIGIR Conference on Research and Development in Information Retrieval*, pages 104–111, 1998.

P. Bille. A survey on tree edit distance and related problems. *Theor. Comput. Sci.*, 337(1–3):217–239, 2005.

Daniel Billsus and Michael J. Pazzani. Learning collaborative information filters. In *ICML '98: Proceedings of the Fifteenth International Conference on Machine Learning*, pages 46–54, 1998.

Alberto Del Bimbo, Enrico Vicario, and Daniele Zingoni. Symbolic description and visual querying of image sequences using spatio-temporal logic. *IEEE Trans. Knowl. Data Eng.*, 7(4):609–622, 1995.

Burton H. Bloom. Space/time trade-offs in hash coding with allowable errors. *Commun. ACM*, 13(7):422–426, 1970.

J. Blustein, C. Fu, and D. L. Silver. Information visualization for an intrusion detection system. In *Proceedings of Hypertext '05*, pages 278–279, 2005.

L. Bolduc, J. Culbert, T. Harada, J. Harward, and E. Schlusselberg, The athenamuse 2. functional specification ceci(mit). report, 1992.

Ravi Boppana and Magnús M. Halldórsson. Approximating maximum independent sets by excluding subgraphs. *BIT*, 32(2):180–196, 1992.

Ravi B. Boppana. Eigenvalues and graph bisection: An average-case analysis. In *IEEE Symposium on Foundations of Computer Science*, pages 280–285, 1987.

Stephan Borzsonyi, Konrad Stocker, and Donald Kossmann. The skyline operator. In *International Conference on Data Engineering*, pages 421–430, 2001.

Bernhard E. Boser, Isabelle M. Guyon, and Vladimir N. Vapnik. A training algorithm for optimal margin classifiers. In *COLT '92: Proceedings of the Fifth Annual Workshop on Computational Learning Theory*, pages 144–152, 1992.

Robert S. Boyer and J. Strother Moore. A fast string searching algorithm. *Commun. ACM*, 20(10):762–772, 1977.

Tolga Bozkaya and Meral Ozsoyoglu. Indexing large metric spaces for similarity search queries. *ACM Trans. Database Syst.*, 24(3):361–404, 1999.

Paul S. Bradley and O. L. Mangasarian. Feature selection via concave minimization and support vector machines. In *ICML '98: Proceedings of the Fifteenth International Conference on Machine Learning*, pages 82–90, 1998.

M. Brand. Fast low-rank modifications of the thin singular value decomposition. *Linear Algebra Appli.*, 415(1):20–30, 2006.

M. Brand. A random walks perspective on maximizing satisfaction and profit. In *SIAM Conference on Optimization*, May 2005.

Matthew Brand. Incremental singular value decomposition of uncertain data with missing values. In *ECCV '02: Proceedings of the 7th European Conference on Computer Vision – Part I*, pages 707–720, 2002.

Ulrik Brandes, Daniel Delling, Marco Gaertler, Robert Gorke, Martin Hoefer, Zoran Nikoloski, and Dorothea Wagner. On modularity clustering. *IEEE Trans. Knowl. Data Eng.*, 20(2):172–188, 2008.

John Breese, David Heckerman, and Carl Kadie. Empirical analysis of predictive algorithms for collaborative filtering. In *Proceedings of the 14th Annual Conference on Uncertainty in Artificial Intelligence (UAI-98)*, pages 43–52, San Francisco, CA, 1998. Morgan Kaufmann.

Leo Breiman. Random forests. *Mach. Learn.*, pages 5–32, 2001.

Leo Breiman. Bagging predictors. *Mach. Learn.*, 24(2):123–140, 1996.

Leo Breiman, Jerome Friedman, Charles J. Stone, and R. A. Olshen. *Classification and Regression Trees*. 1984.

Lee Breslau, Pei Cao, Li Fan, Graham Phillips, and Scott Shenker. Web caching and zipf-like distributions: Evidence and implications. In *INFOCOM*, pages 126–134, 1999.

Richard Brewer and Margaret McCann. *Laboratory and Field Manual of Ecology*. Saunders College Publishing, November 1997.

Sergey Brin. Near neighbor search in large metric spaces. In *VLDB*, pages 574–584, 1995.

Sergey Brin and Lawrence Page. The anatomy of a large-scale hypertextual web search engine. *Comput. Netw. ISDN Syst.*, 30(1–7):107–117, 1998.

Alan J. Broder. Strategies for efficient incremental nearest neighbor search. *Pattern Recogn.*, 23(1–2):171–178, 1990.

Andrei Z. Broder. On the resemblance and containment of documents. In *Compression and Complexity of Sequences (SEQUENCES '97)*, pages 21–29. IEEE Computer Society, 1997.

Andrei Z. Broder, Steven C. Glassman, Mark S. Manasse, and Geoffrey Zweig. Syntactic clustering of the Web. *Comput. Netw. ISDN Syst.*, 29(8–13):1157–1166, 1997.

P. Brucker. On the complexity of clustering problems. *Optim. Operat. Res.*, 1977.

M. Cecelia Buchanan and Polle Zellweger. Scheduling multimedia documents using temporal constraints. In *Proceedings of the Third International Workshop on Network and Operating System Support for Digital Audio and Video*, pages 237–249. Springer-Verlag.

M. Cecelia Buchanan and Polle Zellweger. Automatically generating consistent schedules for multimedia documents. *Multimedia Syst.*, 1(2):55–67, 1993a.

M. C. Buchanan and P.T. Zellweger. Automatic temporal layout mechanisms. In *ACM Multimedia 93*, pages 341–350, 1993b.

Michael Buckland and Fredric Gey. The relationship between recall and precision. *J. Am. Soc. Inf. Sci.*, 45(1):12–19, 1994.

Chris Buckley, Gerard Salton, James Allan, and Amit Singhal. Automatic query expansion using smart: Trec 3. In *Third Text Retrieval Conference (TREC-3)*, pages 69–80, 1995.

H. Bunke. Error correcting graph matching: On the influence of the underlying cost function. *IEEE Trans. Pattern Anal. Mach. Intell.*, 21(9):917–922, 1999.

Christopher J. C. Burges. A tutorial on support vector machines for pattern recognition. *Data Mining Knowl. Discov.*, 2:121–167, 1998.

M. Burgin. Generalized Kolmogorov complexity and duality in theory of computations. *Not. Russian Acad. Sci.*, 25(3):19–23, 1982.

W. A. Burkhard and R. M. Keller. Some approaches to best-match file searching. *Commun. ACM*, 16(4):230–236, 1973.

A. R. Butz. Alternative algorithm for hilbert's space-filling curve. *IEEE Trans. Comput.*, 20(4):424–426, 1971.

Paul B. Callahan and S. Rao Kosaraju. A decomposition of multidimensional point sets with applications to k-nearest-neighbors and n-body potential fields. *J. ACM*, 42(1):67–90, 1995.

Iain Campbell. Interactive evaluation of the ostensive model using a new test collection of images with multiple relevance assessments. *J. Inform. Retri.*, 2:89–114, 2000a.

Iain Campbell. *The Ostensive Model of Developing Information-Needs*. Ph.D. thesis, University of Glasgow, September 2000b.

Iain Campbell. Supporting information needs by ostensive definition in an adaptive information space. In *MIRO*, 1995.

K. Selçuk Candan and Wen-Syan Li. On similarity measures for multimedia database applications. *Knowl. Inform. Syst.*, 3(1):30–51, 2001.

K. Selçuk Candan and Wen-Syan Li. Reasoning for web document associations and its applications in site map construction. *Data Knowl. Eng.*, 43(2):121–150, 2002.

K. Selçuk Candan and Wen-Syan Li. Using random walks for mining web document associations. In *PAKDD '00: Proceedings of the 4th Pacific-Asia Conference on Knowledge Discovery and Data Mining, Current Issues and New Applications*, pages 294–305, 2000.

K. Selçuk Candan and Prakash Yamuna. Similarity-based retrieval of temporal specifications and its application to the retrieval of multimedia documents. *Multimedia Tools Appl.*, 27(1):143–180, 2005.

K. Selçuk Candan, B. Prabhakaran, and V. S. Subrahmanian. Chimp: a framework for supporting distributed multimedia document authoring and presentation. In *Multimedia '96: Proceedings of the Fourth ACM International Conference on Multimedia*, pages 329–340, 1996a.

K. Selçuk Candan, B. Prabhakaran, and V. S. Subrahmanian. Collaborative multimedia documents: authoring and presentation. *Int. J. Intel. Syst. Multimedia Comput. Syst.*, 13:1059–1111, 1996b.

K. Selçuk Candan, P. Venkat Rangan, and V. S. Subrahmanian. Collaborative multimedia systems: synthesis of media objects. *IEEE Trans. Knowl. Data Eng.*, 10(3):433–457, 1998.

K. Selçuk Candan, Eric Lemar, and V. S. Subrahmanian. View management in multimedia databases. *The VLDB Journal*, 9(2):131–153, 2000a.

K. Selçuk Candan, Wen-Syan Li, and M. Lakshmi Priya. Similarity-based ranking and query processing in multimedia databases. *Data Knowl. Eng.*, 35(3):259–298, 2000b.

K. Selçuk Candan, Mehmet E. Dönderler, J. Ramamoorthy, and Jong W. Kim. Clustering and indexing of experience sequences for popularity-driven recommendations. In *CARPE '06: Proceedings of the 3rd ACM Workshop on Continuous Archival and Retrieval of Personal Experiences*, pages 75–84, 2006.

K. Selçuk Candan, Jong Wook Kim, Huan Liu, Reshma Suvarna, and Nitin Agarwal. *Multimedia Data Mining and Knowledge Discovery*, chapter, Exploiting spatial transformations for identifying mappings in hierarchical media data. Springer 2007.

K. Selçuk Candan, Huiping Cao, Yan Qi, and Maria Luisa Sapino. System support for exploration and expert feedback in resolving conflicts during integration of metadata. *VLDB J.*, 17(6):1407–1444, 2008.

K. Selçuk Candan, Mehmet E. Donderler, Terri Hedgpeth, Jong Wook Kim, Qing Li, and Maria Luisa Sapino. Sea: Segment-enrich-annotate paradigm for adapting dialog-based content for improved accessibility. *TOIS ACM Trans. Inform. Syst.*, 27, 3, pages 1–45, May, 2009.

J. Canny. A computational approach to edge detection. *Trans. Pattern Anal. Mach. Intell.*, 8:679–714, 1986.

Huiping Cao, Yan Qi, K. Selçuk Candan, and Maria Luisa Sapino. Feedback-driven result ranking and query refinement for exploring semi-structured data collections. In *EDBT'10: 13th International Conference on Extending Database Technology*, pages 3–14, 2010.

Jianrong Cao and A. Cai. A method for classification of scenery documentary using mpeg-7 edge histogram descriptor. *VLSI Design and Video Technology, 2005. Proceedings of 2005 IEEE International Workshop on*, pages 105–108, 2005.

A. F. Cardenas, I. T. Ieong, R. Barker, R. K. Taira, and C. M. Breant. The knowledge-based object-oriented picquery+ language. *IEEE Trans. Knowl. Data Eng.*, 5(4):644–657, 1993.

Michael J. Carey and Donald Kossmann. Reducing the braking distance of an SQL query engine. In *VLDB '98: Proceedings of the 24rd International Conference on Very Large Data Bases*, pages 158–169, 1998.

Michael J. Carey and Donald Kossmann. On saying "enough already!" in SQL. In *Proceeding of the ACM SIGMOD Conference on Management of Data*, pages 219–230. ACM Press, 1997a.

Michael J. Carey and Donald Kossmann. Processing top n and bottom n queries. *Data Eng. Bull.*, 20(3) 12–19, 1997b.

J. D. Caroll and J. J. Chang. Analysis of individual diferences in multidimensional scaling via an n-way generalization of "Eckart-Young" decomposition. *Psychometrika*, 35:283–319, 1970.

R. G. G. Cattell and Douglas K. Barry, editors. *The Object Data Standard: ODMG 3.0*. Morgan Kauffman, 2000.

Deepayan Chakrabarti, Spiros Papadimitriou, Dharmendra S. Modha, and Christos Faloutsos. Fully automatic cross-associations. In *KDD '04: Proceedings of the Tenth ACM SIGKDD International Conference on Knowledge Discovery and Data Mining*, pages 79–88, 2004.

Kaushik Chakrabarti and Sharad Mehrotra. High dimensional feature indexing using hybrid trees. In *Proceedings of the 15th IEEE International Conference on Data Engineering (ICDE)*, pages 440–447, 1999.

Kaushik Chakrabarti, Venkatesh Ganti, Jiawei Han, and Dong Xin. Ranking objects based on relationships. In *SIGMOD Conference*, pages 371–382, 2006.

Soumen Chakrabarti. *Mining the Web: Discovering Knowledge from Hypertext Data*. Morgan-Kauffman, 2002.

I. M. Chakravarti, R. G. Laha, and J. Roy. *Handbook of Methods of Applied Statistics*, volume I. John Wiley and Sons, 1967.

C.-Y. Chan, M. Garofalakis, and R. Rastogi. Re-tree: An efficient index structure for regular expressions. In *VLDB*, 1994.

Chee-Yong Chan, Pin-Kwang Eng, and Kian-Lee Tan. Efficient processing of skyline queries with partially-ordered domains. In *ICDE '05: Proceedings of the 21st International Conference on Data Engineering*, pages 190–191, 2005a.

Chee-Yong Chan, Pin-Kwang Eng, and Kian-Lee Tan. Stratified computation of skylines with partially-ordered domains. In *SIGMOD '05: Proceedings of the 2005 ACM SIGMOD International Conference on Management of Data*, pages 203–214, 2005b.

S. Chandrasekaran, B. S. Manjunath, Y. F. Wang, J. Winkeler, and H. Zhang. An eigenspace update algorithm for image analysis. *Graph. Models Image Process.*, 59(5):321–332, 1997.

C. C. Chang and S. Y. Lee. Retrieval of similar pictures on pictorial databases. *Pattern Recogn.*, 24(7):675–681, 1991.

C. C. Chang. Spatial match retrieval of symbolic pictures. *J. Inform. Sci. Eng.*, 7: 405–422, 1991.

J. W. Chang, J. H. Lee, and Y. J. Lee. Multikey access methods based on term discrimination and signature clustering. *SIGIR Forum*, 23(SI):176–185, 1989.

J. W. Chang, J. S. Yoo, M. H. Kim, and Y. J. Lee. A signature-based hybrid access scheme for text databases. In *International Symposium on Next Generation Database Systems and Their Applications*, pages 138–144, 1993.

Kevin Chen-Chuan Chang and Seung-won Hwang. Minimal probing: supporting expensive predicates for top-k queries. In *SIGMOD '02: Proceedings of the 2002 ACM SIGMOD International Conference on Management of Data*, pages 346–357, 2002.

Ning-San Chang and King-Sun Fu. Query-by-pictorial-example. *IEEE Trans. Softw. Eng.*, 6(6):519–524, 1980.

S. K. Chang, Q. Y. Shi, and C. W. Yan. Iconic indexing by 2-D strings. *IEEE Trans. Pattern Anal. Mach. Intell.*, 9(3):413–428, 1987.

Shi-Kuo Chang and Eriand Jungert. A spatial knowledge structure for image information systems using symbolic projections. In *ACM '86: Proceedings of 1986 ACM Fall joint computer conference*, pages 79–86, 1986.

Ye-In Chang, Hsing-Yen Ann, and Wei-Horng Yeh. A unique-id-based matrix strategy for efficient iconic indexing of symbolic pictures. *Pattern Recogn.*, 33(8): 1263–1276, 2000a.

Y. I. Chang and B. Y. Yang . A prime-number-based matrix strategy for efficient iconic indexing of symbolic pictures. *Pattern Recogn.*, 30(10):1–13, 1997.

Y. I. Chang, B. Y. Yang, and W. H. Yeh. A generalized prime-number-based matrix strategy for efficient iconic indexing of symbolic pictures. *Pattern Recogn. Lett.*, 22:657–666, 2001.

Y. I. Chang, B. Y. Yang, and W. H. Yeh. A bit-pattern-based matrix strategy for efficient iconic indexing of symbolic pictures. *Pattern Recogn. Lett.*, 24:537–545, 2003.

Yuan-Chi Chang, Lawrence Bergman, Vittorio Castelli, Chung-Sheng Li, Ming-Ling Lo, and John R. Smith. The onion technique: indexing for linear optimization queries. In *SIGMOD '00: Proceedings of the 2000 ACM SIGMOD international conference on Management of data*, pages 391–402, 2000b.

Moses S. Charikar. Similarity estimation techniques from rounding algorithms. In *STOC '02: Proceedings of the Thirty-fourth Annual ACM Symposium on Theory of Computing*, pages 380–388, 2002.

B. B. Chaudhuri and N. Sarkar. Texture segmentation using fractal dimension. *PAMI*, 17(1):72–77, January 1995.

S. Chaudhuri, L. Gravano, and Amlie Marian. Optimizing top-k selection queries over multimedia repositories. *IEEE Trans. Knowl. Data Eng*, 16(8):992–1009, 2004.

Surajit Chaudhuri. An overview of query optimization in relational systems. In *PODS '98: Proceedings of the Seventeenth ACM SIGACT-SIGMOD-SIGART Symposium on Principles of Database Systems*, pages 34–43, 1998.

Surajit Chaudhuri and Luis Gravano. Evaluating top-k selection queries. In *VLDB'99, Proceedings of 25th International Conference on Very Large Data Bases, September 7–10, 1999, Edinburgh, Scotland, UK*, pages 397–410, 1999.

Edgar Chavez, Gonzalo Navarro, Ricardo Baeza-Yates, and Jose L. Marroquin. Searching in metric spaces. *ACM Comput. Surv.*, 33:273–321, 1999.

S. Chawathe. *Comparing Hierarchical Data in External Memory*. In *Twenty-fifth International Conference on Very Large Data Bases*, Edinburgh, Scotland, U.K., 1999.

S. Chawathe and H. Garcia-Molina. Meaningful change detection in structured data. In *Proceedings of the ACM SIGMOD International Conference on Management of Data*, pages 26–37. Tucson, Arizona, May 1997.

R. Chellappa. Two dimensional discrete Gaussian Markov random field models for image processing. In L. N. Kanal and A. Rosenfeld, editors, *Progress in Pattern Recognition*, volume 2, pages 79–122. North Holland, 1986.

H. Chen and T. Ng. An algorithmic approach to concept exploration in a large knowledge network (automatic thesaurus consultation): symbolic branch-and-bound search vs. connectionist Hopfield net activation. *J. Am. Soc. Inf. Sci.*, 46 (5):348–369, 1995.

Peter Pin-Shan Chen. The entity-relationship model – toward a unified view of data. *ACM Trans. Database Syst.*, 1(1):9–36, 1976.

Weimin Chen. More efficient algorithm for ordered tree inclusion. *J. Algorithms*, 26(2):370–385, 1998.

Reynold Cheng, Dmitri V. Kalashnikov, and Sunil Prabhakar. Evaluation of probabilistic queries over imprecise data in constantly-evolving environments. *Inform. Syst.*, 32(1):104–130, 2007.

Venkata S. Cherukuri and K. Selçuk Candan. Propagation-vectors for trees (pvt): Concise yet effective summaries for hierarchical data and trees. In *CIKM Workshop on Large-Scale Distributed Systems for Information Retrieval (LSDS-IR)*, 2008.

David Maxwell Chickering, David Heckerman, and Christopher Meek. A Bayesian approach to learning Bayesian networks with local structure. In *Proceedings of Thirteenth Conference on Uncertainty in Artificial Intelligence*, pages 80–89, 1997.

Jan Chomicki. Preference formulas in relational queries. *ACM Trans. Database Syst.*, 28(4):427–466, 2003.

Jan Chomicki, Parke Godfrey, Jarek Gryz, and Dongming Liang. Skyline with presorting. In *ICDE*, pages 717–719, 2003.

Jan Chomicki, Parke Godfrey, Jarek Gryz, and Dongming Liang. Skyline with presorting: Theory and optimizations. In *Intelligent Information Systems*, pages 595–604, 2005.

Wesley W. Chu, Chih-Cheng Hsu, Ion Tim Ieong, and Ricky K. Taira. Content-based image retrieval using metadata and relaxation techniques. In *Multimedia Data Management*, pages 149–190. 1998.

Fan R. K. Chung. *Spectral Graph Theory*. American Mathematical Society, 1997.

P. Ciaccia, M. Patella, F. Rabitti, and P. Zezula. P. Indexing metric spaces with Mtree. In *Proc. Quinto convegno Nazionale Sistemi Evoluti per Basi di Dati*, pages 67–86, 1997.

Paolo Ciaccia and Marco Patella. Pac nearest neighbor queries: Approximate and controlled search in high-dimensional and metric spaces. In *ICDE*, pages 244–255, 2000.

Rudi Cilibrasi and Paul M. B. Vitanyi. Clustering by compression. *IEEE Trans. Inform. Theory*, 51(4):1523–1545, 2005.

Kenneth L. Clarkson. An algorithm for approximate closest-point queries. In *SCG '94: Proceedings of the Tenth Annual Symposium on Computational Geometry*, pages 160–164, 1994.

E. F. Codd. A relational model of data for large shared data banks. *Commun. ACM*, 13(6):377–387, 1970.

William W. Cohen, Robert E. Schapire, and Yoram Singer. Learning to order things. In *NIPS '97: Proceedings of the 1997 Conference on Advances in Neural Information Processing Systems 10*, pages 451–457, 1998.

Richard Cole. Tight bounds on the complexity of the Boyer–Moore string matching algorithm. *SIAM J. Comput.*, 23(5), 1994.

Allan M. Collins and Elizabeth F. Loftus. A spreading-activation theory of semantic processing. *Psychol. Rev.*, 82(6):407–428, 1975.

Beate Commentz-Walter. A string matching algorithm fast on the average. In *Proceedings of the 6th Colloquium on Automata, Languages and Programming*, pages 118–132, London, UK, 1979. Springer-Verlag.

F. Commoner, A. W. Holt, S. Even, and A. Pnueli. Marked directed graphs. *J. Comp. Syst. Sci.*, 5(5):511–523, 1971.

Thomas H. Cormen, Charles E. Leiserson, Ronald L. Rivest, and Clifford Stein. *Introduction to Algorithms, Second Edition*. McGraw-Hill Science/Engineering/Math, July 2001. ISBN 0070131511.

G. Cormode and S. Muthukrishnan. The string edit distance matching problem with moves. In *ACM-SIAM Symposium on Discrete Algorithms*, 2002.

M. Crochemore and R. Vrin. Direct construction of compact directed acyclic word graphs. In *CPM97*, pages 116–12. LNCS 1264, Springer-Verlag, 1997.

M. Crochemore, A. Czumaj, L. Gasieniec, S. Jarominek, T. Lecroq, W. Plandowski, and W. Rytter. Speeding up two string-matching algorithms. *Algorithmica*, 12 (4/5):247–267, October 1994.

W. B. Croft and D. J. Harper. Using probabilistic models of document retrieval without relevance information. In Readings in information Retrieval, K. Sparck Jones and P. Willett, Eds., Morgan Kaufmann Multimedia Information And Systems Series, Morgan Kaufmann Publishers, San Francisco, CA, pages 339–344, 1997.

W. B. Croft and D. J. Harper. Using probabilistic models of document retrieval without relevance information. *J. Documentation*, 35:285–295, 1979.

G. R. Cross and A. K. Jain. Markov random field texture models. *TransPAMI*, 5: 25–39, 1983.

Nilesh N. Dalvi and Dan Suciu. Management of probabilistic data: foundations and challenges. In *PODS*, pages 1–12, 2007.

N. N. Dalvi and D. Suciu. Efficient query evaluation on probabilistic databases. In *Proceedings of VLDB '04*, pages 864–875, 2004.

Fred J. Damerau. A technique for computer detection and correction of spelling errors. *Commun. ACM*, 7(3):171–176, 1964.

Nabil Hachem Daniel J. Abadi, and Samuel R. Madden. Column-stores vs. row-stores: how different are they really? In *SIGMOD*, Vancouver, Canada, 2008.

George Dantzig. *Linear Programming and Extensions*. Princeton University Press, 1963.

Mayur Datar, Nicole Immorlica, Piotr Indyk, and Vahab S. Mirrokni. Locality-sensitive hashing scheme based on p-stable distributions. In *SCG '04: Proceedings of the Twentieth Annual Symposium on Computational Geometry*, pages 253–262, 2004.

G. Davis. Self-quantized wavelet subtrees: a wavelet-based theory for fractal image compression. *Data Compression Conference*, 232, 1995.

Jesse Davis and Mark Goadrich. The relationship between precision-recall and roc curves. In *ICML '06: Proceedings of the 23rd International Conference on Machine Learning*, pages 233–240, 2006.

Young Francis Day, Serhan Dagtas, Mitsutoshi Iino, Ashfaq A. Khokhar, and Arif Ghafoor. Spatio-temporal modeling of video data for on-line object-oriented query processing. In *ICMCS*, pages 98–105, 1995a.

Young Francis Day, Serhan Dagtas, Mitsutoshi Iino, Ashfaq A. Khokhar, and Arif Ghafoor. An object-oriented conceptual modeling of video data. In *ICDE '95: Proceedings of the Eleventh International Conference on Data Engineering*, pages 401–408. IEEE Computer Society, 1995b.

D. Dasgupta and F. A. Gonzalez. An intelligent decision support system for intrusion detection and response. In *Proceedings of MMM-ACNS'01*, 2001.

Ronaldo Mussauer de Lima, Flavio Paiva Junqueira, Paulo Andre da S. Gonçalves, and Otto Carlos Muniz B. Duarte. Samm: An integrated environment to support multimedia synchronization of pre-orchestrated data. In *ICMCS '99: Proceedings of the IEEE International Conference on Multimedia Computing and Systems, Volume 2*, page 929. IEEE Computer Society, 1999.

H. Debar, M. Dacier, and A. Wespi. Towards a taxonomy of intrusion-detection systems. *Comp. Networks*, 31:805–822, 1999.

Rina Dechter, Itay Meiri, and Judea Pearl. Temporal constraint networks. *Artifi. Intell.*, 49(1–3):61–95, 1991.

S. Deerwester, Susan Dumais, G. W. Furnas, T. K. Landauer, and R. Harshman. Indexing by latent semantic analysis. *J. Am. Soc. Inform. Sci.*, 41(6):391–407, 1990.

A. P. Dempster, N. M. Laird, and D. B. Rubin. Maximum likelihood from incomplete data via the em algorithm. *J. R. Statist. Soc. Ser. B (Methodol.)*, 39(1):1–38, 1977.

P. Desain. A (de)composable theory of rhythm. *Music Perception*, 9(4):439–454, 1992.

Mukund Deshpande and George Karypis. Item based top-n recommendation algorithms. *ACM Trans. Inform. Syst.*, 22:143–177, 2004.

Luc Devroye and Louise Laforest. An analysis of random d-dimensional quad trees. *SIAM J. Comput.*, 19(5):821–832, 1990.

Inderjit S. Dhillon, Subramanyam Mallela, and Dharmendra S. Modha. Information-theoretic co-clustering. In *KDD '03: Proceedings of the Ninth ACM SIGKDD International Conference on Knowledge Discovery and Data Mining*, pages 89–98, 2003.

Thomas G. Dietterich. An experimental comparison of three methods for constructing ensembles of decision trees: bagging, boosting, and randomization. *Mach. Learn.*, 40(2):139–157, 2000.

B. Ding, J. X. Yu, S. Wang, L. Qing, X. Zhang, and X. Lin. Finding top-k min-cost connected trees in databases. In *ICDE*, 2007.

Chris Ding and Xiaofeng He. K-means clustering via principal component analysis. In *ICML '04: Proceedings of the Twenty-first International Conference on Machine Learning*, pages 225–232, 2004.

Ajay Divakaran. An overview of MPEG-7 motion descriptors and their applications. In Proceedings of the 9th International Conference on Computer Analysis of Images and Patterns (CAIP'01), 29–40, 2001.

Donko Donjerkovic and Raghu Ramakrishnan. Probabilistic optimization of top n queries. In *VLDB '99: Proceedings of the 25th International Conference on Very Large Data Bases*, pages 411–422, 1999.

P. Drineas, Alan Frieze, Ravi Kannan, Santosh Vempala, and V. Vinay. Clustering in large graphs and matrices. In *SODA '99: Proceedings of the Tenth Annual ACM-SIAM Symposium on Discrete Algorithms*, pages 291–299, 1999.

Petros Drineas, Ravi Kannan, and Michael W. Mahoney. Fast Monte Carlo algorithms for matrices III: computing a compressed approximate matrix decomposition. *SIAM J. Comput.*, 36(1):184–206, 2006a.

Petros Drineas, Michael W. Mahoney, and S. Muthukrishnan. Subspace sampling and relative-error matrix approximation: column-row-based methods. In *ESA'06: Proceedings of the 14th Annual European Symposium on Algorithms*, pages 304–314, 2006b.

Didier Dubois and Henri Prade. What are fuzzy rules and how to use them. *Fuzzy Sets Syst.*, 84:169–185, 1996.

M. P. Dubuisson and R. C. Dubes. Efficacy of fractal features in segmenting images of natural textures. *PRL*, 15(4):419–431, April 1994.

R. O. Duda and P. E. Hart. Use of the Hough transformation to detect lines and curves in pictures. *Commun. ACM*, 15:11–15, 1972.

Cynthia Dwork, Ravi Kumar, Moni Naor, and D. Sivakumar. Rank aggregation methods for the web. In *WWW '01: Proceedings of the 10th International Conference on World Wide Web*, pages 613–622, 2001.

H. Edelsbrunner. A new approach to rectangle intersections, part i. *Int. J. Computer Mathematics*, 13:209–219, 1983a.

H. Edelsbrunner. A new approach to rectangle intersections, part ii. *Int. J. Computer Mathematics*, 13:221–229, 1983b.

M. Egenhofer. Deriving the composition of binary topological relations. *J. Visual Lang. Comput.*, 5(2):133–149, 1994.

Essam A. El-Kwae and Mansur R. Kabuka. A robust framework for content-based retrieval by spatial similarity in image databases. *ACM Trans. Inf. Syst.*, 17(2): 174–198, 1999.

I. M. Elfadel and R. W. Picard. Gibbs random fields, cooccurrences and texture modeling. *IEEE Trans. Pattern Anal. Mach. Intell.*, 16(1):24–37, 1994.

Daniel P. Ellis. Beat tracking by dynamic programming. *J. New Music Res.*, 36(1): 51–60, 2007.

Dominik M. Endres and Johannes E. Schindelin. A new metric for probability distributions. *IEEE Trans. Inform. Theory*, 49(7):1858–1860, 2003.

P. Erdos and A. Renyi. On random graphs. *Pub. Math.*, 6:290–297, 1959.

Martha Escobar-Molano, David A. Barrett, Zornitza Genova, and Lei Zhang. Retrieval scheduling for multimedia presentations. In *Multimedia Information Systems*, pages 143–152, 2001.

Ronald Fagin. Combining fuzzy information from multiple systems. In *Proceedings of the ACM Symposium on Principles of Database Systems*, pages 216–226, 1996.

Ronald Fagin. Fuzzy queries in multimedia database systems. In *PODS*, pages 1–10, 1998.

Ronald Fagin and Yoelle S. Maarek. Allowing users to weight search terms. In *Proceedings of Recherche d'Informations Assistee par Ordinateur RIAO '2000*, pages 682–700, 2000.

Ronald Fagin and Edward L. Wimmers. Incorporating user preferences in multimedia queries. In *ICDT*, pages 247–261, 1997.

Ronald Fagin, Amnon Lotem, and Moni Naor. Optimal aggregation algorithms for middleware. In *PODS*, 2001.

Ronald Fagin, Amnon Lotem, and Moni Naor. Optimal aggregation algorithms for middleware. *J. Comput. Syst. Sci.*, 66(4):614–656, 2003.

C. Faloutsos, R. Barber, M. Flickner, J. Hafner, W. Niblack, D. Petkovic, and W. Equitz. Efficient and effective querying by image content. *J. Intell. Inform. Syst.*, 3(3–4):231–262, 1994.

Christos Faloutsos. Signature files. Information Retrieval: Data Structures & Algorithms, pages 44–65, 1992.

Christos Faloutsos and Stavros Christodoulakis. Design of a signature file method that accounts for non-uniform occurrence and query frequencies. In *VLDB '1985: Proceedings of the 11th International Conference on Very Large Data Bases*, pages 165–170, 1985.

Christos Faloutsos and H. V. Jagadish. Hybrid index organizations for text databases. In *EDBT '92: Proceedings of the 3rd International Conference on Extending Database Technology*, pages 310–327, 1992.

Christos Faloutsos and King-Ip Lin. FastMap: a fast algorithm for indexing, data-mining and visualization of traditional and multimedia datasets. In *SIGMOD '95: Proceedings of the 1995 ACM SIGMOD International Conference on Management of Data*, pages 163–174, 1995.

Christos Faloutsos and Shari Roseman. Fractals for secondary key retrieval. Technical Report UMIACS-TR-89-47, University of Maryland, 1989.

Christos Faloutsos and Hanghang Tong. Large graph mining: patterns, tools and case studies. Tutorial at ICDE 2009, 2009.

Gunnar Fant. Analysis and synthesis of speech processes. In *Manual of Phonetics*, 1968.

M. Farach and M. Thorup. Sparse dynamic programming for evolutionary-tree comparison. *SIAM J. Comput.*, 26(1):210–230, January 1997.

W. Y. Feng, Y. B. Yan, G. G. Huang, and G. F. Jin. Micro-optical multiwavelet element for hybrid texture segmentation processor. *OptEng*, 37(1):185–188, January 1998.

T. S. Ferguson. A Bayesian analysis of some nonparametric problems. *Ann. Statist.*, 1(2):209–230, 1973.

Hakan Ferhatosmanoglu, Ertem Tuncel, Divyakant Agrawal, and Amr El Abbadi. Vector approximation based indexing for non-uniform high dimensional data sets. In *CIKM '00: Proceedings of the Ninth International Conference on Information and Knowledge Management*, pages 202–209, 2000.

C. M. Fiduccia and R. M. Mattheyses. A linear-time heuristic for improving network partitions. In *25 years of DAC: Papers on Twenty-five Years of Electronic Design Automation*, pages 241–247, 1988.

M. Fiedler. Algebraic connectivity of graphs. *Czech. Math. J.*, 23(98):298–305, 1973.

M. Fiedler. A property of eigenvectors of nonnegative symmetric matrices and its application to graph theory. *Czech. Math. J.*, 25:619–637, 1975.

R. A. Finkel and J. L. Bentley. Quad trees: a data structure for retrieval on composite keys. *Acta Inform.*, 4:1–9, 1974.

G. Fischer. User modeling in human-computer interaction. In *User Modeling and User-Adapted Interaction*, 2001.

Gary W. Flake, Robert E. Tarjan, and Kostas Tsioutsiouliklis. Graph clustering and minimum cut trees. *Internet Math.*, 1(4):385–408, 2004.

Gary William Flake, Steve Lawrence, and C. Lee Giles. Efficient identification of web communities. In *KDD '00: Proceedings of the Sixth ACM SIGKDD International Conference on Knowledge Discovery and Data Mining*, pages 150–160, 2000.

Sergio Flesca, Giuseppe Manco, Elio Masciari, and Luigi Pontieri. Fast detection of XML structural similarity. *IEEE Trans. Knowl. Data Eng.*, 17(2):160–175, 2005. Student Member-Andrea Pugliese.

Myron Flickner, Harpreet Sawhney, Wayne Niblack, Jonathan Ashley, Qian Huang, Byron Dom, Monika Gorkani, Jim Hafner, Denis Lee, Dragutin Petkovic, David Steele, and Peter Yanker. Query by image and video content: The qbic system. *Computer*, 28(9):23–32, 1995.

G. D. Forney. The viterbi algorithm. In *Proceedings of the IEEE*, volume 61, pages 268–278, March 1973.

W. N. Francis and H. Kucera. *Frequency Analysis of English Usage: Lexicon and Grammar*. Houghton Mifflin, 1982.

Edward Fredkin. Trie memory. *Commun. ACM*, 3(9):490–499, 1960.

H. Freeman. Use of incremental curvature for describing and analyzing two-dimensional shape. In *PRIP79*, pages 437–444, 1979.

H. Freeman. Boundary encoding revisited. In *AIU96*, pages 84–91, 1996.

William Freeman and Edward H. Adelson Y. The design and use of steerable filters. *IEEE Trans. Pattern Anal. Mach. Intel.*, 13:891–906, 1991.

Yoav Freund and Robert E. Schapire. Large margin classification using the perceptron algorithm. In *COLT' 98: Proceedings of the Eleventh Annual Conference on Computational Learning Theory*, pages 209–217, 1998.

Yoav Freund and Robert E. Schapire. A decision-theoretic generalization of on-line learning and an application to boosting. In *EuroCOLT '95: Proceedings of the Second European Conference on Computational Learning Theory*, pages 23–37, 1995.

Yoav Freund and Robert E. Schapire. A decision-theoretic generalization of on-line learning and an application to boosting. *J. Comp. Syst. Sci.*, 55(1):119–139, 1997.

Yoav Freund, Raj Iyer, Robert E. Schapire, and Yoram Singer. An efficient boosting algorithm for combining preferences. *J. Mach. Learn. Res.*, pages 170–178, 2003.

Jerome H. Friedman, Jon Louis Bentley, and Raphael Ari Finkel. An algorithm for finding best matches in logarithmic expected time. *ACM Trans. Math. Softw.*, 3 (3):209–226, 1977.

Alan Frieze, Ravi Kannan, and Santosh Vempala. Fast Monte-Carlo algorithms for finding low-rank approximations. In *FOCS '98: Proceedings of the 39th Annual Symposium on Foundations of Computer Science*, pages 370–378, 1998.

Henry Fuchs, Zvi M. Kedem, and Bruce F. Naylor. On visible surface generation by a priori tree structures. *SIGGRAPH Comput. Graph.*, 14(3):124–133, 1980.

Keinosuke Fukunaga and Patrenahalli M. Narendra. A branch and bound algorithms for computing k-nearest neighbors. *IEEE Trans. Comput.*, 24(7):750–753, 1975.

Ombretta Gaggi and Augusto Celentano. Modelling synchronized hypermedia presentations. *Multimedia Tools Appl.*, 27(1):53–78, 2005.

S. I. Gallant. Optimal linear discriminants. In *Eighth International Conference on Pattern Recognition*, pages 849–852, 1986.

N. Garg, G. Konjevod, and R. Ravi. A polylogarithmic approximation algorithm for the group Steiner tree problem. In *Proceedings of the 9th Annual ACM-SIAM Symposium on Discrete Algorithms*, pages 253–259, 1998.

J. Gemmell, G. Bell, and R. Lueder. Mylifebits: a personal database for everything. *CACM*, 49(1):88–95, 2006.

Simon J. Gibbs, Christian Breiteneder, and Dennis Tsichritzis. Audio/video databases: An object-oriented approach. In *Proceedings of the Ninth International Conference on Data Engineering*, pages 381–390, 1993.

David Gibson, Jon Kleinberg, and Prabhakar Raghavan. Inferring web communities from link topology. In *HYPERTEXT '98: Proceedings of the Ninth ACM Conference on Hypertext and Hypermedia: Links, Objects, Time and Space – Structure in Hypermedia Systems*, pages 225–234, 1998.

Rosalba Giugno and Dennis Shasha. Graphgrep: a fast and universal method for querying graphs. In *Proceeding of the IEEE International Conference on Pattern Recognition (ICPR)*, pages 112–115, 2002.

Parke Godfrey, Ryan Shipley, and Jarek Gryz. Maximal vector computation in large data sets. In *VLDB*, pages 229–240, 2005.

Martin Gogolla and Uwe Hohenstein. Towards a semantic view of an extended entity-relationship model. *ACM Trans. Database Syst.*, 16(3):369–416, 1991.

David Goldberg, David Nichols, Brian M. Oki, and Douglas Terry. Using collaborative filtering to weave an information tapestry. *Commun. ACM*, 35(12):61–70, 1992.

R. E. Gomory and T. C. Hu. Multi-terminal network flows. *J. SIAM*, 9:551–570, 1961.

C. Goodall. Procrustes methods in the statistical analysis of shape. *J. R. Statist. Soc. Ser. B (Methodol)*, 53(2):285–339, 1991.

Luc J. Van Gool, Theo Moons, and Dorin Ungureanu. Affine/ photometric invariants for planar intensity patterns. In *ECCV '96: Proceedings of the 4th European Conference on Computer Vision, Volume I*, pages 642–651, 1996.

J. Gower. Generalized Procrustes analysis. *Psychometrika*, 40:33–51, 1975.

Luis Gravano, Amelie Marian, and Surajit Chaudhuri. Optimizing top-*k* selection queries over multimedia repositories. *IEEE Trans. Knowl. Data Eng.*, 16(8):992–1009, 2004.

Todd J. Green and Val Tannen. Models for incomplete and probabilistic information. *IEEE Data Eng. Bull.*, 29, 2006.

S. Grinaker. Edge based segmentation and texture separation. In *Proceedings of the 5th International Conference on Pattern Recognition*, pages 554–557, 1980.

Matthias Gruhne, Ruben Tous, Jaime Delgado, Mario Doeller, and Harald Kosch. Mp7qf: An Mpeg-7 query format. In *AXMEDIS '07: Proceedings of the Third International Conference on Automated Production of Cross Media Content for Multi-Channel Distribution*, pages 15–18, 2007.

Xiaohui Gu and Klara Nahrstedt. Distributed multimedia service composition with statistical qos assurances. *IEEE Transactions on Multimedia*, 8(1):141–151, 2006.

Xiaohui Gu and Philip S. Yu. Toward self-managed media stream processing service overlays. In *ICME*, pages 2054–2057, 2007.

Ming Gu and Stanley C. Eisenstat. Downdating the singular value decomposition. *SIAM J. Matrix Anal. Appl.*, 16(3):793–810, 1995.

Ming Gu and Stanley C. Eisenstat. A stable and fast algorithm for updating the singular value decomposition. Technical report, YALEU/DCS/RR-966, Department of Computer Science, Yale University, New Haven, CT, 1993.

Venkat N. Gudivada. ThetaR-string: a geometry-based representation for efficient and effective retrieval of images by spatial similarity. *IEEE Trans. Knowl. Data Eng.*, 10(3):504–512, 1998.

Venkat N. Gudivada and Vijay V. Raghavan. Design and evaluation of algorithms for image retrieval by spatial similarity. *ACM Trans. Inform. Syst.*, 13:115–144, 1995.

Ulrich Güntzer, Wolf-Tilo Balke, and Werner Kiessling. Optimizing multi-feature queries for image databases. In *VLDB '00: Proceedings of the 26th International Conference on Very Large Data Bases*, pages 419–428, 2000.

Ulrich Güntzer, Wolf-Tilo Balke, and Werner Kiessling. Towards efficient multi-feature queries in heterogeneous environments. In *ITCC '01: Proceedings of the International Conference on Information Technology: Coding and Computing*, pages 622–628, 2001.

Sha Guo, Wei Sun, Yi Deng, Wei Li, Qing Liu, and Weiping Zhang. Panther: an inexpensive and integrated multimedia environment. *Proceedings of the International Conference on Multimedia Computing and Systems, 1994*, pages 382–391, May 1994.

Zhen Guo, Zhongfei Zhang, Eric Xing, and Christos Faloutsos. Enhanced max margin learning on multimodal data mining in a multimedia database. In *KDD '07: Proceedings of the 13th ACM SIGKDD International Conference on Knowledge Discovery and Data Mining*, pages 340–349, 2007.

Peter Gurský and Peter Vojtáš. Speeding up the NRA algorithm. In *SUM '08: Proceedings of the 2nd International Conference on Scalable Uncertainty Management*, pages 243–255, 2008.

Antomn Guttman. R-trees: a dynamic index structure for spatial searching. In *Proceedings of the 1984 ACM SIGMOD International Conference on Management of Data*, pages 47–57, 1984.

A. Haar. Zur theorie der orthogonalen Funktionensysteme. *Math. Ann.*, 69:331–371, 1910.

Peter J. Haas and Joseph M. Hellerstein. Ripple joins for online aggregation. *SIGMOD Rec.*, 28(2):287–298, 1999.

James L. Hafner, Harpreet S. Sawhney, William Equitz, Myron Flickner, and Wayne Niblack. Efficient color histogram indexing for quadratic form distance functions. *IEEE Trans. Pattern Anal. Mach. Intell.*, 17(7):729–736, 1995.

Veli Hakkoymaz and Gültekin Özsoyoglu. A constraint-driven approach to automate the organization and playout of presentations in multimedia databases. *Multimedia Tools Appl.*, 4(2):171–197, 1997.

Veli Hakkoymaz, J. Kraft, and G. Ozsoyoglu. Constraint-based automation of multimedia presentation assembly. *ACM Multimedia Syst. J.*, 7:500–518, 1999.

Rei Hamakawa and Jun Rekimoto. Object composition and playback models for handling multimedia data. In *MULTIMEDIA '93: Proceedings of the First ACM International Conference on Multimedia*, pages 273–281, 1993.

Greg Hamerly and Charles Elkan. Learning the k in k-means. In *Proceedings of the 17th NIPS*, pages 281–288, 2003.

Richard W. Hamming. Error detecting and error correcting codes. *Bell Syst. Tech. J.*, 26(2):147–160, 1950.

J. Han and M. Kamber. *Data Mining: Concepts and Techniques*. Morgan Kauffman, 2001.

Mark H. Hansen and Bin Yu. Model selection and the principle of minimum description length. *J. Am. Statist. Assoc.*, 96(454):746–774, 2001.

Frank Harary and Allen J. Schwenk. The spectral approach to determining the number of walks in a graph. *Pacific J. Math.*, 80(2):443–449, 1979.

Donna Harman, Edward A. Fox, Ricardo A. Baeza-Yates, and Whay C. Lee. Inverted files. In *Information Retrieval: Data Structures & Algorithms*, pages 28–43. 1992.

R. A. Harshman. Foundations of the parafac procedure: models and conditions for an" explanatory" multi-modal factor analysis. *UCLA Working Papers Phonet.*, 16:1–84, 1970.

M. Hassner and J. Sklansky. The use of Markov random fields as models of textures. *Comp. Graph. Image Proc.*, 12:357–370, 1980.

Peter E. Hart, Nils J. Nilsson, and Bertram Raphael. Correction to "a formal basis for the heuristic determination of minimum cost paths." *SIGART Bull.*, (37):28–29, 1972.

Bin He and Kevin Chen-Chuan Chang. Automatic complex schema matching across web query interfaces: A correlation mining approach. *ACM Trans. Database Syst.*, 31(1):346–395, 2006.

D. Hebb. *Organisation of Behaviour*. John Wiley & Sons, 1949.

Nevin Heintze. Scalable document fingerprinting. In *USENIX Workshop on Electronic Commerce*, 1996.

Joseph M. Hellerstein. Optimization techniques for queries with expensive methods. *ACM Trans. Database Syst.*, 23(2):113–157, 1998.

David P. Helmbold and Manfred K. Warmuth. On weak learning. *J. Comput. Syst. Sci.*, 50(3):551–573, 1995.

Sven Helmer. Measuring the structural similarity of semistructured documents using entropy. In *VLDB '07: Proceedings of the 33rd International Conference on Very Large Data Bases*, pages 1022–1032, 2007.

A. Henrich, H. W. Six, and P. Widmayer. The LSD tree: spatial access to multidimensional and non-point objects. In *VLDB '89: Proceedings of the 15th International Conference on Very Large Data Bases*, pages 45–53, 1989.

Andreas Henrich. The lsdh-tree: an access structure for feature vectors. In *ICDE '98: Proceedings of the Fourteenth International Conference on Data Engineering*, pages 362–369, 1998.

Ralf Herbrich, Thore Graepel, and Klaus Obermayer. *Large Margin Rank Boundaries for Ordinal Regression*. MIT Press, Cambridge, MA, 2000.

Melanie Herschel and Felix Naumann. Scaling up duplicate detection in graph data. In *CIKM '08: Proceeding of the 17th ACM Conference on Information and Knowledge Management*, pages 1325–1326, 2008.

Stacie Hibino and Elke A. Rundensteiner. A visual query language for identifying temporal trends in video data. In *Proceedings of the 1995 International Workshop on Multi-Media Database Management Systems*, pages 74–81, 1995.

Stacie Hibino and Elke A. Rundensteiner. A visual multimedia query language for temporal analysis of video data. In *Multimedia Database Systems*, pages 123–159. 1996.

David Hilbert. Über stetige Abbildung einer Linie auf ein Flachenstuck. *Math. Ann.*, 38:459–460, 1891.

Will Hill, Larry Stead, Mark Rosenstein, and George Furnas. Recommending and evaluating choices in a virtual community of use. In *CHI '95: Proceedings of the SIGCHI Conference on Human Factors in Computing Systems*, pages 194–201, 1995.

Klaus Hinrichs. Implementation of the grid file: design concepts and experience. *BIT*, 25(4):569–592, 1985.

Gisli R. Hjaltason and Hanan Samet. Index-driven similarity search in metric spaces (survey article). *ACM Trans. Database Syst.*, 28(4):517–580, 2003.

Gisli R. Hjaltason and Hanan Samet. Incremental similarity search in multimedia databases. Technical report, Computer Science Department, University of Maryland, College Park, 2000.

Gísli R. Hjaltason and Hanan Samet. Distance browsing in spatial databases. *ACM Trans. Database Syst.*, 24(2):265–318, 1999.

Rune Hjelsvold and Roger Midtstraum. Modelling and querying video data. In *VLDB '94: Proceedings of the 20th International Conference on Very Large Data Bases*, pages 686–694, 1994.

Tin Kam Ho. Complexity of classification problems and comparative advantages of combined classifiers. In *Proceedings of the First International Workshop on Multiple Classifier Systems, Lecture Notes in Computer science*, pages 97–106, 2000.

Tin Kam Ho. The random subspace method for constructing decision forests. *IEEE Trans. Pattern Anal. Mach. Intell.*, 20(8):832–844, 1998.

Tin Kam Ho. Random decision forest. In *Proceedings of the 3rd International Conference on Document Analysis and Recognition*, pages 278–282, Montreal, Canada, August 1995.

Thomas Hofmann. Probabilistic latent semantic indexing. In *SIGIR '99: Proceedings of the 22nd Annual International ACM SIGIR Conference on Research and Development in Information Retrieval*, pages 50–57, 1999.

Thomas Hofmann. Learning what people (don't) want. In *EMCL '01: Proceedings of the 12th European Conference on Machine Learning*, pages 214–225, 2001.

N. Holsti and E. Sutinen. Approximate string matching using q-gram places. In *Proceedings of the 7th Finnish Symposium on Computer Science*, pages 16–12. University of Joensuu, 1994.

Andre Holzapfel and Yannis Stylianou. Rhythmic similarity of music based on dynamic periodicity warping. In *ICASSP 2008*, pages 2217–2220, 2008.

Wei Hong and Michael Stonebraker. Optimization of parallel query execution plans in xprs. *Distrib. Parallel Databases*, 1(1):9–32, 1993.

John Hopcroft and Jeffrey Ullman. *Introduction to Automata Theory, Languages, and Computation*. Addison-Wesley, 1979.

P. V. C. Hough. Method and means for recognizing complex patterns. U.S. Patent 3,069,654, Dec. 18, 1962.

Paul G. Howard and Jeffrey Scott Vitter. Analysis of arithmetic coding for data compression. In *Data Compression Conference*, pages 3–12, 1991.

Vagelis Hristidis, Nick Koudas, and Yannis Papakonstantinou. Prefer: a system for the efficient execution of multi-parametric ranked queries. In *SIGMOD Conference*, pages 259–270, 2001.

Yi-Chung Hu, Ruey-Shun Chen, and Gwo-Hshiung Tzeng. Finding fuzzy classification rules using data mining techniques. *Pattern Recogn. Lett.*, 24(1-3):509–519, 2003.

P. W. Huang and Y. R. Jean. Using 2D C+-string as spatial knowledge representation for image database systems. *Pattern Recogn.*, (27):1249–1257, 1994.

Zan Huang, Hsinchun Chen, and Daniel Zeng. Applying associative retrieval techniques to alleviate the sparsity problem in collaborative filtering. *ACM Trans. Inform. Syst.*, 22:116–142, 2004.

D. A. Huffman. A method for the construction of minimum-redundancy codes. *Proc. IRE*, 40(9):1098–1101, 1952.

John E. Hutchinson. Fractals and self similarity. *Indiana Univ. Math. J.*, 30:713–747, 1981.

Eenjun Hwang and V. S. Subrahmanian. Querying video libraries. *J. Visual Commun. Image Representation*, 7(1):44–60, 1996.

A. Hyvärinen. Survey on independent component analysis. *Neural Comput. Surv.*, 2:94–128, 1999.

E. Ide and G. Salton. *New Experiments in Relevance Feedback*, chapter 16, in The Smart Retrieval System – Experiments in Automatic Document Processing, Prentice-Hall, pages 337–354. 1971a.

E. Ide and G. Salton. *Interactive Search Strategies and Dynamic File Organization in Information Retrieval*, chapter 18, in The Smart Retrieval System – Experiments in Automatic Document Processing, Prentic-Hall, pages 373–393. 1971b.

E. Ihler. Bounds on the quality of approximate solutions to the group Steiner tree problem. In *Proceedings of the 16th International Workshop on Graph Theoretic Concepts in Computer Science. Lecture Notes in Computer Science*, pages 109–118, 1991.

Mitsutoshi Iino, Young Francis Day, and Arif Ghafoor. An object-oriented model for spatio-temporal synchronization of multimedia information. In *ICMCS*, pages 110–119, 1994.

N. Ikonomakis, K. N. Plataniotis, and A. N. Venetsanopoulos. Color image segmentation for multimedia applications. *J. Intell. Robotics Syst.*, 28(1–2):5–20, 2000.

Ihab F. Ilyas, Walid G. Aref, and Ahmed K. Elmagarmid. Joining ranked inputs in practice. In *VLDB '02: Proceedings of the 28th International Conference on Very Large Data Bases*, pages 950–961, 2002.

Ihab F. Ilyas, Walid G. Aref, and Ahmed K. Elmagarmid. Supporting top-k join queries in relational databases. In *VLDB*, 2003.

Ihab F. Ilyas, G. Aref, and K. Elmagarmid. Supporting top-k join queries in relational databases. *VLDB J.*, 13(3):207–221, 2004a.

Ihab F. Ilyas, Rahul Shah, Walid G. Aref, Jeffrey Scott Vitter, and Ahmed K. Elmagarmid. Rank-aware query optimization. In *SIGMOD '04: Proceedings of the 2004 ACM SIGMOD International Conference on Management of Data*, pages 203–214, 2004b.

Piotr Indyk and Rajeev Motwani. Approximate nearest neighbors: towards removing the curse of dimensionality. In *STOC '98: Proceedings of the Thirtieth Annual ACM Symposium on Theory of Computing*, pages 604–613, 1998.

H. Ishibuchi, T. Nakashima, and T. Murata. Performance evaluation of fuzzy classifier systems for multidimensional pattern classification problems. *IEEE Trans. SMC-B*, pages 601–618, 1999.

Hemant Ishwaran and Lancelot F. James. Gibbs sampling methods for stick-breaking priors. *J. Am. Statist. Assoc.*, 96:161–173, 2001.

R. Jain. Experiential computing. *CACM*, 46(7):48–55, 2003a.

R. Jain. Multimedia electronic chronicles. *IEEE MultiMedia*, 10(3):111–112, 2003b.

Kristoffer Jensen. Multiple scale music segmentation using rhythm, timbre, and harmony. *EURASIP J. Appl. Signal Process.*, 2007(1):159–159, 2007.

Jing Jiang and Chengxiang Zhai. Extraction of coherent relevant passages using hidden markov models. *ACM Trans. Inform. Syst.*, 24(3):295–319, 2006.

Tao Jiang, Lusheng Wang, and Kaizhong Zhang. Alignment of trees: an alternative to tree edit. *Theor. Comput. Sci.*, 143(1):137–148, 1995.

Thorsten Joachims. Optimizing search engines using clickthrough data. In *Proceedings of the Eighth ACM SIGKDD International Conference on Knowledge Discovery and Data Mining*, pages 133–142, 2002.

Thorsten Joachims. Training linear svms in linear time. In *KDD '06: Proceedings of the 12th ACM SIGKDD International Conference on Knowledge Discovery and Data Mining*, pages 217–226, 2006.

David S. Johnson and Christos H. Papadimitriou. On generating all maximal independent sets. *Inform. Process. Lett.*, 27(3):119–123, 1988.

Petteri Jokinen, Jorma Tarhio, and Esko Ukkonen. A comparison of approximate string matching algorithms. *Softw. Pract. Exper.*, 26(12):1439–1458, 1996.

T. Joseph and A. F. Cardenas. Picquery: a high level query language for pictorial database management. *IEEE Trans. Softw. Eng.*, 14(5):630–638, 1988.

James E. Coolahan and Nick Roussopoulos. Timing requirements for time-driven systems using augmented petri nets. *IEEE Trans. Softw. Eng.*, 9(5):603–616, 1983.

Erland Jungert. Extended symbolic projections as a knowledge structure for spatial reasoning. In *Proceedings of the 4th International Conference on Pattern Recognition*, pages 343–351, 1988.

Varun Kacholia, Shashank Pandit, Soumen Chakrabarti, S. Sudarshan, Rushi Desai, and Hrishikesh Karambelkar. Bidirectional expansion for keyword search on graph databases. In *VLDB*, pages 505–516, 2005.

Peter K. Kaiser and R.M Boynton. *Human Color Vision*, 2nd ed. Optical Society of America, 1996.

Ibrahim Kamel and Christos Faloutsos. On packing R-trees. In *CIKM '93: Proceedings of the Second International Conference on Information and Knowledge Management*, pages 490–499, 1993.

Ibrahim Kamel and Christos Faloutsos. Hilbert R-tree: An improved R-tree using fractals. In *VLDB '94: Proceedings of the 20th International Conference on Very Large Data Bases*, pages 500–509, 1994.

B. Kamgar-Parsi and L. N. Kanal. An improved branch and bound algorithm for computing k-nearest neighbors. *Pattern Recogn. Lett*, 3(1):7–12, 1985.

R. Kannan, S. Vempala, and A. Veta. On clusterings – good, bad and spectral. In *FOCS '00: Proceedings of the 41st Annual Symposium on Foundations of Computer Science*, page 367, 2000.

L. M. Kaplan. Extended fractal analysis for texture classification and segmentation. *IP*, 8(11):1572–1585, November 1999.

L. M. Kaplan and C. C. J. Kuo. Texture segmentation via Haar fractal feature estimation. *JVCIR*, 6(4):387–400, December 1995.

Richard M. Karp and Michael O. Rabin. Pattern-matching algorithms. *IBM J. Res. Dev.*, 31(2):249–260, 1987.

B. Kartikeyan and A. Sarkar. Shape description by time series. *IEEE Trans. Pattern Anal. Mach. Intell.*, 11(9):977–984, 1989.

George Karypis and Vipin Kumar. Multilevel algorithms for multi-constraint graph partitioning. In *Supercomputing '98: Proceedings of the 1998 ACM/IEEE Conference on Supercomputing*, pages 1–13, 1998.

R. Kashyap and R. Chellappa. Estimation and choice of neighbors in spatial-interaction models of images. *IEEE Trans. Inform. Theory*, 29(1):60–72, 1983.

R. Kashyap, R. Chellappa, and A. Khotanzad. Texture classification using features derived from random field models. *Pattern Recogn. Lett.*, 1(1):43–50, 1982.

Robert E. Kass and Larry Wasserman. A reference Bayesian test for nested hypotheses and its relationship to the Schwarz criterion. *J. Am. Statist. Assoc.*, 90:928–934, 1995.

Norio Katayama and Shin'ichi Satoh. The SR-tree: an index structure for high-dimensional nearest neighbor queries. In *SIGMOD '97: Proceedings of the 1997 ACM SIGMOD International Conference on Management of Data*, pages 369–380, 1997.

N. Katzir, M. Lindenbaum, and M. Porat. Curve segmentation under partial occlusion. *IEEE Trans. Pattern Anal. Mach. Intell.*, 16(5):513–519, May 1994.

S. C. Kau and J. Tseng. MQL – a query language for multimedia databases. In *ACM Multimedia*, pages 511–516, 1994.

Yan Ke and Rahul Sukthankar. PCA-sift: A more distinctive representation for local image descriptors. In *Proceedings of the Conference on Computer Vision and Pattern Recognition*, pages 506–513, 2004.

J. M. Keller, S. S. Chen, and R. M. Crownover. Texture description and segmentation through fractal geometry. *CVGIP*, 45(2):150–166, February 1989.

David G. Kendall. Shape manifolds, procrustean metrics, and complex projective spaces. *Bull. London Math. Soc.*, 16(2):81–121, 1984.

M. G. Kendall. A new measure of rank correlation. *Biometrika*, 30(1/2):81–93, 1938.

A. J. Kent, R. Sacks-Davis, and K. Ramamohanarao. A signature file scheme based on multiple organisations for indexing very large text databases. *J. Am. Soc. Inform. Sci.*, 7(41):508–534, 1990.

B. W. Kernighan and S. Lin. An efficient heuristic procedure for partitioning graphs. *Bell Syst. Tech. J.*, 49(2):291–308, 1970.

J. Kiefer. Sequential minimax search for a maximum. In *Proceedings of the American Mathematical Society*, volume 4, pages 502–506, 1953.

Werner Kiessling. Foundations of preferences in database systems. In *VLDB '02: Proceedings of the 28th International Conference on Very Large Data Bases*, pages 311–322, 2002.

Werner Kiessling. Preference queries with sv-semantics. In *COMAD'05*, pages 15–26, 2005.

Pekka Kilpelainen. Tree matching problems with applications to structured text databases. Technical report, University of Helsinki, Finland, 1992.

Pekka Kilpelainen and Heikki Mannila. Ordered and unordered tree inclusion. *SIAM J. Comput.*, 24(2):340–356, 1995.

Jong Wook Kim and K. Selçuk Candan. Cp/cv: concept similarity mining without frequency information from domain describing taxonomies. In *CIKM '06: Proceedings of the 15th ACM International Conference on Information and Knowledge Management*, pages 483–492, 2006.

Jong Wook Kim and K. Selçuk Candan. Skip-and-prune: Cosine-based top-k query processing for efficient context-sensitive document retrieval. In *SIGMOD*, 2009.

Jong Wook Kim, K. Selçuk Candan, and Junichi Tatemura. Efficient overlap and content reuse detection in blogs and online news articles. In *WWW '09: Proceedings of the 18th International Conference on World Wide Web*, pages 81–90, 2009.

Michelle Y. Kim and Junehwa Song. Multimedia documents with elastic time. In *MULTIMEDIA '95: Proceedings of the Third ACM International Conference on Multimedia*, pages 143–154, 1995.

M. Y. Kim and J. Song. Hyperstories: combining time, space and asynchrony in multimedia documents. Technical Report RC19277(83726) (revised 1995), IBM Computer Science/Mathematics Research, 1993.

Carolyn Kimme, Dana Ballard, and Jack Sklansky. Finding circles by an array of accumulators. *Commun. ACM*, 18(2):120–122, 1975.

A. Klapuri. Sound onset detection by applying psychoacoustic knowledge. In *ICASSP '99: Proceedings of the 1999 IEEE International Conference on Acoustics, Speech, and Signal Processing*, pages 3089–3092, 1999.

Philip N. Klein. Computing the edit-distance between unrooted ordered trees. In *ESA '98: Proceedings of the 6th Annual European Symposium on Algorithms*, pages 91–102, 1998.

Jon M. Kleinberg. Two algorithms for nearest-neighbor search in high dimensions. In *STOC '97: Proceedings of the Twenty-ninth Annual ACM Symposium on Theory of Computing*, pages 599–608, 1997.

Jon M. Kleinberg. Authoritative sources in a hyperlinked environment. *J. ACM*, 46 (5):604–632, 1999.

D. E. Knuth, J. H. Morris, and V. R. Pratt. Fast pattern matching in strings. *SIAM J. Comput.*, 6(2):323–350, 1977.

Donald E. Knuth. *Art of Computer Programming, Volume 3: Sorting and Searching (2nd Edition)*. Addison-Wesley Professional, 1998.

J. J. Koenderink and A. J. van Doom. Representation of local geometry in the visual system. *Biol. Cybern.*, 55(6):367–375, 1987.

R. Koenen. Mpeg-4 overview (v.16 la bauleversion), iso/iec jtc1/sc29/wg11 n3747, int'l standards organization, oct. 2000.

Teuvo Kohonen. Self-organized formation of topologically correct feature maps, in Neurocomputing: Foundations of Research, J. A. Anderson and E. Rosenfeld, Eds., MIT Press, Cambridge, MA, pages 509–521, 1988.

Tamara G. Kolda and Brett W. Bader. Tensor decompositions and applications. *SIAM Review*, 51(3):455–500, September 2009.

Flip Korn, Nikolaos Sidiropoulos, Christos Faloutsos, Eliot Siegel, and Zenon Protopapas. Fast nearest neighbor search in medical image databases. In *VLDB*, pages 215–226, 1996.

Donald Kossmann, Frank Ramsak, and Steffen Rost. Shooting stars in the sky: an online algorithm for skyline queries. In *VLDB '02: Proceedings of the 28th International Conference on Very Large Data Bases*, pages 275–286, 2002.

R. Kowalski and M. Sergot. A logic-based calculus of events. *New Generation Comput.*, 4(1):67–95, 1986.

Pieter M. Kroonenberg and Jan De Leeuw. Principal component analysis of three-mode data by means of alternating least squares algorithms. *Psychometrika*, 1(45):69–97, 1980.

J. B. Kruskal. Nonmetric multidimensional scaling: a numerical method. *Psychometrika*, 29(2):115–129, 1964a.

Joseph B. Kruskal. Multidimensional scaling by optimizing goodness of fit to a nonmetric hypothesis. *Psychometrika*, 1(29):1–27, 1964b.

J. B. Kruskal and W. Myron. *Multidimensional Scaling*. Sage Publications, Beverly Hills, CA, 1978.

Ravi Kumar, Prabhakar Raghavan, Sridhar Rajagopalan, and Andrew Tomkins. Extracting large-scale knowledge bases from the web. In *Proceedings of the 25th VLDB Conference*, pages 639–650, 1999.

H. T. Kung, F. Luccio, and F. P. Preparata. On finding the maxima of a set of vectors. *J. ACM*, 22(4):469–476, 1975.

Tony C. T. Kuo and Arbee L. P. Chen. A content-based query language for video databases. In *ICMCS*, pages 209–214, 1996.

S. Kurtz. Approximate string searching under weighted edit distance. In *Proc. WSP'96*, pages 156–170. Carleton University Press, 1996.

John Lafferty and Chengxiang Zhai. Document language models, query models, and risk minimization for information retrieval. In *SIGIR '01: Proceedings of the 24th Annual International ACM SIGIR Conference on Research and Development in Information Retrieval*, pages 111–119, 2001.

L. V. Lakshmanan, N. Leone, R. Ross, and V. S. Subrahmanian. Probview: A flexible probabilistic database system. *ACM Trans. Database Syst.*, 3(22):419–469, 1997.

G. M. Landau and U. Vishkin. Fast string matching with k differences. *J. Comput. Syst. Sci.*, 37:63–78, 1988.

G. M. Landau and U. Vishkin. Fast parallel and serial approximate string matching. *J. Algorithms*, 10(2):157–169, 1989.

Christian A. Lang, Yuan-Chi Chang, and John R. Smith. Making the threshold algorithm access cost aware. *IEEE Trans. Knowl. Data Eng.*, 16(10):1297–1301, 2004.

Soren Larsen and L.N. Kanal. Analysis of k-nearest neighbor branch and bound rules. *Pattern Recogn. Lett.*, 4(2):71–77, 1986.

O. Lassila and R. Swick. Resource description framework (rdf) model and syntax specification. http://www.w3.org/tr/rec-rdf-syntax., 1999.

Lieven De Lathauwer, Bart De Moor, and JoosVandewalle. A multilinearsingular value decomposition. *SIAM J. Matrix Anal. A.*, 21(4):1253–1278, 2000.

J. K. Lawder. The application of space-filling curves to the storage and retrieval of multi-dimensional data. Technical Report JL/1/99, Birkbeck College, University of London, 1999.

Iosif Lazaridis and Sharad Mehrotra. Progressive approximate aggregate queries with a multi-resolution tree structure. In *SIGMOD '01: Proceedings of the 2001 ACM SIGMOD International Conference on Management of Data*, pages 401–412, 2001.

Svetlana Lazebnik, Cordelia Schmid, and Jean Ponce. A sparse texture representation using affine-invariant regions. *IEEE Computer Society Conference on Computer Vision and Pattern Recognition*, Volume 2, page 319, 2003.

Anthony J. T. Lee and Han-Pang Chiu. 2D Z-string: a new spatial knowledge representation for image databases. *Pattern Recogn. Lett.*, 24(16):3015–3026, 2003.

Jeong Ki Lee and Jae Woo Chang. Performance evaluation of hybrid access methods for efficient information retrieval. In *Proceedings of the 20th EUROMICRO Conference*, pages 372–378, 1994.

John A. Lee and Michel Verleysen. *Nonlinear Dimensionality Reduction*. Springer, 2007.

S. Y. Lee and F. J. Hsu. Spatial reasoning and knowledge representation. *Pattern Recogn.*, 25(3):305–318, 1992.

S. Y. Lee, M. C. Yang, and J. W. Chen. 2D B-string: a spatial knowledge representation for image database systems. In *Second International Computer Science Conference (ICSC)*, 1992.

Taekyong Lee, Lei Sheng, Tolga Bozkaya, Nevzat Hurkan Balkir, Meral Özsoyoglu, and Gultekin Özsoyoglu. Querying multimedia presentations based on content, IEEE Transactions on Knowledge and Data Engineering, 11(3), pages 361–385, May/Jun 1999, 2001.

Jure Leskoec, Kevin J. Lang, Anirban Dasgupta, and Michael W. Mahoney. Statistical properties of community structure in large social and information networks. In *WWW '08: Proceeding of the 17th international conference on World Wide Web*, pages 695–704, 2008.

Jure Leskovec and Christos Faloutsos. Sampling from large graphs. In *KDD '06: Proceedings of the 12th ACM SIGKDD International Conference on Knowledge Discovery and Data Mining*, pages 631–636, 2006.

Jure Leskovec, Jon Kleinberg, and Christos Faloutsos. Graph evolution: Densification and shrinking diameters. *ACM Trans. Knowl. Discov. Data*, 1(1):1–41, 2007.

Scott T. Leutenegger, J. M. Edgington, and Mario A. Lopez. Str: A simple and efficient algorithm for r-tree packing. In *ICDE '97: Proceedings of the Thirteenth International Conference on Data Engineering*, pages 497–506, 1997.

V. I. Levenshtein. Binary codes capable of correcting deletions, insertions, and reversals. *Soviet Phy. Dok.*, 10:707–710, 1966.

Hector J. Levesque, Fiora Pirri, and Raymond Reiter. Foundations for the situation calculus. *Electron. Trans. Artif. Intell.*, 2:159–178, 1998.

A. Levy and M. Lindenbaum. Sequential Karhunen-Loeve basis extraction and its application to images. *IEEE Trans. Image Proc.*, 9:1371–1374, 2000.

Chengkai Li, Kevin Chen-Chuan Chang, Ihab F. Ilyas, and Sumin Song. RankSQL: query algebra and optimization for relational top-k queries. In *SIGMOD '05: Proceedings of the 2005 ACM SIGMOD International Conference on Management of Data*, pages 131–142, 2005.

Jian Li and Amol Deshpande. Consensus answers for queries over probabilistic databases. In *PODS '09: Proceedings of the Twenty-eighth ACM SIGMOD-SIGACT-SIGART Symposium on Principles of Database Systems*, pages 259–268, 2009.

John Z. Li, M. Tamer, Duane Szafron, and Vincent Oria. Moql: A multimedia object query language. In *Proceedings of the 3rd International Workshop on Multimedia Information Systems*, 1997a.

Lian Li, Ahmed Karmouch, and Nicolas D. Georganas. Multimedia teleorchestra with independent sources: Part 1 – temporal modeling of collaborative multimedia scenarios. *Multimedia Syst.*, 1(4):143–153, 1994a.

Lian Li, Ahmed Karmouch, and Nicolas D. Georganas. Multimedia teleorchestra with independent sources: Part 2 – synchronization algorithms. *Multimedia Syst.*, 1(4):154–165, 1994b.

Qing Li, K. Selçuk Candan, and Qi Yan. Extracting relevant snippets for web navigation. In *Proceedings of the Twenty-third AAAI Conference on Artificial Intelligence (AAAI)*, pages 1195–1200, 2008.

W.-S. Li and K.S. Candan. Semcog: A hybrid object-based image and video database system and its modeling, language, and query processing. *TAPOS*, 5(3):163–180, 1999a.

Wen-Syan Li and K. Selçuk Candan. Integrating content search with structure analysis for hypermedia retrieval and management. *ACM Comput. Surv.*, 31(4es):13–20, 1999b.

Wen-Syan Li, K. Selçuk Candan, Kyoji Hirata, and Yoshinori Hara. Facilitating multimedia database exploration through visual interfaces and perpetual query reformulations. In *VLDB*, pages 538–547, 1997b.

Wen-Syan Li, K. Selçuk Candan, Kyoji Hirata, and Yoshinori Hara. Ifq: A visual query interface and query generator for object-based media retrieval. In *ICMCS*, pages 353–361, 1997c.

Wen-Syan Li, K. Selçuk Candan, Quoc Vu, and Divyakant Agrawal. Retrieving and organizing web pages by information unit. In *WWW*, pages 230–244, 2001a.

Wen-Syan Li, K. Selçuk Candan, Kyoji Hirata, and Yoshinori Hara. Supporting efficient multimedia database exploration. *VLDB J.*, 9(4):312–326, 2001b.

Wentian Li. Random texts exhibit Zipf's law–like word frequency distribution. *IEEE Trans. Inform. Theory*, 38, 1992.

Z. N. Li and M. S. Drew. *Fundamentals of Multimedia*. Prentice-Hall, 2003.

King Ip Lin, H. V. Jagadish, and Christos Faloutsos. The TV-tree: an index structure for high-dimensional data. *VLDB J.*, 3(4):517–542, 1994.

Jessica Lin, Eamonn J. Keogh, Stefano Lonardi, and Bill Yuan-chi Chiu. A symbolic representation of time series, with implications for streaming algorithms. pages 2–11, June 2003.

Ping Lin and K. Selçuk Candan. Enabling access-privacy for random walk based data analysis applications. *Data Knowl. Eng.*, 63(3):667–683, 2007.

T. D. C. Little and A. Ghafoor. Interval-based conceptual models for time-dependent multimedia data. *IEEE Trans. Knowl. Data Eng.*, 5(4):551–563, 1993.

Thomas D. C. Little and Arif Ghafoor. Synchronization and storage models for multimedia objects. *IEEE J. Sel. Areas Commun.*, 8(3):413–427, 1990.

Nick Littlestone. From on-line to batch learning. In *COLT '89: Proceedings of the Second Annual Workshop on Computational Learning Theory*, pages 269–284, 1989.

Peiya Liu, Amit Chankraborty, and Liang H. Hsu. A predicate logic approach for MPEG-7 XML document queries. *Markup Lang.*, 3(3):365–381, 2001.

Bin Liu, Amarnath Gupta, and Ramesh Jain. Medsman: a streaming data management system over live multimedia. In *Multimedia '05: Proceedings of the 13th annual ACM International Conference on Multimedia*, pages 171–180, 2005.

Bin Liu, Amarnath Gupta, and Ramesh Jain. Medsman: a live multimedia stream querying system. *Multimedia Tools Appl.*, 38(2):209–232, 2008.

S. Lloyd. Least squares quantization in pcm. *IEEE Trans. Inform. Theory*, 28(2):129–137, 1982.

S. P. Lloyd. Least squares quantization in PCM'S. *Bell Tele. Labs Memo*, 1957.

Daniel P. Lopresti and Gordon T. Wilfong. Comparing semi-structured documents via graph probing. In *Multimedia Information Systems*, pages 41–50, 2001.

D. G. Lowe. Three-dimensional object recognition from single two-dimensional images. *Artif. Intell.*, 31(3):355–395, 1987.

David G. Lowe. Object recognition from local scale-invariant features. In *ICCV '99: Proceedings of the International Conference on Computer Vision*, Volume 2, pages 1150–1157, 1999.

David G. Lowe. Distinctive image features from scale-invariant keypoints. *Int. J. Comp. Vision*, 60:91–110, 2004.

F. Luccio and L. Pagli. Approximate matching for two families of trees. *Inform. Comput.*, 123(1):111–120, 1995.

H. P. Luhn. A statistical approach to mechanized encoding and searching of literary information. *IBM J. Res. Dev.*, 1(4):309–317, 1957.

F. Lumbreras and J. Serrat. Wavelet filtering for the segmentation of marble images. *OptEng*, 35(10):2864–2872, October 1996.

Lakshmi Priya Mahalingam and K. Selçuk Candan. Multi-criteria query optimization in the presence of result size and quality tradeoffs. *Multimedia Tools Appl.*, 23(3):167–183, 2004.

Michael W. Mahoney, Mauro Maggioni, and Petros Drineas. Tensor-cur decompositions for tensor-based data. In *KDD '06: Proceedings of the 12th ACM SIGKDD International Conference on Knowledge Discovery and Data Mining*, pages 327–336, 2006.

D. Maier. Comments on the "third-generation database system manifesto." Oregon Graduate Institute Working Paper, 1991.

Nikos Mamoulis, Kit Hung Cheng, Man Lung Yiu, and David W. Cheung. Efficient aggregation of ranked inputs. In *ICDE '06: Proceedings of the 22nd International Conference on Data Engineering*, page 72, 2006.

Udi Manber. Finding similar files in a large file system. In *Proceedings of the USENIX Winter 1994 Technical Conference*, pages 1–10, 1994.

Udi Manber and Eugene W. Myers. Suffix arrays: a new method for on-line string searches. *SIAM J. Comput.*, 22(5):935–948, 1993.

Christopher D. Manning and Hinrich Schtze. *Foundations of Statistical Natural Language Processing*. MIT Press, 1999.

J. Mao and A. K. Jain. Texture classification and segmentation using multiresolution simultaneous autoregressive models. *Pattern Recogn.*, 25(2):173–188, 1992.

Sherry Marcus and V. S. Subrahmanian. Foundations of multimedia database systems. *J. ACM*, 43(3):474–523, 1996.

Amélie Marian, Nicolas Bruno, and Luis Gravano. Evaluating top-k queries over web-accessible databases. *ACM Trans. Database Syst.*, 29(2):319–362, 2004.

Jose L. Marroquin and Federico Girosi. Some extensions of the k-means algorithm for image segmentation and pattern classification. Technical report, Cambridge, MA, USA, 1993.

Andre T. Martins. String kernels and similarity measures for information retrieval. Technical report, Priberam, Lisbon, Portugal, 2006.

C.B. Mayer, K.S. Candan, and V. Sangam. Effects of user request patterns on a multimedia delivery system. *Multimedia Tools Appl.*, 24(3):233–251, 2004.

S. McAdams and A. Bregman. Hearing musical streams. *Comp. Music J.*, 3(4):26–43, 1979.

Edward M. McCreight. A space-economical suffix tree construction algorithm. *J. ACM*, 22(2):262–272, 1976.

G. J. McLachlan and K. E. Basford. *Mixture Models: Inference and Applications to Clustering*. Marcel Dekker, New York, 1988.

F. McSherry. Spectral partitioning of random graphs. In *FOCS '01: Proceedings of the 42nd IEEE Symposium on Foundations of Computer Science*, page 529, 2001.

Christoph Meinel and Thorsten Theobald. *Algorithms and Data Structures in VLSI Design*. Springer-Verlag New York, 1998.

Jim Melton and Andrew Eisenberg. SQL multimedia and application packages (SQL/MM). *SIGMOD Rec.*, 30(4):97–102, 2001.

María Luisa Micó, José Oncina, and Enrique Vidal. A new version of the nearest-neighbour approximating and eliminating search algorithm (AESA) with linear preprocessing time and memory requirements. *Pattern Recogn. Lett.*, 15(1):9–17, 1994.

María Luisa Micó, Jose Oncina, and Rafael C. Carrasco. A fast branch & bound nearest neighbour classifier in metric spaces. *Pattern Recogn. Lett.*, 17:731–739, 1996.

K. Mikolajczyk and C. Schmid. A performance evaluation of local descriptors. *IEEE Computer Society Conference on Computer Vision and Pattern Recognition*, Volume 2, pages 257–263, 2003.

Krystian Mikolajczyk and Cordelia Schmid. A performance evaluation of local descriptors. *IEEE Trans. Pattern Anal. Mach. Intell.*, 27(10):1615–1630, 2005.

David R. Miller, Tim Leek, and Richard M. Schwartz. A hidden Markov model information retrieval system. In *Proceedings of SIGIR-99, 22nd ACM International Conference on Research and Development in Information Retrieval*, pages 214–221, 1999.

I. Mirbel, B. Pernici, and M. Vazirgiannis. Temporal integrity constraints in interactive multimedia documents. In *ICMCS '99: Proceedings of the IEEE International Conference on Multimedia Computing and Systems*, Volume 2, page 867. IEEE Computer Society, 1999.

Mandar Mitra, Amit Singhal, and Chris Buckley. Improving automatic query expansion. In *SIGIR '98: Proceedings of the 21st Annual International ACM SIGIR Conference on Research and Development in Information Retrieval*, pages 206–214, 1998.

Mohamed F. Mokbel, Ming Lu, and Walid G. Aref. Hash-merge join: a non-blocking join algorithm for producing fast and early join results. In *ICDE*, pages 251–263, 2004.

C. L. Monma and J. B. Sidney. Sequencing with series-parallel precedence constraints. *Mathematics of Operations Research*, 1979.

Ugo Montanari. On the optimal detection of curves in noisy pictures. *Commun. ACM*, 14(5):335–345, 1971.

J. W. Moon and L. Moser. On cliques in graphs. *Israel J. Math.*, 3:23–28, 1965.

Raymond J. Mooney and Loriene Roy. Content-based book recommending using learning for text categorization. In *DL '00: Proceedings of the Fifth ACM Conference on Digital Libraries*, pages 195–204, New York, NY, USA, 2000.

Donald R. Morrison. Patricia – practical algorithm to retrieve information coded in alphanumeric. *J. ACM*, 15(4):514–534, 1968.

G.M. Morton. A computer oriented geodetic data base; and a new technique in file sequencing. Technical Report, Ottawa, Canada: IBM Ltd., 1966.

S. Muthukrishnan and H. Ramesh. String matching under a general matching relation. *Inform. Comput.*, 122(1):140–148, 1995.

G. Myers. Incremental alignment algorithms and their applications. tr-8622. Technical report, Deptartment of Computer Science, University of Arizona, 1986.

Mohammad Nabil, Anne H. H. Ngu, and John Shepherd. Picture similarity retrieval using the 2D projection interval representation. *IEEE Trans. Knowl. Data Eng.*, 08(4):533–539, 1996.

Klara Nahrstedt and Wolf-Tilo Balke. A taxonomy for multimedia service composition. In *Multimedia '04: Proceedings of the 12th ACM International Conference on Multimedia*, pages 88–95, 2004.

Atsuyoshi Nakamura and Naoki Abe. Collaborative filtering using weighted majority prediction algorithms. In *ICML '98: Proceedings of the Fifteenth International Conference on Machine Learning*, pages 395–403, San Francisco, CA, USA, 1998. Morgan Kaufmann.

Nathan Srebro Nati and Tommi Jaakkola. Weighted low-rank approximations. In *20th International Conference on Machine Learning*, pages 720–727. AAAI Press, 2003.

Apostol Natsev, Yuan chi Chang, John R. Smith, Chung-Sheng Li, and Jeffrey Scott Vitter. Supporting incremental join queries on ranked inputs. In *VLDB*, pages 281–290, 2001.

D. Nauck and R. Kruse. Obtaing interpretable fuzzy classification rules from medical data. *Artif. Intell. Med.*, pages 149–169, 1999.

G. Navarro and M. Raffinot. A bit-parallel approach to suffix automata: fast extended string matching. In *Proceedings of the 9th Annual Symposium on Combinatorial Pattern Matching*, pages 14–33, 1998.

Gonzalo Navarro. Multiple approximate string matching by counting. In *Proceedings of WSP'97*, pages 125–139. Carleton University Press, 1997.

Gonzalo Navarro. A guided tour to approximate string matching. *ACM Comput. Surv.*, 33(1):31–88, 2001.

Gonzalo Navarro. Searching in metric spaces by spatial approximation. *VLDB J.*, 11(1):28–46, 2002.

Gonzalo Navarro. Searching in metric spaces by spatial approximation. In *SPIRE '99: Proceedings of the String Processing and Information Retrieval Symposium & International Workshop on Groupware*, page 141, 1999.

Surya Nepal and M. V. Ramakrishna. Query processing issues in image (multimedia) databases. In *ICDE '99: Proceedings of the 15th International Conference on Data Engineering*, pages 22–29, 1999.

M. E. J. Newman and M. Girvan. Finding and evaluating community structure in networks. *Phys. Rev. E*, 69(2), 2004.

Hieu Tat Nguyen, Marcel Worring, and Rein van den Boomgaard. Watersnakes: energy-driven watershed segmentation. *IEEE Trans. Pattern Anal. Mach. Intell.*, 25(3):330–342, 2003.

Carlton W. Niblack, Ron Barber, Will Equitz, Myron D. Flickner, Eduardo H. Glasman, Dragutin Petkovic, Peter Yanker, Christos Faloutsos, and Gabriel Taubin. Qbic project: querying images by content, using color, texture, and shape. *Proc. SPIE*, 1908 (173): 1–10, 1993.

Andrew Nierman and H. V. Jagadish. Evaluating structural similarity in XML documents. In *WebDB*, pages 61–66, 2002.

Jürg Nievergelt, Hans Hinterberger, and Kenneth C. Sevcik. The grid file: an adaptable, symmetric multi-key file structure. In *Proceedings of the 3rd Conference of the European Cooperation in Informatics on Trends in Information Processing Systems*, pages 236–251, 1981.

Haruhiko Nishiyama, Sumi Kin, Teruo Yokoyama, and Yutaka Matsushita. An image retrieval system considering subjective perception. In *ACM SIGCHI '94: Conference Companion on Human Factors in Computing Systems*, page 201, 1994.

Albert B. Novikoff. On convergence proofs for perceptrons. In *Proceedings of the Symposium on the Mathematical Theory of Automata*, Volume 12, pages 615–622, 1963.

G. O'Brien. Information management tools for updating an SVD-encoded indexing scheme, Master's Thesis, The University of Konxville, Tennessee, 1994.

Virginia E. Ogle and Michael Stonebraker. Chabot: retrieval from a relational database of images. *Computer*, 28(9):40–48, 1995.

Dan Olteanu and Jiewen Huang. Secondary-storage confidence computation for conjunctive queries with inequalities. In *SIGMOD '09: Proceedings of the 35th SIGMOD International Conference on Management of Data*, pages 389–402, 2009.

Beng Chin Ooi, Kian-Lee Tan, Cui Yu, and Stéphane Bressan. Indexing the edges – a simple and yet efficient approach to high-dimensional indexing. In *Proceedings of the Principles of Database Systems*, pages 166–174, 2000.

Eitetsu Oomoto and Katsumi Tanaka. Ovid: design and implementation of a video-object database system. *IEEE Trans. Knowl. Data Eng.*, 5(4):629–643, 1993.

M. T. Orchard. A fast nearest-neighbor search algorithm. In *IEEE International Conference on Acoustics. Speech, and Signal Processing*, Volume 4, pages 2297–2300, 1991.

J. A. Orenstein. Redundancy in spatial databases. *SIGMOD Rec.*, 18(2):295–305, 1989.

Vincent Oria, M. Tamer Ozsu, Bing Xu, L. Irene Cheng, and Paul J. Iglinski. Visualmoql: The disima visual query language. *ICMCS*, 01:9536, 1999.

Gultekin Özsoyoğlu, Veli Hakkoymaz, and Joel Kraft. Automating the assembly of presentations from multimedia databases. In *ICDE '96: Proceedings of the Twelfth International Conference on Data Engineering*, pages 593–601. IEEE Computer Society, 1996.

Lawrence Page, Sergey Brin, Rajeev Motwani, and Terry Winograd. The pagerank citation ranking: Bringing order to the web. Technical report, Stanford Digital Library Technologies Project, 1998.

Dimitris Papadias, Yufei Tao, Greg Fu, and Bernhard Seeger. Progressive skyline computation in database systems. *ACM Trans. Database Syst.*, 30(1):41–82, 2005.

Christos H. Papadimitriou and Mihalis Yannakakis. Multiobjective query optimization. In *PODS '01: Proceedings of the Twentieth ACM SIGMOD-SIGACT-SIGART Symposium on Principles of Database Systems*, pages 52–59, 2001.

Spiros Papadimitriou, Jimeng Sun, and Christos Faloutsos. Streaming pattern discovery in multiple time-series. In *VLDB '05: Proceedings of the 31st International Conference on Very Large Data Bases*, pages 697–708, 2005.

Apostolos N. Papadopoulos and Yannis Manolopoulos. Structure-based similarity search with graph histograms. In *DEXA '99: Proceedings of the 10th International Workshop on Database & Expert Systems Applications*, page 174, 1999.

Y. Papakonstantinou, H. Garcia-Molina, and J. Widom. Object exchange across heterogeneous information sources. *Proceedings of the Eleventh International Conference on Data Engineering, 1995*, pages 251–260, March 1995.

Panos M. Pardalos and Stephen A. Vavasis. Quadratic programming with one negative eigenvalue is NP-hard. *J. Global Optim.*, 1(1):15–22, 1991.

Dong Kwon Park, Yoon Seok Jeon, and Chee Sun Won. Efficient use of local edge histogram descriptor. In *MULTIMEDIA '00: Proceedings of the 2000 ACM Workshops on Multimedia*, pages 51–54, 2000.

T. Pavlidis and Y.-T. Liow. Integrating region growing and edge detection. *IEEE Trans. Pattern Anal. Mach. Intell.*, 12(3):225–233, 1990.

Manoj M. Pawar, Gaurav N. Pradhan, Kang Zhang, and Balakrishnan Prabhakaran. Content based querying and searching for 3d human motions. In *MMM*, pages 446–455, 2008.

Giuseppe Peano. Sur une courbe, qui remplit toute une aire plane (on a curve which completely fills a planar region). *Math. Ann.*, 36:157–160, 1890.

J. Pearl. Bayesian networks: a model of self-activated memory for evidential reasoning. In *Proceedings of the Conference of the Cognitive Science Society*, pages 329–334, 1985.

Dan Pelleg. X-means: Extending k-means with efficient estimation of the number of clusters. In *Proceedings of the 17th International Conference on Machine Learning*, pages 727–734, 2000.

Lina Peng and K. Selçuk Candan. Data-quality guided load shedding for expensive in-network data processing. In *ICDE*, pages 1325–1328, 2007.

Lina Peng, Gisik Kwon, Yinpeng Chen, K. Selçuk Candan, Hari Sundaram, Karam S. Chatha, and Maria Luisa Sapino. Modular design of media retrieval workflows using aria. In *CIVR*, pages 491–494, 2006.

Lina Peng, K. Selçuk Candan, Christopher Mayer, Karamvir S. Chatha, and Kyung Dong Ryu. Optimization of media processing workflows with adaptive operator behaviors. *Multimedia Tools Appl.*, 33(3), 2007.

Lina Peng, Renwei Yu, K. Selçuk Candan, and Xinxin Wang. Object and combination shedding schemes for adaptive media workflow execution. *IEEE Trans. Knowl. Data Eng.*, 22(1), pages 105–119, 2010.

David Pennock, Eric Horvitz, Steve Lawrence, and C Lee Giles. Collaborative filtering by personality diagnosis: a hybrid memory- and model-based approach. In *Proceedings of the Sixteenth Conference on Uncertainty in Artificial Intelligence*, pages 473–480, 2000.

Haim Permuter, Joseph Francos, and Ian Jermyn. A study of gaussian mixture models of color and texture features for image classification and segmentation. *Pattern Recogn.*, 39(4):695–706, 2006.

E. Persoon and K. S. Fu. Shape discrimination using fourier descriptors. *IEEE Trans. Pattern Anal. Mach. Intell.*, 8(3):388–397, 1986.

G. Petraglia, M. Sebillo, M. Tucci, and G. Tortora. Virtual images for similarity retrieval in image databases. *IEEE Trans. Knowl. Data Eng.*, 13(6):951–967, Nov/Dec 2001.

G. Piatetsky-Shapiro. *Discovery, Analysis, and Presentation of Strong Rules*, pages 229–248. AAAI/MIT Press, 1991.

Claudio Pinhanez and Aaron Bobick. Fast constraint propagation on specialized Allen networks and its application to action recognition and control [electronic version]. Technical report, MIT Media Lab Perceptual Computing Section, 1998.

Claudio S. Pinhanez, Kenji Mase, and Aaron Bobick. Interval scripts: a design paradigm for story-based interactive systems. In *CHI '97: Proceedings of the SIGCHI Conference on Human Factors in Computing Systems*, pages 287–294. ACM, 1997.

Jay M. Ponte and W. Bruce Croft. A language modeling approach to information retrieval. In *SIGIR '98: Proceedings of the 21st Annual International ACM SIGIR Conference on Research and Development in Information Retrieval*, pages 275–281, 1998.

Alex Pothen, Horst D. Simon, and Kan-Pu Liou. Partitioning sparse matrices with eigenvectors of graphs. *SIAM J. Matrix Anal. Appl.*, 11(3):430–452, 1990.

B. Prabhakaran and S. V. Raghavan. Synchronization models for multimedia presentation with user participation. *Multimedia Syst.*, 2(2):53–62, 1994.

Franco P. Preparata and Michael I. Shamos. *Computational Geometry: An Introduction (Monographs in Computer Science)*. Springer, 1985.

William H. Press, Brian P. Flannery, Saul A. Teukolsky, and William T. Vetterling. *Numerical Recipes in C: the Art of Scientific Computing*. Cambridge University Press, New York, 1988.

Foster J. Provost, Tom Fawcett, and Ron Kohavi. The case against accuracy estimation for comparing induction algorithms. In *ICML '98: Proceedings of the Fifteenth International Conference on Machine Learning*, pages 445–453, 1998.

H. Prüfer. Neuer Beweis eines Satzes über Permutationen. *Archiv für Mathematik und Physik*, 27:142–144, 1918.

P. Punitha and D. S. Guru. An effective and efficient exact match retrieval scheme for symbolic image database systems based on spatial reasoning: a logarithmic search time approach. *IEEE Trans. Knowl. Data Eng.*, 18(10):1368–1381, 2006.

Yan Qi, K. Selçuk Candan, and Maria Luisa Sapino. Sum-max monotonic ranked joins for evaluating top-k twig queries on weighted data graphs. In *VLDB*, pages 507–518, 2007.

J. R. Quinlan. Rulequest research: See5/c5.0_2.05. http://www.rulequest.com/, 2008.

J. R. Quinlan. Improved use of continuous attributes in C4.5. *J. Artif. Intell. Res.*, 4: 77–90, 1996.

J. Ross Quinlan. *C4.5: Machine Learning*. Morgan Kaufmann, 1993.

J. Ross Quinlan. *Machine Learning*, Volume 1. 1975.

Lawrence R. Rabiner. A tutorial on hidden Markov models and selected applications in speech recognition, Proceedings of the IEEE, 77(2), pages 267–296, 1990.

R. Rada, H. Mili, E. Bicknell, and M. Blettner. Development and application of a metric on semantic nets. *IEEE Trans. Syst. Man Cybernet.*, 19(1):17–30, 1989.

Davood Rafiei, Daniel L. Moise, and Dabo Sun. Finding syntactic similarities between XML documents. In *DEXA '06: Proceedings of the 17th International Conference on Database and Expert Systems Applications*, pages 512–516. IEEE Computer Society, 2006.

Adrian E. Raftery. Choosing models for cross-classifications. *Am. Sociol. Rev.*, 51 (1):145–146, February 1986.

A. E. Raftery. Bayes factors and BIC-comment on "a critique of the Bayesian information criterion for model selection." *Sociol. Methods Res.*, 27:411–427, 1999.

Praveen Rao and Bongki Moon. Prix: Indexing and querying XML using Prüfer sequences. In *ICDE '04: Proceedings of the 20th International Conference on Data Engineering*, page 288, 2004.

Christopher Re, Nilesh N. Dalvi, and Dan Suciu. Query evaluation on probabilistic databases. *IEEE Data Eng. Bull.*, 29(1):25–31, 2006.

G. Reich and P. Widmayer. Approximate minimum spanning trees for vertex classes. Technical Report, Institut für Informatik, Freiburg University, 1991.

P. Resnick, N. Iacovou, M. Suchak, P. Bergstorm, and J. Riedl. Grouplens: an open architecture for collaborative filtering of netnews. In *Proceedings of ACM 1994 Conference on Computer Supported Cooperative Work*, pages 175–186, 1994.

R. Richardson and A. Smeaton. Using wordnet in a knowledge-based approach to information retrieval. In *BCS-IRSG Colloquium on Information Retrieval*, 1995.

J. Rissanen. Modelling by the shortest data description. *Automatica*, 14:465–471, 1978.

Stephen J. Roberts, Dirk Husmeier, William Penny, and lead Rezek. Bayesian approaches to gaussian mixture modeling. *IEEE Trans. Pattern Anal. Mach. Intell.*, 20(11):1133–1142, 1998.

S. E. Robertson. On term selection for query expansion. *J. Documentation*, 46(4): 359–364, December 1990.

S. E. Robertson and Sparck K. Jones. Relevance weighting of search terms. *J. Am. Soc. Inform. Sci.*, 27(3):129–146, 1976.

S. E. Robertson and K. Karen Spark-Jones. Relevance weighting of search terms. *J. Am. Soc. Inform. Sci.*, 27(3):129–146, 1976.

Stephen E. Robertson and Karen Sparck Jones. Relevance weighting of search terms, in Document Retrieval Systems, P. Willett, Ed. Taylor Graham Series In Foundations Of Information Science, vol. 3, Taylor Graham Publishing, London, UK, pages 143–160, 1988.

John T. Robinson. The k-d-b-tree: a search structure for large multidimensional dynamic indexes. In *SIGMOD '81: Proceedings of the 1981 ACM SIGMOD International Conference on Management of Data*, pages 10–18, 1981.

J. J. Rocchio. *Relevance Feedback in Information Retrieval*, chapter 14, in The Smart Retrieval System – Experiments in Automatic Document Processing, Prentice-Hall, pages 313–323, 1971.

Jos B. T. M. Roerdink and Arnold Meijster. The watershed transform: definitions, algorithms and parallelization strategies. *Fundam. Inform.*, 41(1–2):187–228, 2000.

Frank Rosenblatt. The perceptron: a probabilistic model for information storage and organization in the brain. *Psychol. Rev.*, 65(6):386–408, November 1958.

A. Rosenfeld R. B. Thomas, and Y. H. Lee. Edge and curve enhancement in digital pictures. Tech. Rep. 69-93. Technical Report, University of Maryland, College Park, 1969.

R. Rosenfeld. Two decades of statistical language modeling: where do we go from here? *Proc. IEEE*, 88(8):1270–1278, 2000.

Johannes A. Roubos, Magne Setnes, and János Abonyi. Learning fuzzy classification rules from labeled data. *Inform. Sci.*, 150(1-2):77–93, 2003.

Nick Roussopoulos and Daniel Leifker. Direct spatial search on pictorial databases using packed R-trees. *SIGMOD Rec.*, 14(4):17–31, 1985.

Nick Roussopoulos, Stephen Kelley, and Frederic Vincent. Nearest neighbor queries. In *ACM SIGMOD*, pages 71–79, 1995.

R. Rudzkis and M. Radavicius. Statistical estimation of a mixture of gaussian distributions. *Acta Applicandae Mathematicae*, 38:37–54, 1995.

Y. Rui and T. S. Huang. Relevance feedback techniques in image retrieval. In M.S. Lew, editor, *Principles of Visual Information Retrieval*, pages 219–258. Springer-Verlag, 2001.

Richard Russell and Pawan Sinha. Perceptually-based comparison of image similarity metrics. MIT Technical Report, AIM-2001-014, CBCL-201, 2001.

Stuart Russell and Peter Norvig. *Artificial Intelligence: A Modern Approach*. Prentice Hall, 1995.

I. Ruthven, M. Lalmas, and C. J. van Rijsbergen. Ranking expansion terms using partial and ostensive evidence. In *Proceedings of the 4th International Conference on Conceptions of Library and Information Science. CoLIS 4*, pages 199–220, 2002.

Ian Ruthven and Mounia Lalmas. A survey on the use of relevance feedback for information access systems. *Knowl. Eng. Rev.*, 18(2):95–145, June 2003.

S. K. Chang, E. Jungert, and Y. Li. Representation and retrieval of symbolic pictures using generalized 2-D strings. In *Proc. SPIE: Visual Communication Image Process, IV*, pages 1360–1372, 1989.

R. Sacks-Davis, A. Kent, and K. Ramamohanarao. Multikey access methods based on superimposed coding techniques. *ACM Trans. Database Syst.*, 12(4):655–696, 1987.

Ron Sacks-Davis. Performance of a multi-key access method based on descriptors and superimposed coding techniques. *Inform. Syst.*, 10(4):391–403, 1985.

Ron Sacks-Davis, Alan Kent, Kotagiri Ramamohanarao, James Thom, and Justin Zobel. Atlas: A nested relational database system for text applications. *IEEE Trans. Knowl. Data Eng.*, 7(3):454–470, 1995.

J. A. Saghri and H. Freeman. Analysis of the precision of generalized chain codes for the representation of planar curves. *PAMI*, 3(5):533–539, September 1981.

Mukesh K. Saini, Vivek K. Singh, Ramesh C. Jain, and Mohan S. Kankanhalli. Multimodal observation systems. In *MM '08: Proceeding of the 16th ACM international conference on Multimedia*, pages 933–936, 2008.

P. Saint-Marc, H. Rom, and G. Medioni. B-spline contour representation and symmetry detection. *IEEE Trans. Pattern Anal. Mach. Intell.*, 15(11):1191–1197, 1993.

Hiroaki Sakoe. Dynamic programming algorithm optimization for spoken word recognition. *IEEE Trans. Acoust, Speech, Signal Proc.*, 26:43–49, 1978.

G. Salton and C. Buckley. On the use of spreading activation methods in automatic information retrieval. In *SIGIR '88: Proceedings of the 11th Annual International ACM SIGIR Conference on Research and Development in Information Retrieval*, pages 147–160, 1988a.

Gerard Salton and Chris Buckley. Term weighting approaches in automatic text retrieval. *Inform. Proc. Management*, 24:513–523, 1988b.

Gerard Salton and Chris Buckley. Improving retrieval performance by relevance feedback. *J. Am. Soc. Inform. Sci.*, 41(4):288–297, 1990.

G. Salton, A. Wong, and C. S. Yang. A vector space model for automatic indexing. *Commun. ACM*, 18(11):613–620, November 1975.

H. Samet. Neighbor finding in quadtrees. In *PRIP'81*, pages 68–74, 1981.

H. Samet and C.A. Shaffer. A model for the analysis of neighbor finding in pointer based quadtrees. *PAMI*, 7(6):717–720, November 1985.

Hanan Samet. *Foundations of Multidimensional and Metric Data Structures*. Morgan Kaufmann, San Francisco, CA, USA, 2005.

Hanan Samet. *Applications of Spatial Data Structures: Computer Graphics, Image Processing, and GIS*. Addison-Wesley Longman Publishing Co., Inc., Boston, MA, USA, 1990.

Hanan Samet. The quadtree and related hierarchical data structures. *ACM Comput. Surv.*, 16(2):187–260, 1984.

M. L. Sapino, K. S. Candan, and P. Bertolotti. Log-analysis based characterization of multimedia documents for effective delivery of distributed multimedia presentations. In *Proc. DMS 06*, 2006.

Anish Das Sarma, Omar Benjelloun, Alon Halevy, and Jennifer Widom. Working models for uncertain data. In *ICDE '06: Proceedings of the 22nd International Conference on Data Engineering*, 2006.

Badrul Sarwar, George Karypis, Joseph Konstan, and John Riedl. Analysis of recommendation algorithms for e-commerce. In *Proceedings of the ACM EC'00 Conference*, pages 158–167, 2000.

Badrul Sarwar, George Karypis, Joseph Konstan, and John Reidl. Item-based collaborative filtering recommendation algorithms. In *WWW '01: Proceedings of the 10th International Conference on World Wide Web*, pages 285–295, 2001.

Lawrence Saul and O Pereira. Aggregate and mixed-order Markov models for statistical language processing. In *Proceedings of the Second Conference on Empirical Methods in Natural Language Processing*, pages 81–89, 1997.

Satu Elisa Schaeffer. Graph clustering. *Comp. Sci. Rev.*, 1(1):27–64, 2007.

Frederik Schaffalitzky and Andrew Zisserman. Multi-view matching for unordered image sets, or "How do I organize my holiday snaps?" In *ECCV '02: Proceedings of the 7th European Conference on Computer Vision – Part I*, pages 414–431, 2002.

Cullen Schaffer. Overfitting avoidance as bias. *Mach. Learn.*, 10(2):153–178, 1993.

Robert E. Schapire and Yoram Singer. Improved boosting algorithms using confidence-rated predictions. *Mach. Learn.*, 37(3):297–336, 1999.

Ansgar Scher, Ramesh Jain, and Mohan Kankanhalli. Events in multimedia. In *MM '09: Proceedings of the 17th ACM International Conference on Multimedia*, pages 1147–1148, 2009.

Saul Schleimer, Daniel S. Wilkerson, and Alex Aiken. Winnowing: local algorithms for document fingerprinting. In *SIGMOD '03: Proceedings of the 2003 ACM SIGMOD International Conference on Management of Data*, pages 76–85, 2003.

Ingo Schmitt, Nadine Schulz, and Thomas Herstel. Ws-qbe: A QBE-like query language for complex multimedia queries. In *MMM '05: Proceedings of the 11th International Multimedia Modelling Conference*, pages 222–229. IEEE Computer Society, 2005.

P. H. Schoenemann and R. Carroll. Fitting one matrix to another under choice of a central dilation and a rigid motion. *Psychometrika*, 35(2):245–255, 1970.

Bernhard Schölkopf, Alexander Smola, and Klaus-Robert Müller. Nonlinear component analysis as a kernel eigenvalue problem. *Neural Comput.*, 10(5):1299–1319, 1998.

Peter Schönemann. A generalized solution of the orthogonal Procrustes problem. *Psychometrika*, 31(1):1–10, 1966.

Eddie Schwalb and Rina Dechter. Processing disjunctions in temporal constraint networks. *Artif. Intell.*, 93(1-2):29–61, 1997.

Gideon Schwarz. Estimating the dimension of a model. *Ann. Statist.*, 6(2):461–464, 1978.

E. Di Sciascio, M. Mongiello, F. M. Donini, and L. Allegretti. Retrieval by spatial similarity: an algorithm and a comparative evaluation. *Pattern Recogn. Lett.*, 25 (14):1633–1645, 2004.

Thomas Seidl and Hans-Peter Kriegel. Optimal multi-step *k*-nearest neighbor search. In *SIGMOD Conference*, pages 154–165, 1998.

A. Sekey and B. A. Hanson. Improved 1-bark bandwidth auditory filter. *J. Acoust. Soc. Am.*, 75(6):1902–1904, 1987.

S. Selkow. *The Tree-to-tree Editing Problem. Inform. Proc. Lett.*, 6(6):184–186, 1977.

P. Sellers. The theory and computation of evolutionary distances: pattern recognition. *J. Algorithms*, 1:359–373, 1980.

Timos K. Sellis, Nick Roussopoulos, and Christos Faloutsos. The R+−tree: a dynamic index for multi-dimensional objects. In *VLDB '87: Proceedings of the 13th International Conference on Very Large Data Bases*, pages 507–518, 1987.

J. Sethuraman. A constructive definition of dirichlet priors. *Statist. Sin.*, 4:639–650, 1994.

M. Setnes and J. A. Roubos. Transparent fuzzy modelling using fuzzy clustering and GA's. In *Proceedings of NAFIPS*, pages 198–202, 2000.

Michael Ian Shamos and Dan Hoey. Geometric intersection problems. *17th Annual Symposium on Foundations of Computer Science*, pages 208–215, 1976.

Claude E. Shannon. Prediction and entropy of printed English. *Bell Syst. Tech. J.*, 30:50–64, 1950.

Marvin Shapiro. The choice of reference points in best-match file searching. *Commun. ACM*, 20(5):339–343, 1977.

Vladimir Shapiro. Accuracy of the straight line Hough transform: the non-voting approach. *Comput. Vis. Image Underst.*, 103(1):1–21, 2006.

Upendra Shardanand and Pattie Maes. Social information filtering: algorithms for automating "word of mouth." In *CHI '95: Proceedings of the SIGCHI Conference on Human Factors in Computing Systems*, pages 210–217, 1995.

M. Sharir. Almost tight upper bounds for lower envelopes in higher dimensions. *Discrete Comput. Geom.*, 12:327–345, 1994.

D. Shasha and K. Zhang. Fast algorithms for the unit cost distance between trees. *J. Algorithms*, 11:581–621, 1990.

D. Shasha and K. Zhang. Approximate tree pattern matching. In *Pattern Matching in Strings, Trees and Arrays*, Chapter 14. 1995.

D. Shasha, J. T.-L. Wang, Kaizhong Zhang, and F. Y. Shih. Exact and approximate algorithms for unordered tree matching. *IEEE Trans. Syst. Man Cybernet.*, 24(4): 668–678, 1994.

Dennis Shasha, Jason Wang, and Kaizhong Zhang. Unordered tree comparison based on cousin distance (http://cs.nyu.edu/shasha/papers/cousins.html), downloaded, 2009.

R. Shepard. Circularity in judgements of relative pitch. *J. Acoust. Soc. Am.*, 36:2346–2353, 1964.

A. Prasad Sistla, Clement T. Yu, and R. Haddad. Reasoning about spatial relationships in picture retrieval systems. In *VLDB '94: Proceedings of the 20th International Conference on Very Large Data Bases*, pages 570–581, San Francisco, CA, USA, 1994. Morgan Kaufmann.

A. Prasad Sistla, Clement T. Yu, Chengwen Liu, and King Liu. Similarity based retrieval of pictures using indices on spatial relationships. In *VLDB '95: Proceedings of the 21th International Conference on Very Large Data Bases*, pages 619–629, San Francisco, CA, USA, 1995. Morgan Kaufmann.

John R. Smith and Shih-Fu Chang. Visualseek: a fully automated content-based image query system. In *MULTIMEDIA '96: Proceedings of the Fourth ACM International Conference on Multimedia*, pages 87–98. ACM, 1996.

I. Sobel and G. Feldman. A 3×3 isotropic gradient operator for image processing. Presented as a talk at the Stanford Artificial Project, 1968.

Ian Soboroff and Charles Nicholas. Collaborative filtering and the generalized vector space model. In *SIGIR '00: Proceedings of the 23rd Annual International ACM SIGIR Conference on Research and Development in Information Retrieval*, pages 351–353, 2000.

Junehwa Song, Yurdaer N. Doganata, Michelle Y. Kim, and Asser N. Tantawi. Modeling timed user-interactions in multimedia documents. *ICMCS*, 00, 1996.

Yuqing Song, Markus Mielke, and Aidong Zhang. Netmedia: synchronized streaming of multimedia presentations in distributed environments. *ICMCS*, 585–590, 1999.

Cees Snoek and Marcel Worring. Multimedia event-based video indexing using time intervals. *IEEE Transactions on Multimedia*, 7(4):638–647, 2005.

C. Spearman. The proof and measurement of association between two things. *Am. j. Psychol.*, 15(3-4):72–101, 1904.

Daniel A. Spielman and Shang Hua Teng. Spectral partitioning works: planar graphs and finite element meshes. In *IEEE Symposium on Foundations of Computer Science*, pages 96–105, 1996.

Robert F. Sproull. Refinements to nearest-neighbor searching in k-dimensional trees. *Algorithmica*, 6(4):579–589, 1991.

H. Sridharan, H. Sundaram, and T. Rikakis. Computational models for experiences in the arts, and multimedia. In *ETP '03: Proceedings of the 2003 ACM SIGMM Workshop on Experiential Telepresence*, pages 31–44, 2003.

K. Sripanidkulchai. The popularity of Gnutella queries and its implications on scalability. (Online http://www.cs.cmu.edu/~kunwadee/research/p2p/gnutella.html, February 2001).

H. Steinhaus. Sur la division des corp materiels en parties. *Bull. Acad. Polon. Sci., Cl. III*, IV:801–804, 1956.

M.A. Stephens. EDF statistics for goodness of fit and some comparisons. *J. Am. Statist. Assoc.*, 69(347):730–737, 1974.

S. S. Stevens, J. Volkmann, and E. B. Newman. A scale for the measurement of the psychological magnitude pitch. *J. Acoust. Soc. Am.*, 8(3):185–190, 1937.

William J. Stewart and Wei Wu. Numerical experiments with iteration and aggregation for Markov chains. *ORSA J. Comput.*, 4:336–350, 1992.

G. C. Stockman and A. K. Agrawala. Equivalence of Hough curve detection to template matching. *Commun. ACM*, 20(11):820–822, 1977.

Michael Stonebraker, Lawrence A. Rowe, Bruce G. Lindsay, Jim Gray, Michael J. Carey, Michael L. Brodie, Philip A. Bernstein, and David Beech. Third-generation database system manifesto. *SIGMOD Rec.*, 19(3):31–44, 1990.

Michael Stonebraker, Daniel J. Abadi, Adam Batkin, Xuedong Chen, Mitch Cherniack, Miguel Ferreira, Edmond Lau, Amerson Lin, Samuel R. Madden, Elizabeth J. O'Neil, Patrick E. O'Neil, Alexander Rasin, Nga Tran, and Stan B. Zdonik. C-store: a column-oriented DBMS. In *VLDB*, pages 553–564, Trondheim, Norway, 2005.

Jimeng Sun, Dacheng Tao, and Christos Faloutsos. Beyond streams and graphs: dynamic tensor analysis. In *KDD '06: Proceedings of the 12th ACM SIGKDD International Conference on Knowledge Discovery and Data Mining*, pages 374–383, 2006.

Daniel M. Sunday. A very fast substring search algorithm. *Commun. ACM*, 33(8), 1990.

Erkki Sutinen and Jorma Tarhio. On using q-gram locations in approximate string matching. In *ESA '95: Proceedings of the Third Annual European Symposium on Algorithms*, pages 327–340. Springer-Verlag, 1995.

K.-C. Tai. The tree-to-tree correction problem. *J. ACM*, 26:422–433, 1979.

Tadao Takaoka. Approximate pattern matching with samples. In *ISAAC*, pages 234–242, 1994.

Kian-Lee Tan, Pin-Kwang Eng, and Beng Chin Ooi. Efficient progressive skyline computation. In *VLDB*, pages 301–310, 2001.

Pang-Ning Tan, Vipin Kumar, and Jaideep Srivastava. Selecting the right objective measure for association analysis. *Inform. Syst.*, 29(4):293–313, 2004.

Yufei Tao, Christos Faloutsos, and Dimitris Papadias. The power-method: a comprehensive estimation technique for multi-dimensional queries. In *CIKM*, pages 83–90, 2003.

Yufei Tao, Ke Yi, Cheng Sheng, and Panos Kalnis. Quality and efficiency in high dimensional nearest neighbor search. In *SIGMOD '09: Proceedings of the 35th SIGMOD International Conference on Management of Data*, pages 563–576, 2009.

Yee Whye Teh, Michael I. Jordan, Matthew J. Beal, and David M. Blei. Hierarchical dirichlet processes. *J. Am. Statist. Assoc.*, 101, 2003.

Kengo Terasawa and Yuzuru Tanaka. Spherical LSH for approximate nearest neighbor search on unit hypersphere. In *Workshop on Algorithms and Data Structures (WADS)*, Volume 4619 of *Lecture Notes in Computer Science*, pages 27–38, 2007.

Martin Theobald, Gerhard Weikum, and Ralf Schenkel. Top-k query evaluation with probabilistic guarantees. In *VLDB*, pages 648–659, 2004.

Yannis Theodoridis, Emmanuel Stefanakis, and Timos Sellis. Efficient cost models for spatial queries using R-trees. *IEEE Trans. Knowl. Data Eng.*, 12(1):19–32, 2000.

R. Tibshirani. Regression shrinkage and selection via the lasso. *J. R. Statist. Soc. (Ser. B)*, 58:267–288, 1996.

David A. Tolliver and Gary L. Miller. Graph partitioning by spectral rounding: Applications in image segmentation and clustering. In *CVPR '06: Proceedings of the 2006 IEEE Computer Society Conference on Computer Vision and Pattern Recognition*, pages 1053–1060, 2006.

W. S. Torgerson. Multidimensional scaling: I. Theory and method. *Psychometrika*, 17:401–419, 1952.

Caetano Traina, Jr., Agma Traina, Jr. Agma, Traina Leejay, and Wu Christos Faloutsos. Fast feature selection using fractal dimension. In *XV Brazilian Symposium on Databases (SBBD*, pages 158–171, 2000.

Panayiotis Tsaparas, Themistoklis Palpanas, Yannis Kotidis, Nick Koudas, and Divesh Srivastava. Ranked join indices. In *ICDE*, pages 277–288, 2003.

Charalampos E. Tsourakakis. Fast counting of triangles in large real networks without counting: algorithms and laws. In *ICDM '08: Proceedings of the Eighth IEEE International Conference on Data Mining*, pages 608–617, 2008.

Maurizio Tucci, Gennaro Costagliola, and Shi-Kuo Chang. A remark on NP-completeness of picture matching. *Inf. Process. Lett.*, 39(5):241–243, 1991.

Ledyard R. Tucker. Some mathematical notes on three-mode factor analysis. *Psychometrika*, (31):279–311, 1966.

J. K. Uhlmann. Metric trees. *Appl. Math. Lett.*, 4(5):61–62, 1991.

E. Ukkonen. Finding approximate patterns in strings. *J. Algorithms*, 6:132–137, 1985.

E. Ukkonen. Approximate string-matching with q-grams and maximal matches. *Theoret. Comp. Sci. 92*, pages 191–211, 1992a.

Esko Ukkonen. Constructing suffix trees on-line in linear time. In *Proceedings of the IFIP 12th World Computer Congress on Algorithms, Software, Architecture – Information Processing '92*, Volume 1, pages 484–492. North-Holland, 1992b.

J. R. Ullmann. An algorithm for subgraph isomorphism. *J. ACM*, 23(1):31–42, 1976.

Julian R. Ullmann. A binary n-gram technique for automatic correction of substitution, deletion, insertion and reversal errors in words. *Comput. J.*, 20(2):141–147, 1977.

Tanguy Urvoy, Emmanuel Chauveau, Pascal Filoche, and Thomas Lavergne. Tracking web spam with HTML style similarities. *ACM Trans. Web*, 2(1):1–28, 2008.

Jouko Vaananen. Second-order logic and foundations of mathematics. *Bull. Symbolic Logic*, 7(4):504–520, 2001.

Gabriel Valiente. An efficient bottom-up distance between trees. In *Eighth International Symposium on String Processing and Information Retrieval (SPIRE'01)*, pages 212–219, 2001.

Peter van Beek. Approximation algorithms for temporal reasoning. In *Proceedings of the 11th International Joint Conference on Artificial Intelligence*, pages 1291–1296, 1989.

C. J. van Rijsbergen, D. J. Harper, and M. F. Porter. The selection of good search terms. *Inform. Process. Management*, 17:77–91, 1981.

C. J. van Rijsbergen. *Information Retrieval*, 2nd ed. Butterworths, London, 1979.

V. Vapnik. *Estimation of Dependencies Based on Empirical Data*. Nauka, Moscow, 1979.

M. Vazirgiannis and S. Boll. Events in interactive multimedia applications: modeling and implementation design. In *ICMCS '97: Proceedings of the 1997 International Conference on Multimedia Computing and Systems (ICMCS '97)*, page 244. IEEE Computer Society, 1997.

Sriharsha Veeramachaneni, Diego Sona, and Paolo Avesani. Hierarchical dirichlet model for document classification. In *ICML '05: Proceedings of the 22nd International Conference on Machine Learning*, pages 928–935, 2005.

Enrique Vidal. New formulation and improvements of the nearest-neighbour approximating and eliminating search algorithm (aesa). *Pattern Recogn. Lett.*, 15 (1):1–7, 1994.

Karane Vieira, André Luiz Costa Carvalho, Klessius Berlt, Edleno S. Moura, Altigran S. Silva, and Juliana Freire. On finding templates on web collections. *World Wide Web*, 12(2):171–211, 2009.

M. Vilain and H. Kautz. Constraint propagation algorithms for temporal reasoning. In *Proceedings of AAAI- 86, Artificial Intelligence*, pages 377–382, 1986.

Juan Miguel Vilar. Reducing the overhead of the aesa metric-space nearest neighbour searching algorithm. *Inform. Process. Lett.*, 56(5):265–271, 1995.

Luc Vincent and Pierre Soille. Watersheds in digital spaces: an efficient algorithm based on immersion simulations. *IEEE Trans. Pattern Anal. Mach. Intell.*, 13(6): 583–598, 1991.

S. Vishwanathan and A. Smola. Fast kernels for string and tree matching. In K. Tsuda, B. Scholkopf, and J. P. Vert, editors, *Kernels and Bioinformatics*. MIT Press, 2003.

A. J. Viterbi. Error bounds for convolution codes and an asymptotically optimum decoding algorithm. *IEEE. Trans. Inform. Theory*, 13(2):260–269, 1967.

Willem Waegeman and Luc Boullart. An ensemble of weighted support vector machines for ordinal regression. In *Proceedings of World Academy of Science, Engineering and Technology*, Volume 12, March 2006.

Jason Tsong-Li Wang and Kaizhong Zhang. Finding similar consensus between trees: an algorithm and a distance hierarchy. *Pattern Recogn.*, 34(1):127–137, 2001.

Tsong-Li Wang and Dennis Shasha. Query processing for distance metrics. In *Proceedings of the Sixteenth International Conference on Very Large Databases*, pages 602–613, 1990.

Xuanhui Wang, Hui Fang, and ChengXiang Zhai. Improve retrieval accuracy for difficult queries using negative feedback. In *CIKM '07: Proceedings of the Sixteenth ACM Conference on Information and Knowledge Management*, pages 991–994, 2007.

Xuanhui Wang, Hui Fang, and ChengXiang Zhai. A study of methods for negative relevance feedback. In *SIGIR '08: Proceedings of the 31st annual international ACM SIGIR Conference on Research and Development in Information Retrieval*, pages 219–226, 2008.

Ying-Hong Wang. Image indexing and similarity retrieval based on a new spatial relation model. In *International Conference on Distributed Computing Systems, Workshop,* pages 396 – 401, 2001.

Stanley Wasserman, Katherine Faust, and Dawn Iacobucci. *Social Network Analysis: Methods and Applications (Structural Analysis in the Social Sciences)*. Cambridge University Press, November 1994.

D. J. Watts and S. H. Strogatz. Collective dynamics of "small-world" networks. *Nature*, 393(6684):440–442, June 1998.

David L. Weakliem. A critique of the Bayesian information criterion for model selection. *Sociol. Methods Res.*, 27:359–397, 1999.

Roger Weber and Stephen Blott. A quantitative analysis and performance study for similarity-search methods in high-dimensional spaces. In *Proceedings of the 24th International Conference on Very Large Data Bases (VLDB)*, pages 194–205, 1998.

Ron Weiss, Andrzej Duda, and David K. Gifford. Content-based access to algebraic video. In *International Conference on Multimedia Computing and Systems, IEEE*, pages 140–151, 1994.

L. R. Welch. Hidden Markov models and the Baum-Welch algorithm. *IEEE Inform. Theory Soc. Newsl.*, 53(4), December 2003.

Utz Westermann and Ramesh Jain. Toward a common event model for multimedia applications. *IEEE MultiMedia*, 14(1):19–29, 2007.

David A. White and Ramesh Jain. Similarity indexing with the SS-tree. In *ICDE '96: Proceedings of the Twelfth International Conference on Data Engineering*, pages 516–523, 1996a.

David A. White and Ramesh Jain. Similarity indexing: Algorithms and performance. In *Storage and Retrieval for Image and Video Databases (SPIE)*, 1996b.

Frank Wilcoxon. Individual comparisons by ranking methods. *Biometrics Bull.*, 1(6):80–83, 1945.

Christopher K. I. Williams and Matthias Seeger. Using the Nyström method to speed up kernel machines. In T. Leen, T. Dietterich, and V. Tresp, editors, *Neural Information Processing Systems 13*, pages 682–688. MIT Press, 2001.

Stefan Wirag. Scheduling of adaptive multimedia documents. In *ICMCS '99: Proceedings of the IEEE International Conference on Multimedia Computing and Systems*, Volume 2, page 307. IEEE Computer Society, 1999.

Dian I. Witter and Michael W. Berry. Downdating the latent semantic indexing model for conceptual information retrieval. *Comput. J.*, 41(8):589–601, 1998.

Raymond Chi-Wing Wong, Ada Wai-Chee Fu, Jian Pei, Yip Sing Ho, Tai Wong, and Yubao Liu. Efficient skyline querying with variable user preferences on nominal attributes. *Proc. VLDB*, 1(1):1032–1043, 2008.

M. F. Worboys, H. M. Hearnshaw, and D. J. Maguire. Object-oriented data modelling for spatial databases. *Int. J. Geograph. Inform. Syst.*, 4:369–383, 1990.

G. H. Wu, Y.J. Zhang, and X.G. Lin. Wavelet transform–based texture classification with feature weighting. In *ICIP99*, pages IV:435–439, 1999.

Sun Wu and Udi Manber. Fast text searching with errors. tr 9111. Technical report, Department of Computer Science, University of Arizona., 1991.

Sun Wu and Udi Manber. Fast text searching: allowing errors. *Commun. ACM*, 35 (10):83–91, 1992.

Zhibiao Wu and Martha Palmer. Verbs semantics and lexical selection. In *Proceedings of the 32nd Annual Meeting of the Association for Computational Linguistics*, pages 133–138, 1994.

Dong Xin, Chen Chen, and Jiawei Han. Towards robust indexing for ranked queries. In *VLDB '06: Proceedings of the 32nd International Conference on Very Large Data Bases*, pages 235–246, 2006.

Dong Xin, Jiawei Han, and Kevin C. Chang. Progressive and selective merge: computing top-k with ad-hoc ranking functions. In *SIGMOD '07: Proceedings of the 2007 ACM SIGMOD International Conference on Management of Data*, pages 103–114, 2007.

R. R. Yager. Some procedures for selecting fuzzy set-theoretic operations. *Int. J. General Syst.*, 8:115–124, 1982.

P. Yamuna, N. Cho, K. Selçuk Candan, and M. Wagner. Towards an open repository for VRML. In *International Symposium on Computer and Information Sciences*, 1999.

Prakash Yamuna and K. Selçuk Candan. Efficient similarity-based retrieval of temporal structures. In *SAINT-W '01: Proceedings of the 2001 Symposium on Applications and the Internet-Workshops (SAINT 2001 Workshops)*, pages 133–138, Jan 2001.

Wuu Yang. Identifying syntactic differences between two programs. *Softw. Pract. Exper.*, 21(7):739–755, 1991.

Mihalis Yannakakis. Graph-theoretic methods in database theory. In *PODS '90: Proceedings of the Ninth ACM SIGACT-SIGMOD-SIGART Symposium on Principles of Database Systems*, pages 230–242, 1990.

Peter N. Yianilos. Data structures and algorithms for nearest neighbor search in general metric spaces. In *SODA '93: Proceedings of the Fourth Annual ACM-SIAM Symposium on Discrete Algorithms*, pages 311–321, 1993.

Hujun Yin. Data visualisation and manifold mapping using the visom. *Neural Netw.*, 15(8-9):1005–1016, 2002.

Hujun Yin. *Learning Nonlinear Principal Manifolds by Self-Organising Maps*, in *Principal Manifolds for Data Visualization and Dimension Reduction, Springer*, pages 68–95, 2007.

Xiaoxin Yin, Jiawei Han, and Philip S. Yu. Linkclus: efficient clustering via heterogeneous semantic links. In *VLDB '06: Proceedings of the 32nd International Conference on Very Large Data Bases*, pages 427–438, 2006.

Xiaoxin Yin, Jiawei Han, and Philip S. Yu. Object distinction: Distinguishing objects with identical names. In *ICDE*, pages 1242–1246, 2007.

Man Lung Yiu and Nikos Mamoulis. Efficient processing of top-k dominating queries on multi-dimensional data. In *VLDB '07: Proceedings of the 33rd International Conference on Very Large Data Bases*, pages 483–494, 2007.

C. T. Yu, W. S. Luk, and T. Y. Cheung. A statistical model for relevance feedback in information retrieval. *J. ACM*, 23(2):273–286, 1976.

Clement Yu, Prasoon Sharma, Weiyi Meng, and Yan Qin. Database selection for processing k nearest neighbors queries in distributed environments. In *JCDL '01: Proceedings of the 1st ACM/IEEE-CS Joint Conference on Digital Libraries*, pages 215–222, 2001.

Clement Yu, George Philip, and Weiyi Meng. Distributed top-n query processing with possibly uncooperative local systems. In *VLDB 2003, Proceedings of 29th International Conference on Very Large Data Bases, September 9-12, 2003*, pages 117–128. Morgan Kaufmann, 2003.

Clement T. Yu and Weiyi Meng. *Principles of Database Query processing for Advanced Applications*. Morgan Kaufmann, San Francisco, CA, USA, 1998.

Jie Yu, Jaume Amores, Nicu Sebe, Petia Radeva, and Qi Tian. Distance learning for similarity estimation. *IEEE Trans. Pattern Anal. Mach. Intell.*, 30(3):451–462, 2008.

L. A. Zadeh. Fuzzy sets. *Inform. Control*, 8:338–353, 1965.

L. A. Zadeh. The concept of a linguistic variable and its application to approximate reasoning-i. *Inform. Sci.*, 8:199–249, 1975.

Hongyuan Zha and Horst D. Simon. On updating problems in latent semantic indexing. *SIAM J. Sci. Comput.*, 21(2):782–791, 1999.

Chengxiang Zhai and John Lafferty. Model-based feedback in the language modeling approach to information retrieval. In *CIKM '01: Proceedings of the Tenth*

International Conference on Information and Knowledge Management, pages 403–410, 2001.

Chengxiang Zhai and John Lafferty. A study of smoothing methods for language models applied to information retrieval. *ACM Trans. Inform. Syst.*, 22(2):179–214, 2004.

Chi Zhang and P. Wang. A new method of color image segmentation based on intensity and hue clustering. *ICPR*, volume 3, page 613–616, 2000.

K. Zhang and D. Shasha. Simple fast algorithms for the editing distance between trees and related problems. *SIAM J. Comput.*, 18(6):1245–1262, 1989.

K. Zhang, J. T. L. Wang, and D. Shasha. On the editing distance between undirected acyclic graphs. *Int. J. Comp. Sci.*, 7(1):43–57, 1996.

Kaizhong Zhang, Rick Statman, and Dennis Shasha. On the editing distance between unordered labeled trees. *Inform. Process. Lett.*, 42(3):133–139, 1992.

Q.-L. Zhang. A remark on intractability of picture retrieval by contents. Technical Report, University of Illinois, 1994.

Q.-L. Zhang and S. S.-T. Yau. On intractability of spatial relationships in content-based image database systems. *Commun. Inform. Syst.*, 4(2):181–190, 2005.

Zhen Zhang, Seung-won Hwang, Kevin Chen-Chuan Chang, Min Wang, Christian A. Lang, and Yuan-chi Chang. Boolean + ranking: querying a database by *k*-constrained optimization. In *SIGMOD '06: Proceedings of the 2006 ACM SIGMOD International Conference on Management of Data*, pages 359–370, 2006.

Yi Zhou and T. Murata. Fuzzy-timing Petri net model for distributed multimedia synchronization. In *1998 IEEE International Conference on Systems, Man, and Cybernetics*, Volume 1, pages 244–249, 1998.

George K. Zipf. *Human Behavior and the Principle of Least Effort*. Addison-Wesley, Reading, MA, 1949.

Jacob Ziv and Abraham Lempel. A universal algorithm for sequential data compression. *IEEE Trans. Inform. Theory*, 23:337–343, 1977.

Jacob Ziv and Neri Merhav. A measure of relative entropy between individual sequences with application to universal classification. *IEEE Trans. Inform. Theory*, 39(4):1270–1279, 1993.

J. Zobel and A. Moffat. Inverted files for text search engines. *Computing Surveys*, 38:1–56, 2006.

Justin Zobel, Alistair Moffat, and Kotagiri Ramamohanarao. Inverted files versus signature files for text indexing. *ACM Trans. Database Syst.*, 23(4):453–490, 1998.

A. Zunjarwad, H. Sundaram, and L. Xie. Contextual wisdom: social relations and correlations for multimedia event annotation. In *Proceedings of ACM Multimedia*, pages 615–624, 2007.

CITED LINKS

[X3D], http://www.web3d.org/x3d/specifications/.

[Amazon], Amazon e-commerce site. http://www.amazon.com.

[Facebook]. http://www.facebook.com.

[HyTime], The Hypermedia/Time-based Structuring Language (HyTime) Iso/iec 10744.

[LinkedIn]. http://www.linkedin.com.

[MacromediaDirector], Macromedia Director (now Adobe Director) http://www.adobe.com/.

[MHEG], Iso 13522-5.

[MPEG21] overview v.5. http://www.chiariglione.org/mpeg/standards/mpeg-21/mpeg-21.htm.

[MPEG4] systems, iso/iec 14496-1: Coding of audio-visual objects: Systems, final draft international standard, iso/iec jtc1/sc29/wg11 n2501, Oct. 1998.

[MPEG7] overview. http://www.chiariglione.org/mpeg/standards/mpeg-7/mpeg-7.htm.

[MPEG-7xm] visual part of experimentation model (XM) version 2.0, MPEG-7 output document iso/mpeg, December 1999.

[Netflix]. http://www.netflix.com.

[ODMG]. The Object Database Standard: ODMG-93, Release 1.1. (editor R.G.G. Cattell), Morgan Kaufmann Publishers, San Francisco, 1994.

[Quicktime]. http://www.apple.com/quicktime.

[SGML], standard generalized markup language. http://www.w3.org/markup/sgml/.

[Smil], Synchronized multimedia integration language recommendation (SMIL), http://www.w3.org/tr/rec-smil/, 1998.

[SQL-99], Ansi/iso/iec international standard (is). database language SQL – part 2: Foundation (sql/foundation). ISO Standard, 1999.

[SQL-08] Iso/iec iso/iec 9075(1-4,9-11,13,14):2008; sql:2008 standard. ISO Standard, 2008.

[SQL3], Iso/iec jtc1/sc21 n10489, iso//iec 9075, part 2, committeedraft (cd), database language SQL – part 2: Sql/foundation. ISO Standard, July 1996a.

[SQL3], Objects, Iso/iec jtc1/sc21 n10491, iso//iec 9075, part 8, committeedraft (cd), database language SQL – part 8: Sql/object. ISO Standard, July 1996b.

[SQL03Images], Iso/iec 13249-5:2003; SQL multimedia and application packages – part 5: Still image. ISO Standard, 2003.

[SQL07Multimedia], Iso/iec 13249-[1;2;3;4;5;6;7]:2007; information technology – database languages – SQL multimedia and application packages. ISO Standard, 2007.

[TREC], Text retrieval conference. http://trec.nist.gov/.

[UML], Unified modeling language. http://www.uml.org/.

[Vrml], virtual reality modeling language. http://www.w3.org/markup/vrml/.

[XML], extensible markup language. http://www.w3.org/xml/.

[Yahoo], Yahoo directory. http://dir.yahoo.com/.

Index